The Humanistic Tradition

Volume II

The Early Modern World
to the Present

FOURTH EDITION

The Humanistic Tradition

Volume II

The Early Modern World
to the Present

Gloria K. Fiero

Boston   Burr Ridge, IL   Dubuque, IA   Madison, WI   New York
San Francisco   St. Louis   Bangkok   Bogotá   Caracas   Kuala Lumpur
Lisbon   London   Madrid   Mexico City   Milan   Montreal   New Delhi
Santiago   Seoul   Singapore   Sydney   Taipei   Toronto

McGraw-Hill Higher Education

A Division of The **McGraw-Hill** Companies

THE HUMANISTIC TRADITION, VOLUME II
THE EARLY MODERN WORLD TO THE PRESENT
Published by McGraw-Hill, an imprint of the McGraw-Hill Companies, Inc.
1221 Avenue of the Americas, New York, NY, 10020.

This book is printed on acid-free paper.

2 3 4 5 6 7 8 9 0 QWV/QWV 0 9 8 7 6 5 4 3

ISBN 0-07-288550-5

Permissions Acknowledgments appear on page E1,
and on this page by reference.

Editorial director: *Phillip A. Butcher*
Executive sponsoring editor: *Christopher Freitag*
Marketing manager: *David S. Patterson*
Senior project manager: *Pat Frederickson*
Production supervisor: *Susanne Riedell*
Senior designer: *Jennifer McQueen*
Manager, publication services: *Ira Roberts*
Supplement producer: *Rose Range*
Media technology producer: *Sean Crowley*
Cover designer: *Kiera Cunningham*
Typeface: *10/12 Goudy*
Printer: *Quebecor World Versailles, Inc.*

http://www.mhhe.com

This book was designed and produced by
CALMANN & KING LTD
71 Great Russell Street, London WC1B 3BP
www.calmann-king.com

Senior editor: *Jon Haynes*
Picture researcher: *Peter Kent*
Cartographer: *Andrea Fairbrass*
Typesetter: *Fakenham Photosetting, Norfolk*

Front cover
Main image: Henri de Toulouse-Lautrec, detail of *At The Moulin-Rouge*, 1893–1895.
Oil on canvas, 4 ft. ⅛ in. × 4 ft. 7¼ in. Photograph: © 1993. The Art Institute of
Chicago. All Rights Reserved. Helen Birch Bartlett Memorial Collection
(1928.610).

Insets: (top left) Pieter de Hooch, detail of *Portrait of a Family Making Music*, 1663.
Oil on canvas, 38⅞ × 45¹⁵⁄₁₆ in. © The Cleveland Museum of Art 1998. Gift of the
Hanna Fund (1951.355)
(middle left) Francisco Goya, detail of the *Third of May, 1808: The Execution of the
Defenders of Madrid*, 1814. Oil on canvas, 8 ft. 6 in. × 10 ft. 4 in. Prado, Madrid.
(middle right) Edward Hopper, detail of *Nighthawks*, 1942. Oil on canvas, 33 ⅛ ×
60 ⅛ in. Art Institute of Chicago. Chicago Friends of American Art Collection,
1942.51.
(top right) Detail of *Rejoicing at the Birth of Prince Salim in 1569* Manuscript
illustration from the Akbar-Nama. The Chester Beatty Library Dublin.

Frontispiece: Pierre-Auguste Renoir, detail of *Le Moulin de la Galette*, 1876. Oil on
canvas, 4 ft. × 3½ in × 5 ft. 9 in. Musee d'Orsay, Paris. Photograph: © R.M.N., Paris.

Series Contents

Volume II
Contents

PART TWO
The Age of Enlightenment 601

BOOK FIVE

PART ONE
The romantic era   677

PART TWO
The postmodern turn   909

"It's the most curious thing I ever saw in all my life!" exclaimed Lewis Carroll's Alice in Wonderland, as she watched the Cheshire Cat slowly disappear, leaving only the outline of a broad smile. "I've often seen a cat without a grin, but a grin without a cat!" A student who encounters an ancient Greek epic, a Yoruba mask, or a Mozart opera—lacking any context for these works—might be equally baffled. It may be helpful, therefore, to begin by explaining how the artifacts (the "grin") of the humanistic tradition relate to the larger and more elusive phenomenon (the "cat") of human culture.

The Humanistic Tradition and the Humanities

In its broadest sense, the term *humanistic tradition* refers to humankind's cultural legacy—the sum total of the significant ideas and achievements handed down from generation to generation. This tradition is the product of responses to conditions that have confronted all people throughout history. Since the beginnings of life on earth, human beings have tried to ensure their own survival by achieving harmony with nature. They have attempted to come to terms with the inevitable realities of disease and death. They have endeavored to establish ways of living collectively and communally. And they have persisted in the desire to understand themselves and their place in the universe. In response to these ever-present and universal challenges—*survival, communality,* and *self-knowledge*—human beings have created and transmitted the tools of science and technology, social and cultural institutions, religious and philosophic systems, and various forms of personal expression, the sum total of which we call culture.

Even the most ambitious survey cannot assess all manifestations of the humanistic tradition. This book therefore focuses on the creative legacy referred to collectively as *the humanities*: literature, philosophy, history (in its literary dimension), architecture, the visual arts (including photography and film), music, and dance. Selected examples from each of these disciplines constitute our *primary sources.* Primary sources (that is, works original to the age that produced them) provide first-hand evidence of human inventiveness and ingenuity. The primary sources in this text have been chosen on the basis of their authority, their beauty, and their enduring value. They are, simply stated, the great works of their time and, in some cases, of all time. Universal in their appeal, they have been transmitted from generation to generation. Such works are, as well, the landmark examples of a specific time and place: They offer insight into the ideas and values of the society in which they were produced. The drawings of

Leonardo da Vinci, for example, reveal a passionate determination to understand the operations and functions of nature. And while Leonardo's talents far exceeded those of the average individual of his time, his achievements may be viewed as a mirror of the robust curiosity that characterized his time and place—the age of the Renaissance in Italy. *The Humanistic Tradition* surveys such landmark works, but joins "the grin" to "the cat" by examining them within their political, economic, and social contexts.

The Humanistic Tradition explores a living legacy. History confirms that the humanities are integral forms of a given culture's values, ambitions, and beliefs. Poetry, painting, philosophy, and music are not, generally speaking, products of unstructured leisure or indulgent individuality; rather, they are tangible expressions of the human quest for the good (one might even say the "complete") life. Throughout history, these forms of expression have served the domains of the sacred, the ceremonial, and the communal. And even in the early days of the twenty-first century, as many time-honored traditions come under assault, the arts retain their power to awaken our imagination in the quest for survival, communality, and self-knowledge.

The Scope of the Humanistic Tradition

The humanistic tradition is not the exclusive achievement of any one geographic region, race, or class of human beings. For that reason, this text assumes a global and multicultural rather than exclusively Western perspective. At the same time, Western contributions are emphasized, first, because the audience for these books is predominantly Western, but also because in recent centuries the West has exercised a dominant influence on the course and substance of global history. Clearly, the humanistic tradition belongs to all of humankind, and the best way to understand the Western contribution to that tradition is to examine it in the arena of world culture.

As a survey, *The Humanistic Tradition* cannot provide an exhaustive analysis of our creative legacy. The critical reader will discover many gaps. Some aspects of culture that receive extended examination in traditional Western humanities surveys have been pared down to make room for the too often neglected contributions of Islam, Africa, and Asia. This book is necessarily selective—it omits many major figures and treats others only briefly. Primary sources are arranged, for the most part, chronologically, but they are presented as manifestations of the informing ideas of the age in which they were produced. The intent is to examine the evidence of the humanistic tradition thematically and topically, rather than to compile a series of mini-histories of the individual arts.

Studying the Humanistic Tradition

To study the creative record is to engage in a dialogue with the past, one that brings us face to face with the values of our ancestors, and, ultimately, with our own. This dialogue is (or should be) a source of personal revelation and delight; like Alice in Wonderland, our strange, new encounters will be enriched according to the degree of curiosity and patience we bring to them. Just as lasting friendships with special people are cultivated by extended familiarity, so our appreciation of a painting, a play, or a symphony depends on close attention and repeated contact. There are no short-cuts to the study of the humanistic tradition, but there are some techniques that may be helpful. It should be useful, for instance, to approach each primary source from the triple perspective of its text, its context, and its subtext.

The Text: The *text* of any primary source refers to its *medium* (that is, what it is made of), its *form* (its outward shape), and its *content* (the subject it describes). All literature, for example, whether intended to be spoken or read, depends on the medium of words—the American poet Robert Frost once defined literature as "performance in words." Literary form varies according to the manner in which words are arranged. So poetry, which shares with music and dance rhythmic organization, may be distinguished from prose, which normally lacks regular rhythmic pattern. The main purpose of prose is to convey information, to narrate, and to describe; poetry, by its freedom from conventional patterns of grammar, provides unique opportunities for the expression of intense emotions. Philosophy (the search for truth through reasoned analysis) and history (the record of the past) make use of prose to analyze and communicate ideas and information. In literature, as in most kinds of expression, content and form are usually interrelated. The subject matter or the form of a literary work determines its *genre*. For instance, a long narrative poem recounting the adventures of a hero constitutes an *epic*, while a formal, dignified speech in praise of a person or thing constitutes a *eulogy*.

The visual arts—painting, sculpture, architecture, and photography—employ a wide variety of media, such as wood, clay, colored pigments, marble, granite, steel, and (more recently) plastic, neon, film, and computers. The form or outward shape of a work of art depends on the manner in which the artist manipulates the formal elements of color, line, texture, and space. Unlike words, these formal elements lack denotative meaning. The artist may manipulate form to describe and interpret the visible world (as in such genres as portraiture and landscape painting); to generate fantastic and imaginative kinds of imagery; or to create imagery that is nonrepresentational—without identifiable subject matter. In general, however, the visual arts are spatial, that is, they operate and are apprehended in space.

The medium of music is sound. Like literature, music is durational: It unfolds over the period of time in which it occurs. The formal elements of music are melody, rhythm,

harmony, and tone color—elements that also characterize the oral life of literature. As with the visual arts, the formal elements of music are without symbolic content, but while literature, painting, and sculpture may imitate or describe nature, music is almost always nonrepresentational—it rarely has meaning beyond the sound itself. For that reason, music is the most difficult of the arts to describe in words. It is also (in the view of some) the most affective of the arts. Dance, the artform that makes the human body itself a medium of expression, resembles music in that it is temporal and performance-oriented. Like music, dance exploits rhythm as a formal tool, but, like painting and sculpture, it unfolds in space as well as time.

In analyzing the text of a work of literature, art, or music, we ask how its formal elements contribute to its meaning and affective power. We examine the ways in which the artist manipulates medium and form to achieve a characteristic manner of execution and expression that we call *style*. And we try to determine the extent to which a style reflects the personal vision of the artist and the larger vision of his or her time and place. Comparing the styles of various artworks from a single era, we may discover that they share certain defining features and characteristics. Similarities (both formal and stylistic) between, for instance, golden age Greek temples and Greek tragedies, between Chinese lyric poems and landscape paintings, and between postmodern fiction and pop sculpture, prompt us to seek the unifying moral and aesthetic values of the cultures in which they were produced.

The Context: We use the word *context* to describe the historical and cultural environment. To determine the context, we ask: In what time and place did the artifact originate? How did it function within the society in which it was created? Was the purpose of the piece decorative, didactic, magical, propagandistic? Did it serve the religious or political needs of the community? Sometimes our answers to these questions are mere guesses. Nevertheless, understanding the function of an artifact often serves to clarify the nature of its form (and vice versa). For instance, much of the literature produced prior to the fifteenth century was spoken or sung rather than read; for that reason, such literature tends to feature repetition and rhyme, devices that facilitate memorization. We can assume that literary works embellished with frequent repetitions, such as the *Epic of Gilgamesh* and the Hebrew Bible, were products of an oral tradition. Determining the original function of an artwork also permits us to assess its significance in its own time and place: The paintings on the walls of Paleolithic caves, which are among the most compelling animal illustrations in the history of world art, are not "artworks" in the modern sense of the term but, rather, magical signs that accompanied hunting rituals, the performance of which was essential to the survival of the community. Understanding the relationship between text and context is one of the principal concerns of any inquiry into the humanistic tradition.

The Subtext: The *subtext* of the literary or artistic object refers to its secondary and implied meanings. The subtext embraces the emotional or intellectual messages embedded in, or implied by, a work of art. The epic poems of the ancient Greeks, for instance, which glorify prowess and physical courage in battle, suggest that such virtues are exclusively male. The state portraits of the seventeenth-century French ruler Louis XIV carry the subtext of unassailable and absolute power. In our own century, Andy Warhol's serial adaptations of soup cans and Coca-Cola bottles offer wry commentary on the supermarket mentality of postmodern American culture. Identifying the implicit message of an artwork helps us to determine the values and customs of the age in which it was produced and to assess those values against others.

Beyond *The Humanistic Tradition*

This book offers only small, enticing samples from an enormous cultural buffet. To dine more fully, students are encouraged to go beyond the sampling presented at this table; and for the most sumptuous feasting, nothing can substitute for first-hand experience. Students, therefore, should make every effort to supplement this book with visits to art museums and galleries, concert halls, theaters, and libraries. *The Humanistic Tradition* is designed for students who may or may not be able to read music, but who surely are able to cultivate an appreciation of music in performance. The music logos that appear in the text refer to the Music Listening Selections found on two accompanying compact discs, available from the publishers. Lists of suggestions for further reading are included at the end of each chapter, while a selected general bibliography of electronic humanities resources appears in the Online Learning Center at http://www.mhhe.com/fiero.

The Fourth Edition

The fourth edition of *The Humanistic Tradition* continues to take as its main focus the topical and global themes that have informed the last three editions. Book 1, however, has been restructured: Egypt, Mesopotamia, and the East Asian civilizations now each receive separate chapters, and chapter 7, "The Bipolar Empires of Rome and China," has been divided into two separate chapters. In Book 3, chapters 18 and 19 have been reversed, and in Book 4, chapters 21 to 23 have been reordered. There are new reading selections throughout the text. These range from the poems of Catallus to the lyrics of Derek Walcott and from Saint Francis' *Canticle of Brother Sun* to Mark Twain's *Huckleberry Finn*. Excerpts from Mary Wollstonecraft's *Vindication of the Rights of Women*, two newly translated writings by Renaissance women, the *Scivias* of Hildegard of Bingen, and the narrative of Sojourner Truth give greater dimension to the role of women in the arts. The *Analects* of Confucius appear in a 1997 translation. Greek mythology, slave songs and spirituals, and the nineteenth-century symbolist movement take their places in the appropriate chapters. Excerpts from Shakespeare's *Hamlet* and *Othello* replace the complete text of *Othello*, which is now available in the web-based resources for *The Humanistic Tradition*. Our examination of the twentieth century has been expanded to include film, and each chapter in Book 6 now brings attention to landmark developments in that medium. The contemporary chapters have been updated to include a segment on the quest for ethnic identity, focusing on the Latino voice that has made a significant mark in the arts of the past two decades.

Keymap Indicating Areas Shown as White Highlights on the Locator Maps

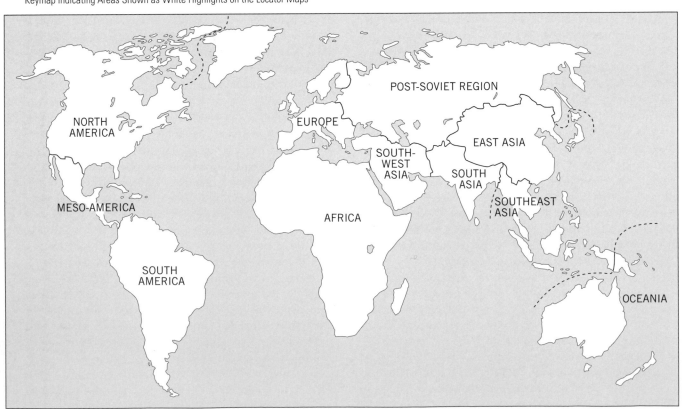

In the newly organized chapter 38, electronic and digital art receive expanded consideration.

This new edition includes more color illustrations than previous editions, as well as new diagrams that assist the reader in understanding the content, function, or construction techniques of various artworks. The Rosetta Stone, the so-called Mask of Agamemnon, the Hellenistic Altar of Zeus, and artwork by Angelica Kauffmann, Henry Ossawa Tanner, Lucca della Robbia, Piero della Francesco, Fernand Léger, and Anselm Kiefer are among the many new illustrations. The treatment of ancient China has been updated to include the information yielded by recent excavations of early dynastic graves in the People's Republic of China. Two new audio compact discs replace the older cassettes. These listening selections illustrate the musical works discussed in the text. Music by Hildegard of Bingen and Aaron Copland, African call-and-response chant, and the Muslim Call to Prayer have been added to the earlier materials, along with an excerpt from Mozart's *Marriage of Figaro*. The revised *Science and Technology Boxes*, along with *Locator Maps* and new *Timelines*, provide useful and popular study aids. The revised timelines are not exhaustive, but show selected key works. Each chapter in the fourth edition opens with a key quotation drawn from the readings and focusing on the theme of the chapter. Updated bibliographies are appended to each individual chapter.

A Note to Instructors

The key to successful classroom use of *The Humanistic Tradition* is *selectivity*. Although students may be assigned to read whole chapters that focus on a topic or theme, as well as complete works that supplement the abridged readings, the classroom should be the stage for a selective treatment of a single example or a set of examples. The organization of this textbook is designed to emphasize themes that cut across geographic boundaries—themes whose universal significance prompts students to evaluate and compare rather than simply memorize and repeat lists of names and places. To assist readers in achieving global cultural literacy, every effort has been made to resist isolating (or "ghettoizing") individual cultures and to avoid the inevitable biases we bring to our evaluation of relatively unfamiliar cultures.

Acknowledgments

Writing *The Humanistic Tradition* has been an exercise in humility. Without the assistance of learned friends and colleagues, assembling a book of this breadth would have been an impossible task. James H. Dormon read all parts of the manuscript and made extensive and substantive editorial suggestions; as his colleague, best friend, and wife, I am most deeply indebted to him.

The following readers and reviewers generously shared their insights in matters of content and style: Professors Jill Carrington (Stephen F. Austin State University), Darrell Bourque (University of Louisiana, Lafayette), Enid Housty (Hampton University), Kim Jones (Seminole Community College), Juergen Pelzer (Occidental College), Denise Rogers (University of Louisiana, Lafayette), Ralph V. Turner (Florida State University), and my colleagues, Donald Liss and Robert Butler.

In the preparation of the fourth edition, I have also benefited from the suggestions and comments generously offered by Roy Barineau (Tallahassee Community College), Carol A. Berger (St. Louis Community College), Rodney Boyd (Collin County Community College), Judith Ann Cohn (West Virginia State College), Janet L. DeCosmo (Florida A&M University), Larry Dorr (University of North Carolina), Edward M. Frame (Valencia Community College), Grant Hardy (University of North Carolina), Cynthia Ho (University of North Carolina), Connie LaMarca-Frankel (Pasco-Hernando Community College), Robert J. G. Lange (University of North Carolina), Sandra Loman (Madison Area Technical College), Susan McMichaels (University of North Carolina), Lois L. McNamara (Valencia Community College), Ann Malloy (Tulsa Community College), Sharon Rooks (Edison Community College), Charlie Schuler (Pensacola Junior College), Gerald Stacy (Central Washington University), Elisabeth Stein (Tallahassee Community College), Patricia Gailah Taylor (Southwest Texas State University), Barbara Tomlinson (Kean University), Camille Weiss (West Virginia University), and Alice Weldon (University of North Carolina).

The burden of preparing the fourth edition has been lightened by the assistance of Christopher Freitag, Executive Editor, and by the editorial vigilance of Jon Haynes, Richard Mason, and Cleia Smith at Calmann & King.

SUPPLEMENTS FOR THE INSTRUCTOR AND THE STUDENT

A number of useful supplements are available to instructors and students using *The Humanistic Tradition*. Please contact your sales representative or call 1-800-338-5371 to obtain these resources, or to ask for further details.

Online Learning Center

A complete set of web-based resources for *The Humanistic Tradition* can be found at www.mhhe.com/fiero. Material for students includes study outlines, self-tests, interactive maps and timelines, and links to other web resources. Instructors will benefit from teaching tips, web activities and assignments, and access to material from the Instructor's Resource Manual. Instructors can also utilize PageOut, McGraw-Hill's own online course management tool. PageOut works seamlessly with the Online Learning Center resources and allows instructors to have complete control over the organization of online course content on their own course website. Instructors can register for this free service at www.pageout.net.

Compact Discs

Two audio compact discs have been designed exclusively for use with *The Humanistic Tradition*. CD One corresponds to the music listening selections discussed in books 1–3 and CD Two contains the music in books 4–6. Instructors may obtain copies of the recordings for classroom use through the local sales representative or by calling 1-800-338-5371. The recordings are also available for individual purchase by students; they can be packaged with any or all of the six texts. Consult your local sales representative for details.

Slide Sets

A set of book-specific slides is available to qualified adopters of *The Humanistic Tradition*. These slides have been especially selected to include many of the less well-known images in the books and will be a useful complement to your present slide resources. Additional slides are available for purchase directly from Universal Color Slides. For further information consult our web site at www.mhhe.com/fiero.

Instructor's Resource Manual

The Instructor's Resource Manual is designed to assist instructors as they plan and prepare for classes. Course outlines and sample syllabi for both semester and quarter systems are included. The chapter summaries emphasize key themes and topics that give focus to the primary source readings. The study questions for each chapter may be removed and copied as handouts for student discussion or written assignments. A Test Item File follows each chapter along with a correlation list that directs instructors to the appropriate supplemental resources. A list of suggested videotapes, recordings, videodiscs, and their suppliers is included.

MicroTest III

The questions in the Test Item File are available on MicroTest III, a powerful but easy-to-use test generating program. MicroTest is available for Windows, and Macintosh personal computers. With MicroTest, an instructor can easily select the questions from the Test Item File and print a test and answer key. You can customize questions, headings, and instructions and add or import questions of your own.

Student Study Guides, Volumes 1 and 2

Written by Gloria K. Fiero, two new Student Study Guides are now available to help students gain a better understanding of subjects found in *The Humanistic Tradition*. Volume 1 accompanies books 1–3 and Volume 2 accompanies books 4–6. Each chapter contains: a Chapter Objective; a Chapter Outline; Key Terms, Names (with pronunciation guides), and Dates; Vocabulary Building; Multiple Choice Questions; and Essay Questions. Many chapters also contain a Visual/Spatial Exercise and Bonus Material. At the end of each Part, Synthesis material helps students draw together ideas from a set of chapters.

CHAPTER NINETEEN

Protest and reform: the waning of the old order

"Now what else is the whole life of mortals but a sort of comedy, in which the various actors, disguised by various costumes and masks, walk on and play each one his part, until the manager waves them off the stage?"
Erasmus

The Temper of Reform

The Impact of Technology

In the transition from medieval to early modern times, technology played a crucial role. Gunpowder, the light cannon, and other military devices made warfare more impersonal and ultimately more deadly. At the same time, Western advances in navigation, shipbuilding, and maritime instrumentation brought Europe into a dominant position in world exploration and colonization. By the end of the sixteenth century, European expansion would change the map of the world.

Another kind of technology, the printing press, revolutionized the future of learning and communication. Block printing originated in China in the ninth century and movable type in the eleventh, but print technology did not reach Western Europe until the fifteenth century. By 1450, in the city of Mainz, the German goldsmith Johannez Gutenberg (ca. 1400–ca. 1468) had perfected a printing press that made it possible to fabricate books more cheaply, more rapidly, and in greater numbers than ever before (Figure **19.1**). As information became a commodity for mass production, vast areas of knowledge—heretofore the exclusive domain of the monastery, the Church, and the university—became available to the public. The printing press facilitated the rise of popular education and encouraged individuals to form their own opinions by reading for themselves. Print technology proved to be the single most important factor in the success of the Protestant Reformation, as it brought the complaints of Church reformers to the attention of all literate folk. And, in the wake of such writers as Dante, Chaucer, Petrarch, and Boccaccio, the printing press nourished the growing interest in vernacular literature, which in turn enhanced national and individual self-consciousness.

Christian Humanism and the Northern Renaissance

The new print technology broadcast an old message of religious protest and reform. For two centuries, critics had attacked the wealth, worldliness, and unchecked corruption of the Church of Rome. During the early fifteenth century, the rekindled sparks of lay piety and anticlericalism spread throughout the Netherlands, where religious leaders launched the movement known as the *devotio moderna* ("modern devotion"). Lay Brothers and Sisters of the Common Life, as they were called, organized houses in which they studied and taught Scripture. Living in the manner of Christian monks and nuns, but taking no monastic vows, these lay Christians cultivated a devotional lifestyle that fulfilled the ideals of the apostles and the church fathers. They followed the mandate of Thomas a Kempis (1380–1471), himself a Brother of the Common Life and author of the *Imitatio Christi* (*Imitation of Christ*), to put the message of Jesus into daily practice.

The *devotio moderna* spread quickly throughout Northern Europe, harnessing the dominant strains of anticlericalism, lay piety, and mysticism, even as it coincided with the revival of classical studies in the newly established universities of Germany. Although Northern humanists, like their Italian Renaissance counterparts, encouraged learning in Greek and Latin, they were more concerned with the study and translation of Early Christian manuscripts than with the classical and largely secular texts that had preoccupied the Italian humanists.

1320	paper adopted for use in Europe (having long been in use in China)
1450	the Dutch devise the first firearm small enough to be carried by a single person
1451	Nicolas of Cusa (German) uses concave lenses to amend nearsightedness
1454	Johannes Gutenberg (German) prints the Bible with movable metal type

Figure 19.1 An early sixteenth century woodcut of a printer at work. Victoria and Albert Museum.

Northern humanists studied the Bible and the writings of the church fathers with the same intellectual fervor that the Italian humanists had brought to their examination of Plato and Cicero. The efforts of these Northern scholars gave rise to a rebirth (or renaissance) that focused on the late classical world and, specifically, on the revival of Church life and doctrine as gleaned from early Christian literature. The Northern Renaissance put Christian humanism at the service of evangelical Christianity.

The leading Christian humanist of the sixteenth century—often called "the Prince of Humanists"—was Desiderius Erasmus of Rotterdam (1466–1536; Figure **19.2**). Schooled among the Brothers of the Common Life and learned in Latin, Greek, and Hebrew, Erasmus was a superb scholar and a prolific writer (see Reading 3.22). The first humanist to make extensive use of the printing press, he once dared a famous publisher to print his words as fast as he could write them. Erasmus was a fervent neoclassicist—he argued that almost everything worth knowing was set forth in Greek and Latin. He was also a devout

Christian who advocated a return to the basic teachings of Christ. He criticized the Church and all Christians whose faith had been jaded by slavish adherence to dogma and ritual. Using four different Greek manuscripts of the Gospels, he produced a critical edition of the New Testament that corrected Jerome's mistranslations of key passages. Erasmus' New Testament became the source of most sixteenth-century German and English vernacular translations of this central text of Christian humanism.

Luther and the Protestant Reformation Medici Leo 10

During the sixteenth century, papal extravagance and immorality reached new heights, and Church reform became an urgent public issue. In the territories of Germany, loosely united under the leadership of the Holy Roman Emperor Charles V (1500–1558), the voices of protest were more strident than anywhere else in Europe. Across Germany, the sale of indulgences for the benefit of the Church of Rome—specifically for the rebuilding of Saint Peter's Cathedral—provoked harsh criticism,

Figure 19.2 ALBRECHT DÜRER. *Erasmus of Rotterdam*, 1526. Engraving. 9¾ × 7½ in. Reproduced by courtesy of the Trustees of the British Museum, London.

Heroic Values — Humanism
New medium — print

especially by those who saw the luxuries of the papacy as a betrayal of apostolic ideals. As with most movements of religious reform, it fell to one individual to galvanize popular sentiment. In 1505, Martin Luther (1483–1546), the son of a rural coal miner, abandoned his legal studies to become an Augustinian monk (Figure 19.3). Thereafter, as a doctor of theology at the University of Wittenberg, he spoke out against the Church. His inflammatory sermons and essays offered radical remedies to what he called "the misery and wretchedness of Christendom."

Luther was convinced of the inherent sinfulness of humankind, but he took issue with the traditional medieval view—as promulgated, for instance, in *Everyman* (see chapter 12)—that salvation was earned through the performance of good works and grace received through the intermediation of the Church and its priesthood. Inspired by the words of Saint Paul, "the just shall live by faith" (Romans 1:17), Luther maintained that salvation could be gained only by faith in the validity of Christ's sacrifice. Human beings were saved by the unearned gift of God's grace, argued Luther, not by their good works on earth. The purchase of indulgences, the veneration of relics, making pilgrimages, and seeking the intercession of the

saints were useless, because only the grace of God could save the Christian soul. Justified by faith alone, Christians should assume full responsibility for their own actions and intentions.

In 1517, in pointed criticism of Church abuses, Luther posted on the door of the cathedral of Wittenberg a list of ninety-five issues he intended for dispute with the leaders of the Church of Rome. The *Ninety-Five Theses*, which took the confrontational tone of the sample below, were put to press and circulated throughout Europe:

27 They are wrong who say that the soul flies out of Purgatory as soon as the money thrown into the chest rattles.

32 Those who believe that, through letters of pardon [indulgences], they are made sure of their own salvation will be eternally damned along with their teachers.

37 Every true Christian, whether living or dead, has a share in all the benefits of Christ and of the Church, given by God, even without letters of pardon.

43 Christians should be taught that he who gives to a poor man, or lends to a needy man, does better than if he bought pardons.

44 Because by works of charity, charity increases, and the man becomes better; while by means of pardons, he does not become better, but only freer from punishment.

45 Christians should be taught that he who sees any one in need, and, passing him by, gives money for pardons, is not purchasing for himself the indulgences of the Pope but the anger of God.

49 Christians should be taught that the Pope's pardons are useful if they do not put their trust in them, but most hurtful if through them they lose the fear of God.

50 Christians should be taught that if the Pope were acquainted with the exactions of the Preachers of pardons, he would prefer that the Basilica of St. Peter should be burnt to ashes rather than that it should be built up with the skin, flesh, and bones of his sheep.

54 Wrong is done to the Word of God when, in the same sermon, an equal or longer time is spent on pardons than on it.

62 The true treasure of the Church is the Holy Gospel of the glory and grace of God.

66 The treasures of indulgences are nets, wherewith they now fish for the riches of men.

67 Those indulgences which the preachers loudly proclaim to be the greatest graces, are seen to be truly such as regards the promotion of gain.

68 Yet they are in reality most insignificant when compared to the grace of God and the piety of the cross.

86 . . . why does not the Pope, whose riches are at this day more ample than those of the wealthiest of the wealthy, build the single Basilica of St. Peter

Figure 19.3 LUCAS CRANACH THE ELDER, *Portrait of Martin Luther.* 1533, panel, 8 × 5¾ in. City of Bristol Museum and Art Gallery.

with his own money rather than with that of poor believers? . . .*

Luther did not wish to destroy Catholicism, but rather to reform it. Gradually he extended his criticism of Church abuses to criticism of Church doctrine. For instance, because he found justification in Scripture for only two of the sacraments dispensed by the Catholic Church—Baptism and Holy Communion—he rejected the other five. He attacked monasticism and clerical celibacy, ultimately marrying a former nun and fathering six children. Luther's boldest challenge to the old medieval order, however, was his unwillingness to accept the pope as the ultimate source of religious authority. He denied that the pope was the spiritual heir to Saint Peter and claimed that the head of the Church, like any other human being, was subject to error and correction. Christians, argued Luther, were collectively a priesthood of believers; they were "consecrated as priests by baptism." The ultimate source of authority in matters of faith and doctrine, held Luther, was Scripture, as interpreted by the individual Christian. To encourage the reading of the Bible among his followers, Luther translated the Old and New Testaments into German.

Luther's assertions were revolutionary because they defied both Church dogma and the authority of the Church of Rome. In 1520, Pope Leo X issued an edict excommunicating the outspoken reformer. Luther promptly burned the edict in the presence of his students at the University of Wittenberg. The following year, he was summoned to the city of Worms in order to appear before the Diet—the German parliamentary council. Charged with heresy, Luther stubbornly refused to recant. His confrontational temperament and down-to-earth style are captured in this excerpt from his *Address to the German Nobility*, a call for religious reform written shortly before the Diet of Worms and circulated widely in a printed edition.

READING 3.21 From Luther's *Address to the German Nobility* (1520)

It has been devised that the Pope, bishops, priests, and monks are called the *spiritual estate*; princes, lords, artificers, and peasants are the *temporal estate*. This is an artful lie and hypocritical device, but let no one be made afraid by it, and that for this reason: that all Christians are truly of the spiritual estate, and there is no difference among them, save of office alone. As St. Paul says (1 Cor.: 12), we are all one body, though each member does its own work, to serve the others. This is because we have one baptism, one Gospel, one faith, and are all Christians alike; for baptism, Gospel, and faith, these alone make spiritual and Christian people. [10]

---

*J. H. Robinson, ed., *Translations and Reprints from the Original Sources of European History*, II. No. 6. Philadelphia: University of Pennsylvania Press, 1894.

As for the unction by a pope or a bishop, tonsure, ordination, consecration, and clothes differing from those of laymen—all this may make a hypocrite or an anointed puppet, but never a Christian or a spiritual man. Thus we are all consecrated as priests by baptism. . . .

And to put the matter even more plainly, if a little company of pious Christian laymen were taken prisoners and carried away to a desert, and had not among them a priest consecrated by a bishop, and were there to agree to elect one of them, born in wedlock or not, and were to order him to baptise, to celebrate the mass, to absolve, and to preach, this man would as truly be a priest, as if all the bishops and all the popes had consecrated him. That is why in cases of necessity every man can baptise and absolve, which would not be possible if we were not all priests. . . . [20]

[Members of the Church of Rome] alone pretend to be considered masters of the Scriptures; although they learn nothing of them all their life. They assume authority, and juggle before us with impudent words, saying that the Pope cannot err in matters of faith, whether he be evil or good, albeit they cannot prove it by a single letter. That is why the canon law contains so many heretical and unchristian, nay unnatural, laws. . . . [30]

. . . And though they say that this authority was given to St. Peter when the keys were given to him, it is plain enough that the keys were not given to St. Peter alone, but to the whole community. Besides, the keys were not ordained for doctrine or authority, but for sin, to bind or loose; and what they claim besides this from the keys is mere invention. . . . [40]

Only consider the matter. They must needs acknowledge that there are pious Christians among us that have the true faith, spirit, understanding, word, and mind of Christ: why then should we reject their word and understanding, and follow a pope who has neither understanding nor spirit? Surely this were to deny our whole faith and the Christian Church. . . .

Therefore when need requires, and the Pope is a cause of offence to Christendom, in these cases whoever can best do so, as a faithful member of the whole body, must do what he can to procure a true free council. This no one can do so well as the temporal authorities, especially since they are fellow-Christians, fellow-priests, sharing one spirit and one power in all things, . . . Would it not be most unnatural, if a fire were to break out in a city, and every one were to keep still and let it burn on and on, whatever might be burnt, simply because they had not the mayor's authority, or because the fire perchance broke out at the mayor's house? Is not every citizen bound in this case to rouse and call in the rest? How much more should this be done in the spiritual city of Christ, if a fire of offence breaks out, either at the Pope's government or wherever it may! The like happens if an enemy attacks a town. The first to rouse up the rest earns glory and thanks. Why then should not he earn glory that decries the coming of our enemies from hell and rouses and summons all Christians? [50] [60]

But as for their boasts of their authority, that no one must oppose it, this is idle talk. No one in Christendom [70] has any authority to do harm, or to forbid others to prevent harm being done. There is no authority in the Church but for reformation. Therefore if the Pope wished to use his power to prevent the calling of a free council, so as to prevent the reformation of the Church, we must not respect him or his power; and if he should begin to excommunicate and fulminate, we must despise this as the doings of a madman, and, trusting in God, excommunicate and repel him as best we may. . . .   **80**

The Spread of Protestantism

Luther's criticism constituted an open revolt against the institution that for centuries had governed the lives of Western Christians. With the aid of the printing press, his "protestant" sermons circulated throughout Europe. Luther's defense of Christian conscience as opposed to episcopal authority worked to justify protest against all forms of dominion. In 1524, under the banner of Christian liberty, German commoners instigated a series of violent uprisings against the oppressive landholding aristocracy. The result was full-scale war, the so-called "Peasant Revolts," that resulted in the bloody defeat of thousands of peasants. Although Luther condemned the violence and brutality of the Peasant Revolts, social unrest and ideological warfare had only just begun. His denunciation of the lower classes rebels brought many of the German princes to his side; and some used their new religious allegiance as an excuse to seize and usurp Church properties and revenues within their own domains. As the floodgates of dissent opened wide, civil wars broke out between German princes who were faithful to Rome and those who called themselves Lutheran. The wars lasted for some twenty-five years, until, by the terms of the Peace of Augsburg in 1555, it was agreed that each German prince should have the right to choose the religion to be practiced within his own domain. But religious wars resumed in the late sixteenth century and devastated German lands for almost a century.

All of Europe was affected by Luther's break with the Church. The Lutheran insistence that enlightened Christians could arrive at truth by way of Scripture led reformers everywhere to interpret the Bible for themselves. The result was the birth of many new Protestant sects, each based on its own interpretation of Scripture. In the independent city of Geneva, Switzerland, the French theologian John Calvin (1509–1564) set up a government in which elected officials, using the Bible as the supreme law, ruled the community. Calvin held that Christians were predestined from birth for either salvation or damnation, a circumstance that made good works irrelevant. The "Doctrine of Predestination" encouraged Calvinists to glorify God by living an upright life, one that required abstention from dancing, gambling, swearing, drunkenness, and from all forms of public display. For, although one's status was known only by God, Christians might manifest that they were among the "elect" by a show of moral rectitude. Finally, since Calvin taught that wealth was a sign of God's favor, Calvinists extolled the "work ethic" as consistent with the divine will.

In nearby Zürich, a radical wing of Protestantism emerged: The Anabaptists (given this name by those who opposed their practice of "rebaptizing" adult Christians) rejected all seven of the sacraments (including infant baptism) as sources of God's grace. Placing total emphasis on Christian conscience and the voluntary acceptance of Christ, the Anabaptists called for the abolition of the Mass and the complete separation of church and state; Holding individual responsibility and personal liberty as fundamental ideals, they were among the first Westerners to offer religious sanction for political disobedience. Many Anabaptist reformers met death at the hands of local governments—the men were burned at the stake and the women were usually drowned. English offshoots of the Anabaptists—the Baptists and the Quakers—would come to follow Anabaptist precepts, including the rejection of religious ritual (and imagery) and a fundamentalist approach to Scripture.

In England, the Tudor monarch Henry VIII (1491–1547) broke with the Roman Catholic Church and established a church under his own leadership. Political expediency colored the king's motives: Henry was determined to leave England with a male heir, but when eighteen years of marriage to Catherine of Aragon produced only one heir (a female), he attempted to annul the marriage and take a new wife. The pope refused, prompting the king—formerly a staunch supporter of the Catholic Church—to break with Rome. In 1526, Henry VIII declared himself head of the Church in England. His actions led to years of dispute and hostility between Roman Catholics and Anglicans (members of the new English Church). By the mid-sixteenth century, the consequences of Luther's protests were evident: The religious unity of Western Christendom was shattered forever. Social and political upheaval had become the order of the day.

Music and the Reformation

Since the Reformation clearly dominated the religious and social history of the sixteenth century, it also touched, directly or indirectly, all forms of artistic endeavor, including music. Luther himself was a student of music, an active performer, and an admirer of Josquin des Prez. Emphasizing music as a source of religious instruction, he encouraged the writing of hymnals and reorganized the German Mass to include both congregational and professional singing. Luther held that all religious texts should be sung in German, so that the faithful might understand their message. The text, according to Luther, should be both comprehensible and appealing. Luther's favorite music was the **chorale**, a congregational hymn that served to enhance the spirit of Protestant worship. Chorales, written in German, drew on Latin hymns and German folk tunes. They were characterized by monophonic clarity and simplicity, features that encouraged performance by untrained congregations. The most famous Lutheran chorale (the melody of which may not have originated with Luther) is *Ein' feste Burg ist unser Gott* (*A Mighty Fortress is our God*)—a hymn that has been called "the anthem of the

Reformation." ♪ Luther's chorales had a major influence on religious music for centuries. And although in the hands of later composers the chorale became a complex polyphonic vehicle for voices and instruments, at its inception it was performed with all voices singing the same words at the same time. It was thus an ideal medium for the communal expression of Protestant piety. Other Protestant sects, such as the Anabaptists and the Calvinists, regarded music as a potentially dangerous distraction to the faithful. In many sixteenth-century churches, the organ was dismantled and sung portions of the service edited or deleted. Calvin, however, who encouraged devotional recitation of psalms in the home, revised church services to include the congregational singing of psalms in the vernacular.

Northern Renaissance Art

The austerity of the Protestant reform cast its long shadow upon Church art. Protestants abandoned the traditional images of medieval piety, rejecting relics and sacred images as sources of superstition and idolatry. In Northern Europe, Protestant **iconoclasts** stripped the stained glass from Catholic churches, shattered statues, whitewashed church

---

♪ This Lutheran chorale inspired Johann Sebastian Bach's Cantata No. 80, an excerpt from which may be heard on CD Two, as Music Listening Selection Number 4.

frescoes, and destroyed altarpieces. At the same time, however, Protestant reformers encouraged the proliferation of private devotional imagery—biblical subjects in particular.

Secular subject matter provided abundant inspiration for Northern artists. Portraiture, a favorite genre of the pre-Reformation master Jan van Eyck (see Figures 17.13, 17.14), remained popular among such sixteenth-century artists as Albrecht Dürer of Nuremberg (1471–1528), Lucas Cranach the Elder (1472–1553), and Hans Holbein the Younger (1497–1543), three of the greatest draftsmen of the Renaissance (see Figures 19.2, 19.3, 19.15). The natural world also intrigued artists: Dürer introduced landscape painting into Western art. His panoramic landscapes, often rendered in watercolors, were to be enjoyed for themselves (Figure **19.4**), rather than as settings for sacred or secular subjects (compare Figures 17.15, 17.28, 17.42). To these landscapes, as well as to his detailed studies of animals, birds, and plants, Dürer brought the eye of a scientific naturalist. Finally, the Flemish painter Pieter Brueghel the Elder (1525–1569) carried the tradition of the cosmic landscape to its peak in large panel paintings that describe the everyday labors of European peasants.

Dürer and Printmaking

Paralleling the invention of movable type, there developed in Northern Europe a technology for reproducing images more cheaply and in greater numbers than ever

Figure 19.4 ALBRECHT DÜRER, *Wire Drawing Mill*, undated, watercolour, Staatliche Museen zu Berlin Photo: B. P. K.

Figure 19.5 ALBRECHT DÜRER, *The Four Horsemen of the Apocalypse*, ca. 1496. Woodcut, 15½ × 11 in. Museum of Fine Arts, Boston.

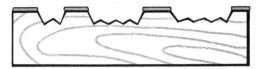

Figure 19.6 Woodcut. A relief printing process created by lines cut into the plank surface of wood. The raised portions of the block are inked and transferred by pressure to the paper by hand or with a printing press.

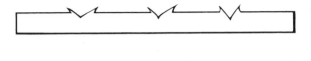

Figure 19.7 Engraving. An intaglio method of printing. The cutting tool, a *burin* or *graver*, is used to cut lines in the surface of metal plates. (a) A cross-section of an engraved plate showing burrs (ridges) produced by scratching a burin into the surface of a metal plate; (b) the burrs are removed and ink is wiped over the surface and forced into the scratches. The plate is then wiped clean, leaving ink deposits in the scratches; the ink is forced from the plate onto paper under pressure in a special press.

Figure 19.8 ALBRECHT DÜRER, *Knight, Death, and the Devil*, 1513. Engraving, 9⅝ × 7½ in. The Metropolitan Museum of Art, New York, Harris Brisbane Dick Fund, 1943.

before. The two new printmaking processes were **woodcut**, the technique of cutting away all parts of a design on a wood surface except those that will be inked and transferred to paper (Figure **19.6**), and **engraving** (Figure **19.7**), the process by which lines are incised on a metal (usually copper) plate that is inked and run through a printing press. These relatively inexpensive techniques of mass-producing images made possible the proliferation of book illustrations and individual prints for private devotional use. Books with printed illustrations became cheap alternatives to the hand-illuminated manuscripts that were prohibitively expensive to all but wealthy patrons.

The unassailed leader in Northern Renaissance printmaking and one of the finest graphic artists of all time was Albrecht Dürer. Dürer earned international fame for his woodcuts and metal engravings. His mastery of the laws of linear perspective and human anatomy and his investigations into classical principles of proportions (enhanced by two trips to Italy) equaled those of the best Italian Renaissance artist-scientists. In the genre of portraiture, Dürer was the match of Raphael but, unlike Raphael, he recorded the features of his sitters with little idealization. His portrait engraving of Erasmus (see Figure 19.2) captures the concentrated intelligence of the Prince of Humanists. Dürer included a Latin inscription confirming that the portrait was executed from life, but added modestly in Greek, "The better image is [found] in his writings."

Dürer brought to the art of his day a profoundly religious view of the world and a desire to embody the spiritual message of Scripture in art. The series of woodcuts he produced to illustrate the last book of the New Testament, *The Revelation* According to Saint John (also called the "Apocalypse"), reveals the extent to which Dürer achieved his purpose. Executed two decades before Luther's revolt, *The Four Horsemen* of the Apocalypse—one of fifteen woodcuts in the series—brings to life the terrify-

ing prophecies described in Revelation 6.1–8 (Figure **19.5**). Amidst billowing clouds, Death (in the foreground), Famine (carrying a pair of scales), War (brandishing a sword), and Pestilence (drawing his bow) sweep down upon humankind; their victims fall beneath the horses' hooves, or, as with the bishop in the lower left, are devoured by infernal monsters. Dürer's image seems a grim prophecy of the coming age, in which 5 million people would die in religious wars.

Dürer was a humanist in his own right and a great admirer of both the moderate Erasmus and the zealous Luther. In one of his most memorable engravings, *Knight, Death, and the Devil*, he depicted the Christian soul in the allegorical guise of a medieval knight (Figure **19.8**), a figure made famous in a treatise by Erasmus entitled *Handbook for the Militant Christian* (1504). The knight, the medieval symbol of fortitude and courage, advances against a dark and brooding landscape. Accompanied by his loyal dog, he marches forward, ignoring his fearsome companions: Death, who rides a pale horse and carries an hourglass, and the devil, a shaggy, cross-eyed, and horned demon. Here is the visual counterpart for Erasmus' message that the Christian must hold to the path of virtue, and in spite of "all of those spooks and phantoms" that come upon him, he must "look not behind." The knight's dignified bearing (probably inspired by heroic equestrian statues Dürer had seen in Italy) contrasts sharply with the bestial and cankerous features of his forbidding escorts. Dürer's engraving is remarkable for its wealth of microscopic detail. In the tradition of Jan van Eyck, but with a precision facilitated by the medium of metal engraving, Dürer records with scientific precision every leaf and pebble, hair and wrinkle; and yet the final effect is not a mere piling up of minutiae but, like nature itself, an astonishing amalgam of organically related substances.

The Paintings of Grünewald, Bosch, and Brueghel

Whether Catholic or Protestant, sixteenth-century Northern artists brought to religious subject matter spiritual intensity and emotional subjectivity that were uncharacteristic of Italian art. With the exception of Dürer, whose monumental paintings betray his admiration for classically proportioned figures and the Italianate unity of design, Northern Renaissance artists shared few of the aesthetic ideals of the Italian Renaissance masters. In the paintings of the German artist Matthias Gothardt Neithardt, better known as "Grünewald" (1460–1528), naturalistic detail and brutal distortion produced a highly expressive style. Grünewald's *Crucifixion* (Figure **19.9**),

the central panel of the multipaneled Isenheim Altarpiece, emphasizes the physical suffering of Christ, a devotional subject that might have provided solace to the disease victims at the hospital for which this work was commissioned. In the manner of his anonymous fourteenth-century German predecessor (compare Figure 15.10), Grünewald rejects harmonious proportion and figural idealization in favor of exaggeration and painfully precise detail: The agonized body of Jesus is lengthened to emphasize its weight as it hangs from the bowed cross, the flesh putrefies with clotted blood and angry thorns, the fingers convulse and curl, while the feet—broken and bruised—contort in a spasm of pain. Grünewald reinforces the mood of lamentation by placing the scene in a darkened landscape. He exaggerates the gestures of the attending figures, including that of John the Baptist, whose oversized finger points to the prophetic Latin inscription that explains his mystical presence: "He must increase and I must decrease" (John 3:30). A comparison of this painting with, for instance, Masaccio's *Trinity* (see Figure 17.18) provides a study in contrasts between German and Italian sensibilities in the age of the Renaissance.

Figure 19.9 MATTHIAS GRÜNEWALD, *Crucifixion*, central panel of the Isenheim Altarpiece, ca. 1510–1515. Oil on panel, 8 ft. × 10 ft. 1 in. Museé d'Unterlinden, Colmar, France. Photo: O. Zimmerman.

More difficult to interpret are the works of the extraordinary Flemish artist Hieronymus Bosch (1460–1516). Like Grünewald, Bosch was preoccupied with matters of sin and salvation. Bosch's *Death and the Miser* (Figure **19.10**), for instance, belongs to the tradition of the *memento mori* (discussed in chapter 12), which works to warn the beholder of the inevitability of death. The painting also shows the influence of popular fifteenth-century handbooks on the art of dying (the *ars moriendi*), designed to remind Christians that they must choose between sinful pleasures and the way of Christ. As Death looms on his threshold, the miser, unable to resist worldly temptations even in his last minutes of life, reaches for the bag of gold offered to him by a demon. In the foreground, Bosch depicts the miser storing gold in his money chest while clutching his rosary. Symbols of worldly power—a helmet, sword, and shield—allude to earthly follies. The depiction of such still-life objects to symbolize earthly vanity, transience, or decay would become a genre in itself among seventeenth-century Flemish artists.

Bosch's most famous work, *The Garden of Earthly Delights*—executed around 1510, the very time that Raphael was painting *The School of Athens*—underscores the enormous contrast between Renaissance art in Italy and in Northern Europe. Whereas Raphael celebrates the nobility and dignity of the human being, Bosch contemplates the inconstancy and degeneracy of humankind. In Bosch's **triptych** (a three-paneled painting), the Creation of Adam and Eve (left) and the Tortures of Hell (right) flank a central panel whose iconographic meaning is obscure (Figure **19.11**). Here, in an imaginary landscape, youthful nude men and women cavort in erotic pastimes, dallying affectionately with each other or with oversized flora and fauna that teeter between the fantastic and the actual. The scene, a veritable "Garden of Delights," may be an exposition on the lustful behavior of the descendants of Adam and Eve. But in this central panel, as in the scenes of Creation and Hell, Bosch has turned his back on convention—a circumstance probably related to the fact that the triptych was commissioned not by the Church but by a private patron. His imagery, the subject of endless scholarly interpretation, derives from many sources, including astrology and alchemy, both pseudosciences of some repute in Bosch's time. Astrology, the study of the influence of heavenly bodies on human affairs, and alchemy, the art of distillation (employed by apothecaries as well as by quacks who sought to transmute base metals into gold), attracted new attention when Islamic writings on both were introduced into late medieval Europe. Both, moreover, became subjects of serious study during the sixteenth century. Symbolic of the Renaissance quest to understand the operations of the material world, astrology (the ancestor of astronomy) and alchemy (precursor to

Ars
Memoria

Figure 19.10 HIERONYMUS BOSCH, *Death and the Miser,* ca. 1485–1490. Oil on oak, 36⅝ × 12⅛ in. © 2000 Board of Trustees, National Gallery of Art, Washington, D.C. Samuel H. Kress Collection.

Figure 19.11 HIERONYMUS BOSCH, *The Creation of Eve: The Garden of Earthly Delights: Hell* (triptych), ca. 1510–1515. Oil on wood, 7 ft. 2⅜ in. × 6 ft. 4¾ in. (center panel), 7 ft. 2⅜ in. × 3 ft. 2¼ in. (each side panel). © Museo del Prado, Madrid.

chemistry) figured frequently in the works of sixteenth-century artists and writers.

In *The Garden of Earthly Delights*, egg-shaped vessels, beakers, transparent tubes, and other alchemical devices reflect Bosch's familiarity with both the equipment and the distillation process that were used in experimental transmutation. Bosch seems to have embraced alchemy—and especially the cyclical process of creation and destruction central to that pseudoscience—as a metaphor for the Christian myth of the Creation and Fall. The creatures of this garden participate in the mysteries of procreation, indulging their physical impulses with little regard for the inevitable consequences of their actions: the devastating punishments of Hell depicted in the right panel.

The fantastic demons in Bosch's Hell are products of an age that found the supernatural in natural and ordinary guises. Indeed, the witch-hunts that infested Europe (and especially Germany) during the sixteenth century were fueled by the popular belief that the devil was actively involved in human affairs. Belief in witches dates back to humankind's earliest communities; however, the business of persecuting witches did not begin until the late fourteenth century. The first massive persecutions occurred at the end of the fifteenth century and reached their peak approximately one hundred years later. In 1484, two theologians published the *Malleus Maleficarum* (*Witches' Hammer*), an encyclopedia that described the nature of witches, their collusion with the devil, and the ways by which they were to be recognized and punished. Since women were traditionally regarded as inherently susceptible to the devil's temptations, they became the primary victims of this mass hysteria. Women—especially single, old, and eccentric women—constituted four-fifths of the witches executed between the fifteenth and early seventeenth centuries. The German artist Hans Baldung, called "Grien" (ca. 1484–1545), was one of a number of Northern Renaissance artists who portrayed the activities of witches in painting and prints (Figure **19.12**). The witchcraft craze of this period dramatizes the prevailing gap between Christian humanism and rationalism on the one hand and barbarism and superstition on the other. Whether viewed as an instrument of post-Reformation political oppression, as the intensification of anti-female sentiment, or as the expression of the darker side of religious fanaticism, the witch-hunts of the early modern era force us to question the very notion of human progress.

The realities of violence, prejudice, and immorality did not go uncriticized among sixteenth-century Northern European artists. Bosch's contemporary, Pieter Brueghel the Elder, produced numerous paintings and prints that were cloaked condemnations of human folly, immorality, and war. Brueghel's *Triumph of Death* (Figure **19.13**), for instance, may be read as an indictment of the brutal wars that plagued sixteenth-century Europe: In a panoramic landscape that resembles the setting for a Last Judgment or a Bosch hell scene, Brueghel depicts armies of skeletons relentlessly slaughtering the living at work and at play. Some are crushed beneath the wheels of a death cart, while others are subjected to torture and execution. Not

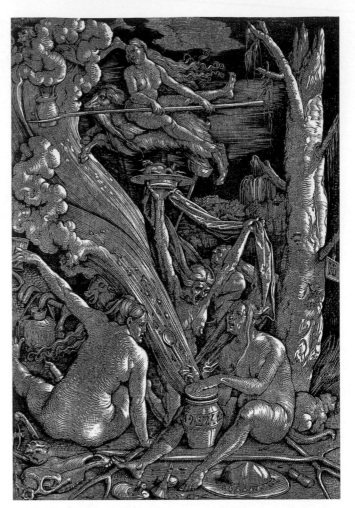

Figure 19.12 HANS BALDUNG ("Grien"), *Witches*, 1510. *Chiaroscuro* woodcut, 15⅛ × 10¼ in. Louvre, Paris. Collection Rothschild. Photo: © R.M.N., Paris.

divine judgment but human destiny rules here. Indeed, in Brueghel's hands, the late medieval Dance of Death (see chapter 15) has become a universal holocaust.

The last of the great sixteenth-century Flemish painters, Brueghel had traveled widely in Renaissance Italy; however, his paintings reflect only a passing interest in classical themes. His preoccupation with the details of rustic life, which earned him the title "Peasant Brueghel," continued the tradition of such medieval illuminators as the Limbourg brothers (see Figure 15.13). However, Brueghel's **genre paintings** (representations of the everyday life of ordinary folk) were not small-scale illustrations, but monumental (and sometimes allegorical) transcriptions of rural activities. *The Wedding Dance* (Figure **19.14**) depicts peasant revelry in a country setting whose earthiness is reinforced by rich tones of russet, tan, and muddy green. At the very top of the panel the bride and groom sit before an improvised dais, while the villagers cavort to the music of the bagpipe (right foreground). Although Brueghel's figures are clumsy and often ill proportioned, they share an ennobling vitality. In Brueghel's art, as in that of many other Northern Renaissance painters, we discover an unvarnished perception of the individual in mundane and unheroic circumstances—a sharp contrast to the idealized image of humankind found in the art of Renaissance Italy.

Figure 19.13 PIETER BRUEGHEL THE ELDER, *Triumph of Death*, ca. 1562–1564. Oil on panel, 3 ft. 10 in. × 5 ft. 3¾ in. © Museo del Prado, Madrid.

Northern Renaissance Literature

Erasmus and More

European literature of the sixteenth century was marked by heightened individualism and a progressive inclination to clear away the last remnants of medieval orthodoxy. It was, in many ways, a literature of protest and reform, and one whose dominant themes reflect the tension between medieval and modern ideas. European writers were especially concerned with the discrepancies between the noble ideals of classical humanism and the ignoble realities of human behavior. Religious rivalries and the horrors of war, witch-hunts, and religious persecution all seemed to contradict the optimistic view that the Renaissance had inaugurated a more enlightened phase of human self-consciousness. Satire, a literary genre that conveys the contradictions between real and ideal situations, was especially popular during the sixteenth century. By means of satiric irony, Northern Renaissance writers held up prevailing abuses to ridicule, thus implying the need for reform.

The scholarly treatises and letters of Desiderius Erasmus won him the respect of scholars throughout Europe; but his single most popular work was *The Praise of Folly*, a satiric oration attacking a wide variety of human foibles, including greed, intellectual pomposity, and pride. *The Praise of Folly*, which went through more than two dozen editions in Erasmus' lifetime, influenced other humanists, including Erasmus' lifelong friend and colleague Thomas More, to whom it was dedicated (in Latin, *moria* means "folly"). A short excerpt from *The Praise of Folly* offers

1540 the Swiss physician Paracelsus (Philippus van Hohenheim) pioneers the use of chemistry for medical purposes

1543 Copernicus (Polish) publishes *On the Revolution of the Heavenly Spheres*, announcing his heliocentric theory

1553 Michael Servetus (Spanish) describes the pulmonary circulation of the blood

Figure 19.14
**PIETER BRUEGHEL
THE ELDER**, *The
Wedding Dance*,
1566. Oil on panel,
3 ft. 11 in. × 5 ft 2 in.
Photo: © 2000 The
Detroit Institute of
Arts. City of Detroit
Purchase. 30.374.

some idea of Erasmus' keen wit as applied to a typical Northern Renaissance theme: the vast gulf between human fallibility and human perfectibility. The excerpt opens with the image of the world as a stage, a favorite metaphor of sixteenth-century painters and poets—not the least of whom was William Shakespeare. Folly, the allegorical figure who is the speaker in the piece, compares life to a comedy in which the players assume various roles: In the course of the drama (she observes), one may come to play the parts of both beggar and king. The lecturer then describes each of a number of roles (or disciplines), such as medicine, law, and so on, in terms of its affinity with folly. Erasmus' most searing words were reserved for theologians and church dignitaries, but his insights expose more generally (and timelessly) the frailties of all human beings.

READING 3.22   From Erasmus' *The Praise of Folly* (1511)

Now what else is the whole life of mortals but a sort of comedy, in which the various actors, disguised by various costumes and masks, walk on and play each one his part, until the manager waves them off the stage? Moreover, this manager frequently bids the same actor go back in a different costume, so that he who has but lately played the king in scarlet now acts the flunkey in patched clothes. Thus all things are presented by shadows; yet this play is put on in no other way. . . .
    [The disciplines] that approach nearest to common   10

sense, that is, to folly, are held in highest esteem. Theologians are starved, naturalists find cold comfort, astrologers are mocked, and logicians are slighted. . . . Within the profession of medicine, furthermore, so far as any member is eminently unlearned, impudent, or careless, he is valued the more, even in the chambers of belted earls. For medicine, especially as now practiced by many, is but a subdivision of the art of flattery, no less truly than is rhetoric. Lawyers have the next place after doctors, and I do not know but that they should   20 have first place; with great unanimity the philosophers— not that I would say such a thing myself—are wont to ridicule the law as an ass. Yet great matters and little matters alike are settled by the arbitrament of these asses. They gather goodly freeholds with broad acres, while the theologian, after poring over chestfuls of the great corpus of divinity, gnaws on bitter beans, at the same time manfully waging war against lice and fleas. As those arts are more successful which have the greatest affinity with folly, so those people are by far the happiest   30 who enjoy the privilege of avoiding all contact with the learned disciplines, and who follow nature as their only guide, since she is in no respect wanting, except as a mortal wishes to transgress the limits set for his status. Nature hates counterfeits; and that which is innocent of art gets along far the more prosperously.
    What need we say about practitioners in the arts? Self-love is the hallmark of them all. You will find that they would sooner give up their paternal acres than any piece of their poor talents. Take particularly actors, singers,   40 orators, and poets; the more unskilled one of them is,

1

the more insolent he will be in his self-satisfaction, the more he will blow himself up. . . . Thus the worst art pleases the most people, for the simple reason that the larger part of mankind, as I said before, is subject to folly. If, therefore, the less skilled man is more pleasing both in his own eyes and in the wondering gaze of the many, what reason is there that he should prefer sound discipline and true skill? In the first place, these will cost him a great outlay; in the second place, they will make him more affected and meticulous; and finally, they will please far fewer of his audience. . . .

In England Erasmus' friend, the scholar and statesman Sir Thomas More (1478–1535), served as chancellor to King Henry VIII at the time of Henry's break with the Catholic Church (Figure **19.15**). Like Erasmus, More was a Christian humanist and a man of conscience. He denounced the modern evils of acquisitive capitalism and religious fanaticism and championed religious tolerance and Christian charity. Unwilling to compromise his position as a Roman Catholic, he opposed the actions of the king and was executed for treason in 1535.

In 1516, More completed his classic political satire on European statecraft and society, a work entitled *Utopia* (the Greek word meaning both "no place" and "a good place"). More's *Utopia*, the first literary description of an ideal state since Plato's *Republic*, was inspired, in part, by accounts of wondrous lands reported by sailors returning

Figure 19.15 HANS HOLBEIN THE YOUNGER, *Sir Thomas More*, ca. 1530. Oil on panel, 29½ × 23¼ in. © The Frick Collection, New York. Holbein's superb portrait reveals a visionary and a man of conscience ("a man for all seasons"), who died at the hands of Henry VIII rather than compromise his religious convictions.

from the "New World" across the Atlantic (see chapter 18). More's fictional island ("discovered" by a fictional explorer-narrator) is a socialistic state in which goods and property are shared, war and personal vanities are held in contempt, learning is available to all citizens (except slaves), and freedom of religion is absolute. In this ideal commonwealth, natural reason, benevolence, and scorn for material wealth ensure social harmony. More's ideal society differs from Plato's in that More gives to each individual, rather than to society's guardians, full responsibility for the establishment of social justice. Like Alberti (and Calvin), More regarded work—limited in Utopia to six hours a day—as essential to moral and communal well-being. Fundamental to *Utopia* as satire is the implicit contrast More draws between his own corrupt Christian society and that of his ideal community; although More's Utopians are not Christians, they are guided by Christian principles of morality and charity. They have little use, for instance, for precious metals, jewels, and the "trifles" that drive men to war.

READING 3.23 From More's *Utopia* (1516)

[As] to their manner of living in society, the oldest man of every family . . . is its governor. Wives serve their husbands, and children their parents, and always the younger serves the elder. Every city is divided into four equal parts, and in the middle of each there is a marketplace; what is brought thither, and manufactured by the several families, is carried from thence to houses appointed for that purpose, in which all things of a sort are laid by themselves; and there every father goes and takes whatsoever he or his family stand in need of, without either paying for it or leaving anything in exchange. There is no reason for giving a denial to any person, since there is such plenty of everything among them; and there is no danger of a man's asking for more than he needs; they have no inducements to do this, since they are sure that they shall always be supplied. It is the fear of want that makes any of the whole race of animals either greedy or ravenous; but besides fear, there is in man a pride that makes him fancy it a particular glory to excel others in pomp and excess. But by the laws of the Utopians, there is no room for this. . . .

[Since the Utopians] have no use for money among themselves, but keep it as a provision against events which seldom happen, and between which there are generally long intervening intervals, they value it no farther than it deserves, that is, in proportion to its use. So that it is plain they must prefer iron either to gold or silver; for men can no more live without iron than without fire or water, but nature has marked out no use for the other metals so essential and not easily to be dispensed with. The folly of men has enhanced the value of gold and silver, because of their scarcity. Whereas, on the contrary, it is their opinion that nature, as an indulgent parent, has freely given us all the best things in great abundance, such as water and earth, but has

1

10

20

30

50

laid up and hid from us the things that are vain and useless. . . .

. . . They eat and drink out of vessels of earth, or glass, which make an agreeable appearance though formed of brittle materials: while they make their chamber-pots and close-stools[1] of gold and silver, and that not only in their public halls, but in their private houses: of the same metals they likewise make chains and fetters for their slaves; to some [slaves], as a badge of infamy, they hang an ear-ring of gold, and [they] make others wear a chain or coronet of the same metal; and thus they take care, by all possible means, to render gold and silver of no esteem. And from hence it is that while other nations part with their gold and silver as unwillingly as if one tore out their bowels, those of Utopia would look on their giving in all they possess of those [metals] but as the parting with a trifle, or as we would esteem the loss of a penny. They find pearls on their coast, and diamonds and carbuncles on their rocks; they do not look after them, but, if they find them by chance, they polish them, and with them they adorn their children, who are delighted with them, and glory in them during their childhood; but when they grow to years, and see that none but children use such baubles, they of their own accord, without being bid by their parents, lay them aside; and would be as much ashamed to use them afterward as children among us, when they come to years, are of their puppets and other toys. . . .

40

50

60

The Wit of Cervantes

While Erasmus and More wrote primarily in Latin—*Utopia* was not translated into English until 1551—other European writers favored the vernacular. The satiric novel and the essay, two new literary genres, were written in the language of everyday speech that sent defiant messages of social criticism. In Spain, Miguel de Cervantes (1547–1616) wrote *Don Quijote*, a novel that satirizes the outworn values of the Middle Ages as personified in a legendary Spanish hero. *Don Quijote* was not the first novel in world literature—the Chinese and Japanese had been writing novels since the eleventh century (see chapter 14)—but it was among the earliest Western examples of prose fiction in which a series of episodes converged on a fundamental theme. A chivalrous knight in an age of statecraft, the fifty-year-old Alonso Quixado, who changes his name to Don Quijote de la Mancha, sets out to defend the ideals glorified in medieval books of chivalry and romance. (Such ideals may have been valued by Cervantes himself, who had fought in the last Crusade against the Muslim Turks.) Seeking to right all wrongs, and misperceiving the ordinary for the sublime, the Don pursues a long series of misadventures, including an armed attack on windmills which he thinks are giants—the episode inspired the expression "to tilt at windmills." After his illusions of grandeur are exposed, the hero laments that the world is "nothing but schemes and plots."

---
[1] A covered chamber pot set in a stool.

The great success won by our brave Don Quijote in his dreadful, unimaginable encounter with two windmills, plus other honorable events well worth remembering

Just then, they came upon thirty or forty windmills, which (as it happens) stand in the fields of Montiel, and as soon as Don Quijote saw them he said to his squire:

"Destiny guides our fortunes more favorably than we could have expected. Look there, Sancho Panza, my friend, and see those thirty or so wild giants, with whom I intend to do battle and to kill each and all of them, so with their stolen booty we can begin to enrich ourselves. This is noble, righteous warfare, for it is wonderfully useful to God to have such an evil race wiped from the face of the earth."

"What giants?" asked Sancho Panza.

"The ones you can see over there," answered his master, "with the huge arms, some of which are very nearly two leagues long."

"Now look, your grace," said Sancho, "what you see over there aren't giants, but windmills, and what seem to be arms are just their sails, that go around in the wind and turn the millstone."

"Obviously," replied Don Quijote, "you don't know much about adventures. Those are giants—and if you're frightened, take yourself away from here and say your prayers, while I go charging into savage and unequal combat with them."

Saying which, he spurred his horse, Rocinante, paying no attention to the shouts of Sancho Panza, his squire, warning him that without any question it was windmills and not giants he was going to attack. So utterly convinced was he they were giants, indeed, that he neither heard Sancho's cries nor noticed, close as he was, what they really were, but charged on, crying:

"Flee not, oh cowards and dastardly creatures, for he who attacks you is a knight alone and unaccompanied."

Just then the wind blew up a bit, and the great sails began to stir, which Don Quijote saw and cried out:

"Even should you shake more arms than the giant Briareus himself, you'll still have to deal with me."

As he said this, he entrusted himself with all his heart to his lady Dulcinea, imploring her to help and sustain him at such a critical moment, and then, with his shield held high and his spear braced in its socket, and Rocinante at a full gallop, he charged directly at the first windmill he came to, just as a sudden swift gust of wind sent its sail swinging hard around, smashing the spear to bits and sweeping up the knight and his horse, tumbling them all battered and bruised to the ground. Sancho Panza came rushing to his aid, as fast as his donkey could run, but when he got to his master found him unable to move, such a blow had he been given by the falling horse.

1

10

20

30

40

50

"God help me!" said Sancho. "Didn't I tell your grace to be careful what you did, that these were just windmills, and anyone who could ignore that had to have windmills in his head?"

"Silence, Sancho, my friend," answered Don Quijote. "Even more than other things, war is subject to perpetual change. What's more, I think the truth is that the same Frestón the magician, who stole away my room and my books, transformed these giants into windmills, in order to deprive me of the glory of vanquishing them, so bitter is his hatred of me. But in the end, his evil tricks will have little power against my good sword."

"God's will be done," answered Sancho Panza.

Then, helping his master to his feet, he got him back up on Rocinante, whose shoulder was half dislocated. After which, discussing the adventure they'd just experienced, they followed the road toward Lápice Pass, for there, said Don Quijote, they couldn't fail to find adventures of all kinds, it being a well-traveled highway. But having lost his lance, he went along very sorrowfully, as he admitted to his squire, saying:

"I remember having read that a certain Spanish knight named Diego Pérez de Vargas, having lost his sword while fighting in a lost cause, pulled a thick bough, or a stem, off an oak tree, and did such things with it, that day, clubbing down so many moors that ever afterwards they nicknamed him Machuca [Clubber], and indeed from that day on he and all his descendants bore the name Vargas y Machuca. I tell you this because, the first oak tree I come to, I plan to pull off a branch like that, one every bit as good as the huge stick I can see in my mind, and I propose to perform such deeds with it that you'll be thinking yourself blessed, having the opportunity to witness them, and being a living witness to events that might otherwise be unbelievable."

"It's in God's hands," said Sancho. "I believe everything is exactly the way your grace says it is. But maybe you could sit a little straighter, because you seem to be leaning to one side, which must be because of the great fall you took."

"True," answered Don Quijote, "and if I don't say anything about the pain it's because knights errant are never supposed to complain about a wound, even if their guts are leaking through it."

"If that's how it's supposed to be," replied Sancho, "I've got nothing to say. But Lord knows I'd rather your grace told me, any time something hurts you. Me, I've got to groan, even if it's the smallest little pain, unless that rule about knights errant not complaining includes squires, too."

Don Quijote couldn't help laughing at his squire's simplicity, and cheerfully assured him he could certainly complain any time he felt like it, voluntarily or involuntarily, since in all his reading about knighthood and chivalry he'd never once come across anything to the contrary. Sancho said he thought it was dinner-time. His master replied that, for the moment, he himself had no need of food, but Sancho should eat whenever he wanted to. Granted this permission, Sancho made himself as comfortable as he could while jogging along on his donkey and, taking out of his saddlebags what he had put in them, began eating as he rode, falling back a good bit behind his master, and from time to time tilting up his wineskin with a pleasure so intense that the fanciest barman in Málaga might have envied him. And as he rode along like this, gulping quietly away, none of the promises his master had made were on his mind, nor did he feel in the least troubled or afflicted—in fact, he was thoroughly relaxed about this adventure-hunting business, no matter how dangerous it was supposed to be.

In the end, they spent that night sleeping in a wood, and Don Quijote pulled a dry branch from one of the trees, to serve him, more or less, as a lance, fitting onto it the spearhead he'd taken off the broken one. Nor did Don Quijote sleep, that whole night long, meditating on his lady Dulcinea—in order to fulfill what he'd read in his books, namely, that knights always spent long nights out in the woods and other uninhabited places, not sleeping, but happily mulling over memories of their ladies. Which wasn't the case for Sancho Panza: with his stomach full, and not just with chicory water, his dreams swept him away, nor would he have bothered waking up, for all the sunlight shining full on his face, or the birds singing—brightly, loudly greeting the coming of the new day—if his master hadn't called to him. He got up and, patting his wineskin, found it a lot flatter than it had been the night before, which grieved his heart, since it didn't look as if they'd be making up the shortage any time soon. Don Quijote had no interest in breakfast, since, as we have said, he had been sustaining himself with delightful memories. They returned to the road leading to Lápice Pass, which they could see by about three that afternoon.

"Here," said Don Quijote as soon as he saw it, "here, brother Sancho Panza, we can get our hands up to the elbows in adventures. But let me warn you: even if you see me experiencing the greatest dangers in the world, never draw your sword to defend me, unless of course you see that those who insult me are mere rabble, people of low birth, in which case you may be permitted to help me. But if they're knights, the laws of knighthood make it absolutely illegal, without exception, for you to help me, unless you yourself have been ordained a knight."

"Don't worry, your grace," answered Sancho Panza. "You'll find me completely obedient about this, especially since I'm a very peaceful man—I don't like getting myself into quarrels and fights. On the other hand, when it comes to someone laying a hand on me, I won't pay much attention to those laws, because whether they're divine or human they permit any man to defend himself when anyone hurts him."

"To be sure," answered Don Quijote. "But when it comes to helping me against other knights, you must restrain your natural vigor."

"And that's what I'll do," replied Sancho. "I'll observe this rule just as carefully as I keep the Sabbath. . . ."

Rabelais and Montaigne

In the earthier spirit of the prose burlesque, the French humanist François Rabelais (1495–1553) mocked the obsolete values of European society. Rabelais drew upon his experiences as a monk, a student of law, a physician, and a specialist in human affairs to produce *Gargantua and Pantagruel*, an irreverent satire filled with biting allusions to contemporary institutions and customs. The world of the two imaginary giants, Gargantua and Pantagruel, is one of fraud and folly drawn to fantastic dimensions. It is blighted by the absurdities of war, the evils of law and medicine, and the failure of scholastic education. To remedy the last, Rabelais advocates education based on experience and action, rather than rote memorization. In the imaginary Abbey of Thélème, the modern version of a medieval monastery, he pictures a coeducational commune in which well-bred men and women are encouraged to live as they please. *Gargantua and Pantagruel* proclaims Rabelais' faith in the ability of educated individuals to follow their best instincts for establishing a society free from religious prejudice, petty abuse, and selfish desire.

The French humanist Michel de Montaigne (1533–1592) was neither a satirist nor a reformer, but an educated aristocrat who believed in the paramount importance of cultivating good judgment. Trained in Latin, Montaigne was one of the leading proponents of classical learning in Renaissance France. But he earned universal acclaim as the father of the personal **essay**, a short piece of expository prose that examines a single subject or idea. The essay—the word comes from the French *essayer* ("to try")—is a vehicle for probing or "trying out" ideas. Indeed Montaigne regarded his ninety-four vernacular French essays as studies in autobiographical reflection—in them, he confessed, he portrayed himself. Addressing such subjects as virtue, friendship, old age, education, and idleness, Montaigne pursued certain fundamentally humanistic ideas: that contradiction is a characteristically human trait, that self-examination is the essence of true education, that education should enable us to live more harmoniously, and that, skepticism and open-mindedness are alternatives to dogmatic opinion. Like Rabelais, Montaigne defended a kind of learning that posed questions rather than provided answers. In his essay on the education of children, he criticized teachers who pour information into students' ears "as though they were pouring water into a funnel" and then demand that students repeat that information instead of exercising original thought.

Reflecting on the European response to overseas expansion (see chapter 18), Montaigne examined the ways in which behavior and belief vary from culture to culture. In his essay *Of Cannibals*, a portion of which appears below, he weighted the reports of "New World" barbarism and savagery against the morals and manners of "cultured" Europeans. War, which he calls the "human disease," he finds less vile among "savages" than among Europeans, whose warfare is motivated by colonial expansion. Balancing his own views with those of classical Latin writers, whom he quotes freely throughout his essays, Montaigne questions the superiority of any one culture over another. Montaigne's essays, an expression of reasoned inquiry into human values, constitute the literary high-water mark of the French Renaissance.

READING 3.25   From Montaigne's *On Cannibals* (1580)

. . . .I had with me for a long time a man who had lived for ten or twelve years in that other world which has been discovered in our century, in the place where Villegaignon landed, and which he called Antarctic France. This discovery of a boundless country seems worthy of consideration. I don't know if I can guarantee that some other such discovery will not be made in the future, so many personages greater than ourselves having been mistaken about this one. I am afraid we have eyes bigger than our stomachs, and more curiosity than capacity. We embrace everything, but we clasp only wind. . . .   1 — 10

This man I had was a simple, crude fellow—a character fit to bear true witness; for clever people observe more things and more curiously, but they interpret them; and to lend weight and conviction to their interpretation, they cannot help altering history a little. They never show you things as they are, but bend and disguise them according to the way they have seen them; and to give credence to their judgment and attract you to it, they are prone to add something to their matter, to stretch it out and amplify it. We need a man either very honest, or so simple that he has not the stuff to build up false inventions and give them plausibility; and wedded to no theory. Such was my man; and besides this, he at various times brought sailors and merchants, whom he had known on that trip, to see me. So I content myself with his information, without inquiring what the cosmographers say about it.   20

We ought to have topographers who would give us an exact account of the places where they have been. But because they have over us the advantage of having seen Palestine, they want to enjoy the privilege of telling us news about all the rest of the world. I would like everyone to write what he knows, and as much as he knows, not only in this, but in all other subjects; for a man may have   30

1556   Georg Agricola (German) publishes *On the Principles of Mining*

1571   Ambroise Paré (French) publishes five treatises on surgery

1587   Conrad Gesner (Swiss) completes his *Historiae Animalum*, the first zoological encyclopedia

1596   Sir John Harington (English) invents the "water closet," providing indoor toilet facilities

---

[1] *La France antartique* was the French term for South America. In 1555, Nicolaus Durard de Villegaignon founded a colony on an island in the Bay of Rio de Janeiro, Brazil. The colony collapsed some years later, and many of those who had lived there returned to France.

some special knowledge and experience of the nature of a river or a fountain, who in other matters knows only what everybody knows. However, to circulate this little scrap of knowledge, he will undertake to write the whole of physics. From this vice spring many great abuses.

Now to return to my subject, I think there is nothing barbarous and savage in that nation, from what I have been told, except that each man calls barbarism whatever is not his own practice; for indeed it seems we have no other test of truth and reason than the example and pattern of the opinions and customs of the country we live in. *There* is always the perfect religion, perfect government, the perfect and accomplished manners in all things. Those people are wild, just as we call wild the fruits that Nature has produced by herself and in her normal course; whereas really it is those that we have changed artificially and led astray from the common order, that we should rather call wild. The former retain alive and vigorous their genuine, their most useful and natural, virtues and properties, which we have debased in the latter in adapting them to gratify our corrupted taste. And yet for all that, the savor and delicacy of some uncultivated fruits of those countries is quite as excellent, even to our taste, as that of our own. It is not reasonable that art should win the place of honor over our great and powerful mother Nature. We have so overloaded the beauty and richness of her works by our inventions that we have quite smothered her. Yet wherever her purity shines forth, she wonderfully puts to shame our vain and frivolous attempts

> *Ivy comes readier without our care;*
> *In lonely caves the arbutus grows more fair;*
> *No art with artless bird song can compare.*
>
> Propertius

All our efforts cannot even succeed in reproducing the nest of the tiniest little bird, its contexture, its beauty and convenience; or even the web of the puny spider. All things, say Plato, are produced by nature, by fortune, or by art; the greatest and most beautiful by one or the other of the first two, the least and most imperfect by the last.

These nations, then, seem to me barbarous in this sense, that they have been fashioned very little by the human mind, and are still very close to their original naturalness. The laws of nature still rule them, very little corrupted by ours, and they are in such a state of purity that I am sometimes vexed that they were unknown earlier, in the days when there were men able to judge them better than we. I am sorry that Lycurgus[2] and Plato did not know of them; for it seems to me that what we actually see in these nations surpasses not only all the pictures in which poets have idealized the golden age and all their inventions in imagining a happy state of man, but also the conceptions and the very desire of philosophy. They could not imagine a naturalness so pure and simple as we see by experience; nor could they believe that our society could be maintained with so little artifice and human solder. This is a nation, I should say to Plato, in which there is no sort of

traffic, no knowledge of letters, no science of numbers, no name for a magistrate or for political superiority, no custom of servitude, no riches or poverty, no contracts, no successions, no partitions, no occupations but leisure ones, no care for any but common kinship, no clothes, no agriculture, no metal, no use of wine or wheat. The very words that signify lying, treachery, dissimulation, avarice, envy, belittling, pardon—unheard of. How far from this perfection would he find the republic that he imagined:

> *Men fresh sprung from the gods*
>
> Seneca

. . . .

They have their wars with the nations beyond the mountains, further inland, to which they go quite naked, with no other arms than bows or wooden swords ending in a sharp point, in the manner of the tongues of our boar spears. It is astonishing what firmness they show in their combats, which never end but in slaughter and bloodshed; for as to routs and terror, they know nothing of either.

Each man brings back as his trophy the head of the enemy he has killed, and sets it up at the entrance to his dwelling. After they have treated their prisoners well for a long time with all the hospitality they can think of, each man who has a prisoner calls a great assembly of his acquaintances. He ties a rope to one of the prisoner's arms, by the end of which he holds him, a few steps away, for fear of being hurt, and gives his dearest friend the other arm to hold in the same way; and these two, in the presence of the whole assembly, kill him with their swords. This done, they roast him and eat him in common and send some pieces to the absent friends. This is not, as people think, for nourishment, as of old the Scythians used to do; it is to betoken an extreme revenge.[3] And the proof of this came when they saw the Portuguese, who had joined forces with their adversaries, inflict a different kind of death on them when they took them prisoner, which was to bury them up to the waist, shoot the rest of their body full of arrows, and afterward hang them. They thought that these people from the other world, being men who had sown the knowledge of many vices among their neighbors and were much greater masters than themselves in every sort of wickedness, did not adopt this sort of vengeance without some reason, and that it must be more painful than their own; so they began to give up their old method and to follow this one.

I am not sorry that we notice the barbarous horror of such acts, but I am heartily sorry that, judging their faults rightly, we should be so blind as to our own. I think there is more barbarity in eating a man alive than in eating him dead; and in tearing by tortures and the rack a body still full of feeling, in roasting a man bit by bit, in having him bitten and mangled by dogs and swine (as we have not only read but seen within fresh memory, not among ancient enemies, but among neighbors and fellow citizens, and what is worse, on the pretext of piety and religion), than in

---

[2]The legendary lawgiver of ancient Sparta.

[3]Montaigne overlooks the fact that ritual cannibalism might also involve the will to consume the power of the opponent, especially if he were a formidable opponent.

roasting and eating him after he is dead.

Indeed, Chrysippus and Zeno, heads of the Stoic sect, thought there was nothing wrong in using our carcasses for any purpose in case of need, and getting nourishment from them; just as our ancestors, when besieged by Caesar in the city of Alésia, resolved to relieve their famine by eating old men, women, and other people useless for fighting.   150

> The Gascons once, 'tis said, their life renewed
> By eating of such food.

Juvenal

And physicians do not fear to use human flesh in all sorts of ways for our health, applying it either inwardly or outwardly. But there never was any opinion so disordered as to excuse treachery, disloyalty, tyranny, and cruelty, which are our ordinary vices.

So we may well call these people barbarians, in respect of the rules of reason, but not in respect of ourselves, who   160
surpass them in every kind of barbarity.

Their warfare is wholly noble and generous, and as excusable and beautiful as this human disease can be; its only basis among them is their rivalry in valor. They are not fighting for the conquest of new lands, for they still enjoy that natural abundance that provides them without toil and trouble with all necessary things in such profusion that they have no wish to enlarge their boundaries. They are still in that happy state of desiring only as much as their natural needs demand; any thing beyond that is superfluous to them.   170

. . . .

The Genius of Shakespeare

No assessment of the early modern era would be complete without some consideration of the literary giant of the age: William Shakespeare (1564–1616) (Figure **19.16**). A poet of unparalleled genius, Shakespeare emerged during the golden age of England under the rule of Elizabeth I. He produced thirty-seven plays—comedies, tragedies, romances, and histories—as well as 154 sonnets and other poems. These works, generally considered to be the greatest examples of English literature, have exercised an enormous influence on the evolution of the English language and the development of the Western literary tradition.*

Little is known about Shakespeare's early life and formal education. He grew up in Stratford-upon-Avon in the English Midlands, married Anne Hathaway (eight years his senior) with whom he had three children, and moved to London sometime before 1585. In London he formed an acting company, the Lord Chamberlain's Company (also called "the King's Men'), in which he was shareholder, actor, and playwright. Like fifteenth-century Florence, sixteenth-century London (and especially the Queen's court) supported a galaxy of artists, musicians, and writers who enjoyed the mutually stimulating interchange of ideas. Shakespeare's theater company performed at the court of Elizabeth I and that of her successor James I. But its main activities took place in the Globe Theatre (Figure **19.17**), one of a handful of playhouses built just outside London's city limits—along with brothels and taverns, theaters were relegated to the suburbs.

While Shakespeare is best known for his plays, he also wrote some of the most beautiful sonnets ever produced in the English language. Indebted to Petrarch, Shakespeare nevertheless devised most of his own sonnets in a form that would come to be called "the English sonnet": **quatrains** (four-line stanzas) with alternate rhymes, followed by a concluding **couplet**. Shakespeare's sonnets employ—and occasionally mock—such traditional Petrarchan themes as blind devotion, the value of friendship, and love's enslaving power. Some, like Sonnet 18, reflect the typically Renaissance (and classical) concern for immortality achieved through art and love. In Sonnet 18, Shakespeare contrives an extended metaphor: Like the summer day, his beloved will fade and die. But, exclaims the poet, she will remain eternal in and through the sonnet; for, so long as the poem survives, so will the object of its inspiration. Stripped of

*The complete works of Shakespeare are available at the following website: http://www-tech.mit.edu/shakespeare/works.html

MR. WILLIAM
SHAKESPEARES
COMEDIES,
HISTORIES, &
TRAGEDIES.
Published according to the True Originall Copies.

To the Reader.

This Figure, that thou here seest put,
    It was for gentle Shakespeare cut;
Wherein the Grauer had a strife
    with Nature, to out-doo the life:
O, could he but haue drawne his wit
    As well in brasse, as he hath hit
His face; the Print would then surpasse
    All, that was euer writ in brasse.
But, since he cannot, Reader, looke
    Not on his Picture, but his Booke.

B. I.

LONDON
Printed by Isaac Iaggard, and Ed. Blount. 1623.

Figure 19.16 DROESHOUT, first Folio edition portrait of William Shakespeare, 1623. By permission of the Folger Shakespeare Library, Washington, D.C.

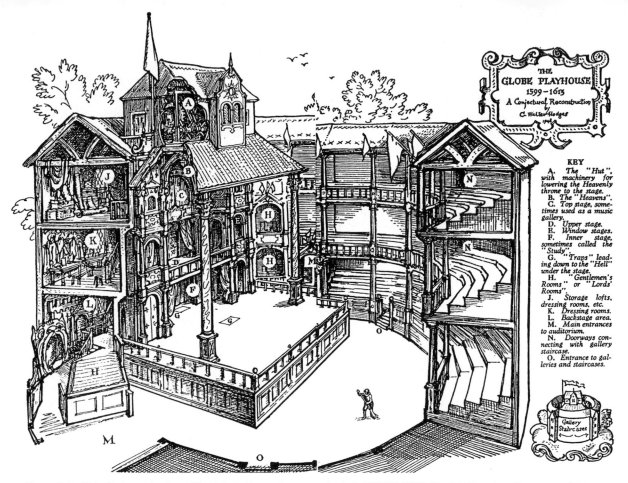

Figure 19.17 Globe Playhouse, London, 1599–1613. Architectural reconstruction by **C. WALTER HODGES**, 1948. Reproduced by courtesy of the Trustees of the British Museum, London.

sentiment, Sonnet 116 states the unchanging nature of love; Shakespeare exalts the "marriage of true minds" that most Renaissance humanists perceived as only possible among men. Sonnet 130, on the other hand, pokes fun at the literary conventions of the Petrarchan love sonnet. Satirizing the fair-haired, red-lipped heroine as object of desire, Shakespeare celebrates the real—though somewhat ordinary—features of his beloved.

READING 3.26   From Shakespeare's Sonnets (1609)

Sonnet 18

Shall I compare thee to a summer's day?   1
Thou art more lovely and more temperate.
Rough winds do shake the darling buds of May,
And summer's lease[1] hath all too short a date.
Sometime too hot the eye[2] of heaven shines,   5
And often is his gold complexion dimm'd;
And every fair from fair sometime declines,[3]
By chance or nature's changing course untrimm'd;[4]
But thy eternal summer shall not fade

---

[1]Allotted time.
[2]The sun.
[3]Beautiful thing from beauty.
[4]Stripped of beauty.

Nor lose possession of that fair thou ow'st,   10
Nor shall Death brag thou wand'rest in his shade,
When in eternal lines to time thou grow'st.[5]
   So long as men can breathe or eyes can see,
   So long lives this[6] and this gives life to thee.

Sonnet 116

Let me not to the marriage of true minds   1
Admit impediments. Love is not love
Which alters when it alteration finds,
Nor bends with the remover to remove.[7]
O, no, it is an ever-fixed mark,[8]   5
That looks on tempests and is never shaken;
It is the star to every wand'ring bark,
Whose worth's unknown, although his height be taken.[9]
Love's not Time's fool, though rose lips and cheeks
Within his bending sickle's compass come;   10
Love alters not with his brief hours and weeks,
But bears it out even to the edge of doom.[10]
   If this be error, and upon me proved,
   I never writ, nor no man ever loved.

---

[5]Your fame will grow as time elapses.
[6]The sonnet itself.
[7]Changes as the beloved changes.
[8]Sea mark, an aid to navigation.
[9]Whose value is beyond estimation.
[10]Endures to the very Day of Judgment.

Sonnet 130

My mistress' eyes are nothing like the sun;   1
Coral is far more red than her lips' red:
If snow be white, why then her breasts are dun;
If hairs be wires, black wires grow on her head.
I have seen roses damasked, red and white,   5
But no such roses see I in her cheeks;
And in some perfumes is there more delight
Than in the breath that from my mistress reeks.
I love to hear her speak, yet well I know
That music hath a far more pleasing sound: 10
I grant I never saw a goddess go,—
My mistress, when she walks, treads on the ground:
   And yet, by heaven, I think my love as rare
   As any she belied with false compare.

The Shakespearean Stage

Secular drama, Renaissance England's most original contribution to the humanistic tradition, was born in an era of high confidence: In 1588, the English navy defeated a Spanish fleet of 130 ships known as the "Invincible Armada." This event, a victory as well for the forces of Protestantism over Catholicism, encouraged a sense of national pride and a renewed confidence in the ambitious policies of the "Protestant Queen" Elizabeth I (1533–1603) (Figure 19.18). In its wake followed a period of high prosperity and commerical expansion. The rebirth of secular drama, stirred by the revival of interest in English history, is a major part of the Elizabethan legacy.

In the centuries following the fall of Rome, the Church condemned all forms of pagan display, including the performance of comedies and tragedies. Tragedy, in the sense that it was defined by Aristotle ("the imitation of an action" involving "some great error" made by an extraordinary man), was philosophically incompatible with the medieval worldview, which held that all events were predetermined by God. If redemption was the goal of Christian life, there was no place for literary tragedy in the Christian cosmos. (Hence Dante's famous journey, though far from humorous, was called a "comedy" in acknowledgment of its "happy" ending in Paradise.) Elizabethan poets adapted classical and medieval literary traditions to the writing of contemporary plays: while the context and the characters might be Christian, the plot and the dramatic action were secular in focus and in spirit. (The same might be said for the culture of the Renaissance in general.) Elizabethan London played host to groups of traveling actors (or "strolling players") who performed in public spaces or for generous patrons. In the late sixteenth century, a number of playhouses were built along the Thames River across from the city of London. Raised in 1599, the Globe, which held between 2,000 and 3,000 spectators, offered all levels of society access to professional theater (Figure 19.17). The open-air structure consisted of three tiers of galleries and standing room for commoners (or "groundlings") at the cost of only a penny—one-sixth of the price for a seat in the covered gallery. The projecting, rectangular stage, some 40 feet wide, included balconies (for musicians and special scenes such as required in *Romeo and Juliet*), exits to dressing areas, and a trap door (used for rising spirits and for burial scenes, such as required in *Hamlet*). Stage props were basic, but costumes were favored, and essential for the male actors who played the female roles—women were not permitted on the public stage. Performances were held in the afternoon and advertised by flying a flag above the theater roof. A globe, the signature logo, embellished the theater, along with a sign that read "*Totus mundus agit histrionem*" (loosely, "All the World's a Stage"). The bustling crowd that attended the theater—some standing through two or more hours of performance—often ate and drank as they enjoyed the most cosmopolitan entertainment of their time.

Shakespeare's Plays

In Shakespeare's time, theater did not rank as high as poetry as a literary genre. As popular entertainment, however, Shakespeare's plays earned high acclaim in London's theatrical community. Thanks to the availability of printed editions, the Bard of Stratford was familiar with the tragedies of Seneca and the comedies of Plautus and Terence. He knew the popular medieval morality plays that addressed the contest between good and evil, as well as the popular improvisational form of Italian comic theater known as the *commedia dell'arte*, which made use of stock or stereotypical characters. All of these resources came to shape the texture of his plays. For his plots, Shakespeare drew largely on classical history, medieval chronicles, and contemporary romances. Like Machiavelli, Shakespeare was an avid reader of ancient and medieval history, as well as a keen observer of his own complex age; but the stories his sources provided became mere springboards for the exploration of human nature. His history plays, such as *Henry V* and *Richard III*, celebrate England's medieval past and its rise to power under the Tudors. The major concerns of these plays, however, are not exclusively historical; rather, they explore the ways in which rulers behave under pressure: the weight of kingly responsibilities on mere humans and the difficulties of reconciling royal obligations and human aspirations. Shakespeare's comedies, which constitute about one half of his plays, deal with such popular themes as the battle of the sexes, rivalry among lovers, and mistaken identities. But here too, in such plays as *Much Ado About Nothing*, *All's Well That Ends Well*, and *The Taming of the Shrew*, it is Shakespeare's characters—their motivations exposed, their weaknesses and strengths laid bare—that command our attention. It is in the tragedies, and especially the tragedies of his mature career—*Hamlet*, *Macbeth*, *Othello*, and *King Lear*—that Shakespeare achieved the concentration of thought and language that have made him the greatest English playwright of all time. Jealousy, greed, ambition, insecurity, and self-deception are among the many human experiences that Shakespeare examined in his plays, but in these last tragedies, they become definitive: they drive the action of the play. Indeed, these plays are the most significant evidence of the Renaissance

Figure 19.18 ANONYMOUS, *The "Armada" Portrait* of Elizabeth I, ca. 1588. Woburn Abbey Collection, by kind permission of the Marquess of Tavistock and the Trustees of the Bedford Estates.

effort to probe the psychological forces that motivate human action.

No discussion of Shakespeare's plays can substitute for the experience of live performance. Yet, in focusing on two of the late tragedies: *Hamlet* and *Othello*, it is possible to isolate Shakespeare's principle contributions to the humanistic tradition. These lie in the areas of character development and in the brilliance of the language with which characters are brought to life. Despite occasional passages in prose and rhymed verse, Shakespeare's plays were written in the current Renaissance verse form known as **blank verse**. This verse form was popular among Renaissance humanists because, like classical poetry, it was unrhymed, and it closely approximated the rhythms of vernacular speech. In Shakespeare's hands, the English language took on a breadth of expression and a majesty of eloquence that has rarely been matched to this day. Shakespeare often used songs to create a special effect or develop the mood of a character. In the chilling scene just prior to her murder by Othello (see Reading 3.28), Desdemona sings a gentle ballad that serves to character-ize her sense of frailty and futility as she anticipates her tragic fate at the hand of her husband, Othello.

Hamlet, the world's most quoted play, belongs to the popular Renaissance genre of revenge tragedy, but the story itself came to Shakespeare from the history of medieval Denmark. Hamlet, the young heir to the throne of Denmark, learns that his uncle has murdered his father and married his mother in order to assume the throne; the burden of avenging his father falls squarely on Hamlet's shoulders. The arc of the play follows his inability to take action—his melancholic lack of resolve that, in the long run, results in the deaths of his mother (Gertrude), his betrothed (Ophelia), her father (Polonius), the king (Claudius), and finally, Hamlet himself. Shakespeare's protagonist differs from the heroes of ancient and medieval times: He lacks the sense of obligation to coun-try and community, the passionate religious loyalties, and the clearly defined spiritual values that drive such heroes as Gilgamesh, Achilles, and Roland. Yet Hamlet repre-sents a new, more modern personality, one whose self-questioning disposition and brooding skepticism more closely resemble a modern existential anti-hero. Though sunk in melancholy, he shares Pico della Mirandola's view (see Reading 3.7) that human nature is freely self-formed by human beings themselves. Hamlet marvels, "What a piece of work is a man! How noble in reason! How infinite in faculty! In form and moving how express and admirable! In action how like an angel! In apprehension how like a god! The beauty of the world! The paragon of animals." Nevertheless he concludes on a note of utter skepticism, "And yet, to me, what is this quintessence of dust?" (Act II, ii, ll. 303–309). It is in the oral examination of his innermost thoughts—the soliloquy—that Hamlet most fully reveals himself. In a painful process of self-examination, Hamlet questions the motives for meaningful action and the impulses that prevent him from action, but at the same time, he suggests the futility of all human action.

READING 3.27 From Shakespeare's *Hamlet*

(1602)   44

Hamlet, Act III, Scene 1

Enter King, Queen, Polonius, Ophelia, Rosencrantz, Guildenstern, lords.

King: And can you by no drift of conference   1
 Get from him why he puts on this confusion,
 Grating so harshly all his days of quiet
 With turbulent and dangerous lunacy?
Rosencrantz: He does confess he feels himself distracted,
 But from what cause 'a will by no means speak.
Guildenstern: Nor do we find him forward to be sounded,
 But with a crafty madness keeps aloof
 When we would bring him on to some confession
 Of his true state.
Queen: Did he receive you well?   10
Rosencrantz: Most like a gentleman.
Guildenstern: But with much forcing of his disposition.
Rosencrantz: Niggard of question, but of our demands
 Most free in his reply.
Queen: Did you assay him
 To any pastime?
Rosencrantz: Madam, it so fell out that certain players
 We o'erraught on the way. Of these we told him,
 And there did seem in him a kind of joy
 To hear of it. They are here about the court,
 And, as I think, they have already order   20
 This night to play before him.
Polonius: 'Tis most true,
 And he beseeched me to entreat Your Majesties
 To hear and see the matter.
King: With all my heart, and it doth much content me
 To hear him so inclined.

3.1. Location: The castle.
1 drift of conference directing of conversation **7 forward** willing.
Sounded questioned **12 disposition** inclination **13 Niggard** stingy
question conversation **14 assay** try to win **17 o'erraught** overtook

Good gentlemen, give him a further edge
And drive his purpose into these delights.
Rosencrantz: We shall, my lord.
          Exeunt Rosencrantz and Guildenstern.
King: Sweet Gertrude, leave us too,
 For we have closely sent for Hamlet hither,
 That he, as 'twere by accident, may here   30
 Affront Ophelia.
 Her father and myself, lawful espials,
 Will so bestow ourselves that seeing, unseen,
 We may of their encounter frankly judge,
 And gather by him, as he is behaved,
 If 't be th' affliction of his love or no
 That thus he suffers for.
Queen: I shall obey you.
 And for your part, Ophelia, I do wish
 That your good beauties be the happy cause
 Of Hamlet's wildness. So shall I hope your virtues   40
 Will bring him to his wonted way again,
 To both your honors.
Ophelia: Madam, I wish it may.
          [*Exit Queen.*]
Polonius: Ophelia, walk you here.—Gracious, so please you,
 We will bestow ourselves. [*To Ophelia.*] Read on this
          book,   [*giving her a book*]
 That show of such an exercise may color
 Your loneliness. We are oft to blame in this—
 'Tis too much proved—that with devotion's visage
 And pious action we do sugar o'er
 The devil himself.
King [*aside*]: O, 'tis too true!   50
 How smart a lash that speech doth give my conscience!
 The harlot's cheek, beautied with plastering art,
 Is not more ugly to the thing that helps it
 Than is my deed to my most painted word.
 O heavy burden!
Polonius: I hear him coming. Let's withdraw, my lord.
          [*The King and Polonius withdraw.*]
          Enter Hamlet. [*Ophelia pretends to read a book.*]
Hamlet: To be, or not to be, that is the question:
 Whether 'tis nobler in the mind to suffer
 The slings and arrows of outrageous fortune,
 Or to take arms against a sea of troubles   60
 And by opposing end them. To die, to sleep—
 No more—and by a sleep to say we end
 The heartache and the thousand natural shocks
 That flesh is heir to. 'Tis a consummation
 Devoutly to be wished. To die, to sleep;

3.1. Location: The castle.
26 edge incitement **29 closely** privately **31 Affront** confront, meet
32 espials spies **41 wonted** accustomed **43 Gracious** Your Grace
(i.e., the King) **44 bestow** conceal **45 exercise** religious exercise
(The book she reads is one of devotion.) **color** give a plausible
appearance to **46 loneliness** being alone **47 too much proved** too
often shown to be true, too often practiced **53 to** compared to **the
thing** i.e., the cosmetic **56 s.d. withdraw** (The King and Polonius
may retire behind an arras. The stage directions specify that they
"enter" again near the end of the scene.) **59 slings** missiles

To sleep, perchance to dream. Ay, there's the rub,
For in that sleep of death what dreams may come,
When we have shuffled off this mortal coil,
Must give us pause. There's the respect
That makes calamity of so long life.   70
For who would bear the whips and scorns of time,
Th' oppressor's wrong, the proud man's contumely,
The pangs of disprized love, the law's delay,
The insolence of office, and the spurns
That patient merit of th' unworthy takes,
When he himself might his quietus make
With a bare bodkin? Who would fardels bear,
To grunt and sweat under a weary life,
But that the dread of something after death,
The undiscovered country from whose bourn   80
No traveler returns, puzzles the will,
And makes us rather bear those ills we have
Than fly to others that we know not of?
Thus conscience does make cowards of us all;
And thus the native hue of resolution
Is sicklied o'er with the pale cast of thought,
And enterprises of great pitch and moment
With this regard their currents turn awry
And lose the name of action.—Soft you now,
The fair Ophelia. Nymph, in thy orisons   90
Be all my sins remembered.

Ophelia: Good my lord,
How does your honor for this many a day?

Hamlet: I humbly thank you; well, well, well.

Ophelia: My lord, I have remembrances of yours,
That I have longèd long to redeliver.
I pray you, now receive them.   *[She offers tokens.]*

Hamlet: No, not I, I never gave you aught.

Ophelia: My honored lord, you know right well you did,
And with them words of so sweet breath composed
As made the things more rich. Their perfume lost,   100
Take these again, for to the noble mind
Rich gifts wax poor when givers prove unkind.
There, my lord.   *[She gives tokens.]*

Hamlet: Ha, ha! Are you honest?

Ophelia: My lord?

Hamlet: Are you fair?

Ophelia: What means your lordship?

Hamlet: That if you be honest and fair, your honesty
should admit no discourse to your beauty.

Ophelia: Could beauty, my lord, have better commerce   110
than with honesty?

Hamlet: Ay, truly, for the power of beauty will sooner
transform honesty from what it is to a bawd than the
force of honesty can translate beauty into his likeness.
This was sometime a paradox, but now the time gives
if proof. I did love you once.

Ophelia: Indeed, my lord, you made me believe so.

Hamlet: You should not have believed me, for virtue
cannot so inoculate our old stock but we shall relish of
it. I loved you not.   120

Ophelia: I was the more deceived.

Hamlet: Get thee to a nunnery. Why wouldst thou be a
breeder of sinners? I am myself indifferent honest, but
yet I could accuse me of such things that it were better
my mother had not borne me: I am very proud,
revengeful, ambitious, with more offenses at my beck
than I have thoughts to put them in, imagination to
give them shape, or time to act them in. What should
such fellows as I do crawling between earth and
heaven? We are arrant knaves all; believe none of us.   130
Go thy ways to a nunnery. Where's your father?

Ophelia: At home, my lord.

Hamlet: Let the doors be shut upon him, that he may
play the fool nowhere but in 's own house. Farewell.

Ophelia: O, help him, you sweet heavens!

Hamlet: If thou dost marry, I'll give thee this plague for
thy dowry: be thou as chaste as ice, as pure as snow,
thou shalt not escape calumny. Get thee to a nunnery,
farewell. Or, if thou wilt needs marry, marry a fool, for
wise men know well enough what monsters you   140
make of them. To a nunnery, go, and quickly too.
Farewell.

Ophelia: Heavenly powers, restore him!

Hamlet: I have heard of your paintings too, well
enough. God hath given you one face, and you make
yourselves another. You jig, you amble, and you
lisp, you nickname God's creatures, and make your
wantonness your ignorance. Go to, I'll no more on 't;
it hath made me made. I say we will have no more
marriage. Those that are married already—all but   150
one—shall live. The rest shall keep as they are. To a
nunnery, go.   *Exit.*

Ophelia: O, what a noble mind is here o'erthrown!
The courtier's, soldier's, scholar's, eye, tongue,
sword,

---

66 rub (Literally, an obstacle in the game of bowls.) **68 shuffled**
sloughed, cast. **Coil** turmoil **69 respect** consideration **70 of . . .**
life so long-lived, something we willingly endure for so long (also
suggesting that long life is itself a calamity) **72 contumely** insolent
abuse **73 disprized** unvalued **74 office** officialdom **spurns**
insults **75 of . . . takes** receives from unworthy persons **76 quietus**
acquitance; here, death **77 a bare bodkin** a mere dagger,
unsheathed. **fardels** burdens **80 bourn** frontier, boundary **85**
native hue natural color, complexion **86 cast** tinge, shade of color
87 pitch height (as of a falcon's flight). **moment** importance **88**
regard respect, consideration **currents** courses **89 Soft you** i.e.,
wait a minute, gently **90 orisons** prayers **104 honest** (1) truthful (2)
chaste **106 fair** (1) beautiful (2) just, honorable **108 your honesty**
your chastity **109 discourse to** familiar dealings with **110–111**
commerce dealings, intercourse **114 his** its **115 sometime**
formerly **a paradox** a view opposite to commonly held opinion
the time the present age **119 inoculate** graft, be engrafted to

119–120 but . . . it that we do not still have about us a taste of the old
stock, i.e., retain our sinfulness **122 nunnery** convent (with possibly
an awareness that the word was also used derisively to denote a
brothel) **123 indifferent honest** reasonably virtuous **126 beck**
command **140 monsters** (An illusion to the horns of a cuckold.) **you**
i.e., you women **146 jig** dance **amble** move coyly **147 you**
nickname . . . creatures i.e., you give trendy names to things in place
of their God-given names **147–148 make . . . ignorance** i.e., excuse
your affectation on the grounds of pretended ignorance **148 on 't** of it

Th' expectancy and rose of the fair state,
The glass of fashion and the mold of form,
Th' observed of all observers, quite, quite down!
And I, of ladies most deject and wretched,
That sucked the honey of his music vows,
Now see that noble and most sovereign reason   160
Like sweet bells jangled out of tune and harsh,
That unmatched form and feature of blown youth
Blasted with ecstasy. O, woe is me,
T' have seen what I have seen, see what I see!

                Enter King and Polonius.

King: Love? His affections do not that way tend;
   Nor what he spake, though it lacked form a little,
   Was not like madness. There's something in his soul
   O'er which his melancholy sits on brood,
   And I do doubt the hatch and the disclose
   Will be some danger; which for to prevent,   170
   I have in quick determination
   Thus set it down: he shall with speed to England
   For the demand of our neglected tribute.
   Haply the seas and countries different
   With variable objects shall expel
   This something-settled matter in his heart,
   Whereon his brains still beating puts him thus
   From fashion of himself. What think you on 't?
Polonius: It shall do well. But yet do I believe
   The origin and commencement of his grief   180
   Sprung from neglected love.—How now, Ophelia?
   You need not tell us what Lord Hamlet said;
   We heard it all.—My lord, do as you please,
   But, if you hold it fit, after the play
   Let his queen-mother all alone entreat him
   To show his grief. Let her be round with him;
   And I'll be placed, so please you, in the ear
   Of all their conference. If she find him not,
   To England send him, or confine him where
   Your wisdom best shall think.
King: It shall be so.   190
   Madness in great ones must not unwatched go. *Exeunt.*

The Tragedy of Othello, the Moor of Venice was based on a story from a collection of tales published in Italy in the sixteenth century. The life of the handsome and distinguished Othello, an African soldier whose leadership in the Venetian wars against the Turks has brought him heroic esteem, takes a tragic turn when his ensign Iago beguiles

---

155 expectancy hope.   **rose** ornament   **156 The glass ... form**
the mirror of true self-fashioning and the pattern of courtly behavior
157 Th' observed ... observers i.e., the center of attention and
honor in the court   **159 music** musical, sweetly uttered   **162 blown**
blooming · **163 Blasted** withered. **estasy** madness   **165 affections**
emotions, feelings   **168 sits on brood** sits like a bird on a nest, about
to *hatch* mischief (line 169)   **169 doubt** fear. **disclose** disclosure,
hatching   **172 set it down** resolved   **173 For ... of** to demand   **175**
variable objects various sights and surroundings to divert him   **176**
This something ... heart the strange matter settled in his heart   **177**
still continually   **178 From ... himself** out of his matural manner
185 queen-mother queen and mother   **186 round** blunt   **188 find**
him not fails to discover what is troubling him

---

him into thinking that his beautiful wife Desdemona has betrayed him with another man. Enraged with jealousy, Othello destroys the person he loves most in the world, his wife; and, in the unbearable grief of his error, he takes his own life as well. No brief synopsis can capture the dramatic impact of this, one of Shakespeare's most sensational plays. While Othello's jealousy is the flaw that brings about his doom, it is Iago whose unmitigated evil drives the action of the plot. Conniving Iago is the Machiavellian villain, "a demi-devil," as he is called in the play. In contrast, Desdemona is the paragon of virtue and beauty. Such characters hark back to the allegorical figures in medieval morality plays, but Shakespeare transforms these figures into complex personalities, allowing them full freedom to falter and fail through their own actions.

That Shakespeare made a black man the hero of one of his tragedies is significant, since his treatment of the character seems to have challenged Elizabethan stereotypes. Medieval and Renaissance literature described blacks as vengeful, hot-blooded, and evil, black being the color traditionally associated with the devil. But in Shakespeare's play, the Moor (the Elizabethan name for any African) is unwitting, ingenuous, and pure, while Iago, the white man who confounds him, is the personification of evil. Perhaps more significant than this irony is Shakespeare's implication that underlying the most untainted acts of heroism and the purest emotions of love is the dark possibility of misguided action that leads to self-defeat. Shakespeare's plays generally preach no explicit moral; rather, they suggest that, in a universe in which order and disorder coexist, human choices play a vital and potentially destructive part. The nihilism that darkens *The Tragedy of Othello, Macbeth,* and *Hamlet* was unthinkable before the modern era.

READING 3.28   From Shakespeare's *Othello*
(1604)   127²⁰

Othello, Act IV, Scene III
Enter Othello, Lodovico, Desdemona, Emilia, and Attendants.

Lodovico: I do beseech you, sir, trouble yourself no further.   1
Othello: O, pardon me; 'twill do me good to walk.
Lodovico: Madam, good night. I humbly thank your
   ladyship.
Desdemona: Your honor is most welcome.
Othello: Will you walk, sir?
   O, Desdemona!
Desdemona: My lord?
Othello: Get you to bed on th' instant; I will be return'd
   forthwith. Dismiss your attendant there. Look 't be done.
Desdemona: I will, my lord.
               Exit [Othello, with Lodovico and Attendants].
Emilia: How goes it now? He looks gentler than he did.   10
Desdemona: He says he will return incontinent,
   And hath commanded me to go to bed,
   And bade me to dismiss you.

IV.iii Location: The citadel.
11 incontinent immediately

Emilia: Dismiss me?

Desdemona: It was his bidding; therefore, good Emilia,
Give me my nightly wearing, and adieu.
We must not now displease him.

Emilia: I would you had never seen him!

Desdemona: So would not I. My love doth so approve him,
That even his stubbornness, his checks, his frowns—
Prithee unpin me—have grace and favor in them.   20

[*Emilia prepares Desdemona for bed.*]

Emilia: I have laid those sheets you bade me on the bed.

Desdemona: All's one. Good faith, how foolish are our
minds!
If I do die before thee, prithee shroud me
In one of those same sheets.

Emilia: Come, come, you talk.

Desdemona: My mother had a maid call'd Barbary.
She was in love, and he she lov'd prov'd mad
And did forsake her. She had a song of "Willow,"
An old thing 'twas, but it express'd her fortune,
And she died singing it. That song tonight
Will not go from my mind; I have much to do   30
But to go hang my head all at one side
And sing it like poor Barbary. Prithee, dispatch.

Emilia: Shall I go fetch your nightgown?

Desdemona: No, unpin me here.
This Lodovico is a proper man.

Emilia: A very handsome man.

Desdemona: He speaks well.

Emilia: I know a lady in Venice would have walk'd barefoot
to Palestine for a touch of his nether lip.

Desdemona [*Singing*]:
"The poor soul sat sighing by a sycamore tree,
Sing all a green willow;   40
Her hand on her bosom, her head on her knee,
Sing willow, willow, willow.
The fresh streams ran by her, and murmur'd her moans;
Sing willow, willow, willow;
Her salt tears fell from her, and soft'ned the stones"—
Lay by these.
[*Singing*]: "Sing willow, willow, willow"—
Prithee, hie thee; he'll come anon.
[*Singing*] "Sing all a green willow must be my garland.
Let nobody blame him; his scorn I approve"—   50
Nay, that's not next.—Hark! Who is 't that knocks?

Emilia: It's the wind.

Desdemona [*Singing*]
"I call'd my love false love; but what said he then?
Sing willow, willow, willow;
If I court moe women, you'll couch with moe men"—
So, get thee gone; good night. Mine eyes do itch;
Doth that bode weeping?

Emilia: 'Tis neither here nor there.

Desdemona: I have heard it said so. O, these men, these
men!
Dost thou in conscience think—tell me, Emilia—
That there be women do abuse their husbands   60
In such gross kind?

Emilia: There be some such, no question.

Desdemona: Wouldst thou do such a deed for all the world?

Emilia: Why, would not you?

Desdemona: No, by this heavenly light!

Emilia: Nor I neither by this heavenly light; I might do
't as well i' th' dark.

Desdemona: Wouldst thou do such a deed for all the
world?

Emilia: The world's a huge thing. It is a great price
For a small vice.

Desdemona: Good troth, I think thou wouldst not.

Emilia: By my troth, I think I should; and undo 't when I
had done. Marry, I would not do such a thing for a joint-   70
ring, nor for measures of lawn, nor for gowns, petticoats,
nor caps, nor any petty exhibition; but, for all the whole
world—'ud's pity, who would not make her husband a
cuckold to make him a monarch? I should venture
purgatory for 't.

Desdemona: Beshrew me if I would do such a wrong for the
whole world.

Emilia: Why, the wrong is but a wrong i' th' world; and
having the world for your labor, 'tis a wrong in your own
world, and you might quickly make it right.   80

Desdemona: I do not think there is any such woman.

Emilia: Yes, a dozen; and as many to th' vantage as
would store the world they play'd for.
But I do think it is their husbands' faults
If wives do fall. Say that they slack their duties,
And pour our treasures into foreign laps,
Or else break out in peevish jealousies,
Throwing restraint upon us? Or say they strike us,
Or scant our former having in despite?
Why, we have galls, and though we have some grace,
Yet have we some revenge. Let husbands know   90
Their wives have sense like them. They see, and smell,
And have their palates both for sweet and sour,
As husbands have. What is it that they do
When they change us for others? Is it sport?
I think it is. And doth affection breed it?
I think it doth. Is 't frailty that thus errs?
It is so too. And have not we affections,
Desires for sport, and frailty, as men have?
Then let them use us well; else let them know,
The ills we do, their ills instruct us so.   100

Desdemona: Good night, good night. God me such uses
send,
Not to pick bad from bad, but by bad mend!   *Exeunt.*

---

48 hie thee hurry   **70–71 joint-ring** a ring made in separate halves
71 lawn fine linen   **72 exhibition** gift   **73 'ud's** i.e., God's   **82 to
th' vantage** in addition, to boot **store** populate   **85 pour . . . laps** i.e.,
are unfaithful, give what is rightfully ours (semen) to other women   **88
scant . . . despite** reduce our allowance to spite us   **89 have galls**
i.e., are capable of resenting injury and insult   **91 sense** physical
sense   **101 uses** habit, practice   **102 Not . . . mend** i.e., not to learn
bad conduct from others' badness (as Emilia has suggested women
learn from men), but to mend my ways by perceiving what badness is,
making spiritual benefit out of evil and adversity

---

19 stubbornness roughness **checks** rebukes   **26 mad** wild, i.e.,
faithless   **30–31 I . . . hang** I can scarcely keep myself from hanging

SUMMARY

The sixteenth century was a time of rapid change marked by growing secularism, advancing technology, and European geographic expansion. It was also an age of profound religious and social upheaval. Northern European humanists, led by Erasmus of Rotterdam, made critical studies of early Christian literature and urged a return to the teachings of Jesus and the early church fathers. Demands for Church reform went hand in hand with the revival of Early Christian writings to culminate in the Protestant Reformation.

Aided by Gutenberg's printing press, Martin Luther contested the authority of the Church of Rome. He held that Scripture was the sole basis for religious interpretation and emphasized the idea of salvation through faith in God's grace rather than through good works. As Lutheranism and other Protestant sects proliferated throughout Europe, the unity of medieval Christendom was shattered.

The music and art of the Northern Renaissance reflect the mood of religious reform. In music, the Lutheran chorale became the vehicle of Protestant piety. In art, the increasing demand for illustrated devotional literature and private devotional art stimulated the production of woodcuts and metal engravings. The works of Dürer and Grünewald exhibit the Northern Renaissance passion for realistic detail and graphic expression, while the fantastic imagery of Hieronymus Bosch suggests a pessimistic and typically Northern concern with sin and death. Bosch's preoccupation with the palpable forces of evil found its counterpart in the witch-hunts of the sixteenth century. In painting, portraiture, landscapes, and scenes of everyday life mirrored the tastes of a growing middle-class audience for an unidealized record of the material world.

Northern Renaissance writers took a generally skeptical and pessimistic view of human nature. Erasmus, More, Cervantes, and Rabelais lampooned individual and societal failings and described the ruling influence of folly in all aspects of human conduct. In France, Montaigne devised the essay as an intimate form of rational reflection. The most powerful form of literary expression to evolve in the late sixteenth century, however, was secular drama. In the hands of William Shakespeare, Elizabethan drama became the ideal vehicle for exposing the psychological forces that motivate human behavior.

By the end of the sixteenth century, national loyalties, religious fanaticism, and commercial rivalries had splintered the European community, rendering ever more complex the society of the West. And yet, on the threshold of modernity, the challenges to the human condition—economic survival, communality, self-knowledge, and the inevitability of death—were no less pressing than they had been two thousand years earlier. If the technology of the sixteenth century gave human beings greater control over nature than ever before, it also provided more devastating weapons of war and destruction. In the centuries to come, the humanistic tradition would be shaped and reshaped by changing historical circumstances and the creative imagination of indomitable humankind.

SUGGESTIONS FOR READING

Bloom, Harold. *Shakespeare: The Invention of the Human*. New York: Riverhead Books, 1998.

Eisenstein, Elizabeth L. *The Printing Press as an Instrument of Change*. Cambridge, U.K. Cambridge University Press, 1979.

Farrell, Kirby. *Play, Death, and Heroism in Shakespeare*. Chapel Hill. N.C.: University of North Carolina Press, 1989.

Harbison, Craig. *The Mirror of the Artist: Northern Renaissance Art in its Historical Context*. New York: Abrams, 1995.

Holden, Anthony. *William Shakespeare: The Man Behind the Genius*. Boston: Little, Brown and Company, 2000.

Holl, Karl. *The Cultural Significance of the Reformation*, translated by K. and B. Herz and J. H. Lichtblau. Cleveland, Ohio: Meridian, 1962.

Kinsman, R. S. *The Darker Vision of the Renaissance: Beyond the Fields of Reason*. Berkeley, Calif.: University of California Press, 1975.

Pettegree, Andrew. *The Reformation World*. New York: Routledge, 2000.

Schoeck, Richard. *Erasmus of Europe: Prince of the Humanists 1501–1536*. New York: Columbia University Press, 1995.

Strong, Roy. *The Cult of Elizabeth: Elizabethan Portraiture and Pageantry*. London: Pimlico, 1999.

Tillyard, E. M. W. *The Elizabethan World Picture*. New York: Random House, 1964.

GLOSSARY

blank verse unrhymed lines of iambic pentameter, that is, lines consisting of ten syllables each with accents on every second syllable

chorale a congregational hymn, first sung in the Lutheran church

couplet two successive lines of verse with similar end-rhymes

engraving the process by which lines are incised on a metal plate, then inked and printed; see Figure 19.6

essay a short piece of expository prose that examines a single subject

genre painting art depicting scenes from everyday life; not to be confused with "genre," a term used to designate a particular category in literature or art, such as the essay (in literature) and portraiture (in painting)

iconoclast one who opposes the use of images in religious worship

quatrain a four-line stanza

triptych a picture or altarpiece with a central panel and two flanking panels; see also "diptych" in Glossary, chapter 9

woodcut a relief printing process by which all parts of a design are cut away except those that will be inked and printed; see Figure 19.5

JAN VAN EYCK, *Man in a Turban* (*Self-Portrait?*), 1433. Tempera and oil on panel, 13⅜ × 10⅛ in. National Gallery, London.

Summary of the Renaissance and the Reformation

The following paragraphs provide an overview of the Renaissance and Reformation, the two movements that ushered in the modern era in the West. This summary of fifteenth- and sixteenth-century culture (dealt with in detail in Book 3) offers some background to the materials contained in books 4, 5, and 6, which deal with the modern era in a global context.

Classical Humanism

The effort to recover, edit, and study ancient Greek and Latin manuscripts, a movement known as classical humanism, first occurred in fourteenth-century Italy, where it marked the beginnings of the Renaissance. This revival of Greco-Roman culture was to spread throughout Western Europe over the following three hundred years. Petrarch, known as the father of humanism, provided the model for Renaissance scholarship and education. He promoted the study of the classic Greek and Latin writers, especially Cicero, encouraged textual criticism, and wrote introspective and passionate sonnets that were revered and imitated for centuries to come.

The city of Florence was the unrivaled center of classical humanism in the first 150 years of the Renaissance. A thriving commercial and financial center dominated by a well-to-do middle class, Florence found political and cultural leadership in such wealthy and sophisticated families as the Medici. Classical humanism helped to cultivate a sense of civic pride, a new respect for oral and written eloquence, and a set of personal values that sustained the ambitions of the rising merchant class.

Fifteenth-century humanists carried on Petrarch's quest to recover the classical past. Ficino translated the entire body of Plato's writings, while Pico's investigations in Hebrew and Arabic led him to believe that the world's great minds shared a single, universal truth. Pico's *Oration on the Dignity of Man* proclaimed the centrality of humankind and defended the unlimited freedom of the individual within the universal scheme.

Renaissance humanists cultivated the idea of the good life. Following Alberti's maxim, "A man can do anything he wants," they applied the moral precepts of the classical past to such contemporary pursuits as diplomacy, politics, and the arts. While Petrarch and his peers were concerned primarily with the recovery of classical manuscripts and the production of critical editions, Alberti, Castiglione, and Machiavelli eagerly infused scholarship with action. Allying their scrutiny of the past to an empirical study of the present, they fostered a heroic ideal of the individual that surpassed all classical models. For Alberti, wealth and authority proceeded from the exercise of *virtù*; for Castiglione, the superior breed of human being was identical with *l'uomo universale*, the well-rounded person; for Machiavelli, only a ruthless master of power politics could ensure the survival of the state. Alberti, Castiglione, and Machiavelli were representative of the larger group of Renaissance humanists who asserted the human capacity for self-knowledge and exalted the role of the individual in the secular world. Their views shaped the modern character of the humanistic tradition in the European West.

Renaissance Artists

Most significant about the artists of the Renaissance is that they were disciples of nature: They brought a scientific curiosity to the study of the natural world and untiringly investigated its operations. Such Early Renaissance artists as Donatello, Pollaiuolo, Masaccio, and Brunelleschi studied the mechanics of the human body, the effects of light on material substances, and the physical appearance of objects in three-dimensional space. At the same time, Renaissance artists were masters of invention: They perfected the technique of oil painting, formulated the laws of perspective, and applied the principles of classical art to the representation of Christian and contemporary subjects. Patronized by a wealthy European middle class, they revived such this-worldly genres as portraiture and gave new attention to the nude body as an object of natural beauty.

The art of the High Renaissance marks the culmination of a hundred-year effort to wed the techniques of naturalistic representation to classical ideals of proportion and harmony. Leonardo da Vinci, the quintessential artist-scientist, tried to reconcile empirical experience with basic principles of balance and order. The compositions of Raphael, with their monumental scale and unity of design, became standards by which Western paintings would be judged for many centuries. The multitalented Michelangelo brought a heroic idealism to the treatment of traditional Christian and classical themes. In Venice, Titian's painterly handling of the reclining female nude represented a new and more sensuous naturalism. In architecture, the centrally planned buildings of Bramante and Palladio fulfilled the quest of such Early Renaissance architects as Brunelleschi and Alberti for an architecture of harmony, balance, and clarity.

The Renaissance produced an equally splendid flowering in music, especially among Franco-Flemish composers. Secular compositions began to outnumber religious ones. The techniques of imitation and word painting infused both religious and secular music with homogeneity and increased expressiveness. Printed sheet music helped to popularize the madrigal and other secular, vernacular song forms. Instrumental music and dance now emerged as independent genres. Like their classical predecessors, Renaissance artists placed human concerns and feelings at the center of a harmonious universe. Such optimism, combined with intellectual curiosity and increasing worldliness, fueled the early modern era in the West.

Shattering the Old Order: Protest and Reform

The sixteenth century was a time of rapid change marked by growing secularism, advancing technology, and European overseas expansion. It was also an age of profound religious and social upheaval. Northern humanists led by Erasmus of Rotterdam made critical studies of early Christian literature and urged a return to the teachings of Jesus and the early church fathers. Demands for church reform went hand in hand with the revival of early Christian writings to culminate in the Protestant Reformation.

Aided by Gutenberg's printing press, Martin Luther contested the authority of the Church of Rome. He held that Scripture was the sole basis for religious interpretation and emphasized the idea of salvation through faith in God's grace rather than through good works. As Lutheranism and other Protestant sects proliferated throughout Europe, the unity of medieval Christendom was shattered.

The music and the art of the Northern Renaissance reflect the mood of religious reform. In music, the Lutheran chorale became the vehicle of Protestant piety. In art, the increasing demand for illustrated devotional literature and private devotional art stimulated the production of woodcuts and metal engravings. The works of Dürer and Grünewald exhibit the Northern Renaissance passion for realistic detail and graphic expression, while the fantastic imagery of Hieronymus Bosch suggests a pessimistic and typically Northern concern with sin and death. Bosch's preoccupation with the palpable forces of evil found its counterpart in the witch-hunts of the sixteenth century. In painting, too, such secular subjects as portraiture, landscapes, and scenes of everyday life mirrored the tastes of a growing middle-class audience for an unidealized record of the visual world.

Northern Renaissance writers took a generally skeptical and pessimistic view of human nature. Erasmus, More, Cervantes, and Rabelais lampooned individual and societal failings and described the ruling influence of folly in all aspects of human conduct. In France, Montaigne devised the essay as an intimate form of rational reflection. The most powerful form of literary expression to evolve in the late sixteenth century, however, was secular drama. In the hands of William Shakespeare, drama became the ultimate expression of the sixteenth-century quest to examine the human personality in its secular and spiritual dimensions. Shakespeare's tragedies (as opposed, for instance, to Montaigne's essays) reveal the human condition through overt action, rather than through private reflection.

By the end of the sixteenth century, national loyalties, religious fanaticism, and commercial rivalries for control of trade with Africa, Asia and the Americas had splintered the European community. These conditions rendered ever more complex the society of the West. And yet, on the threshold of modernity, the challenges to the human condition—economic survival, communality, self-knowledge, and the inevitability of death—were no less pressing than they had been two thousand years earlier. If the technology of the sixteenth century was more sophisticated than that of ancient times—giving human beings greater control over nature than ever before—it also provided more devastating weapons of war and destruction. In the centuries to come, the humanistic tradition would be shaped and reshaped by changing historical circumstances and the creative imagination of indomitable humankind.

PART ONE

The age of the baroque

The period between approximately 1600 and 1800 was an age of contradictions. In Western Europe, deeply felt, even mystical, religious sentiment vied with the rise of science and rational methods of scientific investigation. Newly developed theories of constitutional government contended with firmly entrenched claims to divine right among "absolute" rulers—monarchs who recognized no legal limitations to their authority. The rising wealth of a small segment of the population failed to offset widespread poverty and old aristocratic privilege. In Asia, as well, the seventeenth and eighteenth centuries brought major changes: Muslim rulers united the primarily Hindu peoples of India and proceeded to establish the glorious Mogul dynasty. The Ming emperors of China, who governed an empire larger than any other in the world, fell to Mongol (Manchu) tribes in the early seventeenth century. These foreign rulers secured internal stability through rigid control of Chinese culture.

The early modern era witnessed the beginnings of the European state system and the establishment of the fundamental political, economic, and cultural norms of European and, by extension, American life. Rival religious claims following the Protestant Reformation complicated the scramble for land and power among European states. The first half of the seventeenth century witnessed the Thirty Years' War and other devastating conflicts between Catholics and Protestants. In 1648, however, by the terms of the Treaty of Westphalia, which ended the Thirty Years' War, the principle of national sovereignty was firmly established in the West: By that principle, each European state would exercise independent and supreme authority over its own territories and inhabitants.

In the economic arena, the prosperity of the sixteenth century was followed by marked decline in the seventeenth. Nevertheless, after 1660, commercial capitalism and the production of manufactured goods flourished in the West, where economic growth was tied to a pattern of global commerce. Asia, Africa, and the Americas—lucrative markets for European goods—were frontiers for European traders. And as global perceptions widened, Europeans realized that the "Old World" could no longer live in isolation.

In the West, the years between 1600 and 1750 were closely associated with a style known as "the baroque." Characterized by dramatic expression, theatrical spectacle, and spatial grandeur, the baroque became the hallmark of an age of exuberant expansion. The style also reflected the new, dynamic view of the universe as set forth by proponents of the Scientific Revolution. The baroque encompassed various phases: In Italy, it mirrored the intensely religious mood of the Catholic Reformation; in Northern Europe, it reflected the intimate spirit of Protestant devotionalism as well as the reliance on sensory experience associated with the New Science; and among authoritarian regimes throughout Europe and Asia, it worked to glorify secular power and wealth.

The age of the baroque was fueled by the human ambition to master nature on a colossal scale. This ambition—inspired perhaps by a more detached and objective view of the self in relation to the world—is as evident in Galileo's efforts to understand and explain the operations of nature as it is in Louis XIV's attempts to exert unlimited power over vast territories and peoples. A similar kind of energy is apparent in the complexities of a Bach fugue, the cosmic scope of Milton's *Paradise Lost*, the spectacle of early Italian opera, the panoramic sweep of Dutch landscape paintings, the splendor of the royal palaces at Versailles, Delhi, and Beijing, and the efforts of Ming and Manchu emperors to collect and copy all of China's literary classics. Under King Louis XIV of France, as among the Safavid Persians, the Moguls of India, the Ming and Manchu emperors of China, and the Tokugawa shoguns in Japan, there emerged an aristocratic style that aimed to glorify the majesty and power of the ruler.

(opposite) **EL GRECO**, detail of *The Agony in the Garden,* ca. 1585-1586. Oil on canvas, 6 ft. 1 in. × 9 ft. 1 in. Courtesy of the Toledo Museum of Art, Ohio.

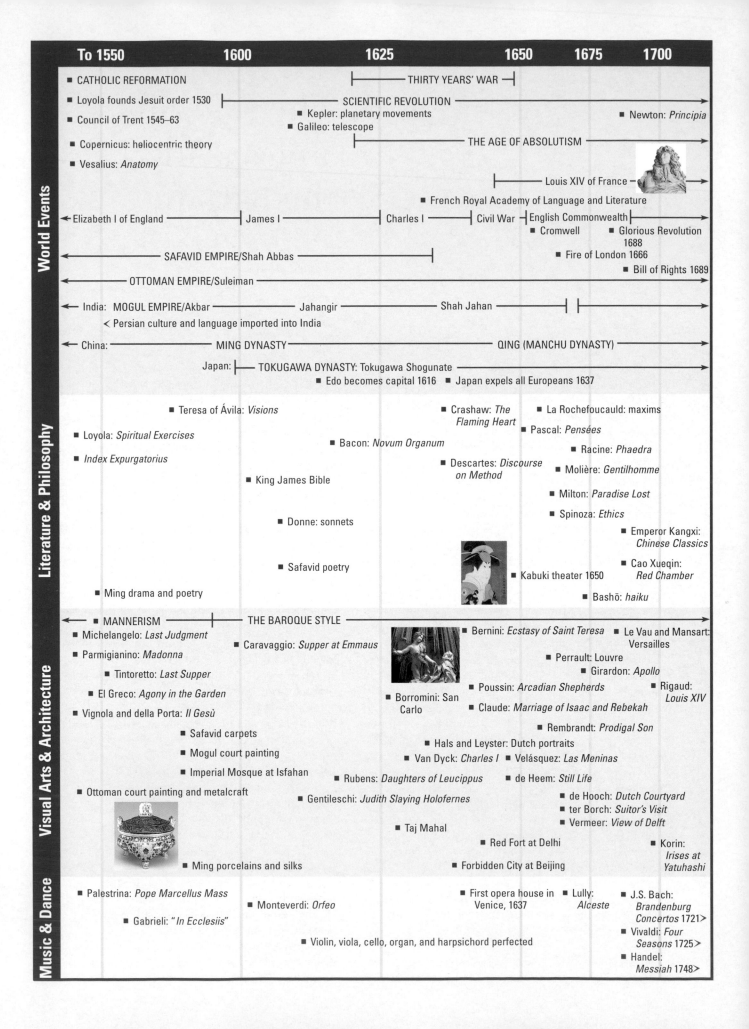

	To 1550	1600	1625	1650	1675	1700

World Events

- CATHOLIC REFORMATION
- ├─ THIRTY YEARS' WAR ─┤
- Loyola founds Jesuit order 1530
- SCIENTIFIC REVOLUTION →
- Council of Trent 1545–63
- Kepler: planetary movements
- Galileo: telescope
- Newton: *Principia*
- Copernicus: heliocentric theory
- THE AGE OF ABSOLUTISM →
- Vesalius: *Anatomy*
- ├── Louis XIV of France →
- French Royal Academy of Language and Literature
- ← Elizabeth I of England ── James I ── Charles I ── Civil War ─┤ English Commonwealth ├─
- Cromwell
- Glorious Revolution 1688
- ← SAFAVID EMPIRE/Shah Abbas ──
- Fire of London 1666
- ── OTTOMAN EMPIRE/Suleiman ──
- Bill of Rights 1689
- ← India: MOGUL EMPIRE/Akbar ── Jahangir ── Shah Jahan ──┤ →
- < Persian culture and language imported into India
- ← China: ── MING DYNASTY ── QING (MANCHU DYNASTY) →
- Japan: ├─ TOKUGAWA DYNASTY: Tokugawa Shogunate ──
- Edo becomes capital 1616
- Japan expels all Europeans 1637

Literature & Philosophy

- Teresa of Ávila: *Visions*
- Crashaw: *The Flaming Heart*
- La Rochefoucauld: maxims
- Loyola: *Spiritual Exercises*
- Pascal: *Pensées*
- Bacon: *Novum Organum*
- *Index Expurgatorius*
- Racine: *Phaedra*
- Descartes: *Discourse on Method*
- Molière: *Gentilhomme*
- King James Bible
- Milton: *Paradise Lost*
- Spinoza: *Ethics*
- Donne: sonnets
- Emperor Kangxi: *Chinese Classics*
- Safavid poetry
- Cao Xueqin: *Red Chamber*
- Kabuki theater 1650
- Ming drama and poetry
- Bashō: *haiku*

Visual Arts & Architecture

- ← MANNERISM ── THE BAROQUE STYLE →
- Michelangelo: *Last Judgment*
- Bernini: *Ecstasy of Saint Teresa*
- Le Vau and Mansart: Versailles
- Caravaggio: *Supper at Emmaus*
- Parmigianino: *Madonna*
- Perrault: Louvre
- Tintoretto: *Last Supper*
- Girardon: *Apollo*
- El Greco: *Agony in the Garden*
- Poussin: *Arcadian Shepherds*
- Rigaud: *Louis XIV*
- Vignola and della Porta: *Il Gesù*
- Borromini: San Carlo
- Claude: *Marriage of Isaac and Rebekah*
- Safavid carpets
- Rembrandt: *Prodigal Son*
- Mogul court painting
- Hals and Leyster: Dutch portraits
- Imperial Mosque at Isfahan
- Van Dyck: *Charles I*
- Velásquez: *Las Meninas*
- Ottoman court painting and metalcraft
- Rubens: *Daughters of Leucippus*
- de Heem: *Still Life*
- Gentileschi: *Judith Slaying Holofernes*
- de Hooch: *Dutch Courtyard*
- ter Borch: *Suitor's Visit*
- Vermeer: *View of Delft*
- Taj Mahal
- Red Fort at Delhi
- Korin: *Irises at Yatuhashi*
- Ming porcelains and silks
- Forbidden City at Beijing

Music & Dance

- Palestrina: *Pope Marcellus Mass*
- First opera house in Venice, 1637
- Lully: *Alceste*
- J.S. Bach: *Brandenburg Concertos* 1721>
- Monteverdi: *Orfeo*
- Gabrieli: "*In Ecclesiis*"
- Vivaldi: *Four Seasons* 1725>
- Violin, viola, cello, organ, and harpsichord perfected
- Handel: *Messiah* 1748>

The Catholic Reformation and the baroque style

"So sweet are the colloquies of love which pass between the soul and God …"
Saint Teresa of Avila

The Protestant Reformation created a religious upheaval unlike any other within the history of Western Christianity. Luther's criticism of the Roman Catholic Church had encouraged religious devotion free of papal authority and had prepared the way for the rise of other Protestant sects (chapter 19). The rival religious beliefs that fragmented Western Europe quickly accelerated into armed combat. The Thirty Years' War (1618–1648), which ended with the establishment of Protestantism throughout most of Northern Europe, caused the death of some five million Christians. During the early sixteenth century, as Protestant sects began to lure increasing numbers of Christians away from Roman Catholicism, the Church undertook a program of internal reform and reorganization known as the Catholic Reformation. Further, by the 1540s, in an effort to win back to Catholicism those who had strayed to Protestantism, the Church launched the evangelical campaign known as the Counter-Reformation. These two interdependent movements gradually introduced a more militant form of Catholicism to all parts of the world. They also encouraged intensely personalized expressions of religious sentiment, particularly in Spain, Italy, and Latin America. In the arts, a vigorous new style—the baroque—became the vehicle for this new, more dynamic outpouring of religious fervor.

The Catholic Reformation

In the face of the Protestant challenge, the Roman Catholic Church pursued a path that ensured its survival in the modern world. Between 1540 and 1565 churchmen undertook papal and monastic reforms that eliminated corruption and restored Catholicism to many parts of Europe. The impetus for renewal came largely from fervent Spanish Catholics, the most notable of whom was Ignatius Loyola (1491–1556). A soldier in the army of King Charles I of Spain (the Holy Roman emperor Charles V), Loyola brought to Catholicism the same iron will he had exercised on the battlefield. After his right leg was fractured by a French cannonball at the siege of Pamplona, Loyola became a religious teacher and a hermit, traveling lame and barefoot to Jerusalem in an effort to convert Muslims to Christianity. In the 1530s he founded the Society of Jesus, the most important of the many new monastic orders associated with the Catholic Reformation. The Society of Jesus, or Jesuits, followed Loyola in calling for a militant return to fundamental Catholic dogma and the strict enforcement of traditional Church teachings. In addition to the monastic vows of celibacy, poverty, and obedience, the Jesuits took an oath of allegiance to the pope, whom they served as soldiers of Christ.

Under Loyola's leadership, the Jesuit order became the most influential missionary society of early modern times. Rigorously trained, its members acted as preachers, confessors, and teachers—leaders in educational reform and moral discipline. Throughout Europe, members of the newly formed order worked as missionaries to win back those who had strayed from "Mother Church." The Jesuits were fairly successful in stamping out Protestantism in much of France, Southern Germany, and other parts of Europe. But their reach extended further: As pioneers in learning the languages and customs of India, China, and Japan, the Jesuits were the prime intermediaries between Europe and Asia from the sixteenth through the nineteenth century. In the Americas, which became prime targets for Jesuit activity, missionaries mastered Native American tribal languages and proceeded to convert thousands to Roman Catholicism. Their success in Mexico, Central and South America has stamped these parts of the world with a distinctive cultural character.

The Jesuit order was a fascinating amalgam of two elements—mysticism and militant religious zeal. The first emphasized the personal and intuitive experience of God, while the second involved an attitude of unquestioned submission to the Church as the absolute source of truth.

These two aspects of Jesuit thinking—mysticism and militancy—are reflected in Loyola's influential handbook, the *Spiritual Exercises*, published in 1548. In his introductory observations, Loyola explains that the spiritual exercises should do for the soul what such physical exercises as running and walking do for the body. As aids to the development of perfect spiritual discipline, these devotional exercises—each of which should occupy a full hour's time—engage the body in perfecting the soul. For example, in the Fifth Exercise, a meditation on Hell, each of the five senses is summoned to heighten the mystical experience:

> FIRST POINT: This will be to *see* in imagination the vast fires, and the souls enclosed, as it were, in bodies of fire.
> SECOND POINT: To *hear* the wailing, the howling, cries, and blasphemies against Christ our Lord and against His saints.
> THIRD POINT: With the sense of *smell* to perceive the smoke, the sulphur, the filth, and corruption.
> FOURTH POINT: To *taste* the bitterness of tears, sadness, and remorse of conscience.
> FIFTH POINT: With the sense of *touch* to feel the flames which envelop and burn the souls.

Loyola also insists on an unswerving commitment to traditional Church teachings. Among the "rules for thinking with the Church" is Loyola's advice that Christians put aside all judgments of their own and remain obedient to the "holy Mother, the hierarchical Church."

READING 4.1   From Loyola's *Spiritual Exercises* (1548)

The following rules should be observed to foster the true attitude of mind we ought to have in the church militant.

1   We must put aside all judgment of our own, and keep the mind ever ready and prompt to obey in all things the true Spouse of Christ our Lord, our holy Mother, the hierarchical Church.

2   We should praise sacramental confession, the yearly reception of the Most Blessed Sacrament, and praise more highly monthly reception, and still more weekly Communion, provided requisite and proper dispositions are present.

3   We ought to praise the frequent hearing of Mass, the singing of hymns, psalmody, and long prayers whether in the church or outside; likewise, the hours arranged at fixed times for the whole Divine Office, for every kind of prayer, and for the canonical hours.[1]

4   We must praise highly religious life, virginity, and continency; and matrimony ought not be praised as much as any of these.

5   We should praise vows of religion, obedience, poverty, chastity, and vows to perform other works . . . conducive to perfection. . . .

6   We should show our esteem for the relics of the saints by venerating them and praying to the saints. We should praise

visits to the Station Churches,[2] pilgrimages, indulgences, jubilees,[3] crusade indults,[4] and the lighting of candles in churches.

7   We must praise the regulations of the Church with regard to fast and abstinence. . . . We should praise works of penance, not only those that are interior but also those that are exterior.

8   We ought to praise not only the building and adornment of churches, but also images and veneration of them according to the subject they represent.

9   Finally, we must praise all the commandments of the Church, and be on the alert to find reasons to defend them, and by no means in order to criticize them. . . .

13 If we wish to proceed securely in all things, we must hold fast to the following principle: What seems to me white, I will believe black if the hierarchical Church so defines. For I must be convinced that in Christ our Lord, the bridegroom, and in His spouse the Church, only one Spirit holds sway, which governs and rules for the salvation of souls. For it is by the same Spirit and Lord who gave the Ten Commandments that our holy Mother Church is ruled and governed.

Loyola's affirmation of Roman Catholic doctrine anticipated the actions of the Council of Trent, the general church council that met intermittently between 1545 and 1563. The Council of Trent reconfirmed all seven of the sacraments and reasserted the traditional Catholic position on all theological matters that had been challenged by the Protestants. It also set clear guidelines for the elimination of abuses among members of the clergy, emphasized preaching to the uneducated laity, and encouraged the regeneration of intellectual life within Catholic monasteries. Church leaders revived the activities of the Inquisition (see chapter 12) and established the *Index Expurgatorius*, a list of books judged heretical and therefore forbidden to Catholic readers. The Catholic Reformation supported a broadly based Catholicism that emphasized the direct and intuitive—hence, mystical—experience of God. And although the Church of Rome would never again reassume the universal authority it had enjoyed during the Middle Ages, its internal reforms and its efforts to rekindle the faith restored its dignity in the minds and hearts of its followers.

Catholicism's Global Reach

The evangelical activities of the Jesuits and other religious orders were widespread, but not uniformly successful. In China, where European traders were regarded as "ocean devils," the Catholic missionaries assumed a cordial relationship with the intellectual classes and succeeded in

---

[1]The eight times of the day appointed for special devotions; see chapters 9 and 15.

[2]Churches with images representing the stages of Christ's Passion.
[3]A time of special solemnity, ordinarily every twenty-five years, proclaimed by the pope; also, special indulgences granted during that time. The jubilee principle is based on a biblical injunction to free slaves, return land to its original owners, and leave fields untilled once every fifty years (Leviticus 25).
[4]Church indulgences granted to Christian Crusaders.

converting a number of Chinese scholars. By the eighteenth century, however, disputes between the Jesuits and the Dominicans over the veneration of Confucius (aggravated by papal condemnation of Confucian rites in 1744) weakened Catholic influence. In Japan, the first Jesuit missionaries, admirers of Tokugawa culture (see chapter 21), diligently mastered the Japanese language and culture. While the Jesuits introduced the Japanese to European styles of painting and music, the Portuguese (and thereafter, Dutch and English) merchants brought imperialistic commercial interests to Japan, thus clouding the evangelical aims of the Jesuits with European material ambitions. The Jesuit efforts at conversion were also frustrated by rival Franciscan missionaries. Over time, the Jesuits fell into disfavor with Japanese Buddhists, who came to view all Christians as potentially subversive to the traditional social order. By 1606, following decades of disruption caused by European efforts to win trading privileges in Japan, the Japanese outlawed Christianity. The country expelled almost all Western foreigners from Japanese soil by 1624, after a wave of brutal persecutions of both European Christians and Japanese converts to Catholicism.

Christian evangelism in the Americas proved to be an entirely different story. In sixteenth-century Latin America, where Spanish political authority went largely unchallenged, Catholicism went hand in hand with colonization. The arrival of the Jesuits in Mexico in 1571 followed that of the Augustinians, the Dominicans, and the Franciscans in a vast program of Christianization. Just as the convergence of Europeans and Indians came to produce a unique new "Latin American" population, so the blend of European Catholic and native religious traditions produced a unique synthesis in the culture of Mexico. A formidable example of this creolizing phenomenon, and one that testifies to the powerful religious impact of Catholicism, is the Miracle of the Virgin of Guadalupe. In 1531, ten years after the conquest of Mexico by Cortés, on the site of a former shrine to the Aztec mother-goddess, a dark-skinned Virgin Mary appeared in a vision before a simple Mexican peasant. The legend of this miraculous apparition of the Mother of God, commemorated in hundreds of carved and painted images (Figure **20.1**), became the basis for the most important religious cult in Mexican history: the cult of the Virgin of Guadalupe. The colonial cult of Guadalupe worships the Virgin in the traditional medieval guise of mother, intercessor, and protector, but it also exalts her as the symbol of Mexican national consciousness. At her shrine—the goal of thousands of pilgrims each year—and at hundreds of chapels throughout Mexico, the faithful pay homage to the Virgin, who is shown standing on a crescent moon, surrounded by a corona of sunrays and angels bearing the colors of the Mexican flag. The significance of the Virgin of Guadalupe as a Christian devotional image, enthusiastically promoted by the Jesuits beginning in the late sixteeth century, and her widespread popularity as protectress of Mexico have persisted even into modern times: In 1910, she was made an honorary general of the Mexican Revolution.

Literature and the Catholic Reformation

The passionate mysticism of the Catholic Reformation infused the arts of the sixteenth and seventeenth centuries. In literature, there appeared a new emphasis on heightened spirituality and on personal visionary experience acquired by way of the senses. One of the most colorful personalities to emerge in forging the new language of mysticism was the Spanish Carmelite nun Teresa of Avila (1515–1582), who was canonized in 1622. Teresa's activities in founding religious houses and in defending groups of Carmelites, who symbolized their humility by going without shoes, took her all over Spain and earned her the nickname "the roving nun." It was not until she was almost forty years old that her life as a visionary began. Teresa's visions, including the one described in the following autobiographical excerpt, marry sensory experience to spiritual contemplation. They address, moreover, the intriguing kinship between physical suffering and psychic bliss and between divine and erotic fulfillment. For Saint Teresa, love is the inspiration for oneness with God. The language by which the saint describes that union is

Figure 20.1 The Virgin of Guadalupe, late seventeenth century. Oil, gilding, and mother-of-pearl on wood, height 74¾ in. Museo Franz Mayer, Mexico City.

charged with passion, for instance, when she relates how God's flaming arrow leaves her "completely afire."

READING 4.2 From Saint Teresa's *Visions* (1611)

It pleased the Lord that I should sometimes see the following vision. I would see beside me, on my left hand, an angel in bodily form—a type of vision which I am not in the habit of seeing, except very rarely. Though I often see representations of angels, my visions of them are of the type which I first mentioned. It pleased the Lord that I should see this angel in the following way. He was not tall, but short, and very beautiful, his face so aflame that he appeared to be one of the highest types of angel who seem to be all afire. They must be those who are called cherubim: they do not tell me their names **10** but I am well aware that there is a great difference between certain angels and others, and between these and others still, of a kind that I could not possibly explain. In his hands I saw a long golden spear and at the end of the iron tip I seemed to see a point of fire. With this he seemed to pierce my heart several times so that it penetrated to my entrails. When he drew it out, I thought he was drawing them out with it and he left me completely afire with a great love for God. The pain was so sharp that it made me utter several moans; and so excessive was the sweetness caused me by this intense pain **20** that one can never wish to lose it, nor will one's soul be content with anything less than God. It is not bodily pain, but spiritual, though the body has a share in it—indeed, a great share. So sweet are the colloquies of love which pass between the soul and God that if anyone thinks I am lying I beseech God, in His goodness, to give him the same experience.

1

The sensuous tone of Teresa's visions enriched the religious verse of the seventeenth century, including that of her Spanish contemporaries, Saint John of the Cross (1542–1591), also a Carmelite, and Luis de Góngora y Argote (1561–1637). Similarly, in the poetry of devout English Catholics such as Richard Crashaw (1613–1649), the language of religious ecstasy swells with brooding desire.

Born into a Protestant family, Crashaw converted to Catholicism early in life. His religious poems, written in Latin and English, reflect the dual influence of Loyola's meditations and Teresa's visions. At least two of his most lyrical pieces are dedicated to Saint Teresa: *A Hymn to the Name and Honor of the Admirable Saint Teresa* and *The Flaming Heart, upon the Book and Picture of the Seraphical Saint Teresa, as She Is Usually Expressed with a Seraphim beside Her.* The latter poem suggests that Crashaw was familiar with Bernini's sculpted version of Teresa's vision before it was publicly unveiled in Rome (Figure **20.2**). Representative of this visionary sensibility, the last sixteen lines of *The Flaming Heart*, reproduced in Reading 4.3, are rhapsodic in their intense expression of personal emotion. Erasing boundaries between erotic and spiritual love, Crashaw pleads that Teresa ravish his soul, even as she has been ravished by God.

READING 4.3 From Crashaw's *The Flaming Heart* (1652)

. . . .

O thou undaunted daughter of desires!
By all thou dower of lights and fires;
By all the eagle in thee, all the dove;
By all thy lives and deaths of love;
By thy large draughts of intellectual day,
And by thy thirsts of love more large than they,
By all thy brim-filled bowls of fierce desire,
By thy last morning's draught of liquid fire;
By the full kingdom of that final kiss
That seized thy parting soul, and sealed thee His;
By all the heavens thou hast in Him,
Fair sister of the seraphim,
By all of Him we have in thee;
Leave nothing of myself in me!
Let me so read thy life that I
Unto all life of mine may die.

The Visual Arts and the Catholic Reformation

Mannerist Painting

The religious zeal of the Catholic reformers inspired a tremendous surge of artistic activity, especially in Italy and Spain. In Venice and Rome, the centers of Italian cultural life, the art of the High Renaissance underwent radical transformation. The clearly defined, symmetrical compositions of High Renaissance painters and the decorum and dignity of the grand style (see chapter 17) gave way to *mannerism*, a style marked by spatial complexity, artificiality, and affectation. Mannerist artists brought a new psychological intensity to visual expression. Their paintings mirrored the self-conscious spirituality and the profound insecurities of an age of religious wars and political rivalry.

The mannerist style is already evident in *The Last Judgment* that the sixty-year-old Michelangelo (see chapter 17) painted on the east wall of the Sistine Chapel (Figure **20.3**). Between 1534 and 1541, only a few years after the armies of the Holy Roman Empire had sacked the city of Rome, Michelangelo returned to the chapel whose ceiling he had painted some twenty years earlier with the optimistic vision of salvation. Now, in a mood of brooding pessimism, he filled the altar wall with agonized, writhing figures that press dramatically against one another. Surrounding the wrathful Christ are the Christian martyrs, who carry the instruments of their torture, and throngs of the resurrected—originally depicted nude but later, in the wake of Catholic reform, draped to hide their genitals. Reflecting the anxieties of his day, Michelangelo has replaced the classically proportioned figures, calm balance, and spatial clarity of High Renaissance painting with a more troubled vision of salvation.

Figure 20.3 MICHELANGELO BUONARROTI, *The Last Judgment* (after restoration), 1536–1540. Fresco, 48 × 44 ft. Altar wall, Sistine Chapel, Vatican, Rome. Nippon Television, Tokyo.

Figure 20.4 PARMIGIANINO,
Madonna of the Long Neck,
1534–1540. Oil on panel, 7 ft. 1 in.
× 4 ft. 4 in. Uffizi Gallery, Florence.
Scala/Art Resource, New York.

The traits of the mannerist style can be seen best in the *Madonna of the Long Neck* (Figure **20.4**) by Parmigianino (1503–1540). In this work the traditional subject of Madonna and Child is given a new mood of theatricality (compare Raphael's *Alba Madonna*; see chapter 17). Perched precariously above a courtyard adorned with a column that supports no superstructure, the unnaturally elongated Mother of God—her spidery fingers affectedly touching her chest—gazes at the oversized Christ child, who seems to slip lifelessly off her lap. Onlookers press into the ambiguous space from the left, while a small figure (perhaps a prophet) at the bottom right corner of the canvas draws our eye into distant space. Cool coloring and an overall smoky hue make the painting seem even more contrived and artificial, yet, by its very contrivance, unforgettable.

The degree to which the mannerists rejected the guiding principles of High Renaissance painting is nowhere better illustrated than by a comparison of *The Last Supper* (Figure **20.5**) by the Venetian artist Jacopo Tintoretto (1518–1594) with the mural of the same subject by Leonardo da

Figure 20.5 JACOPO TINTORETTO, *The Last Supper*, 1592–1594. Oil on canvas, 12 ft × 18 ft. 8 in. San Giorgio Maggiore, Venice. Scala, Florence.

Vinci (see chapter 17) executed approximately a century earlier (Figure **20.6**). In his rendering of the sacred event, Tintoretto renounces the symmetry and geometric clarity of Leonardo's composition. The receding lines of the table and the floor in Tintoretto's painting place the viewer above the scene and draw the eye toward a vanishing point that lies in a distant and uncertain space beyond the canvas. The even texture of Leonardo's fresco gives way in Tintoretto's canvas to vaporous contrasts of dark and light, produced by a smoking oil lamp. Clouds of angels flutter spectrally at the ceiling, and phosphorescent halos seem to electrify the figures of the apostles. At the most concen-

Figure 20.6 LEONARDO DA VINCI, *The Last Supper*, ca. 1485–1498.
Oil and tempera on plaster, 14 ft 5 in × 28 ft. Refectory, Santa Maria delle Grazie, Milan. Scala/Art Resource, New York.

trated burst of light, the Savior is pictured distributing bread and wine to the disciples. While Leonardo focuses on the human element of the Last Supper—the moment when Jesus acknowledges his impending betrayal—Tintoretto illustrates the superhuman and miraculous moment when Jesus initiates the sacrament by which the bread and wine become his flesh and blood. Yet Tintoretto sets the miracle amidst the ordinary activities of household servants, who occupy the entire right-hand portion of the picture.

The mannerist passion for pictorial intensity was most vividly realized in the paintings of Domenikos Theotokopoulos, generally known (because of his Greek origins) as El Greco (1541–1614). A master painter who worked in Italy and Spain in the service of the Church and the devout Philip II, El Greco preferred the dramatic grace of Tintoretto to the more muscular vitality of Michelangelo. With the inward eye of a mystic, he produced visionary canvases marked by bold distortions of form, dissonant colors, and a daring handling of space. His

figures, elongated and flamelike, and often highlighted by ghostly whites and yellow-grays, seem to radiate halos of light—auras that symbolize the luminous power of divine revelation. In *The Agony in the Garden*, the moment of Jesus' final submission to the divine will, El Greco created a moonlit landscape in which clouds, rocks, and fabrics billow and swell with mysterious energy (Figure **20.7**). Below the tempestuous sky, Judas (lower right) leads the arresting officers to the Garden of Gethsemane. The sleeping apostles, tucked away in a cocoonlike envelope, violate rational space: They are too small in relation to the oversized image of Jesus and the angel that hovers above. El Greco's ambiguous spatial fields, which often include multiple vanishing points, his acrid greens and acid yellows, and his "painterly" techniques—his brushstrokes remain engagingly visible on the surface of the canvas—all contribute to the creation of a highly personal and, by our standards, "modern" style that captured the mystical fervor of the new Catholicism.

Figure 20.7 EL GRECO, *The Agony in the Garden*, ca. 1585–1586. Oil on canvas, 6 ft. 1 in. × 9 ft. 1 in. Courtesy of the Toledo Museum of Art, Ohio. Purchased with funds from the Libbey Endowment, Gift of Edward Drummond Libbey.

Baroque Painting in Italy

If mannerism was the vehicle of the Counter-Reformation mysticism, the *baroque style* conveyed the dynamic spirit of an entire age. Derived from the Portuguese word *barocco*, which describes the irregularly shaped pearls often featured in ornamental European decoration, the term *baroque* is associated with such features as ornateness, spatial grandeur, and theatrical flamboyance. In painting, the baroque style is characterized by asymmetric compositions, strong contrasts of light and dark, and bold, illusionistic effects.

The baroque style originated in Italy and came to dominate artistic production in the years between 1600 and 1750 throughout Europe and in those parts of the Americas colonized by Spain. Italian baroque artists worked to increase the dramatic expressiveness of religious subject matter in order to give viewers the sense that they were participating in the action of the scene. They copied nature faithfully and without idealization. Such was the ambition of the North Italian artist Michelangelo Merisi, known as Caravaggio (1573–1610). The leading Italian painter of the seventeenth century, Caravaggio flouted Renaissance artistic conventions, even as he flouted the law—he was arrested for violent acts that ranged from throwing a plate of artichokes in the face of a tavern keeper to armed assault and murder. In his paintings, Caravaggio renounced the grand style of the High Renaissance, which called for dignity, decorum, and the idealization of figures and setting. Rather, he recreated the early Christian past as though its major events were occurring in the local taverns and streets of sixteenth-century Italy. Caravaggio dramatized these events with strong contrasts of light and dark that give his figures a sculptural presence. A golden light bathes Christ and his disciples in *The Supper at Emmaus* (Figure 20.8); Caravaggio "spotlights" Jesus at the moment when, raising his hand to bless the bread, he is recognized as the Christ (Luke 24:30–31). Caravaggio further underscores the moment of recognition by means of vigorous theatrical gestures. Christ's right arm, painted at angles to the picture plane by means of a perspective device known as **foreshortening**, seems to project sharply toward the beholders, as if to bless them as well as the bread. At the moment of recognition, the disciple at the right flings his arms outward along a diagonal axis that draws the viewer into the composition, while the figure at the left grips the arm of his chair as though to rise in astonishment. Unlike the visionary El Greco, Caravaggio brings sacred subjects down to earth with an almost cameralike naturalism. Where El Greco's saints and martyrs are ethereal, Caravaggio's are solid, substantive, and often quite ordinary. Their strong physical presence and frank homeliness transform biblical miracles into human narratives—a bold repudiation of Italian Renaissance conventions of beauty.

Figure 20.8 CARAVAGGIO, *The Supper at Emmaus*, ca. 1600. Oil on canvas, 4 ft 7 in. × 6 ft. 5½ in. National Gallery, London.

Figure 20.9 CARAVAGGIO, *The Crucifixion of Saint Peter*, 1601. Oil on canvas, 7 ft. 6 in. × 5 ft. 9 in. Santa Maria del Popolo, Rome. Scala, Florence.

519

CHAPTER TWENTY   The Catholic Reformation and the baroque style

Caravaggio organized traditional religious compositions with unprecedented theatrical power and daring. In *The Crucifixion of Saint Peter* (Figure **20.9**), he arranged the figures in a tense, off-centered pinwheel that catches the eccentricity of Saint Peter's torment (he was crucified upside down). The saint's powerful physique is belied by the expression of vulnerability on his aging face. By placing the vigorously modeled figures close to the viewer, Caravaggio reduces the psychological distance between viewer and subject. By illuminating them against a darkened background, he "stages" the action so that it seems to take place within the viewer's space—a space whose cruel light reveals such banal details as the executioner's dirty feet. True to the ideals of the Catholic Reformation, Caravaggio's paintings appealed to the senses rather than to the intellect, but they also introduced into European art a new and vigorously lifelike realization of the natural world, one that inventively mingled the sacred and the profane.

Caravaggio's powerful style had considerable impact throughout Europe, but his most talented follower was born in Rome: Artemisia Gentileschi (1593–1653) was the daughter of a highly esteemed painter, himself a follower of Caravaggio. Trained by her father, Artemisia soon outstripped him in technical proficiency and imagination. Since women were not permitted to draw from live male models, they rarely painted large-scale canvases with biblical and mythological themes, which required monumental nude figures; instead, their efforts were confined to the genres of portrait painting and still life. Gentileschi's paintings, however, challenged this tradition. Her canvas *Judith Slaying Holofernes* (Figure **20.10**), which compares in size and impact with Caravaggio's *Crucifixion of Saint Peter* (see Figure 20.9), illustrates the decapitation of an Assyrian general and enemy of Israel at the hands of a clever Hebrew widow. A tale found in the Apocrypha (the non-canonical books of the Bible), the slaying of the tyrannical Holofernes was a favorite Renaissance allegory of liberty and religious defiance. Gentileschi invested this painting with the dramatic techniques of Caravaggio: realistically conceived figures, stark contrasts of light and dark, and a

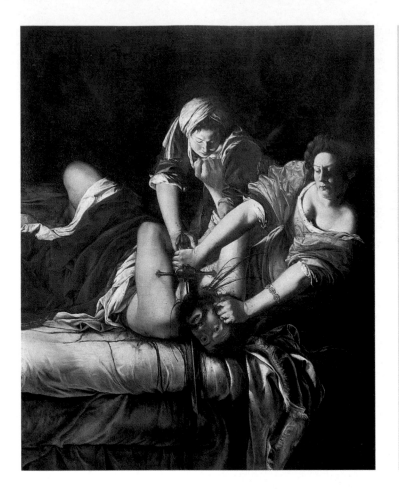

Figure 20.10 ARTEMISIA GENTILESCHI, *Judith Slaying Holofernes*, ca. 1614–1620. Oil on canvas, 6 ft 6⅓ in. × 5 ft. 4 in. Uffizi Gallery, Florence.

composition that brings the viewer painfully close to the event; but she invested her subject with fierce intensity— the pinwheel arrangement of human limbs forces the eye to focus on the gruesome action of the swordblade as it severs head from neck in a shower of blood.

Gentileschi's favorite subjects were biblical heroines— she painted the Judith story some seven times. The violence she brought to these particular subjects may have been influenced by her profound sense of victimization: At the age of eighteen, she was raped by her drawing teacher and (during the sensational trial of her assailant) subjected to torture as a test of the truth of her testimony.

Baroque Sculpture in Italy

Gianlorenzo Bernini (1598–1680), Caravaggio's contemporary, brought the theatrical spirit of baroque painting to Italian architecture and sculpture. A man of remarkable technical virtuosity, Bernini was the chief architect of seventeenth-century Rome, as well as one of its leading

Figure 20.11 GIANLORENZO BERNINI, Fountain of the Four Rivers, 1648–1651. Travertine and marble. Piazza Navona, Rome. Alinari/ Art Resource, New York.

Figure 20.12 Anonymous, Cornaro Chapel, ca. 1644. Oil on canvas, 5 ft. 6¼ in. × 3 ft. 11¼ in. Staatliches Museum, Schwerin, Germany. Photo: E. Walford, Hamburg.

sculptors. Under Bernini's direction, Rome became the "city of fountains," a phenomenon facilitated by the early seventeenth-century revival of the old Roman aqueducts. Richly adorned with dolphins, mermaids, and tritons, the fountain—its waters dancing and sparkling in the shifting wind and light—was the favorite ornamental device of the baroque era (Figure **20.11**).

Bernini's most important contribution to baroque religious sculpture was his multimedia masterpiece *The Ecstasy of Saint Teresa* (see Figure 20.2), executed between 1645 and 1652 for the Cornaro Chapel of Santa Maria della Vittoria in Rome (Figure **20.12**). The piece illustrates Bernini's dazzling skill in bringing to life Saint Teresa's autobiographical description of divine seduction (see Reading 4.2). Bernini depicts the swooning saint with head sunk

back and eyes half closed. A smiling angel, resembling a teenage cupid, gently lifts Teresa's bodice to insert the flaming arrow of divine love. Bold illusionism heightens the sensuous effect: The angel's marble draperies flutter and billow with tense energy, while the slack and heavy gown of Teresa echoes the emotion of ecstatic surrender. The vision takes place on a marble cloud, which floats in heavenly space, while the uncertain juxtaposition of the saint and the cloud on which she reclines suggests the experience of levitation described in her vision. Sweetness and eroticism are the central features of this extraordinary image.

But Bernini's conception goes beyond the sculpture of the two figures to achieve a dramatic unity of figure and setting. To capture the theatrical intensity of Teresa's mystical experience, Bernini engaged the tools of architecture, sculpture, and painting: He situated Teresa beneath a colonnaded marble canopy from which radiate gilded wood rays (heaven's supernatural light). Real light entering through the glazed yellow panes of a concealed window above the chapel bathes the saint in a golden glow—an effect comparable to the spotlighting in a Caravaggio painting. At the ceiling of the chapel a host of angels both painted and sculpted in **stucco** (a light, pliable plaster) miraculously descends from the heavens. Agate and dark green marble walls provide a somber setting for the gleaming white and gold central image. On either side of the chapel, the members of the Cornaro family (conceived in marble) behold Teresa's ecstasy from behind prayer desks that resemble theater boxes. These life-sized figures extend the supernatural space of the chapel and reinforce the viewer's role as witness to an actual event. It is no coincidence that Bernini's illusionistic tour de force appeared contemporaneously with the birth of opera in Italy, for both share the baroque affection for dramatic expression on a monumental scale.

Baroque Architecture in Italy

The city of Rome carries the stamp of Bernini's flamboyant style. Commissioned to complete the *piazza*, the broad public space in front of Saint Peter's Basilica, Bernini designed a trapezoidal space that opens out to a larger oval—the two shapes form, perhaps symbolically, a keyhole. Bernini's courtyard is bounded by a spectacular colonnade that incorporates 284 Doric columns (each 39

feet high) as well as 96 statues of saints (each 15 feet tall). In a manner consistent with the ecumenical breadth of Jesuit evangelism, the gigantic pincerlike arms of the colonnade reach out to embrace an area that can accommodate over 250,000 people (Figure **20.13**)—a vast proscenium on which devotional activities of the Church of Rome are staged to this day. The Saint Peter's of Bernini's time was the locus of papal authority; then, as now, popes used the central balcony of the basilica to impart the traditional blessing: "Urbi et Orbi" ("To the city and to the world"). The proportions of Bernini's colonnade are symbolic of the baroque preference for the grandiose, a preference equally apparent in the artist's spectacular setting for the Throne of Saint Peter and in the immense bronze canopy (*baldacchino*) he raised over the high altar of the basilica (Figure **20.14**).

As with Saint Peter's, Italian baroque churches were designed to reflect the mystical and evangelical ideals of the Catholic Reformation. Il Gesù (the Church of Jesus) in Rome was the mother church of the Jesuit order and the model for hundreds of Counter-Reformation churches

Figure 20.13 (below) **GIANLORENZO BERNINI**, Aerial view of colonnade and Piazza of Saint Peter's, Rome, begun 1656. Travertine, longitudinal axis approx. 800 ft. Copper engraving by Giovanni Piranesi, 1750. Kunstbibliothek, Berlin. The enormous piazza in front of the east façade of Saint Peter's can accommodate over 250,000 people.

Figure 20.14 (opposite) **GIANLORENZO BERNINI**, *Baldacchino*, ca. 1624–1633. Bronze with gilding, height 93 ft. 6 in. Saint Peter's, Rome, Scala/Art Resource, New York.

Figure 20.15 **GIACOMO DA VIGNOLA**, interior of Il Gesù, Rome, 1568–1573. Length approx. 240 ft. Foto Marburg.

Figure 20.16 **GIACOMO DA VIGNOLA** and **GIACOMO DELLA PORTA**, facade of Il Gesù, Rome, ca. 1575–1584. Height 105 ft., width 115 ft. The Conway Library, Courtauld Institute of Art, London.

built throughout Europe and Latin America. Designed by Giacomo da Vignola (1507–1573), Il Gesù bears the typical features of the baroque church interior: a broad Latin cross nave with domed crossing and deeply recessed chapels (Figure 20.15). Lacking side aisles, the 60-foot-wide nave allowed a large congregation to assemble close enough to the high altar and the pulpit to see the ceremony and hear the sermon. The wide nave also provided ample space for elaborate religious processions. Il Gesù's interior, with its magnificent altarpiece dedicated to Ignatius Loyola, exemplifies the baroque inclination to synthesize various media, such as painted stucco, bronze, and precious stones, in the interest of achieving sumptuous and ornate effects.

The exterior of Il Gesù, completed by Giacomo della Porta, is equally dramatic (Figure 20.16). Its design—especially the elegant buttressing scrolls—looks back to Alberti's two-storied facade of Santa Maria Novella (Figure 20.17). But in contrast to the linear sobriety of his Florentine model, della Porta's facade, with its deeply carved decorative elements, has a dynamic sculptural presence. For dramatic effect, the architect added structurally functionless engaged columns topped with Corinthian capitals. An ornate **cartouche** (oval tablet) and a double cornice accentuate the central doorway, inviting the worshiper to enter. While the Renaissance facade was conceived in two dimensions, according to an essentially geometric linear pattern, the baroque churchfront is conceived in three. Like a Caravaggio painting, Il Gesù exploits dramatic contrasts of light and dark and of shallow and deep space.

The most daring of the Italian baroque architects was Francesco Borromini (1599–1667). Borromini designed the small monastic church of San Carlo alle Quattro

Figure 20.17 **LEON BATTISTA ALBERTI**, facade of Santa Maria Novella, Florence, completed 1470. Width approx. 117 ft. Scala, Florence.

Figure 20.18
FRANCESCO BORROMINI,
facade of San Carlo alle Quattro
Fontane, Rome, 1667; Length 52 ft.,
width 34 ft., width of facade 38 ft.
© Araldo de Luca, Rome.

Fontane (Saint Charles at the Four Fountains; Figure **20.18**) to fit a narrow site at the intersection of two Roman streets. Rejecting the rules of classical design, he combined convex and concave units to produce a sense of fluid and undulating movement. The facade consists of an assortment of deeply cut decorative elements: monumental Corinthian columns, a scrolled gable over the doorway,

and life-sized angels that support a cartouche at the roofline. Borromini's aversion to the circle and the square—the "perfect" shapes of Renaissance architecture—extends to the interior of San Carlo, which is oval in plan. The dome, also oval, is lit by hidden windows that flood the interior with light. Carved with geometric motifs that diminish in size toward the apex, the shallow cupola

Figure 20.19 FRANCESCO BORROMINI, interior of dome, San Carlo alle Quattro Fontane, Rome, ca. 1638. Width approx. 52 ft. Alinari/Art Resource, New York.

appears to recede deep into space (Figure **20.19**). Such inventive illusionism, accented by dynamic spatial contrasts, characterized the Roman baroque style of church architecture at its best.

But the theatricality of the baroque style went further still: By painting religious scenes on the walls and ceilings of churches and chapels, baroque artists turned houses of God into theaters for sacred drama. Such is the case with the Church of Sant'Ignazio in Rome, the barrel-vaulted ceiling of which bears a breathtaking *trompe l'oeil* vision of Saint Ignatius' apotheosis—his elevation to divine status (Figure **20.20**). A master of the techniques of linear perspective and dramatic foreshortening, the Jesuit architect and sculptor Andrea Pozzo (1642–1709) made the walls above Sant'Ignazio's clerestory appear to open up, so that the viewer gazes "through" the roof into the heavens

that receive the levitating body of the saint. Pozzo's cosmic rendering—one of the first of numerous illusionistic ceilings found in seventeenth- and eighteenth-century European churches and palaces—may be taken to reflect a new perception of physical space inspired, in part, by European geographic exploration and discovery. Indeed, Pozzo underlines the global ambitions of Roman Catholic evangelism by adding at the four corners of the ceiling the allegorical figures of Asia, Africa, Europe, and America. The vast, illusionistic spatial fields of Italian baroque frescoes also may be seen as a response to the new astronomy of the Scientific Revolution, which presented a view of the universe as spatially infinite and dynamic rather than

Figure 20.20 (opposite) **ANDREA POZZO**, *Apotheosis of Saint Ignatius*, 1691. Fresco. Nave ceiling, Sant'Ignazio, Rome. Scala, Florence.

finite and static (see chapter 23). Whatever its inspiration, the spatial illusionism of baroque painting and architecture gave apocalyptic grandeur to Counter-Reformation ideals.

Baroque Music

In an effort to rid sacred music of secular influence, the Council of Trent condemned complex polyphony and the borrowing of popular tunes, both of which had become popular in religious music since the late Middle Ages. Above all, the reformers stressed the intelligibility of the sacred text: The message of the words was primary. The Italian composer Giovanni di Palestrina (1525–1594) took these recommendations as strict guidelines: His more than one hundred polyphonic masses and 450 motets feature clarity of text, skillful counterpoint, and regular rhythms. The *a cappella* lines of Palestrina's Pope Marcellus Mass flow with the smooth grace of a mannerist painting. Called "the music of mystic serenity," Palestrina's compositions embody the conservative and contemplative side of the Catholic Reformation rather than its inventive, dramatic aspect. In the religious compositions of Palestrina's Spanish contemporary Tomás Luis de Victoria, there is a brooding but fervent mystical intensity. Like El Greco, his colleague at the court of Philip II, Victoria brought passion and drama to religious themes. And, recognizing that the Council of Trent had forbidden Palestrina to compose secular music, Victoria wrote not one note of secular song.

The Genius of Gabrieli

At the turn of the sixteenth century, the opulent city of Venice was the center of European religious musical activity. Giovanni Gabrieli (1555–1612), principal organist at Saint Mark's Cathedral in Venice and one of the greatest composers of his time, ushered in a new and dramatic style of choral and instrumental music. Gabrieli composed expansive **polychoral** religious pieces featuring up to five choruses. Abandoning the *a cappella* style favored in Rome, he included solo and ensemble groups of instruments—especially the trombones and cornets commonly used in Venice's ritual street processions. Gabrieli was the first composer to indicate a specific instrument for each voice part in the musical composition, earning him the name "the father of orchestration." Like baroque painters and sculptors, who sought sharp contrasts of light and shadow and dramatic spatial effects, Gabrieli created coloristic contrasts in sound. He was among the first composers to write into his scores the words *piano* (soft) and *forte* (loud) to govern the **dynamics** (the degree of loudness or softness) of the piece.

Gabrieli was also the first musician to make use of a divided choir employed in *concertato*, that is, in opposing or contrasting bodies of sound. At Saint Mark's, an organ was located on each side of the chancel, and four choirs were stationed on balconies high above the nave. The antiphonal play of chorus, instruments, and solo voices produced exhilarating sonorities (evident in the excerpt from Gabrieli's motet, *In Ecclesiis* 🎵) that met and mingled in the magical space above the heads of the congregation. In some of Gabrieli's compositions, echo effects produced by alternating voices and the use of unseen (offstage) voices achieve a degree of musical illusionism comparable to the visual illusionism of mannerist and baroque art. Like the extremes of light and dark in the paintings of El Greco and Caravaggio, Gabrieli's alternating bodies of sound (chorus versus chorus, solo voice versus chorus, chorus versus instruments) and contrasting musical dynamics (loud and soft) and pitches (high and low) produce strong harmonic textures and rich, dramatic effects. The *concertato* technique was the essence of early seventeenth-century baroque music and, in Gabrieli's hands, it was nothing less than majestic.

Gabrieli explored a type of musical organization that would come to dominate baroque music: *tonality* based on the melodic, harmonic, and rhythmic vocabulary of the major–minor key system. **Tonality** refers to the arrangement of a musical composition around a central note, called the "tonic" or "home tone" (usually designated as the "key" of a given composition). A keynote or tonic can be built on any of the twelve tones of the **chromatic scale** (the twelve tones—seven white and five black keys—of the piano keyboard). In baroque music—as in most music written to this day—all of the tones in the composition relate to the home tone. Tonality provided baroque composers with a way of achieving dramatic focus in a piece of music—much in the way that light served baroque painters to achieve dramatic focus in their compositions. By the mid-seventeenth century, the even progress of Renaissance polyphony, like the even lighting of Renaissance painting, had given way to the dynamic use of individual voices and the inventive combination of choral and instrumental textures.

Monteverdi and the Birth of Opera

The master of baroque vocal expression and the greatest Italian composer of the seventeenth century was Claudio Monteverdi (1567–1643). Monteverdi served the court of Mantua until he became chapel master of Saint Mark's in Venice in 1621, a post he held for the rest of his life. During his long career, he wrote various kinds of religious music, as well as ballets, madrigals, and operas. Like Gabrieli, Monteverdi discarded the intimate dimensions of Renaissance chamber music and cultivated an expansive, dramatic style, makred by vivid contrasts of texture and color. His compositions reflect a typically baroque effort to imbue music with a vocal expressiveness that reflected the emotional charge of poetry. "The [written] text," declared Monteverdi, "should be the master of the music, not the servant." Monteverdi linked "affections" or specific emotional states with appropriate sounds: anger, for instance, with the high voice register, moderation with the middle voice register, and humility with the low voice register. With Monteverdi, the union of music and speech sought in the word painting techniques of Josquin (see

🎵 See Music Listening Selections at end of chapter.

Figure 20.21 P. D. OLIVIER, *The Teatro Regio, Turin*. Painting of the opening night, December 26, 1740. Five tiers of boxes are fitted into the sides of the proscenium, one even perched over the semicircular pediment. Note the orchestra, without a conductor; the girls distributing refreshments; and the armed guard protecting against disorder. Courtesy of the Museo Civico, Turin.

chapter 17) blossomed into full-blown opera: that form of theater that combined all aspects of baroque artistic expression—music, drama, dance, and the visual arts.

Born in Italy, opera emerged out of Renaissance efforts to revive the music-drama of ancient Greek theater. While humanist composers had no idea what Greek music sounded like, they sought to imitate the ancient unity of music and poetry. The earliest performances of Western opera resembled the Renaissance masque, a form of musical entertainment that included dance and poetry, along with rich costumes and scenery. Baroque operas were more musically complex, however, and more dramatically cohesive than most Renaissance masques. The first opera house was built in Venice in 1637, and by 1700 Italy was home to seventeen more such houses, a measure of the vast popularity of the new genre. By the end of the seventeenth century, Italian courts and public theaters boasted all of the essential features of the modern theater: the picture-frame stage, the horseshoe-shaped auditorium, and tiers of galleries or boxes (Figure **20.21**). Interestingly enough, some of these opera houses, resplendent with life-sized sculptures and illusionistic frescoes, are aesthetically indistinguishable from Italian baroque church and chapel interiors (see Figures 20.12 and 20.15).

Monteverdi's *Orfeo*, ♪ composed in 1607 for the duke of Mantua, was Monteverdi's first opera and one of the first full-length operas in music history. The libretto (literally,

♪ See Music Listening Selections at end of chapter.

"little book") or text of the opera was written by Alessandro Striggio and based on a classical theme—the descent of Orpheus, the Greek poet-musician, to Hades. Orfeo required an orchestra of more than three dozen instruments, including ten viols, three trombones, and four trumpets. The instrumentalists performed the **overture**, an orchestral introduction to the opera. They also accompanied vocal music that consisted of **arias** (elaborate solo songs or duets) alternating with **recitatives** (passages spoken or recited to sparse chordal accompaniment). The aria tended to develop a character's feelings or state of mind, while the recitative served to narrate the action of the story or to heighten its dramatic effect.

Monteverdi believed that opera should convey the full range of human passions. To that end, he contrived inventive contrasts between singer and accompaniment, recitative and aria, soloist and chorus. He also employed abrupt changes of key to emphasize shifts in mood and action. And he introduced such novel and expressive instrumental effects as *pizzicato*, the technique of plucking rather than bowing a stringed instrument. A multimedia synthesis of music, drama, and visual display, Italian opera, whether secular or religious in theme, became the ideal expression of the baroque sensibility and the object of imitation throughout Western Europe.

SUMMARY

In the wake of the Protestant Reformation, the Roman Catholic Church launched a reform movement that took late sixteenth-century Europe by storm. Loyola's *Spiritual Exercises* and the autobiographical writings of Saint Teresa of Avila set the tone for a new, more mystical Catholicism. In the spirit of Saint Teresa's ecstatic visions, such Catholic poets as Richard Crashaw wrote rhapsodic lyrics that fused sensual and spiritual yearnings. The arts of the seventeenth century reflect the religious intensity of the Catholic Reformation, even as they mirror the insecurities of the religiously divided and politically turbulent West.

The baroque style, which came to dominate Western Europe between 1600 and 1750, was born in Italy. The mannerist paintings of Parmigianino, Tintoretto, and El Greco anticipated the baroque style by their figural distortions, irrational space, bizarre colors, and general disregard for the "rules" of Renaissance painting. Italian baroque art, as typified by Caravaggio's paintings and Bernini's sculpture, featured dynamic contrasts of light and dark, an expanded sense of space, and the operatic staging of subject matter. Counter-Reformation churches, embellished with visionary paintings and sculptures, were ornate theaters for the performance of Catholic ritual. Bernini's *Ecstasy of Saint Teresa* and Pozzo's ceiling for the Church of Saint Ignatius in Rome achieved new heights of illusionistic theatricality. Addressing the passions rather than the intellect, baroque art broadcast the visionary message of Catholic reform to a vast audience that extended from Europe to the Americas.

Rome and Venice were fountainheads for Italian baroque art and music. Palestrina's polyphonic masses and motets emphasized clarity of text and calm sublimity, while Gabrieli's lofty polychoral compositions, performed at Saint Mark's Cathedral in Venice, featured dynamic contrasts between and among voices and musical nstruments. The daring contrasts, rich color, and sheer volume of Gabrieli's music find their parallel in the canvases of Caravaggio.

The most important development in seventeenth-century European music was the birth of opera. Borrowing themes from classical mythology and history, Claudio Monteverdi integrated text and music to create the new and noble art of music-drama. In its synthesis of all forms of performance—music, literature, and the visual arts—Italian opera became the supreme expression of the theatrical exuberance and spiritual vitality of the baroque style.

GLOSSARY

aria an elaborate solo song or duet, usually with instrumental accompaniment, performed as part of an opera or other dramatic musical composition

cartouche an oval tablet or medallion, usually containing an inscription or heraldic device

chromatic scale a series of twelve tones represented by the seven white and five black keys of the piano keyboard; see also Glossary, chapter 6, "scale"

concertato (Italian, concerto = "opposing" or "competing") an early baroque style in which voices or instruments of different rather than similar natures are used in an opposing or contrasting manner

dynamics the degree of loudness or softness in music

foreshortening a perspective device by which figures or objects appear to recede or project into space

overture an instrumental introduction to a longer musical piece, such as an opera

piazza (Italian) a broad, open public space

pizzicato (Italian) the technique of plucking (with the fingers) rather than bowing a stringed instrument

polychoral music written for two or more choruses, performed both in turn and together

recitative a textual passage recited to sparse chordal accompaniment; a rhythmically free vocal style popular in seventeenth-century opera

stucco a light, pliable plaster made of gypsum, sand, water, and ground marble

tonality the use of a central note, called the *tonic*, around which all other tonal material of a composition is organized, and to which the music returns for a sense of rest and finality

SUGGESTIONS FOR READING

Bantel, Linda, and M. B. Burke. *Spain and New Spain: Mexican Colonial Arts in their European Context*. Corpus Christi, Tex.: Art Museum of South Texas, 1992.

Bianconi, Lorenzo. *Music in the Seventeenth Century*, translated by David Bryant. New York: Cambridge University Press, 1987.

Lavin, Irving. *Bernini and the Unity of the Visual Arts*. New York: Oxford University Press, 1980.

Hammond, Frederick. *Music and Spectacle in Baroque Rome*. New Haven: Yale University Press, 1994.

Marden, T. A. *Bernini and the Art of Architecture*. New York: Abbeville Press, 1999.

Martin, John Rupert. *Baroque*. New York: Harper, 1977.

Mullett, Michael A. *The Catholic Reformation*. New York: Routledge, 1999

Norberg-Schulz, Christian. *Baroque Architecture*. New York: Rizzoli, 1986.

Petersson, Robert T. *The Art of Ecstasy: Teresa, Bernini and Crashaw*. New York: Atheneum, 1970.

Sternfeld, F. W. *The Birth of Opera*. New York: Oxford University Press, 1995.

Wittkower, Rudolf, and Irma B. Jaffe, eds. *Baroque Art: The Jesuit Contribution*. New York: Fordham University Press, 1972.

MUSIC LISTENING SELECTIONS

CD Two Selection 1 Gabrieli, Motet, "In Ecclesiis," excerpt, 1615.
CD Two Selection 2 Monteverdi, *Orfeo*, Aria: "Vi recorda, o boschi ombrosi," 1607.

CHAPTER TWENTY-ONE

Absolute power and the aristocratic style

"Virtue would not go nearly so far if vanity did not keep her company."
La Rochefoucauld

The early modern era in the West is sometimes called the Age of Absolutism. Absolutism, a political theory asserting that unlimited power be vested in one or more rulers, confirmed longstanding theocratic tradition. During the seventeenth and well into the eighteenth century, divine right kings—rulers who were believed to hold their power directly from God—exercised unlimited power within their individual nation-states. But the term "Age of Absolutism" is equally appropriate to the period as it unfolded in the lands beyond Europe, for in China, India, and elsewhere, divine right monarchs also held unlimited control over their own vast states or empires (Map **21.1**).

Absolute rulers maintained their authority by controlling a centralized bureaucracy and a standing army, and by pursuing economic policies designed to maximize the wealth of the state. In Western Europe, the mightiest of

Map 21.1 Empires in the Late Sixteenth and Early Seventeenth Centuries

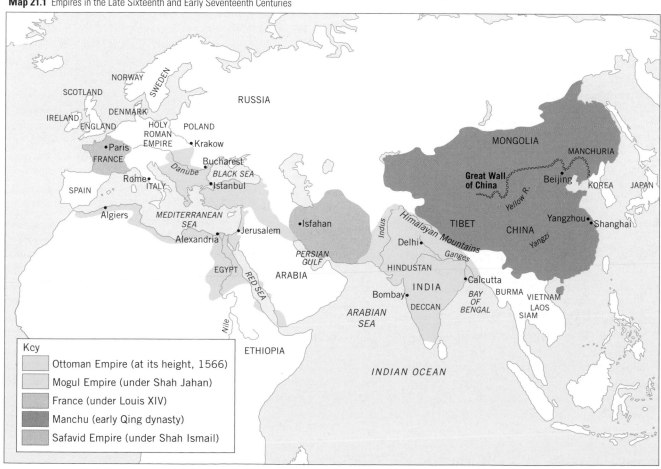

Key

- Ottoman Empire (at its height, 1566)
- Mogul Empire (under Shah Jahan)
- France (under Louis XIV)
- Manchu (early Qing dynasty)
- Safavid Empire (under Shah Ismail)

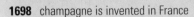

1657 the first fountain pens are manufactured in Paris

1688 the French army introduces bayonets attached to muskets

1698 champagne is invented in France

such potentates was King Louis XIV of France. During the nearly three-quarters of a century that Louis occupied the French throne (1643–1715), he dictated the political, economic, and cultural policies of the country. Under his guidance, France assumed a position of political and military leadership in Western Europe. As cultural arbiter, Louis helped to bring about a phase of the baroque called the *classical baroque*. This style pervaded the arts of seventeenth-century France and became one of the hallmarks of French absolutism. It also impressed its stamp on the rest of Europe and, somewhat later, on an emergent American culture.

Outside of Europe, absolute rulers also held sway: Suleiman the Magnificent (grand vizier of the Ottoman Empire), the Safavids of Persia in Southwest Asia, the Moguls in India, the Ming and Qing emperors in China, and the Tokugawa rulers in Japan. Within each of these territories, as within the European nation-states, the arts flourished as an expression of the majesty of the ruler and of the wealth and strength of his domain.

The Aristocratic Style in France

Louis XIV and French Absolutism

Like the pharaohs of ancient Egypt and in the tradition of his medieval ancestors, Louis XIV (1638–1715) governed France as the direct representative of God on earth (Figure **21.1**). Neither the Church, nor the nobility, nor the will of his subjects limited his power. During his seventy-two years on the throne, the Estates General, France's representative assembly, was never once called into session. As absolute monarch, Louis brought France to a position of political and military preeminence among the European nation-states. He challenged the power of the feudal nobility and placed the Church under the authority of the state, thus centralizing all authority in his own hands. By exempting the nobility and upper middle class from taxation and offering them important positions at court, he turned potential opponents into supporters. Even if Louis never uttered the famous words attributed to him, "I am the state," he surely operated according to that precept. Indeed, as an expression of his unrivaled authority, he took as his official insignia the image of the classical sun god Apollo and referred to himself as *le roi soleil* ("the Sun King").

As ruler of France, Louis was one of the world's most influential figures. Under his leadership, the center of artistic patronage and productivity shifted from Italy to France. French culture in all of its forms—from art and architecture to fashions and fine cuisine—came to dominate European tastes, a condition that prevailed until well into the early twentieth century. Although Louis was not

an intellectual, he was both shrewd and ambitious. He chose first-rate advisers to execute his policies and financed those policies with money from taxes that fell primarily upon the backs of French peasants. Vast amounts of money were spent to make France the undisputed military leader of Western Europe. But Louis, who instinctively recognized the propaganda value of the arts, also used the French treasury to glorify himself and his office. His extravagances left France in a woeful financial condition, a circumstance that contributed to the outbreak of the revolution at the end of the eighteenth century. Incapable of foreseeing these circumstances, Louis cultivated the arts as an adjunct to majesty.

Versailles: Symbol of Royal Absolutism

Architecture played a vital role in the vocabulary of royal power. The French royal family traditionally resided in Paris, at the palace known as the Louvre. But Louis, who detested Paris, moved his capital to a spot from which he might more directly control the nobility and keep them dependent upon him for honors and financial favors. Early in his career he commissioned a massive renovation of his father's hunting lodge at the village of Versailles, some 12 miles from Paris. It took 36,000 workers and nearly twenty years to build Versailles, but, in 1682, the French court finally established itself in the apartments of this magnificent unfortified *château* (castle). More than a royal residence, Versailles was—in its size and splendor—the symbol of Louis' absolute supremacy over the landed aristocracy, the provincial governments, the urban councils, and the Estates General.

The wooded site that constituted the village of Versailles, almost half the size of Paris, was connected to the old capital by a grand boulevard that (following the path of the sun) ran from the king's bedroom—where most state business was transacted—to the Avenue de Paris. Even a cursory examination of the plan of Versailles, laid out by the French architect Louis Le Vau (1612–1670), reveals esteem for the rules of symmetry, clarity, and geometric regularity (Figure **21.2**). These principles, in combination with a taste for spatial grandeur, dramatic contrast, and theatrical display, were the distinguishing features of the classical baroque style.

Shaped like a winged horseshoe, the almost 2,000-foot-long royal residence—best viewed in its entirety from the air—was the focus of an immense complex of parks, lakes, and forest (Figure **21.3**). The central building of the palace was designed by Le Vau, while the two additional wings were added by Jules Hardouin-Mansart (1646–1708). Three levels of vertically aligned windows march across the palace facade like soldiers in a formal procession (Figure **21.4**). Porches bearing freestanding Corinthian columns accent the second level, and ornamental statues at the roofline help to relieve the monotonous horizontality of the structure. In its total effect, the palace is dignified and commanding, a grand synthesis of classical and Palladian elements. Its calm nobility provides a striking contrast to the robust theatricality of most Italian baroque structures (see Figures 20.16 and 20.18).

Figure 21.1 HYACINTHE RIGAUD, *Portrait of Louis XIV*, 1701. Oil on canvas, 9 ft 1 in × 6 ft. 4 in. Louvre, Paris. © R.M.N., Paris.

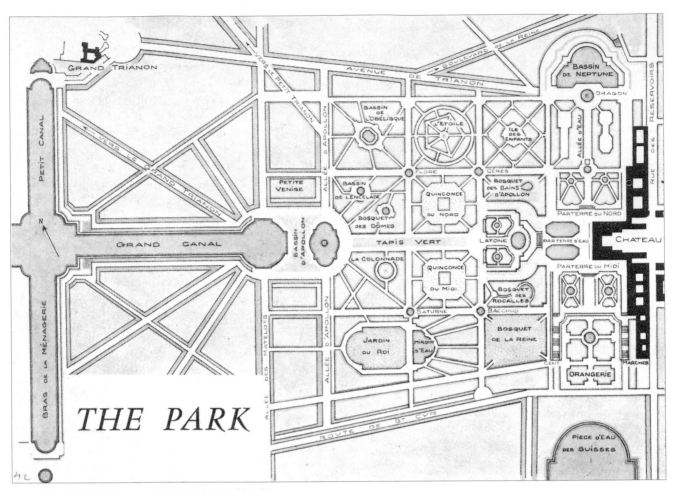

THE PARK

Figure 21.2 LOUIS LE VAU, plan of Versailles. Musée de Versailles.

Figure 21.3 Anonymous seventeenth-century painting of Versailles. © The Bettmann Archive, New York.

Figure 21.4 LOUIS LE VAU and **JULES HARDOUIN-MANSART**, facade of Versailles, viewed from the north flower bed, 1669–1685. Length of facade approx. 2,000 ft. Spectrum, London.

Figure 21.5 CLAUDE PERRAULT, LOUIS LE VAU, and **CHARLES LE BRUN**, east facade of the Louvre, Paris, 1667–1670. Photo: James Austin, Cambridge, U.K.

Figure 21.6 Ornamental Lake and Fountain of Latone, Versailles, Musée de Versailles. © Paul M. R. Maeyaert, Mont de l'Enclus (Orroir), Belgium.

Figure 21.7 JEAN LE PAUTRE, *Marble Court, Versailles*. Engraving showing a performance of Lully's *Alceste*, 1674. The Metropolitan Museum of Art, New York. Harris Brisbane Dick Fund, 1930 (30–22.32[53]).

Figure 21.8 Apartment of the Queen/Salon of the Nobles, Versailles. Length 31 ft.; width 32 ft.; height 24 ft. 8 in. Musée de Versailles. Giraudon/Art Resource, New York.

The grandeur and majesty of Versailles made it the model for hundreds of palace-estates and city planning projects in both Europe and America for the following two centuries. Le Vau's facade became the prototype for the remodeled royal palace in Paris, the Louvre. Designed by Claude Perrault (1613–1688), the east facade of the Louvre echoes the basic classical baroque features of Louis' residence at Versailles: a strong rectilinear organization, paired Corinthian columns, and a gabled entrance that provides dramatic focus (Figure **21.5**).

The palace at Versailles housed Louis' family, his royal mistresses (one of whom bore him nine children), and hundreds of members of the French nobility whose presence was politically useful to Louis. Life at the court of the Sun King was both formal and public—a small army of servants, courtiers, ministers, and pet animals constantly surrounded Louis. All forms of behavior were fixed by protocol. Rank at court determined where one sat at the dinner table and whether one or both panels of Versailles' "French doors" were to be opened upon entering.

Flanking the palace were barracks for honor guards, lodgings for more than fifteen hundred servants, kennels, greenhouses, and an orangery with over 2,000 orange trees. Over 7 square miles of gardens were designed by André Le Nôtre with the same compelling sense of order that Le Vau

brought to the architecture. The great park featured an array of hedges clipped into geometric shapes, sparkling fountains (that favorite of all baroque mechanical devices), artificial lakes, grottoes, a zoo, theaters, and outdoor "rooms" for private gatherings and clandestine meetings. When in bloom, the gardens—some planted with over 4 million tulip bulbs, which Louis imported annually from Holland—were a spectacular sight. They framed and embellished the long walkways that radiate from the central building. On the garden side of the palace, artificial pools reflected sculptures whose subject matter glorified the majesty of the king (Figure **21.6**). Itself a kind of outdoor theater, the royal palace provided the ideal backdrop for the ballets, operas, and plays that were regular features of court life (Figure **21.7**).

If the exterior of Versailles symbolized the grandeur of the king, the interior was a monument to princely self-indulgence (Figure **21.8**). Though now shorn of many of their original furnishings, Versailles' sumptuous *salons* (drawing rooms) still testify to Louis' success at cultivating French trades in such luxury items as crafted silver, clocks, lace, brocades, porcelain, and fine glass. During the seventeenth century, the silk industry reached its peak, French carpets competed with those of Turkey and Persia, the art of **marquetry** (inlaid wood) rivaled that of Italy, and the tapestries produced at the Gobelins factory in Paris out-classed those woven in Flanders. Versailles' *salons* were adorned with illusionistic frescoes, gilded stucco moldings, crystal chandeliers, and huge, ornate mirrors. The rooms housed some of the most lavish ***objets d'art*** (art objects) in Western history, all of which, it is sobering to recall, were enjoyed at a time when the peasant majority of the French population lived in one-room, thatch-roofed houses filled with coarse wooden furniture. Equally sobering is the fact that despite its splendor, the palace lacked any kind of indoor plumbing. Servants carried out the slops, but the unpleasant odor of human waste was difficult to mask, even with the finest French perfumes.

Each of Versailles' rooms illustrates a specific theme: The Salon de Venus was decorated by Charles Le Brun (1619–1690) with ceiling paintings portraying the influence of love on various kings in history. In the Salon de la Guerre (Drawing Room of War) an idealized, equestrian Louis, carved in low-relief marble, is shown receiving the victor's crown (Figure **21.9**)—though, in fact, Louis himself rarely took part in combat. The most splendid room at Versailles, however, is the 240-foot-long Galerie des Glaces (Hall of Mirrors), which once connected the royal apartments with the chapel (Figure **21.10**). Embellished with glorious frescoes, marble pilasters, and gilded bronze capitals, and furnished with ornate candelabra and bejeweled trees (the latter have since disappeared), the hall features a wall of seventeen mirrored arcades that face an equal number of high-arched windows opening on to the garden. Framing this opulent royal passageway, mirrors and windows set up a brilliant counterpoint of image and reflection. Mirrors were to Versailles what fountains were to Rome: vehicles for the theatrical display of changing light in unbounded space.

Louis as Patron of the Arts

At the center of his court, Louis was the arbiter of fashion and manners. Within his dining *salons*, linen napkins came into use, forks replaced fingers for eating, and elaborate dishes were served to suit the royal palate. Graced with an eye for beauty and a passion for aggrandizement, Louis increased the number of paintings in the French

Figure 21.9 JULES HARDOUIN-MANSART, Salon de la Guerre (Drawing Room of War), Versailles. Length and width 33 ft. 8 in; height 37 ft. 9 in. Musée de Versailles. Lauros-Giraudon, Paris.

Figure 21.10 JULES HARDOUIN-MANSART and **CHARLES LE BRUN**, Galerie des Glaces (Hall of Mirrors), Versailles, ca. 1680. Length 240 ft. Musée de Versailles.
© Paul M. R. Maeyaert, Mont de l'Enclus (Orroir), Belgium & R.M.N., Paris.

royal collection from the two hundred he inherited upon his accession to the throne to the two thousand he left at his death. These paintings formed the basis of the permanent collection at the Louvre, now a world-renowned art museum.

On a grander scale Louis dictated the standards for all forms of artistic production. Following in the tradition of his father, Louis XIII, who had instituted the French Royal Academy of Language and Literature in 1635, he created and subsidized government-sponsored institutions in the arts, appointing his personal favorites to oversee each. In 1648, Louis founded the Academy of Painting and Sculpture; in 1661 he established the Academy of Dance; in 1666, the Academy of Sciences; in 1669, the Academy of Music; and in 1671, the Academy of Architecture. The creation of the academies was a symptom of royal efforts to fix standards, but Louis had something more personal in mind: He is said to have told a group of academicians, "Gentlemen, I entrust to you the most precious thing on earth— my fame." His trust was well placed, for the

academies brought glory to the king and set standards that would govern the arts for at least two centuries. These standards were enshrined in "rules" inspired by the legacy of ancient Greece and Rome, thus *neoclassicism*— the revival of classical style and subject matter—became the accepted style of academic art.

In the early days of his reign, when Italy was the leader in artistic style, Louis invited Italian artists to execute royal commissions. Among these artists was the master architect-sculptor Gianlorenzo Bernini (see chapter 20). Bernini had submitted designs for a remodeled Louvre, and although his plans were rejected ultimately in favor of Perrault's, his vigorous style survives in such works as the life-sized marble portrait bust of Louis completed in 1665 (Figure **21.11**). Originally designed to stand on a gilded enamel globe inscribed with a message celebrating the king's lofty position, this sculpture—with its billowing draperies, elaborate coiffure, and idealized features— glorifies the ruler in typically baroque fashion. Bernini's theatrical exuberance contrasts sharply with the sober neoclassicism of the French academician François Girardon (1628–1715). Girardon drew on Hellenistic models for the ideally proportioned statues that he arranged in graceful tableaux for the gardens of Versailles. In one such tableau, Girardon's neoclassical nymphs are seen entertaining the sun god Apollo—an obvious reference to Louis as *roi soleil* (Figure **21.12**).

Poussin and the Academic Style in Painting

Girardon's compositions owed much to the paintings of the leading exponent of French academic art, Nicolas Poussin (1594–1665). Poussin spent most of his life in Rome, absorbing the rich heritage of the classical and Renaissance past. He revered Raphael, master of the High Renaissance, as the leading proponent of the classical style, and, like many neoclassicists, he shared Raphael's esteem for lofty subjects drawn from Greco-

Figure 21.11 (right) **GIANLORENZO BERNINI**, *Louis XIV*, 1665. Marble, height 33⅛ in. Musée de Versailles. Photo: © R.M.N., Paris.

Figure 21.12 (below) **FRANÇOIS GIRARDON**, *Apollo Attended by the Nymphs*, ca. 1666–1672. Marble, life-sized. Musée de Versailles. Giraudon, Paris.

Roman mythology and Christian legend. In an influential treatise on painting, Poussin formalized the rules that would govern academic art for centuries. These principles, drawn largely from the aesthetic theories of seventeenth-century Italian painters, would come to characterize the Grand Manner in Western art: Artists should choose only serious and elevated subjects (such as battles, heroic actions, and miraculous events) drawn from classical or Christian history, and reject crude, bizarre, and ordinary subject matter. As to the manner of representation, artists should make the physical action suit the mood of the narrative, avoiding, at all cost, the gross aspects of ordinary existence and any type of exaggeration. They should present their subjects clearly and evenly in harmonious compositions that were free of irrelevant and sordid details. Restraint, moderation, and decorum—that is, propriety and good taste—should govern all aspects of pictorial representation.

Poussin faithfully practiced the rules of the academic or Grand Manner. His *Arcadian Shepherds*, completed in 1639, transports us to the idyllic region in ancient Greece known as Arcadia, a place where men and women were said to live in perfect harmony with nature (Figure **21.13**). Three shepherds have come upon an ancient tomb, a symbol of death; on the right, the stately Muse of History meditates upon the tomb's inscription: "*Et in Arcadia Ego*," ("I [death] also dwell in Arcadia"), that is, death reigns even in this most perfect of places. Poussin's moral allegory, at once a pastoral elegy and a *memento mori*, instructs us that death is universal. Cool, bright colors and even lighting enhance the elegiac mood, while sharp contours and the sure use of line provide absolute clarity of design. But the real power of the painting lies in its rigorous composition. Poussin arrived at this composition by arranging and rearranging miniature wax models of his figures within a small rectangular box. He then posed these figures—statuesque, heroically proportioned, and idealized—so that their every gesture served to narrate the story. Indeed, all of the elements in the painting, from the Muse's feet (which parallel the horizontal picture plane) to the trees in the landscape and at the right edge of the tomb (which parallel the vertical picture plane) contribute to the geometric order of the pictorial structure.

Despite the grand theatricality of Poussin's paintings, order dominates over spontaneity. Both in form and in content, Poussin's canvases are intellectual; that is, they appeal to the mind rather than to the senses. In contrast to Italian baroque painters such as Caravaggio, whose works he detested, Poussin soberly advanced the aesthetics of neoclassicism.

Figure 21.13 NICOLAS POUSSIN, *Arcadian Shepherds*, 1638–1639. Oil on canvas, 33½ × 47⅝ in. Louvre, Paris. R.M.N., Paris.

Figure 21.14 CLAUDE LORRAIN (CLAUDE GELLÉE). *The Marriage of Isaac and Rebekah (The Mill)*, 1642. Oil on canvas, 4 ft. 11 in × 6 ft. 5 in. National Gallery, London.

Poussin and his contemporary, Claude Gellée (1600–1682), known as Claude Lorrain, were responsible for creating the genre known as the "ideal landscape," a landscape painted in the high-minded, idealized style usually found in traditional moral subjects. For such paintings, academic artists made careful renderings of the countryside around Rome. They then deliberately assembled and combined the contents of their sketches according to the classical ideals of balance and clarity. Lorrain's landscapes, characterized by haunting qualities of light, were tranquil settings for lofty mythological or biblical subjects (Figure **21.14**). Unlike the Dutch landscape painters, who rendered nature with forthright realism (see Figure 23.10), academic artists imposed a preconceived, rationalized order upon the natural world.

The Aristocratic Portrait

The Age of the Baroque was the great period of aristocratic portraiture. Commissioned by the hundreds by Louis XIV and the members of his court, aristocratic portraits differ dramatically from the portraits of such artists as Hals, Leyster, and Rembrandt (see chapter 23). Whereas Dutch artists investigated the personalities of their sitters, bringing to their portraits a combination of psychological intimacy and forthrightness, French artists were concerned primarily with outward appearance. The classic example of French aristocratic portraiture is the image of Louis XIV shown at the beginning of this chapter (see Figure 21.1), painted in 1701 by Hyacinthe Rigaud (1659–1743). Rigaud shows the aging monarch in his coronation garments, with the royal paraphernalia: the scepter, the crown (on the cushion at the left), and the sword of state. He is adorned with ermine-lined coronation robes, silk stockings, lace cravat, high-heeled shoes, and a well-manicured wig—all but the first were fashionable hallmarks of upper-class wealth. Louis' mannered pose, which harks back to classical models, reflects self-conscious pride in status. Rigaud employed special devices to enhance the themes of authority and regality: Satin curtains theatrically dignify the king, and a lone column compositionally and metaphorically underscores his rectitude. Such devices would become standard conventions in European and American portraits of the eighteenth century (see Figure 26.24).

The Aristocratic Style in Europe

Velázquez, Rubens, and van Dyck

In Spain, Diego Velázquez (1599–1660), court painter to King Philip IV, became that country's most prestigious artist. Velázquez excelled at modeling forms so that they conveyed the powerful presence of real objects in atmospheric space. For the Spanish court, Velázquez painted a variety of classical and Christian subjects, but his greatest enterprise was the informal group portrait known as *Las Meninas* (*The Maids of Honor*; Figure **21.15**). In this painting, Velázquez depicted himself at his easel, alongside the members of the royal court: the *infanta* (the five-year-old daughter of the king), her maids of honor, her dwarf, a mastiff hound, and the royal escorts. In the background is a mirror that reflects the images of the king and queen of Spain—presumably the subjects of the large canvas Velázquez shows himself painting in the left foreground. Superficially, this is a group portrait of the kind painted by the Dutch artist Rembrandt (see Figure 23.15), but it is far more complex in composition and in content—its "meaning" has been for decades the subject of extensive debate among art historians. Indisputably, however, *Las Meninas* comments intriguingly on the relationship between the perceived and the perceiver. Almost all of the characters in the painting, including the painter himself, are shown gazing at the royal couple, who must be standing outside of the picture space in the very spot occupied by the viewer. With baroque inventiveness, Velázquez expands the spatial field to invite the beholder to "enter" the space from a variety of vantage points. The painting becomes a "conceit" that provokes a visual dialogue between viewer and viewed and between patron and artist.

A contemporary of Velázquez, the internationally renowned Flemish painter Peter Paul Rubens (1577–1640) established his reputation in the courts of Europe. Fluent in six languages, he traveled widely as a diplomat and art dealer for royal patrons in Italy, England, and France. He also headed a large studio workshop that trained scores of assistants to help fill his many commissions—a total lifetime production of some 1800 paintings. For the Luxembourg Palace of Paris, Rubens and his studio executed twenty-one monumental canvases that glorified Marie de' Medici, Louis XIV's grandmother, and her late

Figure 21.15 DIEGO VELÁZQUEZ, *Las Meninas (The Maids of Honor)* 1656. Oil on canvas, 10 ft. 5 in. × 9 ft. Prado, Madrid.

Figure 21.16 PETER PAUL RUBENS, *Rape of the Daughters of Leucippus*, ca. 1618. Oil on canvas, 7 ft. 3 in. × 6 ft. 10 in. Alte Pinakothek, Munich.

husband, King Henry IV of France. Like Poussin, Rubens studied in Italy and was familiar with both classical and High Renaissance art. Rubens deeply admired the flamboyant colorists Titian and Tintoretto, and he developed a style that, by comparison with Poussin's, was painterly in technique and dynamic in composition.

One of Rubens' most memorable canvases, the *Rape of the Daughters of Leucippus* (Figure **21.16**), depicts the abduction of two mortal women by the Roman heroes Castor and Pollux. Rubens' portrayal of the classical story brims with vigor and imagination: Pressing against the picture plane are the fleshy bodies of the nude maidens, their limbs arranged in the pattern of a slowly revolving pinwheel. The masterful paintstrokes exploit sensuous contrasts of luminous pink flesh, burnished armor, gleaming satins, and dense horsehide. Probably commissioned to commemorate the double marriage of Louis XIII of France to a Spanish princess and Philip IV of Spain to a French princess (and, thus, to celebrate the diplomatic alliance of France and Spain), the subtext of the painting is a message of (male) power over (female) privilege—and, by extension, of political absolutism. Images of subjugation by force, whether in the form of lion hunts (as in ancient

Assyrian reliefs; see chapter 3) or in paintings and sculptures depicting mythological stories of rape, were metaphors for the sovereign authority of the ruler over his subjects, hence a veiled expression of political absolutism.

In England, the most accomplished seventeenth-century portraitist was the Flemish master Anthony van Dyck (1599–1641). Born in Antwerp, van Dyck had been an assistant to Rubens and may have worked with him on the *Rape of the Daughters of Leucippus*. Unwilling to compete with Rubens, van Dyck moved to Genoa and then to London, where he became the court painter to King Charles I of England. Van Dyck's many commissioned portraits of European aristocrats are striking for their polished elegance and idealized grandeur, features that are especially evident in his equestrian portrait of King Charles I (see Figure 22.1). In this painting, which revives the traditional motif of ruler-on-horseback (see chapters 6, 11, and 17), van Dyck shows the king, who was actually short and undistinguished looking, as handsome and regal. The combination of fluid composition and naturalistic detail, and the shimmering vitality of the brushwork make this one of the most memorable examples of aristocratic baroque portraiture.

Music and Dance at the Court of Louis XIV

The court at Versailles was the setting for an extraordinary outpouring of music, theater, and dance. To provide musical entertainments for state dinners, balls, and operatic performances, Louis established a permanent orchestra, the first in European history. Its director, the Italian-born (but French-educated) Jean-Baptiste Lully (1632–1687), also headed the French Academy of Music. Often called the father of French opera, Lully oversaw all phases of musical performance, from writing scores and conducting the orchestra to training the chorus and staging operatic productions. Many of Lully's operas were based on themes from classical mythology. Their semidivine heroes, prototypes of Louis himself, flattered his image as ruler.

Lully's operas shared the pomp and splendor of Le Brun's frescoes, the strict clarity of Poussin's paintings, and the formal correctness of classical drama. Though Lully's compositions were generally lacking in spontaneity and warmth of feeling, they were faithful to the neoclassical unity of words and music. Lully modified the music of the

Figure 21.17 King Louis XIV as the sun in the 1653 *Ballet de la Nuit.* Bibliothèque Nationale, Paris.

recitative to follow precisely and with great clarity the inflections of the spoken word. He also introduced to opera the "French overture," an instrumental form that featured contrasts between a slow first part in homophonic texture and a fast, contrapuntal second part. Under Lully's leadership, French opera also developed its most characteristic feature: the inclusion of formal dance.

At the court of Louis XIV, dancing and fencing were the touchstones of aristocratic grace. All members of the upper class were expected to perform the basic court dances, including the very popular *minuet*, and the courtier who could not dance was judged rude and inept. Like his father, Louis XIII, who had commissioned and participated in extravagantly expensive ballets, Louis XIV was a superb dancer. Dressed as the sun, he danced the lead in the 1653 performance of the *Ballet de la Nuit* (Figure **21.17**). Of lasting significance was Louis' contribution to the birth of professional dance and the transformation of court dance into an independent art form. During the late seventeenth century, French ballet masters of the Royal Academy of Dance established rules for the five positions that have become the basis for classical dance. Clarity, balance, and proportion, along with studied technique—elements characteristic of classicism in general—became the ideals of the classical ballet.

By 1685 female dancers were permitted to join the previously all-male French dance ensembles in staged performances. And in 1700 Raoul Auget Feuillet published a system of abstract symbols for recording specific dance steps and movements, thus facilitating **choreography**. Ballet, itself a metaphor for the strict etiquette and ceremony of court life, enriched all aspects of the French theater. However, since classical ballet demanded a rigorous attention to proper form, it soon became too specialized for any but professionals to perform, and so there developed the gap between performer and audience that exists to this day in the art of dance.

Seventeenth-Century French Literature

As with most forms of artistic expression in seventeenth-century France, in literature neoclassical precepts of form and content held sway. French writers addressed questions of human dignity and morality in a language that was clear, polished, and precise. Their prose is marked by refinement, good taste, and the concentrated presentation of ideas.

One literary genre that typified the neoclassical spirit was the **maxim**. A maxim is a short, concise, and often witty saying, usually drawn from experience and offering some practical advice. Witty sayings that distilled wisdom into a few words were popular in many cultures, including those of the Hebrews, the Greeks, and the Africans. But in seventeenth-century France, the cautionary or moralizing aphorism was exalted as the ideal means of teaching good sense and decorum. Terse and lean, the maxim exalted precision of language and thought. France's greatest maxim writer was François de La Rochefoucauld (1613–1680), a nobleman who had participated in a revolt against Louis XIV early in his reign. Withdrawing from court society, La Rochefoucauld wrote with a cynicism that reflected his conviction that self-interest, hypocrisy, and greed motivated the behavior of most human beings—including and especially the aristocrats of his day. As the following maxims illustrate, however, La Rochefoucauld's insights into human behavior apply equally well to individuals of all social classes and to any age.

READING 4.4 From La Rochefoucauld's Maxims (1664)

Truth does less good in the world than its appearances do harm.

Love of justice in most men is only a fear of encountering injustice.

We often do good that we may do harm with impunity.

As it is the mark of great minds to convey much in few words, so small minds are skilled at talking at length and saying little.

Virtue would not go nearly so far if vanity did not keep her company.

We confess to small faults to create the impression that we have no great ones.

To be rational is not to use reason by chance, but to recognize it, distinguish it, appreciate it.

We all have strength enough to endure the misfortunes of others.

We are never so happy or so unhappy as we imagine we are.

Our minds are lazier than our bodies.

Quarrels would not last long were the wrong all on one side.

Like La Rochefoucauld's maxims, but on a larger scale, French drama, too, reflected the neoclassical effort to restrain passionate feeling by means of cool objectivity and common sense. The leading French tragedian of the seventeenth century, Jean Racine (1639–1699), wrote plays that treated high-minded themes in an elevated language. Racine added to Aristotle's unities of action and time (see chapter 4) a strict unity of place, thus manifesting his abiding commitment to intellectual control. In the play *Phèdre* (1677), itself based on Greek models, Racine explored the conflict between human passions (Phaedra's "unnatural" infatuation with her stepson) and human reason (Phaedra's sense of duty as the wife of Theseus, king of Athens). As in all of Racine's tragedies of passion, *Phèdre* illustrates the disastrous consequences of emotional indulgence—a weakness especially peculiar to Racine's female characters. Indeed, while Racine created some of the most dramatic female roles in neoclassical theater, he usually pictured women as weak, irrational, and cruel.

Molière's Human Comedy

Jean-Baptiste Poquelin (1622–1673), whose stage name was Molière, was France's leading comic dramatist. The son of a wealthy upholsterer, he abandoned a career in law in favor of acting and play writing. He learned much from the *commedia dell'arte*, a form of improvised Italian street theater that depended on buffoonery, slapstick humor, and pantomime. Molière's plays involve simple story lines that bring to life the comic foibles of such stock characters as the miser, the hypochondriac, the hypocrite, the misanthrope, and the would-be gentleman. The last of these is the subject of one of Moliére's last plays, *Le Bourgeois Gentilhomme* ("The Tradesman Turned Gentleman"). The plot involves a wealthy tradesman (Monsieur Jourdain) who, aspiring to nobility, hires a variety of tutors to school him in the trappings of upper-class respectability. The play's fabric of deception and self-deception is complicated by Jourdain's refusal to accept his daughter's choice of a partner, the handsome but poor Cléonte. Only after Cléonte appears disguised as the son of the Grand Turk does the unwitting merchant bless the betrothal. Essentially a farce or comedy-of-manners, Molière's play (like La Rochefoucauld's maxims) holds up to ridicule the fundamental flaws of human behavior, which might be corrected by applying the classical norms of reason and moderation. By contrasting incidents of hypocrisy, pomposity, and greed with the solid, good sense demonstrated, for instance, by M. Jourdain's wife, Molière probes the excesses of passion and vanity that enfeeble human dignity. *Le Bourgeois Gentilhomme* was designed as a **comédie-ballet**, a dramatic performance that incorporated interludes of song and dance (in a manner similar to modern musical comedy). Lully provided the music, choreographed the ballet, and directed the entire production, which, like many other of Molière's plays, was well received by the king and his court, a court that lavishly and regularly received the ambassadors of "exotic" countries, such as Turkey.

But even beyond Versailles, Molière's hilarious comedy had wide appeal. French aristocrats, convinced that they were above imitation, embraced the play. So did upper-middle-class patrons who, while claiming an increasingly prominent place in the social order, refused to see themselves as merchants longing to be aristocrats. Women found themselves endowed in Molière's play with confidence and guile, while servants discovered themselves invested with admirable common sense. The comedy, for all its farce, reflected the emerging class structure of early modern European society, with its firmly drawn lines between the sexes. In a single stroke, *Le Bourgeois Gentilhomme* captured the spirit of the seventeenth century—its class tensions and social contradictions, along with its ambitions and high expectations. Yet, for all its value as a mirror of a particular time and place, *Le Bourgeois Gentilhomme* is universal and timeless. The portions of the first and second acts of the play included here offer a representative sampling of Molière's rollicking exposition of human nature.

READING 4.5 From Molière's *Le Bourgeois Gentilhomme* (1670)

Characters

Mr. Jourdain	His Scholar
Mrs. Jourdain, *his wife*	A Dancing-Master
Lucile, *his daughter*	A Fencing-Master
Cléonte, *suitor of Lucile*	A Philosophy-Master
Dorimene, *a marquise*	A Master-Tailor
Dorante, *a count, in love with*	A Journeyman-Tailor
Dorimene	Two lackeys
Nicole, *servant to*	Musicians, Dancers, Cooks,
Mr. Jourdain	Journeymen Tailors, and other
Coveille, valet to Cléonte	characters to dance in the
A Music-Master	interludes

The scene is at Paris

ACT I

Overture, played by a full orchestra; in the middle of the stage the Music-Master's Scholar, seated at a table, is composing the air for a serenade which Mr. Jourdain has ordered.

Scene I

Music-Master, Dancing-Master, Three Singers, Two Violinists, Four Dancers

Music-Master (*To the singers*): Here, step inside, and wait   1
until he comes.

Dancing-Master (*To the dancers*): And you too, this way.

Music-Master (*To his scholar*): Is it finished?

Scholar: Yes.

Music-Master: Let's see . . . That's good.

Dancing-Master: Is it something new?

Music-Master: Yes, 'tis the air for a serenade which I have
had him compose, while waiting for our gentleman to wake up.

Dancing-Master: May I see it?   10

Music-Master: You shall hear it, with the words, when he
comes. He won't be long.

Dancing-Master: You and I have no lack of occupation now.

Music-Master: That's true. We have found a man here who
is just what we both needed. He's a nice little source of income
for us, this Mr. Jourdain, with his visions of nobility and
gallantry that he has got into his noddle. And 'twould be a fine
thing for your dancing and my music if everybody were like
him.

Dancing-Master: No, no, not quite; I could wish, for his   20
sake, that he had some true understanding of the good things
we bring him.

Music-Master: 'Tis true he understands them ill, but he
pays for them well; and that is what the arts need most
nowadays.

Dancing-Master: For my part, I'll own, I must be fed
somewhat on fame. I am sensitive to applause, and I feel that
in all the fine arts 'tis a grievous torture to show one's talents
before fools, and to endure the barbarous judgments of a
dunce upon our compositions. There's great pleasure, I tell you,   30
in working for people who are capable of feeling the
refinements of art, who know how to give a flattering
reception to the beauties of your work, and recompense your
toil by titillating praise. Yes, the most agreeable reward
possible for what we do, is to see it understood, to see it
caressed by applause that honors us. Nothing else, methinks,
can pay us so well for all our labors; and enlightened praise
gives exquisite delight.

Music-Master: I grant you that, and I relish it as you do.
There is surely nothing more gratifying than such praise as you   40
speak of; but man cannot live on applause. Mere praise won't
buy you an estate; it takes something more solid. And the best
way to praise, is to praise with open hands. Our fellow, to be
sure, is a man of little wit, who discourses at random about
anything and everything, and never applauds but at the wrong
time. But his money sets right the errors of his mind; there is
judgment in his purse; his praises pass current; and this
ignorant shopkeeper is worth more to us, as you very well see,
than the enlightened lord who introduced us to his house.

Dancing-Master: There is some truth in what you say; but   50
methinks you set too much store by money; and self-interest is
something so base that no gentleman should ever show a
leaning towards it.

Music-Master: Yet I haven't seen you refuse the money our
fellow offers you.

Dancing-Master: Certainly not; but neither do I find
therein all my happiness; and I could still wish that with his
wealth he had good taste to boot.

Music-Master: I could wish so too; and 'tis to that end that
we are both working, as best we may. But in any case, he gives   60
us the means to make ourselves known in the world; he shall
pay for others, and others shall praise for him.

Dancing-Master: Here he comes.

[Act I, Scene II: Mr. Jourdain converses with his music- and dancing-masters, who dispute as to which is the more important art: music or dance. A dialogue in music, written by the music-master, follows, then a ballet choreographed by the dancing-master.

Act II, Scene I: Mr. Jourdain dances the minuet for the dancing-master, and then learns how to make a "proper" bow.]

ACT II, Scene II

Mr. Jourdain, Music-Master, Dancing-Master, Lackey

Lackey: Sir, here is your fencing-master.   1

Mr. Jourdain: Tell him to come in and give me my lesson
here. (*To the music-master and dancing-master*) I want you to
see me perform.

Scene III

Mr. Jourdain, Fencing-Master, Music-Master, Dancing-Master,
a Lackey with two foils

Fencing-Master (*Taking the two foils from the lackey and
giving one of them to Mr. Jourdain*): Now, sir, your salute.
The body erect. The weight slightly on the left thigh. The legs
not so far apart. The feet in line. The wrist in line with the
thigh. The point of your sword in line with your shoulder.
The arm not quite so far extended. The left hand on a level   10
with the eye. The left shoulder farther back. Head up. A
bold look. Advance. The body steady. Engage my sword in

quart[1] and finish the thrust. One, two. Recover. Again, your feet firm. One, two. Retreat. When you thrust, sir, your sword must move first, and your body be held well back, and sideways. One, two. Now, engage my sword in tierce,[2] and finish the thrust. Advance. Your body steady. Advance. Now, from that position. One, two. Recover. Again. One, two. Retreat. On guard, sir, on guard (*the fencing-master gives him several thrusts*), on guard.

Mr. Jourdain: Well?

Music-Master: You do wonders.

Fencing-Master: I've told you already: the whole secret of arms consists in two things only: hitting and not being hit. And as I proved to you the other day by demonstrative logic, it is impossible that you should be hit if you know how to turn aside your adversary's sword from the line of your body; and that depends merely on a slight movement of the wrist, inwards or outwards.

Mr. Jourdain: So, then, without any courage, one may be sure of killing his man and not being killed?

Fencing-Master: Certainly. Didn't you see the demonstration of it?

Mr. Jourdain: Yes.

Fencing-Master: And by this you may see how highly our profession should be esteemed in the State; and how far the science of arms excels all other sciences that are of no use, like dancing, music . . .

Dancing-Master: Softly, Mr. Swordsman; don't speak disrespectfully of dancing.

Music-Master: Learn, pray, to appreciate better the excellences of music.

Fencing-Master: You are absurd fellows, to think of comparing your sciences with mine.

Music-Master: Just see the man of consequence!

Dancing-Master: The ridiculous animal, with his padded stomacher![3]

Fencing-Master: My little dancing-master, I will make you dance to a tune of my own, and you, little songster, I will make you sing out lustily.

Dancing-Master: Mr. Ironmonger,[4] I'll teach you your own trade.

Mr. Jourdain (*To the dancing-master*): Are you mad, to pick a quarrel with him, when he knows tierce and quart and can kill a man by demonstrative logic?

Dancing-Master: A fig for his demonstrative logic, and his tierce and his quart.

Mr. Jourdain (*To the dancing-master*): Softly, I tell you.

Fencing-Master (*To the dancing-master*): What, little Master Impudence!

Mr. Jourdain: Hey! my dear fencing-master.

Dancing-Master (*To the fencing-master*): What, you great cart-horse!

Mr. Jourdain: Hey, my dear dancing-master.

Fencing-Master: If I once fall upon you . . .

Mr. Jourdain (*To the fencing-master*): Gently.

Dancing-Master: If I once lay hands on you . . .

Mr. Jourdain (*To the dancing-master*): So, so.

Fencing-Master: I will give you such a dressing . . .

Mr. Jourdain (*To the fencing-master*): I beg you.

Dancing-Master: I will give you such a drubbing[5] . . .

Mr. Jourdain (*To the dancing-master*): I beseech you . . .

Music-Master: Let us teach him manners a little.

Mr. Jourdain: Good Heavens! do stop.

Scene IV

Professor of Philosphy, Mr. Jourdain, Music-Master, Dancing-Master, Fencing-Master, Lackey

Mr. Jourdain: Oho! Mr. Philosopher, you've arrived in the nick of time with your philosophy. Do come and set these people here at peace.

The Philosopher: How now? What is the matter, gentlemen?

Mr. Jourdain: They have put themselves in a passion about the precedence of their professions, and even insulted each other and almost come to blows.

The Philosopher: O fie, gentlemen! Should a man so lose his self-control? Have you not read the learned treatise which Seneca composed, *Of Anger*?[6] Is there anything more base or shameful than this passion, which of a man makes a savage beast? Should not reason be mistress of all our emotions?

Dancing-Master: How, how, sir! Here he comes and insults us both, by condemning dancing, which I practise, and music, which is his profession.

The Philosopher: A wise man is above all the insults that can be offered him; and the chief answer which we should make to all offences, is calmness and patience.

Fencing-Master: They both have the insolence to think of comparing their professions with mine!

The Philosopher: Should that move you? 'Tis not for vainglory and precedence that men should contend; what really distinguishes us from each other is wisdom and virtue.

Dancing-Master: I maintain to his face that dancing is a science which cannot be too highly honored.

Music-Master: And I, that music is a science which all ages have reverenced.

Fencing-Master: And I maintain, against both of them, that the science of fencing is the finest and most indispensable of all sciences.

The Philosopher: But what then becomes of philosophy? I think you are all three mighty impertinent to speak with such arrogance before me, and impudently to give the name of science to things which ought not even to be honored with the name of art, and which may best be classed together as pitiful trades, whether of prize-fighters, ballad-mongers, or mountebanks.[7]

Fencing-Master: Go to, dog of a philosopher.

Music-Master: Go to, beggarly pedagogue.

Dancing-Master: Go to, past master pedant.

The Philosopher: What, you rascally knaves! . . .

(*He falls upon them, and they all three belabor him with blows.*)

---

[1]A defensive posture in the art of fencing.
[2]Another fencing posture.
[3]Protection used in fencing.
[4]A dealer in hardware.

[5]A beating
[6]A treatise by the first-century Roman stoic, Lucius Annaeus Seneca (see chapter 7).
[7]Charlatans or quacks.

Mr. Jourdain: Mr. Philosopher!

The Philosopher: Villains! varlets! insolent vermin!

Mr. Jourdain: Mr. Philosopher!

Fencing-Master: Plague take the beast!

Mr. Jourdain: Gentlemen!

The Philosopher: Brazen-faced ruffians! 120

Mr. Jourdain: Mr. Philosopher!

Dancing-Master: Deuce take the old pack-mule!

Mr. Jourdain: Gentlemen!

The Philosopher: Scoundrels!

Mr. Jourdain: Mr. Philosopher!

Music-Master: Devil take the impertinent puppy!

Mr. Jourdain: Gentlemen!

The Philosopher: Thieves! vagabonds! rogues! impostors!

Mr. Jourdain: Mr. Philosopher! Gentlemen! Mr. Philosopher!

Gentlemen! Mr. Philosopher! 130

(*Exit fighting.*)

Scene V
Mr. Jourdain, Lackey

Mr. Jourdain: Oh! fight as much as you please; I can't help it, and I won't go spoil my gown trying to part you. I should be mad to thrust myself among them and get some blow that might do me a mischief.

Scene VI
The Philosopher, Mr. Jourdain, Lackey

The Philosopher (*Straightening his collar*): Now for our lesson.

Mr. Jourdain: Oh! sir, I am sorry for the blows you got.

The Philosopher: That's nothing. A philosopher knows how to take things aright; and I shall compose a satire against them 140 in Juvenal's manner,[8] which will cut them up properly. But let that pass. What do you want to learn?

Mr. Jourdain: Everything I can; for I have the greatest desire conceivable to be learned; it throws me in a rage to think that my father and mother did not make me study all the sciences when I was young.

The Philosopher: That is a reasonable sentiment; *nam, sine doctrina, vita est quasi mortis imago.* You understand that, for of course you know Latin.

Mr. Jourdain: Yes; but play that I don't know it; and explain 150 what it means.

The Philosopher: It means that, *without learning, life is almost an image of death.*

Mr. Jourdain: That same Latin's in the right.

The Philosopher: Have you not some foundations, some rudiments of knowledge?

Mr. Jourdain: Oh! yes, I can read and write.

The Philosopher: Where will you please to have us begin? Shall I teach you logic?

Mr. Jourdain: What may that same logic be? 160

The Philosopher: 'Tis the science that teaches the three operations of the mind.

Mr. Jourdain: And who are they, these three operations of the mind?

The Philosopher: The first, the second, and the third. The first is to conceive aright, by means of the universals; the second, to judge aright, by means of the categories; and the third, to draw deductions aright, by means of the figures: *Barbara, Celarent, Darii, Ferio, Baralipton.*[9]

Mr. Jourdain: There's a pack of crabbed words. This logic 170 doesn't suit me at all. Let's learn something else that's prettier.

The Philosopher: Will you learn ethics?

Mr. Jourdain: Ethics?

The Philosopher: Yes.

Mr. Jourdain: What is your ethics about?

The Philosopher: It treats of happiness, teaches men to moderate their passions, and . . .

Mr. Jourdain: No; no more of that. I am choleric as the whole pack of devils, ethics or no ethics; no, sir, I'll be angry to my heart's content, whenever I have a mind to it. 180

The Philosopher: Is it physics you want to learn?

Mr. Jourdain: And what has this physics to say for itself?

The Philosopher: Physics is the science which explains the principles of natural phenomena, and the properties of bodies; which treats of the nature of the elements, metals, minerals, stones, plants, and animals, and teaches us the causes of all such things as meteors, the rainbow, St. Elmo's fire,[10] comets, lightning, thunder, thunderbolts, rain, snow, hail, winds, and whirlwinds.

Mr. Jourdain: There's too much jingle-jangle in that, too 190 much hurly-burly.

The Philosopher: Then what to do you want me to teach you?

Mr. Jourdain: Teach me spelling.

The Philosopher: With all my heart.

Mr. Jourdain: And afterward, you shall teach me the almanac, so as to know when there's a moon, and when there isn't.

The Philosopher: Very well. To follow up your line of thought logically, and treat this matter in true philosophic 200 fashion, we must begin, according to the proper order of things, by an exact knowledge of the nature of the letters, and the different method of pronouncing each one. And on that head I must tell you that the letters are divided into vowels, so called—*vowels*—because they express the sounds of the voice alone; and consonants, so called—*con-sonants*—because they sound with the vowels, and only mark the different articulations of the voice. There are five vowels, or voices: A, E, I, O, U.

Mr. Jourdain: I understand all that. 210

The Philosopher: The vowel A is formed by opening the mouth wide: A.

Mr. Jourdain: A, A. Yes.

The Philosopher: The vowel E is formed by lifting the lower jaw nearer to the upper: A, E.

---

[8]A Roman satirist of the early second century (see chapter 6).

[9]Part of a series of Latin names used by medieval logicians to help remember the valid forms of syllogisms.

[10]Electrical discharges seen by sailors before and after storms at sea and named after the patron saint of sailors.

Mr. Jourdain: A, E; A, E. On my word, 'tis so. Ah! how fine!

The Philosopher: And the vowel I, by bringing the jaws still nearer together, and stretching the corners of the mouth toward the ears: A, E, I.

Mr. Jourdain: A, E, I, I, I, I. That is true. Science forever! 220

The Philosopher: The vowel O is formed by opening the jaws, and drawing in the lips at the corners: O.

Mr. Jourdain: O, O. Nothing could be more correct: A, E, I, O, I, O. 'Tis admirable! I, O; I, O.

The Philosopher: The opening of the mouth looks exactly like a little circle, representing an O.

Mr. Jourdain: O, O, O. You are right. O. Ah! What a fine thing it is to know something!

The Philosopher: The vowel U is formed by bringing the teeth together without letting them quite touch, and thrusting 230 out the lips, at the same time bringing them together without quite shutting them: U.

Mr. Jourdain: U, U. Nothing could be truer: U.

The Philosopher: Your lips are extended as if you were pouting; therefore if you wish to make a face at anyone, and mock at him, you have only to say U.

Mr. Jourdain: U, U. 'Tis true. Ah! would I had studied sooner, to know all that!

The Philosopher: To-morrow, we will consider the other letters, namely the consonants. 240

Mr. Jourdain: Are there just as curious things about them as about these?

The Philosopher: Certainly. The consonant D, for instance, is pronounced by clapping the tip of the tongue just above the upper teeth: D.

Mr. Jourdain: D, D. Yes! Oh! what fine things! what fine things!

The Philosopher: The F, by resting the upper teeth on the lower lip: F.

Mr. Jourdain: F, F. 'Tis the very truth. Oh! father and mother 250 of me, what a grudge I owe you!

The Philosopher: And the R by lifting the tip of the tongue to the roof of the mouth; so that being grazed by the air, which comes out sharply, it yields to it, yet keeps returning to the same point, and so makes a sort of trilling: R, Ra.

Mr. Jourdain: R, R, Ra, R, R, R, R, R, R, Ra. That is fine. Oh! what a learned man you are, and how much time I've lost! R, R, R, Ra.

The Philosopher: I will explain all these curious things to you thoroughly. 260

Mr. Jourdain: Do, I beg you. But now, I must tell you a great secret. I am in love with a person of very high rank, and I wish you would help me to write her something in a little love note which I'll drop at her feet.

The Philosopher: Excellent!

Mr. Jourdain: 'Twill be very gallant, will it not?

The Philosopher: Surely. Do you want to write to her in verse?

Mr. Jourdain: No, no; none of your verse.

The Philosopher: You want mere prose? 270

Mr. Jourdain: No, I will have neither prose nor verse.

The Philosopher: It must needs be one or the other.

Mr. Jourdain: Why?

The Philosopher: For this reason, that there is nothing but prose or verse to express oneself by.

Mr. Jourdain: There is nothing but prose or verse?

The Philosopher: No, sir. All that is not prose is verse, and all that is not verse is prose.

Mr. Jourdain: But when we talk, what is that, say?

The Philosopher: Prose. 280

Mr. Jourdain: What! When I say: "Nicole, bring me my slippers and give me my nightcap," that's prose?

The Philosopher: Yes, sir.

Mr. Jourdain: Oh my word, I've been speaking prose these forty years, and never knew it; I am infinitely obliged to you for having informed me of this. Now I want to write to her in a note: *Fair Marquise,*[11] *your fair eyes make me die of love*; but I want it to be put in gallant fashion, and neatly turned.

The Philosopher: Say that the fires of her eyes reduce your heart to ashes; that night and day you suffer for her all the 290 tortures of a. . .

Mr. Jourdain: No, no, no, I want none of all that. I will have nothing but what I told you: *Fair Marquise, your fair eyes make me die of love.*

The Philosopher: You must enlarge upon the matter a little.

Mr. Jourdain: No, I tell you. I'll have none but those very words in the note, but put in a fashionable way, arranged as they should be. Pray tell me over the different ways they can be put, so that I may see.

The Philosopher: You can first of all put them as you said: 300
Fair Marquise, your fair eyes make me die of love.
Or else: *Of love to die me make, fair Marquise, your fair eyes.*
Or else: *Your fair eyes of love me make, fair Marquise, to die.*
Or else: *To die your fair eyes, fair Marquise, of love me make.*
Or else: *Me make your fair eyes die, fair Marquise, of love.*

Mr. Jourdain: But which of all these ways is the best?

The Philosopher: The way you said it: *Fair Marquise, your fair eyes make me die of love.*

Mr. Jourdain: And yet I never studied, and I did it at the first try. I thank you with all my heart, and beg you to come 310 again to-morrow early.

The Philosopher: I shall not fail to.

Scene VII
Mr. Jourdain, Lackey

Mr. Jourdain (*To the lackey*): What! Haven't my clothes come yet?

Lackey: No, sir.

Mr. Jourdain: That cursed tailor makes me wait a long while, on a day when I'm so busy. I am furious. May the quartan ague[12] wring this villain of a tailor unmercifully! To the devil with the tailor! Plague choke the tailor! If I had him here now, that wretch of a tailor, that dog of a tailor, that scoundrel 320 of a tailor, I'd. . .

---

[11]The wife of a nobleman ranking below a duke and above an earl or count.
[12]An intermittent fever.

Scene VIII

Mr. Jourdain, A Master-Tailor; A Journeyman-Tailor, *carrying Mr. Jourdain's suit*; Lackey

Mr. Jourdain: Ah! so there you are! I was just going to get angry with you.

Master-Tailor: I could not come sooner. I had twenty men at work on your clothes.

Mr. Jourdain: You sent me some silk stockings so tight that I had dreadful work getting them on, and there are two stitches broke in them already.

Master-Tailor: If anything, they will grow only too loose.

Mr. Jourdain: Yes, if I keep on breaking out stitches. And you made me some shoes that pinch horribly.   330

Master-Tailor: Not at all, sir.

Mr. Jourdain: What! Not at all?

Master-Tailor: No, they do not pinch you.

Mr. Jourdain: I tell you they do pinch me.

Master-Tailor: You imagine it.

Mr. Jourdain: I imagine it because I feel it. A fine way of talking!

Master-Tailor: There, this is one of the very handsomest and best matched of court costumes. 'Tis a masterpiece to   340 have invented a suit that is dignified, yet not of black; and I'd give the most cultured tailors six trials and defy them to equal it.

Mr. Jourdain: What's this? You have put the flowers upside down.

Master-Tailor: You didn't tell me you wanted them right end up.

Mr. Jourdain: Was there any need to tell you that?

Master-Tailor: Why, of course. All persons of quality wear them this way.   350

Mr. Jourdain: Persons of quality wear the flowers upside down?

Master-Tailor: Yes, sir.

Mr. Jourdain: Oh! that's all right then.

Master-Tailor: If you wish, I will put them right end up.

Mr. Jourdain: No, no.

Master-Tailor: You have only to say the word.

Mr. Jourdain: No, I tell you; you did rightly. Do you think the clothes will fit me?

Master-Tailor: A pretty question! I defy any painter, with   360 his brush, to make you a closer fit. I have in my shop a fellow that is the greatest genius in the world for setting up a pair of German breeches; and another who is the hero of our age for the cut of a doublet.[13]

Mr. Jourdain: Are the wig and the feathers just as they should be?

Master-Tailor: Everything is just right.

Mr. Jourdain (*Looking at the tailor's suit*): Ah! ah! Mr. Tailor here is some of the cloth from my last suit you made me. I know it perfectly.   370

Master-Tailor: The cloth seemed to me so fine that I thought well to cut a suit for myself out of it.

---

[13]A man's close-fitting jacket.
[14]Stolen or filched.

Mr. Jourdain: Yes; but you ought not to have cabbaged[14] it out of mine.

Master-Tailor: Will you put on your suit?

Mr. Jourdain: Yes; let me have it.

Master-Tailor: Wait. That is not the way to do things. I have brought my men with me to dress you to music; clothes such as these must be put on with ceremony. Ho! enter, you fellows.

Scene IX

Mr. Jourdain, Master-Tailor, Journeyman-Tailor; Dancers, *in the costume of journeymen-tailors*; Lackey

Master-Tailor (*To his journeymen*): Put on the gentleman's   380 suit, in the style you use for persons of quality.

First Ballet

Enter four journeymen-tailors, two of whom pull off Mr. Jourdain's breeches that he has on for his exercise, and the other two his jacket; then they put on his new suit; and Mr. Jourdain walks about among them, showing off his suit, to see if it is all right. All this to the accompaniment of full orchestra.

Journeyman-Tailor: Noble Sir, please give the tailor's men something to drink.

Mr. Jourdain: What did you call me?

Journeyman-Tailor: Noble Sir.   390

Mr. Jourdain: Noble Sir! That is what it is to dress as a person of quality! You may go clothed as a tradesman all your days, and nobody will call you Noble Sir. (*Giving him money*) There, that's for Noble Sir.

Journeyman-Tailor: My Lord, we are greatly obliged to you.

Mr. Jourdain: My Lord! Oh! oh! My Lord! Wait, friend; My Lord deserves something, 'tis no mean word, My Lord! There, there's what His Lordship gives you.

Journeyman-Tailor: My Lord, we will all go and drink Your Grace's health.   400

Mr. Jourdain: Your Grace! Oh! oh! oh! wait; don't go. Your Grace, to me! (*Aside*) Faith, if he goes as far as Your Highness he'll empty my purse. (*Aloud*) There, there's for Your Grace.

Journeyman-Tailor: My Lord, we thank you most humbly for your generosity.

Mr. Jourdain: He did well to stop. I was just going to give it all to him.

Absolute Power and the Aristocratic Style Beyond Europe

Fueled by curiosity and commercial ambition, cross-cultural contacts between Europe and Asia flourished during the early modern era. In the 1700s, ambassadors of the Shah (the word means "king") of Persia and of other Asian potentates were splendidly received at Versailles, while, at the same time, Christian missionaries and official representatives of the European monarchs found their way to Hindu, Buddhist, and Muslim lands. France had long maintained diplomatic ties with the Ottoman Turks, the Muslim successors of the Seljuk Turks in Southwest Asia, North Africa, and parts of southeastern Europe (see Map

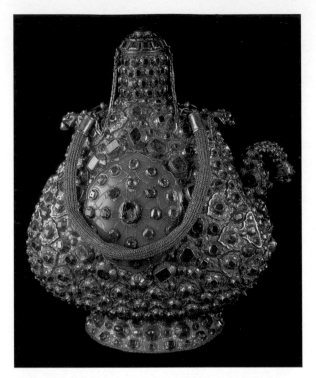

Figure 21.18 Ceremonial canteen, Ottoman Empire, second half of the sixteenth century. Gold decorated with jade plaques and gems. Topkapi Sarayi Museum, Istanbul.

21.1). So powerful were the Ottoman forces and so vast were their territories that one of Louis' ancestors, Francis I, had attempted to tip the balance of power in Western Europe by forming, in 1536, an "unholy" alliance with the great Muslim leader Suleiman (1494–1566).

Under Suleiman's rule the Ottoman Empire became a model of Muslim absolutism. Unlimited power in matters political and religious lay in Suleiman's hands. Known in Turkish history as the "Lawgiver," Suleiman oversaw the establishment of a legal code that fixed specific penalties for routine crimes and introduced the concept of balanced financial budgets. State revenues some eighty times those of France permitted Suleiman to undertake an extensive program of architectural and urban improvement in Mecca, Constantinople, and Jerusalem. A goldsmith and a poet of some esteem, Suleiman initiated a golden age of literature and art. Pomp and luxury characterized Suleiman's court, and the arts that flourished under his patronage shared with those of seventeenth-century France a taste for the ornate and a high degree of technical skill (Figure **21.18**). Suleiman, whom Europeans called "the magnificent," personally oversaw the activities of official court poets, painters, architects, and musicians. He established a model for imperial patronage that ensured the triumph of the aristocratic style not only in Turkish lands but in all parts of his multiethnic empire.

Neither absolutism nor its manifestation in the arts were the invention of Suleiman, any more than they were the creation of Louis XIV. Suleiman's ancestors, as well as his successors and their rivals, were equally autocratic. During the seventeenth century, as the Ottoman Empire fell into decline, Muslims of the Safavid dynasty rose to power in Persia under the astute leadership of Shah Abbas (1557–1629). Shah Abbas united a multiethnic population to make theocratic Persia (present-day Iran) the political, economic, and cultural leader of Asia. By the year 1600, Persian silk rivaled that of China at European markets. Carpet weaving became a

Figure 21.19 Kirman shrub rug, Persia, seventeenth century. Silk and wool, 10 ft. 1 in. × 4 ft. 7 in. Philadelphia Museum of Art: The Joseph Lees Williams Memorial Collection.

553 CHAPTER TWENTY-ONE Absolute power and the aristocratic style

Figure 21.20 Imperial Mosque, Isfahan, Iran, 1637. Surface decorated with colored glazed tiles, height of dome 177 ft. © E. Böhm, Mainz.

national industry which employed over twenty-five thousand people in the capital city of Isfahan alone. Persian tapestries, intricately woven in silk and wool (Figure **21.19**), and finely ornamented ceramics were avidly sought across the world, and Persian manuscripts embellished with brightly printed illustrations came to be imitated throughout Asia. The arts were as much an adjunct to the majesty of Shah Abbas as they had been to Suleiman and would be to Louis XIV.

In the field of architecture, the outstanding monument to Safavid wealth and power was the Imperial Mosque, commissioned by Shah Abbas for the city of Isfahan

(Figure **21.20**). Completed in 1637, this magnificent structure, flanked by two minarets, encloses a square main hall covered by a splendid dome which rises to 177 feet. The surfaces of the mosque, both inside and out, are covered with colored glazed tiles (compare the Ishtar Gate from Babylon, 604–562 B.C.E., illustrated in chapter 2) ornamented with delicate blue and yellow blossoms. French aristocrats in the service of Louis XIV brought back to France enthusiastic reports of the Imperial Mosque—a fact that has led scholars to detect the influence of Persian art on some of Louis' more lavish enterprises at Versailles.

Absolute Power and the Aristocratic Style in India

Muslims had ruled parts of India for almost a thousand years, but it was not until the sixteenth century that a Muslim dynasty, known as the Moguls (the name derives from "Mongol"), actually succeeded in uniting all of India (see Map 21.1). Distant cousins of the Safavid princes, the Moguls created an Indian empire and ruled India as absolute monarchs from 1526 to 1707. They imported Persian culture and language into India in much the same way that Louis XIV brought Italian culture into France. The creators of a cultural style that blended Muslim, Hindu, Turkish, Persian, Arabic, and African traditions, the Moguls encouraged the development of an aristocratic style, which—like that of the Sun King—served as an adjunct to majesty.

The founder of the Mogul empire, Akbar (1542–1605), came to the throne at the age of thirteen and laid the foundations for a luxurious court style that his son and grandson would perpetuate. India's most dynamic ruler since Emperor Asoka of the third century B.C.E., Akbar ruled over a court consisting of thousands of courtiers, servants, wives, and concubines. He exercised political control over feudal noblemen and court officials who, unlike their French counterparts, received paid salaries. Amidst the primarily Hindu population, Akbar tirelessly pursued a policy of religious toleration, a position that complemented his own quest for a synthesis of faiths that would surpass the teaching of any one religion. To this end, he brought to his court learned representatives of Christianity, Judaism, Hinduism, and other religions to debate with Muslim theologians. He also made every effort to rid India of such outmoded traditions as the immolation of wives on their husbands' funeral pyres. Despite Akbar's reforms, however, the lower classes and especially the peasants were taxed heavily (as were the French peasants under Louis) to finance the luxuries of the upper-class elite.

In the seventeenth century, the Moguls governed the wealthiest state in the world, a state whose revenues were ten times greater than those of France. Akbar commissioned magnificent works of music, poetry, painting, and architecture—the tangible expressions of princely affluence and taste. As was the case in Louis' court, most of

Figure 21.21 *Rejoicing at the Birth of Prince Salim in 1569.* Manuscript illustration from the Akbar-Nama. The Chester Beatty Library, Dublin.

1717 inoculation against smallpox is introduced in Europe (from Ottoman Turkey)

1736 expansion of the Indian shipbuilding industry in Bombay

1780 a European version of Chinese silk-reeling machines is introduced in Bengal

1781 Turkish methods for producing high-quality cloth are copied in England

1790 India uses military rockets based on Ottoman technology in warfare

these exquisite objects were designed for domestic, not liturgical, use. A state studio of more than one hundred artists working under Persian masters created a library of over 24,000 illuminated manuscripts, the contents of which ranged from love poetry to Hindu epics and religious tales. Mogul paintings reveal the brilliant union of delicate line, vivid color, and strong surface patterns—features that also appear in Asian carpets. A miniature celebrating the birth of Akbar's son, Jahangir, shows members of the court rejoicing: Dancers perform to the rhythms of an elaborate musical ensemble, while bread and alms are distributed outside the palace gate (Figure 21.21). Bright colors and the absence of Western perspective give the scene a strong decorative quality.

The Patronage of Jahangir and Shah Jahan

Under the rule of Akbar's son, Jahangir (ruled 1605–1627), aristocratic court portraiture came into fashion in India. The new genre reflects the influence of European painting, which had been eagerly embraced by the Moguls, and suggests the gradual relaxation of Muslim prohibition against the representation of the human figure. Relatively small in comparison with the aristocratic portraits executed by Rigaud or van Dyck (see Figures 21.1, 22.1), the painted likeness of Jahangir (the name means "world seizer") reflects, nevertheless, the will to glorify royalty in a realistic and psychologically probing style (Figure **21.22**). The artist Bichitr (fl. 1625), whose self-portrait appears in the lower left corner, shows the Shah enthroned atop an elaborate hourglass throne, a reference to the brevity of life and possibly an allusion to Jahangir's declining health. Jahangir welcomes a sufi (a Muslim mystic), who stands in the company of a Turkish dignitary and the European King James I of England. Four Western-style angels frame the scene: The upper two seem to lament the impermanence of worldly power (as suggested in the inscription above them), while the bottom two inscribe the base of the hourglass with the prayer, "O Shah, may the span of your life be a thousand years." Just as Louis XIV assumed the guise of the Sun King, so Jahangir—as notorious for his overconsumption of wine and opium as Louis was for fine food and sex—is apotheosized by a huge halo consisting of the sun and the moon.

Well before the seventeenth century, Mogul rulers had initiated the tradition of building huge ceremonial and administrative complexes, veritable cities in themselves. Such complexes symbolized Muslim wealth and authority in India, but, as in France, they were also political manifestations of the cult of royalty. Akbar had personally overseen the construction of a palace complex near Agra, which, comparable with Versailles, featured an elaborate residence surrounded by courtyards and mosques, as well as by formal gardens and fountains watered by means of artificial conduits. The garden, a this-worldly counterpart of the Garden of Paradise described in the Quran (see chapter 10) and a welcome refuge from India's intense heat, was a characteristic feature of the Mogul palace complex.

Inspired by the elaborate ceremonial centers built by his father and his grandfather, Shah Jahan (1627–1666) commissioned the most sumptuous of all Mogul palaces,

Figure 21.22 (above) *Jahangir Preferring a Sufi Shaikh to Kings*, from the *Leningrad Album of Bichitr*, seventeenth century. Color and gold, 10 × 7⅛ in. Courtesy of the Freer Gallery of Art, Smithsonian Institution, Washington, D.C. (42.15V).

the Shahjahanabad (present-day Old Delhi). The red sandstone walls of the Shahjahanabad (nicknamed the "Red Fort") enclosed a palatial residence of white marble, flanked by magnificent gardens, public and private audience halls, courtyards, pavilions, baths, and the largest mosque in India (Figure **21.23**). The Red Fort's 3:4 rectangular plan was bisected by an axis that led through successive courts to the public audience hall, a pattern that anticipated the rigid symmetry of Versailles (compare Figure 21.2).

Figure 21.23 Anonymous Delhi artist, *The Red Fort*, ca. 1820. The building dates from the Shah Jahan period, after 1638. Courtesy of the British Library, London.

The hot Indian climate inclined Mogul architects to open up interior space by means of foliated arcades (see chapter 10) and latticed screens through which breezes might blow uninterrupted. These graceful architectural features distinguish the Shah's palace at the Red Fort (Figure 21.24). The most ornate of all Mogul interiors, Shah Jahan's audience hall consists of white marble arcades and ceilings decorated with geometric and floral patterns popular in Mogul embroidery, a craft traditionally dominated by women. The rich designs consist of inlaid precious and semiprecious stones (*pietra dura*), a type of mosaic work that the Moguls had borrowed from Italy (Figure 21.25). At the center of the hall, the Shah once sat on the prized (but no longer existing) Peacock Throne, fashioned in solid gold and studded with emeralds, rubies, diamonds, and pearls. Above the throne (which served as

Figure 21.24 Foliated arcades and perforated monolithic screens in the Red Fort (Shahjahanabad), Delhi, Shah Jahan period, after 1638.

Figure 21.25 *Pietra dura* inlay in the Mussamman Burj, Red Fort, Agra Mogul, Shah Jahan period, ca. 1637. Spectrum, London.

the imperial throne of India until it was plundered by Persian warriors in 1732) was a canopy on which stood two gold peacocks, and above the canopy, around the ceiling of the hall, were inscribed the words, "If there is a paradise on the face of the earth, It is this, oh! it is this, oh! it is this."

Surpassing the splendor of the palace at Delhi (badly damaged by the British army during the nineteenth century) is Shah Jahan's most magnificent gift to world architecture: the Taj Mahal (Figure **21.26**). Shah Jahan built the Taj Mahal as a mausoleum to honor the memory of his favorite wife, Mumtaz Mahal (the name means "light of the world"). When Mumtaz died giving birth to their fourteenth child, her husband, legend has it, was inconsolable. He directed his architects to construct alongside the Jumna River a glorious tomb, a twin to one he planned for himself on the adjoining riverbank. Fabricated in cream-colored marble, the Taj rises majestically above a tree-lined pool which mirrors its elegant silhouette so that the mausoleum seems to be floating in air. Although the individual elements of the building—minarets, bulbous domes, and octagonal base—recall Byzantine and Persian prototypes (see chapter 9 and Figure 21.20), the total effect is unique: Shadowy voids and bright solids play against one another on the surface of the exterior, while delicate patterns of light and dark are repeated in the latticed marble screens and exquisitely carved walls of the interior. The garden complex, divided into quadrants by waterways and broad footpaths, is an earthly recreation of the Muslim garden of paradise. The Taj Mahal is the product of some twenty thousand West Asian builders and craftsmen working under the direction of a Persian architect. It is a brilliant fusion of the best aspects of Byzantine, Muslim, and Hindu traditions and, hence, an emblem of Islamic cohesion. But it is also an extravagant expression of conjugal devotion and, to generations of Western visitors, an eloquent symbol of romantic love.

Figure 21.26 Taj Mahal, Agra, India, 1623–1643. Scala, Florence.

Absolute Power and the Aristocratic Style in China

From the earliest days of Chinese history, Chinese emperors—the "Sons of Heaven"—ruled on earth by divine authority, or, as the Chinese called it, "the Mandate of Heaven" (see chapter 3). In theory, all of China's emperors were absolute rulers. Nevertheless, over the centuries, their power was frequently contested by feudal lords, military generals, and government officials. In 1368, native Chinese rebels drove out the last of the Mongol rulers (see chapter 14) and established the Ming dynasty, which ruled China until 1644. The Ming dynasty governed the largest and most sophisticated empire on earth, an empire of some 120 million people. In the highly centralized Chinese state, Ming emperors oversaw a bureaucracy that included offices of finance, laws, military affairs, and public works. They rebuilt the Great Wall (see chapter 7) and revived the ancient Chinese tradition of the examination system, which had been suspended by the Mongols. By the seventeenth century, however, the Ming had become autocrats who, like the foreigners they had displaced, took all power into their own hands. They transformed the civil service into a non-hereditary bureaucracy that did not dare to threaten the emperor's authority. The rigid court protocol that developed around the imperial rulers of the late Ming dynasty symbolized this shift toward autocracy. Officials, for instance, knelt in the presence of the emperor, who, as the Son of Heaven, sat on an elevated throne in the center of the imperial precinct.

Beset by court corruption and popular revolts, the Ming fell prey to the invading hordes of East Asians (descendants of Mongols, Turks, and other tribes) known as the Manchu. Under the rule of the Manchu, who established the Qing dynasty (1644–1911), the conditions of imperial autocracy intensified. As a symbol of submission, every Chinese male was required to adopt the Manchu hairstyle, by which one shaved the front of the head and wore a plaited pigtail at the back. Qing rulers retained the administrative traditions of their predecessors, but government posts were often sold rather than earned by merit. When the Qing dynasty reached its zenith—during the very last years that Louis XIV ruled France—it governed the largest, most populous, and one of the most unified states in the world (see Map 21.1). Despite internal peace, however, uprisings were common. They reflected the discontent of peasant masses beset by high taxes and rents and periodic famines. Like the lower classes of France and India, Chinese villagers and urban workers supported the luxuries of royal princes, government officials, and large landholders, who (as in France and India) were themselves exempt from taxation. The early Manchu rulers imitated their predecessors

Figure 21.27 XU YANG *Bird's-Eye View of the Capital,* 1770. Hanging scroll, ink and color on paper, 8 ft. 4¼ in. × 7 ft. 8 in. The Palace Museum.

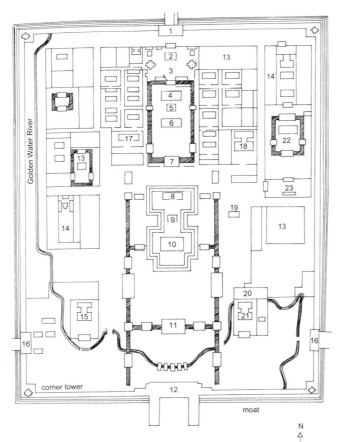

Figure 21.28 (above) Plan of the imperial palace, Forbidden City, Beijing, China.

1 Gate of Divine Pride
2 Pavilion of Imperial Peace
3 Imperial Garden
4 Palace of Earthly Tranquillity
5 Hall of Union
6 Palace of Heavenly Purity
7 Gate of Heavenly Purity
8 Hall of the Preservation of Harmony
9 Hall of Perfect Harmony
10 Hall of Supreme Harmony
11 Gate of Supreme Harmony
12 Meridian Gate
13 Kitchens
14 Gardens
15 Former Imperial Printing House
16 Flower Gate
17 Palace of the Culture of the Mind
18 Hall of the Worship of the Ancestors
19 Pavilion of Arrows
20 Imperial Library
21 Palace of Culture
22 Palace of Peace and Longevity
23 Nine Dragon Screen

Figure 21.29 Three-tiered stone terrace and Hall of Supreme Harmony, Forbidden City, Beijing, China, Ming dynasty. Hall approx. 200 × 100 ft. Robert Harding, London.

as royal sponsors of art and architecture. Like Louis XIV and Shah Jahan, the Chinese emperor and his huge retinue resided in an impressive ceremonial complex (Figure **21.27**). This metropolis, the symbol of entrenched absolutism and the majesty of the ruler, was known as the Forbidden City—so-called because of its inaccessibility to ordinary Chinese citizens.

The Forbidden City Comparable in size and conception to Versailles in the West and to the Mogul palaces of India, the Forbidden City—a walled complex of palaces, tombs, and gardens located in Beijing—was the most elaborate imperial monument of the Ming and Qing eras. Construction on the imperial palace began under fifteenth-century Ming emperors and was continued by the Manchus. For almost 500 years, this vast ceremonial complex—which, like Versailles, is now a park and museum—was the administrative center of China and the home of Chinese emperors, their families, and the members of their courts. By the eighteenth century, some 9,000 people, including guards and domestic servants, resided within the complex.

Inside the walls of the Forbidden City are grand avenues, broad courtyards, government offices, mansions of princes and dignitaries, artificial lakes, lush gardens, spacious temples, theaters, a library, and a printing house (Figure **21.28**). Entering from the south, one passes under the majestic, five-towered entranceway through a succession of courtyards and gates reminiscent of the intriguing boxes within boxes at which Chinese artisans excel. At the heart of the rectangular complex, one proceeds up the three-tiered stone terrace (Figure **21.29**), into the Hall of Supreme Harmony (approximately 200 by 100 feet), where the Sons of Heaven once sat (see Figure 21.27), and beyond, to the imperial living quarters at the rear of the complex. Fragrant gardens, watered by fountains and artificial pools, once graced the private quarters of the royal

officials who lived here. During the seventeenth century, courtyard gardening itself developed into a fine art. Often flanked by a covered walkway from which it could be viewed, the garden was an arrangement of seemingly random (but actually carefully placed) rocks, plants, and trees—a miniature version of the natural world. Like the Chinese landscape scroll, the Chinese garden was designed to be enjoyed progressively, as an object of gentle contemplation. Such gardens, with their winding, narrow paths, delicate ferns, and quivering bamboos, have become a hallmark of East Asian culture.

The Forbidden City was the nucleus of imperial power and the symbol of Chinese absolutism. Laid out with a gridiron regularity that rivaled Mogul and French palatial complexes, the arrangement of buildings, courtyards, gates, and terraces was nevertheless uniquely Chinese. This ceremonial arrangement reflects an adherence to ancient Confucian principles of correctness and to the Chinese taste for self-enclosure. Buildings are lined up along the traditional north/south axis and their relative sizes and functions determined by the rigors of Chinese court procedure, a strict protocol based on rank, age, and gender. During the Ming Era, for instance, imperial legislation prescribed nine rooms for the emperor, seven for a prince, five for a court official, and three for an ordinary citizen. Most of the buildings of the Forbidden City are no more than a single story high, their walls serving only as screens that divide interior space. What the Chinese sacrificed in monumentality, however, they recovered in ornamental splendor and in the creation of an architecture that sought harmony with (rather than dominance over) nature. Chinese architects deliberately preserved such traditional features as the rectangular hall with fully exposed wooden rafters and the pitched roof with projecting eaves and glazed yellow tiles—the latter symbolic of the mantle of heaven. Bronze lions and gilded dragons (symbols of royal power) guard the great halls and entrances. In the Forbidden City, as in all Chinese culture prior to the twentieth century, elaborate court ritual enhanced the majesty of the ruler.

Imperial Patronage of the Arts The Ming and Manchu emperors were great patrons of the arts. They encouraged the traditional schools of landscape painting and oversaw the production of such luxury items as inlaid bronze vessels, carved ivories and jades, lacquer ware, embroidered silk, and painted ceramics. Chinese porcelains had been much sought-after since the seventh century; by the seventeenth century they were world famous, so much so that in the West the word "Ming" became synonymous with porcelain. (More generally, the word "china" has come to signify fine ceramics and tableware.)

Qing artists used bright colors more freely than in earlier times. Vessels with solid color glazes of ox-blood red and peach-blossom pink (Figure **21.30**) alternated with colorful landscapes filled with songbirds, flowering trees, human figures, and mythical animals. One Qing bowl ornamented with a rich five-color palette shows a group of elegantly attired men, women, and servants in a luxurious

Figure 21.30 Flower vase, Qing dynasty. Chinese pottery, "peach-bloom" glaze, height 7¾ in. Courtesy of the Freer Gallery of Art, Smithsonian Institution, Washington, D.C. (42.20).

interior (Figure **21.31**). As this delightful scene suggests, neither in the porcelains nor in the paintings of this period did the Chinese develop any interest in the kinds of heroic and moralizing themes that dominated baroque art in the West. This difference notwithstanding, imperial tastes dictated the style of aristocratic art in China every bit as much as the royal academies of France influenced seventeenth-century French style. By 1680, there were over thirty official palace workshops serving the imperial

Figure 21.31 *Famille verte*, Qing dynasty, early eighteenth century. Foliated porcelain bowl, diameter 6½ in. Ashmolean Museum, Oxford, Department of Eastern Art.

Figure 21.32 Incense burner in the shape of a *li* (tripod), Ming dynasty, fifteenth or possibly early sixteenth century. *Cloisonné* enamel. Courtesy of the Freer Gallery of Art, Smithsonian Institution, Washington, D.C. (F61.12).

court. Out of these workshops poured increasingly flamboyant works of art: exotic jewelry, painted enamels, *cloisonné* vessels (Figure **21.32**), intricate jade carvings, and lavishly embroidered silk and gold tapestries (Figure **21.33**). Many of these objects found their way into Europe, where they inspired ***chinoiserie***, a style reflecting the influence of Chinese art and a taste for Chinese items that, in the 1700s, developed into something of a mania. From China, by way of the Dutch, tea ("the Chinese drink") came into use in England, often smuggled into the country to avoid the high import tax. Fashionable tea service became the object of imitation in the West, most notably in the blue and white wares of Delft, Holland. Cultural exchange between East and West, however, was mutual: Delegations of Jesuits, who arrived in China in 1601, introduced the rules of linear perspective to Chinese art, even as they transmitted to Europe (often by means of prints and engravings) a knowledge of Chinese techniques and materials. And French prints in turn prompted early Manchu rulers to build a Chinese version of Versailles, complete with fountains, at the imperial summer palace northwest of Beijing.

Chinese Literature and the Theater Arts Ming and Manchu rulers worked hard to preserve the rich literary heritage of China. Under Ming patronage, a group of two thousand scholars began the enormous task of collecting and copying the most famous of

Figure 21.33 Section of a screen panel, Ming dynasty (1368–1644). Tapestry weave with silk and gold thread, 78 × 26 in. © The Cleveland Museum of Art 1998. Gift of Mr. & Mrs. J. H. Wade (CMA 1916.1334).

Figure 21.34 UNKNOWN ARTIST, portrait of Emperor Kangxi reading. Imperial Palace Museum, Beijing.

China's literary and historical works. The Manchu contemporary of Louis XIV, Emperor Kangxi (1662–1722; Figure **21.34**), hired 15,000 calligraphers and 360 editors to compile a vast assortment of dictionaries, encyclopedias, and a thirty-six-volume anthology of the Chinese classics. Increasing numbers of literate middle-class men and women in China's growing cities demanded printed books for everyday use. These included almanacs, guides to letter writing, short stories, collections of proverbs and maxims, chronicles, ballads, and romances. Novels, long works of fiction in the colloquial style, had emerged as early as the twelfth century in China and even earlier in Japan (see chapter 14); but in the Ming and Qing eras, this literary genre became ever more popular. The typical Chinese novel recounted historical events and often made fun of religious and secular authorities. In the early eighteenth century, Cao Xueqin produced China's greatest novel, *The Dream of the Red Chamber* (also known as *The Story of the Stone*). This 4,000-page work, which was to become the most popular example of Chinese fiction, is a love story involving two noble Beijing families. Filled with realistic detail as well as fantastic dream sequences, the novel provides a fascinating picture of upper-class Qing society.

Plots drawn from popular novels such as *The Dream of the Red Chamber* provided the themes for staged performances, which always included mime, dance, and vocal and instrumental music. This type of theatrical performance—which Westerners would call "opera"—was the only form of drama that existed in China prior to the twentieth century (when, imitating Western drama, Chinese writers began to produce exclusively spoken plays). In the Chinese theater, performers were exclusively male, and male actors would play the parts of such stock characters as the coquette or the virtuous maid. Since troupes of players moved from city to city, elaborate costumes and stage scenery might be minimal. In place of costumes and scenery, a system of conventions arose in the performance of Chinese plays to indicate setting or circumstance: A chair might represent a mountain, a whip might signify that the actor was on horseback, and a black cloth might be used to indicate that a character was invisible. Colors symbolized conventional character types: Red represented loyalty and dignity, white symbolized villainy or treachery, and so on. During the Ming Era, when sumptuous costumes and masklike makeup became popular, such earlier stage symbols and conventions were still preserved. Indeed, to this day, Chinese theater retains traditional, highly stylized features.

Despite the differences in their origins, Chinese and European opera developed at roughly the same time—the seventeenth century. And, by the late eighteenth century (when the first permanent Chinese opera company appeared in the capital city of Beijing), both appealed to an increasingly wealthy social class. Both employed many artificial conventions and both employed male performers for female roles. Chinese music, however, sounded distinctly different from Western music. Rich in melodic and rhythmic nuances, Chinese opera 🎵 shunned the dramatic contrasts in texture and timbre that have characterized Western opera (and Western music in general since the Renaissance). Elaborately staged (and usually many hours long), Chinese opera might be said to have greater popular appeal than European opera. While European operas usually borrowed themes from Greco-Roman mythology and biblical history—themes often employed to glorify a royal patron or flatter upper-class tastes—Chinese operas mainly drew on a traditional repertory of love stories, social events, and the adventures of folk heroes. Such operas often featured stock characters resembling those of Molière's plays, and, like Molière's plays, they had wide and lasting popularity.

Absolute Power and the Aristocratic Style in Japan

By the seventeenth century, feudal Japan (see chapter 11) had taken the direction of a unified and centralized state led by members of the Tokugawa dynasty (1600–1868). In contrast to China, whose aristocracy consisted of a scholarly elite recruited through civil service examinations, Japan had an aristocracy that consisted of a warrior elite (the *samurai*) recruited in battle. In the style of Louis XIV, the Tokugawa *shogun* (general-in-chief) demanded that his feudal lords attend his court in Edo (modern-day Tokyo), from which center he enforced court etiquette as faithfully as he solidified political and economic control. Unique to

🎵 See Music Listening Selection 14, CD One, an excerpt from a Chinese opera described in chapter 14.

Japan was its policy of isolation from the West. In the 1630s Tokugawa rulers initiated a policy of national seclusion. Determined to maintain internal stability and peace, they expelled foreigners and forbade citizens to travel abroad, thus sealing off Japan from the outside world.

While a large segment of Japan's peasantry led barely subsistent lives, the pleasure-loving court at Edo (a city of 1 million people by the year 1700) and the rising commercial classes of the towns enjoyed one of the most creative periods in Japanese history. In the Tokugawa court, the traditional Japanese decorative style reached new heights in multipaneled screens (used to divide interior space), hand-painted scrolls, ceramics (including the decorative porcelains known as "Imari ware"), and lacquer boxes used for the tea ceremony. Japan's aristocratic style is epitomized in the Edo Era's brightly painted multifold screens, adorned with stylized flowers, birds, or landscape motifs. In the large six-paneled screen by Ogata Korin (ca. 1657–1716), pictured in Figure **21.35**, the Japanese love of bold, decorative shapes organized by means of a subtle balance of figures and ground (positive and negative space) evokes an astonishing purity of design. Such screens reveal a unique blend of elegant simplicity and luxury (the ground of the screen is gold leaf) which distinguishes the Japanese court style at its best.

Parallel with the flowering of the aristocratic style in Tokugawa Japan was the rise of popular culture and popular art. Between the mid-seventeenth and mid-eighteenth centuries, three of Japan's best-known modes of artistic expression emerged: *kabuki* theater, the woodblock print, and the light verse form known as the **haiku**. Kabuki theater evolved out of the popular dances and skits presented by troupes of female performers. Although women's kabuki was banned after 1629, male actors continued to work this popular form of urban entertainment (Figure **21.36**).

Kabuki drama—whose domestic, historical, and contemporary themes called for elaborate scenery and magnificent costumes—featured tales of romance marked by violent passions and "love suicides." It provided an alternative to the classical drama of Japan, the Nō play, whose stylized action, traditional literary subjects, choral interludes, and masked players resembled Greek drama.

Often mirroring the expressive moods of kabuki, seventeenth- and eighteenth-century woodblock prints, with their actors (see chapter 31), courtesans, and leisure-time entertainments, capture the "floating world" (*ukiyo*)—the world of fugitive urban pleasures and delights, often marked by bawdy entertainment. Executed in black and white, or colored by hand or with inked blocks, such prints are evidence of Japanese virtuosity in calligraphic design. As with Korin's screens, these prints display a rare unity of simplicity, elegance, and control.

The Way of Tea and Zen A classic expression of the Japanese aesthetic of elegance and simplicity is the ritual tea ceremony—a unique synthesis of art, theater, and everyday ritual. Introduced into Japan from China during the ninth century, tea served as an aid to Buddhist meditation. The tea ceremony developed in sixteenth-century Japan in conjunction with Zen Buddhism, a strand of Buddhism that stresses the attainment of spiritual enlightenment through intuitive illumination (see chapter 8). With the cultivation of better types of tea plants in Japan, the Way of Tea (as the philosophy of tea-drinking was called) became widely practiced in Japanese society and gradually came to symbolize the elite conservatism of the Japanese aristocracy. A mainstay of Zen monastic life, tea and the etiquette of tea-drinking coincided with a revival of Zen painting among eighteenth-century artist-monks. Zen calligraphers did not consider their paintings as works of

Figure 21.35 OGATA KORIN, *Irises at Yatuhashi*, from the *Tale of Ise (Ise Monogatari)*, Edo Period. One of a pair of six-paneled screens, ink and color and gilded paper, with black lacquered frames, each screen 4 ft. 11½ in. × 11 ft. 3¼ in. Nezu Institute of Fine Arts, Tokyo.

Figure 21.36 TOSHUSAI SHARAKU, *Bust Portrait of the Actor Segawa Tomisaburo as Yadorigi, the Wife of Ogishi Kurando*, 1794–1795. Woodblock print, 14½ × 9¼ in. Photograph © 1997, The Art Institution of Chicago, All Rights Reserved. Clarence Buckingham Collection, 1928.1056.

art, but as acts of meditation involving intense concentration and focus. Absence of detail invited the beholder to complete the painting, and thus partake of the meditative process. One of the greatest Zen masters was Hakuin Ekaku (1685–1768), whose magnificent ink scrolls are noted for their vigorous yet subtle brush drawing. In *Two Blind Men Crossing a Log Bridge* (Figure **21.37**), Hakuin illustrates his vision of the precarious nature of the human journey to spiritual enlightenment: Two monks, one with his sandals hanging on his staff so as to grasp the log's surface more directly, make their way unsteadily across the narrow bridge, which, like each Japanese character, is executed with a single, confident calligraphic brushstroke. Hakuin adds the accompanying poem:

Both inner life and the floating world outside us
Are like the blind man's round log bridge—
An enlightened mind is the best guide.

In their improvisational brushwork, the ink scrolls of the Zen master differ from the stylized and elegantly patterned Edo screens. Yet, both share the Japanese preference for a

stripped style of the utmost simplicity. Controlled simplicity also characterizes Tokugawa lyric verse forms, the most notable of which is the *haiku*. The *haiku*—a seventeen-syllable poem arranged in three lines of 5/7/5/ syllables—depends for its effectiveness on the pairing of contrasting images. The unexpected contrast does not describe a condition or event, but rather, evokes a mood or emotion. Much like the art of the Zen calligrapher, the *haiku* creates a provocative void between what is stated and what is left unsaid. In this void there lies an implied "truth," one that aims to close the gap between the world of things and the world of feelings. Witness the following five compositions by Japan's most famous *haiku* poet and Zen monk, Matsuo Bashō (1644–1694):

The beginning of all art
  a song when planting a rice field
    in the country's inmost part.

◆

The first day of the year:
  thoughts come—and there is loneliness;
    the autumn dusk is here.

◆

Oh, these spring days!
  A nameless little mountain,
    wrapped in morning haze!

◆

I'd like enough drinks
  to put me to sleep—on stones
    covered with pinks.

◆

Leaning upon staves
  and white-haired—a whole family
    visiting the graves.*

SUMMARY

The aristocratic style in the arts of the seventeenth century reflects the influence of absolutism in the political history of the West, as well as in Central and East Asia. In Europe, the most notable figure of the Age of Absolutism was Louis XIV. Under Louis' leadership, the arts worked to serve the majesty of the crown. At Versailles, the classical baroque style—an amalgam of Greco-Roman subject matter, classical principles of design (often derived from Renaissance models), and baroque theatricality—became the vehicle of French royal authority. Luxury, grandeur, and technical refinement became the hallmarks of elitism.

Louis XIV was instrumental in founding most of the royal academies of France, whose members established neoclassical guidelines for painting, sculpture, music, literature, and dance. Poussin's canvases, Girardon's sculptures, La Rochefoucauld's maxims, Lully's operas, Racine's tragedies, and Molière's comedies all assert the neoclassical

*Henderson, Harold G. *An Introduction to Haiku.* Garden City, NY: Doubleday, 1958. Pages 25, 33, 23, 44, 49.

Figure 21.37 HAKUIN EKAKU, *Two Blind Men Crossing a Log Bridge,* Edo Period (1615–1868). Hanging scroll, ink on paper, 11¹⁄₁₆ × 33 in. Kurt and Millie Gitter Collection.

view that the mind must prevail over the passions. Under Louis' leadership, the ballet emerged as an independent art form and one that epitomized neoclassical order and grace. Outside of France, Velázquez and van Dyck painted elegant portraits that flattered aristocratic patrons, while Rubens produced dramatic allegories of royal authority.

In Southwest Asia, the Ottoman Emperor Suleiman established a pattern of princely patronage that was imitated by Muslim rulers for at least two centuries. The Persian Shah Abbas and the Mogul rulers of India—Akbar, Jahangir, and Shah Jahan—were great patrons of the arts and commissioned some of the most magnificent monuments in architectural history. Like Versailles in France, the Imperial Mosque at Isfahan, the Red Fort at Old Delhi, and the Taj Mahal—though serving different functions—epitomize the wealth, absolute authority, and artistic vision of a privileged minority. So too, the imperial complex at the Forbidden City in Beijing stands as a symbol of the absolutism of China's rulers. Finally, in the sheltered society of Tokugawa Japan, the decorative tradition in the arts reached new heights of sophistication and refinement.

Though the aristocratic style has a rich history whose origins may be traced back to the pharaohs of Egypt, that style held a particularly important place in the seventeenth century, when it served to legitimize and glorify the power of the ruling elite throughout Europe and Asia. Flamboyant and lavish, the aristocratic style touched all forms of intellectual and artistic expression, including drama, opera, architecture, and dance. And although the artists of Asia tapped a heritage that was essentially different from that of Europeans, the East produced works of art that in every way rivaled those of the West.

SUGGESTIONS FOR READING

Asher, Catherine B. *Architecture of Mughal India.* New York: Cambridge University Press, 1992.

Delay, Nelly. *The Art and Culture of Japan.* New York: Abrams, 1998.

Howarth, W. D. Molière: *A Playwright and his Audience.* Cambridge: Cambridge University Press, 1982.

Lablaude, Pierre A. *The Gardens of Versailles.* New York: Scala, 1996.

Lewis, W. H. *The Splendid Century: Life in the France of Louis XIV.* New York: Waveland Press, 1997.

Michell, George. *The Royal Palaces of India.* London: Thames and Hudson, 1994.

Mitford, Nancy. *The Sun King: Louis XIV at Versailles.* New York: Rpt. edn. Penguin USA, 1995. Harper and Row, 1966.

Singer, Robert T. et al. *Edo: Art in Japan 1615–1868.* New Haven, Conn.: Yale University Press, 1999.

Spence, Jonathan D. *Emperor of China: Self-Portrait of K'ang Hsi.* New York: Vintage, 1988.

Walker, Hallam. *Molière.* Boston: Twayne, 1990.

Wright, Christopher. *The French Painters of the Seventeenth Century.* New York: New York Graphic Society, 1986.

Yu Zhuoyen, ed. *Palaces of the Forbidden City,* translated by Ng Mau-Sang and others. New York: Viking, 1984.

GLOSSARY

chinoiserie European imitation of Chinese art, architecture, and decorative motifs; also any objects that reflect such imitation

choreography the art of composing, arranging, and/or notating dance movements

comédie-ballet (French) a dramatic performance that features interludes of song and dance

haiku a light verse form consisting of seventeen syllables (three lines of five, seven, and five)

marquetry a decorative technique in which patterns are created on a wooden surface by means of inlaid wood, shell, or ivory

maxim a short, concise, and often witty saying

objet d'art (French) art object

pietra dura (Italian, "hard stone") an ornamental technique involving inlaid precious and semiprecious stones

salon (French, "drawing room") an elegant apartment or drawing room

CHAPTER TWENTY-TWO

The baroque in the Protestant north

"No man is an island entire of itself, every man is a piece of the continent, a part of the main."
John Donne

Throughout France, Italy, Spain, and other parts of the West, the baroque style mirrored the spirit of the Catholic Reformation; but in Northern Europe, where Protestant loyalties remained strong, another phase of the style emerged. The differences between the two are easily observed in the arts: In Italy, church interiors were ornate and theatrical; but in England, the Netherlands, and Northern Germany, where Protestants as a matter of faith were committed to private devotion rather than public ritual, churches were stripped of ornamentation, and the mood was more somber and intimate. Protestant devotionalism shared with Catholic mysticism an anti-intellectual bias, but Protestantism shunned all forms of theatrical display. In Northern Europe, where a largely Protestant population valued personal piety and private devotion, the Bible exercised an especially significant influence on the arts. Pietism, a seventeenth-century religious movement that originated in Germany, encouraged Bible study as the principal means of cultivating the "inner light" of religious truth.

If the Bible was a shaping influence on the arts of the Protestant North, so too was the patronage of a rising middle class. Having benefited financially from worldwide commerce, middle-class merchants demanded an art that reflected their keen interests in secular life. And while princely patronage in the North did not slacken during the seventeenth century, the landmark examples of Northern European art pay tribute to the vitality of this wealthy commercial class.

The Rise of the English Commonwealth

In England, Queen Elizabeth I (1558–1603) was succeeded by the first Stuart monarch James I (1566–1625). A Scot, and a committed proponent of absolute monarchy, James claimed, "There are no privileges and immunities which can stand against a divinely appointed King." His son, Charles I (1600–1649; Figure **22.1**), shared his father's view

that kings held a God-given right to rule. Charles alienated Parliament by governing for more than a decade without its approval and antagonized the growing number of Puritans (English Calvinists who demanded church reform and greater strictness in religious observance). Allying with antiroyalist factions, mostly of the emergent middle class, the Puritans constituted a powerful political group. With the support of the Puritans, leaders in Parliament raised an army to oppose King Charles, ultimately defeating the royalist forces in a civil war that lasted from 1642 to 1648 and executing the king on charges of treason. The government that followed this civil war, led by the Puritan general Oliver Cromwell (1599–1658), was known as the "Commonwealth." Bearing the hallmarks of a republic, the new government issued a written constitution that proposed the formation of a national legislature elected by universal manhood suffrage. The Commonwealth, however, was unable to survive without military support. When Cromwell died, Stuart monarchs were invited to return to the throne; however, when the Stuart king James II (1633–1701) attempted to fill a new Parliament with his Catholic supporters, the opposition rebelled again. They expelled the king and offered the crown of England to William of Orange, ruler of the Netherlands, and his wife Mary, the Protestant daughter of James II. Following the "Glorious Revolution" of 1688, Parliament enacted a Bill of Rights prohibiting the king from suspending parliamentary laws or interfering with the ordinary course of justice. The Bill of Rights was followed by the Toleration Act of 1689, which guaranteed freedom of worship to non-Anglican sects. By 1689, Parliament's authority to limit the power of the English monarch was firmly established. The "bloodless revolution" reestablished constitutional monarchy and won a victory for popular sovereignty.

The King James Bible

These dramatic political events, so closely tied to religious issues, occurred in the years following one of the most

Figure 22.1 ANTHONY VAN DYCK, *Charles I on Horseback*, ca. 1638. Oil on canvas, 12 ft. × 9 ft. 7in. National Gallery, London

influential cultural events of the seventeenth century: the new English translation of the Bible. If, indeed, tradition is formed by the perpetuation of systems of ideas, then, surely, English tradition and Western European culture in general owe a major debt to the 1611 publication of the King James version of the Bible. Drawing on a number of earlier English translations of Scripture made during the sixteenth century, a committee of fifty-four scholars recruited by James I of England produced an "authorized" English-language edition of the Old and New Testaments. This edition of Scripture emerged during the very decades in which Shakespeare was writing his last major dramas (see chapter 19)—a time when the English language reached its peak in eloquence. Along with the writings of Shakespeare, the King James Bible had a shaping influence on the English language and on all of English literature.

The new translation of Scripture preserved the spiritual fervor of the Old Testament Hebrew and the narrative vigor of the New Testament Greek. Like Shakespeare's poetry, the language of the King James Bible is majestic and compelling. Some appreciation of these qualities may be gleaned from comparing the two following translations. The first, a sixteenth-century translation based on Saint Jerome's Latin Vulgate edition and published in the city of Douay in France in 1609, lacks the concise language, the poetic imagery, and the lyrical rhythms of the King James version (the second example), which, though deeply indebted to a number of sixteenth-century English translations, drew directly on manuscripts written in the original Hebrew.

READING 4.6 The Twenty-Third Psalm

From the Douay Bible (1609)

Our Lord ruleth me, and nothing shall be wanting to me; in place of pasture there he hath placed me.

Upon the water of refection he hath brought me up; he hath converted my soul.

He hath conducted me upon the paths of justice, for his name.

For although I shall walk in the midst of the shadow of death, I will not fear evils; because thou art with me.

Thy rod and thy staff, they have comforted me.

Thou hast prepared in my sight a table against them that trouble me.

Thou hast fatted my head with oil, and my chalice inebriating, how goodly is it!

And thy mercy shall follow me all the days of my life.

And that I may dwell in the house of our Lord in longitude of days.

From the King James Bible (1611)

The Lord is my shepherd; I shall not want.

He maketh me to lie down in green pastures: he leadeth me beside the still waters.

He restoreth my soul: he leadeth me in the paths of righteousness for his name's sake.

Yea, though I walk through the valley of the shadow of death, I will fear no evil: for thou art with me; thy rod and thy staff they comfort me.

Thou preparest a table before me in the presence of mine enemies: thou anointest my head with oil; my cup runneth over.

Surely goodness and mercy shall follow me all the days of my life: and I will dwell in the house of the Lord for ever.

English Literature of the Seventeenth Century

John Donne

One of the most eloquent voices of religious devotionalism in the Protestant North was that of the poet John Donne (1571–1631). Born and raised as a Roman Catholic, Donne studied at Oxford and Cambridge, but renounced Catholicism when he was in his twenties. He traveled widely, entered Parliament in 1601, and converted to Anglicanism fourteen years later, soon becoming a priest of the Church of England. A formidable preacher as well as a man of great intellectual prowess, Donne wrote eloquent sermons that challenged the parishioners at Saint Paul's Cathedral in London (Figure **22.2**), where he acted as dean. At Saint Paul's, Donne developed the sermon as a vehicle for philosophic meditation. In *Meditation 17* (an excerpt from which follows), Donne pictures humankind—in typically baroque terms—as part of a vast, cosmic plan. His image of human beings as "chapters" in the larger "book" of God's design is an example of Donne's affection for unusual, extended metaphors.

READING 4.7 From Donne's *Meditation 17* (1623)

All mankind is of one author, and is one volume; when one man   1
dies, one chapter is not torn out of the book, but translated into
a better language; and every chapter must be so translated. God
employs several translators; some pieces are translated by age,
some by sickness, some by war, some by justice; but God's hand   5
is in every translation, and his hand shall bind up all our
scattered leaves again for that library where every book shall lie
open to one another. As therefore the bell that rings to a
sermon calls not upon the preacher only but upon the
congregation to come, so this bell calls us all. . . . No man is an   10
island entire of itself; every man is a piece of the continent, a
part of the main. If a clod be washed away by the sea, Europe is
the less, as well as if a promontory were, as well as if a manor
of thy friend's or of thine own were. Any man's death diminishes
me, because I am involved in mankind, and therefore never send   15
to know for whom the bell tolls; it tolls for thee.

The tolling bell that figures so powerfully in the last lines of Donne's *Meditation* makes reference to an age-old tradition (perpetuated at Saint Paul's) of ringing the church bells to announce the death of a parishioner. Donne's poetry was as unconventional as his prose: Both abound in "conceits," that is, elaborate metaphors that compare two apparently dissimilar objects or emotions, often with the intention of shocking or surprising. In that the conceits of

breadth and to narrate (as Mi
tempted yet in prose or rhyr
convey some sense of the po
verse. In the first twenty-si
announces the subject of th
kind's spiritual innocence. Tl
Book I, relates the manner i
from Hell's burning lake and
ruler of the fallen legions. In t
IX), Adam resolves to peris
Eve, by imitating her in e
Milton's description of "the
trespass" (l. 71) perpetuatec
flawed womankind well into
Finally, in the passage from
angel Michael's prophetic des
tiny and prepares to leave Pa

READING 4.9 From Mil
(Books I,

Of man's first disobedience, and th
Of that forbidden tree, whose mor
Brought death into the world, and
With loss of Eden, till one greater
Restore us, and regain the blissful
Sing Heav'nly Muse, that on the s
Of Oreb, or of Sinai,² didst inspire
That shepherd, who first taught th
In the beginning how the heav'ns ;
Rose out of chaos: or if Sion hill
Delight thee more, and Siloa's bro
Fast by the oracle of God; I thence
Invoke thy aid to my advent'rous s
That with no middle flight intends
Above th' Aonian mount,⁴ while it
Things unattempted yet in prose o
And chiefly thou O Spirit, that dost
Before all temples th' upright hear
Instruct me, for thou know'st; thou
Wast present, and with mighty wi
Dove-like sat'st brooding on the va
And mad'st it pregnant: what in m
Illumine, what is low raise and sup
That to the highth of this great arg
I may assert Eternal Providence,
And justify the ways of God to me

· · · · ·

¹Christ.
²As was the case with epic poets of
source of inspiration. Milton's muse
Judeo-Christian wisdom, identified
at Mount Horeb (Deut. 4.10) or on M
³A spring near Mount Zion in Jerusa
God spoke to his people.
⁴In Greece, the Muses were thought
known as the "Aonian mountain."

Figure 22.2 CHRISTOPHER WREN, West facade of Saint Paul's Cathedral, London, 1675–1710. Width approx. 90 ft. Photo: A. F. Kersting, London.

Donne (and other seventeenth-century writers) borrowed words and images from the new science (see chapter 23), critics called these devices and the poetry they embellished "metaphysical." Metaphysical poetry reflects the baroque affection for dramatic contrast, for frequent and unexpected shifts of viewpoint, and for the dramatic synthesis of discordant images. These features are apparent in some of Donne's finest works, including the group of religious poems known as the *Holy Sonnets*. In the first of the following two sonnets, Donne challenges Death in conceiving itself as powerful and influential. Instead of regard-

ing Death, according to convention, as a "mighty and dreadful" ruler, Donne demeans Death as a slave who keeps bad company ("poison, war, and sickness"); he concludes with the artful device of Death itself "dying." Donne's defiance of Death stands in contrast to the submissive tone of medieval preachers (see chapter 12), but his view of physical death as "a short sleep" from which "we wake eternally" is confidently Christian.

In the second sonnet, Donne compares himself to a fortress that has been seized by the enemies of the Lord. Donne describes Reason as the ruler ("Your viceroy in

me") who has failed to defend
with God to "ravish" and "
abounds in intriguing paradox
deliverance, conquest with lil
with freedom. Donne's unex
paradoxical images are typic:
poetry, but his rejection of co
in favor of a conversational
modern poets) represents a re'
European literature.

READING 4.8   From Don

Death be not proud, though some ha
Mighty and dreadful, for thou art no
For those whom thou think'st thou d
Die not, poor Death, nor yet canst th
From rest and sleep, which but thy ¡
Much pleasure, then from thee muc
And soonest our best men with thee
Rest of their bones and souls' delive
Thou art slave to fate, chance, kings
And dost with poison, war, and sick
And poppy, or charms can make us :
And better than thy stroke; why swe
One short sleep past, we wake eter
And Death shall be no more; Death,

. . . . .

Batter my heart, three-personed Go
As yet but knock, breath, shine, and
That I may rise, and stand, o'erthrov
Your force, to break, blow, burn, anc
I, like an usurped town to another d
Labour to admit You, but oh! to no e
Reason, Your viceroy in me, me sho
But is captived and proves weak or
Yet dearly I love You, and would be
But am betrothed unto Your enemy.
Divorce me, untie, or break that kno
Take me to You, imprison me, for I
Except You enthrall me, never shall
Nor ever chaste, except You ravish

The Genius of John Milton

John Milton (1608–1674) w
defender of the Cromwellian
lapsed in 1658. His career as a
Cambridge University and
eleven-year tenure as secretar
State. Though shy and retirin;
activist and a persistent defenc
intellectual freedom. He chal
expository prose essays on :
subjects. In one pamphlet, he

---
[1]Willingly.

"O fairest of creation, last and best
Of all God's works, creature in whom excelled
Whatever can to sight or thought be formed,   80
Holy, divine, good, amiable, or sweet!
How art thou lost, how on a sudden lost,
Defaced, deflow'red, and now to death devote?[10]
Rather how hast thou yielded to transgress
The strict forbiddance, how to violate
The sacred fruit forbidd'n! some cursèd fraud
Of enemy hath beguiled thee, yet unknown,
And me with thee hath ruined, for with thee
Certain my resolution is to die;
How can I live without thee, how forgo   90
Thy sweet converse and love so dearly joined,
To live again in these wild woods forlorn?
Should God create another Eve, and I
Another rib afford, yet loss of thee
Would never from my heart; no no, I feel
The link of nature draw me: flesh of flesh,
Bone of my bone thou art, and from thy state
Mine never shall be parted, bliss or woe."
    So having said, as one from sad dismay
Recomforted,[11] and after thoughts disturbed   100
Submitting to what seemed remédiless,
Thus in calm mood his words to Eve he turned.
    "Bold deed thou hast presumed, advent'rous Eve,
And peril great provoked, who thus hast dared
Had it been only coveting to eye
That sacred fruit, sacred to abstinence,
Much more to taste it under ban to touch.
But past who can recall, or done undo?
Not God omnipotent, nor fate; yet so
Perhaps thou shalt not die, perhaps the fact[12]   110
Is not so heinous now, foretasted fruit,
Profaned first by the serpent, by him first
Made common and unhallowed ere our taste;
Nor yet on him found deadly, he yet lives,
Lives, as thou saidst, and gains to live as man
Higher degree of life, inducement strong
To us, as likely tasting to attain
Proportional ascent, which cannot be
But to be gods, or angels demi-gods.
Nor can I think that God, Creator wise,   120
Though threat'ning, will in earnest so destroy
Us his prime creatures, dignified so high,
Set over all his works, which in our fall,
For us created, needs with us must fail,
Dependent made; so God shall uncreate,
Be frustrate, do, undo, and labor lose,
Not well conceived of God, who though his power
Creation could repeat, yet would be loath
Us to abolish, lest the Adversary
Triumph and say; 'Fickle their state whom God   130
Most favors, who can please him long? Me first
He ruined, now mankind; whom will he next?'

---
[10]Devoted, doomed.
[11]Comforted, refreshed.
[12]Crime, deed.

Matter of scorn, not to be given the Foe.
However I with thee have fixed my lot,
Certain to undergo like doom; if death
Consort with thee, death is to me as life;
So forcible within my heart I feel
The bond of nature draw me to my own.
My own in thee, for what thou art is mine;
Our state cannot be severed, we are one,   140
One flesh: to lose thee were to lose myself."

. . . .

[. . . to the Angel] Adam last replied.
"How soon hath thy prediction, seer blest,
Measured this transient world, the race of time,
Till time stand fixed: beyond is all abyss,
Eternity, whose end no eye can reach.
Greatly instructed I shall hence depart,
Greatly in peace of thought, and have my fill
Of knowledge, what this vessel can contain;
Beyond which was my folly to aspire.   150
Henceforth I learn, that to obey is best,
And love with fear the only God, to walk
As in his presence, ever to observe
His providence, and on him sole depend,
Merciful over all his works, with good
Still overcoming evil, and by small
Accomplishing great things, by things deemed weak
Subverting worldly strong, and worldly wise
By simply meek; that suffering for truth's sake
Is fortitude to highest victory,   160
And to the faithful death the gate of life;
Taught this by his example whom I now
Acknowledge my Redeemer ever blest."
    To whom thus also th' angel last replied:
"This having learnt, thou hast attained the sum
Of wisdom; hope no higher, though all the stars
Thou knew'st by name, and all th' ethereal powers,
All secrets of the deep, all nature's works,
Or works of God in heav'n, air, earth, or sea,
And all the riches of this world enjoy'dst,   170
And all the rule, one empire; only add
Deeds to thy knowledge answerable, add faith,
Add virtue, patience, temperance, add love,
By name to come called charity, the soul
Of all the rest: then wilt thou not be loath
To leave this Paradise, but shalt possess
A paradise within thee, happier far.
Let us descend now therefore from this top
Of speculation; for the hour precise
Exacts our parting hence; and see the guards,   180
By me encamped on yonder hill, expect
Their motion,[13] at whose front a flaming sword,
In signal of remove,[14] waves fiercely round;
We may no longer stay: go, waken Eve;
Her also I with gentle dreams have calmed
Portending good, and all her spirits composed

---
[13]Await their marching orders.
[14]Departure.

To meek submission: thou at season fit
Let her with thee partake what thou hast heard,
Chiefly what may concern her faith to know,
The great deliverance by her seed to come
(For by the Woman's Seed) on all mankind.
That ye may live, which will be many days,
Both in one faith unanimous though sad,
With cause for evils past, yet much more cheered
With meditation on the happy end."

190

The London of Christopher Wren

London at the time of Donne and Milton was a city of vast extremes. England's commercial activities in India and the Americas made London a center for stock exchanges, insurance firms, and joint-stock companies. Amongst the wealthy Londoners, a great number of people remained poor. While one-fourth of London's inhabitants (among a population of a quarter of a million people) could neither read nor write, intellectuals advanced scientific learning. For some time Londoners enjoyed some of the finest libraries and theaters in Western Europe, but, under the Puritan-dominated Parliament of the 1640s, stage plays were suppressed, and many old theaters, including Shakespeare's Globe, were torn down. The restoration of the monarchy in 1660 brought with it a revived interest in drama and in the construction of indoor theaters (as opposed to the open-air theaters of Shakespeare's time).

Figure 22.3 Cross section of Saint Paul's showing Wren's three domes.

ST. PAUL'S CATHEDRAL

In 1666, a devastating fire tore through London and destroyed three-quarters of the city, including 13,000 homes, eighty-seven parish churches, and the cathedral church of Saint Paul's, where John Donne had served as dean some decades earlier. Following the fire, there was an upsurge of large-scale building activity and a general effort to modernize London. The architect Christoper Wren (1632–1723) played a leading role in this effort. A child prodigy in mathematics, an experimental scientist, and professor of astronomy at London and Oxford, Wren was one of the founding fathers of the Royal Society of London for Improving Natural Knowledge. Following the Great Fire, Wren prepared designs for the reconstruction of London. Although his plans for new city streets (based on Rome) were rejected, he was commissioned to rebuild more than fifty churches, including Saint Paul's—the first church in Christendom to be completed in the lifetime of its architect. Wren's early designs for Saint Paul's featured the Greek-cross plan that Michelangelo had proposed for Saint Peter's in Rome (see chapter 17). However, the clergy of Saint Paul's preferred a Latin-cross structure. The final church was a compromise that combined classical, Gothic, Renaissance, and baroque architectural features. Saint Paul's dramatic two-story facade, with its ornate twin clock towers and its strong surface contrasts of light and dark (see Figure 22.2), looks back to Borromini (see Figure 20.18), but its massive scale and overall design—a large dome set upon a Latin-cross basilica—are reminiscent of Saint Peter's (see Figure 20.13). As at Saint Peter's, Wren's dome, which physically resembles Bramante's Tempietto (see chapter 17), is equal in its diameter to the combined width of the nave and side aisles. And the dimensions of Saint Paul's are colossal: 366 feet from ground level to the top of the lantern cross (Saint Peter's reaches 405 feet).

Wren envisioned a dome that was both impressive from the outside and easily visible from the inside. He came up with an inventive and complex device: Two domes, one exterior (made of timber covered with lead) and the other interior (made of light brick), are supported by a third, cone-shaped, middle dome, which is hidden between the other two (Figure **22.3**). The monumental silhouette of Wren's exterior dome, some 102 feet in diameter, remains an impressive presence on the London skyline. From within the church, there is the equally impressive illusionism of the *trompe l'oeil* heavens painted on the inner surface of the central cupola. Like Milton's *Paradise Lost*, Wren's Saint Paul's is a majestic synthesis of classical and Christian traditions, while its huge size, dramatic exterior, and light-filled interior are baroque in conception and effect.

Rembrandt and Protestant Devotionalism

In the Netherlands, developments in painting rivaled those in English architecture. Among the great artists of the Protestant North, Rembrandt van Rijn (1606–1669) stands out as a man of towering stature and talent. His contribution to the humanistic tradition is better understood in the context of his time and place.

Figure 22.4 REMBRANDT VAN RIJN, *The Return of the Prodigal Son*, ca. 1662–1668. Oil on canvas, 8 ft. 8 in. × 6 ft. 8 in. Hermitage Museum, Saint Petersburg. Bridgeman Art Library, London.

Since 1560, when Spain had invaded the Dutch Lowlands, the seventeen provinces of the Netherlands had been engaged in a bitter struggle against the Catholic forces of the Spanish king Philip II. In 1579, after years of bloodshed, the Dutch forced Philip's armies to withdraw. In 1581, the seven provinces of the North Netherlands declared their independence. By the end of the century the predominantly Calvinist Dutch Republic (later called "Holland") was a self-governing state and one of the most commercially active territories in Western Europe. Dutch shipbuilders produced some of the finest trading vessels on the high seas, while skilled Dutch seamen brought those vessels to all parts of the world. In Amsterdam, as in hundreds of other Dutch towns, merchants and crafts-people shared the responsibilities of local government, profiting handsomely from the smooth-running, primarily maritime economy.

The autonomous towns of the North Netherlands, many of which supported fine universities, fostered free-dom of thought and a high rate of literacy. Hardworking, thrifty, and independent minded, the seventeenth-century Dutch enjoyed a degree of independence and material prosperity unmatched elsewhere in the world. Their proletarian tastes, along with a profound appreciation for the physical comforts of home and hearth, inspired their calls for such secular subjects as portraits, still lifes, landscapes, and scenes of domestic life (see chapter 23). While the arts in Italy reflected the Mediterranean love for outdoor display, in the North, where a harsher climate prevailed, artistic expression cen-tered on the domestic interior. And, in the North, where the remains of ancient Greece and Rome were fewer, the classical heritage figured less visibly in the arts.

Since Calvinism strongly discouraged the use of reli-gious icons, sculpture was uncommon in the Protestant North. But paintings, especially those with scriptural sub-jects, were favored sources of seventeenth-century moral knowledge and instruction. The Old Testament was espe-cially popular among the Dutch, who viewed themselves as God's "chosen" people, elected to triumph over Spain. From this milieu emerged Amsterdam's leading painter, Rembrandt van Rijn. The Leyden-born Rembrandt rose to fame as a painter of biblical subjects that were uncommon in Catholic art. His moving representation of *The Return of the Prodigal Son* (Figure **22.4**), for instance, shows the moment when the wayward son in Jesus' parable returns home in rags and, humbly kneeling before his father, receives forgiveness (Luke 15:11–32). The figures of father and son, bathed in golden light, form an off-center trian-gle balanced by the sharply lit vertical figure to the right. The composition is thus "open" and asymmetrical, rather than "closed" and symmetrical in the manner of High Renaissance art (see chapter 17). As if to symbolize spiri-tual revelation itself, Rembrandt "pulls" figures out of the shadowy depths of the background. His rich contrasts between bright **impasto** areas (produced by building up thick layers of paint) and dark, brooding passages work to increase the dramatic impact of the composition. Rembrandt learned much about theatrical staging from

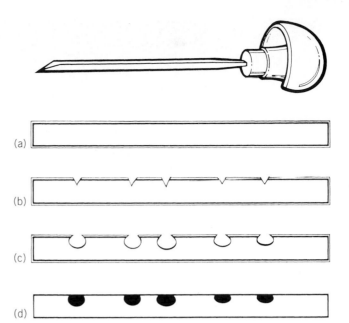

Figure 22.5 Etching is an intaglio printing process. A metal plate is coated with resin (a) then images are scratched through the coating with a burin, or graver (b). Acid is applied, which "eats" or etches the metal exposed by the scratches (c). The resin is then removed and ink is rubbed into the etched lines on the metal plate (d). After the plate is wiped clean, it is pressed onto the paper and the ink-filled lines are deposited on the paper surface. Other intaglio processes include engraving and acquatint. From Richard Phipps and Richard Wink, *Invitation to the Gallery.* Copyright © 1987 Wm. C. Brown Publishers, Dubuque, Iowa. All rights reserved. Reprinted by permission.

Caravaggio, but, in his simpler, more restrained composi-tions, Rembrandt reaches further below surface appear-ances to explore the psychological depths of his subjects.

Rembrandt's unidealized treatment of sacred subject matter belonged to a long tradition of Northern European religious devotionalism (see chapter 15), but his sympa-thetic depiction of the poor and the persecuted was uniquely Protestant. His Anabaptist upbringing, with its fundamentalist approach to Scripture and its solemn attention to the role of individual conscience in daily life, surely contributed to Rembrandt's preference for portray-ing biblical subjects in literal, human terms. The people of the streets provided him with a cast of characters, and his Bible narratives abound with the faces of Spanish and Jewish refugees, whom he regularly sketched in the ghet-tos of Amsterdam.

Rembrandt's technical virtuosity as a draftsman made him more famous in his own time as a printmaker than as a painter. Like the woodcuts and engravings of his Northern Renaissance predecessors Dürer and Holbein (see chapter 19), Rembrandt's **etchings** met the demands of middle-class patrons who sought private devotional images that—by comparison with paintings—were inex-pensive. A consummate printmaker, Rembrandt used the **burin** (a steel cutting tool) to develop dramatic contrasts of rich darks and emphatic lights (Figure **22.5**). *Christ Preaching* (Figure **22.6**)—also known as "The Hundred-Guilder Print," because it sold for one hundred Dutch guilders in a seventeenth-century auction—illustrates parts of the Gospel of Matthew. In the etching,

Figure 22.6 (above)
REMBRANDT VAN RIJN, *Christ Preaching* ("The Hundred-Guilder Print"), ca. 1648–1650, 11 × 15½ in. Rijksmuseum, Amsterdam.

Figure 22.7 (right) **REMBRANDT VAN RIJN**, detail of *Christ Preaching* ("The Hundred-Guilder Print"), ca. 1648–1650. Etching.

Rembrandt depicts Jesus addressing the members of the Jewish community: the sick and the lame (foreground), "the little children" (middle left), the ill and infirm (right), and an assembly of Pharisees (far left). With an extraordinary economy of line—no more than a few deft strokes of the pen—the artist brings to life the woes of the poor, the downtrodden, and the aged (Figure 22.7). So colloquial is Rembrandt's handling of the biblical story that it seems an event that might have taken place in Rembrandt's time and place, or in ours.

The Music of the Protestant North

Handel and the English Oratorio

In the same way that the Protestant North produced memorable works of religious literature and art, it also generated great works of music. The careers of two extraordinary German composers, George Frederick Handel (1685–1756) and Johann Sebastian Bach (1685–1750), represent the culmination of the baroque style in Northern European music.

Born in the Lutheran trading city of Halle, Germany, George Frederick Handel was determined to pursue his childhood musical talents. When his father, who intended for him a career in law, refused to provide him with a musical instrument, he smuggled a small clavichord into the attic. After proving himself at the keyboard and as a successful violinist and composer in the courts of Hamburg, Rome, Paris, Naples, and Venice, he migrated to London in 1710 and became an English citizen in 1726. Like many of his contemporaries, Handel began his career as a student of Italian opera. He composed forty-six operas in Italian and four in his native German. He also produced a prodigious number of instrumental works. But it was for his development of the **oratorio** that he earned fame among the English, who called him "England's greatest composer."

An oratorio is the musical setting of a long text that is performed in concert by a narrator, soloists, chorus, and orchestra (Figure 22.8). Like operas, oratorios are large in scale and dramatic in intent but, unlike opera, they are performed without scenery, costumes, or dramatic action. Soloists and chorus assume the roles of the main characters in the narrative. The word "oratorio" refers to a church chapel, and most oratorios were religious in content; however, they were never intended for church services. Rather, they were performed in public concert halls.

Figure 22.8 Performance of an oratorio; Handel (far right) is conducting. Woodcut.

With the oratorio came the shift from music written and performed for church or court to music composed for concert halls (or opera houses) and enjoyed by the general public. Appropriately, in the late seventeenth century, public concerts (and entrance fees) made their first appearance in the social history of music.

In his lifetime, Handel composed more than thirty oratorios. Like Rembrandt and Milton (whose verses he borrowed for the oratorio *Samson*), Handel brought Scripture to life. The most famous of Handel's oratorios is *Messiah*, which was written in the English of the King James Bible. Composed, remarkably enough, in twenty-four days, it was performed for the first time in Dublin in 1742. It received instant acclaim. One of the most moving pieces of choral music ever written, *Messiah* celebrates the birth, death, and resurrection of Jesus. Unlike most of Handel's oratorios, *Messiah* is not a biblical dramatization but rather a collection of verses from the Old and New Testaments. The first part of the piece recounts Old Testament prophecies of a Savior, the second relates the suffering and death of Jesus, and the third rejoices in the redemption of humankind through Christ's resurrection.

Messiah is typical of the baroque sensibility: Indeed, the epic proportions of its score and libretto call to mind Milton's *Paradise Lost*. It is also baroque in its style, which features vigorous contrasts of tempo and dynamics and dramatic interaction between participating ensembles—solo voices, chorus, and instruments. A master of theatrical effects, Handel employed word painting and other affective devices throughout the piece. For example, the

music for the last words of the sentence, "All we, like sheep, have gone astray," consists of deliberately divergent melodic lines. The best loved choral work in the English language, *Messiah* has outlasted its age. Indeed, in many Christian communities, it has become traditional to perform Handel's *Messiah* during both the Christmas and Easter seasons. The jubilant "Hallelujah Chorus" ♪ (which ends the second of the three parts of the oratorio) still brings audiences to their feet, as it did King George II of England, who introduced this tradition by rising from his seat when he first heard it performed in London in 1743.

Handel's *Messiah* features polyphonic textures at the start of many of the choruses, such as the "For unto us, a Child is born." Nevertheless, like Handel's other oratorios, much of *Messiah* is essentially **homophonic**; that is, its musical organization depends on the use of a dominant melody supported by chordal accompaniment. The homophonic organization of melody and chords differed dramatically from the uninterrupted polyphonic interweaving of voices that characterized most music prior to the seventeenth century. The chords in a homophonic composition serve to support—or, in the visual sense, to "spotlight"—a primary melody. In the seventeenth century, there evolved a form of musical shorthand that allowed musicians to fill in the harmony for a principal melody. The **figured bass**, as this shorthand was called, consisted of a line of music with numbers written below it to indicate the harmony accompanying the primary melody. The use of the figured bass (also called the "continuo," since it played throughout the duration of the piece) was one of the main features of baroque music.

Bach and Religious Music

Johann Sebastian Bach (Figure **22.9**) was born in the small town of Eisenach, very near the castle in which Martin Luther—hiding from the wrath of the Roman papacy—had first translated the Bible into German. Unlike the cosmopolitan Handel, Bach never strayed more than a couple of hundred miles from his birthplace; the last twenty-seven years of his career were spent in nearby Leipzig. Nor did he depart from his Protestant roots: Luther's teachings and Lutheran hymn tunes were Bach's major sources of religious inspiration, and the organ—the principal instrument of Protestant church music—was one of his favorite instruments. The Germans were the masters of the organ at this period, and Bach was acknowledged to be the finest of organ virtuosi. He even served as a consultant in the construction of baroque organs, whose ornately embellished casings made them the glory of many Protestant churches (Figure **22.10**). As organ master and choir director of the Lutheran Church of Saint Thomas in Leipzig, Bach assumed the responsibility of composing music for each of the Sunday services and for holy days. A pious Lutheran, who, in the course of two marriages, fathered twenty children (five of whom became notable musicians), Bach humbly dedicated his compositions "to the glory of God."

Figure 22.9 ELIAS GOTTLOB HAUSSMAN, *Johann Sebastian Bach*, 1746. Oil on canvas.
William H. Scheide Library, Princeton University.

♪ See Music Listening Selections at end of chapter.

At the apex of Bach's achievement in vocal music is the *Passion According to Saint Matthew*, an oratorio written for the Good Friday service at the Church of Saint Thomas in Leipzig. This majestic piece of religious music consists of the sung texts of chapters 26 and 27 of Matthew's Gospel, which describe Christ's Passion: the events between the Last Supper and the Resurrection. The biblical verses alternate with narrative commentary from a text written by a local German poet. Bach's combination of Bible and moral commentary dramatizes Scripture with eloquence and expressive power.

The *Passion According to Saint Matthew* is written for a double chorus whose members take the parts of the disciples, the Pharisees, and other characters in the biblical account. The chorus alternates with soloists (representing Matthew, Jesus, Judas, and others) who sing the arias and recitatives. Two orchestras accompany the voices. The three-and-a-half-hour-long piece consists of two parts, the first originally to be sung before the Vespers sermon and the second after it. In Bach's time, the church congregation participated in the performance of the choral portions, thus adding to the sheer volume of sound produced by choirs and orchestras. Performed today in the church or in the concert hall, Bach's oratorio still conveys the devotional spirit of the Protestant North. In its imaginative use of Scripture, as well as in its vivid tonal color and dramatic force, the *Passion According to Saint Matthew* compares with the best of Rembrandt's Bible narratives, Handel's *Messiah*, and Milton's *Paradise Lost*.

SUMMARY

In seventeenth-century Northern Europe, a unique set of circumstances shaped the progress of the baroque style. These circumstances featured the dominance of Protestantism, with its strong scriptural and devotional

Bach's religious vocal music included such forms as the oratorio, the Mass, and the **cantata**. The cantata is a multimovement work with a text in verse sung by chorus and soloists and accompanied by a musical instrument or instruments. Like the oratorio, the cantata may be sacred or secular in subject matter and lyric or dramatic in style. Bach composed cantatas as musical commentaries on the daily scriptural lessons of the Lutheran church service. Extraordinary in their florid counterpoint, Bach's 195 surviving cantatas were usually inspired by the simple melodies of Lutheran chorales. Cantata No. 80 ♪ is based on Luther's "A Mighty Fortress is Our God," the most important hymn of the Lutheran church (see chapter 19). Bach used Protestant chorales, with their regular rhythms and rugged melodies, not only for his cantatas but as the basis for many of his instrumental compositions (see chapter 23), including the 170 organ **preludes** that he composed to precede and set the mood for congregational singing.

♪ See Music Listening Selections at end of chapter.

emphasis, rising commercialism, and—especially in England and Holland—passionate antiauthoritarian efforts to sustain personal rights and political liberties. The study of sacred Scripture was central to the ideals of Pietism and Protestant belief. Consequently, Northern baroque artistic expression turned inward to the personal and subjective, rather than outward to spectacular forms of religious display.

In the literary domain, the King James translation of the Bible brought the English language to new heights of eloquence. The Anglican John Donne and the Puritan John Milton produced poetry that reflected Protestant perspectives of morality, evil, and death. Donne's metaphysical poetry featured ingenious conceits and paradoxes. Milton's *Paradise Lost*, the last great epic poem in Western literature, recast the heritage of the Hebrew Bible according to Puritan views of sin and salvation. The poem's cosmic scope, colossal proportions, and majestic language exemplify the baroque spirit in the Protestant North.

The religious works of the Dutch master Rembrandt van Rijn present a visual parallel to these literary landmarks. Rembrandt illustrated the contents of Holy Scripture in paintings, drawings, and etchings that were at once realistic, theatrical, and psychologically profound. With bold compositions and an inventive use of light, he described sacred events as though they had occurred in his own time and place.

The genius of Rembrandt was matched in music by the German masters Johann Sebastian Bach and George Frederick Handel. Handel dramatized scriptural narrative by means of the oratorio, a new musical form that typified the baroque taste for rich color and dramatic effect. Handel's *Messiah*, an early landmark in homophonic composition, remains one of the most stirring examples of baroque music. Handel's Lutheran contemporary, Johann Sebastian Bach, dedicated much of his life to composing music that honored God. His cantatas and his preludes employ melodies borrowed largely from Lutheran hymns. In the *Passion According to Saint Matthew*, Bach brought polyphonic choral music to new heights of dramatic grandeur. Like Milton's *Paradise Lost* and the paintings of Rembrandt, Bach's music invested Protestant Christianity with a sublime and deeply personal sense of human tragedy. In all, the contributions of Milton, Rembrandt, Handel, and Bach constitute the crowning achievements of the baroque style in the Protestant North.

GLOSSARY

burin a steel tool used for engraving and incising

cantata (Italian, *cantare* = "to sing") a multimovement composition for voices and instrumental accompaniment; smaller in scale than the *oratorio*

etching a kind of engraving in which a metal plate is covered with resin, then incised with a *burin*; acid is applied to "eat" away the exposed lines, which are inked before the plate is wiped clean and printed; see Figure 22.5

figured bass in baroque music, the line of music with numbers written below (or above) it to indicate the required harmonies, usually improvised in the form of keyboard chords accompanying the melody; also called "continuo"

homophony a musical texture consisting of a dominant melody supported by chordal accompaniment that is far less important than the melody; compare monophony (see Glossary, chapter 5) and polyphony (see Glossary, chapter 13)

impasto a style in painting in which the paint is applied thickly or heavily

oratorio (Latin, *oratorium* = "church chapel") a musical setting of a long text, either religious or secular, for soloists, chorus, narrator, and orchestra; usually performed without scenery, costumes, or dramatic action

prelude a piece of instrumental music that introduces either a church service or another piece of music

SUGGESTIONS FOR READING

Arnold, Denis. *Bach*. New York: Oxford University Press, 1984.

Bukofzer, Manfred. *Music in the Baroque Era*. New York: Norton, 1947.

Clark, Kenneth. *An Introduction to Rembrandt*. New York: Harper, 1978.

Kahr, Madlyn M. *Dutch Painting in the Seventeenth Century*. New York: Harper, 1978.

Palisca, C. V. *Baroque Music*, 3rd ed. Englewood Cliffs, N.J.: Prentice Hall, 1991.

Price, J. L. *Culture and Society in the Dutch Republic during the Seventeenth Century*. New York: Scribners, 1974.

Schama, Simon. *An Embarrassment of Riches: An Interpretation of Dutch Art*. New York: Knopf, 1987.

Schwendowlus, Barbara, and Wolfgang Dömling, eds. *Johann Sebastian Bach: Life, Times, Influence*. Basel: Bärenreiter Kassell, 1997.

Wallace, Robert. *The World of Rembrandt 1606–1669*. Library of Art Series. New York: Time-Life Books, 1968.

Wolff, Christoph. *Johann Sebastian Bach: The Learned Musician*. New York: Norton, 2000.

MUSIC LISTENING SELECTIONS

CD Two Selection 3 Handel, *Messiah*, "Hallelujah Chorus," 1742.

CD Two Selection 4 Bach, Cantata No. 80, "Ein feste Burg ist unser Gott" ("A Mighty Fortress is Our God"), Chorale, 1724.

The scientific revolution and the new learning

"Human knowledge and human power meet in one; for where the cause is not known, the effect cannot be produced."
Francis Bacon

While the seventeenth century was a period of religious turbulence and heightened spirituality, it was also an age of scientific discovery and development. The Scientific Revolution that occurred in Europe between approximately 1600 and 1750 was not entirely sudden, nor were its foundations exclusively European. It owed much to a long history of science and technology that reached back to ancient Egypt, China, and Islam, to the construction of pyramids and cathedrals, the formulation of Euclidean geometry, and the invention of the windmill, the magnetic compass, and the printing press. As Renaissance artist-scientists diligently investigated the visible world, the will to control nature by means of practical knowledge gained impetus in the West. Following the pioneering efforts of Leonardo da Vinci, the Flemish physician

Andreas Vesalius (1514–1574) dissected cadavers to make an accurate record of the human anatomy. The Swiss alchemist Philippus Ambrosius Paracelsus (1493–1541) compounded medical remedies from minerals rather than from the older, botanical substances. And the Polish humanist, physician, and astronomer Nicolas Copernicus (1473–1543) opposed the traditional **geocentric** (earth-centered) explanation of the cosmos with the **heliocentric** (sun-centered) theory according to which the earth and all the other planets circle around the sun (Figure **23.1**).

The Scientific Revolution

Those who launched the Scientific Revolution differed from their Asian and European predecessors in effectively

Figure 23.1 The cosmos on the left, dating from the sixteenth century, shows a geocentric universe. The version, on the right, from Copernicus' *De revolutionibus orbium coelestium* (1543), shows a heliocentric universe.

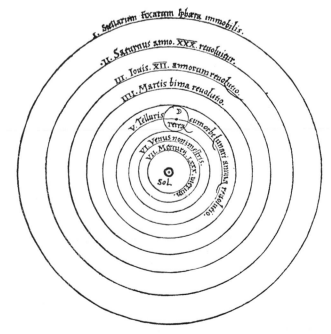

combining the tools of mathematics and experimentation. They invented new instruments with which to measure more precisely natural phenomena, to test scientific hypotheses, and to predict the operations of nature (Figure 23.2). They also differed from their predecessors in asserting that *scientia* (the Latin word for "knowledge") existed separate and apart from divine power and authority. If medieval intellectuals viewed the universe as the extension of an absolute and eternal God, modern scientists regarded it as a mechanism that operated according to its own laws. Modern scientists took nature out of the hands of poets and priests and put it inside the laboratory.

Kepler and Galileo

Even before the second century C.E., when the Greek geographer Ptolemy published his theory of a geometric universe, learned individuals regarded the earth as fixed in space and spherical in shape. They envisioned the earth at the center of a series of endlessly turning crystalline spheres, one for each of the celestial bodies: the Moon, Mercury, Venus, the Sun, Mars, Jupiter, and Saturn—a cosmology enshrined in Dante's *Divine Comedy* (see chapter 12). According to Aristotle, movement in nature was the work of a *prime mover* or, in the later, Christian view, of some supernatural force. During the one hundred years following the publication of Copernicus' treatise *On the Revolution of the Heavenly Spheres* in 1543, these earlier theories came under scrutiny. Early in the seventeenth century, the German mathematician Johannes Kepler (1571–1630) made detailed records of the planets' movements which substantiated the heliocentric theory. Challenging the conventional assumption that the planetary orbits had to be perfectly circular, Kepler also showed that the five known planets moved around the sun in elliptical paths. He argued that the magnetic force emitted by the sun determined the movements of the planets and their distances from the sun. Kepler's new physics, which advanced the idea of a universe in motion, contradicted the Aristotelian notion of a fixed and unchanging cosmos. It also stood in opposition to the Bible—where, for example, the Hebrew hero Joshua is described as making the sun stand still, a miraculous event that could have occurred only if the sun normally moved around the earth. Although Catholics and Protestants were at odds on many theological matters, in defending the inviolable truth of Scripture against the claims of the new science, they were one.

In Italy, Kepler's contemporary Galileo Galilei (1564–1642) was experimenting with matters of terrestrial motion. His assertions concerning motion and gravity

stood contrary to long-held opinions based on Aristotle. Whether or not Galileo actually dropped different-sized weights from the top of the leaning Tower of Pisa—as legend has it—in an effort to determine rates of speed relative to mass, the Florentine astronomer formulated the *law of falling bodies*, which proclaimed that the earth's gravity attracts all objects—regardless of shape, size, or density—at the same rate of acceleration. In 1608, shortly after the publication of this theorem, a Dutch lensmaker invented an instrument that magnified objects seen at a great distance. Perfected by Galileo, the telescope literally revealed new worlds. Through its lens, one could see the craters of the moon, the rings of Saturn, and the moons of Jupiter, which, Galileo observed, operated exactly like earth's moon. The telescope turned the heliocentric theory into fact.

Galileo's discoveries immediately aroused opposition from Catholics and Protestants committed to maintaining orthodox Christian beliefs, especially as set forth in Scripture. Not only did the theory of a heliocentric universe contradict God's word and challenge the Christian concept of a stable and finite universe, it also deprived human beings of their central place in that universe. The heliocentric theory made humanity seem incidental to God's plan and the heavens seem material and "corruptible." Such an idea did not go unchallenged. The first institutional attack on "the new science" had occurred in 1600, when the Catholic Inquisition tried, condemned, and publicly executed the Italian astronomer Giordano Bruno, who had asserted that the universe was infinite and without center. Bruno had also suggested that other solar systems might exist in space. Sixteen years after Bruno was burned at the stake, Rome issued an edict that condemned Copernican astronomy as "false and contrary to Holy Scripture" and the writings of Copernicus were put on the Catholic Index of Forbidden Books. Galileo added to the controversy by making his own findings public; and more so because he wrote in the everyday Italian rather than in Latin, the traditional language of Western authority.

More inflammatory still in the eyes of the Church was the publication of Galileo's *Dialogue Concerning the Two Principal Systems of the World* (1632), a fictional conversation between a Copernican and the defenders of the old order, one of whom resembled the pope. Earlier in his career, when it had become evident that his gravitational theories contradicted Aristotle, Galileo had been forced to give up his position as mathematics professor at the University of Pisa. Now, ill with kidney stones and arthritis, he was dragged to Rome and brought before the Inquisition. After a long and unpleasant trial, Church officials, threatening torture, forced the aging astronomer to "admit his errors." Legend has it that after publicly denying that the earth moved around the sun, he muttered under his breath, "Eppur si muove" ("But it *does* move!"). Though condemned to indefinite imprisonment, Galileo was permitted to reside—under "house arrest"—in a villa outside of Florence. Imprisonment, however, did not daunt his ingenuity or his sense of awe. On developing the compound microscope, he marveled, "I have observed

1608	the telescope is invented in the Netherlands; in Italy, Galileo improves the design to provide three-power magnification
1610	Johannes Kepler perfects the compound microscope
1619	William Harvey accurately describes the circulation of the blood

Figure 23.2 JAN VERMEER,
The Geographer, ca. 1668.
Oil on canvas, 20⅛ × 18¼ in.
Städelsches Kunstinstitut,
Frankfurt. Courtesy
Blauel/Gramm—Arthotek,
Peissenberg.

many tiny animals. . . among which the flea is quite horrible, the gnat and the moth very beautiful; and with great satisfaction I have seen how flies and other little animals can walk attached to mirrors, upside down." His books banned by the Church, Galileo continued to receive personal visits from eminent figures, including the English poet, John Milton.

Despite unrelenting Church opposition, scientists pressed on to devise new instruments for measurement and new procedures for experimentation and analysis. The slide rule, the magnet, the microscope, the mercury barometer, and the air pump were among the many products of the European quest to calculate, investigate, predict, and ultimately master nature. Seventeenth-century Western scientists investigated the workings of the human eye and explored the genesis and propagation of light, thus advancing the science of optics beyond the frontiers of Islamic and Renaissance scholarship. They accurately described the action of gases and the circulation of the blood. And they devised the branches of higher mathematics known as coordinate geometry, trigonometry, and infinitesimal calculus, by means of which modern scientists might analyze the phenomena of space and motion.

The New Learning
Bacon and the Empirical Method

One of the most characteristic features of the Scientific Revolution was its glorification of the empirical method, a manner of inquiry that depended on direct observation and experimentation. Natural phenomena, argued seventeenth-century scientists, provided evidence from which one might draw general conclusions or axioms, according to a process known as **inductive reasoning**. The leading spokesman for the new learning was the English scientist and politician Francis Bacon (1561–1626). In 1620, Bacon published his *Novum Organum* ("New

Royal Society of London for Improving Natural Knowledge. The first of many such European and American societies for scientific advancement, the Royal Society has attracted, over the centuries, thousands of members. Their achievements have confirmed one nineteenth-century historian's assessment of Bacon as "the man that moved the minds that moved the world."

While Bacon wrote his scientific treatises in Latin, he used English for essays on law, rhetoric, and intellectual life. In *The Advancement of Learning* (1605), a sketch of his key ideas concerning methods for acquiring and classifying knowledge, and in the essay *Of Studies*, Bacon demonstrated the masterful use of prose as a tool for theorizing. Written in the poetic prose of the early seventeenth century, *Of Studies* describes the ways in which books serve the individual and society at large. In the excerpt that follows, Bacon eloquently defends reading as a source of pleasure, but, equally important, as a source of practical knowledge and power.

Figure 23.3 FRANS HALS, *Portrait of René Descartes*, 1649. Oil on wood, 7½ × 5½ in. Royal Museum of Fine Arts, Copenhagen.

READING 4.11 From Bacon's *Of Studies* from *Essays* (1625)

Studies serve for delight, for ornament, and for ability. Their chief use for delight is in privateness and retiring; for ornament, is in discourse; and for ability, is in the judgment and disposition of business. For expert men can execute, and perhaps judge of particulars, one by one; but the general counsels and the plots and marshalling of affairs come best from those that are learned. To spend too much time in studies is sloth; to use them too much for ornament is affectation; to make judgment wholly by their rules is the humor of a scholar. They perfect nature, and are perfected by experience: for natural abilities are like natural plants, that need pruning by study; . . . Read not to contradict and confute; nor to believe and take for granted; nor to find talk and discourse, but to weigh and consider. Some books are to be tasted, others to be swallowed, and some few to be chewed and digested; that is, some books are to be read only in parts; others to be read, but not curiously; and some few to be read wholly, and with diligence and attention. . . . Reading maketh a full man; conference a ready man; and writing an exact man. And therefore, if a man write little, he had need have a great memory; if he confer little, he had need have a present wit; and if he read little, he had need have much cunning, to seem to know that he does not. Histories make men wise; poets witty; mathematics subtile; natural philosophy deep; moral [philosophy] grave; logic and rhetoric able to contend. . . .

1

10

20

Descartes and the Birth of Modern Philosophy

Born in France, René Descartes (1596–1650; Figure **23.3**) is regarded as the founder of modern Western philosophy and the father of analytic geometry. His writings revived the ancient Greek quest to discover how one knows what one knows, and his methods made the discipline of philosophy wholly independent of theology.

Whereas Bacon gave priority to knowledge gained through the senses, Descartes, the supreme rationalist, valued abstract reasoning and mathematical speculation. Descartes did not deny the importance of the senses in the search for truth, but he observed that our senses might deceive us. As an alternative to inductive reasoning, he championed a procedure for investigation called **deductive reasoning**. The reverse of the inductive method, the deductive process began with clearly established general premises and moved toward the establishment of particular truths. Among the rules Descartes set forth were the following: Never accept anything as true that you do not clearly know to be true; dissect a problem into as many parts as possible; reason from simple to complex knowledge; and finally, draw complete and exhaustive conclusions. In the *Discourse on the Method of Rightly Conducting the Reason and Seeking for Truth in the Sciences*, perhaps the most important of all his philosophic works, Descartes began by systematically calling everything into doubt. He then proceeded to identify the first thing that he could not doubt—his existence as a thinking individual. This one clear and distinct idea of himself as a "thinking thing," expressed in the proposition "Cogito, ergo sum" ("I think, therefore I am"), became Descartes' "first principle" and the premise for all of his major arguments.

For Descartes, the clear and unbiased mind was the source of all natural understanding. "Except [for] our own thoughts," he insisted, "there is nothing absolutely in our power." Having established rational consciousness as the only sure point of departure for knowledge, Descartes proceeded to examine the world. He made a clear distinction between physical and psychical phenomena, that is, between matter and mind, and between body and soul. According to this dualistic model, the human body operates much like a computer, with the immaterial mind (the software) "informing" the physical components of the body (the hardware). The **Cartesian** view of the human mind as a thinking substance distinct from the human body dominated European philosophic thought until the end of the nineteenth century and still has some strong adherents today.

READING 4.12 From Descartes' *Discourse on Method* (Part IV) (1637)

. . . I do not know that I ought to tell you of the first meditations there made by me, for they are so metaphysical and so unusual that they may perhaps not be acceptable to everyone. And yet at the same time, in order that one may judge whether the foundations which I have laid are sufficiently secure, I find myself constrained in some measure to refer to them. For a long time I had remarked that it is sometimes requisite in common life to follow opinions which one knows to be most uncertain, exactly as though they were indisputable, as has been said above. But because in this case I wished to give myself entirely **10** to the search after Truth, I thought that it was necessary for me to take an apparently opposite course, and to reject as absolutely false everything as to which I could imagine the least ground of doubt, in order to see if afterwards there remained anything in my belief that was entirely certain. Thus, because our senses sometimes deceive us, I wished to suppose that nothing is just as they cause us to imagine it to be; and because there are men who deceive themselves in their reasoning and fall into paralogisms,[1] even concerning the simplest matters of geometry, and judging that I was as subject to error as was any **20** other, I rejected as false all the reasons formerly accepted by me as demonstrations. And since all the same thoughts and conceptions which we have while awake may also come to us in sleep, without any of them being at that time true, I resolved to assume that everything that ever entered into my mind was no more true than the illusions of my dreams. But immediately afterwards I noticed that whilst I thus wished to think all things false, it was absolutely essential that the "I" who thought this should be somewhat, and remarking that this truth "*I think, therefore I am*" was so certain and so assured that all the most **30** extravagant suppositions brought forward by the sceptics were incapable of shaking it, I came to the conclusion that I could receive it without scruple as the first principle of the Philosophy for which I was seeking.

And then, examining attentively that which I was, I saw that I could conceive that I had no body, and that there was no world nor place where I might be; but yet that I could not for all that conceive that I was not. On the contrary, I saw from the very

fact that I thought of doubting the truth of other things, it very evidently and certainly followed that I was; on the other hand if **40** I had only ceased from thinking, even if all the rest of what I had ever imagined had really existed, I should have no reason for thinking that I had existed. From that I knew that I was a substance the whole essence or nature of which is to think, and that for its existence there is no need of any place, nor does it depend on any material thing; so that this "me," that is to say, the soul by which I am what I am, is entirely distinct from body, and is even more easy to know than is the latter; and even if body were not, the soul would not cease to be what it is.

After this I considered generally what in a proposition is **50** requisite in order to be true and certain; for since I had just discovered one which I knew to be such, I thought that I ought also to know in what this certainly consisted. And having remarked that there was nothing at all in the statement "*I think, therefore I am*" which assures me of having thereby made a true assertion, excepting that I see very clearly that to think it is necessary to be, I came to the conclusion that I might assume, as a general rule, that the things which we conceive very clearly and distinctly are all true—remembering, however, that there is some difficulty in ascertaining which are those that we **60** distinctly conceive.

Following upon this, and reflecting on the fact that I doubted, and that consequently my existence was not quite perfect (for I saw clearly that it was a greater perfection to know than to doubt), I resolved to inquire whence I had learnt to think of anything more perfect than I myself was; and I recognised very clearly that this conception must proceed from some nature which was really more perfect. As to the thoughts which I had of many other things outside of me, like the heavens, the earth, light, heat, and a thousand others, I had **70** not so much difficulty in knowing whence they came, because, remarking nothing in them which seemed to render them superior to me, I could believe that, if they were true, they were dependencies upon my nature, in so far as it possessed some perfection; and if they were not true, that I held them from nought, that is to say, that they were in me because I had something lacking in my nature. But this could not apply to the idea of a Being more perfect than my own, for to hold it from nought would be manifestly impossible; and because it is no less contradictory to say of the more perfect that it is what **80** results from and depends on the less perfect, than to say that there is something which proceeds from nothing, it was equally impossible that I should hold it from myself. In this way it could but follow that it had been placed in me by a Nature which was really more perfect than mine could be, and which even had within itself all the perfections of which I could form any idea—that is to say, to put it in a word, which was God. . . .

Religion and the New Learning

The new learning, a composite of scientific method and rational inquiry, presented its own challenge to traditional religion. From "self-evident" propositions, Descartes arrived at conclusions to which empirical confirmation was irrelevant. His rationalism—like Plato's—involved a process of the mind independent of the senses. Reasoning that the concept of perfection ("something more perfect

---

[1]Fallacious arguments.

than myself") had to proceed from "some Nature which in reality was more perfect," Descartes "proved" the existence of God as Absolute Substance. Since something cannot proceed from nothing, argued Descartes, the idea of God held by human beings must come from God. Moreover, the idea of Perfection (God) embraces the idea of existence, for, if something is perfect, it must exist. Raised by Jesuits, Descartes believed in the existence of a Supreme Creator, but he shared with many seventeenth-century intellectuals the view that God was neither Caretaker nor personal Redeemer. Indeed, Descartes identified God with "the mathematical order of nature." The idea that God did not interfere with the laws of humanity and nature was central to **deism**, a system of thought advocating a "natural" religion based on human reason rather than revelation. Deists purged religion of superstition, myth, and ritual. They viewed God as a master mechanic who had created the universe, then stepped aside and allowed his World-Machine to run unattended.

Unlike Bacon, Descartes did not envision any conflict between science and religion. He optimistically concluded that "all our ideas or notions contain in them some truth; for otherwise it could not be that God, who is wholly perfect and veracious, should have placed them in us." Like other deists of his time, Descartes held that to follow reason was to follow God.

In Amsterdam, a city whose reputation for freedom of thought attracted Descartes—he lived there between 1628 and 1649—the Jewish philosopher Baruch Spinoza (1632–1677) addressed the question of the new science versus the old faith. Stripping God of his traditional role as Creator (and consequently finding himself ousted from the local synagogue), Spinoza claimed "God exists only philosophically"; hence, God was neither behind, nor beyond, nor separate from nature but, rather, identical with nature. Every physical thing, including human beings, was an expression of God in some variation of mind combined with matter. In a pantheistic spirit reminiscent of Hinduism and Daoism, Spinoza held that the greatest good was the union of the human mind with the whole of nature.

For the French physicist-mathematician Blaise Pascal (1623–1662), on the other hand, science and religion were irreconcilable. Having undergone a mystical experience that converted him to devout Roman Catholicism, he believed that the path to God was through the heart rather than through the head. Although reason might yield a true understanding of nature, it could in no way prove God's existence. We are capable, wrote Pascal, of "certain knowledge and of absolute ignorance." In his collected meditations on human nature, called simply *Pensées* ("Thoughts"), Pascal proposed a wager that challenged the indifference of skeptics: If God does *not* exist, skeptics lose nothing by believing in him, but if God *does* exist, they reap eternal life. The spiritual quest for purpose and value in a vast, impersonal universe moved the precision-minded Pascal—inventor of a machine that anticipated the digital calculator—to confess: "The eternal silence of these infinite spaces frightens me."

Locke and the Culmination of the Empirical Tradition

The writings of the English philosopher and physician John Locke (1632–1704) firmly defended the empirical tradition in seventeenth-century thought and provided a clearly reasoned basis for centuries of philosophic debate. Written seventy years after Bacon's *Novum Organum*, Locke's *Essay Concerning Human Understanding* (1690) confirmed his predecessor's thesis that everything one knows derives from sensory experience. According to Locke, the human mind at birth is a *tabula rasa* ("blank slate") upon which experience—consisting of sensation, followed by reflection—writes the script. No innate moral principles or ideas exist; rather, human knowledge consists of the progressive accumulation of the evidence of the senses.

The implications of Locke's principles of knowledge strongly affected European and (later) American thought and helped to shape an optimistic view of human destiny. For, if experience influenced human knowledge and behavior, argued the empiricists, then, surely, improving the social environment would work to perfect the human condition. Locke's ideas became basic to eighteenth-century liberalism, as well as to all political ideologies that held that human knowledge, if properly applied, would produce happiness for humankind (see chapter 24).

READING 4.13 From Locke's *Essay Concerning Human Understanding* (1690)

Idea is the Object of Thinking.—Every man being conscious to himself that he thinks, and that which his mind is applied about whilst thinking, being the ideas that are there, it is past doubt that men have in their minds several ideas, such as are those expressed by the words whiteness, hardness, sweetness, thinking, motion, man, elephant, army, drunkenness, and others. It is in the first place then to be inquired how he comes by them. I know it is a received doctrine that men have native ideas and original characters stamped upon their minds in their very first being. This opinion I have at large examined already; 10 and I suppose what I have [already] said . . . will be much more easily admitted when I have shown whence the understanding may get all the ideas it has, and by what ways and degrees they may come into the mind; for which I shall appeal to every one's own observation and experience.

All Ideas come from Sensation or Reflection.—Let us then suppose the mind to be, as we say, white paper, void of all characters, without any ideas; how comes it to be furnished? Whence comes it by that vast store which the busy and boundless fancy of man has painted on it with an almost endless 20 variety? Whence has it all the materials of reason and knowledge? To this I answer in one word, from experience; in that all our knowledge is founded, and from that it ultimately derives itself. Our observation employed either about external sensible objects, or about the internal operations of our minds, perceived and reflected on by ourselves, is that which supplies our understandings with all the materials of thinking. These two are the fountains of knowledge from whence all the ideas we have or can naturally have do spring.

The Objects of Sensation, one Source of Ideas.—First, our senses, conversant about particular sensible objects, do convey into the mind several distinct perceptions of things, according to those various ways wherein those objects do affect them: and thus we come by those ideas we have, of yellow, white, heat, cold, soft, hard, bitter, sweet, and all those which we call sensible qualities; which when I say the senses convey into the mind, I mean, they from external objects convey into the mind what produces there those perceptions. This great source of most of the ideas we have, depending wholly upon our senses, and derived by them to the understanding, I call Sensation.

The Operations of our Minds, the other Source of them.—Secondly, the other fountain, from which experience furnishes the understanding with ideas, is the perception of the operations of our own mind within us, as it is employed about the ideas it has got; which operations, when the soul comes to reflect on and consider, do furnish the understanding with another set of ideas, which could not be had from things without; and such are perception, thinking, doubting, believing, reasoning, knowing, willing, and all the different actings of our own minds; which we being conscious of, and observing in ourselves, do from these receive into our understandings as distinct ideas, as we do from bodies affecting our senses. This source of ideas every man has wholly in himself; and though it be not sense, as having nothing to do with external objects, yet it is very like it, and might properly enough be called internal sense. But as I call the other Sensation, so I call this Reflection, the ideas it affords being such only as the mind gets by reflecting on its own operations within itself. By reflection then, in the following part of this discourse, I would be understood to mean that notice which the mind takes of its own operations, and the manner of them; by reason whereof there come to be ideas of these operations in the understanding. These two, I say, *viz.*, external material things, as the objects of sensation; and the operations of our own minds within, as the objects of reflection; are to me the only originals from whence all our ideas take their beginnings. . . .

All our Ideas are of the one or the other of these.— The understanding seems to me not to have the least glimmering of any ideas which it doth not receive from one of these two. External objects furnish the mind with the ideas of sensible qualities, which are all those different perceptions they produce in us; and the mind furnishes the understanding with ideas of its own operations.

These, when we have taken a full survey of them, and their several modes, combinations, and relations, we shall find to contain all our whole stock of ideas; and that we have nothing in our minds, which did not come in one of these two ways. Let any one examine his own thoughts, and thoroughly search into his understanding; and then let him tell me, whether all the original ideas he has there, are any other than of the objects of his senses, or of the operations of his mind, considered as objects of his reflection: and how great a mass of knowledge soever he imagines to be lodged there, he will, upon taking a strict view, see that he has not any idea in his mind, but what one of these two have imprinted. . . .

Newton's Scientific Synthesis

The work of the great English astronomer and mathematician Isaac Newton (1642–1727) represents a practical synthesis of seventeenth-century physics and mathematics and the union of the inductive and deductive methods. Newton advanced the new science from its speculative and empirical phases (represented by Copernicus and Galileo, respectively) to the stage of codification. He brought Kepler's laws of celestial mechanics and Galileo's terrestrial law of falling bodies into an all-embracing theory of universal gravitation that described every physical movement in the universe—from the operation of the tides to the effects of a planet upon its moons. In 1687 Newton published his monumental treatise on gravitation and the three laws of motion: the *Philosophiae Naturalis Principia Mathematica* ("Mathematical Principles of Natural Philosophy").[1] Newton's *Principia*, the fundamentals of which went unchallenged until the late nineteenth century, promoted the idea of a uniform and intelligible universe that operated as systematically as a well-oiled machine. Newton not only desanctified nature; he proved that nature's laws applied equally to terrestrial and celestial matter. He replaced Aristotle's description of the physical world with simple mathematical equations that would become the basis of modern physics. Essentially, Newton confirmed that by means of mathematical analysis and scientific observation, enlightened individuals might comprehend and control their world more completely than had ever before been possible. Newton's shaping influence on the spirit of the age is best described in the lines of his admiring British contemporary, Alexander Pope (see chapter 24), who wrote: "Nature and Nature's Laws lay hid in Night./ God said, *Let Newton be*! And All was Light."

The Impact of the Scientific Revolution on Art

Northern Baroque Painting

If the new science engendered a spirit of objective inquiry in literature, it also had a profound influence on the visual arts. In the cities of seventeenth-century Holland, where Dutch lensmakers had produced the first telescopes and microscopes, there evolved a style of painting that reflected an obsessive attention to the appearance of the natural world. In still lifes, portraits, landscape, and scenes

---

[1]The term "natural philosophy" meant primarily physics, astronomy, and the science of matter.

1666 Isaac Newton uses a prism to analyze light

1671 Gottfried Wilhelm Leibniz invents a calculating machine that multiplies and divides

1684 Leibniz publishes his first paper on differential calculus

1687 Newton publishes his *Principia Mathematica*

Figure 23.4 JAN DAVIDSZ DE HEEM, *Still Life with View of the Sea*, 1646. Oil on canvas, 23⅜ × 36½ in.
Courtesy of the Toledo Museum of Art, Ohio. Purchased with funds from the Libbey Endowment. Gift of Edward Drummond Libbey.

Figure 23.5 MARIA VAN OOSTERWYCK, *Vanitas Still Life*, 1668. Oil on canvas, 29 × 35 in. Kunsthistorisches Museum, Vienna.

Figure 23.6 PIETER DE HOOCH, *A Dutch Courtyard*, 1658–1660. Oil on canvas, 26¾ × 23 in.
© 1998 Board of Trustees, National Gallery of Art, Washington, D.C. Andrew W. Mellon Collection.

look back upon a long tradition perpetuated by such Netherlanders as Jan van Eyck, whose realistically depicted imagery carried secondary, symbolic intent (see chapter 17). Van Oosterwyck brings the naturalist's passion for detail to every object: the radiant flowers (including a magnificent Dutch tulip), the microscopically precise fly, the worn book, the rotting skull, the meticulously detailed globe, and the minute self-portrait (reflected in the carafe on the left). The still life thus serves a double function: it is decorative, yet it moralizes on the realities it depicts. Van Oosterwyck is only one of a number of outstanding female still-life artists who flourished in the seventeenth-century Dutch Republic. Some, such as Rachel Ruysch (1664–1750), the mother of ten children, served an international circle of patrons. Her precisely executed flower pieces reflect the influence of newly available botanical prints, yet another indication of the close relationship between the scientific impulse of the time and the world of art.

In addition to still-life subjects, genre paintings—scenes of everyday life and especially family life—were in high demand in the Netherlands in the seventeenth century, generating a virtual "Golden Age" of Dutch art. The domestic scenes painted by Pieter de Hooch (1629–1684) show Dutch art to be societal—an art concerned with conviviality and companionship. In one painting, de Hooch uses a spacious courtyard filled with cool, bright light as the setting for such ordinary pleasures as pipe smoking and beer drinking (Figure 23.6). He captures a mood of domestic intimacy in his loving attention to humble fact: the crumbling brick wall, the gleaming tankard, the homely matron, and the pudgy child. The strict verticals and horizontals of the composition—established with Cartesian clarity and precision—create a sense of tranquillity and order.

Amateur musical performances, one of the major domestic entertainments of the seventeenth century, are the subject of many Northern baroque paintings, including de Hooch's *Portrait of a Family Making Music* (Figure 23.7). The popularity of musical subjects reflects the emphasis on musical education and the rising number of private musical societies in the towns of the Dutch Republic. In the belief that music-listening and music-making were morally edifying (and thus more desirable than the all too popular pastime of drinking), many churches required musical recitals before and after services and encouraged instrumental and choral expression

of everyday life—all secular subjects—Dutch masters practiced the "art of describing."[2] The almost photographic realism of such paintings as Jan Davidsz de Heem's *Still Life with View of the Sea* (Figure 23.4) is typical of the new "Baconian" attention to the natural world: Plump oysters and crabs, a succulent ham, ripe melons and peaches, a gleaming tankard are all rendered with keen precision and detail. A distant view of the sea and a storm-tossed vessel in the background of the painting are less than subtle reminders that Dutch maritime activity financed the bounties of the dinner table.

While de Heem's fruits and meats celebrate robust material pleasures, the objects in Maria van Oosterwyck's realistic *Still Life* of 1668—a skull, insects (the moth and the fly), a tiny mouse nibbling at some grain—make cloaked reference to the transience of earthly existence (Figure 23.5). Van Oosterwyck's *Still Life* belongs to a category of European **vanitas** paintings, the contents of which suggest the corruptibility of worldly goods, the futility of riches, and the inevitability of death. Such paintings

---

[2]See Svetlana Alpers, *The Art of Describing: Dutch Art in the Seventeenth Century.* Chicago: University of Chicago Press, 1983.

among members of the congregation. Holland was a center for the manufacture of musical instruments; the Dutch household pictured by de Hooch would have owned the bass viol, recorder, cittern (a type of lute), and violin on which the family performed, their rhythms closely measured by the portly, no-nonsense matron of the house.

Music making also figures in the delightful painting called *The Suitor's Visit* by Gerard ter Borch (1617–1681). The narrative is staged like a scene from a play: A well-dressed gentleman, who has just entered the parlor of a well-to-do middleclass family, bows before a young woman whose coy apprehension suggests that she is the object of courtship (Figure **23.8**). The father and the family dog take note of the tense moment, while a younger woman, absorbed in playing the lute, ignores the interruption. Ter Borch was famous for his virtuosity in painting silk and satin fabrics that subtly gleam from within the shadowy depths of domestic interiors. Equally impressive, however, was his ability to dignify an inconsequential social event with profound human meaning.

Vermeer and Dutch Painting

Seventeenth-century Dutch artists developed the naturalistic landscape (the very word derives from the Dutch *landschap*) as a major artistic subject. In landscape painting as in genre subjects, Dutch artists described nature with a close attention to detail and a sensitivity to atmosphere that rivaled the landscapes of their Northern European predecessors, Dürer and Brueghel (see chapter 19). Unlike their seventeenth-century French contemporaries, Poussin and Claude Lorrain (see chapter 21), Dutch landscape painters depicted nature free of moralizing narratives; they focused instead on the spirit and sense of place. Holland's leading artists shared an interest in the optical research of scientists such as Galileo and Newton. Indeed, the Delft artist Jan Vermeer (1632–1675) is thought to have conceived his paintings with the use of the *camera obscura* (Figure **23.9**), an optical device that anticipated the modern pinhole camera (though it lacked the means of capturing the image on film). Vermeer's *View of Delft*, a topographical study of the artist's native city, reveals a typically Dutch affection for the visible world and its all-embracing light (Figure **23.10**). Vermeer lowers the

Figure 23.9 A *camera obscura*; the image formed by the lens and reflected by the mirror on the ground glass is traced by the artist.

Figure 23.10 JAN VERMEER, *View of Delft*, 1658. Oil on canvas, 3 ft. 2¾ in. × 3 ft. 10 in. Mauritshuis, The Hague.

horizon line of the painting to give increased attention to the sky—a reflection perhaps of his interest in the new astronomy. Unlike the great landscape painters of China (see chapter 14), who employed multiple vanishing points to create vistas that unfold only gradually, Vermeer fixes a single point of view at a single moment in time. Nevertheless, the broad horizon in the Vermeer painting seems to reach beyond the limits of the frame to embrace a world that exceeds the mundane boundaries of seventeenth-century Delft. Dwarfed by their setting, two groups of tiny figures (artfully placed in the left foreground) behold the cityscape from within the painting as we do from without.

The exemplar of an age of observation, Vermeer brought to his compositions a keen sensitivity to light. Small beads of light, an effect produced by the *camera obscura*, twinkle on the surface of his canvases. In *The Geographer*, a warm golden light highlights the scientist's face and hands, while it creates a unifying atmosphere for the scholarly tools and instruments of his studio-laboratory (see Figure 23.2). In *Woman Holding a Balance* (Figure **23.11**), light transforms a mundane subject—the weighing of gold—into an allegory that suggests

Figure 23.11 JAN VERMEER, *Woman Holding a Balance*, ca. 1664. Oil on canvas, 16¾ × 15 in.
© 1998 Board of Trustees, National Gallery of Art, Washington, D.C. The Widener Collection, 1962.

the balance between material prosperity (symbolized by the jewels on the table) and spiritual destiny (represented by the painting of the Last Judgment that hangs on the wall). With cool intellectualism, Vermeer balances the negative space of the background against the positive figure of the pregnant woman. He weighs light against dark as he sets realistic details against broadly generalized shapes. These formal devices, conceived with painstaking technical precision, reinforce the allegorical theme of balance. Whether or not Vermeer intended the painting as an allegory, the affective power of the painting lies in its exquisite intimacy and in the meditative mood created by light, which, entering from a nearby window, subtly illuminates the face and body of the young woman. (Vermeer's Netherlandish ancestor, Jan van Eyck, had captured a similar mood in the Arnolfini marriage portrait executed two centuries earlier—see chapter 17.) Women, usually self-contained and self-possessed, and always without children, were one of Vermeer's favorite subjects. He pictured them in comfortable domestic interiors, playing musical instruments, reading letters, and enjoying the company of men.

Dutch Portraiture

The vogue of portraiture in Northern baroque art reflected the self-conscious materialism of a rising middle class. Like the portraits of wealthy Renaissance aristocrats (see chapter 17), the painted likenesses of seventeenth-century Dutch burghers fulfilled the desire to immortalize one's worldly self. But in contrast to Italian portraits, the painted images of middle-class Dutch men and women are usually unidealized and often even unflattering. They capture a truth to nature reminiscent of late Roman portraiture (see chapter 6) but surpass even these in their self-scrutiny and probing, self-reflective character.

Two contemporaries, Frans Hals (1581–1666) and Rembrandt van Rijn (the latter introduced in chapter 22), dominated the genre of portraiture in seventeenth-century Dutch painting. Hals was the leading painter of Haarlem and one of the great realists of the Western portrait tradition. His talent lay in capturing the fleeting expressions that characterized the personality and physical presence of his sitters. Hals rendered the jaunty self-confidence of a courtly Dutch soldier (Figure **23.12**) with the same fidelity to nature that he used to convey the dour solemnity of the scholar-philosopher Descartes (see Figure 23.3). A master of the brush, Hals brought his forms to life by means of quick, loose, staccato brushstrokes and impasto high-lights. Immediacy, spontaneity, and impulsive movement—features typical of baroque art—are captured in Hals' vigorous portraits.

These qualities also appear in the work of Judith Leyster (1609–1660), a Netherlandish artist from the province of Utrecht, whose can-vases until the twentieth century were usually attributed to her colleague, Frans Hals. Leyster established a workshop in Haarlem and was elected to the painters' guild of that city. Almost all her known paintings date from before her marriage at the age of twenty-six. Leyster's *Self-Portrait* achieves a sense of informality through the casual manner in which the artist turns away from her canvas as if to greet the viewer (Figure **23.13**). The laughing violinist that is the sub-ject of the painting-within-the-painting pro-vides an exuberant counterpoint to Leyster's robust visage, which conveys the self-confidence

Figure 23.12 (below) **FRANS HALS**, *The Laughing Cavalier*, 1624. Oil on canvas, 33¾ × 27 in. Reproduced by permission of the Trustees, the Wallace Collection, London.

Figure 23.13 (above) **JUDITH LEYSTER**, *Self-Portrait*, ca. 1630. Oil on canvas, 29⅜ × 25⅛ in. © 1998 Board of Trustees, National Gallery of Art, Washington, D.C. Gift of Mr. and Mrs. Robert Woods Bliss.

of a middle-class woman who held membership in the largely male artists' guild, trained stu-dents, and turned her art to profit. Leyster's por-trait is a personal comment on the role of the artist as muse and artisan.

Hals' and Leyster's portraits are astute records of surface appearance and the social milieu. By comparison, Rembrandt's portraits are studies of the inner life of his sitters, uncompromising explorations of flesh and blood, rather than flat-tering accounts of rich costumes and grandiose architectural settings. A keen observer of human character and a master technician, Rembrandt became the leading portrait painter in the city of Amsterdam. The commissions he received at the beginning of his career exceeded his ability to fill them. But after a meteoric rise to fame, he saw his fortunes decline. Accumulated debts led to poverty, bankruptcy, and psychological depres-sion—the last compounded by the loss of his beloved wife in 1642. The history of Rembrandt's career is mirrored in his self-portraits, over sixty of which survive; these are a kind of visual diary, a lifetime record of the artist's passionate enter-prise in self-scrutiny. His *Self-Portrait* of 1661, with its slackened facial muscles and furrowed

Figure 23.14 REMBRANDT VAN RIJN, *Self-Portrait as Saint Paul*, 1661. Oil on canvas, 35⅞ × 30⅜ in. Rijksmuseum, Amsterdam.

brow, directly engages the viewer with the image of a noble and yet utterly vulnerable personality (Figure **23.14**). Portraiture of this kind, which has no equivalent in any non-Western culture, may be considered among the outstanding examples of probing individualism.

Among the most lucrative of Rembrandt's commissions was the group portrait, a uniquely Dutch genre which commemorated the achievements of wealthy families, guild members, and militia officers. Some of these paintings, which measure more than 12 by 14 feet, reflect the baroque taste for colossal proportion and theatrical setting. But Rembrandt skillfully fused dramatic effect with sober, unidealized characterization. These features are especially obvious in *The Anatomy Lesson of Dr. Nicolaes Tulp* (1632), the painting that established Rembrandt's reputation as a master portraitist (Figure **23.15**). Rembrandt eliminated the posed look of the conventional group portrait by staging the scene as a dissection in progress. Here, as in his religious compositions (compare Figure 22.4), he manipulates light for dramatic purposes: He spotlights the dissected corpse in the foreground and balances the darker area on the right, dominated by the figure of the doctor, with a triangle formed by the illuminated heads of the students (whose names appear on the piece of paper held by the central figure). The faces of Tulp's students carry the force of individual personalities and capture the spirit of inquisitiveness peculiar to the Age of Science.

Figure 23.15 REMBRANDT VAN RIJN, *The Anatomy Lesson of Dr. Nicolaes Tulp*, 1632. Oil on canvas, 5 ft. 3⅜ in. × 7 ft. 1¼ in. Mauritshuis, The Hague.

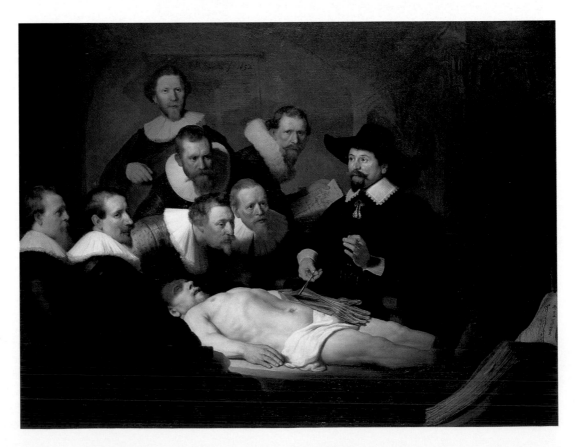

Baroque Instrumental Music

Until the sixteenth century, almost all music was written for the voice rather than for musical instruments. Even during the Renaissance, instrumental music was, for the most part, the result of substituting an instrument for a voice in music written for singing or dancing. The seventeenth century marked the rise of music that lacked extramusical meaning. Like a mathematical equation or a geometric formula, the instrumental music of the early modern era carried no explicit narrative content—it was neither a vehicle of religious expression nor a means of supporting a secular vocalized text. Such music was written without consideration for the associational content traditionally provided by a set of sung lyrics. The idea of music as an aesthetic exercise, composed for its own sake rather than to serve a religious or communal purpose, was a notable feature of the seventeenth century and one that has distinguished modern Western European music from the musical traditions of Asia and Africa.

Not surprisingly, the rise of instrumental music was accompanied by improvements in instruments and refinements in tuning. Indeed, instrumental music came to dominate musical composition at the very moment that Western musicians were perfecting such stringed instruments as the violin, viola, and cello (see Figure 23.7) and such keyboard instruments as the organ and harpsichord (Figure **23.16**). By the early eighteenth century, musicians were adopting the system of tuning known as **equal temperament**, whereby the octave was divided into twelve half-steps of equal size. Equal temperament made the chromatic scale uniform among instruments. Johann Sebastian Bach's *Well-Tempered Keyboard* (1722) was an attempt to popularize this system to a skeptical musical public. The new attention paid to improving instruments and systematizing key mirrored the efforts of scientists and philosophers to bring precision and uniformity to the tools and methods for scientific inquiry.

In the seventeenth century, Northern Italy was the world center for the manufacture of violins. The Amati, Guarneri, and Stradivari families of Cremona, Italy, established the techniques of making quality violins that were sought in all of the great courts of Europe. Transmitted from father to son, the construction techniques used to produce these instruments were guarded so secretly that modern violinmakers have never successfully imitated them. Elsewhere, around 1650, earlier instruments were standardized and refined. The ancient double-reed wind instrument known as the shawm, for instance, developed into the modern oboe. While amateur music making was widespread, professional performance also took a great leap forward, as a new breed of virtuosi inspired the writing of treatises on performance techniques.

Three main types of composition—the sonata, the suite, and the concerto—dominated seventeenth-century instrumental music. All three reflect the baroque taste for dramatic contrasts in tempo and texture. The **sonata** (from the Italian word for "sounded," that is, music played and not sung) is a piece written for a few instruments—

Figure 23.16 JOHANNES COUCHET (maker), Flemish Harpsichord-double-banked; compass, four octaves, and a fifth F to C (each keyboard), ca. 1650. Case decorated with carving and gilt gesso work. The Metropolitan Museum of Art, New York. The Crosby Brown Collection of Musical Instruments, 1889 (89.4.2363).

often no more than one or two. It usually consisted of three **movements** of contrasting tempo—fast/slow/fast—each based on a song or dance form of the time. The **suite**, written for any combination of instruments, is a sequence or series of movements derived from various European court or folk dances—for example, the sarabande, the pavane, the minuet, and the gigue, or jig. Henry Purcell (1659–1695) in England, François Couperin (1668–1733) in France (see chapter 26), and Johann Sebastian Bach (1685–1750) in Germany all contributed to the development of the suite as a musical genre. Finally, the **concerto** (from the same root as *concertato*, which describes opposing or contrasting bodies of sound; see chapter 20) is a composition consisting of two groups of instruments, one small and the other large, playing in "dialogue." The typical baroque concerto, the **concerto grosso** ("large concerto") featured several movements, whose number and kind varied considerably.

The leading Italian instrumental composer of the baroque era was Antonio Vivaldi (1678–1741), a Roman Catholic priest and the son of a prominent violinist at Saint Mark's Cathedral in Venice. Vivaldi wrote some 450 concertos. He systematized the concerto grosso into a three-movement form (fast/slow/fast) and increased the distinctions between solo and ensemble groups in each movement. Of the many exciting compositions Vivaldi wrote for solo violin and ensemble, the most glorious is *The Four Seasons*, ♪ a group of four violin concertos, each of which musically describes a single season. Vivaldi intended that this piece be "programmatic," that is, that it carry meaning outside of the music itself. As if to ensure that the music duplicate the descriptive power of the traditional vocal lines, he added poems at appropriate passages in the score for the instruction of the performers. At the section called "Spring," for instance, Vivaldi's verses describe "flowing streams" and "singing birds." While the music offers listeners the challenge of detecting such extramusical references to nature, the brilliance of this instrumental masterpiece lies not in its programmatic innovations but, rather, in its vibrant rhythms, its lyrical solos, and its exuberant "dialogues" between violin and small orchestra.

Rivaling Vivaldi's *Four Seasons* in their spiraling melodies and expansive rhythms are Bach's Brandenburg Concertos, which Bach completed in 1721 on commission from Christian Ludwig, the Margrave of Brandenburg. Though there is no record that the six concertos were ever performed during Bach's lifetime, they were probably intended for performance by the Brandenburg court orchestra. The Brandenburg Concertos employ as soloists most of the principal instruments of the baroque orchestra: violin, oboe, recorder, trumpet, and harpsichord. Totally unconcerned with extramusical meaning, Bach applied himself to developing rich contrasts of tone and texture between the two "contending" groups of instruments—note especially the massive sound of the entire ensemble versus the lighter sounds of the small sections in the first movement of the fourth concerto. ♪ Here, tightly drawn webs of counterpoint are spun between upper and lower instrumental parts, while musical lines, driven by an unflagging rhythm and energy, unfold majestically.

Only one year before he died, in 1749, Bach undertook one of the most monumental works of his career, a compelling example of baroque musical composition that came to be called *The Art of Fugue*. ♪ A **fugue** (literally "flight") is a polyphonic composition in which a single musical theme (or subject) is restated in sequential phrases. As in the more familiar canon known as a "round"—for instance, "Three Blind Mice"—a melody in one voice part is imitated in other voice parts, so that melody and repetitions overlap. The musical subject can be arranged to appear backward or inverted (or both), augmented (the time value of the notes doubled, so that the melody moves twice as slowly), or diminished (note values halved, so that the melody moves twice as fast). In the hands of a great composer, this form of imitative counterpoint might become a majestic tapestry of sound. Such is the case with Bach's *Art of Fugue*, in the last portion of which he went so far as to sign his name with a musical motif made up of the letters of his name—B flat, A, C, and B natural (pronounced as an H in German). Bach produced this *summa* of seventeenth-century musical science as a tool for instruction in the writing of fugues. However, even the

listener who cannot read music or analyze the intricacies of Bach's inventions is struck by the concentrated brilliance of each of his fugues. No less than Newton's codification of the laws of nature, *The Art of Fugue* was a triumphant expression of the Age of Science.

SUMMARY

During the seventeenth century, European scientists advanced a new picture of the cosmos. They showed that the earth, like the other planets, follows an elliptical and therefore irregular path around the sun, which stands at the center of the solar system. Clearly, the planet earth and its human inhabitants could no longer be regarded as the hub of a motionless universe. The progress of the Scientific Revolution moved from the stage of methodical speculation (represented by Copernicus and Kepler) to that of empirical confirmation (provided by Galileo's telescope) and, ultimately with Newton's *Principia*, to codification. Between 1600 and 1750, many new scientific instruments were invented, and the sciences of physics and astronomy, along with the language of higher mathematics, were firmly established.

While the new science demystified nature, the new learning provided a methodology for more accurately describing and predicting the operations of nature. Francis Bacon championed induction and the empirical method, which gave priority to knowledge gained through the senses. John Locke, the most influential philosopher of the age, defended the empirical tradition by claiming that all ideas came from sensation and reflection. René Descartes opposed such views; he gave priority to deductive reasoning and mathematical analysis. Despite their differences, seventeenth-century intellectuals shared the deist notions of God as a master mechanic and the universe as a great machine that operated independent of divine intervention.

The Scientific Revolution and the new learning ushered in a phase of the baroque style marked by an empirical attention to detail, a fascination with light and space, and an increased demand for such subjects as still life, landscape, portraiture, and genre painting. The many examples of each produced in this era testify to the secular preoccupations of middle-class patrons. In seventeenth-century art, cosmic landscapes such as Vermeer's *View of Delft* are balanced by the genre paintings of de Hooch and ter Borch, which explore the intimate pleasures of house and home, and by the portraits of Hals, Leyster, and Rembrandt, which give clear evidence of the robust confidence of the age.

Modern science also touched the art of music. During the seventeenth century, the violin and the organ were perfected, and keyboard instruments (and musical performance in general) benefited from the development of a uniform system of tuning. Treatises on the art of instrumental performance became increasingly popular. The seventeenth century saw the rise of wholly instrumental music and of such instrumental forms as the sonata, the suite, and the concerto. Vivaldi and Bach perfected the concerto grosso, while Bach exploited the art of the fugue in musical compositions whose complexity and intricacy remain unrivaled. These instrumental forms captured the exuberance of the baroque spirit, just as they summed up the dynamic intellectualism of the age.

GLOSSARY

Cartesian of or relating to René Descartes or his philosophy

concerto (Italian, "opposing" or "competing") an instrumental composition consisting of one or more solo instruments and a larger group of instruments playing in "dialogue"

concerto grosso a "large concerto," the typical kind of baroque concerto, consisting of several movements

deductive reasoning a method of inquiry that begins with clearly established general premises and moves toward the establishment of particular truths

deism a movement or system of thought advocating natural religion based on human reason rather than revelation; deists describe God as Creator, but deny that God interferes with the laws of the universe

equal temperament a system of tuning that originated in the seventeenth century, whereby the octave is divided into twelve half-steps of equal size; since intervals have the same value in all keys, music may be played in any key, and a

musician may change from one key to another with complete freedom.

fugue ("flight") a polyphonic composition in which a theme (or subject) is imitated, restated, and developed by successively entering voice parts

geocentric earth-centered

heliocentric sun-centered

inductive reasoning a method of inquiry that begins with direct observation and experimentation and moves toward the establishment of general conclusions or axioms

movement a major section in a long instrumental composition

sonata an instrumental composition consisting of three movements of contrasting tempo, usually fast/slow/fast; see also Glossary, chapter 26

suite an instrumental composition consisting of a sequence or series of movements derived from court or folk dances

vanitas (Latin, "vanity") a type of still life consisting of objects that symbolize the brevity of life and the transience of earthly pleasures and achievements

SUGGESTIONS FOR READING

Alpers, Svetlana. *The Art of Describing: Dutch Art in the Seventeenth Century*. Chicago: University of Chicago Press, 1983.

——*Rembrandt's Enterprise: The Studio and the Market*. Chicago: University of Chicago Press, 1990.

Chapman, H. P. *Rembrandt's Self-Portraits: A Study in Seventeenth-Century Identity*. Princeton, N.J.: Princeton University Press, 1990.

Donington, Robert. *Baroque Music: Style and Performance*. New York: Norton, 1982.

Edgerton. Samuel Y. *The Heritage of Giotto's Geometry: Art and Science on the Eve of the Scientific Revolution*. Ithaca: Cornell University Press, 1994.

Hall, A. Rupert. *The Revolution in Science: 1500–1750*. New York: Longman, 1983.

Jacob, Margaret C. *The Cultural Meaning of the Scientific Revolution*. New York: Knopf, 1988.

Montias, John M. *Vermeer and His Milieu*. Princeton, N.J.: Princeton University Press, 1991.

Shapin, Steven. *The Scientific Revolution*. Chicago: University of Chicago Press, 1996.

Stechow, Wolfgang. *Dutch Landscape Painting of the Seventeenth Century*. London: Phaidon, 1966.

Wheelock, Arthur K., Jr. *Vermeer and the Art of Painting*. New Haven: Yale University Press, 1995.

MUSIC LISTENING SELECTIONS

CD Two Selection 5 Vivaldi, *The Four Seasons*, "Spring," Concerto in E Major, Op. 8, No. 1; first movement, 1725.

CD Two Selection 6 Bach, Brandenburg Concerto No. 4 in G Major, first movement, excerpt, 1721.

CD Two Selection 7 Bach, *The Art of Fugue*, Canon in the 12th, harpsichord, 1749–1750.

PART TWO

The Age of Enlightenment

The Age of Enlightenment, as the eighteenth century is often called, was a time of buoyant optimism. Educated Europeans envisioned themselves as the most civilized people in history: Having survived a millennium of darkness, they now ushered in a new era of light—the light of reason. Reason, they optimistically predicted, would dispel the mists of human ignorance, superstition, and prejudice.

Eighteenth-century intellectuals were the heirs to Newtonian science. They viewed the universe as a great machine that operated according to unchanging "natural" laws. Just as Newton had systematized the laws of the physical universe, so these rationalists tried to regulate the laws of human behavior. Such practical powers, they argued, were not only attainable, but also essential to the progress and betterment of humankind. Enlightenment theorists—John Locke and Adam Smith in Great Britain, Jean-Jacques Rousseau in France, and Thomas Jefferson in America—articulated the fundamental concepts of natural law, political freedom, free enterprise, and the social contract between ruler and ruled; while other thinkers, such as Antoine Nicolas de Condorcet and Mary Wollstonecraft championed social equality and human progress. And although the major intellectual and cultural ideals of the Enlightenment did not directly touch the lives of millions of eighteenth-century peasants and villagers, these ideals profoundly influenced the course of modern history, not only in the West, but, more recently, throughout the world.

During the eighteenth century, learning freed itself from the Church, and literacy became widespread. Among middle-class Europeans, ninety to one hundred percent of the males and almost seventy-five percent of the females could read and write. This new, more literate middle class competed with a waning aristocracy for social and political prestige. The public interest in literature and the arts spurred the rise of the newspaper, the novel, and the symphony. Satire became a popular vehicle for dramatizing the contradictions between the polite society of the upper classes and the poverty and illiteracy of the lower classes. In educated circles, debate raged over the powers of rulers versus those of the ruled. And in France and North America, visionary treatises defended the unalienable rights of citizens and fanned the flames of revolt, culminating in violent revolutions. None of the age-old certitudes were left unexamined: The church hierarchy, the autocratic rule of kings and despots, the very social order—all fell under close scrutiny. By the pen and by the musket, the new order would be launched.

At the same time, the Age of Enlightenment was rich in the production of works of art and architecture, now increasingly commissioned by secular patrons. While the visual arts of the Enlightenment reflect some of the intellectual ideals of the era, they more closely mirror the shifting tastes and values of eighteenth-century society. The rococo style was an expression of aristocratic luxury and the delight in physical pleasure, while the neoclassical revival, inspired by a wealth of archeological discoveries, responded to the tempered rationalism and political idealism of reformers in France and the young American republic. The portrait, the visual counterpart of literary biography, continued to hold a prized place in Western art. Finally, in the birth of the symphony orchestra and in the development of classical forms of Western instrumental music, the eighteenth century made a lasting contribution to the humanistic tradition, one that continues to influence modern musical history.

(opposite) **JEAN-AUGUSTE-DOMINIQUE INGRES**, detail of *The Apotheosis of Homer*, 1827. Oil on canvas, 12 ft. 8 in. x 16 ft. 10 ¾ in. Louvre, Paris. © R. M. N., Paris.

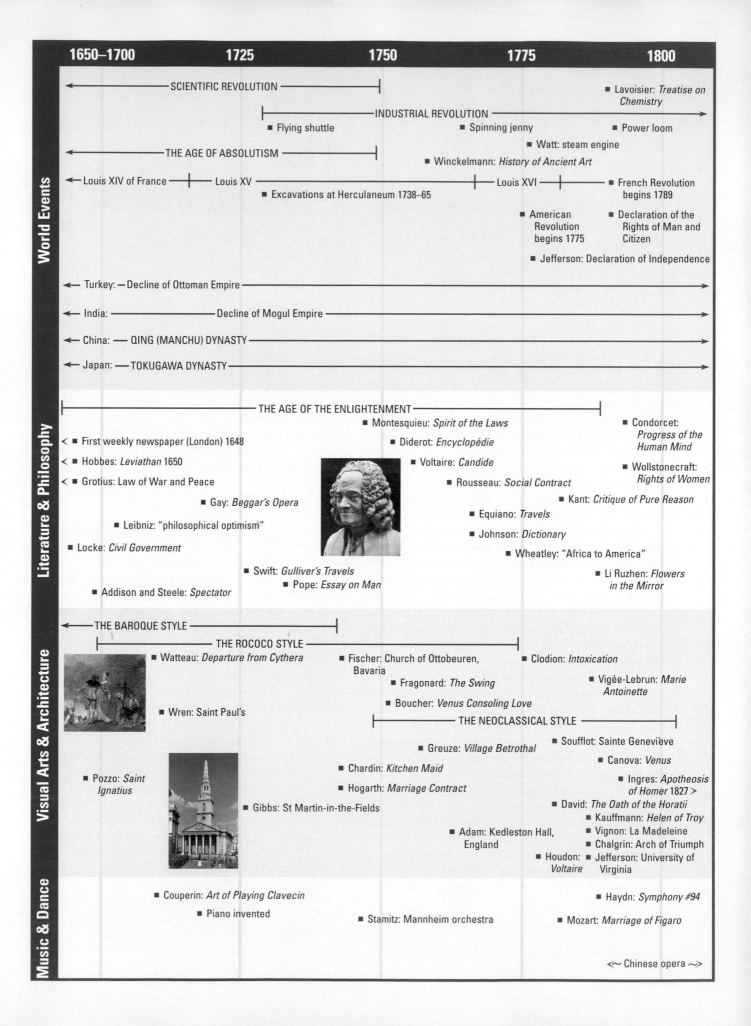

	1650–1700	1725	1750	1775	1800

World Events

◄—————— SCIENTIFIC REVOLUTION ——————►

■ Lavoisier: *Treatise on Chemistry*

◄—— INDUSTRIAL REVOLUTION ——————►

■ Flying shuttle ■ Spinning jenny ■ Power loom

■ Watt: steam engine

◄———— THE AGE OF ABSOLUTISM ————►

■ Winckelmann: *History of Ancient Art*

◄— Louis XIV of France —┤— Louis XV ————┤— Louis XVI —┤— ■ French Revolution begins 1789

■ Excavations at Herculaneum 1738–65

■ American Revolution begins 1775

■ Declaration of the Rights of Man and Citizen

■ Jefferson: Declaration of Independence

◄— Turkey: — Decline of Ottoman Empire ————————►

◄— India: ————— Decline of Mogul Empire ——————►

◄— China: — QING (MANCHU) DYNASTY ——————————►

◄— Japan: — TOKUGAWA DYNASTY ———————————►

Literature & Philosophy

◄———————— THE AGE OF THE ENLIGHTENMENT ————————►

■ Montesquieu: *Spirit of the Laws*

■ Condorcet: *Progress of the Human Mind*

< ■ First weekly newspaper (London) 1648

■ Diderot: *Encyclopédie*

< ■ Hobbes: *Leviathan* 1650

■ Voltaire: *Candide*

■ Wollstonecraft: *Rights of Women*

< ■ Grotius: Law of War and Peace

■ Rousseau: *Social Contract*

■ Gay: *Beggar's Opera*

■ Kant: *Critique of Pure Reason*

■ Leibniz: "philosophical optimism"

■ Equiano: *Travels*

■ Locke: *Civil Government*

■ Johnson: *Dictionary*

■ Wheatley: "Africa to America"

■ Swift: *Gulliver's Travels*

■ Li Ruzhen: *Flowers in the Mirror*

■ Pope: *Essay on Man*

■ Addison and Steele: *Spectator*

Visual Arts & Architecture

◄— THE BAROQUE STYLE ————————►

◄———— THE ROCOCO STYLE ————————►

■ Watteau: *Departure from Cythera*

■ Fischer: Church of Ottobeuren, Bavaria

■ Clodion: *Intoxication*

■ Fragonard: *The Swing*

■ Vigée-Lebrun: *Marie Antoinette*

■ Boucher: *Venus Consoling Love*

■ Wren: Saint Paul's

◄———— THE NEOCLASSICAL STYLE ————————►

■ Greuze: *Village Betrothal*

■ Soufflot: Sainte Geneviève

■ Chardin: *Kitchen Maid*

■ Canova: *Venus*

■ Pozzo: *Saint Ignatius*

■ Hogarth: *Marriage Contract*

■ Ingres: *Apotheosis of Homer* 1827 >

■ Gibbs: St Martin-in-the-Fields

■ David: *The Oath of the Horatii*

■ Kauffmann: *Helen of Troy*

■ Adam: Kedleston Hall, England

■ Vignon: La Madeleine

■ Chalgrin: Arch of Triumph

■ Houdon: *Voltaire*

■ Jefferson: University of Virginia

Music & Dance

■ Couperin: *Art of Playing Clavecin*

■ Haydn: *Symphony #94*

■ Piano invented

■ Stamitz: Mannheim orchestra

■ Mozart: *Marriage of Figaro*

<~ Chinese opera ~>

CHAPTER TWENTY-FOUR

The promise of reason

"The time will … come when the sun will shine only on free men who know no other master but their reason."
Antoine Nicolas de Condorcet

In the year 1680, a comet blazed across the skies over Western Europe. The English astronomer Edmund Halley (1656–1742) observed the celestial body, calculated its orbit, and predicted its future appearances. Stripped of its former role as a portent of catastrophe or a harbinger of natural calamity, Halley's comet now became merely another natural phenomenon, the behavior of which invited scientific investigation. This new, objective attitude toward nature and the accompanying confidence in the liberating role of reason were hallmarks of the Enlightenment—the period between 1687 (the date of Newton's *Principia*) and 1789 (the beginning of the French Revolution). Indeed, the eighteenth century marks the divide between the essentially medieval view of the world as controlled by an omnipotent God and governed by the principles of faith, and the modern, secular view of the world as dominated by humankind and governed by the principles of reason. It also marks the beginning of an optimistic faith in the human ability to create a kind of happiness on earth that in former ages had been thought to exist only in heaven.

One of the principal preoccupations of Enlightenment thinkers was the comprehension of human nature in scientific terms—without reference to divine authority. "Theology," wrote one Enlightenment skeptic, "is only ignorance of natural causes." Just as Halley explained the operations of the celestial bodies as a logical part of nature's mechanics, so eighteenth-century intellectuals explained human nature in terms of *natural law*. The unwritten and divinely sanctioned law of nature, or natural law, held that there are certain principles of right and wrong that all human beings, by way of reason, can discover and apply in the course of creating a just society. "Natural rights" included the right to life, liberty, property, and just treatment by the ruling order. Moreover, Enlightenment thinkers argued that a true understanding of the human condition was the first step toward progress,

that is, toward the gradual betterment of human life. It is no wonder, then, that the eighteenth century saw the formation of the social sciences: anthropology, sociology, economics, and political science. These new disciplines, devoted to the study of humankind, optimistically confirmed that the promise of reason was the realization of an enlightened social order.

The Political Theories of Hobbes and Locke

An enlightened social order required a redefinition of the role of government and the rights of citizens. Not since the Golden Age of Athens had the relationship between the ruler and the ruled received so much intellectual attention as in the early modern era, the age of the rising European nation-state. During the sixteenth century, the political theorist Machiavelli had argued that the survival of the state was more important than the well-being of its citizens. Later in that century, the French lawyer Jean Bodin (1530–1596) had used biblical precepts and long-standing tradition to defend theories of divine right monarchy. In the seventeenth century, the Dutch statesman Hugo Grotius (1583–1645) proposed an all-embracing system of international law based on reason, which he identified with nature. Grotius' idea of a political contract based in natural law profoundly influenced the thinking of two of England's finest philosophers, Thomas Hobbes (1588–1679) and John Locke, the latter of whom we met in chapter 23 as a champion of the empirical method.

Hobbes and Locke took up the urgent question of human rights versus the sovereignty of the ruler. Shaken by the conflict between royalist and antiroyalist factions that had fueled the English Civil War (see chapter 22), both thinkers rejected the principle of divine right monarchy. Instead, they advanced the idea that government must be based in a **social contract**. For Hobbes, the social contract was a covenant among individuals who willingly surrendered a portion of their freedom to a governing authority or ruler, in whose hands should rest ultimate authority. Some forty years later, Locke agreed with Hobbes that government must be formed by a contract that laid the basis for social order and individual happiness. But he believed that power must remain with the ruled.

The divergent positions of Hobbes and Locke proceeded from their contrasting perceptions of human nature. Whereas Locke described human beings as naturally equal, free, and capable (through reason) of defining the common good, Hobbes viewed human beings as selfish, greedy, and warlike. Without the state, he argued, human life was "solitary, poor, nasty, brutish, and short." Bound by an irrevocable and irreversible social contract, government under one individual or a ruling assembly was, according to Hobbes, society's only hope for peace and security. The collective safety of society lay in its willingness to submit to a higher authority, which Hobbes dubbed the "Leviathan," after the mythological marine monster described in the Bible. Hobbes aired these views in a treatise called the *Leviathan*, which he published in 1651—only two years after England's antiroyalist forces had beheaded the English monarch, Charles I.

READING 4.14 From Hobbes' *Leviathan* (1651)

Part I   Chapter 13: Of the Natural Condition of Mankind as Concerning their Felicity and Misery

Nature has made men so equal in the faculties of the body and mind as that, though there be found one man sometimes manifestly stronger in body or of quicker mind than another, yet, when all is reckoned together, the difference between man and man is not so considerable as that one man can thereupon claim to himself any benefit to which another may not pretend as well as he. For as to the strength of body, the weakest has strength to kill the strongest, either by secret machination or by confederacy with others that are in the same danger with himself. . . . ⁵¹⁰

From this equality of ability arises equality of hope in the attaining of our ends. And therefore if any two men desire the same thing, which nevertheless they cannot both enjoy, they become enemies; and in the way to their end, which is principally their own conservation, and sometimes their delectation[1] only, endeavor to destroy or subdue one another. And from hence it comes to pass that where an invader has no more to fear than another man's single power, if one plant, sow, build, or possess a convenient seat, others may probably be expected to come prepared with forces united to dispossess ²⁰ and deprive him, not only of the fruit of his labor, but also of his life or liberty. And the invader again is in the like danger of another. . . .

So that in the nature of man we find three principal causes of quarrel: first, competition; secondly, diffidence;[2] thirdly, glory.

_____
[1]Enjoyment; delight
[2]Lack of confidence

The first makes men invade for gain, the second for safety, and the third for reputation. The first use violence to make themselves masters of other men's persons, wives, children, and cattle; the second, to defend them; the third, for trifles, as a word, a smile, a different opinion, and any other sign of undervalue, either direct in their persons or by reflection in their kindred, their friends, their nation, their profession, or their name. ³⁰

Hereby it is manifest that, during the time men live without a common power to keep them all in awe, they are in that condition which is called war, and such a war as is of every man against every man. For WAR consists not in battle only, or the act of fighting, but in a tract of time wherein the will to contend by battle is sufficiently known; and therefore the notion of *time* is ⁴⁰ to be considered in the nature of war as it is in the nature of weather. For as the nature of foul weather lies not in a shower or two of rain but in an inclination thereto of many days together, so the nature of war consists not in actual fighting but in the known disposition thereto, during all the time there is no assurance to the contrary. All other time is PEACE.

Whatsoever, therefore, is consequent to a time of war where every man is enemy to every man, the same is consequent to the time wherein men live without other security than what their own strength and their own invention shall furnish them ⁵⁰ withal. In such condition there is no place for industry, because the fruit thereof is uncertain; and consequently no culture of the earth; no navigation nor use of the commodities that may be imported by sea; no commodious building; no instruments of moving and removing such things as require much force; no knowledge of the face of the earth; no account of time; no arts; no letters; no society; and, which is worst of all, continual fear and danger of violent death; and the life of man solitary, poor, nasty, brutish, and short. . . .

Part II   Chapter 17: Of the Causes, Generation, and Definition of a Commonwealth

The final cause, end, or design of men, who naturally love ⁶⁰ liberty and dominion over others, in the introduction of that restraint upon themselves in which we see them live in commonwealths, is the foresight of their own preservation, and of a more contented life thereby—that is to say, of getting themselves out from that miserable condition of war which is necessarily consequent . . . to the natural passions of man when there is no visible power to keep them in awe and tie them by fear of punishment to the performance of their covenants and observations of [the] laws of nature. . . .

For the laws of nature—as *justice, equity, modesty, mercy*, ⁷⁰ and, in sum, *doing to others as we would be done to*—of themselves, without the terror of some power to cause them to be observed, are contrary to our natural passions, that carry us to partiality, pride, revenge, and the like. And covenants without the sword are but words, and of no strength to secure a man at all. Therefore, notwithstanding the laws of nature . . ., if there be no power erected, or not great enough for our security, every man will—and may lawfully—rely on his own strength and art for caution against all other men. . . .

The only way to erect such a common power as may be able ⁸⁰ to defend them from the invasion of foreigners and the injuries of one another, and thereby to secure them in such sort as that by their own industry and by the fruits of the earth they may nourish themselves and live contentedly, is to confer all their power and strength upon one man, or upon one assembly of men that may reduce all their wills, by plurality of voices, unto one will; which is as much as to say, to appoint one man or assembly of men to bear their person, and everyone to own and acknowledge to himself to be author of whatsoever he that so bears their person shall act or cause to be acted in those things which concern the common peace and safety, and therein to submit their wills every one to his will, and their judgments to his judgment. This is more than consent or concord; it is a real unity of them all in one and the same person, made by covenant of every man with every man, in which manner as if every man should say to every man, *I authorize and give up my right of governing myself to this man, or to this assembly of men, on this condition, that you give up your right to him and authorize all his actions in like manner.* This done, the multitude so united in one person is called a COMMONWEALTH, in Latin CIVITAS. This is the generation of that great LEVIATHAN (or rather, to speak more reverently, of that *mortal god*) to which we owe, under the *immortal God*, our peace and defense. For by this authority, given him by every particular man in the commonwealth, he has the use of so much power and strength conferred on him that, by terror thereof, he is enabled to form the wills of them all to peace at home and mutual aid against their enemies abroad. And in him consists the essence of the commonwealth, which, to define it, is *one person, of whose acts a great multitude, by mutual covenants one with another, have made themselves every one the author, to the end he may use the strength and means of them all as he shall think expedient for their peace and common defense.* And he that carries this person is called SOVEREIGN and said to have *sovereign power*: and everyone besides, his SUBJECT.

The attaining to this sovereign power is by two ways. One, by natural force. . . . The other is when men agree among themselves to submit to some man or assembly of men voluntarily, on confidence to be protected by him against all others. This latter may be called a political commonwealth, or commonwealth by *institution*, and the former a commonwealth by *acquisition*. . . .

Part II   Chapter 30: Of the Office of the Sovereign Representative

The office of the sovereign, be it a monarch or an assembly, consists in the end for which he was trusted with the sovereign power, namely, the procuration of the *safety of the people*; to which he is obliged by the law of nature, and to render an account thereof to God, the author of that law, and to none but him. But by safety here is not meant a bare preservation but also all other contentments of life which every man by lawful industry, without danger or hurt to the commonwealth, shall acquire to himself.

And this is intended should be done, not by care applied to individuals further than their protection from injuries when they shall complain, but by a general providence contained in public instruction, both of doctrine and example, and in the making and executing of good laws, to which individual

persons may apply their own cases.

And because, if the essential rights of sovereignty . . . be taken away, the commonwealth is thereby dissolved and every man returns into the condition and calamity of a war with every other man, which is the greatest evil that can happen in this life, it is the office of the sovereign to maintain those rights entire, and consequently against his duty, first, to transfer to another or to lay from himself any of them. For he that deserts the means deserts the ends. . . .

Locke's Government of the People

Locke (Figure **24.1**) disagreed with Hobbes' view of humankind as self-serving and aggressive. He held that since human beings were born without any preexisting qualities, their natural state was one of perfect freedom. Whether people became brutish or otherwise depended solely upon their experiences and their environment. People have, by their very nature as human beings, said Locke, the right to life, liberty, and estate (or "property"). Government must arbitrate between the exercise of one person's liberty and that of the next. The social contract thus preserves the natural rights of the governed. And, although individuals may willingly consent to give up some of their liberty in return for the ruler's protection, they may never relinquish their ultimate authority. If a ruler is tyrannical or oppressive, the people have not only the right but the obligation to rebel and seek a new ruler. Locke's defense of political rebellion in the face of tyranny served as justification for the "Glorious Revolution" of

Figure 24.1 JOHN GREENHILL, *Portrait of John Locke*, ca. 1672–1676. Oil on canvas, 22⅛ × 18½ in. © National Portrait Gallery, London.

1688, as well as inspiration for the revolutions that took place in America and in France toward the end of the eighteenth century.

If for Hobbes the state was sovereign, for Locke sovereignty rested with the people, and government existed only to protect the natural rights of its citizens. In his first treatise, *On Government* (1689), Locke argued that individuals might attain their maximum development only in a society free from the unnatural restrictions imposed by absolute rulers. In his second treatise, *Of Civil Government* (an excerpt from which follows), Locke expounded the idea that government must rest upon the consent of the governed. While Locke's views were basic to the development of modern liberal thought, Hobbes' views provided the justification for all forms of tyranny, including the enlightened despotism of such eighteenth-century rulers as Frederick of Prussia and Catherine II of Russia, who claimed that their authority was founded in the general consent of the people. Nevertheless, the notion of government as the product of a social contract between the ruler and the ruled has become one of the dominating ideas of modern Western—and more recently of Eastern European and Asian—political life.

READING 4.15 From Locke's *Of Civil Government* (1690)

Book II   Chapter II: Of the State of Nature

To understand political power right and derive it from its original, we must consider what state all men are naturally in, and that is a state of perfect freedom to order their actions and dispose of their possessions and persons as they think fit, within the bounds of the law of nature without asking leave or depending upon the will of any other man.   1

A state also of equality, wherein all the power and jurisdiction is reciprocal, no one having more than another; there being nothing more evident than that creatures of the same species and rank, promiscuously born to all the same advantages of nature and the use of the same faculties, should   10 also be equal one amongst another without subordination or subjection; unless the Lord and Master of them all should, by any manifest declaration of his will, set one above another and confer on him, by an evident and clear appointment, an undoubted right to dominion and sovereignty. . . .

Chapter V: Of Property

God, who hath given the world to men in common, hath also given them reason to make use of it to the best advantage of life and convenience. The earth and all that is therein is given to men for the support and comfort of their being. And though   20 all the fruits it naturally produces and beasts it feeds belong to mankind in common . . ., there must of necessity be a means to appropriate them some way or other before they can be of any use, or at all beneficial to any particular man. . . .

Though the earth and all inferior creatures be common to all men, yet every man has a property in his own person: this nobody has any right to but himself. The labor of his body, and

the work of his hands we may say, are properly his. Whatsoever then he removes out of the state that nature has provided and left it in, he has mixed his labor with and joined   30 to it something that is his own, and thereby makes it his property. . . .

Chapter VIII: The Beginning of Political Societies

Men being, as has been said, by nature all free, equal, and independent, no one can be put out of this estate and subjected to the political power of another without his own consent. The only way whereby any one divests himself of his natural liberty and puts on the bonds of civil society is by agreeing with other men to join and unite into a community for their comfortable, safe, and peaceable living one amongst another, in a secure enjoyment of their properties, and a   40 greater security against any that are not of it. This any number of men may do, because it injures not the freedom of the rest; they are left as they were in the liberty of the state of nature. When any number of men have so consented to make one community or government, they are thereby presently incorporated and make one body politic, wherein the majority have a right to act and conclude the rest.

For when any number of men have, by the consent of every individual, made a community, they have thereby made that community one body, with a power to act as one body, which is   50 only by the will and determination of the majority: . . . And therefore we see that in assemblies empowered to act by positive laws, where no number is set by that positive law which empowers them, the act of the majority passes for the act of the whole and of course determines; as having, by the law of nature and reason, the power of the whole.

And thus every man, by consenting with others to make one body politic under one government, puts himself under an obligation to every one of that society to submit to the determination of the majority and to be concluded by it; or else   60 this original compact whereby he with others incorporate into one society, would signify nothing and be no compact if he be left free and under no other ties than he was in before in the state of nature. . . .

Chapter IX: Of the Ends of Political Society and Government

If man in the state of nature be so free as has been said; if he be absolute lord of his own person and possessions, equal to the greatest, and subject to nobody, why will he part with his freedom, why will he give up this empire and subject himself to the dominion and control of any other power? To which it is obvious to answer that though in the state of nature he has   70 such a right, yet the enjoyment of it is very uncertain and constantly exposed to the invasion of others; for all being kings as much as he, every man his equal and the greater part no strict observers of equity and justice, the enjoyment of the property he has in this state is very unsafe, very unsecure. This makes him willing to quit a condition, which, however free, is full of fears and continual dangers: and it is not without reason that he seeks out and is willing to join in society with others who are already united or have a mind to unite for the mutual preservation of their lives, liberties, and estates, which I call by   80 the general name property.

The great and chief end, therefore, of men's uniting into commonwealths, and putting themselves under government, is the preservation of their property. . . .

Chapter XVIII: Of Tyranny

As usurpation is the exercise of power, which another hath a right to, so tyranny is the exercise of power beyond right, which nobody can have a right to. And this is making use of the power any one has in his hands, not for the good of those who are under it, but for his own private, separate advantage— when the governor, however entitled, makes not the law, but   **90**
his will, the rule; and his commands and actions are not directed to the preservation of the properties of his people, but [to] the satisfaction of his own ambition, revenge, covetousness, or any other irregular passion. . . .

Wherever law ends, tyranny begins, if the law be transgressed to another's harm; and whosoever in authority exceeds the power given him by the law, and makes use of the force he has under his command, . . . ceases in that to be a [magistrate]; and, acting without authority, may be opposed as any other man who by force invades the right of another. . . .   **100**

"May the commands then of a prince be opposed? may he be resisted as often as any one shall find himself aggrieved, and but imagine he has not right done him? This will unhinge and overturn all politics, and, instead of government and order, leave nothing but anarchy and confusion."

To this I answer that force is to be opposed to nothing but to unjust and unlawful force; whoever makes any opposition in any other case, draws on himself a just condemnation both from God and man. . . .

The Influence of Locke on Montesquieu and Jefferson

Locke's political treatises were read widely. So too, his defense of religious toleration (issued even as Louis XIV forced all Calvinists to leave France), his plea for equality of education among men and women, and his arguments for the use of modern languages in place of Latin won the attention of many intellectuals. Published during the last decade of the seventeenth century, Locke's treatises became the wellspring of the Enlightenment in both Europe and America.

In France, the keen-minded aristocrat Charles Louis de Secondat Montesquieu (1689–1755) championed Locke's views on political freedom and expanded on his theories. Intrigued by the ways in which nature seemed to govern social behavior, the Baron de Montesquieu investigated the effects of climate and custom on human conduct, thus pioneering the field of sociology. In his elegantly written thousand-page treatise *The Spirit of the Laws* (1748), Montesquieu defended liberty as the free exercise of the will and condemned slavery as fundamentally "unnatural and evil." A proponent of constitutional monarchy, he advanced the idea of a separation of powers among the executive, legislative, and judicial agencies of government, advising that each monitor the activities of the

others in order to ensure a balanced system of government. He warned that when legislative and executive powers were united in the same person (or body of magistrates), or when judicial power was inseparable from legislative and executive powers, human liberty might be gravely threatened. Montesquieu's system of checks and balances was later enshrined in the Constitution of the United States of America (1787).

Across the Atlantic, the most eloquent expression of Locke's ideas appeared in the preamble to the statement declaring the independence of the North American colonies from the rule of the British king George III. Written by the leading American apostle of the Enlightenment, Thomas Jefferson (1743–1826; see Figure 26.21), and adopted by the Continental Congress on July 4, 1776, the American Declaration of Independence echoes Locke's ideology of revolt as well as his view that governments derive their just powers from the consent of the governed. Following Locke and Montesquieu, Jefferson justified the establishment of a social contract between ruler and ruled as the principal means of fulfilling natural law—the "unalienable right" to life, liberty, and the pursuit of happiness. While Jefferson did not include "property" among the unalienable rights, he was, as well, fully committed to the individual's natural right to property.

READING 4.16 From Jefferson's Declaration of Independence (1776)

When, in the course of human events, it becomes necessary   **1**
for one people to dissolve the political bands which have connected them with another, and to assume among the powers of the earth, the separate and equal station to which the laws of nature and of nature's God entitle them, a decent respect to the opinions of mankind requires that they should declare the causes which impel them to separation.

We hold these truths to be self-evident: That all men are created equal; that they are endowed by their Creator with certain unalienable rights; that among these are life, liberty   **10**
and the pursuit of happiness; that to secure these rights governments are instituted among men, deriving their just powers from the consent of the governed; that whenever any form of government becomes destructive of these ends, it is the right of the people to alter or to abolish it, and to institute new government, laying its foundation on such principles and organizing its powers in such form, as to them shall seem most likely to effect their safety and happiness. . . .

The Declaration of Independence made clear the belief of America's "founding fathers" in equality among men. Equality between the sexes was, however, another matter: Although both Locke and Jefferson acknowledged that women held the same natural rights as men, they did not consider women—or slaves, or children, for that matter— capable of exercising such rights. Recognizing this bias, Abigail Adams (d. 1818) wrote to her husband, John, who was serving as a delegate to the Second Continental Congress (1777), as follows:

> I . . . hear that you have declared an independency, and, by the way, in the new code of laws which I suppose it will be necessary for you to make, I desire you would remember the ladies and be more generous and favorable to them than were your ancestors. Do not put such unlimited power into the hands of husbands. Remember all men would be tyrants if they could. If particular care and attention are not paid to the ladies we are determined to foment a rebellion, and will not hold ourselves bound to obey any laws in which we have no voice or representation.*

Despite the future First Lady's spirited admonitions, however, American women did not secure the legal right to vote or to hold political office until well into the twentieth century.

If the Declaration of Independence constituted a clear expression of Enlightenment theory in justifying revolution against tyrannical rule, the Constitution of the new United States of America represented the practical outcome of the Revolution: the creation of a viable new nation with its government based ultimately on Enlightenment principles. The U.S. Constitution, framed in 1787 and ratified by popular vote in 1788–1789, articulated the mechanics of self-rule. First, it created a form of government new to the modern world: a system of representative government embodying the principal of "Republicanism," that is, government by the elected representatives of the people. Second, following the precepts of Montesquieu, the framers of the Constitution divided the new government into three branches—legislative, executive, and judicial—each to be "checked and balanced" by the others to prevent the possible tyranny of any one branch. Third, the new republic was granted sufficient power to govern primarily through the authority granted the president to execute national laws and constitutional provisions. Withal, the U.S. Constitution would prove effective for over two centuries, and would serve as the model for the constitutions of all the new-born republics to be created throughout the world, even until today.

Adam Smith and the Birth of Economic Theory

While Enlightenment thinkers were primarily concerned with matters of political equality, they also addressed questions related to the economy of the modern European state. The Scottish philosopher Adam Smith (1723–1790) applied the idea of natural law to the domains of human labor, productivity, and the exchange of goods. In his

epoch-making synthesis of ethics and economics, *An Inquiry into the Nature and Causes of the Wealth of Nations*, published in 1776, Smith set forth the "laws" of labor, production, and trade with an exhaustiveness reminiscent of Newton's *Principia Mathematica* (see chapter 23). Smith contended that labor, a condition natural to humankind (as Locke had observed), was the foundation for prosperity. A nation's wealth is not its land or its money, said Smith, but its labor force. In the "natural" economic order, individual self-interest guides the progress of economic life, and certain natural forces, such as the "law of supply and demand," motivate a market economy. Since government interference would infringe on this order, reasoned Smith, such interference is undesirable. He thus opposed all artificial restraints on economic progress and all forms of government regulation and control. The modern concepts of free enterprise and **laissez-faire** (literally, "allow to act") economics spring from Smith's incisive formulations. In the following excerpt, Smith examines the origin of the division of labor among human beings and defends the natural and unimpeded operation of trade and competition among nations.

> **READING 4.17** From Smith's *An Inquiry into the Nature and Causes of the Wealth of Nations* (1776)

Book I   Chapter II: The Principle which Occasions the Division of Labor

[The] division of labor, from which so many advantages are derived, is not originally the effect of any human wisdom, which foresees and intends that general opulence to which it gives occasion. It is the necessary, though very slow and gradual, consequence of a certain propensity in human nature which has in view no such extensive utility; the propensity to truck, barter, and exchange one thing for another.   1

. . . . [This propensity] is common to all men, and to be found in no other race of animals, which seem to know neither this nor any other species of contracts. Two greyhounds, in running   10 down the same hare, have sometimes the appearance of acting in some sort of concert. Each turns her towards his companion, or endeavors to intercept her when his companion turns her towards himself. This, however, is not the effect of any contract, but of the accidental concurrence of their passions in the same object at that particular time. Nobody ever saw a dog make a fair and deliberate exchange of one bone for another with another dog. . . . In almost every other race of animals each individual, when it is grown up to maturity, is entirely independent, and in its natural state has occasion for the   20 assistance of no other living creature. But man has almost constant occasion for the help of his brethren, and it is in vain for him to expect it from their benevolence only. He will be more likely to prevail if he can interest their self-love in his favor, and show them that it is for their own advantage to do for him what he requires of them. Whoever offers to another a bargain of any kind, proposes to do this. Give me that which I want, and you shall have this which you want, is the meaning of every such

*Letter of March 31, 1776, in *Familiar Letters of John Adams and His Wife Abigail Adams During the Revolution*, ed. Charles Francis Adams (New York: Hurd and Houghton, 1876. Reprint: Freeport, N.Y.: Books for Library Press, 1970), p. 148.

offer; and it is in this manner that we obtain from one another the far greater part of those good offices which we stand in need of. It is not from the benevolence of the butcher, the brewer, or the baker, that we expect our dinner, but from their regard to their own interest. We address ourselves, not to their humanity, but to their self-love; and never talk to them of our own necessities, but of their advantages. . . .

As it is by treaty, by barter, and by purchase, that we obtain from one another the greater part of those mutual good offices which we stand in need of, so it is this same trucking disposition which originally gives occasion to the division of labor. In a tribe of hunters or shepherds a particular person makes bows and arrows, for example, with more readiness and dexterity than any other. He frequently exchanges them for cattle or for venison with his companions; and he finds at last that he can in this manner get more cattle and venison, than if he himself went to the field to catch them. From a regard to his own interest, therefore, the making of bows and arrows grows to be his chief business. . . .

Book IV   Chapter III, Part II: Of the Unreasonableness of Restraints [on Trade]

Nations have been taught that their interest consisted in beggaring all their neighbors. Each nation has been made to look with an invidious eye upon the prosperity of all the nations with which it trades, and to consider their gain as its own loss. Commerce, which ought naturally to be, among nations as among individuals, a bond of union and friendship, has become the most fertile source of discord and animosity. The capricious ambition of kings and ministers has not, during the present and the preceding century, been more fatal to the repose of Europe, than the impertinent jealousy of merchants and manufacturers. The violence and injustice of the rulers of mankind is an ancient evil, for which, I am afraid, the nature of human affairs can scarce admit of a remedy. But the mean rapacity, the monopolizing spirit of merchants and manufacturers, who neither are, nor ought to be, the rulers of mankind, though it cannot perhaps be corrected, may very easily be prevented from disturbing the tranquility of anybody but themselves.

That it was the spirit of monopoly which originally both invented and propagated this doctrine, cannot be doubted; and they who first taught it were by no means such fools as they who believed it. In every country it always is and must be the interest of the great body of the people to buy whatever they want of those who sell it cheapest. The proposition is so very manifest, that it seems ridiculous to take any pains to prove it; nor could it ever have been called in question had not the interested sophistry of merchants and manufacturers confounded the common sense of mankind. Their interest is, in this respect, directly opposed to that of the great body of the people. . . .

The wealth of a neighboring nation, though dangerous in war and politics, is certainly advantageous in trade. In a state of hostility it may enable our enemies to maintain fleets and armies superior to our own; but in a state of peace and commerce it must likewise enable them to exchange with us to a greater value and to afford a better market, either for the

immediate produce of our own industry or for whatever is purchased with that produce. As a rich man is likely to be a better customer to the industrious people in his neighborhood, than a poor, so is likewise a rich nation. . . .

The Philosophes

When Louis XIV died in 1715, the French nobility fled the Palace of Versailles and settled in townhouses in Paris, often decorated in the latest fashion. Socially ambitious noblewomen, many of whom championed a freer and more public role for their gender, organized gatherings in the *salons*, where nobility and middle-class thinkers met to exchange views on morality, politics, science, and religion and to voice opinions on everything ranging from diet to the latest fashions in theater and dress (Figure **24.2**). Inevitably, new ideas began to circulate in these meetings, and Paris became the hub of intellectual activity.

A small circle of well-educated individuals came to be known as **philosophes** (the French word for "philosophers"). Intellectuals rather than philosophers in the strictest sense of the word, the *philosophes* dominated the intellectual activity of the Enlightenment. Like the humanists of fifteenth-century Florence, their interests were mainly secular and social. Unlike their Renaissance counterparts, however, the *philosophes* scorned all forms of authority—they believed that they had surpassed the ancients, and they looked beyond the present state of knowledge to the establishment of a superior moral and social order.

Most *philosophes* held to the deist view of God as Creator and providential force behind nature and natural law, rather than as personal Redeemer. They believed in the immortality of the soul, not out of commitment to any religious doctrine, but because they saw human beings as fundamentally different from other living creatures. They viewed the Bible as mythology rather than as revealed truth, and scorned Church hierarchy and ritual. Their antipathy to irrationality, superstition, and religious dogma (as reflected, for instance, in the Catholic doctrine of original sin) alienated them from the Church and set them at odds with the established authorities—a position memorably expressed in the acerbic pronouncement that "men will not be free until the last king is strangled with the entrails of the last priest." The quest for a nonauthoritarian, secular morality led the *philosophes* to challenge all existing forms of intolerance, inequality, and injustice. The banner cry of the *philosophes*, "Ecrasez l'infame" ("Wipe

1702 the world's first daily newspaper is published in England

1704 the first alphabetical encyclopedia in English is printed

1714 a London engineer patents the first known typewriter

1765 Diderot's *Encyclopédie* is issued in seventeen volumes

out all evils"), sparked a commitment to social reforms that led to the French Revolution (see chapter 25).

Diderot and the *Encyclopédie*

The basic ideals of the Enlightenment were summed up in a monumental literary endeavor to which many of the *philosophes* contributed: the thirty-five-volume *Encyclopédie* (including eleven volumes of engraved plates), published between 1751 and 1772 and edited by Denis Diderot (1713–1784; Figure **24.3**). Modeled on the two-volume Chambers' Encyclopedia printed in England in 1751, Diderot's *Encyclopédie*—also known as *The Analytical Dictionary of the Sciences, Arts, and Crafts*—was the largest compendium of contemporary social, philosophic, artistic, scientific, and technological knowledge ever produced in the West. A collection of "all the knowledge scattered over the face of the earth," as Diderot explained, it manifested the zealous desire of the *philosophes* to dispel human ignorance and transform society. It was also, in part, a response to rising literacy and to the widespread public interest in the facts of everyday life. Not all members of society welcomed the enterprise, however: King Louis XV, who claimed that the *Encyclopédie* was doing "irreparable dam-age to morality and religion," twice banned its printing; some volumes were published and distributed secretly.

Diderot's *Encyclopédie* was the most ambitious and influential literary undertaking of the eighteenth century. Some two hundred individuals contributed seventy-two thousand entries on subjects ranging from political theory, cultural history, and art criticism to the technology of theater machinery, the making of silk stockings, and the varieties of wigs (Figure **24.4**). Articles on Islam, India, and China indicate a more than idle curiosity about civilizations that remained to most Westerners remote and exotic. Diderot enlisted as contributors to the *Encyclopédie* the most progressive minds of the Enlightenment: François Marie Arouet (1694–1778), known as Voltaire, wrote on "matters of nature and art"; the French philosopher and educator Jean-Jacques Rousseau (1712–1778; see chapter 25) provided articles on music; François Quesnay wrote on political economy; Montesquieu (whose articles were published posthumously) examined the different types of governments; Jean Le Rond d'Alembert (1717–1783) treated the subject of higher education; and Diderot himself prepared numerous entries on art and politics.

Although women contributed moral and financial support to the *Encyclopédie*, none was invited to participate in its production. Moreover, not one of the thirty-one entries on women makes reference to the contributions of exceptional eighteenth-century women such as Gabrielle-

Figure 24.2 FRANÇOIS DEQUEVAUVILLER after **N. LAVRÉINCE**, *Assembly in a Salon*, 1745–1807. Engraving, 15¹³⁄₁₆ × 19⅝ in. The Metropolitan Museum of Art, New York. Harris Brisbane Dick Fund, 1935 (35.100.17).

Figure 24.3 JEAN-ANTOINE HOUDON, *Diderot*, 1773. Marble, height 20⅞ in. The Metropolitan Museum of Art, New York. Gift of Mr. and Mrs. Charles Wrightsman, 1974 (1974.291).

Émilie Le Tonnelier de Breteuil, the Marquise du Châtelet (1706–1749; Figure **24.5**). An impeccable scholar and a brilliant mathematician, Madame du Châtelet produced an annotated French translation of Newton's *Principia*—a monumental achievement that was almost finished when she died, a few days after giving birth to her fourth child. Proficient in Latin, Italian, and English, the Marquise also translated the works of Virgil, Horace, and Ovid into eloquent French; she wrote original poetry and conducted experiments in physics and chemistry. She was a reckless gambler, a feminist, a champion of the fashionably low-cut neckline, and the mistress of Voltaire, who lived at her *château* until her death in 1749. Voltaire confessed that he could hardly live without the Marquise, whom he regarded as "a great man." In their assessment of the abilities and the rights of women, the *philosophes* were ambivalent at best, their personal sentiments characterized by Rousseau's self-scorning complaint that one of his greatest misfortunes was "always to be connected with some literary woman." Nevertheless, the *Encyclopédie* remains a monument to secular knowledge and to the Enlightenment faith in the promise of reason—a spirit summed up in Voltaire's proclamation, "Let the facts prevail." The following excerpts come from the entry on natural law written by the French lawyer Antoine-Gaspart Boucher d'Argis and from the long article on black Africans written by Le Romain (first name and dates unknown).

READING 4.18 From the *Encyclopédie* (1751–1772)

Law of Nature or Natural Law

In its broadest sense the term is taken to designate certain principles which nature alone inspires and which all animals as well as all men have in common. On this law are based the union of male and female, the begetting of children as well as their education, love of liberty, self-preservation, concern for self-defense. 1

It is improper to call the behavior of animals natural law, for, not being endowed with reason, they can know neither law nor justice.

More commonly we understand by natural law certain laws of justice and equity which only natural reason has established among men, or better, which God has engraved in our hearts. 10

The fundamental principles of law and all justice are: to live honestly, not to give offense to anyone, and to render unto each whatever is his. From these general principles derive a great many particular rules which nature alone, that is, reason and equity, suggest to mankind.

Since this natural law is based on such fundamental principles, it is perpetual and unchangeable: no agreement can debase it, no law can alter it or exempt anyone from the obligation it imposes. . . . 20

Figure 24.4 *Wigs*, a plate from the *Encylopédie* illustrating the varieties of men's wigs that were fashionable in Europe in the 1750s. Thomas J. Watson Library, The Metropolitan Museum of Art, New York.

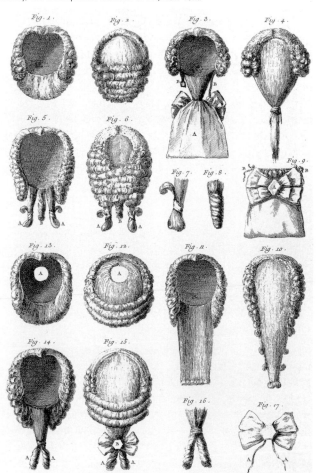

The principles of natural law, therefore, form part of the law of nations, particularly the primitive law of nations; they also form part of public and of private law: for the principles of natural law, which we have stated, are the purest source of the foundation of most of private and public law. . . .

The authority of natural laws stems from the fact that they owe their existence to God. Men submit to them because to observe them leads to the happiness of men and society. This is a truth demonstrated by reason. It is equally true that virtue by itself is a principle of inner satisfaction whereas vice is a principle of unrest and trouble. It is equally certain that virtue produces great external advantage, while vice produces great ills. . . .

Negroes[1]

For the last few centuries the Europeans have carried on a trade in Negroes whom they obtain from Guinea and other coasts of Africa and whom they use to maintain the colonies established in various parts of America and in the West Indies. To justify this loathsome commerce, which is contrary to natural law, it is argued that ordinarily these slaves find the salvation of their souls in the loss of their liberty, and that the Christian teaching they receive, together with their indispensable role in the cultivation of sugar cane, tobacco, indigo, etc., softens the apparent inhumanity of a commerce where men buy and sell their fellow men as they would animals used in the cultivation of the land.

Trade in Negroes is carried on by all the nations which have settlements in the West Indies, and especially by the French, the English, the Portuguese, the Dutch, the Swedes, and the Danes. The Spaniards, in spite of the fact that they possess the greatest part of the Americas, have no direct way of acquiring slaves but have concluded treaties with other nations to furnish them with Negroes. . . .

As soon as the trade is completed no time must be lost in setting sail. Experience has shown that as long as these unfortunates are still within sight of their homeland, they are overcome by sorrow and gripped by despair. The former is the cause of many illnesses from which a large number perish during the crossing; the latter inclines them to suicide, which they effect either by refusing nourishment or by shutting off their breathing. This they do in a way they know of turning and twisting their tongues which unfailingly suffocates them. Others again shatter their head against the sides of the ship or throw themselves into the sea if the occasion presents itself. . . .

Punishment of the Negroes, policing, and regulations concerning these matters:

If the Negro commits a slight offense the overseer may on his own responsibilty punish him with a few strokes of the whip. If, however, it is a serious matter, the master has the culprit clapped in irons and then decides the number of strokes with which he will be punished. If all men were equally just, these necessary punishments would be kept within limits, but it

[1] A term originally used by the Spanish and Portuguese to identify black Africans.

often happens that certain masters abuse the authority which they claim over their slaves and chastise these unfortunates too harshly. Yet the masters themselves may be responsible for the situation which led to the offense. To put an end to the cruelties of these barbarous men who would be capable of leaving their slaves without the basic necessities of life while driving them to forced labor, the officers of His Majesty, who are resident in the colonies, have the responsibility of enforcing the edict of the king, which is called the Black Code. In the French islands of America this code regulates the governing and the administration of justice and of the police, as well as the discipline of the slaves and the slave-trade. . . .

The Encyclopedic Cast of Mind

The *Encyclopédie* had an enormous impact on eighteenth-century culture. Although few individuals actually read or understood all of it, it fostered an encyclopedic cast of mind. Indeed, the emphasis on the accumulation, codification, and systematic preservation of knowledge linked the eighteenth century to the Scientific Revolution and to that other Enlightenment "bible," Newton's *Principia*.

Eighteenth-century scientists made notable advances in the fields of chemistry, electricity, biology, and the medical sciences. They produced the mercury thermometer and the stethoscope and introduced the science of immunology to the West—some seven centuries after the Chinese had invented the first inoculations against smallpox. Antoine Lavoisier (1743–1794) published the *Elementary Treatise of Chemistry* (1789) and launched chemistry as an exact science. The Swede Carolus Linnaeus (1707–1778) produced a systematic method for classifying plants, and the French naturalist Georges Louis Leclerc, Comte de Buffon (1707–1788), made landmark advances in zoology.

Valuable efforts to accumulate and classify knowledge took place in the arts as well. The English critic and poet Samuel Johnson (1709–1784) published the first dictionary of the English language and Rousseau produced the first Western dictionary of music. In the social sciences, Voltaire's seven-volume general history (published in 1756), which included a monumental account of the age of Louis XIV, provided a model for a new universal and rationalist kind of history-writing. Voltaire was among the first to recognize Europe's debt to Arab science and Asian thought. He rejected all explanations of the past as the workings of divine Providence and was generally critical of the role played by the Catholic Church in Western history. But it fell to the English historian Edward Gibbon (1737–1794) to provide the rationale that attacked Christianity for the collapse of Rome. *The Decline and Fall of the Roman Empire* (1776) was the product of Gibbon's unique interpretation of the sociological forces at work within ancient cultures.

Eighteenth-century China lay beyond the immediate influence of the European Enlightenment; nevertheless, in the East an encyclopedic impulse similar to that prevailing in the West came to a climax at this time. Qing rulers followed their Ming predecessors in directing groups of

Figure 24.5 NICOLAS DE LARGILLIÈRE, *Gabrielle-Emilie Le Tonnelier de Breteuil, Marquise du Châtelet*, ca. 1740. Oil on canvas, 4 ft. 3½ in. × 3 ft. 4¼ in. Columbus Museum of Art, Ohio. Bequest of Frederick W. Schumacher.

scholars to assemble exhaustive collections of information, some filling as many as 36,000 manuscript volumes. These "encyclopedias" were actually anthologies of the writings of former Chinese artists and scholars, rather than comprehensive collections of contemporary knowledge. Nevertheless, as in France, some of China's rulers deemed the indiscriminate accumulation of information itself dangerous, and at least one eighteenth-century Qing emperor authorized the official burning of thousands of books.

The Crusade for Progress

Among European intellectuals, the belief in the reforming powers of reason became the basis for a progressive view of human history. The German mathematician and philosopher Gottfried Wilhelm Leibniz (1646–1716) systematically defended the view that human beings live in perfect harmony with God and nature. Leibniz linked optimism to the logic of probability: His *principle of sufficient reason* held, simply, that there must be a reason or purpose for everything in nature. In response to the question, Why does evil exist in a world created by a good God? Leibniz answered that all events conformed to the preestablished harmony of the universe. Even evil, according to Leibniz, was necessary in a world that was "better than any other possible world"—a position that came to be called "philosophic optimism."

For the *philosophes*, the key to social reform lay in a true understanding of human nature, which, they argued, might best be acquired by examining human history. They interpreted the transition from Paleolithic hunting and gathering to the birth of civilization as clear evidence of the steady march toward social improvement. Faith in that steady march motivated the Enlightenment crusade for progress. The Italian lawyer and social reformer Cesare de Beccaria (1738–1794) enlisted in this crusade when he wrote his treatise *On Crimes and Punishments*, in which he suggested that torturing criminals did not work to deter crime. Rather, argued Beccaria, society should seek methods by which to rehabilitate those who commit crimes. Although Beccaria's book generated no immediate changes, it went through six editions in eighteen months and ultimately contributed to movements for prison reform in Europe and the United States. The questions that Beccaria raised concerning the value of punishment are still being debated today.

The most passionate warrior in the Enlightenment crusade for progress was the French aristocrat Antoine Nicolas de Condorcet (1743–1794). Condorcet was a mathematician, a social theorist, and a political moderate amidst revolutionary extremists. His *Sketch for a Historical Picture of the Progress of the Human Mind*, written during the early days of the French Revolution, was the preface to a longer work he never completed, for he committed suicide shortly after being imprisoned as an "enemy" of the Revolution. Condorcet believed that human nature could be perfected through reason. All errors in politics and morals, he argued, were based in philosophic and scientific errors. "There is not a religious system nor a supernatural extravagance," wrote Condorcet, "that is not founded on ignorance of the laws of nature." Fiercely optimistic about the future of humankind, Condorcet was one of the first modern champions of sexual equality. He called for the "complete annihilation of the prejudices that have brought about an inequality of rights between the sexes, an inequality fatal even to the party in whose favor it works." Such inequality, he protested, "has its origin solely in an abuse of strength, and all the later sophistical attempts that have been made to excuse it are vain."

In his *Sketch*, the visionary Condorcet traced the "progress" of humankind through ten stages, from ignorance and tyranny to the threshold of enlightenment and equality. The utopian tenth stage, subtitled "The Future Progress of the Human Mind" (an excerpt of which follows), sets forth ideas that were well ahead of their time, such as a guaranteed livelihood for the aged, a universal

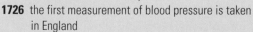

1714 the mercury thermometer and the Fahrenheit scale are invented in Germany
1726 the first measurement of blood pressure is taken in England
1751 the first mental hospital opens in London
1774 Franz Mesmer (Austrian) uses hypnotism to aid in curing disease

system of education, fewer work hours, and the refinement of a technology for the accumulation of knowledge. (How computers would have delighted this prophet of the Information Age!) The educational goals that Condorcet outlines toward the end of the excerpt still carry the force of sound judgment.

READING 4.19 From Condorcet's *Sketch for a Historical Picture of the Progress of the Human Mind* (1793)

If man can, with almost complete assurance, predict phenomena when he knows their laws, and if, even when he does not, he can still, with great expectation of success, forecast the future on the basis of his experience of the past, why, then, should it be regarded as a fantastic undertaking to sketch, with some pretense to truth, the future destiny of man on the basis of his history? The sole foundation for belief in the natural sciences is this idea that the general laws directing the phenomena of the universe, known or unknown, are necessary and constant. Why should this principle be any less true for the development of the intellectual and moral faculties of man than for the other operations of nature? Since beliefs founded on past experience of like conditions provide the only rule of conduct for the wisest of men, why should the philosopher be forbidden to base his conjectures on these same foundations, so long as he does not attribute to them a certainty superior to that warranted by the number, the constancy, and the accuracy of his observations? . . . 10

The time will therefore come when the sun will shine only on free men who know no other master but their reason; when tyrants and slaves, priests and their stupid or hypocritical instruments will exist only in works of history and on the stage; and when we shall think of them only to pity their victims and their dupes; to maintain ourselves in a state of vigilance by thinking on their excesses; and to learn how to recognize and so to destroy, by force of reason, the first seeds of tyranny and superstition, should they ever dare to reappear among us. 20

In looking at the history of societies we shall have had occasion to observe that there is often a great difference between the rights that the law allows its citizens and the rights that they actually enjoy, and, again, between the equality established by political codes and that which in fact exists among individuals. . . . 30

These differences have three main causes: inequality in wealth, inequality in status between the man whose means of subsistence are hereditary and the man whose means are dependent on the length of his life, or, rather, on that part of his life in which he is capable of work; and, finally, inequality in education.

We therefore need to show that these three sorts of real inequality must constantly diminish without however disappearing altogether: for they are the result of natural and necessary causes which it would be foolish and dangerous to wish to eradicate. . . . 40

[As to education] we can teach the citizen everything that he needs to know in order to be able to manage his household, administer his affairs, and employ his labor and his faculties in freedom; to know his rights and to be able to exercise them; to be acquainted with his duties and fulfill them satisfactorily; to judge his own and other men's actions according to his own lights and to be a stranger to none of the high and delicate feelings which honor human nature; not to be in a state of blind dependence upon those to whom he must entrust his affairs or the exercise of his rights; to be in a proper condition to choose and supervise them; to be no longer the dupe of those popular errors which torment man with superstitious fears and chimerical hopes; to defend himself against prejudice by the strength of his reason alone; and, finally, to escape the deceits of charlatans who would lay snares for his fortune, his health, his freedom of thought, and his conscience under the pretext of granting him health, wealth, and salvation. . . . 50 60

The real advantages that should result from this progress, of which we can entertain a hope that is almost a certainty, can have no other term than that of the absolute perfection of the human race; since, as the various kinds of equality come to work in its favor by producing ampler sources of supply, more extensive education, more complete liberty, so equality will be more real and will embrace everything which is really of importance for the happiness of human beings. . . .

Enlightenment and the Rights of Women

While Condorcet was among the first moderns to champion the equality of the sexes, his efforts pale before the impassioned defense of women launched by Mary Wollstonecraft (1759–1797; Figure **24.6**). This self-educated British intellectual applied Enlightenment principles of natural law, liberty, and equality to forge a radical rethinking of the roles and responsibilities of women in Western society. In *A Vindication of the Rights of Woman*, Wollstonecraft attacked the persistence of the female stereotype (docile, domestic, and childlike) as formulated by misguided, misogynistic, and tyrannical males, who, as she complained, "try to secure the good conduct of women by attempting to keep them in a state of childhood." Calling for a "revolution of female manners," she criticized the "disorderly kind of education" received by women, who, owing to their domestic roles, learn "rather by snatches."

Wollstonecraft emphasized the importance of reason in the cultivation of virtue, observing that, "it is a farce to call any being virtuous whose virtues do not result from the exercise of its own reason." Though she condemned women for embracing their roles in "the great art of pleasing [men]," Wollstonecraft seems to have been deeply conflicted by her own personal efforts to reconcile her sexual passions, her need for independence, and her free-spirited will. Her affair with an American speculator and timbermerchant produced an illegitimate child and at least two attempts at suicide; and her marriage to the novelist William Godwin (subsequent to her becoming pregnant by him) proved no less turbulent. She died at the age of thirty-eight, following the birth of their daughter, the future Mary Shelley (see chapter 28). In contrast with her short and troubled life, Wollstonecraft's treatise has enjoyed sustained and significant influence; it stands at the threshold of the modern movement for female equality.

After considering the historic page, and viewing the living world with anxious solicitude, the most melancholy emotions of sorrowful indignation have depressed my spirits, and I have sighed when obliged to confess, that either nature has made a great difference between man and man, or that the civilization which has hitherto taken place in the world has been very partial. I have turned over various books written on the subject of education, and patiently observed the conduct of parents and the management of schools; but what has been the result?—a profound conviction that the neglected education of [10] my fellow-creatures is the grand source of the misery I deplore; and that women, in particular, are rendered weak and wretched by a variety of concurring causes, originating from one hasty conclusion. The conduct and manners of women, in fact, evidently prove that their minds are not in a healthy state; for, like the flowers which are planted in too rich a soil, strength and usefulness are sacrificed to beauty; and the flaunting leaves, after having pleased a fastidious eye, fade, disregarded on the stalk, long before the season when they ought to have arrived at maturity.—One cause of this barren [20] blooming I attribute to a false system of education, gathered from the books written on this subject by men who, considering females rather as women than human creatures, have been more anxious to make them alluring mistresses than affectionate wives and rational mothers and the understanding of the sex has been so bubbled by this specious homage, that the civilized women of the present century, with a few exceptions, are only anxious to inspire love, when they ought to cherish a nobler ambition, and by their abilities and virtues exact respect. [30]

In a treatise, therefore, on female rights and manners, the works which have been particularly written for their improvement must not be overlooked; especially when it is asserted, in direct terms, that the minds of women are enfeebled by false refinement; that the books of instruction, written by men of genius, have had the same tendency as more frivolous productions; and that, in the true style of Mahometanism,[1] they are treated as a kind of subordinate beings, and not as a part of the human species, when improveable reason is allowed to be the dignified distinction [40] which raises men above the brute creation, and puts a natural sceptre in a feeble hand.

Yet, because I am a woman, I would not lead my readers to suppose that I mean violently to agitate the contested question respecting the equality or inferiority of the sex; but as the subject lies in my way, and I cannot pass it over without subjecting the main tendency of my reasoning to misconstruction, I shall stop a moment to deliver, in a few

Figure 24.6 **JOHN OPIE**, *Mary Wollstonecraft*, ca. 1797. Oil on canvas, 29½ in. × 24½ in. © National Portrait Gallery, London.

words, my opinion.—In the government of the physical world it is observable that the female in point of strength is, [50] in general, inferior to the male. This is the law of nature; and it does not appear to be suspended or abrogated in favour of woman. A degree of physical superiority cannot, therefore, be denied—and it is a noble prerogative! But not content with this natural preeminence, men endeavour to sink us still lower, merely to render us alluring objects for a moment; and women, intoxicated by the adoration which men, under the influence of their senses, pay to them, do not seek to obtain a durable interest in their hearts, or to become the friends of the fellow creatures who find [60] amusement in their society. . . .

My own sex, I hope, will excuse me, if I treat them like rational creatures, instead of flattering their *fascinating* graces, and viewing them as if they were in a state of perpetual childhood, unable to stand alone. I earnestly wish to point out in what true dignity and human happiness consists—I wish to persuade women to endeavour to acquire strength, both of mind and body, and to convince them that the soft phrases, susceptibility of heart, delicacy of sentiment, and refinement of taste, are almost [70] synonymous with epithets of weakness, and that those beings who are only the objects of pity and that kind of love, which has been termed its sister, will soon become objects of contempt.

Dismissing then those pretty feminine phrases, which the men condescendingly use to soften our slavish dependence, and despising that weak elegancy of mind, exquisite sensibility, and sweet docility of manners, supposed to be the sexual characteristics of the weaker vessel, I wish to

---

[1]A reference to the widespread Christian misconception that Islam denied that women had souls.

shew that elegance is inferior to virtue, that the first object of laudable ambition is to obtain a character as a human being, regardless of the distinction of sex; and that secondary views should be brought to this simple touchstone. . . .

The education of women has, of late, been more attended to than formerly; yet they are still reckoned a frivolous sex, and ridiculed or pitied by the writers who endeavour by satire or instruction to improve them. It is acknowledged that they spend many of the first years of their lives in acquiring a smattering of accomplishments; meanwhile strength of body and mind are sacrificed to libertine notions of beauty, to the desire of establishing themselves,—the only way women can rise in the world,—by marriage. And this desire making mere animals of them, when they marry they act as such children may be expected to act:—they dress; they paint, and nickname God's creatures.—Surely these weak beings are only fit for a seraglio! Can they be expected to govern a family with judgment, or take care of the poor babes whom they bring into the world?

If then it can be fairly deduced from the present conduct of the sex, from the prevalent fondness for pleasure which takes place of ambition and those nobler passions that open and enlarge the soul; that the instruction which women have hitherto received has only tended, with the constitution of civil society, to render them insignificant objects of desire—mere propagators of fools!—if it can be proved that in aiming to accomplish them, without cultivating their understandings, they are taken out of their sphere of duties, and made ridiculous and useless when the short-lived bloom of beauty is over, I presume that *rational* men will excuse me for endeavouring to persuade them to become more masculine and respectable. . . .

In the present state of society it appears necessary to go back to first principles in search of the most simple truths, and to dispute with some prevailing prejudice every inch of ground. To clear my way, I must be allowed to ask some plain questions, and the answers will probably appear as unequivocal as the axioms on which reasoning is built; though, when entangled with various motives of action, they are formally contradicted, either by the words or conduct of men.

In what does man's pre-eminence over the brute creation consist? The answer is as clear as that a half is less than the whole; in Reason.

What acquirement exalts one being above another? Virtue; we spontaneously reply.

For what purpose were the passions implanted? That man by struggling with them might attain a degree of knowledge denied to the brutes; whispers Experience.

Consequently the perfection of our nature and capability of happiness, must be estimated by the degree of reason, virtue, and knowledge, that distinguish the individual, and direct the laws which bind society: and that from the exercise of reason, knowledge and virtue naturally flow, is equally undeniable, if mankind be viewed collectively.

The rights and duties of man thus simplified, it seems almost impertinent to attempt to illustrate truths that appear so incontrovertible; yet such deeply rooted prejudices have clouded reason, and such spurious qualities have assumed the name of virtues, that it is necessary to pursue the course of

reason as it has been perplexed and involved in error, by various adventitious circumstances, comparing the simple axiom with casual deviations. Men, in general, seem to employ their reason to justify prejudices, which they have imbibed, they can scarcely trace how, rather than to root them out. The mind must be strong that resolutely forms its own principles; for a kind of intellectual cowardice prevails which makes many men shrink from the task, or only do it by halves. . . .

Many are the causes that, in the present corrupt state of society, contribute to enslave women by cramping their understandings and sharpening their senses. One, perhaps, that silently does more mischief than all the rest, is their disregard of order.

To do every thing in an orderly manner, is a most important precept, which women, who, generally speaking, receive only a disorderly kind of education, seldom attend to with that degree of exactness that men, who from their infancy are broken into method, observe. This negligent kind of guesswork, for what other epithet can be used to point out the random exertions of a sort of instinctive common sense, never brought to the test of reason? prevents their generalizing matters of fact—so they do to-day, what they did yesterday, merely because they did it yesterday.

This contempt of the understanding in early life has more baneful consequences that is commonly supposed; for the little knowledge which women of strong minds attain, is, from various circumstances, of a more desultory kind than the knowledge of men, and it is acquired more by sheer observations on real life, than from comparing what has been individually observed with the results of experience generalized by speculation. Led by their dependent situation and domestic employments more into society, what they learn is rather by snatches; and as learning is with them, in general, only a secondary thing, they do not pursue any one branch with that persevering ardour necessary to give vigour to the faculties, and clearness to the judgment. In the present state of society, a little learning is required to support the character of a gentleman; and boys are obliged to submit to a few years of discipline. But in the education of women, the cultivation of the understanding is always subordinate to the acquirement of some corporeal accomplishment; even while enervated by confinement and false notions of modesty, the body is prevented from attaining that grace and beauty which relaxed half-formed limbs never exhibit. Besides, in youth their faculties are not brought forward by emulation; and having no serious scientific study, if they have natural sagacity it is turned too soon on life and manners. . . .

Strengthen the female mind by enlarging it, and there will be an end to blind obedience; but, as blind obedience is ever sought for by power, tyrants and sensualists are in the right when they endeavour to keep women in the dark, because the former only want slaves, and the latter a play-thing. The sensualist, indeed, has been the most dangerous of tyrants, and women have been duped by their lovers, as princes by their ministers, whilst dreaming that they reigned over them. . . .

It appears to me necessary to dwell on these obvious truths, because females have been insulated, as it were; and, while they have been stripped of the virtues that should clothe humanity, they have been decked with artificial graces that enable them to exercise a short-lived tyranny. Love, in their bosoms, taking place of every nobler passion, their sole ambition is to be fair, to raise emotion instead of inspiring respect; and this ignoble desire, like the servility in absolute monarchies, destroys all strength of character. Liberty is the mother of virtue, and if women be, by their very constitution, slaves, and not allowed to breathe the sharp invigorating air of freedom, they must ever languish like exotics, and be reckoned beautiful flaws in nature. . . . **200**

Make [women] free, and they will quickly become wise and virtuous, as men become more so; for the improvements must be mutual, or the injustice which one half of the human race are obliged to submit to, retorting on their oppressors, the **210** virtue of men will be worm-eaten by the insects whom he keeps under his feet.

Let men take their choice, man and woman were made for each other, though not to become one being; and if they will not improve women, they will deprave them!

. . . .

The Journalistic Essay and the Birth of the Modern Novel

As the writings of Condorcet and Wollstonecraft suggest, social criticism assumed an important place in Enlightenment literature. Such criticism now also manifested itself in a new literary genre known as the journalistic essay. Designed to address the middle-class reading public, prose essays and editorials were the stuff of magazines and daily newspapers. The first daily emerged in London during the eighteenth century, although a weekly had been published since 1642. At this time, London, with a population of some three-quarters of a million people, was the largest European city. With the rise of newspapers and periodicals, the "poetic" prose of the seventeenth century—characterized by long sentences and magisterial phrases (see Bacon's *Of Studies*, Reading 4.11)—gave way to a more informal prose style, one that reflected the conversational chatter of the *salons* and the cafés. Journalistic essays brought "philosophy out of the closets and libraries, schools and colleges, to dwell in clubs and assemblies, at tea-tables and in coffee houses," explained Joseph Addison (1672–1719), the leading British prose stylist of his day. In collaboration with his lifelong friend, Richard Steele (1672–1729), Addison published two London periodicals, the *Tatler* and the *Spectator*, which featured penetrating commentaries on current events and social behavior. The *Spectator* had a circulation of some twenty-five thousand readers. Anticipating modern news magazines, eighteenth-century broadsheets and periodicals offered the literate public timely reports and diverse opinions on all aspects of popular culture. They provided entertainment as they also helped to shape popular opinion and cultivate an urban chauvinism best expressed by the English pundit, Samuel Johnson (1709–1784): "When a man is tired of London, he is tired of life: for there is in London all that life can afford."

The most important new form of eighteenth-century literary entertainment, however, was the novel. The novel first appeared in world literature in China and Japan (see chapters 14 and 21). The most famous of the early Japanese novels, *The Tale of Genji*, was written by an unknown eleventh-century author known as Lady Shikibu Murasaki. In China, where the history of the novel reached back to the twelfth century, prose tales of travel, love, and adventure were popular sources for operas and plays. Neither Japanese nor Chinese prose fiction had any direct influence on Western writers. Nevertheless, the vernacular novel became a popular form of social entertainment in both East Asia and the West during the eighteenth century. In both East and West, the rise of the novel occurred at a moment of increasing urbanization. Its popularity reflected the demands of a larger reading public, although, in China, literacy was still confined to the educated elite—only ten percent of Chinese women, for instance, could read and write.

The modern novel made its appearance in England at the beginning of the eighteenth century with the publication of the popular adventure story *Robinson Crusoe* (1719), by Daniel Defoe (1660–1731). Defoe's novel, based on actual experience, was sharply realistic and thus quite different from the fantasy-laden prose of his sixteenth-century predecessors, Cervantes and Rabelais (see chapter 19). The novels of Defoe and his somewhat later contemporaries Samuel Richardson (1689–1761) and Henry Fielding (1707–1754) featured graphic accounts of the personalities and daily lives of the lower and middle classes. With an exuberance reminiscent of Chaucer, these prose narratives brought to life tales of criminals, pirates, and prostitutes. Not surprisingly, such novels appealed to the tastes of the same individuals who enjoyed the spicy realism and journalistic prose of contemporary broadsheets.

Pope: Poet of the Age of Reason

If any single poet typified the spirit of the Enlightenment, it was surely Alexander Pope (1688–1744), the greatest English poet of the eighteenth century. Pope, a semi-invalid from the age of twelve, was a great admirer of Newton and a champion of the scientific method. He was also a staunch neoclassicist who devotedly revived the wit and polish of the Golden-Age Roman poets Virgil and Horace. Largely self-taught (in his time Roman Catholics were barred from attending English universities), Pope defended the value of education in Greek and Latin, and his own love of the classics inspired him to produce new translations of Homer's *Iliad* and *Odyssey*. "A *little learning* is a dangerous thing," warned Pope in pleading for a broader and more thorough survey of the past.

Pope's poems are as controlled and refined as a Poussin painting or a Bach fugue. His epigrammatic verses, written in **heroic couplets**, ring with concentrated brilliance. Pope's choice of the heroic couplet for most of his numerous satires, as well as for his translations of Homer, reflects his commitment to the qualities of balance and order; and his mastery of the polished two-rhymed line bears out his claim that "True ease in writing comes from art, not chance,/As those move easiest who have learned to dance."

Pope's most famous poem was his *Essay on Man*. Like Milton's *Paradise Lost*, but on a smaller scale, the *Essay* tried to explain humankind's place in the universal scheme. But whereas Milton had explained evil in terms of human will, Pope—a Catholic turned deist—asserted that evil was simply part of God's design for the universe, a universe that Pope described as "A mighty maze! but not without a plan." According to Pope (and to Leibniz, whom he admired), whatever occurs in nature has been "programmed" by God and is part of God's benign and rational order. Pope lacked the reforming zeal of the *philosophes*, but he caught the optimism of the Enlightenment in a single statement: "Whatever is, is right." In the *Essay on Man*, Pope warns that we must not presume to understand the whole of nature. Nor should we aspire to a higher place in the great "chain of being." Rather, he counsels the reader, "Know then thyself, presume not God to scan;/The proper study of Mankind is Man."

READING 4.21 From Pope's *Essay on Man* (1773–1774)

Epistle I

. . . .

IX What if the foot, ordain'd the dust to tread, 1
Or hand, to toil, aspir'd to be the head?
What if the head, the eye, or ear repin'd[1]
To serve mere engines to the ruling Mind?
Just as absurd for any part to claim
To be another, in his gen'ral frame:
Just as absurd, to mourn the tasks or pains.
The great directing Mind of All ordains.

All are but parts of one stupendous whole,
Whose body Nature is, and God the soul; 10
That, chang'd thro' all, and yet in all the same;
Great in the earth, as in th' ethereal frame;
Warms in the sun, refreshes in the breeze,
Glows in the stars, and blossoms in the trees,
Lives thro' all life, extends thro' all extent,
Spreads undivided, operates unspent;
Breathes in our soul, informs our mortal part,
As full, as perfect, in a hair as heart:
As full, as perfect, in vile Man that mourns,
As the rapt Seraph[2] that adores and burns: 20
To him no high, no low, no great, no small;
He fills, he bounds, connects, and equals all.

X Cease then, nor Order Imperfection name:
Our proper bliss depends on what we blame.
Know thy own point: This kind, this due degree
Of blindness, weakness, Heav'n bestows on thee.

_____
[1]Complained
[2]A member of the highest order of angels.

Submit—In this, or any other sphere,
Secure to be as blest as thou canst bear:
Safe in the hand of one disposing Pow'r,
Or in the natal, or the mortal hour. 30
All Nature is but Art,[3] unknown to thee;
All Chance, Direction, which thou canst not see;
All Discord, Harmony not understood;
All partial Evil, universal Good:
And, spite of Pride, in erring Reason's spite,
One truth is clear, WHATEVER IS, IS RIGHT.

Epistle II

I Know then thyself, presume not God to scan;[4]
The proper study of Mankind is Man.
Plac'd on this isthmus of a middle state,[5]
A Being darkly wise, and rudely great: 40
With too much knowledge for the Sceptic side,
With too much weakness for the Stoic's pride,
He hangs between; in doubt to act, or rest;
In doubt to deem himself a God, or Beast;
In doubt his Mind or Body to prefer,
Born but to die, and reas'ning but to err;
Alike in ignorance, his reason such.
Whether he thinks too little, or too much:
Chaos of Thought and Passion, all confus'd;
Still by himelf abus'd, or disabus'd; 50
Created half to rise, and half to fall;[6]
Great lord of all things, yet a prey to all;
Sole judge of Truth, in endless Error hurl'd:[7]
The glory, jest, and riddle of the world!

. . . .

SUMMARY

The Age of the European Enlightenment marks the beginning of the Western notion of social progress and human perfectibility. In political thought, Thomas Hobbes and John Locke advanced the idea of government based on a social contract between ruler and ruled. While Hobbes envisioned this contract as a bond between individuals who surrendered some portion of their freedom to a sovereign authority, Locke saw government as an agent of the people—bound to exercise the will of the majority. According to Locke, government must operate according to the consent of the governed.

Locke's writings provided the intellectual foundation for the Enlightenment faith in reason as the sure guide to social progress. Jefferson, Montesquieu, and Adam Smith adapted Locke's views on natural law to political and

_____
[3]Compare Hobbes: "Nature is the art whereby God governs the world."
[4]Investigate.
[5] Between the angels (above) and the animal kingdom (below). Compare Pico della Mirandola's view of human beings as creatures who partake of both earthly and celestial qualities and can therefore ascend or descend the great "chain of being" (chapter 16).
[6]See note 5.
[7]Cast back and forth.

economic life. The idea that human beings, free from the bonds of ignorance and superstition and operating according to the principles of reason, might achieve the good life here on earth inspired the philosophic optimism of Leibniz in Germany, the progressive theories of Beccaria in Italy and Condorcet in France, and the eloquent defense of womankind by Wollstonecraft in England.

The prime symbol of the Enlightenment zeal for knowledge was the *Encyclopédie*, produced by Diderot with the assistance of the *philosophes*. A similar zeal for the ordering of socially useful information inspired the writing of dictionaries, biographies, and histories. The journalistic essay and the early modern novel entertained the new reading public, just as they offered an intimate examination of everyday, secular life. And in poetry, the elegant verbal tapestries of Alexander Pope optimistically pictured human beings as the enlightened inhabitants of an orderly and harmonious universe.

The promise of reason and the gospel of progress—two fundamental ideas of the Enlightenment—have shaped the course of modern Western culture. Imported to America during the eighteenth century, they became the informing ideals of a new order of society. They served a "cult of utility," which promoted the idea that rational thought and its application in science and technology would advance and improve the quality of life for all members of society. More recently, the promise of reason and the gospel of progress have worked to challenge tyranny and injustice in many other parts of the world, including Africa and Asia—a sign of the durability of Enlightenment thought within the humanistic tradition.

SUGGESTIONS FOR READING

Becker, Carl L. *The Heavenly City of the Eighteenth-Century Philosophers.* New Haven: Yale University Press, 1959.

Gay, Peter. *The Enlightenment: An Interpretation.* 2 vols. New York: Norton, 1977.

Goodman, Dana. *The Republic of Letters: A Cultural History of the French Enlightenment.* Ithaca: Cornell University Press, 1996.

Havens, George R. *The Age of Ideas.* New York: Henry Holt, 1955.

Krieger, Leonard. *Kings and Philosophies 1689–1789.* Vol. 3 of *The Norton History of Modern Europe.* New York: Norton, 1970.

Outram, Dovinda. *The Enlightenment.* New York: Cambridge University Press, 1995.

Porter, Roy. *The Creation of the Modern World: The British Enlightenment.* New York: W. W. Norton, 2000.

Richard, Carl J. *The Founders and the Classics: Greece, Rome, and the American Enlightenment.* Cambridge, Mass.: Harvard University Press, 1994.

Vyverberg, Henry. *Human Nature, Cultural Diversity, and the French Enlightenment.* New York: Oxford University Press, 1989.

Watt, Ian. *The Rise of the Novel: Studies in Defoe, Richardson, and Fielding.* Berkeley, Calif.: University of California Press, 1957.

GLOSSARY

heroic couplet a pair of rhymed iambic pentameter lines that reach completion in structure and in sense at the end of the second line

laissez-faire (French, "allow to act") a general policy of noninterference in the economy, defended by such classical economists as Adam Smith

philosophes (French, "philosophers") the intellectuals of the European Enlightenment

social contract an agreement made between citizens leading to the establishment of the state

CHAPTER TWENTY-FIVE

The limits of reason

"'What does it matter,' said the dervish, 'whether there be good or evil [in the world]?'"
Voltaire

Even that most enthusiastic optimist, Alexander Pope, acknowledged in his *Essay on Man* that human beings were "Born but to die and reas'ning but to err"—that is, that people were finite and fallible. Pope and other eighteenth-century champions of reason were, in fact, ambivalent: While generally committed to the belief in human perfectibility and the rational potential of humankind, they observed that people often acted in ways that were wholly irrational. Reason was all too frequently ignored or abandoned altogether. Moreover, the critical exercise of reason, when taken to an extreme, often deteriorated into bitter skepticism and cynicism.

Perhaps the greatest obstacle to the belief in the promise of reason lay, however, in the hard realities of everyday life. In eighteenth-century Europe, where Enlightenment intellectuals were exalting the ideals of human progress, there was clear evidence of human ignorance, depravity, and despair. Upon visiting the much-acclaimed city of Paris, Jean-Jacques Rousseau lamented its "dirty, stinking streets, filthy black houses, an air of slovenliness" and alleys filled with beggars. Indeed, outside the elegant drawing rooms of Paris and London lay clear signs of poverty, violence, and degradation. Science and technology spawned a new barbarism in the form of machines that were as potentially destructive as they were beneficial. In England, the invention of the "flying shuttle" (1733), the "spinning jenny" (1765), and the power loom (1785)—machines for the manufacture of textile goods—encouraged the rise of the factory system and sparked the Industrial Revolution. James Watt's steam engine (1775) provided a new power source for textiles and other industries. But such technological achievements, allied with unregulated capitalism, gave rise to dangerous working conditions and the exploitation of labor. In many of London's factories, children tended the new machines for twelve- to fourteen-hour shifts, following which they were boarded in shabby barracks. And in the mines of Cornwall and Durham, women and children were paid a pittance to labor like animals, pulling carts laden with coal. Some miners worked such long hours that they never saw the light of day.

The Transatlantic Slave Trade

In human terms, however, the most glaring evidence of the failure of the Enlightenment to achieve immediate social reforms was the perpetuation of the slave trade, which, despite the condemnation of many of the *philosophes*, flourished until the mid-nineteenth century. Begun by the Portuguese in the fifteenth century (see chapter 18), the transatlantic slave trade, by which millions of Africans were bought and shipped against their will to colonies in the "New World," reached its peak in the eighteenth century. As England—lured by the lucrative sugar trade—became the leading player in the transatlantic traffic, some six to seven million slaves were transported to work on sugar plantations in the West Indies and elsewhere in the Americas. To feed this market, Africans, including African children, were frequently kidnapped by unscrupulous natives who profited handsomely by selling their captives to white slave traders. The fate of the African slave who survived the perilous "Middle Passage" between Africa and the Americas—it is estimated that roughly one-third perished in transit—was a life of unspeakable suffering (Figure **25.1**).

A first-hand account of this inhumane system is central to the autobiographical narrative of Olaudah Equiano (1745–1797), who was born in the West African kingdom of Benin and kidnapped and enslaved at the age of eleven. Both as a slave and after his release from slavery in 1766, Equiano traveled widely; during his stay in England (as one of only thirty thousand blacks in mid-eighteenth-century England), he mastered the English language and became an outspoken abolitionist (Figure **25.2**). The following excerpt from Equiano's autobiographic narrative recounts with dramatic simplicity the traumatic experience of an eleven-year-old child who was rudely sold into bondage.

READING 4.22 From Equiano's *Travels* (1789)

That part of Africa known by the name of Guinea to which the trade for slaves is carried on extends along the coast above 3,400 miles, from the Senegal to Angola, and includes a variety of kingdoms. Of these the most considerable is the kingdom of Benin, both as to extent and wealth, the richness and cultivation of the soil, the power of its king, and the number and warlike disposition of the inhabitants. . . . This kingdom is divided into many provinces or districts, in one of the most remote and fertile of which, called Eboe, I was born in the year 1745, situated in a charming fruitful vale, named Essaka. The distance of this province from the capital of Benin and the sea coast must be very considerable, for I had never heard of white men or Europeans, nor of the sea, and our subjection to the king of Benin was little more than nominal; for every transaction of the government, as far as my slender observation extended, was conducted by the chiefs or elders of the place. . . .

My father, besides many slaves, had a numerous family of which seven lived to grow up, including myself and a sister who was the only daughter. As I was the youngest of the sons I became, of course, the greatest favourite with my mother and was always with her; and she used to take particular pains to form my mind. I was trained up from my earliest years in the art of war, my daily exercise was shooting and throwing javelins, and my mother adorned me with emblems[1] after the manner of

—————
[1]Body decorations, such as scarification

our greatest warriors. In this way I grew up till I was turned the age of 11, when an end was put to my happiness in the following manner. Generally when the grown people in the neighbourhood were gone far in the fields to labour, the children assembled together in some of the neighbours' premises to play, and commonly some of us used to get up a tree to look out for any assailant or kidnapper that might come upon us, for they sometimes took those opportunities of our parents' absence to attack and carry off as many as they could seize. One day, as I was watching at the top of a tree in our yard, I saw one of those people come into the yard of our next neighbour but one to kidnap, there being many stout young people in it. Immediately on this I gave the alarm of the rogue and he was surrounded by the stoutest of them, who entangled him with cords so that he could not escape till some of the grown people came and secured him. But alas! ere long it was my fate to be thus attacked and to be carried off when none of the grown people were nigh. One day, when all our people were gone out to their works as usual and only I and my dear sister were left to mind the house, two men and a woman got over our walls, and in a moment seized us both, and without giving us time to cry out or make resistance they stopped our mouths and ran off with us into the nearest wood. Here they tied our hands and continued to carry us as far as they could till night came on, when we reached a small house where the robbers halted for refreshment and spent the night. We were then unbound but were unable to take any food, and being quite overpowered by fatigue and grief, our only relief was some sleep, which allayed our misfortune for a short time. The next morning we left the house and continued travelling all the day.

Figure 25.1 **JOHANN MORITZ RUGENDAS**, *The Hold of a Slave Ship*, 1827, from J. M. Rugendas, *Voyage pittoresque dans le Brésil*, 1827–1835. Lithograph, 6 × 10 in.

For a long time we had kept to the woods, but at last we came into a road which I believed I knew. I had now some hopes of being delivered, for we had advanced but a little way before I discovered some people at a distance, on which I began to cry out for their assistance: but my cries had no other effect than to make them tie me faster and stop my mouth, and then they put me into a large sack. They also stopped my sister's mouth and tied her hands, and in this manner we proceeded till we were out of the sight of these people. . . . It was in vain that we besought them not to part us; she was torn from me and immediately carried away, while I was left in a state of distraction not to be described. I cried and grieved continually, and for several days I did not eat anything but what they forced into my mouth. At length, after many days' travelling, during which I had often changed masters, I got into the hands of a chieftain in a very pleasant country. . . . 70

[Equiano describes his tenure with African masters; he is sold a number of times (during a period of six to seven months) before he is taken to the sea coast.]

The first object which saluted my eyes when I arrived on the coast was the sea, and a slave ship which was then riding at anchor and waiting for its cargo. These filled me with astonishment, which was soon converted into terror when I was carried on board. I was immediately handled and tossed up to see if I were sound by some of the crew, and I was now persuaded that I had gotten into a world of bad spirits and that they were going to kill me. Their complexions too differing so much from ours, their long hair and the language they spoke (which was very different from any I had ever heard) united to confirm me in this belief. Indeed such were the horrors of my views and fears at the moment that, if ten thousand worlds had been my own, I would have freely parted with them all to have exchanged my condition with that of the meanest slave in my own country. When I looked round the ship too and saw a large furnace or copper boiling and a multitude of black people of every description chained together, every one of their countenances expressing dejection and sorrow, I no longer doubted of my fate; and quite overpowered with horror and anguish, I fell motionless on the deck and fainted. When I 90 recovered a little I found some black people about me, who I believed were some of those who had brought me on board and had been receiving their pay; they talked to me in order to cheer me, but all in vain. I asked them if we were not to be eaten by those white men with horrible looks, red faces, and loose hair. They told me I was not, and one of the crew brought me a small portion of spirituous liquor in a wine glass, but being afraid of him I would not take it out of his hand. One of the blacks therefore took it from him and gave it to me, and I took a little down my palate, which instead of reviving me, as they thought 100 it would, threw me into the greatest consternation at the strange feeling it produced, having never tasted any such liquor before. Soon after this the blacks who brought me on board went off, and left me abandoned to despair.

I now saw myself deprived of all chance of returning to my native country or even the least glimpse of hope of gaining the shore, which I now considered as friendly; and I even wished for my former slavery in preference to my present situation, which was filled with horrors of every kind, still heightened by my

ignorance of what I was to undergo. I was not long suffered to 110 indulge my grief; I was soon put down under the decks, and there I received such a salutation in my nostrils as I had never experienced in my life: so that with the loathsomeness of the stench and crying together, I became so sick and low that I was not able to eat, nor had I the least desire to taste anything. I now wished for the last friend, death, to relieve me; but soon, to my grief, two of the white men offered me eatables, and on my refusing to eat, one of them held me fast by the hands and laid me across I think the windlass,[2] and tied my feet while the other flogged me severely. I had never experienced anything of 120 this kind before, and although, not being used to the water, I naturally feared that element the first time I saw it, yet nevertheless could I have got over the nettings I would have jumped over the side, but I could not; and besides, the crew used to watch us very closely who were not chained down to the decks, lest we should leap into the water: and I have seen some of these poor African prisoners most severely cut for attempting to do so, and hourly whipped for not eating. This indeed was often the case with myself. In a little time after, amongst the poor chained men I found some of my own nation,[3] 130 which in a small degree gave ease to my mind. I inquired of these what was to be done with us; they gave me to understand we were to be carried to these white people's country to work for them. I then was a little revived, and thought if it were no worse than working, my situation was not so desperate: but still I feared I should be put to death, the white people looked and acted, as I thought, in so savage a manner; for I had never seen among my people such instances of brutal cruelty, and this not only shewn towards us blacks but also to some of the whites themselves. One white man in particular I saw, when we were 140 permitted to be on deck, flogged so unmercifully with a large rope near the foremast that he died in consequence of it; and they tossed him over the side as they would have done a brute. This made me fear these people the more, and I expected nothing less than to be treated in the same manner. I could not help expressing my fears and apprehensions to some of my countrymen: I asked them if these people had no country but lived in this hollow place (the ship): they told me they did not, but came from a distant one. "Then," said I, "how comes it in all our country we never heard of them?" They told me because 150 they lived so very far off. I then asked where were their women? had they any like themselves? I was told they had: "and why," said I, "do we not see them?" They answered, because they were left behind. . . . The stench of the hold while we were on the coast was so intolerably loathsome that it was dangerous to remain there for any time, and some of us had been permitted to stay on the deck for the fresh air; but now that the whole ship's cargo were confined together it became absolutely pestilential. The closeness of the place and the heat of the climate, added to the number in the ship, which was so 160 crowded that each had scarcely room to turn himself, almost suffocated us. This produced copious perspirations, so that the air soon became unfit for respiration from a variety of loathsome smells, and brought on a sickness among the slaves, of which many died, thus falling victims to the improvident

---

[2]The device that works the ship's anchor.
[3]Ethnic group.

avarice, as I may call it, of their purchasers. This wretched situation was again aggravated by the galling of the chains, now become insupportable, and the filth of the necessary tubs, into which the children often fell and were almost suffocated. The shrieks of the women and the groans of the dying rendered the whole a scene of horror almost inconceivable. Happily perhaps for myself I was soon reduced so low here that it was thought necessary to keep me almost always on deck, and from my extreme youth I was not put in fetters. In this situation I expected every hour to share the fate of my companions, some of whom were almost daily brought upon deck at the point of death, which I began to hope would soon put an end to my miseries. Often did I think many of the inhabitants of the deep much more happy than myself. I envied them the freedom they enjoyed, and as often wished I could change my condition for theirs. Every circumstance I met with served only to render my state more painful, and heighten my apprehensions and my opinion of the cruelty of the whites. One day they had taken a number of fishes, and when they had killed and satisfied themselves with as many as they thought fit, to our astonishment who were on the deck, rather than give any of them to us to eat as we expected, they tossed the remaining fish into the sea again, although we begged and prayed for some as well as we could, but in vain; and some of my countrymen, being pressed by hunger, took an opportunity when they thought no one saw them of trying to get a little privately; but they were discovered, and the attempt procured them some very severe floggings. One day, when we had a smooth sea and moderate wind, two of my wearied countrymen who were chained together (I was near them at the time), preferring death to such a life of misery, somehow made through the nettings and jumped into the sea: immediately another quite dejected fellow, who on account of his illness was suffered to be out of irons, also followed their example; and I believe many more would very soon have done the same if they had not been prevented by the ship's crew, who were instantly alarmed. Those of us that were the most active were in a moment put down under the deck, and there was such a noise and confusion amongst the people of the ship as I never heard before, to stop her and get the boat out to go after the slaves. However two of the wretches were drowned, but they got the other and afterwards flogged him unmercifully for thus attempting to prefer death to slavery. In this manner we continued to undergo more hardships than I can now relate, hardships which are inseparable from this accursed trade. . . . At last we came in sight of the island of Barbados, at which the whites on board gave a great shout and made many signs of joy to us. We did not know what to think of this, but as the vessel drew nearer we plainly saw the harbour and other ships of different kinds and sizes, and we soon anchored amongst them off Bridgetown. Many merchants and planters now came on board, though it was in the evening. They put us in separate parcels[4] and examined us attentively. They also made us jump,[5] and pointed to the land, signifying we were to go there. We thought by this we should be eaten by these ugly men, as they appeared to us; and when soon after we were all put down under the deck

170

180

190

200

210

220

---

[4]Groups.

[5]In order to determine whether they were healthy.

Figure 25.2 *Olaudah Equiano*, 1789. Engraving.

again, there was much dread and trembling among us, and nothing but bitter cries to be heard all the night from these apprehensions, insomuch that at last the white people got some old slaves from the land to pacify us. They told us we were not to be eaten but to work, and were soon to go on land where we should see many of our countrypeople. This report eased us much; and sure enough soon after we were landed there came to us Africans of all languages. We were conducted immediately to the merchant's yard, where we were all pent up together like so many sheep in a fold without regard to sex or age. . . . We were not many days in the merchant's custody before we were sold after their usual manner, which is this: On a signal given, (as the beat of a drum) the buyers rush at once into the yard where the slaves are confined, and make choice of that parcel they like best. The noise and clamour with which this is attended and the eagerness visible in the countenances of the buyers serve not a little to increase the apprehensions of the terrified Africans, who may well be supposed to consider them as the ministers of that destruction to which they think themselves devoted. In this manner, without scruple, are relations and friends separated, most of them never to see each other again. I remember in the vessel in which I was brought over, in the men's apartment there were several brothers who, in the sale, were sold in different lots; and it was very moving on this occasion to see and hear their cries at parting. O, ye nominal Christians! might not an African ask you, Learned you this from your God who says unto you, Do unto all men as you would men should do unto you? Is it not enough that we are torn from our country and friends to toil for your

230

240

250

luxury and lust of gain? Must every tender feeling be likewise sacrificed to your avarice? Are the dearest friends and relations, now rendered more dear by their separation from their kindred, still to be parted from each other and thus prevented from cheering the gloom of slavery with the small comfort of being together and mingling their sufferings and sorrows? Why are parents to lose their children, brothers their sisters, or husbands their wives? Surely this is a new refinement in cruelty which, while it has no advantage to atone for it, thus aggravates distress and adds fresh horrors even to the wretchedness of slavery. . . . **260**

As Equiano suggests, the "gloom of slavery" itself left slaves little opportunity for self-expression. It is therefore notable that one particular slave would become America's first black woman poet. Phillis Wheatley (1754?–1784) was kidnapped from Senegal and sold at auction in Boston at the age of seven. She was educated along with the children of her master, John Wheatley, and learned to read and write English, as well as Greek and Latin. Producing her first poem at the age of thirteen, Wheatley went on to publish a collection: *Poems on Various Subjects; Religious and Moral* (1773), which won acclaim in both America and Europe. John Wheatley emancipated Phillis in 1773, giving her the opportunity to travel to London and continue writing. The poem that follows, written in heroic couplets—the favorite meter of Chaucer and Pope—is a terse and eloquent appeal to the Christian promise of equality before God and the enlightenment promise of reason.

READING 4.23 Wheatley's "On Being Brought from Africa to America" (1772)

'TWAS mercy brought me from my *Pagan* land,
Taught my benighted soul to understand
That there's a God, that there's a *Saviour* too:
Once I redemption neither sought nor knew.
Some view our sable[1] race with scornful eye,
"Their colour is a diabolic die."
Remember, *Christians*, *Negros*, black as *Cain*,
May be refin'd, and join the' angelic train.

If slavery and industrialization in the West generated material conditions that were contrary to Enlightenment ideals, other factors served as serious obstacles to their realization. Ignorance, for example, the foundation for bias and (in many cases) unwitting prejudice, clouded the perceptions and judgments of some of the most educated *philosophes*. Diderot himself, who had no first-hand knowledge of the Moslem world, described Arabs (in his *Encyclopédie*) as "thievish and bellicose." Voltaire, who wrote a universal history that charted the customs of nations (including Russia and Africa), brought to his

[1]Black or dark brown.

analysis an anti-Church, anti-Semitic, and anti-black bias. And in America the leading Enlightenment thinker, Thomas Jefferson, believed Africans to be intellectually inferior, and he defended the institution of slavery as a "necessary evil." His perception of African–American slaves was colored by prejudices that are shocking to modern sensibilities. In his *Notes on the State of Virginia*, Jefferson wrote: "Comparing [blacks] by their faculties of memory, reason, and imagination, it appears to me that in memory they are equal to the whites; in reason much inferior . . . I advance it . . . as a suspicion only, that the blacks, whether originally a distinct race, or made distinct by time and circumstances, are inferior to the whites in the endowments both of body and mind . . . This unfortunate difference of color, and perhaps of faculty, is a powerful obstacle to the emancipation of these people."* In such opinions, shared by most of his fellow *philosophes*, Jefferson provided an implicit rationale for enslaving African people. Clearly, such thinkers were all too capable of finding rationalizations for policies in which political or social advantage for the privileged few overrode the abstract ideals of liberty and equality. Thus slavery persisted in the Western hemisphere (and elsewhere) for nearly a century beyond the Age of Enlightenment.

Satire: Weapon of the Enlightenment

The discrepancies between the sordid realities of eighteenth-century life and the progressive ideas of the Enlightenment provoked indignant protests, and none so potent as those couched in literary satire. The eighteenth century was history's greatest age of satire. The favorite weapon of many Enlightenment intellectuals, satire fused wit and irony to underscore human folly and error. The genre that had served Juvenal in imperial Rome (see chapter 6) and Erasmus in the age of the Reformation (see chapter 19) now became the favorite tool of social reformers, who drew attention to the vast contradictions between morals and manners, intentions and actions, and, more generally, between Enlightenment aspirations and contemporary injustice.

The Satires of Jonathan Swift

The premier British satirist of the eighteenth century was Jonathan Swift (1667–1745). Unlike the *philosophes*, this Dublin-born Anglican priest took a pessimistic view of human nature. He once confided (in a letter to the poet Alexander Pope) that he hated the human race, whose misuse of reason produced, in his view, an irredeemably corrupt society. Such negativism accompanied Swift's self-acclaimed "savage

*David A. Hollinger and Charles Capper, eds. *The American Intellectual Tradition: A Sourcebook: 1630–1865*, vol. 1 (New York, third edition, Oxford University Press, 1997), 177.

indignation." Yet, Swift was not a man of despair, for no despairing personality could have produced such a profoundly moralizing body of literature. In 1726, Swift published his most famous work, *Gulliver's Travels*. At the simplest level, *Gulliver's Travels* is a story of travel and adventure that (somewhat like Equiano's true-to-life travels) describes the fortunes of a hero in imaginary lands peopled with midgets, giants, and other fabulous creatures. At a second, symbolic level, however, it is a social statement on the vagaries of human behavior. In one chapter, Gulliver visits the Lilliputians, "little people" whose moral pettiness and inhumanity seem to characterize humankind at its worst; in another, he meets noble horses whose rational behavior contrasts with the bestiality of their human-looking slaves, the Yahoos. An immediate popular sensation, *Gulliver's Travels* has become a landmark in fantasy literature and social satire.

Swift also wrote many pamphlets and letters protesting social and political ills. Among the most famous is an essay publicizing the wretched condition of the Irish peasants, who were exploited unmercifully by the British government. In his satirical treatise *A Modest Proposal*, Swift observed that many Irish peasants were too poor to feed their families; he proposed with deadpan frankness that Irish children should be bred and butchered for the English dining table, thus providing income for the poor and alleviating the miseries of all. While *Gulliver's Travels* attacks conditions that are universal and timeless, *A Modest Proposal* mocks a specific crisis of Swift's own time.

READING 4.24 From Swift's *A Modest Proposal* (1729)

for Preventing the Children of Poor People in Ireland from Being a Burden to Their Parents or Country, and for Making Them Beneficial to the Public

It is a melancholy object to those who walk through this great town,[1] or travel in the country, when they see the streets, the roads, and cabin-doors, crowded with beggars of the female sex, followed by three, four, or six children, all in rags, and importuning every passenger for an alms.[2] These mothers, instead of being able to work for their honest livelihood, are forced to employ all their time in strolling to beg sustenance for their helpless infants: who, as they grow up, either turn thieves for want of work, or leave their dear native country to fight . . . in Spain, or sell themselves to the Barbadoes.[3]

I think it is agreed by all parties, that this prodigious number of children in the arms, or on the backs, or at the heels of their mothers, and frequently of their fathers, is, in the present deplorable state of the kingdom, a very great additional grievance; and, therefore, whoever could find out a fair, cheap, and easy method of making these children sound, useful members of the commonwealth, would deserve so well of the public, as to have his statue set up for a preserver of the nation.

But my intention is very far from being confined to provide only for the children of professed beggars; it is of a much greater extent, and shall take in the whole number of infants at a certain age, who are born of parents in effect as little able to support them, as those who demand our charity in the streets.

As to my own part, having turned my thoughts for many years upon this important subject, and maturely weighed the several schemes of our projectors,[4] I have always found them grossly mistaken in their computation. It is true, a child, just born, may be supported by its mother's milk for a solar year, with little other nourishment; at most, not above the value of two shillings, which the mother may certainly get, or the value in scraps, by her lawful occupation of begging; and it is exactly at one year old that I propose to provide for them in such a manner, as, instead of being a charge upon their parents, or the parish, or wanting food and raiment[5] for the rest of their lives, they shall, on the contrary, contribute to the feeding, and partly to the clothing, of many thousands.

There is likewise another great advantage in my scheme, that it will prevent those voluntary abortions, and that horrid practice of women murdering their bastard children, alas, too frequent among us! sacrificing the poor innocent babes, I doubt more to avoid the expense than the shame, which would move tears and pity in the most savage and inhuman breast.

The number of souls in this kingdom being usually reckoned one million and a half, of these I calculate there may be about two hundred thousand couple whose wives are breeders; from which number I subtract thirty thousand couple, who are able to maintain their own children (although I apprehend there cannot be so many, under the present distresses of the kingdom); but this being granted, there will remain a hundred and seventy thousand breeders. I again subtract fifty thousand, for those women who miscarry, or whose children die by accident or disease within the year. There only remain a hundred and twenty thousand children of poor parents annually born. The question therefore is, How this number shall be reared and provided for? which, as I have already said, under the present situation of affairs, is utterly impossible by all the methods hitherto proposed. For we can neither employ them in handicraft or agriculture; we neither build houses (I mean in the country), nor cultivate land: they can very seldom pick up a livelihood by stealing, till they arrive at six years old, except where they are of towardly[6] parts; although I confess they learn the rudiments[7] much earlier. . . .

I am assured by our merchants, that a boy or a girl before twelve years old is no saleable commodity; and even when they come to this age they will not yield above three pounds or three pounds and half-a-crown at most, on the exchange; which cannot turn to account either to the parents or kingdom, the charge of nutriment and rags having been at least four times that value.

I shall now, therefore, humbly propose my own thoughts, which I hope will not be liable to the least objection.

[1]Dublin.
[2]Charity.
[3]As slaves in the West Indies.
[4]Speculators.
[5]Clothing.
[6]Handsome.
[7]Fundamentals; first principles.

I have been assured by a very knowing American of my acquaintance in London, that a young healthy child, well nursed, is, at a year old, a most delicious, nourishing, and wholesome food, whether stewed, roasted, baked, or boiled; and I make no doubt that it will equally serve in a fricassee or a ragout.

I do therefore humbly offer it to public consideration, that of the hundred and twenty thousand children already computed, twenty thousand may be reserved for breed, whereof only one-fourth part to be males; which is more than we allow to sheep, black-cattle, or swine; and my reason is, that these children are seldom the fruits of marriage, a circumstance not much regarded by our savages, therefore one male will be sufficient for four females. That the remaining hundred thousand may, at a year old, be offered in sale to the persons of quality and fortune through the kingdom; always advising the mother to let them suck[8] plentifully in the last month, so as to render them plump and fat for a good table. A child will make two dishes at an entertainment for friends; and when the family dines alone, the fore or hind quarter will make a reasonable dish, and, seasoned with a little pepper or salt, will be very good boiled on the fourth day, especially in winter.

I have reckoned, upon a medium,[9] that a child just born will weigh twelve pounds, and in a solar year, if tolerably nursed, will increase to twenty-eight pounds.

I grant this food will be somewhat dear, and therefore very proper for landlords, who, as they have already devoured most of the parents, seem to have the best title to the children.

Infants' flesh will be in season throughout the year, but more plentifully in March, and a little before and after: for we are told by a grave author,[10] an eminent French physician, that fish being a prolific diet, there are more children born in Roman Catholic countries about nine months after Lent, than at any other season; therefore, reckoning a year after Lent, the markets will be more glutted than usual, because the number of Popish infants is at least three to one in this kingdom; and therefore it will have one other collateral advantage, by lessening the number of Papists[11] among us.

I have already computed the charge of nursing a beggar's child (in which list I reckon all cottagers, labourers, and four-fifths of the farmers) to be about two shillings per annum, rags included; and I believe no gentleman would repine to give ten shillings for the carcass of a good fat child, which, as I have said, will make four dishes of excellent nutritive meat, when he has only some particular friend, or his own family, to dine with him. Thus the squire will learn to be a good landlord, and grow popular among his tenants; the mother will have eight shillings net profit, and be fit for work till she produces another child.

Those who are more thrifty (as I must confess the times require) may flay the carcass; the skin of which, artificially dressed, will make admirable gloves for ladies, and summer-boots for fine gentlemen. As to our city of Dublin, shambles[12] may be appointed for this purpose in the most convenient parts of it, and butchers we may be assured will not be wanting;

although I rather recommend buying the children alive, then dressing them hot from the knife, as we do roasting pigs.

A very worthy person, a true lover of his country, and whose virtues I highly esteem, was lately pleased, in discoursing on this matter, to offer a refinement upon my scheme. He said that many gentlemen of this kingdom, having of late destroyed their deer, he conceived that the want of venison might be well supplied by the bodies of young lads and maidens, not exceeding fourteen years of age, nor under twelve; so great a number of both sexes in every country being now ready to starve for want of work and service; and these to be disposed of by their parents, if alive, or otherwise by their nearest relations. But, with due deference to so excellent a friend, and so deserving a patriot, I cannot be altogether in his sentiments; for as to the males, my American acquaintance assured me, from frequent experience, that their flesh was generally tough and lean, like that of our schoolboys, by continual exercise, and their taste disagreeable; and to fatten them would not answer the charge. Then as to the females, it would, I think, with humble submission, be a loss to the public, because they soon would become breeders themselves: and besides, it is not improbable that some scrupulous people might be apt to censure such a practice (although indeed very unjustly), as a little bordering upon cruelty; which, I confess, has always been with me the strongest objection against any project, how well soever intended. . . .

I think the advantages by the proposal which I have made are obvious and many, as well as of the highest importance.

For first, as I have already observed, it would greatly lessen the number of Papists, with whom we are yearly over-run, being the principal breeders of the nation, as well as our most dangerous enemies; and who stay at home on purpose to deliver the kingdom to the Pretender, hoping to take their advantage by the absence of so many good Protestants, who have chosen rather to leave their country, than stay at home and pay tithes against their conscience to an Episcopal curate.

Secondly, The poorer tenants will have something valuable of their own, which by law may be made liable to distress, and help to pay their landlord's rent; their corn and cattle being already seized, and money a thing unknown.

Thirdly, Whereas the maintenance of a hundred thousand children, from two years old and upward, cannot be computed at less than ten shillings a piece per annum, the nation's stock will be thereby increased fifty thousand pounds per annum, beside the profit of a new dish introduced to the tables of all gentlemen of fortune in the kingdom, who have any refinement in taste. And the money will circulate among ourselves, the goods being entirely of our own growth and manufacture.

Fourthly, The constant breeders, beside the gain of eight shillings sterling per annum by the sale of their children, will be rid of the charge of maintaining them after the first year.

Fifthly, This food would likewise bring great custom to taverns; where the vintners will certainly be so prudent as to procure the best receipts for dressing it to perfection, and, consequently, have their houses frequented by all the fine gentlemen, who justly value themselves upon their knowledge in good eating: and a skilful cook, who understands how to oblige his guests, will contrive to make it as expensive as they please.

---

[8]To nurse at the breast.
[9]On an average.
[10]François Rabelais (see chapter 18).
[11]Roman Catholics, especially those who ardently support the pope.
[12]Slaughterhouses.

Sixthly, This would be a great inducement to marriage, which all wise nations have either encouraged by rewards, or enforced by laws and penalties. It would increase the care and tenderness of mothers toward their children, when they were sure of a settlement for life to the poor babes, provided in some sort by the public, to their annual profit or expense. We should see an honest emulation among the married women, which of **190** them could bring the fattest child to the market. Men would become as fond of their wives during the time of their pregnancy, as they are now of their mares in foal, their cows in calf, their sows when they are ready to farrow; nor offer to beat or kick them (as is too frequent a practice) for fear of a miscarriage.

Many other advantages might be enumerated. For instance, the addition of some thousand carcasses in our exportation of barrelled beef; the propagation of swine's flesh, and improvement in the art of making good bacon, so much wanted **200** among us by the great destruction of pigs, too frequent at our table; which are no way comparable in taste or magnificence to a well-grown, fat, yearling child, which, roasted whole, will make a considerable figure at a lord mayor's feast, or any other public entertainment. But this, and many others, I omit, being studious of brevity.

Supposing that one thousand families in this city would be constant customers for infants' flesh, beside others who might have it at merry-meetings, particularly at weddings and christenings, I compute that Dublin would take off annually **210** about twenty thousand carcasses; and the rest of the kingdom (where probably they will be sold somewhat cheaper) the remaining eighty thousand.

I can think of no one objection, that will possibly be raised against this proposal, unless it should be urged, that the number of people will be thereby much lessened in the kingdom. This I freely own, and it was indeed one principal design in offering it to the world. I desire the reader will observe, that I calculate my remedy for this one individual kingdom of Ireland, and for no other that ever was, is, or I think **220** ever can be, upon earth. Therefore let no man talk to me of other expedients: of taxing our absentees at five shillings a pound: of using neither clothes, nor household-furniture, except what is our own growth and manufacture: of utterly rejecting the materials and instruments that promote foreign luxury: of curing the expensiveness of pride, vanity, idleness, and gaming in our women; of introducing a vein of parsimony, prudence, and temperance: of learning to love our country, in the want of which we differ even from Laplanders, and the inhabitants of Topinamboo: of quitting our animosities and **230** factions, nor acting any longer like the Jews, who were murdering one another at the very moment their city was taken: of being a little cautious not to sell our country and conscience for nothing: of teaching landlords to have at least one degree of mercy towards their tenants: lastly, of putting a spirit of honesty, industry, and skill into our shopkeepers; who, if a resolution could now be taken to buy only our native goods, would immediately unite to cheat and exact upon us in the price, the measure, and the goodness, nor could ever yet be brought to make one fair proposal of just dealing, though **240** often and earnestly invited to it. . . .

Figure 25.3 JEAN-ANTOINE HOUDON, *Voltaire in Old Age*, 1781. Marble, height 20 in. Musée de Versailles. © Corbis/Bettmann, London.

Voltaire and *Candide*

Swift's satires were an inspiration to that most scintillating of French *philosophes* and leading intellectual of French society, François Marie Arouet (1694–1778), who used the pen name Voltaire (Figure **25.3**). Born into a rising Parisian middle-class family and educated by Jesuits, Voltaire rose to fame as poet, playwright, critic, and as the central figure of the French *salons*. His historical and expository works attacked bigotry as manmade evil and injustice as institutional evil. On two separate occasions, his controversial verse-satires led to his imprisonment in the Bastille (the French state prison). His period of exile in England instilled in him high regard for constitutional government, the principles of toleration, and the concepts of equality found in the writings of John Locke—all of which ideas he championed in his writings.

More than any of the *philosophes*, Voltaire extolled the traditions of non-Western cultures, faiths, and moralities: Having read the works of Confucius in Jesuit translations, he esteemed the ancient teacher as a philosopher-sage. Voltaire was also the first modern intellectual to assess the role of Russia in world society. In his *Essay on Manners*, a universal history that examines the customs of nations around the world, Voltaire gave thoughtful attention to the history of the Russian state. His fascination with Russia as a curious blend of Asian and European traditions became the basis for a lifelong pursuit of things Russian, including a long correspondence with Catherine the Great, who ruled as Empress of Russia from 1762 to 1796.

Like most of the *philosophes*, Voltaire condemned organized religion and all forms of religious fanaticism. A declared deist, he compared human beings to mice, who, living in the recesses of an immense ship, had no cognizance of its captain or its destination. Any confidence Voltaire might have had in beneficent Providence was dashed by the terrible Lisbon earthquake and tidal wave of 1755, which took the lives of more than 20,000 people. For Voltaire, the realities of natural disaster and human cruelty were not easily reconciled with the belief that a good God created the universe or the idea that humans were by nature good—views basic to Enlightenment optimism. In the satirical tale *Candide* (subtitled *Optimism*), Voltaire addressed the age-old question of how evil could exist in a universe created and governed by the forces of good. More important, he leveled a major blow at the optimistic credo postulated by the German philosopher Gottfried Wilhelm Leibniz (see chapter 24) that this was "the best of all possible worlds." A parody of the adventure romances and travel tales (Equiano and Swift both come to mind) in vogue in Voltaire's time, *Candide* describes the exploits of a naive and unsophisticated young man whose blissful optimism is daunted by a series of terrible (and hilarious) experiences. Initially, the youthful Candide (literally, "candid" or "frank") approaches life with the glib optimism taught to him by Dr. Pangloss ("all tongue"), Voltaire's embodiment of Leibniz. But Candide soon discovers the folly of believing that "all is for the best in this best of all possible worlds." He experiences the horrors of war (the consequences of two equally self-righteous opposing armies), the evils of religious fanaticism (as manifested by the Spanish Inquisition), the disasters of nature (the Lisbon earthquake), and the dire effects of human greed (an affliction especially prevalent among the aristocracy and derived, according to Voltaire, from boredom). Experience becomes the antidote to the comfortable fatalism of Pope's "Whatever is, is right." After a lifetime of sobering misadventures, Candide ends his days settled on a farm (in Turkey) in the company of his long-lost friends. (Not coincidentally, the aging Voltaire penned *Candide* while living on his farm retreat just outside Geneva.) "We must cultivate our garden," he concludes. This metaphor for achieving personal satisfaction in a hostile world relieves the otherwise devastating skepticism that underlies *Candide*. It is Voltaire's answer to blind optimism and the foolish hope that human reason can allay evil.

Voltaire's genius, and the quality that separates his style from that of Goldsmith or Swift, is his penetrating wit. Like the marksman's sword, Voltaire's satire is sharply pointed, precise in its aim, and devastating in its effect. With a sure hand, Voltaire manipulates the principal satirical devices: irony, understatement, and overstatement. Using irony—the contradiction between literal and intended meanings—he mocks serious matters and deflates lofty pretensions; he calls war, for instance, "heroic butchery" and refers to Paquetta's venereal disease as a "present" she received from "a very learned Franciscan."

He exploits understatement when he notes, for example, that Pangloss "only lost one eye and one ear" (as the result of syphilis). And he uses overstatement for moral effect: The 350-pound baroness of Westphalia is "greatly respected"; thus corpulence—actually an indication of self-indulgence—becomes a specious sign of dignity and importance.

Voltaire's mock optimism, dispatched by Candide's persistent view that this is "the best of all possible worlds" even as he encounters repeated horrors, underscores the contradiction between the ideal and the real that lies at the heart of all satire. Although *Candide* was censored in many parts of Europe, the book was so popular that it went through forty editions in Voltaire's lifetime. A classic of Western satire, *Candide* has survived numerous adaptations, including a superb twentieth-century version as a comic-operetta with lyrics by the American poet Richard Wilber and music by the American composer Leonard Bernstein.* Approximately one-third of Voltaire's philosophical tale is included in the following excerpt.

READING 4.25 From Voltaire's *Candide* (1759)

Chapter 1

How Candide Was Brought Up in a Fine Castle, and How He Was Expelled From Thence

There lived in Westphalia,[1] in the castle of my Lord the Baron   1
of Thunder-ten-tronckh, a young man, on whom nature had
bestowed the most agreeable manners. His face was the index
to his mind. He had an upright heart, with an easy frankness;
which, I believe, was the reason he got the name of *Candide*.
He was suspected, by the old servants of the family, to be the
son of my Lord the Baron's sister, by a very honest gentleman
of the neighborhood, whom the young lady declined to marry,
because he could only produce seventy-one armorial
quarterings,[2] the rest of his genealogical tree having been   10
destroyed through the injuries of time.

The Baron was one of the most powerful lords in
Westphalia; his castle had both a gate and windows; and his
great hall was even adorned with tapestry. The dogs of his
outer yard composed his hunting pack upon occasion, his
grooms were his huntsmen, and the vicar of the parish was his
chief almoner. He was called My Lord by everybody, and
everyone laughed when he told his stories.

My Lady the Baroness, who weighed about three hundred
and fifty pounds, attracted, by that means, very great   20
attention, and did the honors of the house with a dignity that
rendered her still more respectable. Her daughter Cunegonde,
aged about seventeen years, was of a ruddy complexion, fresh,
plump, and well calculated to excite the passions. The Baron's
son appeared to be in every respect worthy of his father. The

---

*The 1985 New York City Opera House version is available on cassette and CD, New World label: NW–340/41.

[1]A province in Germany.
[2]Genealogical degrees of noble ancestry; since each quartering represents one generation, the family "tree" is over two thousand years old—an obvious impossibility.

preceptor, Pangloss,[3] was the oracle of the house, and little Candide listened to his lectures with all the simplicity that was suitable to his age and character.

Pangloss taught metaphysico-theologo-cosmoloonigology.[4] He proved most admirably, that there could not be an effect without cause; that, in this best of possible worlds,[5] my Lord the Baron's castle was the most magnificent of castles, and my Lady the best of Baronesses that possibly could be.

"It is demonstrable," said he, "that things cannot be otherwise than they are: for things having been made for some end, they must necessarily be for the best end. Observe well, that the nose has been made for carrying spectacles; therefore we have spectacles. The legs are visibly designed for stockings, and therefore we have stockings. Stones have been formed to be hewn, and make castles; therefore my Lord has a very fine castle; the greatest baron of the province ought to be the best accommodated. Swine were made to be eaten; therefore we eat pork all the year round: consequently, those who have merely asserted that all is good, have said a very foolish thing; they should have said all is the best possible."

Candide listened attentively, and believed implicitly; for he thought Miss Cunegonde extremely handsome, though he never had the courage to tell her so. He concluded, that next to the good fortune of being Baron of Thunder-ten-tronckh, the second degree of happiness was that of being Miss Cunegonde, the third to see her every day, and the fourth to listen to the teachings of Master Pangloss, the greatest philosopher of the province, and consequently of the whole world.

One day Cunegonde having taken a walk in the environs of the castle, in a little wood, which they called a park, espied Doctor Pangloss giving a lesson in experimental philosophy to her mother's chambermaid; a little brown wench, very handsome, and very docile. As Miss Cunegonde had a strong inclination for the sciences, she observed, without making any noise, the reiterated experiments that were going on before her eyes; she saw very clearly the sufficient reason of the Doctor, the effects and the causes; and she returned greatly flurried, quite pensive, and full of desire to be learned; imagining that she might be a sufficient reason for young Candide, who also, might be the same to her.

On her return to the castle, she met Candide, and blushed; Candide also blushed; she wished him good morrow with a faltering voice, and Candide answered her, hardly knowing what he said. The next day, after dinner, as they arose from table, Cunegonde and Candide happened to get behind the screen. Cunegonde dropped her handkerchief, and Candide picked it up; she, not thinking any harm, took hold of his hand; and the young man, not thinking any harm neither, kissed the hand of the young lady, with an eagerness, a sensibility, and grace, very particular; their lips met, their eyes sparkled, their knees trembled, their hands strayed.—The Baron of Thunder-ten-tronckh happening to pass close by the screen, and observing this cause and effect, thrust Candide out of the castle, with lusty kicks [to the behind]. Cunegonde fell into a swoon and as soon as she came to herself, was heartily cuffed on the ears by my Lady the Baroness. Thus all was thrown into confusion in the finest and most agreeable castle possible.

Chapter 2

What Became of Candide Among the Bulgarians[6]

Candide being expelled the terrestrial paradise, rambled a long while without knowing where, weeping, and lifting up his eyes to heaven, and sometimes turning them towards the finest of castles, which contained the handsomest of baronesses. He laid himself down, without his supper, in the open fields, between two furrows, while the snow fell in great flakes. Candide, almost frozen to death, crawled next morning to the neighboring village, which was called Waldber-ghoff-trarbk-dikdorff. Having no money, and almost dying with hunger and fatigue, he stopped in a dejected posture before the gate of an inn. Two men, dressed in blue,[7] observing him in such a situation, "Brother," says one of them to the other, "there is a young fellow well built, and of a proper height." They accosted Candide, and invited him very civilly to dinner.

"Gentlemen," replied Candide, with an agreeable modesty, "you do me much honor, but I have no money to pay my share."

"O sir," said one of the blues, "persons of your appearance and merit never pay anything; are you not five feet five inches high?"

"Yes, gentlemen, that is my height," returned he, making a bow.

"Come, sir, sit down at table; we will not only treat you, but we will never let such a man as you want money; men are made to assist one another."

"You are in the right," said Candide; "that is what Pangloss always told me, and I see plainly that everything is for the best."

They entreated him to take a few crowns, which he accepted, and would have given them his note; but they refused it, and sat down to table.

"Do not you tenderly love—"

"O yes," replied he, "I tenderly love Miss Cunegonde."

"No," said one of the gentlemen; "we ask you if you do tenderly love the King of the Bulgarians?"

"Not at all," said he, "for I never saw him."

"How! he is the most charming of kings, and you must drink his health."

"O, with all my heart, gentlemen," and drinks.

"That is enough," said they to him; "you are now the bulwark, the support, the defender, the hero of the Bulgarians; your fortune is made, and you are certain of glory." Instantly they put him in irons, and carried him to the regiment. They made him turn to the right, to the left, draw the ramrod, return the ramrod, present, fire, step double; and they gave him thirty blows with a cudgel. The next day, he performed his exercises not quite so

---

[3]The tutor's name is (literally) "all-tongue."
[4]Note the French *nigaud* ("booby") included in the elaborate title of this pompous-sounding discipline.
[5]One of many allusions in *Candide* to the philosophic optimism systematized by Leibniz and popularized by Pope (see chapter 24).

[6]Voltaire's name for the troops of Frederick the Great, King of Prussia, who, like their king, were widely regarded as Sodomites; the association between the name and the French *bougre* ("to bugger") is patent.
[7]The color of the uniforms worn by the soldiers of Frederick the Great.

badly, and received but twenty blows; the third day the blows were restricted to ten, and he was looked upon by his fellow-soldiers, as a kind of prodigy.

Candide, quite stupefied, could not well conceive how he had become a hero. One fine Spring day he took it into his head to walk out, going straight forward, imagining that the human, as well as the animal species, were entitled to make whatever use they pleased of their limbs. He had not travelled two leagues, when four other heroes, six feet high, came up to him, bound him, and put him into a dungeon. He is asked by a Court-martial, whether he chooses to be whipped six and thirty times through the whole regiment, or receive at once twelve bullets through the forehead? He in vain argued that the will is free, and that he chose neither the one nor the other; he was obliged to make a choice; he therefore resolved, in virtue of God's gift called *freewill*, to run the gauntlet six and thirty times. He underwent this discipline twice. The regiment being composed of two thousand men, he received four thousand lashes, which laid open all his muscles and nerves, from the nape of the neck to the back. As they were proceeding to a third course, Candide, being quite spent, begged as a favor that they would be so kind as to shoot him; he obtained his request; they hoodwinked him, and made him kneel; the King of the Bulgarians passing by, inquired into the crime of the delinquent; and as this prince was a person of great penetration, he discovered from what he heard of Candide, that he was a young metaphysician, entirely ignorant of the things of this world; and he granted him his pardon, with a clemency which will be extolled in all histories, and throughout all ages. An experienced surgeon cured Candide in three weeks, with emollients prescribed by no less a master than Dioscorides.[8] His skin had already began to grow again, and he was able to walk, when the King of the Bulgarians gave battle to the King of the Abares.

Chapter 3

How Candide Made His Escape From the Bulgarians, and What Afterwards Befell Him

Nothing could be so fine, so neat, so brilliant, so well ordered, as the two armies.[9] The trumpets, fifes, hautboys, drums, and cannon, formed an harmony superior to what hell itself could invent. The cannon swept off at first about six thousand men on each side; afterwards, the musketry carried away from the best of worlds, about nine or ten thousand rascals that infected its surface. The bayonet was likewise the sufficient reason of the death of some thousands of men. The whole number might amount to about thirty thousand souls. Candide, who trembled like a philosopher, hid himself as well as he could, during this heroic butchery.

At last, while each of the two kings were causing *Te Deum*—glory to God—to be sung in their respective camps, he resolved to go somewhere else, to reason upon the effects and causes.

He walked over heaps of the dead and dying; he came at first to a neighboring village belonging to the Abares, but found it in ashes; for it had been burnt by the Bulgarians, according to the law of nations. Here were to be seen old men full of wounds, casting their eyes on their murdered wives, who were holding their infants to their bloody breasts. You might see in another place, virgins outraged after they had satisfied the natural desires of some of those heroes, whilst breathing out their last sighs. Others, half-burnt, praying earnestly for instant death. The whole field was covered with brains, and with legs and arms lopped off.

Candide betook himself with all speed to another village. It belonged to the Bulgarians, and had met with the same treatment from the Abarian heroes. Candide, walking still forward over quivering limbs, or through rubbish of houses, got at last out of the theatre of war, having some small quantity of provisions in his knapsack, and never forgetting Miss Cunegonde. His provisions failed him when he arrived in Holland;[10] but having heard that every one was rich in that country, and that they were Christians, he did not doubt but he should be as well treated there as he had been in my Lord the Baron's castle, before he had been expelled thence on account of Miss Cunegonde's sparkling eyes.

He asked alms from several grave looking persons, who all replied, that if he continued that trade, they would confine him in a house of correction, where he should learn to earn his bread.

He applied afterwards to a man, who for a whole hour had been discoursing on the subject of charity, before a large assembly. This orator, looking at him askance, said to him:

"What are you doing here? are you for the good cause?"

"There is no effect without a cause," replied Candide, modestly; "all is necessarily linked, and ordered for the best. A necessity banished me from Miss Cunegonde; a necessity forced me to run the gauntlet; another necessity makes me beg my bread, till I can get into some business by which to earn it. All this could not be otherwise."

"My friend," said the orator to him, "do you believe that the Anti-Christ is alive?"

"I never heard whether he is or not," replied Candide; "but whether he is, or is not, I want bread!"

"You do not deserve to eat any," said the other; "get you gone, you rogue; get you gone, you wretch; never in thy life come near me again!"

The orator's wife, having popped her head out of the chamber window, and seeing a man who doubted whether Anti-Christ was alive, poured on his head a full vessel of. . . . Oh heavens! to what excess does religious zeal transport the fair sex!

A man who had not been baptized, a good Anabaptist,[11] named *James*, saw the barbarous and ignominious manner with which they treated one of his brethren, a being with two feet,

[8]A famous Greek physician of the first century C.E. whose book on medicine was for centuries a standard text.
[9]A mocking reference to the Seven Years' War (1756–63) fought between the Prussians (Bulgars) and the French–Austrian coalition, to whom Voltaire gives the name Abares—a tribe of semicivilized Scythians.

[10]Holland, a mecca of religious freedom for over two centuries, had given asylum to the Anabaptists and other radical religious sects.
[11]A Protestant sect (originating in Zürich in 1524) advocating the baptism of adult believers and the practice of simplicity, mutual help, the exercise of individual conscience, and the separation of Church and state.

Chapter 6

How a Fine *Auto-da-Fé*[18] Was Celebra[...] Earthquakes, and How Candide Was [...]

After the earthquake, which had destroyed [...]
the sages of the country could not find a[...]
to prevent a total destruction, than to giv[...]
auto-da-fé. It had been decided by the un[...]
that the spectacle of some persons burnt [...]
with great ceremony, was an infallible an[...]

In consequence of this resolution, they [...]
Biscayan, convicted of having married his [...]
Portuguese, who, in eating a pullet, had s[...]
After dinner, they came and secured Dr. F[...]
disciple Candide; the one for having spok[...]
other for having heard with an air of appr[...]
both conducted to separate apartments, [...]
never incommoded with the sun.[21] Eight [...]
both clothed with a gown[22] and had their [...]
paper crowns. Candide's crown and gow[...]
inverted flames, and with devils that had [...]
claws; but Pangloss' devils had claws an[...]
were pointed upwards. Being thus dress[...]
procession, and heard a very pathetic sp[...]
music on a squeaking organ. Candide wa[...]
in cadence, while they were singing; the [...]
men who would not eat lard, were burnt [...]
it was contrary to custom, was hanged. [...]
shook anew,[23] with a most dreadful nois[...]

Candide, affrighted, interdicted, aston[...]
panting, said to himself: "If this is the be[...]
what then are the rest? Supposing I had [...]
I have been so, among the Bulgarians; b[...]
Pangloss; thou greatest of philosophers, [...]
fate to see thee hanged without knowin[...]
Anabaptist! thou best of men, that it sh[...]
drowned in the harbor! Oh! Miss Cunego[...]
that it should be thy fate to have been o[...]

He returned, with difficulty, supportin[...]
lectured, whipped, absolved, and blesse[...]
accosted him, and said: "Child, take cou[...]

Chapter 7

How an Old Woman Took Care of Ca[...] How He Found the Object He Loved [...]

Candide did not take courage, but he fo[...]
a ruinated house. She gave him a pot of [...]

---

[18]The public ceremony (literally, "act of fai[...]
guilty of heresy were punished.
[19]A swipe at papal efforts to condemn as i[...]
the parties might be bound by family relat[...]
[20]Unwittingly revealing that they were sec[...]
laws prohibit the eating of pork. Under th[...]
and Portuguese Inquisitions, many Iberian[...]
Christianity.
[21]Prison cells.
[22]Yellow penitential garments worn by the[...]
[23]A second earthquake occurred in Lisbon[...]
[24]Ointment.

---

without feathers, and endowed with a rational soul.[12] He took him home with him, cleaned him, gave him bread and beer, made him a present of two florins,[13] and offered to teach him the method of working in his manufactories of Persian stuffs, which are fabricated in Holland. Candide, prostrating himself almost to the ground, cried out, "Master Pangloss argued well when he said, that everything is for the best in this world; for I am infinitely more affected with your very great generosity, than by the hard-heartedness of that gentleman with the cloak, and the lady his wife." **230**

Next day, as he was taking a walk, he met a beggar, all covered over with sores, his eyes half dead, the tip of his nose eaten off, his mouth turned to one side of his face, his teeth black, speaking through his throat, tormented with a violent cough, with gums so rotten, that his teeth came near falling out every time he spit. **240**

Chapter 4

How Candide Met His Old Master of Philosophy, Dr. Pangloss, and What Happened to Them

Candide, moved still more with compassion than with horror, gave this frightful mendicant the two florins which he had received of his honest Anabaptist James. The spectre fixed his eyes attentively upon him, dropt some tears, and was going to fall upon his neck. Candide, affrighted, drew back.

"Alas!" said the one wretch to the other, "don't you know your dear Pangloss?"

"What do I hear! Is it you, my dear master! you in this dreadful condition! What misfortune has befallen you? Why are you no longer in the most magnificent of castles? What has become of Miss Cunegonde, the nonpareil of the fair sex, the master-piece of nature?" **250**

"I have no more strength," said Pangloss.

Candide immediately carried him to the Anabaptist's stable, where he gave him a little bread to eat. When Pangloss was refreshed a little, "Well," said Candide, "what has become of Cunegonde?"

"She is dead," replied the other.

Candide fainted away at this word; but his friend recovered his senses, with a little bad vinegar which he found by chance in the stable. **260**

Candide, opening his eyes, cried out, "Cunegonde is dead! Ah, best of worlds, where art thou now? But of what distemper did she die? Was not the cause, her seeing me driven out of the castle by my Lord, her father, with such hard kicks on the breech?"

"No," said Pangloss, "she was gutted by some Bulgarian soldiers, after having been barbarously ravished.[14] They knocked my Lord the Baron on the head, for attempting to protect her; **270** my Lady the Baroness was cut in pieces; my poor pupil was treated like his sister; and as for the castle, there is not one stone left upon another, nor a barn, nor a sheep, nor a duck, nor a tree. But we have been sufficiently revenged; for the Abarians

---

[12]The minimalist definition of man ascribed to the philosopher Plato and used here to suggest James' sympathy with all humankind.
[13]Gold coins.
[14]Raped.

---

have done the very same thing to a neighboring barony, which belonged to a Bulgarian Lord."

At this discourse, Candide fainted away a second time; but coming to himself, and having said all that he ought to say, he enquired into the cause and the effect, and into the sufficient reason that had reduced Pangloss to so deplorable a **280** condition. "Alas," said the other, "it was love; love, the comforter of the human race, the preserver of the universe, the soul of all sensible beings, tender love." "Alas!" said Candide, "I know this love, the sovereign of hearts, the soul of our soul; yet it never cost me more than a kiss, and twenty kicks. But how could this charming cause produce in you so abominable an effect?"

Pangloss made answer as follows: "Oh my dear Candide, you knew Paquetta, the pretty attendant on our noble Baroness; I tasted in her arms the delights of Paradise, which **290** produced those torments of hell with which you see me devoured. She was infected,[15] and perhaps she is dead. Paquetta received this present from a very learned Franciscan, who had it from an old countess, who received it from a captain of horse, who was indebted for it to a marchioness, who got it from one of the companions of Christopher Columbus. For my part, I shall give it to nobody, for I am dying."

"Oh Pangloss!" cried Candide, "what a strange genealogy! Was not the devil at the head of it?" "Not at all," replied the great man; "it was a thing indispensable; a necessary **300** ingredient in the best of worlds; for if Columbus had not caught, in an island of America, this disease, we should have had neither chocolate nor cochineal. It may also be observed, that to this day, upon our continent, this malady is as peculiar to us, as is religious controversy. The Turks, the Indians, the Persians, the Chinese, the Siamese, and the Japanese, know nothing of it yet. But there is sufficient reason why they, in their turn, should become acquainted with it, a few centuries hence. In the mean time, it has made marvellous progress among us, and especially in those great armies composed of honest hirelings, well **310** disciplined, who decide the fate of states; for we may rest assured, that when thirty thousand men in a pitched battle fight against troops equal to them in number, there are about twenty thousand of them on each side who have the pox.

"This is admirable," said Candide; "but you must be cured." "Ah! how can I?" said Pangloss; "I have not a penny, my friend; and throughout the whole extent of this globe, we cannot get any one to bleed us, or give us a glister, without paying for it, or getting some other person to pay for us."

This last speech determined Candide. He went and threw **320** himself at the feet of his charitable Anabaptist James, and gave him so touching a description of the state his friend was reduced to, that the good man did not hesitate to entertain Dr. Pangloss, and he had him cured at his own expense. During the cure, Pangloss lost only an eye and an ear. As he wrote well, and understood arithmetic perfectly, the Anabaptist made him his bookkeeper. At the end of two months, being obliged to go to Lisbon on account of his business, he took the two

---

[15]With veneral disease; syphilis, which entered Europe in the late fifteenth century, was one of the most virulent legacies of the Euro-American exchange.

philosophers along with him, in his ship. P[...]
him how every thing was such as it could [...]
James was not of this opinion. "Mankind,["]
somewhat corrupted their nature; for they [...]
wolves, and yet they have become wolves; [...]
neither cannon of twenty-four pounds, nor [...]
they have made cannon and bayonets to d[...]
might throw into the account bankrupts; ar[...]
seizes on the effects of bankrupts only to b[...]
"All this was indispensable," replied the o[...]
private misfortunes constitute the general [...]
more private misfortunes there are, the wh[...]
While he was thus reasoning, the air grew [...]
from the four quarters of the world, and th[...]
by a dreadful storm, within sight of the ha[...]

Chapter 5

Tempest, Shipwreck, Earthquake and [...]
Dr. Pangloss, Candide and James the [...]

One half of the passengers being weaken[...]
breathe their last, with the inconceivable [...]
rolling of the ship conveyed through the n[...]
humors of the body, which were quite dis[...]
capable of being alarmed at the danger th[...]
half uttered cries and made prayers; the s[...]
masts broken, and the ship became leaky.[...]
that was able, nobody cared for any thing [...]
kept. The Anabaptist contributed his assi[...]
ship. As he was upon deck, a furious sailo[...]
and laid him sprawling on the planks; but [...]
gave him, he himself was so violently jolt[...]
overboard with his head foremost, and re[...]
a piece of broken mast. Honest James ra[...]
and helped him on deck again; but in the [...]
the sea, in the sight of the sailor, who su[...]
without deigning to look upon him. Candi[...]
saw his benefactor, one moment emergin[...]
swallowed up for ever. He was just going [...]
the sea after him, when the philosopher [...]
by demonstrating to him, that the road to [...]
on purpose for this Anabaptist to be drov[...]
proving this, *a priori*, the vessel foundere[...]
except Pangloss, Candide, and the brutal [...]
the virtuous Anabaptist. The villain luckil[...]
whither Pangloss and Candide were carr[...]

When they had recovered themselves [...]
towards Lisbon. They had some money le[...]
hoped to save themselves from hunger, a[...]
from the storm.

Scarce had they set foot in the city, be[...]
their benefactor, when they perceived th[...]
under their feet,[16] and saw the sea swell[...]
dash to pieces the ships that were at an[...]
flames and ashes covered the streets an[...]

---

[16]The first Lisbon earthquake and fire took [...]
It destroyed much of the city and took ove[...]

death of the good Anabaptist, and of Pangloss; after which she thus related her adventures to Candide, who lost not a word, but looked on her, as if he would devour her with his eyes.

Chapter 8

The History of Cunegonde

"I was in my bed and fast asleep, when it pleased heaven to send the Bulgarians to our fine castle of Thunder-ten-tronckh; they murdered my father and my brother, and cut my mother to pieces. A huge Bulgarian, six feet high, perceiving the horrible sight had deprived me of my senses, set himself to ravish me. This abuse made me come to myself; I recovered my senses, I cried, I struggled, I bit, I scratched, I wanted to tear out the huge Bulgarian's eyes, not considering that what had happened in my father's castle, was a common thing in war. The brute gave me a cut with his knife, the mark of which I still bear about me." "Ah! I anxiously wish to see it," said the simple Candide. "You shall," answered Cunegonde; "but let me finish my story." "Do so," replied Candide.

She then resumed the thread of her story, as follows: "A Bulgarian captain came in, and saw me bleeding; but the soldier was not at all disconcerted. The Captain flew into a passion at the little respect the brute showed him, and killed him upon my body. He then caused me to be dressed, and carried me as a prisoner of war to his own quarters. I washed the scanty linen he had, and cooked his meals. He found me very pretty, I must say it; and I cannot deny but he was well shaped, and that he had a white, soft skin; but for the rest, he had little sense or philosophy; one could plainly see that he was not bred under Dr. Pangloss. At the end of three months, having lost all his money, and being grown out of conceit with me, he sold me to a Jew, named *Don Issachar*, who traded to Holland and Portugal, and had a most violent passion for women. This Jew laid close siege to my person, but could not triumph over me; I have resisted him better than I did the Bulgarian soldier. A woman of honor may be ravished once, but her virtue gathers strength from such rudeness. The Jew, in order to render me more tractable, brought me to this country-house that you see. I always imagined hitherto, that no place on earth was so fine as the castle of Thunder-ten-tronckh; but I am now undeceived.

"The grand inquisitor observing me one day ogled me very strongly, and sent me a note, saying he wanted to speak with me upon private business. Being conducted to his palace, I informed him of my birth; upon which he represented to me, how much it was below my family to belong to an Israelite. A proposal was then made by him to Don Issachar, to yield me up to my Lord. But Don Issachar, who is the court-banker, and a man of credit, would not come into his measures. The inquisitor threatened him. At last, my Jew, being affrighted, concluded a bargain, by which the house and myself should belong to them both in common; the Jew to have possession Monday, Friday, and Saturday, and the inquisitor, the other days of the week. This agreement has now continued six months. It has not, however, been without quarrels; for it has been often disputed whether Saturday night or Sunday belonged to the old, or to the new law. For my part, I have

hitherto disagreed with them both; and I believe that this is the reason I am still beloved by them.

"At length, to avert the scourge of earthquakes and to intimidate Don Issachar, it pleased his Lordship the inquisitor to celebrate. He did me the honor to invite me to it. I got a very fine seat, and the ladies were served with refreshments between the ceremonies. I was seized with horror at seeing them burn the two Jews, and the honest Biscayan who married his godmother; but how great was my surprise, my consternation, my anguish, when I saw in a sanbenito and mitre, a person that somewhat resembled Pangloss! I rubbed my eyes, I looked upon him very attentively, and I saw him hanged. I fell into a swoon, and scarce had I recovered my senses, when I saw you stripped stark naked; this was the height of horror, consternation, grief, and despair. I will frankly own to you, that your skin is still whiter, and of a better complexion than that of my Bulgarian captain. This sight increased all the sensations that oppressed and distracted my soul. I cried out, I was going to say stop, barbarians; but my voice failed me, and all my cries would have been to no purpose. When you had been severely whipped: How is it possible, said I, that the amiable Candide, and the sage Pangloss, should both be at Lisbon;—the one to receive a hundred lashes and the other to be hanged by order of my Lord the Inquisitor, by whom I am so greatly beloved? Pangloss certainly deceived me most cruelly, when he said that everything was for the best in this world.

"Agitated, astonished, sometimes beside myself, and sometimes ready to die with weakness; my head filled with the massacre of my father, my mother, and my brother, the insolence of the vile Bulgarian soldier, the stab he gave me with his hanger, my abject servitude, and my acting as a cook to the Bulgarian captain; the rascal Don Issachar, my abominable inquisitor; the execution of Dr. Pangloss, the grand music on the organ while you were whipped, and especially the kiss I gave you behind the screen, the last day I saw you. I praised the Lord for having restored you to me after so many trials. I charged my old woman to take care of you, and to bring you hither as soon as she could. She has executed her commission very well; I have tasted the inexpressible pleasure of seeing you, hearing you, and speaking to you. You must have a ravenous appetite, by this time; I am hungry myself, too; let us, therefore, sit down to supper."

On this, they both sat down to table; and after supper, they seated themselves on the fine couch before mentioned. They were there, then Signor Don Issachar, one of the masters of the house, came in. It was his Sabbath day, and he came to enjoy his right, and to express his tender love.

[*Candide, Cunegonde and the old woman travel to Cadiz. The old woman recounts her past misfortunes. They sail to America, where Candide finds a South American paradise, El Dorado, filled with kind and reasonable people; however, he loses Cunegonde to a Spanish colonial nobleman. On his way back to Europe, Candide meets the disillusioned pessimist, Martin, who opens Candide's eyes to the evil in the world. Following various adventures in Europe, Candide travels to Turkey and encounters Pangloss, whom he had thought dead.*]

Chapter 29

How Candide Found Cunegonde and the Old Woman Again

While Candide, the Baron, Pangloss, Martin, and Cacambo were relating their adventures to each other, and disputing about the contigent and non-contigent events of this world, and while they were arguing upon effects and causes, on moral and physical evil, on liberty and necessity, and on the consolations a person may experience in the galleys in Turkey, they arrived on the banks of the Propontis, at the house of the Prince of Transylvania. The first objects which presented themselves were Cunegonde and the old woman, hanging out some table-linen on the line to dry. 640

The Baron grew pale at this sight. Even Candide, the affectionate lover, on seeing his fair Cunegonde awfully tanned, with her eye-lids reversed, her neck withered, her cheeks wrinkled, her arms red and rough, was seized with horror, jumped near three yards backwards, but afterwards advanced to her, but with more politeness than passion. She embraced Candide and her brother, who, each of them, embraced the old woman, and Candide ransomed them both. 650

There was a little farm in the neighborhood, which the old woman advised Candide to hire, till they could meet with better accommodations for their whole company. As Cunegonde did not know that she had grown ugly, nobody having told her of it, she put Candide in mind of his promise to marry her, in so peremptory a manner, that he durst not refuse her. But when this thing was intimated to the Baron, "I will never suffer," said he, "such meanness on her part, nor such insolence on yours. With this infamy I will never be reproached. The children of my sister shall never be enrolled in the chapters[25] of Germany. No; my sister shall never marry any but a Baron of the empire." Cunegonde threw herself at her brother's feet, and bathed them with her tears, but he remained inflexible. "You ungrateful puppy, you," said Candide to him, "I have delivered you from the galleys; I have paid your ransom; I have also paid that of your sister, who was a scullion here, and is very homely; I have the goodness, however, to make her my wife, and you are fool enough to oppose it; I have a good mind to kill you again, you make me so angry." "You may indeed kill me again," said the Baron; "but you shall never marry my sister, while I have breath." 660 670

Chapter 30

Conclusion

Candide had no great desire, at the bottom of his heart, to marry Cunegonde. But the extreme impertinence of the Baron determined him to conclude the match, and Cunegonde pressed it so earnestly, that he could not retract. He advised with Pangloss, Martin, and the trusty Cacambo. Pangloss drew up an excellent memoir, in which he proved, that the Baron had no right over his sister, and that she might, according to all the laws of the empire, espouse Candide with her left hand.[26] 640

Martin was for throwing the Baron into the sea: Cacambo was of opinion that it would be best to send him back again to the Levant captain, and make him work at the galleys. This advice was thought good; the old woman approved it, and nothing was said to his sister about it. The scheme was put in execution for a little money, and so they had the pleasure of punishing the pride of a German Baron.

It is natural to imagine that Candide, after so many disasters, married to his sweetheart, living with the philosopher Pangloss, the philosopher Martin, the discreet Cacambo, and the old woman, and especially as he had brought so many diamonds from the country of the ancient Incas, must live the most agreeable life of any man in the whole world. But he had been so cheated by the Jews,[27] that he had nothing left but the small farm; and his wife, growing still more ugly, turned peevish and insupportable. The old woman was very infirm, and worse humored than Cunegonde herself. Cacambo, who worked in the garden, and went to Constantinople to sell its productions, was worn out with labor, and cursed his fate. Pangloss was ready to despair, because he did not shine at the head of some university in Germany. As for Martin, as he was firmly persuaded that all was equally bad throughout, he bore things with patience. Candide, Martin, and Pangloss disputed sometimes about metaphysics and ethics. They often saw passing under the windows of the farmhouse boats full of effendis, bashaws, and cadis,[28] who were going into banishment to Lemnos, Mitylene, and Erzerum. They observed that other cadis, other bashaws, and other effendis succeeded in the posts of those who were exiled, only to be banished themselves in turn. They saw heads nicely impaled, to be presented to the Sublime Porte. These spectacles increased the number of their disputations; and when they were not disputing, their *ennui* was so tiresome that the old woman would often say to them, "I want to know which is the worst;—to be ravished an hundred times by negro pirates, to run the gauntlet among the Bulgarians, to be whipped and hanged, to be dissected, to row in the galleys; in a word, to have suffered all the miseries we have undergone, or to stay here, without doing anything?" "That is a great question," said Candide. 690 700 710 720

This discourse gave rise to new reflections, and Martin concluded upon the whole, that mankind were born to live either in the distractions of inquietude, or in the lethargy of disgust. Candide did not agree with that opinion, but remained in a state of suspense. Pangloss confessed, that he had always suffered dreadfully; but having once maintained that all things went wonderfully well, he still kept firm to his hypothesis, though it was quite opposed to his real feelings.

What contributed to confirm Martin in his shocking principles, to make Candide stagger more than ever, and to embarrass Pangloss, was, that one day they saw Paquetta and Girofflee, who were in the greatest distress, at their farm. They had quickly squandered away their three thousand piastres,[29] had parted, were reconciled, quarrelled again, had been 730

---

[25]Noble assemblies.
[26]A marriage that denies noble status to the party of the lower rank.

[27]Voltaire's anti-semitism seems to have been the result of financial losses he suffered from the bankruptcies of Jewish moneylenders.
[28]Highranking members of the Turkish nobility.
[29]Spanish dollars; piece of eight.

confined in prison, had made their escape, and Giroflee had at length turned Turk. Paquetta continued her trade wherever she went, but made nothing by it. "I could easily foresee," said Martin to Candide, "that your presents would soon be squandered away, and would render them more miserable. You and Cacambo have spent millions of piastres, and are not a bit happier than Giroflee and Paquetta." "Ha! ha!" said Pangloss to Paquetta, "has Providence then brought you amongst us again, my poor child? Know, then, that you have cost me the tip of my nose, one eye, and one of my ears, as you see. What a world this is!" This new adventure set them a philosophizing more than ever.

There lived in the neighborhood a very famous dervish, who passed for the greatest philosopher in Turkey. They went to consult him. Pangloss was chosen speaker, and said to him, "Master, we are come to desire you would tell us, why so strange an animal as man was created."

"What's that to you?" said the dervish; "is it any business of yours?" "But, my reverend father," said Candide, "there is a horrible amount of evil in the world." "What does it matter," said the dervish, "whether there be good or evil? When his Sublime Highness sends a vessel to Egypt, does it trouble him, whether the mice on board are at their ease or not?" "What would you have one do then?" said Pangloss. "Hold your tongue," said the dervish. "I promised myself the pleasure," said Pangloss, "of reasoning with you upon effects and causes, the best of possible worlds, the origin of evil, the nature of the soul, and the pre-established harmony."—The dervish, at these words, shut the door in their faces.

During this conference, news was brought that two viziers and a mufti were strangled at Constantinople, and a great many of their friends impaled. This catastrophe made a great noise for several hours. Pangloss, Candide, and Martin, on their way back to the little farm, met a good-looking old man, taking the air at his door, under an arbor of orange trees. Pangloss, who had as much curiosity as philosophy, asked him the name of the mufti who was lately strangled. "I know nothing at all about it," said the good man; "and what's more, I never knew the name of a single mufti, or a single vizier, in my life. I am an entire stranger to the story you mention; and presume that, generally speaking, they who trouble their heads with state affairs, sometimes die shocking deaths, not without deserving it. But I never trouble my head about what is doing at Constantinople; I content myself with sending my fruits thither, the produce of my garden, which I cultivate with my own hands!" Having said these words, he introduced the strangers into his house. His two daughters and two sons served them with several kinds of sherbet, which they made themselves, besides caymac, enriched with the peels of candied citrons, oranges, lemons, bananas, pistachio nuts, and Mocha coffee, unadulterated with the bad coffee of Batavia and the isles. After which, the two daughters of this good Muslim perfumed the beards of Candide, Pangloss, and Martin.

"You must certainly," said Candide to the Turk, "have a very large and very opulent estate!" "I have only twenty acres," said the Turk; "which I, with my children, cultivate. Labor keeps us free from three of the greatest evils; boredom, vice, and need."

As Candide returned to his farm, he made deep reflections on the discourse of the Turk. Said he to Pangloss and Martin,

"The condition of this good old man seems to me preferable to that of the six kings with whom we had the honor to dine." "The grandeurs of royalty," said Pangloss, "are very precarious, in the opinion of all philosophers. For, in short, Eglon, king of the Moabites, was assassinated by Ehud; Absalom was hung by the hair of his head, and pierced through with three darts; King Nadab, the son of Jeroboam, was killed by Baasha; King Elah by Zimri; Ahaziah by Jehu; Athaliah by Jehoiadah; the kings Joachim, Jechonias, and Zedekias, were carried into captivity. You know the fates of Croesus, Astyages, Darius, Dionysius of Syracuse, Pyrrhus, Perseus, Hannibal, Jugurtha, Ariovistus, Caesar, Pompey, Nero, Otho, Vitellius, Domitian, Richard II, Edward II, Henry VI, Richard III, Mary Stuart, Charles I of England, the three Henrys of France, and the Emperor Henry IV.[30] You know—" "I know very well," said Candide, "that we ought to look after our garden." "You are in the right," said Pangloss, "for when man was placed in the garden of Eden, he was placed there, *ut operatur cum*, to cultivate it; which proves that mankind are not created to be idle." "Let us work," said Martin, "without disputing; it is the only way to render life supportable."

All their little society entered into this laudable design, according to their different abilities. Their little piece of ground produced a plentiful crop. Cunegonde was indeed very homely, but she became an excellent pastry cook. Paquetta worked at embroidery, and the old woman took care of the linen. There was no idle person in the company, not excepting even Giroflee; he made a very good carpenter, and became a very honest man.

As to Pangloss, he evidently had a lurking consciousness that his theory required unceasing exertions, and all his ingenuity, to sustain it. Yet he stuck to it to the last; his thinking and talking faculties could hardly be diverted from it for a moment. He seized every occasion to say to Candide, "All the events in this best of possible worlds are admirably connected. If a single link in the great chain were omitted, the harmony of the entire universe would be destroyed. If you had not been expelled from that beautiful castle, with those cruel kicks, for your love to Miss Cunegonde; if you had not been imprisoned by the inquisition; if you had not travelled over a great portion of America on foot; if you had not plunged your sword through the baron; if you had not lost all the sheep you brought from that fine country, Eldorado, together with the riches with which they were laden, you would not be here to-day, eating preserved citrons, and pistachio nuts."

"That's very well said, and may all be true," said Candide; "but let's cultivate our garden."

Satire in Chinese Literature

While the satires of Voltaire and Swift drew enthusiastic audiences in the West, satire came into vogue as an important genre elsewhere in the world. Following the Manchu conquest of China in the mid-seventeenth century, Chinese writers indulged

---

[30] All rulers who came to a bad end.

740
750
760
770
780
790
800
810
820
830
840

in writing bitter fictional tales that satirized a wide variety of contemporary social practices, including Buddhist rituals, commercial banditry, and homosexual unions. One of the cruelest satires of the eighteenth century consisted of a collection of stories attacking the absurdities of China's traditional civil service examination system by which talented individuals were brought into government service. *The Scholars*, as the novel is titled, written around 1750 by Wu Jingzi (1701–1754), reflects Wu's own failure to pass the highly competitive exams, which often brought pseudo-scholars to positions of great wealth and power in China. The satire emphasized the unpopular and anti-Confucian truth that the morally unscrupulous often gain great prizes in the world, while the virtuous do not always flourish.

Chinese satire was also effective in attacking some of the more socially inhibiting practices of traditional Chinese culture, such as female footbinding. Beginning in the eleventh century, upper-class Chinese parents bound the feet of their young daughters (thus breaking the arch and stunting the feet to half the normal size) in order to exempt them from common labor, hence make them more physically attractive as marriage partners to wealthy men. Toward the end of the great age of Chinese prose fiction, the philologist Li Ruzhen (1763–1830) boldly attacked this practice in a satire entitled *Flowers in the Mirror*. An adventure story on the model of *Gulliver's Travels* or *Candide*, *Flowers* is a series of loosely woven stories which recount the travels of a hero to many strange lands, including the Country of Two-Faced People, the Country of Long-Armed People, and the Country of Women. In the last of these fictional lands, the traditional roles of the sexes are reversed, and the ruling women of the country set upon the hero to prepare him as "royal concubine": They plait his hair, apply lipstick and powder to his face, pierce his ears, and, to his ultimate dismay, they bind his feet in the traditional Chinese manner. Li Ruzhen's blunt social criticism and his bold assertion of equal rights for women fell on deaf ears, for despite the fact that Manchu rulers censured the old Chinese custom, footbinding continued in many parts of China until the early twentieth century.

READING 4.26 From Li Ruzhen's *Flowers in the Mirror* (1828)

When Tang Ao heard that they had arrived at the Country of Women, he thought that the country was populated entirely by women, and was afraid to go ashore. But Old Tuo said, "Not at all! There are men as well as women, only they call men women, and women men. The men wear the skirts and take care of the home, while the women wear hats and trousers and manage affairs outside. If it were a country populated solely by women, I doubt that even Brother Lin here would dare to venture ashore, although he knows he always makes a good profit from sales here!"

"If the men dress like women, do they use cosmetics and bind their feet?" asked Tang Ao.

"Of course they do!" cried Lin, and took from his pocket a list of the merchandise he was going to sell, which consisted of huge quantities of rouge, face powder, combs and other women's notions. "Luckily I wasn't born in this country," he said. "Catch me mincing around on bound feet!"

When Tang Ao asked why he had not put down the price of the merchandise, Lin said, "The people here, no matter rich or poor, from the 'King' down to the simplest peasant, are all mad about cosmetics. I'll charge them what I can. I shall have no difficulty selling the whole consignment to rich families in two or three days."

Beaming at the prospect of making a good profit, Lin went on shore with his list.

Tang Ao and Old Tuo decided to go and see the city. The people walking on the streets were small of stature, and rather slim, and although dressed in men's clothes, were beardless and spoke with women's voices, and walked with willowy steps.

"Look at them!" said Old Tuo. "They are perfectly normal-looking women. Isn't it a shame for them to dress like men?"

"Wait a minute," said Tang Ao. "Maybe when they see us, they think, 'Look at them, isn't it a shame that they dress like women'?"

"You're right. 'Whatever one is accustomed to always seems natural,' as the ancients say. But I wonder what the men are like?"

[*Invited to sell his wares at the court of the "King," Lin visits the Palace.*]

In a little time, Merchant Lin was ushered to a room upstairs where victuals of many kinds awaited him. As he ate, however, he heard a great deal of noise downstairs. Several palace "maids" ran upstairs soon, and calling him "Your Highness", kowtowed to him and congratulated him. Before he knew what was happening, Merchant Lin was being stripped completely bare by the maids and led to a perfumed bath. Against the powerful arms of these maids, he could scarcely struggle. Soon he found himself being anointed, perfumed, powdered and rouged, and dressed in a skirt. His big feet were bound up in strips of cloth and socks, and his hair was combed into an elaborate braid over his head and decorated with pins. These male "maids" thrust bracelets on his arms and rings on his fingers, and put a phoenix headdress on his head. They tied a jade green sash around his waist and put an embroidered cape around his shoulders.

Then they led him to a bed, and asked him to sit down.

Merchant Lin thought that he must be drunk, or dreaming, and began to tremble. He asked the maids what was happening, and was told that he had been chosen by the "King" to be the Imperial Consort, and that a propitious day would be chosen for him to enter the "King's" chambers.

Before he could utter a word, another group of maids, all tall and strong and wearing beards, came in. One was holding a threaded needle. "We are ordered to pierce your ears," he said, as the other four "maids" grabbed Lin by the arms and legs. The white-bearded one seized Lin's right ear, and after rubbing the lobe a little, drove the needle through it.

"Ooh!" Merchant Lin screamed.

The maid seized the other ear, and likewise drove the needle through it. As Lin screamed with pain, powdered lead was smeared on his earlobes and a pair of "eight-precious" earrings was hung from the holes.

Having finished what they came to do, the maids retreated, and a black-bearded fellow came in with a bolt of white silk. Kneeling down before him, the fellow said, "I am ordered to bind Your Highness's feet."

Two other maids seized Lin's feet as the black-bearded one sat down on a low stool, and began to rip the silk into ribbons. Seizing Lin's right foot, he set it upon his knee, and sprinkled white alum powder between the toes and the grooves of the foot. He squeezed the toes tightly together, bent them down so that the whole foot was shaped like an arch, and took a length of white silk and bound it tightly around it twice. One of the others sewed the ribbon together in small stitches. Again the silk went around the foot, and again, it was sewn up.

Merchant Lin felt as though his feet were burning, and wave after wave of pain rose to his heart. When he could stand it no longer, he let out his voice and began to cry. The "maids" had hastily made a pair of soft-soled red shoes, and these they put on both his feet.

"Please, kind brothers, go and tell Her Majesty that I'm a married man," Lin begged. "How can I become her Consort? As for my feet, please liberate them. They have enjoyed the kind of freedom which scholars who are not interested in official careers enjoy! How can you bind them? Please tell your 'King' to let me go. I shall be grateful, and my wife will be very grateful."

But the maids said, "The King said that you are to enter his chambers as soon as your feet are bound. It is no time for talk of this kind."

When it was dark, a table was laid for him with mountains of meat and oceans of wine. But Merchant Lin only nibbled, and told the "maids" they could have the rest.

Still sitting on the bed, and with his feet aching terribly, he decided to lie down in his clothes for a rest.

At once a middle-aged "maid" came up to him and said, "Please, will you wash before you retire?"

No sooner was this said than a succession of maids came in with candles, basins of water and spittoon, dressing table, boxes of ointment, face powder, towels, silk handkerchiefs, and surrounded him. Lin had to submit to the motions of washing in front of them all. But after he had washed his face, a maid wanted to put some cream on it again.

Merchant Lin stoutly refused.

"But night time is the best time to treat the skin," the white-bearded maid said. "This powder has a lot of musk in it. It will make your skin fragrant, although I dare say it is fair enough already. If you use it regularly your skin will not only seem like white jade, but will give off a natural fragrance of its own. And the more fragrant it is, the fairer it will become, and the more lovely to behold, and the more lovable you will be. You'll see how good it is after you have used it regularly."

But Lin refused firmly, and the maids said, "If you are so stubborn, we will have to report this, and let Matron deal with you tomorrow."

Then they left him alone. But Lin's feet hurt so much that he could not sleep a wink. He tore at the ribbons with all his might, and after a great struggle succeeded in tearing them

off. He stretched out his ten toes again, and luxuriating in their exquisite freedom, finally fell asleep.

The next morning, however, when the black-bearded maid discovered that he had torn off his foot-bandages, he immediately reported it to the "King", who ordered that Lin should be punished by receiving twenty strokes of the bamboo from the "Matron". Accordingly, a white-bearded "Matron" came in with a stick of bamboo about eight feet long, and when the others had stripped him and held him down, raised the stick and began to strike Lin's bottom and legs.

Before five strokes had been delivered, Lin's tender skin was bleeding, and the Matron did not have the heart to go on. "Look at her skin! Have you ever seen such white and tender and lovable skin? Why, I think indeed her looks are comparable to Pan An and Sung Yu!" the Matron thought to himself. "But what am I doing, comparing her bottom and not her face to them? Is that a compliment?"

The foot-binding maid came and asked Lin if he would behave from now on.

"Yes, I'll behave," Lin replied, and they stopped beating him. They wiped the blood from his wounds, and special ointment was sent by the "King" and ginseng soup was given him to drink.

Merchant Lin drank the soup, and fell on the bed for a rest. But the "King" had given orders that his feet must be bound again, and that he should be taught to walk on them. So with one maid supporting him on each side, Merchant Lin was marched up and down the room all day on his bound feet. When he lay down to sleep that night, he could not close his eyes for the excruciating pain.

But from now on, he was never left alone again. Maids took turns to sit with him. Merchant Lin knew that he was no longer in command of his destiny. . . .

The Visual Satires of William Hogarth

Like Li Ruzhen in China and his European forebears Goldsmith, Swift, and Voltaire, the English artist William Hogarth (1697–1764) was a master of satire. Hogarth's paintings and prints are a record of the ills of eighteenth-century British society. He illustrated the novels of Defoe and Swift, including *Gulliver's Travels*, and executed a series of paintings based on John Gay's *Beggar's Opera*—a mock-heroic comedy that equated low-class crime with high-class corruption. Popular novels and plays provided inspiration for what Hogarth called his "modern moral subjects"; while the theater itself prompted many of the devices he used for pictorial representation: boxlike staging, lighting from below, and a wealth of "props." "I have endeavored," he wrote, "to treat my subjects as a dramatic writer: my picture is my stage, and men and women my actors."

Hogarth made engraved versions of his paintings and sold them, just as Diderot sold the volumes of the *Encyclopédie*, by subscription. So popular were these prints that they were pirated and sold without his authorization (a practice that continued even after Parliament passed the first copyright law in 1735). Especially successful were two series of prints based on his paintings. The first ("The Harlot's Progress") illustrates the misfortunes of a young woman who becomes a London prostitute; the second ("The Rake's Progress") reports the comic misadventures of an antihero and ne'er-do-well named Tom Rakewell. Following these, Hogarth published a series of six engravings entitled "Marriage à la Mode" (1742–1746), which depicts the tragic consequences of a marriage of convenience between the son of a poverty-stricken nobleman and the daughter of a wealthy and ambitious merchant. The first print in the series, *The Marriage Transaction*, shows the two families transacting the terms of the matrimonial union (Figure **25.4**). The scene unfolds as if upon a stage: The corpulent Lord Squanderfield, victim of the gout (an ailment traditionally linked with rich food and drink), sits pompously in his ruffled velvet waistcoat, pointing to his family tree, which springs from the loins of William the Conqueror. Across the table, the wealthy merchant and father of the bride carefully peruses the

financial terms of the marriage settlement. On a settee in the corner of the room, the pawns of this socially expedient match turn away from each other in attitudes of mutual dislike. The earl's son, young Squanderfield, sporting a beauty patch, opens his snuffbox and vainly gazes at himself in a mirror, while his bride-to-be idly dangles her betrothal ring on a kerchief. She leans forward to hear the honeyed words of her future seducer, a lawyer named Lord Silvertongue. A combination of **caricature** (exaggeration of peculiarities or defects), comic irony, and symbolic detail, Hogarth's "stylish marriage" is drawn with a stylus every bit as sharp as Voltaire's pen.

Like Voltaire's Paris, Hogarth's London was not yet an industrial city, but it was plagued by some of the worst urban conditions of the day. It lacked sewers, streetlights, and adequate law enforcement. A city of vast contrasts between rich and poor, it was crowded with thieves, drunks, and prostitutes, all of whom threatened the jealously guarded privileges of the rich. Hogarth represented mid-eighteenth-century London at its worst in the famous

Figure 25.4 WILLIAM HOGARTH, *The Marriage Transaction*, from the "Marriage à la Mode" series, 1742–1746. Engraving. Reproduced by courtesy of the Trustees of the British Museum, London.

Figure 25.5 WILLIAM HOGARTH, *Gin Lane*, 1751. Engraving. Reproduced by courtesy of the Trustees of the British Museum, London.

engraving *Gin Lane* (Figure **25.5**). This devastating attack on the combined evils of urban poverty and alcoholism portrays poor, ragged, and drunk men and women in various stages of depravity. Some pawn their possessions to support their expensive addictions (lower left); others commit suicide (upper right corner); and one pours gin down the throat of a babe-in-arms, following the common practice of using liquor and other drugs to quiet noisy infants (far right). In the center of the print is the figure of a besotted mother—her leg covered with syphilitic sores—

who carelessly allows her child to fall over the edge of the stair rail. Hogarth's visual satirization of gin addiction was a heroic attack on the social conditions of his time and on drug abuse in general. But even Parliament's passage of the Gin Law in 1751, which more than doubled the gin tax, did little to reduce the widespread use of gin in eighteenth-century England. While Hogarth's prints failed to reduce the ills and inequities of his society, they remain an enduring condemnation of human hypocrisy, cruelty, vanity, and greed.

Rousseau's Revolt Against Reason

Jean-Jacques Rousseau, introduced in chapter 24 as a contributor to Diderot's *Encyclopédie*, was one of the Enlightenment's most outspoken critics. A playwright, composer, and educator, Rousseau took issue with some of the basic precepts of Enlightenment thought, including the idea that the progress of the arts and sciences might improve human conduct. Human beings may be good by nature, argued Rousseau, but they are ultimately corrupted by society and its institutions. "God makes all things good," wrote Rousseau; "man meddles with them and they become evil." Rousseau condemned the artificiality of civilized life and, although he did not advocate that humankind should return to a "state of nature," he exalted the "noble savage" as the model of the uncorrupted individual. Rousseau's philosophy of the heart elevated the role of instinct over reason and encouraged a new appreciation of nature and the natural—principles that underlay the romantic movement of the early nineteenth century (see chapters 27 to 29). In the following excerpt from the *Discourse on the Origin of Inequality among Men* (1755), Rousseau gives an eloquent account of how, in his view, human beings came to lose their freedom and innocence.

READING 4.27 From Rousseau's *Discourse on the Origin of Inequality among Men* (1755)

The first man who, having enclosed a piece of land, thought   **1**
of saying "This is mine" and found people simple enough to
believe him, was the true founder of civil society. How many
crimes, wars, murders; how much misery and horror the human
race would have been spared if someone had pulled up the
stakes and filled in the ditch and cried out to his fellow men:
"Beware of listening to this impostor. You are lost if you forget
that the fruits of the earth belong to everyone and that the
earth itself belongs to no one!" But it is highly probable that by
this time things had reached a point beyond which they could   **10**
not go on as they were; for the idea of property, depending on
many prior ideas which could only have arisen in successive
stages, was not formed all at once in the human mind. It was
necessary for men to make much progress, to acquire much
industry and knowledge, to transmit and increase it from age
to age, before arriving at this final stage of the state of nature.
Let us therefore look farther back, and try to review from a
single perspective the slow succession of events and
discoveries in their most natural order.

Man's first feeling was that of his existence, his first   **20**
concern was that of his preservation. The products of the earth
furnished all the necessary aids; instinct prompted him to make
use of them. While hunger and other appetites made him
experience in turn different modes of existence, there was one
appetite which urged him to perpetuate his own species; and
this blind impulse, devoid of any sentiment of the heart,
produced only a purely animal act. The need satisfied, the two

sexes recognized each other no longer, and even the child meant
nothing to the mother, as soon as he could do without her.

Such was the condition of nascent[1] man; such was the life   **30**
of an animal limited at first to mere sensation; and scarcely
profiting from the gifts bestowed on him by nature, let alone
was he dreaming of wresting anything from her. But difficulties
soon presented themselves and man had to learn to overcome
them. The height of trees, which prevented him from reaching
their fruits; the competition of animals seeking to nourish
themselves on the same fruits; the ferocity of animals who
threatened his life—all this obliged man to apply himself to
bodily exercises; he had to make himself agile, fleet of foot,
and vigorous in combat. Natural weapons—branches of trees   **40**
and stones—were soon found to be at hand. He learned to
overcome the obstacles of nature, to fight when necessary
against other animals, to struggle for his subsistence even
against other men, or to indemnify[2] himself for what he was
forced to yield to the stronger.

[*Rousseau then describes how people devised a technology for
hunting and fishing, invented fire, and developed superiority
over other creatures.*]

Instructed by experience that love of one's own wellbeing is the
sole motive of human action, he found himself in a position to
distinguish the rare occasions when common interest justified
his relying on the aid of his fellows, and those even rarer
occasions when competition should make him distrust them.   **50**
In the first case, he united with them in a herd, or at most in a
sort of free association that committed no one and which lasted
only as long as the passing need which had brought it into being.
In the second case, each sought to grasp his own advantage,
either by sheer force, if he believed he had the strength, or by
cunning and subtlety if he felt himself to be the weaker. . . .

. . . the habit of living together generated the sweetest
sentiments known to man, conjugal love and paternal love. Each
family became a little society, all the better united because
mutual affection and liberty were its only bonds; at this stage   **60**
also the first differences were established in the ways of life of
the two sexes which had hitherto been identical. Women
became more sedentary and accustomed themselves to looking
after the hut and the children while men went out to seek their
common subsistence. The two sexes began, in living a rather
softer life, to lose something of their ferocity and their strength;
but if each individual became separately less able to fight wild
beasts, all, on the other hand, found it easier to group together
to resist them jointly. . . .

To the extent that ideas and feelings succeeded one   **70**
another, and the heart and mind were exercised, the human race
became more sociable, relationships became more extensive
and bonds tightened. People grew used to gathering together in
front of their huts or around a large tree; singing and dancing,
true progeny[3] of love and leisure, became the amusement, or
rather the occupation, of idle men and women thus assembled.
Each began to look at the others and to want to be looked at
himself; and public esteem came to be prized. He who sang or
danced the best; he who was the most handsome, the

---

[1]Early, developing.   [2]Compensate.   [3]Offspring.

strongest, the most adroit[4] or the most eloquent became the most highly regarded, and this was the first step toward inequality and at the same time toward vice. From those first preferences there arose, on the one side, vanity and scorn, on the other, shame and envy, and the fermentation produced by these new leavens[5] finally produced compounds fatal to happiness and innocence.

As soon as men learned to value one another and the idea of consideration was formed in their minds, everyone claimed a right to it, and it was no longer possible for anyone to be refused consideration without affront. This gave rise to the first duties of civility, even among savages: and henceforth every intentional wrong became an outrage, because together with the hurt which might result from the injury, the offended party saw an insult to his person which was often more unbearable than the hurt itself. Thus, as everyone punished the contempt shown him by another in a manner proportionate to the esteem he accorded himself, revenge became terrible, and men grew bloodthirsty and cruel. This is precisely the stage reached by most of the savage peoples known to us; and it is for lack of having sufficiently distinguished between different ideas and seen how far those peoples already are from the first state of nature that so many authors have hastened to conclude that man is naturally cruel and needs civil institutions to make him peaceable, whereas in truth nothing is more peaceable than man in his primitive state. Placed by nature at an equal distance from the stupidity of brutes[6] and the fatal enlightenment of civilized man, limited equally by reason and instinct to defending himself against evils which threaten him, he is restrained by natural pity from doing harm to anyone, even after receiving harm himself: for according to the wise Locke: "Where there is no property, there is no injury."

But it must be noted that society's having come into existence and relations among individuals having been already established meant that men were required to have qualities different from those they possessed from their primitive constitution. . . .

As long as men were content with their rustic huts, as long as they confined themselves to sewing their garments of skin with thorns or fishbones, and adorning themselves with feathers or shells, to painting their bodies with various colors, to improving or decorating their bows and arrows; and to using sharp stones to make a few fishing canoes or crude musical instruments; in a word, so long as they applied themselves only to work that one person could accomplish alone and to arts that did not require the collaboration of several hands, they lived as free, healthy, good and happy men. . . .

. . . but from the instant one man needed the help of another, and it was found to be useful for one man to have provisions enough for two, equality disappeared, property was introduced, work became necessary, and vast forests were transformed into pleasant fields which had to be watered with the sweat of men, and where slavery and misery were soon seen to germinate and flourish with the crops. . . .

---

[4]Skillful.
[5]Significant changes.
[6]Beasts.

Rousseau was haunted by contradictions within the social order and within his own mind (he suffered acute attacks of paranoia during the last fifteen years of his life). The opening words of his treatise, *The Social Contract* (1762), "Man is born free, and everywhere he is in chains," reflect his apprehension concerning the inhibiting role of institutional authority. In order to safeguard individual liberty, said Rousseau, people should form a contract among themselves. Unlike Hobbes, whose social contract involved transferring absolute authority from the citizens to a sovereign ruler, or Locke, whose social contract gave limited power to the ruler, Rousseau defined the state as nothing more than "the general will" of its citizens. Sovereignty, for Rousseau, was nothing but the exercise of the general will. "The general will alone," he explained, "can direct the State according to the object for which it was instituted, that is, the common good." Rousseau insisted, moreover, that whoever refused to obey the general will should be constrained to do so by the whole society; that is, all humans should "be forced to be free." "As nature gives each man absolute power over all his members," wrote Rousseau, "the social compact gives the body politic absolute power over all its members also." Such views might have contributed to newly developed theories of democracy, but they were equally effective in justifying totalitarian constraints leveled in the name of the people.

Rousseau's wish to preserve the natural also led him to propose revolutionary changes in education. If society is indeed hopelessly corrupt, then let children grow up in accord with nature, argued Rousseau. In *Emile* (1762), his treatise on education, Rousseau advanced the hypothesis—unheard of in his time—that the education of a child begins at birth. He divided childhood development into five stages over a twenty-five-year span and outlined the type of rearing desirable for each stage. "Hands-on" experience was essential to education, according to Rousseau, especially in the period just prior to the development of reason and intellect, which he placed between the ages of twelve and fifteen. "Nature provides for the child's growth in her own fashion, and this should never be thwarted. Do not make him sit still when he wants to run about, nor run when he wants to be quiet." Rousseau also made a clear distinction between the education of men and that of women. Arguing that a woman's place was in the home and beside the cradle, he proposed for her a domestic education that cultivated modesty, obedience, and other virtues agreeable to her mate. Describing Emile's ideal mate, Rousseau writes, "Her education is in no way exceptional. She has taste without study, talents without art, judgment without knowledge. Her mind is still vacant but has been trained to learn; it is a well-tilled land only waiting for the grain. What a pleasing ignorance! Happy is the man destined to instruct her." Thus Rousseau's views on female education were less "enlightened" (by the standards of Mary Wollstonecraft, for one) than those advanced by Castiglione some two hundred years earlier in *The Book of the Courtier* (see chapter 16). Nevertheless, *Emile* became a landmark in educational theory, and Rousseau's new approach to education—particularly his emphasis on the cultivation of natural inquisitiveness over and above rote learning—influenced modern teaching methods such as those developed by the Italian educator Maria Montessori (1870–1952). Ironically, however, Rousseau saw fit to put all five of his own children in a foundling hospital rather than raise them himself.

Kant's Mind/World Revolution

The German philosopher Immanuel Kant (1724–1804) was "awakened from his slumber," as he put it, when he read the treatises of the Scottish philosopher David Hume (1711–1776). Hume had maintained that genuine knowledge was limited to two sorts: statements of logical relationships ("Bachelors are unmarried") and statements of sense perception ("This chalk is yellow"). Hume concluded that all other statements described belief, not true knowledge. Provoked by the arguments of "the gentle skeptic," as Hume was called, Kant rejected Hume's conclusions. Offering his own analysis of the relationship between the perceiver and the perceived, Kant explained the mind *not* as a passive recipient of information (Locke's "blank slate") but, rather, as a participant in the knowledge process. As Kant put it, "though our knowledge begins *with* experience, it does not follow that [all knowledge] arises *out of* experience." Concepts such as time, space, and causality are not (as Hume had it) mere habits of the mind, but the innate conditions of experience itself. The forms of intuition (space and time) and the categories of thought (quantity, quality, relationship, and modality) exist in the mind from birth; they shape the data of the senses into a consistent picture of the world.

Kant's argument altered the relationship between mind and world as radically as Copernicus had changed the relationship between earth and sun. Shifting the focus of philosophic debate from the nature of objective reality to the question of cognition itself—the process by which the mind comprehends experience—Kant described the mind as not merely reflecting experience, but as organizing experience into a coherent pattern. Knowledge, argued Kant, is a synthetic product of the logical self. In 1781, in the *Critique of Pure Reason*, Kant unfolded his revolutionary view of mind and world. The preeminence Kant gave to the role of the mind in constructing our idea of the world laid the basis for transcendental **idealism**, the doctrine that holds that reality consists of the mind and its forms of perception and understanding.

A giant in the field of modern ethics, Kant assessed the limits of reason with regard to morality. In contrast to Descartes and Locke, who held that knowledge was the key to humanity's advancement, Kant viewed knowledge only as a means to enlightenment of a moral nature. In *An Answer to the Question: What is Enlightenment*" (1784), he wrote, "Enlightenment is man's emergence from his self-imposed immaturity. Immaturity is the inability to use one's understanding without guidance from another." In other words, rules and formulas, along with traditional patterns of thoughts and beliefs, were "shackles" that prevented individuals from thinking for themselves. "*Sapere*

Aude!" ("Have courage to use your own reason!") was Kant's motto for enlightenment. At the same time, Kant exalted reason as the keystone for human conduct. Recognizing that notions of good and evil varied widely among different groups of people, Kant proposed an ethical system that transcended individual circumstances. In the *Critique of Practical Reason* (1788), he proposed a general moral law called the "categorical imperative": namely, that we should act as if we could will that the maxim of our actions should become the law for all humankind. The basis of this moral law is the recognition of our duty to act rationally, that is, to act in ways justified by reasons so universal that they are good for all people at all times. It is not enough that our acts have good effects; it is necessary that we *will* the good. Kant's notion of "good will" is not, however, identical with Christian charity. Nor is it the same as Jesus' commandment to "Do to others as you would wish them do to you," since for Kant ethical conduct is based not on love for humankind (which, after all, one may lack), but on respect for the imperative to act rationally, a condition essential to human dignity.

The Revolutions of the Late Eighteenth Century

The American and French Revolutions drew inspiration from the Enlightenment faith in the reforming power of reason. Both, however, demonstrated the limits of reason in achieving social change. As early as 1776, America's thirteen colonies had rebelled against the longstanding political control of the British government. In the Declaration of Independence (see chapter 24), Jefferson restated Locke's assertion that government must protect its citizens' rights to life, liberty, and property. The British government, however, in making unreasonable demands for revenues, threatened colonial liberty, igniting the passions of fervent populists who sought democratic reform. In 1783, following some seven years of armed conflict, several thousand battle deaths, and a war expense estimated at over $100 million, the thirteen North American colonies achieved their independence. And, in 1789, they began to function under the Constitution of the United States of America. The British political theorist Thomas Paine (1737–1809) observed that the Revolution had done more to enlighten the world and diffuse a spirit of freedom among humankind than any event that had preceded it.

1752 Benjamin Franklin proves that lightning is a form of electricity

1768 James Watt patents the steam engine

1783 the first parachute is used in France

1783 the French make the first manned hot-air balloon flight

1795 the Springfield flintlock musket is developed in the United States

Figure 25.6 BRIFFAULT DE LA CHARPRAIS and **MME. ESCLAPART**, *The Siege of the Bastille, July 14*, 1789. 1791–1796. Engraving, 18¼ × 12 in. Pierpont Morgan Library, New York. Bequest of Gordon N. Ray, GNR 78 (plate #16). Art Resource, New York.

The American Revolution did not go unnoticed in France. French intellectuals followed its every turn; the French government secretly aided the American cause and eventually joined in the war against Britain. However, the revolution that began on French soil in 1789 involved circumstances that were quite different from those in America. In France, the lower classes sought to overturn longstanding social and political institutions and end upper-class privilege. The French Revolution was, in the main, the product of two major sets of problems: class inequality and a serious financial crisis, brought about by some five hundred years of costly wars and royal extravagances (see chapter 21). With his nation on the verge of bankruptcy, King Louis XVI sought new measures for raising revenue.

Throughout French history, taxes had fallen exclusively on the shoulders of the lower and middle classes, the so-called Third Estate. Almost four-fifths of the average peasant's income went to pay taxes, which supported the privileged upper classes. In a population of some 25 million people, the First Estate (the clergy) and the Second Estate (the nobility)—a total of only two hundred thousand citizens—controlled nearly half the land in France;

yet they were exempt from paying taxes. Peasant grievances were not confined to matters of taxation: Population growth and rising prices led to severe shortages of bread, the principal food of the lower classes. When, in 1789, in an effort to obtain public support for new taxes, King Louis XVI called a meeting of the Estates General—its first meeting in 175 years—the Third Estate withdrew and, declaring itself representative of the general will of the people, formed a separate body claiming the right to approve or veto all taxation. This daring act set the Revolution in motion. No sooner had the Third Estate declared itself a national assembly than great masses of peasants and laborers began to riot throughout France.

The crowds that stormed the Bastille prison destroyed the visible symbol of the old French regime (Figure **25.6**). Less than one month later, on August 4, the National Assembly—as the new body established by the Third Estate called itself—issued decrees that abolished the last remnants of medieval feudalism, including manorial courts, feudal duties, and church tithes. It also made provisions for a limited monarchy and an elected legislative assembly. The decrees of the National Assembly became part of the Constitution of 1791. It was prefaced by the 1789

Declaration of the Rights of Man and Citizen, which was modeled on the American Declaration of Independence. A Declaration of the Rights of Woman and Citizen, drafted in 1791 by a butcher's daughter, Olympe de Gouges (1748–1793), demanded equal rights for women, the sex de Gouges described as "superior in beauty and courage." (Indeed, in October of 1789 6,000 courageous women had marched on Versailles to protest the lack of bread in Paris.) For the first time in history women constituted a collective revolutionary force, making demands for equal property rights, government employment for women, and equal educational opportunities—demands guaranteed by the Constitution of 1793 but lost less than two years later by the terms of a new Constitution.

Enlightenment idealism, summed up in Rousseau's slogan "Liberty, Equality, Fraternity," had inflamed popular passions and inspired armed revolt. Nevertheless, from the storming of the Bastille through the rural revolts and mass protests that followed, angry, unreasoning mobs controlled the course of the Revolution. Divisions among the revolutionaries themselves led to a more radical phase of the Revolution, called the Reign of Terror. This phase ensured the failure of the government established in 1793 and sent Louis XVI and his queen to the guillotine. Between 1793 and 1794, over 40,000 people (including Olympe de Gouges) met their deaths at the guillotine. In 1794, a National Convention devised a system of government run by two legislative chambers and a five-man executive body of directors, one of whom, Napoleon Bonaparte, would turn France into a military dictatorship some five years later. If, indeed, the French Revolution defended the Enlightenment bastions of liberty and equality, its foundations of reason and rationality ultimately crumbled under the forces of extremism and violence. The radicals of this and many other world-historical revolutions to follow rewrote the words of the *philosophes* in blood.

SUMMARY

The Enlightenment faith in the promise of reason, the cornerstone of eighteenth-century optimism, was tempered by an equally enlightened examination of the limits of reason. Olaudah Equiano's autobiography protested the inhumane trade in African slaves that persisted throughout the eighteenth century. In England, the keenest critic of Enlightenment idealism was Jonathan Swift, while in France, the acerbic writings of Voltaire described human folly as a universal condition. These three masters of satire found their Asian counterpart in Li Ruzhen, whose witty prose attacked long-standing Chinese traditions. Voltaire's *Candide* remains the classic statement of comic skepticism in Western literature. Voltaire's contemporary, William Hogarth, brought the bitter invective of the satirist to the visual arts. His engravings exposed the social ills and class discrepancies of British society, even as they mocked universal human pretensions.

Questioning the value of reason for the advancement of the human condition, Jean-Jacques Rousseau argued that society itself corrupted the individual. He rejected the artificiality of the wig-and-silk-stocking culture in which he lived and championed "man in his primitive state." Rousseau's treatises on social history, government, and education explored ways in which individuals might retain their natural goodness and remain free and self-determining. In Germany, the philosopher Immanuel Kant examined the limits of the mind in the process of knowing. He argued that human beings have knowledge of the world through certain innate capabilities of mind. Kant appealed to "good will" as the basis for moral action.

While Enlightenment ideals fueled armed revolt in both America and France, the revolutions themselves blazed with antirational sentiment. In France especially, the men and women who fired the cannons of revolt abandoned reason as inadequate to the task of effecting social and political reform. Operating according to the dictates of their passions and their will, they gave dramatic evidence of the limits of reason to create a heaven on earth. The shift away from reason and the rational was to have major repercussions in the centuries to follow.

GLOSSARY

caricature exaggeration of peculiarities or defects to produce comic or burlesque effects

idealism in philosophy, the theory that holds that reality consists of the mind and its ideas; transcendental (or critical) idealism is Kant's name for the doctrine that knowledge is a synthetic product of the logical self

SUGGESTIONS FOR READING

Adams, F. D. and Barry Sanders, eds. *Three Black Writers in Eighteenth-Century England.* Belmont, Calif.: Wadsworth, 1971.

Babbitt, Irving. *Rousseau and Romanticism.* New York: Meridian, 1977.

Bernier, Olivier. *Words of Fire, Deeds of Blood: The Mob, the Monarchy, and the French Revolution.* Boston: Little, Brown, 1989.

Dunn, Susan. *Sister Revolutions: French Lightning, American Light.* New York: Faber & Faber, 1999.

Gershoy, Leo. *From Despotism to Revolution*, 1763–1789. Westport, Conn.: Greenwood Press, 1983.

Hallett, Mark. *The Spectacle of Difference: Graphic Satire in the Age of Hogarth.* New Haven, Conn.: Yale University Press, 1999.

Leith, James A. *The Idea of Art as Propaganda in France 1750–1799: A Study in the History of Ideas.* Toronto: University of Toronto Press, 1965.

Lindsay, Jack. *Hogarth: His Art and His World.* New York: Taplinger, 1979.

Richter, Peyton, and Ilona Ricardo. *Voltaire.* Boston: Twayne, 1980.

Thomas, Hugh. *The Slave Trade: The Story of the Atlantic Slave Trade, 1440–1870.* New York: Simon & Schuster, 1997.

Eighteenth-century art, music, and society

"In the presence of this miracle of [ancient Greek] art, I forget the whole universe and my soul acquires a loftiness appropriate to its dignity."
Johann Joachim Winckelmann

The dynamics of class and culture had a shaping influence on the arts of eighteenth-century Europe. European aristocrats of the period between 1715 and 1750 found pleasure in an elegant and refined style known as the *rococo.* Toward the end of the century, middle-class bonds to Enlightenment idealism and revolutionary reform, along with a new archeological appreciation of ancient Greece and Rome, ushered in the *neoclassical* style. In music, too, the era witnessed notable turns: from the ponderous baroque to the more delicate and playful rococo, and then, in the 1780s, to the formal and measured sounds of the *classical* symphony and the string quartet. An increased demand for secular entertainment called forth new genres in instrumental music and a wide range of subject matter in the visual arts. Despite their stylistic diversity, the arts shared a spirit of buoyant optimism and vitality that ensured their endurance beyond the Age of the Enlightenment.

The Rococo Style

The rococo style was born in France among members of the leisured nobility who had outlived Louis XIV. At Versailles and in the elegant urban townhouses (or *hôtels,* as they were called) of Paris, where the wealthy gathered

Figure 26.1 GERMAIN BOFFRAND, Salon de la Princesse, Hôtel de Soubise, Paris, ca. 1740. Oval shaped, 33 × 26 ft. Scala/Art Resource, New York.

Figure 26.2 MARTIN CARLIN (master 1766–1785), Lady's desk, ca. 1775. Decorated with Sèvres porcelain plaques; tulipwood, walnut, and hardwood veneered on oak, height 31⅞ in., width 25⅞ in., depth 16 in. The Metropolitan Museum of Art, New York. Gift of Samuel H. Kress Foundation, 1958 (58.75.49).

to enjoy the pleasures of dancing, dining, and conversing, the rococo provided an atmosphere of elegant refinement. The word "rococo" derives from *rocaille*, French for the fancy rock- or shell-work that was commonly used to ornament aristocratic gardens and grottoes. Rococo interiors display the organic vitality of seashells, plants, and flowers. And while rococo artists preserved the ornate and luxuriant features of the baroque style, they favored elements of play and intimacy that were best realized in works of a small scale, such as porcelain figurines, furniture, and paintings suitable for domestic quarters.

The Salon de la Princesse in the Hôtel de Soubise in Paris typifies the rococo style (Figure **26.1**): Its interior is airy and fragile by comparison with a Louis XIV salon (see Figure 21.9). Brilliant white walls accented with pastel tones of rose, pale blue, and lime replace the ruby reds and royal blues of the baroque *salon*. The geometric regularity of the baroque interior has given way to an organic medley of curves and countercurves, echoed in elegant mirrors and chandeliers. The walls, ornamented with gilded tendrils, playful cupids, and floral garlands, melt into sensuously painted ceiling vaults crowned with graceful moldings.

Rococo furnishings are generally more delicate than baroque furnishings, and chairs are often fully upholstered—an innovation of the eighteenth century. Bureaus and tables may be fitted with panels of porcelain (Figure **26.2**)—a Chinese technique that Marie Antoinette, the consort of Louis XVI, introduced at Versailles. Aristocratic women, especially such notable females as Marie Antoinette in France, Catherine the Great in Russia, and

Maria Theresa in Austria, eagerly embraced the rococo style. Indeed, the rococo, whose widespread commercialization made it popular throughout most of Europe, may be said to reflect the distinctive influence of eighteenth-century women of taste.

Beyond the *salon*, the garden was the favorite setting for the leisured elite. Unlike the geometrically ordered garden parks at Versailles, rococo gardens imitated the calculated naturalism of Chinese gardens. They featured undulating paths that gave false impressions of scale and distance. They also often included artificial lakes, small colonnaded temples, ornamental pagodas, and other architectural "follies." Both outdoors and in, the fascination with Chinese objects and motifs, which began as a fashion in Europe around 1720, promoted the cult of *chinoiserie* (see chapter 21).

Although the rococo style originated in France, it reached spectacular heights in the courts of secular princes at Würzburg, Munich, Salzburg, and Vienna. In Austria and the German states, it became the favorite style for the ornamentation of rural pilgrimage churches. In the Benedictine Church of Ottobeuren in Bavaria, designed by the eighteenth-century German architect Johann Michael Fischer, walls seem to disappear beneath a riot of stucco "frosting" as rich and sumptuous as any wedding cake. The more restrained elegance of French rococo interiors here gives way to a dazzling array of organic forms that sprout from the moldings and cornices like unruly flora (Figure **26.3**). Shimmering light floods into the white-walled interior through oval windows, and pastel-colored frescoes turn ceilings and walls into heavenly

Figure 26.3 Cherubs, Benedictine church, Ottobeuren, Bavaria, 1736–1766. Stucco. Foto Marburg, Germany.

Figure 26.4 JOHAN MICHAEL FISCHER, interior, Benedictine abbey, Ottobeuren, Bavaria, 1736–1766. Painted and gilded wood and stucco. Vanni/Art Resource, New York.

antechambers. Illusionism reigns: Wooden columns and stucco cornices are painted to look like marble; angels and cherubs, tendrils and leaves, curtains and clouds—all made of wood and stucco that have been painted and gilded—come to life as props in a theater of miracles (Figure **26.4**). At Ottobeuren, the somber majesty of the Roman baroque church has given way to a sublime vision of paradise that is also a feast for the senses.

Rococo Painting in France

The pursuit of pleasure—a major eighteenth-century theme—dominates the paintings of the four great rococo masters: Antoine Watteau (1684–1721), François Boucher (1703–1770), Marie-Louise-Elisabeth Vigée-Lebrun (1775–1842), and Jean-Honoré Fragonard (1732–1806). The first of these artists, the Flemish-born Watteau, began his career by painting theatrical scenes. In 1717, he submitted to the French Academy his *Departure from the Island of Cythera* (Figure **26.5**), a painting that pays tribute to the fleeting nature of romantic love. The painting shows a group of fashionable men and women preparing to board a golden boat by which they will leave the island of Cythera. According to legend, Cythera was the birthplace of Venus, and on this outing—a *fête galante* (literally, "elegant entertainment")—aristocrats pay homage to the Goddess of Love, whose rose-bedecked shrine appears at the far right. Amidst fluttering cupids, the pilgrims of love linger in pairs as they wistfully take leave of their florid

hideaway. Watteau repeats the serpentine line formed by the figures in the delicate arabesques of the trees and rolling hills. And he bathes the entire panorama in a misty, golden light. Not since the sixteenth-century artists Giorgione and Titian had any painter indulged so deeply in the pleasures of nature or the voluptuous world of the senses.

Watteau's fragile forms and delicate colors, painted with feathery brushstrokes reminiscent of Rubens, evoke a mood of reverie and nostalgia. His doll-like men and women provide sharp contrast with Rubens' physically powerful figures (see Figure 21.16) or, for that matter, with Poussin's idealized heroes (see Figure 21.13). Watteau's art conveys no noble message; rather, it explores the world of familiar but transitory pleasures.

If Watteau's world was wistful and poetic, that of his contemporary François Boucher was sensual and indulgent. Boucher, a specialist in designing mythological scenes, became head of the Gobelins tapestry factory in 1755 and director of the Royal Academy ten years later. He was First Painter to King Louis XV and a good friend of the king's favorite mistress, Jeanne Antoinette Poisson, the Marquise de Pompadour (1721–1764). A woman of remarkable beauty and intelligence—she owned two telescopes, a microscope, and a lathe that she installed in her apartments in order to carve cameos—Madame de Pompadour influenced state policy and dominated fashion and the arts at Versailles for almost twenty years. In the

Figure 26.5 ANTOINE WATTEAU, *Departure from the Island of Cythera*, 1717. Oil on canvas, 4 ft. 3 in. × 6 ft. 4 in. Louvre, Paris. Photo: © R.M.N., Paris.

Fashion and fashionableness— clear expressions of self-conscious materialism—were major themes of rococo art. Marie-Louise Elisabeth Vigée-Lebrun, the most famous of a number of eighteenth-century female artists, produced refined portrait paintings for an almost exclusively female clientele. Vigée-Lebrun's travels in the Low Countries allowed her to study the works of Rubens and van Dyck, whose painterly style she admired. Her glamorous likeness of Marie Antoinette is a tribute to the European fashion industry (Figure 26.8). Plumed headdresses and low-cut gowns bedecked with lace, ribbons, and tassels turned the aristocratic female into a conspicuous ornament; the size of her billowing skirt required that she turn sideways to pass through open doors. In response to the upper-class infatuation with pastoral and idyllic themes, Vigée-Lebrun also painted portraits of more modestly dressed women in muslin skirts and straw hats. Unlike

Figure 26.7 (below) Sèvres porcelain potpourri vase, mid-eighteenth century. Gondola-shaped body, scrolled handles, 4-lobed cover, height 14⅛ in., length 14½ in., width 8 in. This vase, purchased by Madame de Pompadour, is one of the finest products of the Sèvres porcelain factory, which she sponsored and patronized. The Metropolitan Museum of Art, New York. Gift of Samuel H. Kress Foundation, 1958 (58.75.88 a, b, c).

Figure 26.6 (above) **FRANÇOIS BOUCHER**, *Venus Consoling Love*, 1751. Oil on canvas, 42⅛ × 33⅜ in. © 1998 Board of Trustees. National Gallery of Art, Washington, D.C. Chester Dale Collection.

idyllic *Venus Consoling Love*, Boucher flattered his patron by portraying her as Goddess of Love (Figure **26.6**). Surrounded by attentive doves and cupids, the nubile Venus reclines on a bed of sumptuous rose and satin draperies laid amidst a bower of leafy trees and windswept grasses. Boucher delighted in sensuous contrasts of flesh, fabric, feathers, and flowers. And his girlish women, with their unnaturally tiny feet, rosebud-pink nipples, and wistful glances, were coy symbols of erotic pleasure.

Boucher also designed sets and costumes for the Royal Opera and motifs for tapestries and porcelains. From the Sèvres porcelain factory, located near Paris and founded by Madame de Pompadour, came magnificent porcelains ornamented with gilded wreaths, arabesque cartouches, and playful cupids floating on fleecy clouds (Figure 26.7). Outside of France, in Germany and Austria, porcelain figurines of shepherds and shepherdesses advertised the eighteenth-century enthusiasm for the pastoral life.

Figure 26.8 **MARIE-LOUISE ELISABETH VIGÉE-LEBRUN**, *Marie Antoinette*, 1788. Oil on canvas, 12 ft. 1½ in. × 6ft. 3½ in. Musée de Versailles. Giraudon/Art Resource, New York.

651

CHAPTER TWENTY-SIX   Eighteenth-century art, music, and society

Boucher, Vigée-Lebrun did not cast her subjects as goddesses, but she imparted to them a chic sweetness and artless simplicity. These talents earned her the equivalent of over $200,000 a year and allowed her an independence uncommon among eighteenth-century women.

Jean-Honoré Fragonard, the last of the great rococo artists, was the undisputed master of translating the art of seduction into paint. In the works he completed shortly before the French Revolution, he captured the pleasures of a waning aristocracy, especially the pleasures of courtship and romantic love. In 1766, a wealthy aristocrat commissioned Fragonard to paint a scene that showed the patron's mistress seated on a swing being pushed by a friendly old clergyman. *The Swing* depicts a flirtatious encounter that takes place in a garden bower filled with frothy trees, classical statuary, and delicate light. The young woman, dressed in yards of satin and lace, kicks her tiny shoe into the air in the direction of a statue of Cupid, while her lover, hiding in the bushes below, peers delightedly beneath her billowing skirts (Figure **26.9**). Whether or not the young lady is aware of her lover's presence, her coy gesture and the irreverent behavior of the *ménage à trois* (lover, mistress, and cleric) create a mood of erotic intrigue similar to that found in the comic operas of this period, as well as in

The French sculptor Claude Michel, known as Clodion (1738–1814), who worked almost exclusively for private patrons, was among the favorite rococo artists of the late eighteenth century. His *Intoxication of Wine* revived a classical theme—a celebration honoring Dionysus, the Greek god of wine and fertility (Figure **26.10**). Flushed with wine and revelry, the **satyr** (a semi-bestial woodland creature symbolic of Dionysus) embraces a **bacchante**, an attendant of Dionysus. Clodion made the piece in terra-cotta, a clay medium that requires rapid modeling, thus inviting the artist to capture a sense of spontaneity. Rococo painters sought similar effects through the use of loose and rapid brushstrokes and by sketching with pastels. The expressive impact of *The Intoxication of Wine* belies its tiny size—it is just under 2 feet high.

Figure 26.9 JEAN-HONORÉ FRAGONARD, *The Swing*, 1768. Oil on canvas, 32 × 35 in. Reproduced by permission of the Trustees, the Wallace Collection, London.

Figure 26.10 (right) **CLODION** (Claude Michel), *The Intoxication of Wine*, ca. 1775. Terra-cotta, height 23¼ in. The Metropolitan Museum of Art, New York. Bequest of Benjamin Altman, 1913 (14.40.687).

the pornographic novel, which developed as a genre in eighteenty-century France. Fragonard's deft brushstrokes caress the figures and render the surrounding foliage in delicate pastel tones. Although Fragonard immortalized the union of wealth, privilege, and pleasure enjoyed by the upper classes of the eighteenth century, he captured a spirit of sensuous abandon that has easily outlived the particulars of time, place, and social class.

Rococo Sculpture

The finest examples of eighteenth-century sculpture are small in scale, intimate in mood, and almost entirely lacking in the dramatic urgency and religious fervor of baroque art. Intended for the boudoir or the drawing room, rococo sculpture usually depicted elegant dancers, wooing couples, and other lighthearted subjects.

Eighteenth-Century French Genre Painting

Many of the *philosophes* found the works of Boucher, Clodion, and other rococo artists trivial and morally degenerate. Diderot, for example, denounced rococo boudoir imagery and demanded an art that made "virtue attractive and vice odious." The French artists Jean-Baptiste Greuze (1725–1805) and Jean-Baptiste-Siméon Chardin (1699–1779) heeded the plea for art with a moral purpose. These artists abandoned the indulgent sensuality and frivolity of the rococo; instead they painted realistic scenes of everyday life among the middle and lower classes. This shift in focus mirrored the transition from a society dominated by royal absolutism and religious dogma to one guided by the secular morality of the Enlightenment.

Greuze, Diderot's favorite artist, exalted the natural virtues of ordinary people. He painted such moralizing subjects as *The Father Reading the Bible to His Children*, *The Well-Beloved Mother*, and *The Effects of Drunkenness*. In the manner of Hogarth (whose works Greuze admired), he chose engaging narratives that might require a series of paintings. Greuze's *Village Betrothal* (Figure **26.11**) of 1761

tells the story of an impending matrimony among hard-working, simple-living rustics: The father, who has just given over the dowry to the humble groom, blesses the couple; the mother laments losing a daughter; while the other members of the household, including the hen and chicks (possibly a symbol of the couple's prospective progeny), look on approvingly. Greuze's painting could easily have been an illustration of a scene from a popular eighteenth-century novel. Greuze shunned the intellectualism of Poussin, the sensuality of Fragonard, and the satirical acrimony of Hogarth. His melodramatic representations appealed to common emotion and sentiment. Understandably, they were among the most popular images of the eighteenth and nineteenth centuries.

The art of Greuze's contemporary Chardin was less steeped in sentimentality. Chardin painted humble still lifes and genre scenes showing nurses, governesses, and kitchen maids at work (Figure **26.12**). Unlike Greuze, who illustrated his moral tales as literally as possible, Chardin avoided both explicit moralizing and anecdotal themes. Yet Chardin's paintings bear a deep concern for commonplace humanity, and they carry an implicit message—that of the ennobling dignity of work and the

Figure 26.11 JEAN-BAPTISTE GREUZE, *Village Betrothal*, 1761. Oil on canvas, 3 ft. 10½ in. × 3 ft. Louvre, Paris. © R.M.N., Paris.

Figure 26.12 JEAN-BAPTISTE-SIMÉON CHARDIN, *The Kitchen Maid*, 1738. Oil on canvas, 18⅛ x 14¾ in.
© 1998 Board of Trustees, National Gallery of Art, Washington, D.C. Samuel H. Kress Collection.

virtues of domesticity. The forthright qualities of Chardin's subjects are echoed in his style: His figures are simple and monumental, and his compositions reveal an uncanny sense of balance reminiscent of the works of de Hooch and Vermeer. Each object in the spatial field seems to assume its proper and predestined place. Executed in mellow, creamy tones, Chardin's paintings evoke a mood of gentility and gravity.

Greuze and Chardin brought painting out of the drawing room and into the kitchen. Their canvases were in such high demand that they were sold widely in engraved copies. Ironically, while Chardin's subjects were humble and commonplace, his patrons were often bankers, foreign ambassadors, and royalty itself—Louis XV owned at least two of Chardin's paintings.

1775 the flush toilet is patented in Britain
1777 steam heat is used in France for the first time since the Roman era
1779 the first bicycles appear in Paris

Eighteenth-Century Neoclassicism

Neoclassicism—the self-conscious revival of Greco-Roman culture—belonged to a tradition that stretched at least from the early Renaissance through the age of Louis XIV. During the seventeenth century, Poussin and other artists of the European Academies (see chapter 21) had resurrected the classical ideals of clarity, simplicity, balance, and restraint, following the model of Raphael, the High Renaissance standard-bearer of the Greco-Roman style. The neoclassicism of the eighteenth century was inspired for the most part by archeological excavations of Greek and Roman sites—most specifically, the scientific investigation of two Roman towns, Herculaneum and Pompeii. Greek and Roman artifacts, which had previously been seen only by the nobility and rulers, became available to the general public. Study of these works enabled artists and antiquarians, for the first time in history, to make clear distinctions between the artifacts of Greece and those of Rome. The result was a more austere and archeologically correct neoclassicism than any that had flourished previous to the eighteenth century.

Rome had been a favorite attraction for well-educated tourists and students of art since Renaissance times. But during the eighteenth century, Rome and its monuments came under new scrutiny. Architects studied the monuments of antiquity (see chapter 6), and artists made topographic sketches, often reproduced in copper engravings that were sold cheaply—in the manner of modern-day postcards. In 1740 the Venetian architect and engineer Giovanni Battista Piranesi (1720–1778) established himself in Rome as a printmaker. Piranesi's engravings of Rome were widely bought and appreciated (see Figure 9.9), while his studies of Roman monuments, with their precisely rendered technical details and inscriptions, exerted considerable influence on French and English architects of his time (Figure **26.13**). Piranesi's later works—nightmarish visions of dungeons inspired by the Roman sewer system—abandoned all classical canons of objectivity and emotional restraint. Nevertheless, with European artists more eager than ever to rediscover antiquity through the careful study of its remains, the neoclassical revival was under way.

A major factor for the widespread interest in antiquity, and one that made eighteenth-century neoclassicism unique, was the scientific uncovering of ancient classical ruins. In 1738, the king of Naples sponsored the first archeological excavations at Herculaneum, one of the two Roman cities in Southern Italy buried under volcanic ash by the eruption of Mount Vesuvius in 79 C.E. The excavations at Pompeii would follow in 1748. These enterprises, followed by European archeological expeditions to Greece

Figure 26.13 GIOVANNI BATTISTA PIRANESI, *The Pantheon*, from *Views of Rome*, ca. 1748–1778. Etching. The towers flanking the portico, which were added in the seventeenth century when the Pantheon functioned as a church, have since been removed. Reproduced by Courtesy of the Trustees of the British Museum, London.

Figure 26.14 GIOVANNI PAOLO PANINI (copy after), *Picture Gallery (Roma Antica)*, 1691–1765. Pen and black ink with brush and gray wash and watercolor over graphite on ivory laid paper, 17¼ × 27⅜ in. © 1998 The Art Institute of Chicago. All Rights Reserved. Emily Crane Chadbourne Collection (1955.7.45).

and Asia Minor in 1750, inspired scholars to assemble vast collections of Greek and Roman artifacts (Figure **26.14**). Both the Louvre and the Vatican became museum repositories that housed the treasures of these expeditions. Shortly after the first English expeditions to Athens, the German scholar Johann Joachim Winckelmann (1717–1768) began to study Greek and Roman antiquities. He published an eloquent assessment of these objects in his magnificently illustrated *History of Ancient Art* (1764). These and other of Winckelmann's widely circulated texts, which offered a critical analysis of art objects (rather than a biographical history of artists), established Winckelmann as the father of modern art historical scholarship.

Although Winckelmann himself never visited Greece, he was infatuated with Hellenic and Hellenistic sculpture. He argued that artists of his time could become great only by imitating the ancient Greeks, whose best works, he insisted, betrayed "a noble simplicity and a quiet grandeur." Of his favorite ancient statue, the *Apollo Belvedere* (see Figure 26.17, left), Winckelmann proclaimed, "In the presence of this miracle of art, I forget the whole universe and my soul acquires a loftiness appropriate to its dignity." Winckelmann's reverence for antiquity typified the eighteenth-century attitude toward classicism as a vehicle for the elevation of human consciousness. Here, finally, was the ideal mode of expression for the

Enlightenment program of reason, clarity, and order—a style that equated Beauty with Goodness, Virtue, and Truth. Winckelmann's publications became an inspiration for artists and aesthetes all over Europe. In Britain, Sir Joshua Reynolds (1723–1792), the painter and founder of the Royal Academy of Art in London, lectured on the Grand Manner; his *Discourses* were translated into French, German, and Italian. The lofty vision of a style that captured the nobility and dignity of the Greco-Roman past fired the imagination of intellectuals across Western Europe and America.

Neoclassical Architecture

The classical revival of the eighteenth century was unique in its accuracy of detail and its purity of design. Neoclassical architects made careful distinctions between Greek and Roman buildings and between the various Renaissance and post-Renaissance styles modeled upon antiquity. Simple geometric masses—spheres, cubes, and cylinders—became the bases for a new, more abstract and austere classicism. Neoclassical architects rejected the illusionistic theatricality of the baroque style with its broken pediments, cartouches, and ornamental devices. They also turned their backs on the stucco foliage, cherubic angels, and "wedding-cake" fantasies of the rococo. The ideal neoclassical exterior was free of frivolous ornamentation,

Figure 26.15 (above) **JACQUES-GERMAIN SOUFFLOT**, Sainte Geneviève (renamed the "Panthéon" during the French Revolution), Paris, 1757–1792. Photo: A. F. Kersting, London.

Figure 26.16 (right) **JACQUES-GERMAIN SOUFFLOT**, interior of Sainte Geneviève ("Panthéon"), Paris, 1757–1792. Photo: A. F. Kersting, London.

while its interior consisted of clean and rectilinear wall planes, soberly accented with engaged columns or pilasters, geometric motifs, and shallow niches that housed copies of antique statuary (see Figure 26.17).

In France, the leading architect of the eighteenth century was Jacques-Germain Soufflot (1713–1780). Soufflot's Church of Sainte Geneviève (Figure **26.15** and Figure 26.13), the patron saint of Paris, follows a strict central plan with four shallow domes covering each of the arms. A massive central dome, supported entirely on pillars, rises over the crossing (compare Saint Paul's in London; Figure 22.2). The facade of Sainte Geneviève resembles the portico of the Pantheon in Rome (see chapter 6, and Figure 26.13), while the interior of the church (Figure **26.16**)—which entombs, among others, Voltaire and Rousseau—recalls the grandeur of Saint Peter's in Rome. As the "Panthéon" illustrates, Soufflot did not slavishly imitate any single classical structure; rather, he selected specific features from a variety of notable sources and combined them with clarity and reserve. In contrast with its baroque and rococo ancestors, the Church of Sainte Geneviève was no theater of miracles but rather a rationally ordered, this-worldly shrine.

Some of the purest examples of the classical revival are found in late eighteenth-century English country homes. The interiors of these sprawling symbols of wealth and prestige reflect close attention to archeological drawings of Greek and Roman antiquities. Kedleston Hall in Derbyshire, England, designed by the Scottish architect Robert Adam (1728–1792), reflects a pristine taste for crisp contours and the refined synthesis of Greco-Roman motifs (Figure **26.17**). In such estates as this, the neoclassical spirit touched everything from sculpture (Figure **26.18**) and furniture to tea services and tableware. Among the most popular items of the day were the ceramics of the English potter Josiah Wedgwood (1730–1795).

Wedgwood's wares were modeled on Greek and Roman vases and embellished with finely applied, molded white clay surface designs (Figure **26.19**).

The austerity and dignity of neoclassicism made it the ideal style for public monuments and offices of state. In Paris, Berlin, and Washington, D.C., neoclassical architects borrowed Greek and Roman temple designs for public and private buildings, especially banks, where the modern-day gods of money and materialism took the place of the ancient deities. In some instances, the spirit of revival produced daring architectural hybrids. In England, for instance, the Scottish architect James Gibbs (1682–1754) designed churches that combined a classical portico with a Gothic spire (Figure **26.20**). This scheme, which united the baroque love of contrast with the neoclassical rule of symmetry, became extremely popular in America, especially in the congregational churches built across New England.

Figure 26.17 ROBERT ADAM, Marble Hall, Kedleston Hall, Derbyshire, England, 1763–1777. (Note copy of the *Apollo Belvedere* in niche at left.) 67 × 42 ft., height 40 ft. Photo: A. F. Kersting, London.

Figure 26.18 (left) **ANTONIO CANOVA**, *Pauline Borghese as Venus*, 1808. Marble, life-sized. Galleria Borghese, Rome. Alinari/Art Resource, New York.

Figure 26.19 (below, left) **WEDGWOOD & SONS**, Copy of Portland Vase (#7) with stand, ca. 1790. Black and white jasperware, height 10 in. Courtesy Museum of Fine Arts, Boston. Gift of Dr. Lloyd E. Hawes.

Neoclassicism in America

A tour of the city of Washington in the District of Columbia will convince any student of the impact of neoclassicism on the architecture of the United States. The neoclassical movement in America did not originate, however, in the capital city, whose major buildings date only from the nineteenth century, but, rather, among the Founding Fathers. One of the most passionate devotees of Greco-Roman art and life was the Virginia lawyer and statesman Thomas Jefferson (1743–1826), whose Declaration of Independence was discussed in chapter 24. Farmer, linguist, educator, inventor, architect, musician, and politician, the man who served as third president of the United States was an eighteenth-century *uomo universale* (Figure **26.22**). Jefferson was a student of ancient and Renaissance treatises on architecture and an impassioned apostle of neoclassicism. In 1786, he designed the Virginia State Capitol (see chapter 7) modeled on the Maison Carrée (see Figure 26.32). For the design of his own country estate in Monticello and for the University of Virginia—America's first state university—he drew on the Pantheon in Rome, the most admired of all ancient Roman buildings (see Figure 26.13). Jefferson reconstructed this ancient temple at two-thirds its original size in the Rotunda, which housed the original library of the

University of Virginia (Figure **26.21**). Considerably smaller than Soufflot's "Panthéon," the stripped-down Rotunda is also purer in form. Jefferson's tightly organized and geometrically correct plan for the campus of the University of Virginia reflects the basic sympathy between neoclassical design and the rationalist ideals of the Enlightenment. The "academical village," as Jefferson described it, was a community of the free-thinking elite—exclusively white, wealthy, and male, yet it provided both a physical and a spiritual model for non-sectarian education in the United States.

The young American nation drew on the heritage of the ancients (and especially the history of the Roman Republic) to symbolize its newly forged commitment to the ideals of liberty and equality. The leaders of the American Revolution regarded themselves as descendants of ancient Roman heroes and some even adopted Latin names, much as the Italian Renaissance humanists had done. On the Great Seal of the United States, the Latin phrase "E pluribus unum" ("out of many, one") and the bundle of arrows in the grasp of the American eagle (suggesting the Roman fasces: a bundle of rods surrounding an ax—the ancient symbol for power and authority) identified America as heir to republican Rome (Figure **26.23**).

Neoclassical Sculpture

Neoclassical sculptors heeded the Enlightenment demand for an art that perpetuated the memory of illustrious men. Jean-Antoine Houdon (1741–1828), the leading portrait sculptor of Europe, immortalized in stone the features of his contemporaries. His portrait busts, which met the popular demand for achieving a familiar likeness, revived the realistic tradition in sculpture that had reached its highwater mark among the Romans. Houdon had a special

Figure 26.20 (above) **JAMES GIBBS**, Saint Martin-in-the-Fields, London, 1721–1726. Photo: A. F. Kersting, London.

Figure 26.21 (right) **THOMAS JEFFERSON**, Rotunda, University of Virginia, Charlottesville, 1822–1826. Prints Collection, Special Collections Department, University Archives, University of Virginia Library.

talent for catching characteristic gestures and expressions: Diderot, shown without a wig, surveys his world with inquisitive candor (see Figure 24.3), while the aging Voltaire addresses us with a grim and knowing smile (see Figure 25.3). While visiting America, Houdon carved portraits of Jefferson (see Figure 26.22), Franklin, and other "virtuous men" of the republic. His life-sized statue of George Washington renders the first president of the United States as country gentleman and eminent statesman (Figure **26.24**). Resting his hand on a columnar *fasces*, the poised but slightly potbellied Washington recalls (however faintly) the monumental dignity of the Greek gods and the Roman emperors.

While Houdon invested neoclassicism with a strong taste for realism, most of his contemporaries followed the Hellenic impulse to idealize the human form. Such was the case with the Italian-born sculptor Antonio Canova (1757–1822). Canova's life-sized portrait of Napoleon Bonaparte's sister, Pauline

Figure 26.24 JEAN-ANTOINE HOUDON, *George Washington*, 1786–1796. Marble, height 6 ft. 2 in. State capitol, Richmond, Virginia. Virginia State Library and Archives.

Figure 26.22 (above) **JEAN-ANTOINE HOUDON**, *Thomas Jefferson*, 1789. Marble, height 21½ in. Library of Congress, Washington, D.C.

Figure 26.23 Great Seal of the United States. Courtesy of the Bureau of Printing and Engraving, U.S. Treasury Department.

Borghese, is a sublime example of neoclassical refinement and restraint (see Figure 26.18). Canova casts Pauline in the guise of a reclining Venus. Perfectly proportioned and flawless, she shares the cool elegance of classical statuary and Wedgwood reliefs. In contrast to the vigorously carved surfaces of baroque sculpture (recall, for instance, Bernini's *Ecstasy of Saint Teresa*, Figure 20.2), Canova's figure is smooth and neutral—even stark. A comparison of Canova's *Pauline Borghese as Venus* with Clodion's *Intoxication of Wine* (see Figure 26.10) is also revealing: Both depend on classical themes and models, but whereas Clodion's piece is intimate, sensuous, and spontaneous, Canova's seems remote, controlled, and calculated. Its aesthetic distance is intensified by the ghostlike whiteness of the figure and its "blank" eyes—eighteenth-century sculptors seem to have been unaware that classical artists painted parts of their statues to make them look more lifelike.

Neoclassical Painting and Politics: The Art of David

During the last decades of the eighteenth century, as the tides of revolution began to engulf the indulgent lifestyles of the French aristocracy, the rococo style in painting gave way to a soberminded new approach to picturemaking. The pioneer of the new style was the French artist Jacques-Louis David (1748–1825). David's early canvases were executed in the rococo style of his teacher and distant cousin, Boucher. But after winning the coveted Prix de Rome, which sent him to study in the foremost city of antiquity, David found his place among the classicists. In 1784 he completed one of the most influential paintings of the late eighteenth century: *The Oath of the Horatii* (Figure **26.25**). The painting was commissioned by the French king some five years before the outbreak of the Revolution; ironically, however, it became a symbol of the very spirit that would topple the royal crown.

The Oath of the Horatii illustrates a dramatic event recorded by Livy in his *History of Rome*. It depicts the moment when the three sons of the noble patriarch Horatius Proclus swear to oppose the treacherous Curiatii family in a win-or-die battle that would determine the future of Rome. In France, Livy's story had become especially popular as the subject of a play by the French dramatist

Figure 26.25 JACQUES-LOUIS DAVID, *The Oath of the Horatii*, 1784. Oil on canvas, 10 ft. 10 in. × 14 ft. Louvre, Paris. Photo: © R.M.N., Paris.

Figure 26.26 JACQUES-LOUIS DAVID, *The Death of Socrates*, 1787. Oil on canvas, 4 ft. 3 in. × 6 ft. 5¼ in. The Metropolitan Museum of Art, New York. Catharine Lorillard Wolfe Collection. Wolfe Fund, 1931 (31.45).

Pierre Corneille (1606–1684). David captured the spirit of the story in a single potent image: Resolved to pursue their destiny as defenders of liberty, the Horatii lift their arms in a dramatic military salute. Bathed in golden light, the statuesque figures stand along the strict horizontal line of the picture plane. The body of the warrior on the far left forms a rigid triangular shape that is subtly repeated throughout the composition—in the arches of the colonnade, for instance, and in the group of grieving women (one of whom represents the fiancée of a Curiatius). According to the tale, her victorious brother, the sole survivor of the combat, returned home to find her mourning for her dead lover and murdered her in a fit of rage.

David's painting was an immediate success: People lined up to see it while it hung in the artist's studio in Rome, and the city of Paris received it enthusiastically when it arrived there in 1785. The huge canvas (over 10 by 14 feet) came to be perceived as a clear denunciation of aristocratic pastimes. In place of the lace cuffs, silk suits, and powdered wigs of the rococo drawing room, David had detailed the trappings of war. His painting presented life as serious drama: It proclaimed the importance of reason and the intellect over and above feeling and sentiment, and it defended the ideals of male heroism and self-sacrifice in the interest of one's country. Stylistically, too, the painting was revolutionary: David rejected the luxuriant sparkle of rococo art for sober simplicity. He replaced the pliant forms, sensuous textures, and pastel tones of the rococo with rectilinear shapes, hard-edged contours, and somber colors—features that recalled the art of Poussin (whom David deeply admired). His technique was austere, precise, and realistic—witness the archeologically correct Roman helmets, sandals, and swords.

Three years after painting *The Oath of the Horatii*, David conceived the smaller but equally popular *Death of Socrates* (Figure **26.26**). The scene is a fifth-century B.C.E. Athenian prison. It is the moment before Socrates, the father of Greek philosophy, drinks the fatal hemlock. Surrounding Socrates are his students and friends, posed in various expressions of lament, while the apostle of reason himself—illuminated in the style of Caravaggio—rhetorically lifts his hand to heaven. Clarity and intellectual control dominate the composition: Figures and objects are arranged as if plotted on a grid of lines horizontal and vertical to the picture plane. This ideal geometry, a metaphor for the ordering function of reason, complements the grave and noble message of the painting: Reason guides human beings to live and, if need be, to die for their moral principles. In *The Death of Socrates*, as in *The Oath of the Horatii*, David put neoclassicism at the service of a morality based on Greco-Roman Stoicism, self-sacrifice, and stern patriotism.

Figure 26.27 JEAN-AUGUSTE-DOMINIQUE INGRES, *The Apotheosis of Homer*, 1827. Oil on canvas, 12 ft. 8 in. × 16 ft. 10¾ in. Louvre, Paris. © R.M.N., Paris.

Figure 26.28 Plan of *The Apotheosis of Homer*, 1827. Following Emilio Radius, *L'opera complete di Ingres*, the following figures are identified:

1 Virgil	18 Dante
2 Raphael	19 Iliad
3 Sappho	20 Odyssey
4 Euripides	21 Aesop
5 Demosthenes	22 Shakespeare
6 Sophocles	23 La Fontaine
7 Herodotus	24 Tasso
8 Orpheus	25 Mozart
9 Pindar	26 Poussin
10 Hesiod	27 Corneille
11 Plato	28 Racine
12 Socrates	29 Molière
13 Pericles	30 Glück
14 Michelangelo	31 Apelles
15 Aristotle	32 Phidias
16 Aristarchus	
17 Alexander the Great	

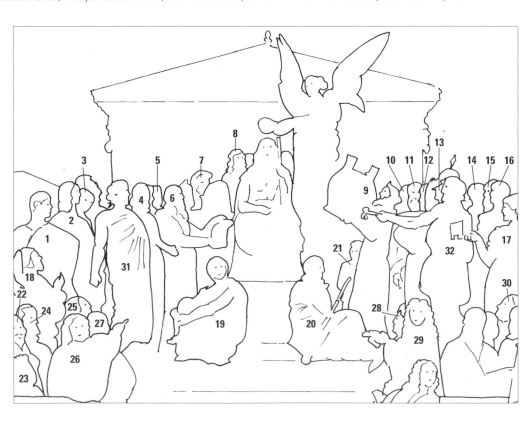

Ingres and Academic Neoclassicism

David's most talented pupil was Jean-Auguste-Dominique Ingres (1780–1867). The son of an artist-craftsman, Ingres rose to fame with his polished depictions of classical history and mythology and with his accomplished portraits of middle- and upper-class patrons. He spent much of his career in Italy, where he came to prize (as he himself admitted), "Raphael, his century, the ancients, and above all the divine Greeks." Ingres shunned the weighty realism of David in favor of the purity of line he admired in Greek vase painting, in the published drawings of the newly unearthed classical artifacts, and in the engraved book illustrations for the works of Homer and Hesiod.

Commissioned to paint a ceiling mural for the Louvre, Ingres produced a visual testament to Europe's infatuation with its classical heritage. The monumental *Apotheosis of Homer* shows the ancient Greek bard enthroned amidst forty-six notables of classical and modern times, and "deified" with a laurel crown bestowed by a winged figure of Victory (Figure **26.27**). Surrounding Homer is an academic assembly that includes Plato, Dante, Raphael, Poussin, Racine, and other Western "luminaries" (thirty of whom are identified in Figure **26.28**). Ingres' Homer sits at the apex of a compositional pyramid; at his feet are the allegorical figures of his epics, the *Iliad* and the *Odyssey*, while behind him is a neoclassical temple facade, not unlike that of "La Madeleine," which was then under construction in Paris (see Figure 26.31). Both in composition and in conception, the *Apotheosis* looks back to Raphael (see *The School of Athens*, Figure 17.29), but Ingres has brought self-conscious rigor to his application of neo-

classical clarity and symmetry. Frozen and iconic, this rationalized tribute to Western culture reveals Ingres as a neoclassical artist—a painter of polished historical, allegorical, and mythological subjects.

Later in his career, however, Ingres turned his nostalgia for the past to exotic themes that would come to preoccupy artists of the romantic style (see chapter 29). Intrigued, for instance, by Turkish culture (publicized by Napoleon's campaigns into North Africa), Ingres painted languorous harem slaves, such as *La Grande Odalisque* (Figure **26.29**). A revisualization of both Titian's *Venus of Urbino* (see chapter 17) and Canova's *Pauline Borghese as Venus* (see Figure 26.18), Ingres' nude turns in a self-consciously seductive manner: both away from and toward the beholder. The fine line and polished brushstrokes are typically neoclassical; but Ingres rejected neoclassical canons of proportion by elongating the limbs in the tradition of the Italian Mannerists (see, for instance, Figure 20.4). The "incorrect" anatomy of the figure drew strong criticism from Ingres' contemporaries, who claimed that his subject had three too many vertebrae. Nevertheless (or perhaps because of its bold departures from both real and ideal norms), *La Grande Odalisque* remains one of the most arresting images of womanhood in Western art.

Kauffmann and Academic Neoclassicism

Well into the eighteenth century, the painting of large-scale historical, mythological, and religious subjects was dominated by male artists, primarily because propriety dictated that women be excluded from studio classes that traditionally utilized the male nude model. Female artists,

Figure 26.29 JEAN-AUGUSTE-DOMINIQUE INGRES, *La Grande Odalisque*, 1814. Oil on canvas, 2 ft. 11¼ in. × 5 ft. 3¾ in. Louvre, Paris. Photo: © R.M.N., Paris.

Figure 26.30 ANGELICA KAUFFMANN, *Zeuxis Selecting Models for His Painting of Helen of Troy*, ca. 1765. Oil on canvas, 32⅛ x 44⅛ in. The Annmary Brown Memorial, Brown University, Providence, Rhode Island.

such as Maria van Oosterwyck (see Figure 23.5) and Judith Leyster (see Figure 23.13), confined their talents to still-life subjects and portrait painting, genres considered of lesser importance among academicians. Nevertheless, the Italian-trained Angelica Kauffmann (1741–1807), like Artemisia Gentileschi (see Figure 20.10), established a glowing reputation as a skilled painter of historical subjects. Kauffmann, the daughter of a Swiss artist who schooled her in music, history, and the visual arts, was one of the founding members of England's Royal Academy of Arts, to which she contributed many critically successful paintings based on classical subjects. Commissioned to paint portrait likenesses of many of her contemporaries (including Johann Winckelmann) during her sojourns in Rome, Florence, and London, she also became one of the most sought-after and highly paid portrait painters of her day. Kauffmann's history subjects, many of which served as models for wall and ceiling designs in the neoclassical interiors of Robert Adam (see Figure 26.17), reveal her familiarity with the figure types found in the wall paintings of Pompeii and Herculaneum, her love of lyrical linear compositions, and her skillful, fluent brushwork. These features are especially apparent in the painting, *Zeuxis Selecting Models for His Painting of Helen of Troy* (Figure 26.30), in which the Greek artist is shown (as described by ancient historians) choosing the finest features of his various female models, so as to combine them in an idealized image of Helen of Troy. Kauffmann herself may have served as the model for the figure at the far right.

Neoclassicism under Napoleon

While neoclassicism was the "official" style of the French Revolution, it soon became the vehicle of French imperialism. Under the leadership of Napoleon Bonaparte (1769 –1821), the imagery of classical Greece and republican Rome was abandoned for the more appropriate imagery of Augustan Rome. Like the Roman emperors, Napoleon used the arts to magnify his greatness. He appointed David to commemorate his military achievements and he commissioned architects to redesign Paris in the spirit of ancient Rome. Paris became a city of straight, wide avenues and huge, impressive squares. Imaginary axes linked the various monuments raised to honor the emperor, and older buildings were remodeled in the new Empire style. Alexandre-Pierre Vignon (1763–1828) redesigned the Church of Saint Mary Magdalene (called "La Madeleine") as a Roman temple dedicated to the glory of the French army (Figure 26.31). Fifty-two Corinthian columns, each 66 feet tall, surround the temple, which rises on a 23-foot-high podium, like a gigantic version of the Maison Carrée in Nîmes (Figure 26.32) Vignon's gloomy interior—a nave crowned with three domes—falls short of reflecting

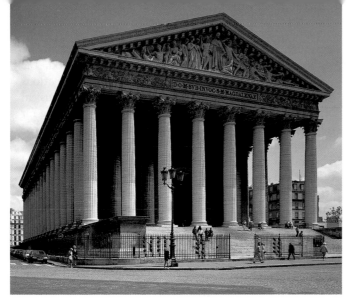

Figure 26.31 ALEXANDRE-PIERRE VIGNON, Church of Mary Magdalene ("La Madeleine"), Paris, 1807–1842. Length 350 ft., width 147 ft., height of podium 23 ft. © Paul M. R. Maeyaert, Mont de l'Enclus (Orroir), Belgium.

Figure 26.32 Maison Carrée, Nîmes, France, 16 B.C.E. © Paul M. R. Maeyaert, Mont de l'Enclus (Orroir), Belgium.

the majesty of the exterior, despite his use of the Corinthian and Ionic orders in the decorative scheme.

Elsewhere, Napoleon's neoclassicism was more precise. The Arc du Carrousel, which stands adjacent to the Louvre, is faithful to its Roman model, the Arch of Constantine in Rome. And the grandest of Paris'

triumphal arches, which occupies the crossing of twelve avenues at the end of the famous Avenue des Champs-Elysées (Figure **26.33**), closely resembles the Arch of Titus in the Roman Forum (see chapter 6). The 164-foot-high commemorative monument—which was dedicated to the French army—was larger than any arch built in ancient

Figure 26.33 JEAN-FRANÇOIS THÉRÈSE CHALGRIN AND OTHERS, Arc de Triomphe, Paris, 1806–1836. Height 164 ft. © Paul M. R. Maeyaert, Mont de l'Enclus (Orroir), Belgium.

Mozart had a special talent for shaping personalities by way of music. While the characters in the operas of Monteverdi and Lully were allegorical stick figures, Mozart's appeal to us as real human beings. They convey a wide range of human expression, from grief and despair to hope and joy. Mozart's vocal music is never sentimental; it retains the precision and clarity of the classical style and invests it with unparalleled melodic grace. Only by listening to his music can one appreciate the reason why Haydn called Mozart "the greatest composer known to me either in person or by name."

Beethoven: The Early Years

Generally considered the third of the great classical composers, Ludwig van Beethoven (1770–1827) spanned the era between the classical and romantic styles in music. Born in Bonn, in northern Germany, Beethoven spent the greater part of his life in Vienna, where he studied briefly with Haydn. His earliest works, mainly keyboard pieces composed between 1782 and 1792, reveal his debt to Mozart, as well as his facility with classical form and style. Between 1793 and 1803, his first years in Vienna, Beethoven made his name as a virtuoso pianist and a composer of piano pieces, as well as a master of the string quartet. By 1799, however, Beethoven began to break with the more formal aspects of the classical style: his compositions, which include the first two of his nine symphonies, anticipate the tension and vigor, the emphasis on rhythm rather than melody, and the forceful instrumental language that would stretch classical form, and, ultimately, challenge the classical style (see chapter 29).

Mozart was more interested in music than in political reform—he even agreed to temper Beaumarchais' scolding satire by way of Lorenzo da Ponte's Italian libretto. But his scorn for the upper classes—perhaps stemming from his own personal difficulties with aristocratic patrons—is readily apparent in the piece.

Politics aside, the enduring beauty of *The Marriage of Figaro* lies in its lyrical force and its expressive ingenuity.

SUMMARY

Eighteenth-century European art and music reflected the changing character and tastes of its various social classes. The fashionable rococo style reflected the aristocratic affection for ornamental delicacy, intimacy, and playful elegance. The rococo style dominated the salons of Paris and the courts and churches of Austria and Germany. In France, Watteau, Boucher, Vigée-Lebrun, Fragonard, and Clodion produced art that evoked a world of physical pleasure and sensuous delight.

By mid-century, a reaction against the rococo style occurred among members of a growing middle class, who identified their interests with the rational ideals of the European Enlightenment. Encouraged by the *philosophes*' demand for an art of moral virtue, Greuze and Chardin produced genre paintings that gave dignity to the life and work of ordinary individuals. At the same time, archeological investigations in Greece and Southern Italy encouraged new interest in the classical past. The neoclassical style swept away the rococo in the same way that the French Revolution swept away the Old Regime. David's stirring pictorial recreations of Greek and Roman history invoked a message of self-sacrifice and moral purpose.

The neoclassical style symbolized the Enlightenment ideals of reason and liberty. In America neoclassicism was best expressed in the architectural achievements of Thomas Jefferson. In Europe, neoclassicism influenced all the arts, from Adam's English country houses and Soufflot's "Panthéon" to the portraits of Houdon and the ceramics of Wedgwood. During the reign of Napoleon, neoclassicists drew on the arts of imperial Rome to glorify Paris and the emperor himself.

The period between 1760 and approximately 1820 witnessed the birth of the orchestra and the development of the classical forms of Western instrumental music. Classical music was characterized by balance, symmetry, and intellectual control—features similar to those admired by neoclassical writers, painters, sculptors, and architects. Composers used the sonata form to govern the composition of the symphony, the string quartet, the sonata, and the concerto. Haydn shaped the character of the classical symphony and the string quartet; Mozart moved easily between rococo and classical styles, investing both with extraordinary melodic grace. In his operas, as well as in his symphonies, Mozart achieved a balance between lyrical invention and technical control that brought the classical style to its peak. In the decades to follow, the polite formalism of the European Enlightenment would yield to the seductive embrace of the Romantic Era.

GLOSSARY

allegro (Italian, "cheerful") a fast tempo in music

andante (Italian, "going," i.e., a normal walking pace) a moderate tempo in music

bacchante a female attendant or devotee of Dionysus

brass a family of wind instruments that usually includes the French horn, trumpet, trombone, and tuba

coda (Italian, "tail") a passage added to the closing section of a movement or musical composition in order to create the sense of a definite ending

concerto see Glossary, chapter 23; the classical concerto, which made use of *sonata form*, usually featured one or more solo instruments and orchestra

fête galante (French, "elegant entertainment") a festive diversion enjoyed by aristocrats, a favored subject in rococo art

fortissimo (Italian, "very loud") a directive indicating that the music should be played very loud; its opposite is *pianissimo* ("very soft")

largo (Italian, "broad") a very slow tempo; the slowest of the conventional tempos in music

opera buffa a type of comic opera usually featuring stock characters

percussion a group of instruments that are sounded by being struck or shaken, used especially for rhythm

satyr a semi-bestial woodland creature symbolic of Dionysus

score the musical notation for all of the instruments or voices in a particular composition; a composite from which the whole piece may be conducted or studied

sonata a composition for an unaccompanied keyboard instrument or for another instrument with keyboard accompaniment; see also Glossary, chapter 23

sonata form (or **sonata allegro form**) a structural form commonly used in the late eighteenth century for the first and fourth movements of symphonies and other instrumental compositions

string quartet a composition for four stringed instruments, each of which plays its own part

strings a family of instruments that usually includes the violin, viola, cello, and double bass (which are normally bowed); the harp, guitar, lute, and zither (which are normally plucked) can also be included, as can the viol, a bowed instrument common in the sixteenth and seventeenth centuries and a forerunner of the violin family

symphony an independent instrumental composition for orchestra

woodwinds a family of wind instruments, usually consisting of the flute, oboe, clarinet, and bassoon

SUGGESTIONS FOR READING

Bernier, Olivier. *The Eighteenth-Century Woman*. New York: Doubleday, 1981.

Conisbee, Philip. *Painting in Eighteenth-Century France*. Ithaca, N.Y.: Cornell University Press, 1981.

Gutman, Robert W. *Mozart: A Cultural Biography*. New York: Harcourt Brace, 1999.

Harries, Karsten. *The Bavarian Rococo Church: Between Faith and Aestheticism*. New Haven: Yale University Press, 1983.

Honour, Hugh. *Neoclassicism*. New York: Harper, 1979.

Irwin, David. *Neoclassicism*. London: Phaidon, 1997.

Jones, Stephen. *The Eighteenth Century*. Cambridge: Cambridge University Press, 1985.

Levey, Michael. *From Rococo to Revolution: Major Trends in Eighteenth-Century Painting*. New York: Norton, 1985.

Park, William. *The Idea of Rococo*. Cranbury, N.J.: University of Delaware Press, 1992.

Rosen, Charles. *The Classical Style: Haydn, Mozart, Beethoven*. New York: Norton, 1997.

Sheriff, Mary D. *The Exceptional Woman: Elizabeth Vigée-LeBrun and the Cultural Politics of Art*. Chicago: University of Chicago Press, 1996.

Solomon, Maynard. *Mozart*. New York: Harper, 1995.

Till, Nicolas, ed. *Mozart and the Enlightenment: Truth, Virtue, and Beauty in Mozart's Operas*. New York: Norton, 1993.

MUSIC LISTENING SELECTIONS

CD Two Selection 8   Couperin, "Le Croc-en-jambe" from Ordre No. 22, harpsichord, 1730.

CD Two Selection 9   Haydn, Symphony No. 94 in G Major, "Surprise," second movement, excerpt, 1791.

CD Two Selection 10   Mozart, Serenade No. 3 in G Major, K. 525, "Eine kleine Nachtmusik," first movement, excerpt, 1787.

CD Two Selection 11   Mozart, *Le nozze di Figaro*, "Dove sono" aria, 1786.

JAN VERMEER, *The Geographer*, ca. 1668. Oil on canvas, 20⅞ × 18¼ in. Städelsches Kunstinstitut, Frankfurt. Courtesy Blauel/Gramm—Aʀᴛʜᴏᴛᴇᴋ, Peissenberg.

PART ONE

The romantic era

Two fundamental developments influenced the cultural vitality of the nineteenth century. The first was the transformation of the West from an agricultural to an industrially based society. The second was the extension of European dominion over much of the rest of the world. This controlling presence of Europeans in Asia and Africa contributed to an eclipsing of native cultural expression in those areas. With the exception of Japan, the regions beyond the West generated few new forms of artistic expression in the nineteenth century and certainly none comparable to those produced in previous centuries. This circumstance also explains why our examination of the nineteenth century assumes a Western focus.

During the nineteenth century, the population of Europe doubled in size, and material culture changed more radically than it had in the previous one thousand years. The application of science to practical invention had already sparked the beginnings of the Industrial Revolution—the mass production of material goods by machines. The first phase of this revolution occurred in mid-eighteenth-century England, with the development of the steam engine and the machinery for spinning and weaving textiles. As the increased production of coal, iron, and steel encouraged the further expansion of industry and commerce, the revolution gained momentum. Industrialization involved a shift from the production of goods in homes and workshops to manufacture in factories, mills, and mines. It demanded enormous investments of capital and the efforts of a large labor force; it stimulated growth in Europe's urban centers. And clearly, industrialism provided the basis for the West's controlling influence over the rest of the world.

If industrialism was the primary force that shaped nineteenth-century Western culture, the second was nationalism. Nationalism—the exaltation of the state—involved the patriotic identification of individuals with a territory that embraced a common language and history. As people began to identify political sovereignty with the nation rather than with the person of the ruler, they sought greater freedom from the autocratic political and economic restraints of the old ruling orders. They also rejected the efforts of other nations to control their destiny. Such sentiments underlay the revolutionary outbursts that were chronic and continuous throughout the nine-

teenth century. European nationalism spurred the drive toward unification of the Germanies and among the Italian provinces and gave rise to a pervasive militarism in the individual states of the West. In the course of the century, England, France, Germany, Belgium, and the United States increased in political, economic, and military strength; and Germany and Italy finally reached the status of unified nation-states.

The nineteenth century is often called "the romantic era." *Romanticism* may be defined as a movement in the history of culture, as an aesthetic style, and as an attitude or spirit. As a movement, romanticism involved a revolt against convention and authority and a search for freedom in personal, political, and artistic life. The romantics reacted against the the rationalism of Enlightenment culture and the impersonality of growing industrialism. Estranged from traditional religious beliefs, the romantics looked upon nature as the dwelling place of God. They worked to revive their nations' history and to liberate the oppressed peoples of the earth.

As an artistic style, romanticism was a reaction against the neoclassical quest for order and intellectual control. Romantics favored the free expression of the imagination and the liberation of the emotions. In preference to aesthetic objectivity and formalism, romantics chose subjectivity and the spontaneous outpouring of feeling. They cultivated a taste for the exotic, the ecstatic, and the fantastic. Finally, as an attitude, romanticism may be seen as an effort to glorify the self by way of intuition and the senses. Romantics did not reject the value of reason; they regarded the emotions as equally important to human experience. Sentimentality, nostalgia, melancholy, and longing were all characteristic of the romantic cast of mind.

The romantics saw themselves as the heroes and visionaries of their time. They freed themselves from exclusive dependence on the patronage of Church and state and tended to pursue fiercely individualistic paths to creativity—paths that often alienated them from society. The lives and works of the romantics were marked by deep subjectivity—one might even say by self-indulgence. If the perceptions and passions of the romantics were intense, their desire to devise a language adequate to that intensity of feeling often drove them to frustration, despair, and, in the case of an unusual number of them, to an early death—the painters Gros and Géricault, the composers Chopin and Schubert, and the poets Byron, Shelley, and Keats all died before the age of forty.

(opposite) **ALBERT BIERSTADT**, detail of *The Rocky Mountains, Lander's Peak*, 1863. Oil on canvas, 6 ft. 1 in. × 10 ft. ¾ in. The Metropolitan Museum of Art, New York. Rogers Fund, 1907 (07.123). © 1979 The Metropolitan Museum of Art.

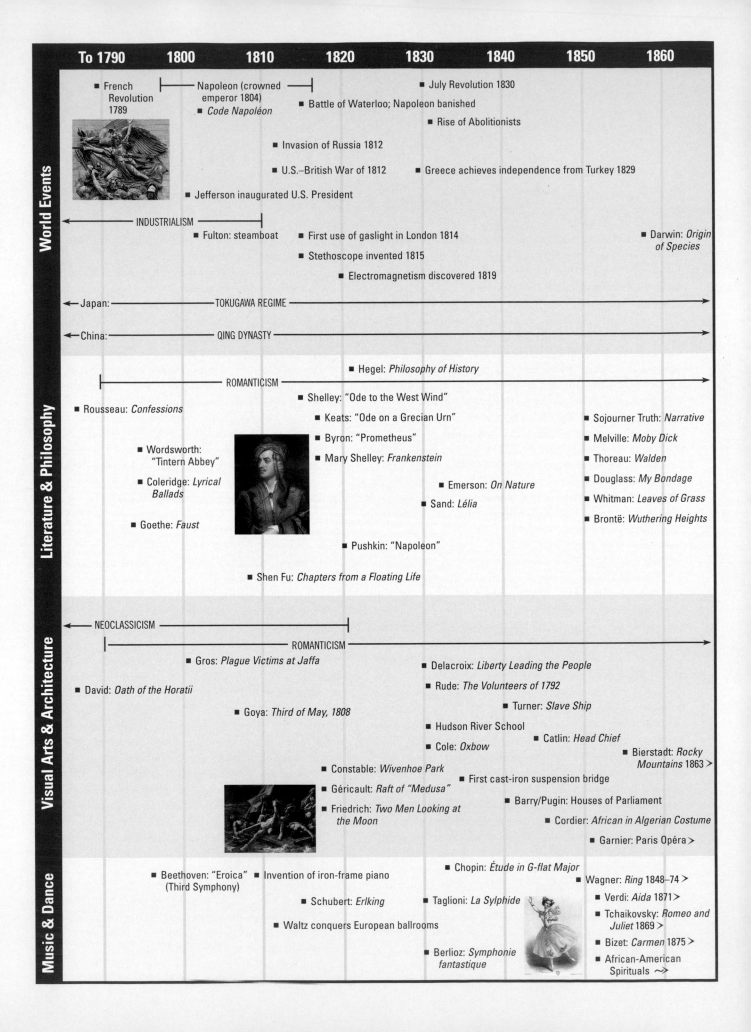

	To 1790	1800	1810	1820	1830	1840	1850	1860

World Events

- French Revolution 1789
- Napoleon (crowned emperor 1804)
- Code Napoléon
- Battle of Waterloo; Napoleon banished
- July Revolution 1830
- Rise of Abolitionists
- Invasion of Russia 1812
- U.S.–British War of 1812
- Greece achieves independence from Turkey 1829
- Jefferson inaugurated U.S. President

← INDUSTRIALISM —

- Fulton: steamboat
- First use of gaslight in London 1814
- Stethoscope invented 1815
- Electromagnetism discovered 1819
- Darwin: *Origin of Species*

← Japan: ——— TOKUGAWA REGIME ——— →

← China: ——— QING DYNASTY ——— →

Literature & Philosophy

← ROMANTICISM →

- Hegel: *Philosophy of History*
- Shelley: "Ode to the West Wind"
- Rousseau: *Confessions*
- Keats: "Ode on a Grecian Urn"
- Byron: "Prometheus"
- Mary Shelley: *Frankenstein*
- Sojourner Truth: *Narrative*
- Melville: *Moby Dick*
- Wordsworth: "Tintern Abbey"
- Thoreau: *Walden*
- Coleridge: *Lyrical Ballads*
- Emerson: *On Nature*
- Sand: *Lélia*
- Douglass: *My Bondage*
- Whitman: *Leaves of Grass*
- Brontë: *Wuthering Heights*
- Goethe: *Faust*
- Pushkin: "Napoleon"
- Shen Fu: *Chapters from a Floating Life*

Visual Arts & Architecture

← NEOCLASSICISM —

← ——— ROMANTICISM ——— →

- Gros: *Plague Victims at Jaffa*
- Delacroix: *Liberty Leading the People*
- Rude: *The Volunteers of 1792*
- David: *Oath of the Horatii*
- Turner: *Slave Ship*
- Goya: *Third of May, 1808*
- Hudson River School
- Catlin: *Head Chief*
- Cole: *Oxbow*
- Bierstadt: *Rocky Mountains* 1863 >
- Constable: *Wivenhoe Park*
- First cast-iron suspension bridge
- Géricault: *Raft of "Medusa"*
- Barry/Pugin: Houses of Parliament
- Friedrich: *Two Men Looking at the Moon*
- Cordier: *African in Algerian Costume*
- Garnier: Paris Opéra >

Music & Dance

- Beethoven: "Eroica" (Third Symphony)
- Invention of iron-frame piano
- Chopin: *Étude in G-flat Major*
- Wagner: *Ring* 1848–74 >
- Verdi: *Aida* 1871 >
- Schubert: *Erlking*
- Taglioni: *La Sylphide*
- Tchaikovsky: *Romeo and Juliet* 1869 >
- Waltz conquers European ballrooms
- Bizet: *Carmen* 1875 >
- Berlioz: *Symphonie fantastique*
- African-American Spirituals ↝

CHAPTER TWENTY-SEVEN

The romantic view of nature

"Beauty in art is truth bathed in an impression received from nature."
Corot

One of the central features of nineteenth-century romanticism was its love affair with nature and the natural. The romantics generally reacted against the artificiality of Enlightenment culture and the dismal effects of growing industrialism. In rural nature, they found a practical refuge from urban blight, smoke-belching factories, and poverty-ridden slums. Aesthetically, they perceived in nature, with all its shifting moods and rhythms, a metaphor for the romantic imagination. They looked to nature as the source of solace, inspiration, and self-discovery. In a broader sense, the romantic view of nature was nothing short of religious. With Rousseau, the romantics held that humans were by nature good but were corrupted by society (see chapter 25). "Natural man" was one who was close to nature and unspoiled by social institutions. To such Enlightenment figures as Locke, Pope, and Jefferson, nature had meant universal order, but to nineteenth-century romantics, nature was the source of divine ecstasy and the medium of the mystical bond that united God with the human soul. Romantics perceived unspoiled nature as the wellspring of all truth; many even viewed God and the natural universe as one. Such **pantheism**—more typical of Asian than of Western religious philosophy—characterized the writings of many European and American romantics, but it is most clearly exemplified in the poetry of William Wordsworth.

Nature and the Natural in European Literature

Wordsworth and the Poetry of Nature

Born in the Lake District of England, William Wordsworth (1770–1850) was the leading nature poet of the nineteenth century. Wordsworth dated the beginning of his career as a poet from the time—at age fourteen—he was struck by the image of tree boughs silhouetted against a bright evening sky. Thereafter, "the infinite variety of natural appearances" became the principal source of his inspiration and the primary subject of his poetry. Wordsworth's exaltation of nature sustained his belief that, through the senses, the individual could commune with elemental and divine universal forces. Nature, in Wordsworth's view, might restore to human beings their untainted, childhood sense of wonder.

In 1798, Wordsworth and his British contemporary Samuel Taylor Coleridge (1772–1834) produced the *Lyrical Ballads*, the literary work that marked the birth of the romantic movement in England. When the *Lyrical Ballads* appeared in a second edition in 1800, Wordsworth added a preface that formally explained the aims of romantic poetry. In this manifesto, Wordsworth defined poetry as "the spontaneous overflow of powerful feelings," which takes its origin "from emotion recollected in tranquillity." According to Wordsworth, the object of the poet was "to choose incidents and situations from common life [and] to throw over them a certain colouring of the imagination . . . and above all, to make these incidents and situations interesting by tracing in them, truly though not ostentatiously, the primary laws of our nature." Wordsworth championed a poetic language that resembled "the real language of men in a state of vivid sensation." Although he did not always abide by his own precepts, his rejection of the artificial diction of neoclassical verse in favor of "the real language of men" anticipated a new, more natural voice in poetry—one informed by childhood memories and deeply felt experiences recollected in tranquillity. Wordsworth's verse reflects the romantic poet's fondness for **lyric poetry**, which—like art song—describes deep personal feeling.

One of the most inspired poems in the *Lyrical Ballads* is "Lines Composed a Few Miles Above Tintern Abbey," the product of Wordsworth's visit to the ruins of a medieval monastery situated on the banks of the Wye River in Southwest England (Figure **27.1**). The 159-line poem constitutes a paean to nature. Wordsworth begins by describing the sensations evoked by the countryside itself;

Figure 27.1 J. M. W. TURNER, *Interior of Tintern Abbey*, 1794. Watercolor, 12⅝ × 9⅞ in.© The Board of Trustees of the Victoria and Albert Museum, London.

he then muses on the pleasures and the solace that these memories provide as they are called up in recollection. The heart of the poem, however, is a joyous celebration of nature's moral value: Nature allows the poet to "see into the life of things" (line 49), infuses him with "the still, sad music of humanity" (line 91), and ultimately brings him into the presence of the divine spirit. Nature, he exults, is the "anchor" of his purest thoughts, the "nurse" and "guardian" of his heart and soul (lines 109–110). In the final portion of the extract (lines 111–134), Wordsworth shares with his "dearest Friend," his sister Dorothy, the joys of his mystical communion with nature and humankind. In "Tintern Abbey," Wordsworth established three of the key motifs of nineteenth-century romanticism: the redemptive power of nature, the idea of nature's sympathy with humankind, and the view that one who is close to nature is close to God.

READING 5.1 From Wordsworth's "Lines Composed a Few Miles Above Tintern Abbey" (1798)

Five years have passed; five summers, with the length   1
Of five long winters! and again I hear
These waters, rolling from their mountain-springs
With a soft inland murmur. Once again
Do I behold these steep and lofty cliffs,   5
That on a wild secluded scene impress
Thoughts of more deep seclusion; and connect
The landscape with the quiet of the sky.
The day is come when I again repose
Here, under this dark sycamore, and view   10
These plots of cottage-ground, these orchard tufts,
Which at this season, with their unripe fruits,
Are clad in one green hue, and lose themselves
'Mid groves and copses. Once again I see
These hedge-rows, hardly hedge-rows, little lines   15
Of sportive wood run wild: these pastoral farms,
Green to the very door; and wreaths of smoke
Sent up, in silence, from among the trees!
With some uncertain notice, as might seem
Of vagrant dwellers in the houseless woods,   20
Or of some Hermit's cave, where by his fire
The hermit sits alone.
                          These beauteous forms,
Through a long absence, have not been to me
As is a landscape to a blind man's eye;
But oft, in lonely rooms, and 'mid the din   25
Of towns and cities, I have owed to them
In hours of weariness, sensations sweet,
Felt in the blood, and felt along the heart;
And passing even into my purer mind,
With tranquil restoration:—feelings too   30
Of unremembered pleasure: such, perhaps,
As have no slight or trivial influence
On that best portion of a good man's life,
His little, nameless, unremembered acts
Of kindness and of love. Nor less, I trust,   35

To them I may have owed another gift,
Of aspect more sublime; that blessed mood,
In which the burthen[1] of the mystery,
In which the heavy and the weary weight
Of all this unintelligible world,   40
Is lightened—that serene and blessed mood,
In which the affections gently lead us on—
Until, the breath of this corporeal frame
And even the motion of our human blood
Almost suspended, we are laid asleep   45
In body, and become a living soul;
While with an eye made quiet by the power
Of harmony, and the deep power of joy,
We see into the life of things.
                          If this
Be but a vain belief, yet, oh! how oft—   50
In darkness and amid the many shapes
Of joyless daylight; when the fretful stir
Unprofitable, and the fever of the world,
Have hung upon the beatings of my heart—
How oft, in spirit, have I turned to thee,   55
O sylvan[2] Wye! thou wanderer through the woods,
How often has my spirit turned to thee!

     And now, with gleams of half-extinguished thought,
With many recognitions dim and faint,
And somewhat of a sad perplexity,   60
The picture of the mind revives again;
While here I stand, not only with the sense
Of present pleasure, but with pleasing thoughts
That in this moment there is life and food
For future years. And so I dare to hope,   65
Though changed, no doubt, from what I was when first
I came among these hills; when like a roe
I bounded o'er the mountains, by the sides
Of the deep rivers, and the lonely streams,
Wherever nature led: more like a man   70
Flying from something that he dreads than one
Who sought the thing he loved. For nature then
(The coarser pleasures of my boyish days,
And their glad animal movements all gone by)
To me was all in all—I cannot paint   75
What then I was. The sounding cataract[3]
Haunted me like a passion; the tall rock,
The mountain, and the deep and gloomy wood,
Their colours and their forms, were then to me
An appetite; a feeling and a love,   80
That had no need of a remoter charm,
By thought supplied, nor any interest
Unborrowed from the eye. That time is past,
And all its aching joys are now no more,
And all its dizzy raptures. Not for this   85
Faint I, nor mourn nor murmur; other gifts
Have followed; for such loss, I would believe,
Abundant recompense. For I have learned

-----
[1]Burden.
[2]Wooded.
[3]A descent of water over a steep surface.

To look on nature, not as in the hour
Of thoughtless youth; but hearing oftentimes   90
The still, sad music of humanity,
Nor harsh nor grating, though of ample power
To chasten and subdue. And I have felt
A presence that disturbs me with the joy
Of elevated thoughts; a sense sublime   95
Of something far more deeply interfused,
Whose dwelling is the light of setting suns,
And the round ocean and the living air,
And the blue sky, and in the mind of man:
A motion and a spirit, that impels   100
All thinking things, all objects of all thought,
And rolls through all things. Therefore am I still
A lover of the meadows and the woods,
And mountains; and of all that we behold
From this green earth; of all the mighty world   105
Of eye, and ear—both what they half create,
And what perceive; well pleased to recognize
In nature and the language of the sense,
The anchor of my purest thoughts, the nurse,
The guide, the guardian of my heart, and soul   110
Of all my moral being.
                        Nor perchance,
If I were not thus taught, should I the more
Suffer my genial spirits to decay:
For thou art with me here upon the banks
Of this fair river; thou my dearest Friend,[4]   115
My dear, dear Friend; and in thy voice I catch
The language of my former heart, and read
My former pleasures in the shooting lights
Of thy wild eyes. Oh! yet a little while
May I behold in thee what I was once,   120
My dear, dear Sister! and this prayer I make,
Knowing that Nature never did betray
The heart that loved her; 'tis her privilege,
Through all the years of this our life, to lead
From joy to joy: for she can so inform   125
The mind that is within us, so impress
With quietness and beauty, and so feed
With lofty thoughts, that neither evil tongues,
Rash judgments, nor the sneers of selfish men,
Nor greetings where no kindness is, nor all   130
The dreary intercourse of daily life,
Shall e'er prevail against us, or disturb
Our cheerful faith, that all which we behold
Is full of blessings. . . .

The Poetry of Shelley

Like Wordsworth, the British poet Percy Bysshe Shelley
(1792–1822) embraced nature as the source of sublime
truth, but his volcanic personality led him to engage the
natural world with greater intensity and deeper melancholy than his older contemporary. A prolific writer and a
passionate champion of human liberty, Shelley led a life
that had all the features of the romantic hero (see chapter

---

[4]Wordsworth's sister, Dorothy.

28). Defiant and unconventional even in his youth,
Shelley provoked the reading public with a treatise entitled *The Necessity of Atheism* (1811), the circulation of
which led to his expulsion from Oxford University. He was
outspoken in his opposition to marriage, a union that he
viewed as hostile to human happiness. Moreover, he was as
unconventional in his deeds as in his discourse: While
married to one woman (Harriet Westbrook), with whom
he had two children, he ran off with another (Mary
Godwin). A harsh critic of England's rulers, he went into
permanent exile in Italy in 1818 and died there four years
later in a boating accident.

Shelley's *Defence of Poetry* (1821), a manifesto of the
poet's function in society, hails poets as "the unacknowl-
edged legislators of the world." According to Shelley, poets
take their authority from nature, the fountainhead of
inspiration. Shelley finds in nature's moods, metaphors for
insubstantial, yet potent, human states. In "Ode to the West
Wind" he appeals to the wind, a symbol of creativity, to
drive his visions throughout the universe, as the wind drives leaves over the earth (stanza 1), clouds through the air
(stanza 2), and waves on the seas (stanza 3). In the final
stanza, Shelley compares the poet to a lyre, whose "mighty
harmonies," stirred by the wind of creativity, will awaken
the world. By means of language that is itself musical,
Shelley defends the notion of poetry as the music of the soul.
Consider, for instance, his frequent use of the exclamatory
"O" and the effective use of **assonance** and **tone color** in
lines 38 to 40: "while far below/The sea-blooms and the oozy
woods which wear/The sapless foliage of the ocean, know."

READING 5.2   Shelley's "Ode to the West Wind" (1819)

1

O wild West Wind, thou breath of Autumn's being,   1
Thou, from whose unseen presence the leaves dead
Are driven, like ghosts from an enchanter fleeing,

Yellow, and black, and pale, and hectic red,
Pestilence-stricken multitudes: O thou,   5
Who chariotest to their dark wintry bed

The wingéd seeds, where they lie cold and low,
Each like a corpse within its grave, until
Thine azure sister of the spring shall blow

Her clarion o'er the dreaming earth, and fill   10
(Driving sweet buds like flocks to feed in air)
With living hues and odours plain and hill:

Wild Spirit, which art moving everywhere;
Destroyer and preserver; hear, oh, hear!

2

Thou on whose stream, 'mid the steep sky's commotion,   15
Loose clouds like earth's decaying leaves are shed,
Shook from the tangled boughs of Heaven and Ocean,

Angels of rain and lightning: there are spread
On the blue surface of thine aëry surge,
Like the bright hair uplifted from the head   20

Of some fierce Maenad,[1] even from the dim verge
Of the horizon to the zenith's height,
The locks of the approaching storm. Thou dirge

Of the dying year, to which this closing night
Will be the dome of a vast sepulchre,[2]   25
Vaulted with all thy congregated might

Of vapours, from whose solid atmosphere
Black rain, and fire, and hail will burst: O, hear!

3

Thou who didst waken from his summer dreams
The blue Mediterranean, where he lay,   30
Lulled by the coil of his crystalline streams,

Beside a pumice isle in Baiae's bay,[3]
And saw in sleep old palaces and towers
Quivering within the wave's intenser day,

All overgrown with azure moss and flowers   35
So sweet, the sense faints picturing them! Thou
For whose path the Atlantic's level powers

Cleave themselves into chasms, while far below
The sea-blooms and the oozy woods which wear
The sapless foliage of the ocean, know   40

Thy voice, and suddenly grow grey with fear,
And tremble and despoil themselves: O, hear!

4

If I were a dead leaf thou mightest bear;
If I were a swift cloud to fly with thee;
A wave to pant beneath thy power, and share   45

The impulse of thy strength, only less free
Than thou, O uncontrollable! If even
I were as in my boyhood, and could be

The comrade of thy wanderings over heaven,
As then, when to outstrip thy skiey speed   50
Scarce seemed a vision; I would ne'er have striven

As thus with thee in prayer in my sore need.
Oh! lift me as a wave, a leaf, a cloud!
I fall upon the thorns of life! I bleed!

A heavy weight of hours has chained and bowed   55
One too like thee: tameless, and swift, and proud.

5

Make me thy lyre, even as the forest is:
What if my leaves are falling like its own!
The tumult of thy mighty harmonies

Will take from both a deep, autumnal tone,   60
Sweet though in sadness. Be thou, spirit fierce,
My spirit! Be thou me, impetuous one!

[1] A female attendant of Dionysus; a bacchante (see chapter 26).
[2] Tomb
[3] An ancient resort in Southwest Italy.

Drive my dead thoughts over the universe
Like withered leaves to quicken a new birth!
And, by the incantation of this verse,   65

Scatter, as from an unextinguished hearth
Ashes and sparks, my words among mankind!
Be through my lips to unawakened earth

The trumpet of a prophecy! O, Wind,
If Winter comes, can Spring be far behind?   70

The Poetry of Keats

The poetry of John Keats (1795–1821), the third of the great British nature poets, shares the elegiac mood of romantic landscape painting. Keats lamented the transience of life's pleasures, even as he contemplated the brevity of life. He lost both his mother and his brother to tuberculosis, and he himself succumbed to that disease at the age of twenty-five. The threat of imminent death seems to have produced in Keats a heightened awareness of the virtues of beauty, human love, and friendship. Keats perceived these phenomena as fleeting forms of a higher reality that might be made permanent only in art. For Keats, art is the great balm of the poet. Art is more than a response to the human experience of love and nature; it is the transmuted product of the imagination, a higher form of nature that triumphantly outreaches the mortal lifespan. These ideas are central to Keats' "Ode on a Grecian Urn." The poem was inspired by ancient Greek artifacts Keats had seen among those brought to London by Lord Elgin in 1816 and placed on display in the British Museum (see chapter 5).

In the "Ode," Keats contemplates a Greek vase (much like the one pictured in Figure **27.2**), whose delicately drawn figures immortalize life's fleeting pleasures. The boughs of trees pictured on such a vase will never shed their leaves, the fair youths will never grow old, the music of the pipes and timbrels will never cease to play, and the lovers will never cease to love. The "little town by river" and the other pastoral vignettes in the poem probably did not belong to any one existing Greek vase; yet Keats describes the imaginary urn (his metaphoric "Cold Pastoral") as a symbol of all great works of art, which, because of their unchanging beauty, remain eternally "true." The poem concludes with the joyous pronouncement that beauty and truth are one.

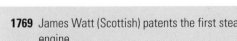

1769 James Watt (Scottish) patents the first steam engine

1787 the first power loom revolutionizes the weaving industry

1805 earliest use of morphine (extracted from opium) to relieve pain

1814 coal is transported by locomotive for the first time in England

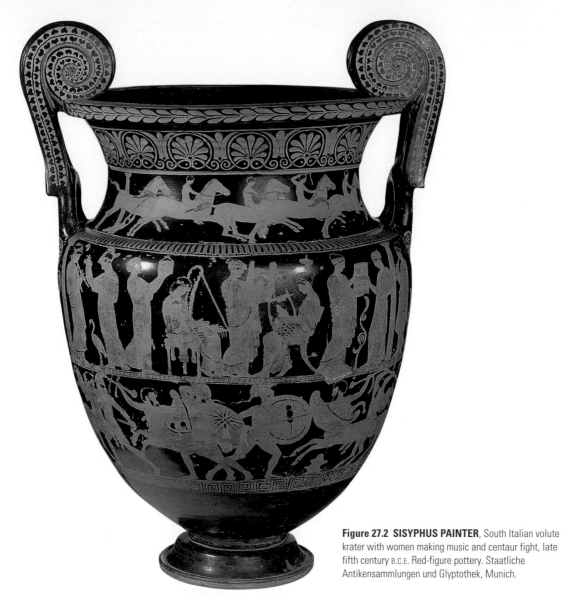

Figure 27.2 SISYPHUS PAINTER, South Italian volute krater with women making music and centaur fight, late fifth century B.C.E. Red-figure pottery. Staatliche Antikensammlungen und Glyptothek, Munich.

READING 5.3   Keats' "Ode on a Grecian Urn"
(1818)

1

Thou still unravished bride of quietness,   1
   Thou foster-child of Silence and slow Time,
Sylvan historian, who canst thus express
   A flowery tale more sweetly than our rhyme:
What leaf-fringed[1] legend haunts about thy shape   5
   Of deities or mortals, or of both,
     In Tempe[2] or the dales of Arcady?[3]
   What men or gods are these? What maidens loth?
What mad pursuit? What struggle to escape?
     What pipes and timbrels? What wild ecstasy?   10

---

[1] A reference to the common Greek practice of bordering the vase with stylized leaf forms (see Figure 27.2).
[2] A valley sacred to Apollo between Mounts Olympus and Ossa in Thessaly, Greece.
[3] Arcadia, the pastoral regions of ancient Greece (see Poussin's *Arcadian Shepherds*, in chapter 21).

2

Heard melodies are sweet, but those unheard
   Are sweeter; therefore, ye soft pipes, play on;
Not to the sensual ear, but, more endeared,
   Pipe to the spirit ditties of no tone:
Fair youth, beneath the trees, thou canst not leave   15
   Thy song, nor ever can those trees be bare;
   Bold Lover, never, never canst thou kiss,
Though winning near the goal—yet, do not grieve;
   She cannot fade, though thou hast not thy bliss,
   For ever wilt thou love, and she be fair!   20

3

Ah, happy, happy boughs! that cannot shed
   Your leaves, nor ever bid the Spring adieu;
And, happy melodist, unweariéd,
   For ever piping songs for ever new;
More happy love! more happy, happy love!   25
   For ever warm and still to be enjoyed,
   For ever panting, and for ever young;
All breathing human passion far above,
   That leaves a heart high-sorrowful and cloyed,
   A burning forehead, and a parching tongue.   30

4

Who are these coming to the sacrifice?
  To what green altar, O mysterious priest,
Lead'st thou that heifer lowing at the skies,
  And all her silken flanks with garlands drest?
What little town by river or sea shore,   35
  Or mountain-built with peaceful citadel,
    Is emptied of this folk, this pious morn?
And, little town, thy streets for evermore
  Will silent be; and not a soul to tell
    Why thou art desolate, can e'er return.   40

5

O Attic[4] shape! Fair attitude! with brede[5]
  Of marble men and maidens overwrought,
With forest branches and the trodden weed;
  Thou, silent form, dost tease us out of thought
As doth eternity: Cold Pastoral!   45
  When old age shall this generation waste,
    Thou shalt remain, in midst of other woe
Than ours, a friend to man, to whom thou say'st,
  "Beauty is truth, truth beauty,"—that is all
    Ye know on earth, and all ye need to know.   50

---

[4]Attica, a region in Southeastern Greece dominated by Athens.
[5]Embroidered border.

Nature and the Natural in Asian Literature

Wordsworth, Shelley, and Keats made nature a major theme in European romantic poetry; however, nature and the natural landscape had dominated the literary arts of East Asia for centuries (see chapter 14). Asian writers, immersed in Buddhist pantheism (the belief that a divine spirit pervades all things in the universe), valued the natural landscape as a symbol of the oneness of man and nature. Chinese poets of the Tang dynasty (618–907 C.E.), a Golden Age of Chinese poetry, embraced nature as a source of solitary joy and private meditation. They exalted China's mountainous landscape and changing seasons as metaphors for human moods and feelings. In poems that resemble intimate diary entries (often inscribed directly on landscape scrolls or album leaves), Chinese poets cultivated the art of nature poetry—an art that has survived well into modern times. These lines were written in the late fifteenth century by Shen Zhou (1427–1509), on a landscape that he himself painted (Figure **27.3**):

Figure 27.3 SHEN ZHOU, *Poet on a Mountain Top*, from the "Landscape Album" series, ca. 1495–1500. Album leaf mounted as a handscroll: ink on paper or ink and light color on paper, 15¼ × 23¾ in. The Nelson-Atkins Museum of Art, Kansas City, Missouri. Purchase: Nelson Trust.

White clouds encircle the waist of the hills like a
    belt;
A stony ledge soars into the void, a narrow path into
    space.
Alone, I lean on my thornwood staff and gaze calmly
    into the distance,
About to play my flute in reply to the song of this
    mountain stream.*

Although Asian poets anticipated the romantic engagement with nature, Eastern and Western styles of poetry
differed considerably. Asian poets translated nature's
moods by way of only a few carefully chosen words, evoking the subtlest of analogies between the natural landscape
and the human condition. The European romantics, on
the other hand, generally built up a series of richly detailed
pictorial images through which they might explore the
redemptive or affective powers of nature. Whereas
Chinese poets tried to record natural appearance with
some immediacy, the English romantics felt bound to dis-
till the experience of the senses by way of the intellect, to
discover moral analogues, and to put personal feelings at
the service of human instruction and improvement. But
despite the differences, the nature poetry of both East and
West addresses an enduring theme in the humanistic tradition: the value of nature in helping human beings escape
the artificial confines of the material world. Moreover,
such poetry suggests that humans and human life processes are extensions of the patterns and rhythms that govern
the cosmos itself.

   Although no literary movement in Chinese history has
been designated "romantic," there are clear examples of
the romantic sensibility in Chinese literature of the nineteenth century, especially in those works that exalt the
emotional identification of the individual with nature.
The Chinese writer Shen Fu (1763–1809) shares with
Wordsworth, Shelley, and Keats the reflective view of
nature and a heightened sensitivity to its transient moods.
A bohemian spirit, Shen Fu failed the district civil examinations that guaranteed financial success for Chinese
intellectuals. Often in debt and expelled from his family
by an overbearing father, he found brief but profound joy
in his marriage to a neighbor's daughter, Zhen Yuen. Shen
Fu's autobiography, Six Chapters from a Floating Life (1809),
is a confessional record of their life together, a life in
which poverty is balanced by the pleasures of married love
and an abiding affection for nature. In the following
excerpt from Shen's autobiography—a favorite with
Chinese readers to this day—the writer describes the simple pleasures he and Zhen Yuen derived from growing
flowers and designing "rockeries": natural arrangements of
rocks and soil which resemble miniature gardens. These
find kinship in China's delicate jade floral pieces (Figure
27.4); they also prefigure the ever popular Japanese bonsai,
the art of dwarfing and shaping trees, which, along with
rocks and other natural substances, are placed in shallow
pots to create miniature landscapes. The tender story of

*Translated by Daniel Bryant.

Figure 27.4 Chinese water pot, probably eighteenth century. Jade, 6 × 4½ in.
© The Board of Trustees of the Victoria and Albert Museum, London.

the destruction of the "Place of Falling Flowers," the couple's tiny version of the natural landscape, anticipates the
central event of Shen's intimate life history: the death of
his beloved wife. The story also functions as a reminder
that all of nature is fragile and impermanent.

READING 5.4 From Shen Fu's *Six Chapters
from a Floating Life* (1809)

As a young man I was excessively fond of flowers and loved to   1
prune and shape potted plants and trees. When I met Chang
Lan-p'o he began to teach me the art of training branches and
supporting joints, and after I had mastered these skills, he
showed me how to graft flowers. Later on, I also learned the
placing of stones and designing of rockeries.

   The orchid we considered the peerless flower, selecting it as
much for its subtle and delicate fragrance as for its beauty and
grace. Fine varieties of orchids were very difficult to find,
especially those worthy of being recorded in the Botanical   10
Register. When Lan-p'o was dying he gave me a pot of spring
orchids of the lotus type, with broad white centres, perfectly
even "shoulders," and very slender stems. As the plant was a
classic specimen of its type, I treasured its perfection like a
piece of ancient jade. Yuen took care of it whenever my work
as yamen secretary[1] called me away from home. She always
watered it herself and the plant flourished, producing a
luxuriant growth of leaves and flowers.

   One morning, about two years later, it suddenly withered
and died. When I dug up the roots to inspect them, I saw that   20
they were as white as jade, with many new shoots beginning
to sprout. At first, I could not understand it. Was I just too
unlucky, I wondered, to possess and enjoy such beauty?
Sighing despondently, I dismissed the matter from my mind.
But some time later I found out what had really happened. It
seemed that a person who had asked for a cutting from the

[1]A government clerk.

plant and had been refused, had then poured boiling water on it and killed it. After that, I vowed never to grow orchids again.

Azaleas were my second choice. Although the flowers had no fragrance they were very beautiful and lasted a long time. The plants were easy to trim and to train, but Yuen loved the green of the branches and leaves so much that she would not let me cut them back, and this made it difficult for me to train them to correct shapes. Unfortunately, Yuen felt this way about all the potted plants that she enjoyed. 30

Every year, in the autumn, I became completely devoted to the chrysanthemum. I loved to arrange the cut flowers in vases but did not like the potted plants. Not that I did not think the potted flowers beautiful, but our house having no garden, it was impossible for me to grow the plants myself, and those for 40 sale at the market were overgrown and untrained; not at all what I would have chosen.

One day, as I was sweeping my ancestral graves in the hills, I found some very unusual stones with interesting streaks and lines running through them. I talked to Yuen about them when I went home.

"When Hsüan-chou stones are mixed with putty and arranged in white-stone dishes, the putty and stones blend well and the effect is very harmonious," I remarked. "These yellow stones from the hills are rugged and old-looking, but if 50 we mix them with putty the yellow and white won't blend. All the seams and gaps will show up and the arrangement will look spotty. I wonder what else we could use instead of putty?"

"Why not pick out some of the poor, uninteresting stones and pound them to powder," Yuen said. "If we mix the powdered stones with the putty while it is still damp, the colour will probably match when it dries."

After doing as she suggested, we took a rectangular I-hsing pottery dish and piled the stones and putty into a miniature 60 mountain peak on the left side of it, with a rocky crag jutting out towards the right. On the surface of the mountain, we made criss-cross marks in the style of the rocks painted by Ni Tsan[2] of the Yuan dynasty. This gave an effect of perspective and the finished arrangement looked very realistic—a precipitous cliff rising sharply from the rocks at the river's edge. Making a hollow in one corner of the dish, we filled it with river mud and planted it with duckweed. Among the rocks we planted "clouds of the pine trees," bindweed. It was several days before the whole thing was finished. 70

Before the end of autumn the bindweed had spread all over the mountain and hung like wistaria from the rocky cliff. The flowers, when they bloomed, were a beautiful clear red. The duckweed, too, had sprouted luxuriantly from the mud and was now a mass of snowy white. Seeing the beauty of the contrasting red and white, we could easily imagine ourselves in Fairyland.

Setting the dish under the eaves, we started discussing what should be done next, developing many themes: "Here there should be a lake with a pavilion—" "This spot calls for a 80 thatched summerhouse—" "This is the perfect place for the six-character inscription 'Place of Falling Flowers and Flowing

Water' "—"Here we could build our house—here go fishing—here enjoy the view"; becoming, by this time, so much a part of the tiny landscape, with its hills and ravines, that it seemed to us as if we were really going to move there to live.

One night, a couple of mis-begotten cats, fighting over food, fell off the eaves and hit the dish, knocking it off its stand and smashing it to fragments in an instant. Neither of us could help crying. 90

"Isn't it possible," I sighed, "to have even a little thing like this without incurring the envy of the gods?"

Romantic Landscape Painting

Like nature poetry, landscape painting originated in China, where it acquired specific stylistic and pictorial conventions (see chapter 14). By the thirteenth century it had overtaken figure painting in popularity and had spread to Japan and other parts of East Asia (see Figure 31.12). Throughout the history of Chinese art, the natural landscape remained an independent genre, that is, a subject *in and of itself*. Chinese landscape painting thus holds a unique place in the history of world art.

Generally speaking, portrayals of the Chinese landscape are not literal imitations of reality, but expressions of a benign natural harmony. Typically their vast and sweeping composition dwarfs all human figures and suggests the cosmic unity of air, earth, and water (see Figure 27.3). Whether vertical or horizontal in format, the composition may be "read" from various viewpoints, rather than (as is usual in the West) from a single vantage point. Often executed by scholar-officials in monochrome ink on silk, bamboo, or paper scrolls, such landscapes—like modern-day hiking expeditions—were intended as sources of personal pleasure and private retreat.

By contrast with the East, the landscape in the West developed quite late as an independent subject. Although Roman artists created elaborate landscape settings for mythological subjects, it was not until the Renaissance—among such painters as Leonardo da Vinci, Dürer, and Brueghel—that the natural landscape became a subject in its own right. During the seventeenth century, the French academicians Poussin and Lorrain devised the ideal landscape, a genre in which nature became the theater for mythological and biblical subjects (see chapter 21). The design or composition of the painting was conceived in the studio, and key elements, such as a large foreground tree, a distant sunset, and a meandering road or stream (which might be drawn from nature), were then organized according to the prearranged design. The seventeenth-century Dutch masters Vermeer and Rembrandt, however, rejected the ideal landscape. They preferred instead empirically precise views of the physical world, thus advancing landscape painting as an independent genre (see chapter 23). Nevertheless, it was not until the nineteenth century that landscape painting became a primary vehicle for recording the artist's shifting moods and private emotions. Romantic painters translated their native affection for the countryside into scenes that ranged from the picturesque

---

[2]A famous landscape painter (1301–1374) of the Yuan dynasty (1279–1368).

to the sublime. Like Wordsworth and Shelley, these artists discovered in nature a source of inspiration and a mirror of their own sensibilities.

Constable and Turner

Of the many landscape painters of nineteenth-century Britain, two figures stand out: John Constable (1776–1837) and Joseph Mallord William Turner (1775–1851). Constable owed much to the Dutch masters; yet his approach to nature was uncluttered by tradition. "When I sit down to make a sketch from nature," he wrote, "the first thing I try to do is to forget that I have ever seen a picture." Constable's freshly perceived landscapes celebrate the physical beauty of the rivers, trees, and cottages of his native Suffolk countryside even as they describe the mundane labors of its inhabitants (Figure 27.5). Like Wordsworth, who tried to illustrate "incidents and situations from common life," Constable chose to paint ordinary and humble subjects— "water escaping from mill-dams, willows, old rotten planks, slimy posts, and brickwork"—as he described them. And like Wordsworth, Constable drew on his childhood experiences as sources of inspiration. "Painting," Constable explained, "is with me but another word for feeling and I associate 'my careless boyhood' with all that

lies on the banks of the Stour [River]; those scenes made me a painter, and I am grateful."

Constable brought to his landscapes a sensitive blend of empirical detail and freedom of form. Fascinated by nineteenth-century treatises on the scientific classifications of clouds, he made numerous oil studies of cloud formations, noting on the reverse of each sketch the time of the year, hour of the day, and direction of the wind. "The sky," he wrote, "is the source of light in nature, and governs everything." He confessed to an "over-anxiety" about his skies and feared that he might destroy "that easy appearance which nature always has in all her movements." In order to capture the "easy appearance" of nature and the fugitive effects of light and atmosphere, Constable often stippled parts of the landscape with white dots (compare Vermeer; see chapter 23)—a device critics called "Constable's snow." His finished landscapes thus record not so much the "look" of nature as its fleeting moods. In *Wivenhoe Park, Essex*, Constable depicts cattle grazing on English lawns which typically resemble well-manicured gardens (Figure 27.6). From the distant horizon, the residence of the owners overlooks a verdant estate. Brilliant sunshine floods through the trees and across the fields onto a lake that is shared by swans and fishermen. But the real subject of the painting is the sky, which, with its windblown clouds, preserves the spontaneity of Constable's oil sketches.

Figure 27.5 JOHN CONSTABLE, *The Haywain*, 1821. Oil on canvas, 4 ft. 3½ in. × 6 ft. 1 in. National Gallery, London.

Figure 27.6 JOHN CONSTABLE, *Wivenhoe Park, Essex*, 1816. Oil on canvas, 22⅛ × 39⅞ in. © 1998 Board of Trustees, National Gallery of Art, Washington, D.C. Widener Collection.

If Constable's landscapes describe nature in its humble and contemplative guises, Turner's render nature at its most sublime. Turner began his career making topographical drawings of picturesque and architectural subjects; these he sold to engravers, who, in turn, mass-produced and marketed them in great numbers. One of these early drawings, the ruined monastery of Tintern Abbey, calls attention to the transience of worldly beauty and reflects the romantic artist's nostalgia for the Gothic past (see Figure 27.1). Between 1814 and 1830, Turner traveled extensively throughout England and the Continent, making landscape studies of the mountains and lakes of Switzerland, the breathtaking reaches of the Alps, and the picturesque cities of Italy. His systematic tours inspired hundreds of rapid pencil sketches and luminous, intimate studies executed in the spontaneous (and portable) medium of watercolor.

In contrast with the peaceful lyricism of his early landscapes, Turner's mature style investigated nature's more turbulent moods. As subjects for large-sized canvases, Turner frequently seized on natural disasters—great storms and Alpine avalanches—and human catastrophes such as shipwrecks and destructive fires. Many of Turner's seascapes treat the sea as a symbol for nature's indomitable power—a favorite romantic theme, and one that prevails in Coleridge's *Rime of the Ancient Mariner* (1798), Théodore Géricault's painting, *The Raft of the "Medusa"* (see Figure 29.4), and Herman Melville's monumental sea novel, *Moby Dick* (1851), to name only three examples. In *The Slave Ship* of 1840 (Figure 27.7), the aesthetic orchestration of the glowing sunset, turbulent seas, impending storm, and fantastic fish (that appear to devour the remains of the shackled body in the right foreground) distract the viewer from the complex social issue boldly described in the original title: *Slavers Throwing Overboard the Dead and Dying: Typhoon Coming On.* While Britain had finally abolished slavery throughout the British colonies in 1838, popular literature on the history of the slave trade published in 1839 described in some detail the notorious activity that inspired Turner's painting: the transatlantic traders' practice of throwing overboard the dead and dying bodies of African slaves, and then collecting insurance money on "goods lost" at sea. On the eve of rising British commercialism (see chapter 30), Turner seems to suggest that the human capacity for evil rivals nature's cruelest powers.

Two years later, in *Snowstorm* (Figure **27.8**), Turner explored his own romantic engagement with nature: The 67-year-old artist claimed that, at his request, sailors lashed him to the mast of a ship caught for hours in a storm at sea so that he might "show what such a scene was like." He subtitled the painting "Steamboat off a Harbour's Mouth making Signals in Shallow Water . . . the Author was in this Storm on the Night the Ariel left Harwich." Since no ship by that name is listed in the records of the port of Harwich, Turner's imagination may have exceeded his experience. Nevertheless, as with many of Turner's late works, *Snowstorm* is an exercise in sensation and intuition. It is the imaginative transformation of an intense physical experience, which, recollected thereafter, evokes—as Wordsworth declared—"a sense sublime/Of something far more deeply interfused,/ Whose dwelling place is the light of setting suns,/And the round ocean and the living air,/And the blue sky, and in the mind of man." Indeed, Turner's "landscapes of the sublime" come closer to

Figure 27.7 (opposite, top) **J. M. W. TURNER**, *The Slave Ship (Slavers Throwing Overboard the Dead and Dying: Typhoon Coming On)*, 1840. Oil on canvas, 35¾ × 48¼ in. The Museum of Fine Arts, Boston. Henry Lillie Pierce Fund.

Figure 27.8 (opposite, below) **J. M. W. TURNER**, *Snowstorm: Steamboat off a Harbour's Mouth*, 1842. Oil on canvas, 3 × 4 ft. Tate Gallery, London.

capturing the spirit of Wordsworth's nature mysticism than do Constable's gentler views of the physical landscape. Their expanding and contracting forms, their swirling masses of paint, and their startling bursts of color are also comparable to the impassioned rhythms and brilliant dynamics of much romantic music.

Turner's late paintings are daringly innovative. His luminous landscapes, haunted by suggestive, "empty" spaces, have more in common with Chinese landscapes than with traditional Western ones. Critics disparagingly called Turner's transparent veils of color—resembling his beloved watercolors—"tinted steam" and "soapsuds." Nevertheless, in dozens of canvases that he never dared to exhibit during his lifetime, Turner all but abandoned recognizable subject matter; these experiments in light and color anticipated (and even outreached) the French impressionists by more than three decades.

Landscape Painting in Germany and France

Outside of England, German landscape artists took a profoundly spiritual view of nature. The paintings of Constable's contemporary, Caspar David Friedrich (1774–1840), which often include ruined Gothic chapels and wintry graveyards, are elegiac remnants of a vanished world. In *Two Men Looking at the Moon* (Figure **27.9**), Friedrich silhouettes a craggy, half-uprooted tree against a glowing, moonlit sky. At the brink of a steep cliff, overlooking the perilous edge of the earth, stand two male figures. Somber colors add to the mood of poetic loneliness in a universe whose vast mysteries might be contemplated by what Friedrich called "our spiritual eye." As a comment on the eternal dialogue between man and nature, the painting has much in common with traditional Chinese landscapes (compare Figure 27.3).

In contrast to Friedrich, French landscape painters made unsentimental but poetic renderings of the local countryside. The artists of the Barbizon school—named after the picturesque village on the edge of the Forest of Fontainebleau near Paris—were the first to take their easels out of doors. Working directly from nature (though usually finishing the canvas in the studio), they painted modest landscapes and scenes of rural life that evoked the realists' unembellished vision of the world; the romantic-realists of the Barbizon school were highly successful in capturing nature's moods. The greatest French landscape painter of the mid-nineteenth century, Jean-Baptiste-Camille Corot (1796–1875), shared the Barbizon preference for working outdoors, but he brought to his landscapes a breathtaking sense of harmony and tranquillity. Corot's early landscapes, executed for the most part in Italy, are as formally composed as the paintings of Poussin and David, but they are at once simpler, more personal, and more serene. In his late canvases, Corot created luminescent landscapes that are intimate and contemplative (Figure **27.10**). He called them "souvenirs," that is,

Figure 27.9 CASPAR DAVID FRIEDRICH, *Two Men Looking at the Moon*, 1819–1820. Oil on panel, 13¾ × 17¼ in. Gemäldegalerie Neue Meister, Dresden.

Figure 27.10 JEAN-BAPTISTE-CAMILLE COROT, *Ville d'Avray*, 1870. Oil on canvas, 21⅝ × 31½ in. The Metropolitan Museum of Art, New York. Catharine Lorillard Wolfe Collection. Bequest of Catharine Lorillard Wolfe, 1887 (87.15.141). © 1980 The Metropolitan Museum of Art.

remembrances, to indicate that they were recollections of previous visual experiences, rather than on-the-spot accounts. Like many artists, Corot kept notebooks in which he jotted his everyday thoughts. One passage perfectly captures the romantic point of view: "Be guided by feeling alone. We are only simple mortals, subject to error, so listen to the advice of others, but follow only what you understand and can unite in your own feeling . . . Beauty in art is truth bathed in an impression received from nature." Corot's poetic landscapes, filled with feathery trees and misty rivers, and bathed in nuances of silver light, became so popular in France and elsewhere that he was able to sell as many canvases as he could paint. Even in his own time, forgeries of Corot's work abounded.

American Romanticism

Transcendentalism

Across the Atlantic, along the eastern shores of the rapidly industrializing American continent, romanticism took hold both as an attitude of mind and as a style. Romanticism infused all aspects of nineteenth-century American culture: It distinguished the frontier tales of James Fenimore Cooper (1789–1851), the mysteries of Edgar Allan Poe

(1809–1849), and the novels of Nathaniel Hawthorne (1804–1864) and Herman Melville (1819–1891). But it found its purest expression in a movement known as *transcendentalism*. The transcendentalists were a group of New England intellectuals who held that knowledge gained by way of intuition transcended or surpassed knowledge based on reason and logic. They believed that the direct experience of nature united one with God. They exalted individualism and self-reliance and urged that human beings discover their higher spiritual selves through sympathy with nature. Reacting against the material excesses of advancing industrialism, the transcendentalists embraced such antimaterialistic philosophies as neoplatonism (see chapter 16), Asian mysticism (see chapters 2 and 14), and German idealism (see chapter 25). Though the transcendentalists were the descendants of English Puritans, they sought spiritual instruction in Eastern religious philosophies that had reached the Boston area in the early nineteenth century. From Hinduism and Buddhism, the transcendentalists adopted a holistic philosophy based in pantheism: the belief that all aspects of the universe are infused with spiritual divinity. It followed as well that all living things derived their being from the same universal source and therefore shared a "universal brotherhood"—the unity of humanity, nature, and God.

The prime exemplar of the transcendentalists was Ralph Waldo Emerson (1803–1882), whose essays powerfully influenced nineteenth-century American thought. The son and grandson of clergymen, Emerson was ordained as a Unitarian minister when he was in his twenties. Like Wordsworth, Emerson courted nature to "see into the life of things" and to taste nature's cleansing power. In the essay entitled *Nature* (1836), Emerson sets forth his pantheistic credo:

> In the woods is perpetual youth. Within these plantations of God, a decorum and sanctity reign, a perennial festival is dressed, and the guest sees not how he should tire of them in a thousand years. In the woods, we return to reason and faith. There I feel that nothing can befall me in life—no disgrace, no calamity (leaving my eyes), which nature cannot repair. Standing on the bare ground—my head bathed by the blithe air and uplifted into infinite space—all mean egotism vanishes. I become a transparent eyeball; I am nothing; I see all; the currents of the Universal Being circulate through me; I am part or parcel of God.*

Although best known for his essays, Emerson was a poet of considerable talent. He shared with Coleridge and Wordsworth (both of whom he had met in England) a mystic reverence for nature; but he also brought to his poetry a unique appreciation of Asian philosophy, which he had acquired by reading some of the central works of Hindu literature, including the *Bhagavad Gita* (see chapter 3). In Emerson's short poem "Brahma," the voice of the Absolute Spirit and World Creator reminds the reader that a single identity—Brahma him/her/itself—underlies all apparent differences in nature. All universal forces, explains Brahma—even death and birth ("shadow and sunlight") —are one, the knowledge of which supersedes Heaven.

READING 5.5 Emerson's "Brahma" (1856)

If the red slayer[1] think he slays,   1
  Or if the slain think he is slain,
They know not well the subtle ways
  I keep, and pass, and turn again.

Far or forgot to me is near;   5
  Shadow and sunlight are the same;
The vanished gods to me appear;
  And one to me are shame and fame.

They reckon ill who leave me out;
  When me they fly, I am the wings;   10
I am the doubter and the doubt,
  And I the hymn the Brahmin[2] sings.

---

* *The Complete Essays and Other Writings of Ralph Waldo Emerson*, ed. Brooks Atkinson. New York: The Modern Library, 1950, 6.

[1] Siva, the Hindu god who represents the destructive (and also the recreative) force in nature; with Brahma and Vishnu, one of the three central deities in the Hindu pantheon.

[2] Hindu priest.

The strong gods[3] pine for my abode,
  And pine in vain the sacred Seven;[4]
But thou, meek lover of the good!   15
  Find me, and turn thy back on heaven.

Emerson's friend Henry David Thoreau (1817–1862) carried transcendentalism to its logical end by literally returning to nature. Thoreau had completed a degree at Harvard University and made his way in the world by tutoring, surveying, and making pencils. An avid opponent of slavery, he was jailed briefly for refusing to pay a poll tax to a pro-slavery government. In an influential essay on civil disobedience, he described the philosophy of passive resistance and moral idealism that he himself practiced—a philosophy embraced by the twentieth-century leaders Mohandas Karamchand Gandhi and Martin Luther King. In 1845 Thoreau abandoned urban society to live in the Massachusetts woods near Walden Pond—an experiment that lasted twenty-six months. He described his love of the natural world, his nonconformist attitude toward society, and his deep commitment to monkish simplicity in his "handbook for living," called *Walden, or Life in the Woods*. In this intimate yet forthright diary, from which the following excerpts are drawn, Thoreau glorifies nature as innocent and beneficent—a source of joy and practical instruction.

READING 5.6 From Thoreau's *Walden* (1854)

Near the end of March, 1845, I borrowed an axe and went   1
down to the woods by Walden Pond, nearest to where I
intended to build my house, and began to cut down some tall,
arrowy white pines, still in their youth, for timber. . . . It was a
pleasant hillside where I worked, covered with pine woods,
through which I looked out on the pond, and a small open field
in the woods where pines and hickories were springing up. The
ice in the pond was not yet dissolved, though there were some
open spaces, and it was all dark-colored and saturated with
water. There were some slight flurries of snow during the days   10
that I worked there; but for the most part when I came out on
to the railroad, on my way home, its yellow sand-heap
stretched away gleaming in the hazy atmosphere, and the rails
shone in the spring sun, and I heard the lark and pewee and
other birds already come to commence another year with us.
They were pleasant spring days, in which the winter of man's
discontent was thawing as well as the earth, and the life that
had lain torpid began to stretch itself. One day, when my axe
had come off and I had cut a green hickory for a wedge, driving
it with a stone, and had placed the whole to soak in a pond-   20
hole in order to swell the wood, I saw a striped snake run into
the water, and he lay on the bottom, apparently without
inconvenience, as long as I stayed there, or more than a
quarter of an hour; perhaps because he had not yet fairly come
out of the torpid state. It appeared to me that for a like reason
men remain in their present low and primitive condition; but if

---

[3] *Devas* or angelic beings.
[4] The seven highest Hindu saints.

they should feel the influence of the spring of springs arousing them, they would of necessity rise to a higher and more ethereal life. I had previously seen the snakes on frosty mornings in my path with portions of their bodies still numb and inflexible, waiting for the sun to thaw them. On the 1st of April it rained and melted the ice, and in the early part of the day, which was very foggy, I heard a stray goose groping about over the pond and cackling as if lost, or like the spirit of the fog. . . .

I went to the woods because I wished to live deliberately, to front only the essential facts of life, and see if I could not learn what it had to teach, and not, when I came to die, discover that I had not lived. I did not wish to live what was not life, living is so dear; nor did I wish to practice resignation, unless it was quite necessary. I wanted to live deep and suck out all the marrow of life, to live so sturdily and Spartan-like as to put to rout all that was not life, to cut a broad swath and shave close, to drive life into a corner, and reduce it to its lowest terms, and, if it proved to be mean, why then to get the whole and genuine meanness of it, and publish its meanness to the world; or if it were sublime, to know it by experience, and be able to give a true account of it in my next excursion. For most men, it appears to me, are in a strange uncertainty about it, whether it is of the devil or of God, and have *somewhat hastily* concluded that it is the chief end of man here to "glorify God and enjoy him forever." . . .

Figure 27.11 THOMAS EAKINS, *Walt Whitman*, 1888. Oil on canvas, 30⅛ × 24¼ in. Courtesy of the Museum of American Art of the Pennsylvania Academy of the Fine Arts, Philadelphia. General Fund 1917.1.

Simplicity, simplicity, simplicity! I say, let your affairs be as two or three, and not a hundred or a thousand; instead of a million count half a dozen, and keep your accounts on your thumb-nail. . . . Instead of three meals a day, if it be necessary eat but one; instead of a hundred dishes, five; and reduce other things in proportion. . . .

The indescribable innocence and beneficence of Nature,—of sun and wind and rain, of summer and winter,—such health, such cheer, they afford forever! and such sympathy have they ever with our race, that all Nature would be affected, and the sun's brightness fade, and the winds would sigh humanely, and the clouds rain tears, and the woods shed their leaves and put on mourning in midsummer, if any man should ever for a just cause grieve. Shall I not have intelligence with the earth? Am I not partly leaves and vegetable mould myself? . . .

Walt Whitman's Romantic Individualism

Though technically not a transcendentalist, Walt Whitman (1818–1892; Figure **27.11**) gave voice to the transcendental worldview in his euphoric poetry. Whitman followed Emerson's advice and lived according to the motto of self-reliance. He served as a male nurse in an American Civil War hospital and wrote articles and poems that celebrated his affection for the American landscape. Like Wordsworth, Whitman took everyday life as his theme, but he rejected artificial poetic diction more completely than Wordsworth had. His natural voice bellowed a "barbaric yawp" that found ideal expression in **free verse** (poetry based on irregular rhythmic patterns rather than on the conventional use of meter). Whitman molded his unmetrical rhythms and sonorous cadences by means of standard poetic devices, such as **alliteration**, assonance, and repetition. Whitman loved Italian opera, and his style often simulates the musical grandeur of that genre. But the prevailing themes in Whitman's poetry are nationalism and democracy. Whitman exalted the ordinary individual and sympathized with marginal people, such as felons and prostitutes. Claiming to be a poet of the body as well as the soul, he assumed an honest recognition of the sexual, physical self. The American scene was the source of endless inspiration for the sprawling, cosmic images that dominate his autobiographical masterpiece, *Leaves of Grass* (1855). The first edition of this collection of poems was met with strident criticism for its freewheeling verse forms and its candid celebration of all forms of sexuality—one reviewer attacked the book as "a mixture of Yankee transcendentalism and New York rowdyism." In "Song of Myself," the longest of the lyric poems included in *Leaves of Grass*, we come face to face with the expansive individualism that typified the romantic movement. At the same time, we are struck by Whitman's impassioned quest for unity with nature and with all humankind.

READING 5.7 From Whitman's "Song of Myself" (1855)

1

I celebrate myself, and sing myself,   1
And what I assume you shall assume,
For every atom belonging to me as good belongs to you.

I loaf and invite my soul,
I learn and loaf at my ease observing a spear of summer grass.   5

My tongue, every atom of my blood, form'd from this soil, this
     air,
Born of parents born here from parents the same, and their
     parents the same,
I, now thirty-seven years old in perfect health begin,
Hoping to cease not till death.

Creeds and schools in abeyance,   10
Retiring back a while suffced at what they are, but never
     forgotten,
I harbor for good or bad, I permit to speak at every hazard,
Nature without check with original energy.

24

Walt Whitman, a kosmos, of Manhattan the son,   1
Turbulent, fleshy, sensual, eating, drinking and breeding,
No sentimentalist, no stander above men and women or apart
     from them,
No more modest than immodest.

Unscrew the locks from the doors!   5
Unscrew the doors themselves from their jambs!
Whoever degrades another degrades me,
And whatever is done or said returns at last to me.
Through me the afflatus surging and surging, through me the
     current and index.

I speak the pass-word primeval, I give the sign of democracy,   10
By God! I will accept nothing which all cannot have their
     counterpart of on the same terms.

Through me many long dumb voices,
Voices of the interminable generations of prisoners and slaves,
Voices of the diseas'd and despairing and of thieves and
     dwarfs,
Voices of cycles of preparation and accretion,   15
And of the threads that connect the stars, and of wombs and
     of the father-stuff,
And of the rights of them the others are down upon,
Of the deform'd, trivial, flat, foolish, despised,
Fog in the air, beetles rolling balls of dung.

Through me forbidden voices,   20
Voices of sexes and lusts, voices veil'd and I remove the veil,
Voices indecent by me clarified and transfigur'd.

I do not press my fingers across my mouth,
I keep as delicate around the bowels as around the head and
     heart,
Copulation is no more rank to me than death is.   25

I believe in the flesh and the appetites,
Seeing, hearing, feeling, are miracles, and each part and tag of
     me is a miracle.

Divine am I inside and out, and I make holy whatever I touch or
     am touch'd from,
The scent of these arm-pits aroma finer than prayer,
This head more than churches, bibles, and all the creeds.   30

52

The spotted hawk swoops by and accuses me, he complains of
     my gab and my loitering.   1

I too am not a bit tamed, I too am untranslatable,
I sound my barbaric yawp over the roofs of the world.

The last scud of day holds back for me,
It flings my likeness after the rest and true as any on the
     shadow'd wilds,   5
It coaxes me to the vapor and the dusk.

I depart as air, I shake my white locks at the runaway sun,
I effuse my flesh in eddies, and drift it in lacy jags.
I bequeath myself to the dirt to grow from the grass I love,
If you want me again look for me under your boot-soles.   10

You will hardly know who I am or what I mean,
But I shall be good health to you nevertheless,
And filter and fibre your blood.

Failing to fetch me at first keep encouraged,
Missing me one place search another,   15
I stop somewhere waiting for you.

American Landscape Painting

Landscape painters in America mirrored the sentiments of the transcendentalists by capturing on canvas "the indescribable innocence and beneficence of nature" (Thoreau). As with the paintings of Constable and Corot, American landscapes reveal a clear delight in natural beauty and a fascination with nature's fleeting and dramatic moods. But American artists bring to their art a nationalistic infatuation with one of their young nation's unique features—its unspoiled and resplendent terrain. Every detail of a vast panorama is captured on canvas, as if the artist felt compelled to record with photographic precision the majesty and moral power of the American continent and, at the same time, capture the magnitude of its untamed wilderness. Panorama and painstaking

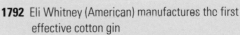

1790 the cotton mill inaugurates the Industrial
     Revolution in America

1792 Eli Whitney (American) manufactures the first
     effective cotton gin

1803 Robert Fulton (American) produces the first steam-
     powered ship

1831 Cyrus McCormick (American) introduces the horse-drawn
     reaper for harvesting

precision are features found in the topographic landscapes of the Hudson River school—a group of artists who worked chiefly in the region of upstate New York during the 1830s and 1840s. One of the leading figures of the Hudson River school was the British-born Thomas Cole (1801–1848), whose *Oxbow* offers a view of the Connecticut River near Northampton, Massachusetts (Figure 27.12). In this landscape, Cole achieved a dramatic mood by framing the brightly lit hills and curving river of the distant vista with the darker motifs of a departing thunderstorm and a blighted tree.

Intrigued by America's drive to settle the West, nineteenth-century artists made panoramic depictions of that virginal territory. Albert Bierstadt's landscape of the Rocky Mountains, which includes a Native American encampment in the foreground, reflects the German-born artist's fascination with the templelike purity of America's vast, rugged spaces along the Western frontier (Figure 27.13). The isolated settlement, dwarfed and enshrined by snowcapped mountains, a magnificent waterfall, and a looking-glass lake—all bathed in golden light—is an American Garden of Eden, inhabited by tribes of unspoiled "noble savages." Bierstadt, who like Keats and Shelley (and numerous American artist/tourists) had toured Italy, gave new meaning to the ancient image of the idyllic landscape, in which man and nature flourish in per-

fect harmony. At the same time, the painting gave public evidence of the American taste for expansion and empire-building, a visible reflection of nineteenth-century American nationalism. Significantly, the size of Bierstadt's painting (some 6 × 10 feet) heralded the official establishment of landscape as a genre: Academic tradition had dictated that large canvases were appropriate only for the representation of serious themes.

Panoramic landscapes with views of exotic, faraway places were popular nineteenth-century substitutes for actual travel, and viewers were known to carry binoculars to their showings, admission to which usually required entrance fees. Such was in fact the case with the paintings of Frederic Edwin Church (1826–1900), a pupil of Thomas Cole. Church's cosmic landscapes, which regularly featured tropical storms, dazzling sunsets, erupting volcanos, and gigantic icebergs, transported gallery patrons to the remote and exotic places—Brazil, Ecuador, Newfoundland—that Church himself had visited. Called by his contemporaries "the Michelangelo of landscape art," Church invested his vistas with a heroic and quasi-religious spirit: In *Rainy Season in the Tropics* (Figure 27.14), for instance, which he painted at the end of the American Civil War, Church uses a rainbow—the symbol of divine benevolence and restored harmony—as the unifying motif. Much like the other nineteenth-century

Figure 27.12 THOMAS COLE, *The Oxbow (View from Mount Holyoke, Northampton, Massachusetts, After a Thunderstorm)*, 1836. Oil on canvas, 4 ft. 3½ in. × 6 ft. 4 in. The Metropolitan Museum of Art, New York. Gift of Mrs. Russell Sage, 1908 (08.228).© 1986 The Metropolitan Museum of Art.

Figure 27.13 **ALBERT BIERSTADT**, *The Rocky Mountains, Lander's Peak*, 1863. Oil on canvas, 6 ft. 1 in. × 10 ft. ¾ in. The Metropolitan Museum of Art, New York. Rogers Fund, 1907 (07.123). © 1979 The Metropolitan Museum of Art.

Figure 27.14 **FREDERIC EDWIN CHURCH**, *Rainy Season in the Tropics*, 1866. Oil on canvas, 4 ft. 8¼ in. × 7 ft. ⅛ in. Fine Arts Museums of San Francisco. Mildred Anna Williams Collection, 1970.9.

romantics, Church conceived the landscape as the vehicle for a moralizing message—here a political one.

America and Native Americans

The romantic fascination with unspoiled nature and "natural man" also inspired documentary studies of Native Americans (Figure **27.15**), such as those executed by the artist/ethnologist George Catlin (1796–1872). During the 1830s, Catlin went to live among the Native Americans of the Great Plains. Moved by what he called the "silent and stoic dignity" of America's tribal peoples, he recorded their lives and customs in literature, as well as in hundreds of drawings and paintings. Catlin's "Gallery of Indians," exhibited widely in mid-nineteenth-century Europe, drew more acclaim abroad than it did in his native country. Catlin popularized the image of Native Americans as people who deeply respected nature and the natural world (see chapter 19). He described native rituals designed to honor the Great Spirit (or Great Sun) and promote health and fertility. Observing that most tribes killed only as much game as was actually needed to feed themselves, Catlin brought attention to the Indians as the first ecologists.

Harmony with nature and its living creatures was central to Native American culture, whose pantheistic idealism is eloquently conveyed in the proverbial teachings of the Northwestern tribes: "The Earth does not belong to us; we belong to the earth . . . We did not weave the web of life; we are merely a strand in it. Whatever we do to the web, we do to ourselves." Following ancestral tradition, Native Americans of the nineteenth century looked upon living things—plants, animals, and human beings—as sacred parts of an all-embracing, spiritually-charged environment. Their arts, which for the most part served religious and communal purposes, reflect their need, at the same time, to protect the balance between these natural forces, and to take spiritual advantage of their transformative and healing powers. Woodcarving, pottery, basket-weaving, beadwork embroidery, sandpainting, and other crafts make significant use of natural imagery, but do so in ways that are profoundly different from the artistic enterprises of European and American romantics: Whereas Western artists perceived nature from "without," as a source of moral and aesthetic inspiration, Native American artists perceived nature from "within," as a resource to be harnessed and appeased. While Western artists recreated the physical appearance of the natural world as a stage for powerful human actions and emotional states, Native Americans stylized individual natural elements to adorn functional and ceremonial objects that embodied the spiritual bond between animals, plants, and humans. A polychrome water jar from the Zuni Pueblos of the American Southwest, for instance, is treated as a living being whose spirit or breath may escape from the bowl by means of an opening in the

Figure 27.15 GEORGE CATLIN, *The White Cloud, Head Chief of the Iowas*, 1844–1845. Oil on canvas, 28 × 22⅞ in. © 1998 Board of Trustees, National Gallery of Art, Washington, D.C. Paul Mellon Collection.

path (the double line) painted around the vessel's shoulder (Figure **27.16**). Likewise, the deer represented on the bowl bears a line that links heart and mouth—a convention that, like the spirit line, derives from prehistoric pottery decoration.

Not the panoramic landscape, but the natural forces and living creatures immediate to that landscape, preoccupied native artists. As Catlin observed while living with the Plains Indians, natural forms embellished all ceremonial objects, one of the most important of which was the carved stone pipe. Pipes were often presented as gifts to seal tribal alliances. They were believed to be charged with supernatural power, and pipe smoking—both public and private—was a sacred act. Among the Plains Indians, pipes were considered supernaturally "activated" when the stem (symbolic of male power) was joined to the bowl (symbolic of the maternal earth). Often produced jointly by men and women, Plains pipes were carved of catlinite, a red-colored stone quarried in southwestern Minnesota (and so-named because Catlin was the first to bring East samples of this distinctive mineral). Legend identified the stone variously as the flesh of a tribal people or the congealed blood of all dead Indians and dead buffalo. Catlinite pipes served in rituals for healing. They usually bear effigies of mythologically important birds, bears, or water creatures (Figure **27.17**), while those executed after the European introduction of the horse often incorporate that animal as well.

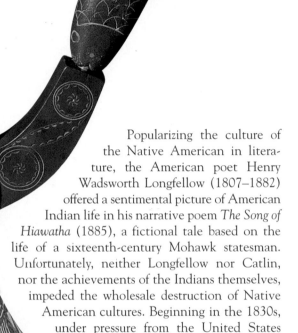

Figure 27.17 Catlinite pipe (possibly a specialized medicine pipe or one for women's use) representing a fanged and crested water spirit, with fish effigy stem, 1850–1860. Sioux tribe, carved in Minnesota. Length 8⅝ in. Private collection. Photo: Peter T. Furst, Albany, New York.

Figure 27.16 Zuni water jar, nineteenth century. Height 9½ in. Smithsonian Institution, Washington, D.C. Photo: Peter T. Furst, Albany, New York.

Popularizing the culture of the Native American in literature, the American poet Henry Wadsworth Longfellow (1807–1882) offered a sentimental picture of American Indian life in his narrative poem *The Song of Hiawatha* (1885), a fictional tale based on the life of a sixteenth-century Mohawk statesman. Unfortunately, neither Longfellow nor Catlin, nor the achievements of the Indians themselves, impeded the wholesale destruction of Native American cultures. Beginning in the 1830s, under pressure from the United States government, tribes were forced to cede their homelands and their hunting grounds to white settlers and to move into unoccupied lands in the American West. The perception of the Native American as the "devil savage" ultimately prevailed over the romantic notion of the "noble savage" and came to justify America's effort to "civilize" its "savage" populations through policies (strongly criticized by Catlin and others) that forced them to take up residence on "reservations" and, more often than not, to abandon their native languages, religions, and traditions. Persecution, humiliation, outright physical attack, and the continuing effects of disease further accelerated the decline and near extinction of America's indigenous peoples.

Figure 27.18 SARAH ANNE WHITTINGTON LANKFORD,
probably Mary Evans, and possibly others,
Baltimore Albion Quilt, ca. 1850. Appliqué, 7 ft. × 8 ft. 3 in.
Abby Aldrich Rockefeller Folk Art Center, Williamsburg, Virginia.

American Folk Art

Nineteenth-century America produced professionally trained artists like Cole and Church, and an impressive body of Native American art. This era also witnessed the rise of "folk" art, the creative achievements of ordinary people who were inspired by practical and personal motives to embellish their everyday surroundings. Folk artists were painters, sculptors, and craftspeople who had no technical training in the academic traditions of Western art, but whose sensitivity to design and affection for natural detail often resulted in the production of works of high artistic quality. One of the most distinctive of nineteenth-century folk art genres was the hand-stitched quilt, a utilitarian object produced (throughout nineteenth-century America) almost exclusively by women. Unlike academic art objects, quilts were often communal projects. Several women embroidered or appliquéd designs onto individual fabric patches salvaged from leftover sewing materials. Then, at popular quilting "bees," they assembled the patches into bed covers some 9 by 8 feet in size. Quilt motifs, frequently drawn from nature, were stylized and brightly colored (Figure **27.18**). These motifs, which eventually became standardized patterns, were passed from mother to daughter and from household to household. Patchwork quilts might commemorate religious or family occasions (such as weddings) or public events (the quilt pictured in Figure 27.18 includes a war memorial and a schematic rendering of the newly completed United States Capitol); but they rarely pictured or narrated a story. Rather, quilt designs conveyed meaning through abstract signs and symbols. A folk record of nature and the natural environment, quilt-making and related textile arts constitute a decorative yet intimate form of nineteenth-century American expression.

Early Nineteenth-Century Thought

Romanticism found its formal philosophers largely among nineteenth-century German intellectuals. Gottlieb Fichte (1762–1814), Georg Wilhelm Friedrich Hegel (1770–1831), and Arthur Schopenhauer (1788–1860) followed the philosophic idealism of Immanuel Kant (see chapter 25) by exalting the role of the human mind in constructing an idea of the world. According to these thinkers, the truths of empirical experience were not self-evident, as Locke had argued, and the truths of the mind were not clear and distinct, as Descartes had held. The German idealists shared Rousseau's belief in the power of human instinct. And, much like Rousseau and the romantic poets, they viewed nature in deeply subjective terms. Schopenhauer defended the existence of a "life-will," a blind and striving impersonal force whose operations are without purpose or design, and whose activities give rise to disorder and delusion. In Schopenhauer's view, the only escape from malignant reality was selfless contemplation of the kind described in Hindu literature and the mystical treatises of Meister Eckhart (see chapter 15). Welcoming the influence of Indian religious philosophy on European intellectuals, Schopenhauer wrote, "Sanskrit literature will be no less influential for our time than Greek literature was in the fifteenth century for the Renaissance."

While Schopenhauer perceived existence as devoid of reason and burdened by constant suffering, other nineteenth-century metaphysicians moved in the direction of mysticism. Some allied with notable visionaries, such as Friedrich von Hardenberg, better known as Novalis (1772–1801). Novalis shaped the German romantic movement through poems and essays that—like the paintings of Caspar David Friedrich—expressed longing for the lost mythic past and a spiritually inspired future. "If God could become man," wrote Novalis, "then He can also become stone, plant, animal, and element and perhaps in this way there is redemption in Nature." The romantic reawakening of religion embraced the doctrines of mysticism, confessional emotionalism, and pantheism, the last of which stressed (as we have seen with Emerson and Whitman) unity of god, man, and nature. According to the foremost German Protestant theologian and preacher, Friedrich E. D. Schleiermacher (1768–1834), the object of religion was "to love the spirit of the world" and "to become one with the infinite." As sentiments of spiritual fervor came to flourish, the once closely allied domains of religion, philosophy, and science moved in independent directions.

Hegel and the Hegelian Dialectic

The most influential philosopher of the nineteenth century was Hegel. A professor of philosophy at the University of Berlin, Hegel taught that the world consisted of a single divine nature, which he termed "absolute mind" or "spirit." According to Hegel, spirit and matter were involved in an evolutionary process impelled by spirit seeking to know its own nature. Hegel explained the operation of that process, or **dialectic**, as follows: Every condition (or "thesis") confronts its opposite condition (or "antithesis"), which then generates a synthesis. The synthesis in turn produces its opposite, and so on, in a continuing evolution that moves, explained Hegel, toward the ultimate goal of spiritual freedom. For Hegel, all reality was a process that operated on the principle of the dialectic—thesis, antithesis, and synthesis—a principle that governed the realm of ideas, artistic creation, philosophic understanding . . . indeed, history itself. "Change in nature, no matter how infinitely varied

1799 paleontologist William Smith (British) theorizes that rock strata may be identified by fossils characteristic to each

1830 Charles Lyell (British) provides foundations for the modern study of geology in his *Principles of Geology*

1859 Darwin publishes *The Origin of Species*

it is," wrote Hegel, "shows only a cycle of constant repetition. In nature, nothing new happens under the sun."

In the dense prose work entitled *The Philosophy of History* (1807), actually a compilation of his own and his students' lecture notes, Hegel advanced the idea that the essence of spirit is freedom, which finds its ultimate expression in the state. According to Hegel, human beings possess free will (thesis), which, though freely exercised over property, is limited by duty to the universal will (antithesis). The ultimate synthesis is a stage that is reached as individual will comes into harmony with universal duty. This last stage, which represents real freedom, manifests itself in the concrete institutions of the state and its laws. Hegel's view of the state (and the European nation-state in particular) as the last stage in the development of spirit and the Hegelian dialectic in general had considerable influence on late nineteenth-century nationalism, as well as on the economic theories of Karl Marx (see chapter 30).

Darwin and the Theory of Evolution

Like Hegel, the British scientist Charles Darwin (1809–1882) perceived nature as constantly changing. A naturalist in the tradition of Aristotle, Darwin spent his early career amassing enormous amounts of biological and geological data, partly as the result of a five-year voyage to South America aboard the research vessel HMS *Beagle*. Darwin's study of fossils confirmed the view of his predecessors that complex forms of life evolved from a few extremely simple organic forms. The theory of evolution did not originate with Darwin—Goethe, for example, had already suggested that all forms of plant life had evolved from a single primeval plant, and the French biologist Jean-Baptiste de Lamarck (1744–1829) showed that fossils gave evidence of perpetual change in all species. Darwin, however, substantiated the theory of evolution by explaining the process by which evolution occurred. Observing the tendency of certain organisms to increase rapidly over time while retaining traits favorable to their survival, Darwin concluded that evolution operated by means of natural selection.

By natural selection, Darwin meant a process whereby nature "pruned away" unfavorable traits in a given species, permitting the survival of those creatures most suited to the struggle for life and for reproduction of their species. The elephant's trunk, the giraffe's neck, and the human brain were evidence of adaptations made by each of these species to its environment and proof that any trait that remained advantageous to a species' continuity would prevail in the species. Failure to develop such advantageous traits meant the ultimate extinction of less developed species; only the "fittest" survived.

In 1859 Darwin published his classic work, *The Origin of Species by Means of Natural Selection, or the Preservation of the Favored Races in the Struggle for Life*. Less than a year later, a commentator observed, "No scientific work that has been published within this century has excited so much general curiosity." But curiosity was among the milder responses to this publication, for Darwin's law of evolution,

like Newton's law of gravity, challenged traditional ideas about nature and the world order. For centuries, most Westerners held to the account of the Creation described in Scripture. Some, indeed, accepted the chronology advanced by the Irish Catholic Bishop James Ussher (1581–1656), which placed earthly creation at 4004 B.C.E. Most scholars, however, perceived the likelihood of a far greater age for the earth and its species. Darwin's theory of evolution by natural selection did not deny the idea of a divine Creator—indeed, Darwin initially agreed that "it is just as noble a conception of the Deity to believe that He created a few original forms capable of self-development into other and needful forms, as to believe that He required a fresh act of creation to supply the voids caused by the action of His laws." But Darwin's theory implied that natural selection, not divine will, governed natural processes. By the implication that nature and its operations were impersonal, continuous and, indeed, the only source of design in nature, the theory of natural selection challenged the creationist view (supported by the Bible) that God had brought into being a fixed and unchanging number of species. Equally troubling was Darwin's argument (clarified in his later publication, *The Descent of Man*, 1871) that the differences between humans and less complex orders of life were differences of degree, not kind, and that all creatures were related to one another by their kinship to lower forms of life. The most likely ancestor for *homo sapiens*, explained Darwin, was "a hairy, tailed quadruped, probably arboreal in its habits . . ." (Figure **27.19**).

Clearly, Darwin's conclusions (which nurtured his own reluctant agnosticism) toppled human beings from their elevated place in the hierarchy of living creatures. If the cosmology of Copernicus and Galileo had displaced earth from the center of the solar system, Darwin's theory robbed human beings of their pre-eminence on that planet. At a single blow, Darwin shattered the harmonious worldviews of both Renaissance humanists and Enlightenment *philosophes*.

Yet, the theory of evolution by natural selection complemented a view of nature in keeping with romanticism, with transcendentalism, and with Asian philosophy, which presupposed an intrinsic unity of all living things. As Thoreau mused, "Am I not partly leaves and vegetable mould myself?" And numerous passages from the writings of Wordsworth, Shelley, Emerson, and Whitman exhibit a similar sort of pantheism. At the same time, Darwin's ideas encouraged the late nineteenth-century movement of "scientism" (the proposition that the methods of the natural sciences should be applied in all areas of rational investigation). Darwin's work also stimulated the rise of natural history museums, which, unlike the random collections of previous centuries, gave evidence of the common order of living things.

The consequences of Darwin's monumental theory were far-reaching, but his ideas were often oversimplified or misinterpreted, especially by social Darwinists, who applied his theories freely to political, economic, and social life. In the context of European efforts to colonize non-Western territories, for instance, social Darwinists

molecular genetics (the study of the digital information preserved in DNA), has provided direct evidence for the validity of Darwin's theories. Yet, to date, scientific explanations for the origins of the first life—where and how it came into being—remain uncertain and are the object of continued research and debate.

Beyond the impact of the theory of evolution by natural selection, Darwin's importance lay in the curiosity and intelligence he brought to his assessment of nature and the natural. Like the romantic poets, Darwin was an eager observer of nature, which he described as vast, energetic, and unceasingly dynamic. In *The Origin of Species*, he exults:

> When we no longer look at an organic being as a savage looks at a ship, as something wholly beyond his comprehension; when we regard every production of nature as one which has had a long history; when we contemplate every complex structure and instinct as the summing up of many contrivances, each useful to the possessor, in the same way as any great mechanical invention is the summing up of the labor, the experience, the reason, and even the blunders of numerous workmen; when we thus view each organic being, how far more interesting . . . does the study of natural history become!

And in the final paragraph of his opus, Darwin brings romantic fervor to his eloquent description of nature's laws:

> It is interesting to contemplate a tangled bank, clothed with many plants of many kinds, with birds singing on the bushes, with various insects flitting about, and with worms crawling through the damp earth, and to reflect that these elaborately constructed forms, so different from each other, and dependent upon each other in so complex a manner, have all been produced by laws acting around us. These laws, taken in the largest sense, being Growth and Reproduction; Inheritance which is almost implied by reproduction; Variability from the indirect and direct action of the conditions of life, and from use and disuse; a Ratio of Increase so high as to lead to a Struggle for Life, and as a consequence to Natural Selection, entailing Divergence of Character and the Extinction of less-improved forms. Thus, from the war of nature, from famine and death, the most exalted object which we are capable of conceiving, namely, the production of the higher animals, directly follows. There is grandeur in this view of life, with its several powers, having been originally breathed by the Creator into a few forms or into one; and that, whilst this planet has gone cycling on according to the fixed law of gravity, from so simple a beginning endless forms most beautiful and most wonderful have been, and are being evolved.*

Figure 27.19 Spoofing evolution, a cartoon of the day portrays an apelike Charles Darwin explaining his controversial theory of evolution to an ape with the help of a mirror. The work appeared in the *London Sketch Book* in May 1874, captioned by two suitable quotations from the plays of Shakespeare: "This is the ape of form" and "Four or five descents since." A.K.G. London.

justified the rapacious efforts of powerful groups of people who, seeing themselves as the "fittest," asserted their right to rule over the less powerful peoples of the world. Further, the theory of evolution provided the basis for analyzing civilizations as living organisms with stages of growth, maturity, and decline. However, since Darwin meant by "fitness" the reproductive success of the species, not simply its survival, most nineteenth-century applications of his work to social conditions represented a distortion, if not a vulgarization, of his ideas. In the course of the twentieth century, modern biology, and particularly the science of

---

*Charles Darwin, *The Origin of Species by means of Natural Selection, or the Preservation of the Favored Races in the Struggle for Life*, 6th ed. New York: Appleton, 1892, II, 280, 306.

SUMMARY

Nature provided both a metaphor for the romantic sensibility and a refuge from the evils of nineteenth-century industrialism and urbanization. William Wordsworth, the leading nature poet of the nineteenth century, emphasized the redemptive power of nature and characterized the English landscape as the source of sublime inspiration and moral truth. Wordsworth and his contemporaries initiated the romantic movement in England. The romantics stressed the free exercise of the imagination, the liberation of the senses, and the cultivation of a more natural language of poetic expression. Shelley compared the elemental forces of nature with the creative powers of the poet, while Keats rejoiced that nature's fleeting beauty might forever dwell in art. American romantics endowed the quest for natural simplicity with a robust spirit of individualism. The transcendentalists Emerson and Thoreau sought a union of self with nature; Walt Whitman proclaimed his untamed and "untranslatable" ego in sympathy with nature's energy.

The romantic embrace of nature and natural imagery was not confined to the West: In Chinese literature, as reflected in Shen Fu's confessional prose, and in painting, nature was a source of inspiration and personal solace. But it was among Western romantics that the landscape became an independent and publicly acclaimed subject in the visual arts. Constable's contemplative scenes of English country life and Turner's sublime vistas are the visual counterparts of the poems of Wordsworth and Shelley. The elegiac landscapes of Friedrich in Germany and Corot in France reflect the efforts of romantic artists to explore nature's moods as metaphors for human feeling. In the American landscapes of Cole, Bierstadt, and Church, nature becomes the symbol of an unspoiled and rapidly vanishing world; and in the art of George Catlin, the native populations of America are lovingly documented. Among these tribal people, yet another (less romantic but equally mystical) view of nature was at work, as evidenced in the production of magnificent nineteenth-century ceremonial objects.

The romantic view of nature extended to intellectual inquiry: German philosophers, influenced by Asian philosophy and Western mysticism, described the world in terms of powerful organic forces. Hegel proposed a dialectical model according to which all reality, all history, and all ideas moved toward perfect freedom. Darwin's *Origin of Species* argued that, by means of natural selection, all living things including man evolved from a few simple forms and that species evolved into higher forms of life or failed to survive. While the theory of natural selection displaced human beings from their central place in nature, it confirmed the romantic view of the unity of nature and humankind.

GLOSSARY

alliteration a literary device involving the repetition of initial sounds in successive or closely associated words or syllables

assonance a literary device involving similarity in sound between vowels followed by different consonants

dialectic in Hegelian philosophy, the process by which every condition (or "thesis") confronts an opposite condition (or "antithesis") to resolve in synthesis

free verse poetry that is based on irregular rhythmic patterns rather than on the conventional and regular use of meter

lyric poetry "lyric" means accompanied by the lyre, hence, verse that is meant to be sung rather than spoken; poetry marked by individual and personal emotion (see also chapter 6)

pantheism the belief that a divine spirit pervades all things in the universe

tone color the distinctive quality of musical sound made by a voice, a musical instrument, or a combination of instruments; also called "timbre"

SUGGESTIONS FOR READING

Clark, Kenneth. *Landscape into Art*. Boston: Beacon Press, 1972.

Furst, Peter T., and Jill L. Furst. *North American Indian Art*. New York: Rizzoli, 1982.

Green, Nicholas. *The Spectacle of Nature: Landscape and Bourgeois Culture in Nineteenth-Century France*. New York: St. Martin's Press, 1993.

Heffernan, James A. W. *The Recreation of Landscape: A Study of Wordsworth, Coleridge, Constable and Turner*. Hanover, Mass.: University Press of New England, 1985.

Himmelfarb, Gertrude. *Darwin and the Darwinian Revolution*. New York: Elephant/Ivan R. Dee, 1996.

Jones, Steve. *Darwin's Ghost: "The Origin of Species" Updated*. New York: Random House, 2000.

Loving, James. *Walt Whitman: The Song of Himself*. Berkeley: University of California Press, 1999.

McIntish, James. *Thoreau as Romantic Naturalist: His Shifting Stance Toward Nature*. Ithaca, N.Y.: Cornell University Press, 1974.

Rosenthal, Michael. *Constable: The Painter and his Landscape*. New Haven: Yale University Press, 1983.

Schenk, H. G. *The Mind of the European Romantics*. Garden City, N.Y.: Doubleday, 1969.

Schwab, Raymond. *The Oriental Renaissance: Europe's Rediscovery of India and the East 1680–1880*. New York: Columbia University Press, 1984.

Shanes, Eric. *Turner's Human Landscape*. London: Heinemann, 1990.

Wordsworth, Jonathan, and others. *William Wordsworth and the Age of English Romanticism*. New Brunswick, N.J.: Rutgers University Press, 1989.

CHAPTER TWENTY-EIGHT

The romantic hero

"O hero, with whose bloodied story
Long, long the earth will resound . . ."
Pushkin

As the romantics idealized nature and the natural, so they exalted the creative singularity of the individual in the person of the hero. Heroes, whether mortal or semidivine, traditionally symbolized humanity at its best, most powerful, and most godlike. The heroes of such classics as the *Epic of Gilgamesh*, the *Mahabharata*, the *Iliad*, the *Aeneid*, the *Song of Roland*, and *Sundiata* were larger-than-life male figures with extraordinary expectations, abilities, and goals. The heroes of old embodied the shared values of the culture they represented. Likewise, the romantic hero was a figure of superhuman ambitions and extraordinary achievements. But romantic heroes differed from traditional literary heroes in that they tended to challenge rather than champion the social and moral values of their time.

Nationalism and the Hero

Nationalism, one of the shaping forces of the nineteenth century, inspired much of the art of this era, as the following chapters testify. While the beginnings of the modern nation-state go back at least to the fourteenth century (see chapter 15), modern nationalism, an ideology (or belief system) grounded in a people's sense of cultural and political unity, did not gain widespread acceptance until roughly 1815. Modern nationalism flourished in the wake of the French Revolution and, thereafter, in resistance to the imperialistic expansion of Napoleonic France. One after another, European states, as well as some in Africa and in Latin America, rose up against foreign rulers. Love of nation and love of liberty became synonymous with the ideals of self-determination and political freedom. In its positive aspects, nationalism cultivated the revival and celebration of a common language, common customs, and a shared national history, as expressed in poetry, music, and art. The collection of German fairy tales (1812–1815) by the brothers Jacob and Wilhelm Grimm serves as an example. But nationalism also manifested a malignant aspect: Well into the twentieth century, nationalism and patriotic chauvinism motivated policies of imperialism and ignited warfare, not only between nations, but among the ethnic populations of various regions. Indeed, as these chapters reveal, much of the art of the nineteenth century is a visceral response to brutal events associated with nascent nationalism.

Nineteenth-century intellectuals celebrated the heroic personality, especially in its dedication to the causes of liberty and equality. The British historian and essayist Thomas Carlyle (1795–1881) published a series of lectures, *On Heroes and Hero-Worship*, in which he glorified hero-gods, prophets, poets, priests, men of letters, and the quasi-legendary Napoleon Bonaparte. Walter Scott (1771–1832) and Alexandre Dumas (1802–1870) wrote historical novels that described the heroic adventures of swashbuckling soldiers and maidens in distress, while Victor Hugo (1802–1885) made sentimental heroes out of egalitarian patriots in the novel *Les Misérables*. Real-life heroes challenged literary heroes in color and daring; Shaka (1787–1828), the Zulu warrior chief, changed the destiny of Southern Africa by aggressive campaigns that united all of the clans in the region to form the Zulu nation.

In America, too, the hero occupied the attention of artists: The novelists Nathaniel Hawthorne (1804–1864) and Herman Melville (1819–1891) created brooding, melancholic fictional heroes whose moral strength was tested by the forces of evil. At the same time, the Americas produced some notable real-life heroes and champions of political freedom, such as Simón Bolívar (1783–1830)—whose victories over the Spanish forces in South America won independence for Bolivia, Colombia, Ecuador, Peru, and Venezuela—and Frederick Douglass (1817–1895), the leading antislavery spokesman, whose autobiography details a heroic life of oppression and struggle.

The nineteenth century did not produce more heroes than other centuries, but it visibly exalted heroic achievement and glorified the role of the heroic imagination. While Enlightenment writers studied the social animal, the romantics explored the depths of their own souls. Egocentric and occasionally misanthropic, the heroes of the romantic era were unique personalities, whose powers of self-invention exalted their public and private image.

Intrigued by European folklore, medieval legend, and Asian customs, romantic artists modeled themselves after the heroes of "exotic" cultures. They passionately defended the notion that artists both create and are created by their art. With a subjectivity bordering on egotism, the romantics saw *themselves* as heroes—the champions of a cult of the senses and of the heart. They eagerly embraced all means of heightening imaginative experience, including those induced by such hallucinogens as opium. "Exister, pour nous, c'est sentir" ("For us, to exist is to feel"), Rousseau had proclaimed in the late eighteenth century. And, on the first page of his *Confessions* (1781), the prophet of romanticism anticipated the sentiments of self-conscious individualism that would drive artists of the next two generations: "I am made unlike anyone I have ever met: I will even venture to say that I am like no one in the whole world. I may be no better, but at least I am different."

Napoleon as a Romantic Hero

In 1799 the thirty-year-old Corsican army general Napoleon Bonaparte (1769–1821) seized control of the government of France. "The Revolution is ended," announced Napoleon when he proclaimed himself emperor in 1804. In the following ten years, Napoleon pursued a policy of conquest that brought continental Western Europe to his feet. Throughout much of the West Napoleon abolished serfdom, expropriated Church possessions, curtailed feudal privileges, and introduced French laws, institutions, and influence. Napoleon spread the revolutionary ideals of liberty, fraternity, and equality throughout the empire (Map 28.1). He championed popular sovereignty and kindled the sentiments of nationalism. In France, Napoleon ended civil strife, reorganized the educational system, and institutionalized the system of civil law known as the *Code Napoléon*.

Map 28.1 The Empire of Napoleon at Its Greatest Extent, 1812.

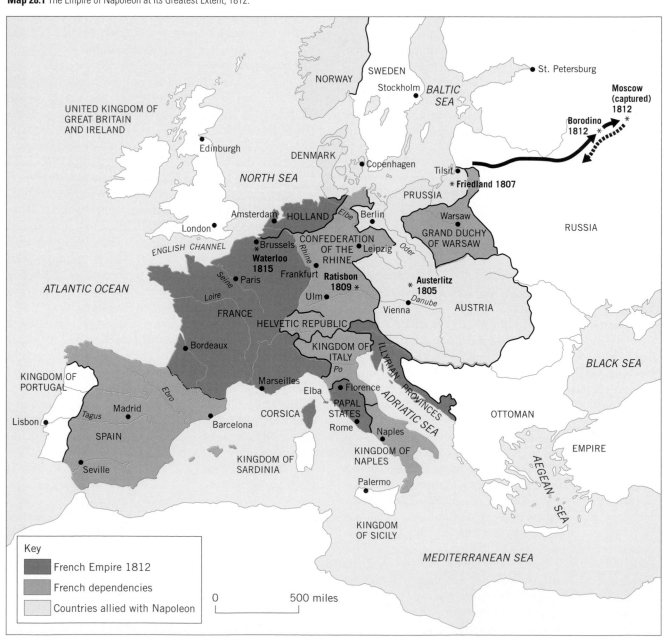

Figure 28.1 JACQUES-LOUIS DAVID, *Napoleon Crossing the Great Saint Bernard Pass*, 1800. Oil on canvas, 8 ft. 6 in. × 7 ft. 3 in. Musée National du Château de la Malmaison, Rueil-Malmaison, France. Photo: © R.M.N., Paris.

If Napoleon's ambitions were heroic, his military campaigns were stunning. Having conquered Italy, Egypt, Austria, Prussia, Portugal, and Spain, he pressed on to Russia where, in 1812, bitter weather and lack of food forced his armies to retreat. Only 100,000 of his army of 600,000 survived. In 1813, a coalition of European powers forced his defeat and exile to the island of Elba off the coast of Italy. A second and final defeat occurred after he escaped in 1814, raised a new army, and met the combined European forces led by the English Duke of Wellington at

the battle of Waterloo. The fallen hero spent the last years of his life in exile on the barren island of Saint Helena off the west coast of Africa.

Napoleon, the first of the modern European dictators, left a distinctly neoclassical stamp upon the city of Paris (see chapter 26). However, he also became the nineteenth century's first romantic hero, as envisioned in numerous European poems and paintings, and especially in the majestic portraits of Jacques-Louis David, Napoleon's favorite artist. David's equestrian portrait of Napoleon (Figure **28.1**), which clearly draws on Roman traditions of heroic glorification, shows an idealized Napoleon who is following the path of ancient generals such as Charlemagne and Hannibal (whose names are carved in stone in the foreground). David suggests in this painting—one of five identical versions of the subject—that Napoleon's rule was one of glory and achievement. Napoleon's ideas, as expressed in his diary, were equally significant in cultivating the image of a romantic hero. The diary—an intimate record of personal reflections and feelings—became a favorite mode of expression for such nineteenth-century romantics as Delacroix, Beethoven, George Sand, and Mary Shelley. Napoleon's diary entries of 1800, 1802, and 1817, quoted in Reading 5.8, reveal some of the typical features of the romantic personality: self-conscious individualism, a sense of personal power, unbridled egotism, and a high regard for the life of the imagination.

READING 5.8 From Napoleon's *Diary* (1800–1817)

Milan, June 17, 1800: . . . What a thing is imagination! Here are men who don't know me, who have never seen me, but who only knew of me, and they are moved by my presence, they would do anything for me! And this same incident arises in all centuries and in all countries! Such is fanaticism! Yes, imagination rules the world. The defect of our modern institutions is that they do not speak to the imagination. By that alone can man be governed; without it he is but a brute.   1

December 30, 1802: My power proceeds from my reputation, and my reputation from the victories I have won. My power would fall if I were not to support it with more glory and more victories. Conquest has made me what I am; only conquest can maintain me. . . .   10

Saint Helena, March 3, 1817: In spite of all the libels, I have no fear whatever about my fame. Posterity will do me justice. The truth will be known; and the good I have done will be compared with the faults I have committed. I am not uneasy as to the result. Had I succeeded, I would have died with the reputation of the greatest man that ever existed. As it is, although I have failed, I shall be considered as an extraordinary man: my elevation was unparalleled, because unaccompanied by crime. I have fought fifty pitched battles, almost all of which I have won. I have framed and carried into effect a code of laws that will bear my name to the most distant posterity. I raised myself from nothing to be the most powerful monarch in the world. Europe was at my feet. I have always been of [the] opinion that the sovereignty lay in the people.   20

The Promethean Hero

The Promethean Myth in Literature

If Napoleon Bonaparte was nineteenth-century Europe's favorite real-life hero, Prometheus was its favorite fictional hero. Prometheus (the name means "forethought") was one of the primordial deities of Greek mythology. According to legend, Prometheus challenged the other Greek gods by stealing from their home on Mount Olympus the sacred fire, source of divine wisdom and creative inspiration, and bestowing this great gift upon humankind. As punishment, Zeus chained him to a lonely rock, where an eagle fed daily on his liver, which was restored each night. A second, less dramatic aspect of the Prometheus story, more popular among the Romans than the Greeks, credited Prometheus with having fashioned human beings out of clay, in the manner of the Babylonian hero-god Marduk (see chapter 2).

Romantic poets embraced the figure of Prometheus as the suffering champion of humanity—a symbol of freedom and a deliverer whose noble ambitions had incurred the wrath of the gods. Percy Bysshe Shelley, whom we met in chapter 27, made Prometheus the savior-hero of his four-act play *Prometheus Unbound* (1820). In this drama, Prometheus frees the universe from the tyranny of the gods. Two years earlier, in 1818, Shelley's second wife, Mary Godwin Shelley (1797–1851), had explored yet another aspect of the Promethean legend in her novel *Frankenstein; or, The Modern Prometheus*. The daughter of William Godwin and the feminist writer Mary Wollstonecraft (see chapter 24), Mary Shelley began to write *Frankenstein* at the age of eighteen. Framed as a series of letters, the novel relates the astonishing tale of the scientist–philosopher Victor Frankenstein, who, having discovered the secret of imparting life to inanimate matter, produces a monster endowed with supernatural strength (Figure **28.2**). A modern Prometheus, Frankenstein suffers

Figure 28.2 The first illustration of the *Frankenstein* monster, frontispiece from the 1831 Standards Novel edition. Mary Evans Picture Library, London.

the punishment for his ambitious designs when the creature, excluded from the normal life of ordinary mortals, betrays its creator: "I was benevolent and good," he protests, "misery made me a fiend." Like the fallen Lucifer, Frankenstein's creature becomes a figure of heroic evil. *Frankenstein* belongs to a literary genre known as the Gothic novel, a type of entertainment that features elements of horror and the supernatural. Such novels, the earliest of which was Horace Walpole's *The Castle of Otranto* (1767), reflect the rising tide of anti-rationalism and a revived interest in the medieval past. Shelley's novel, actually a scientific horror tale, has become a modern classic. It has inspired numerous science fiction "spin-offs," as well as cinematic and video interpretations. Ironically, however, it is not the Promethean scientist but the monster that has captured the modern imagination, even to the point of usurping the name of his creator.

READING 5.9   From Mary Shelley's *Frankenstein* (Chapters 4 and 5) (1818)

. . . One of the phenomena which had peculiarly attracted my attention was the structure of the human frame, and, indeed, any animal endued with life. Whence, I often asked myself, did the principle of life proceed? It was a bold question, and one which has ever been considered as a mystery: yet with how many things are we upon the brink of becoming acquainted, if cowardice or carelessness did not restrain our enquiries. I revolved these circumstances in my mind and determined thenceforth to apply myself more particularly to those branches of natural philosophy which relate to physiology. Unless I had been animated by an almost supernatural enthusiasm, my application to this study would have been irksome and almost intolerable. To examine the causes of life, we must first have recourse to death. I became acquainted with the science of anatomy, but this was not sufficient; I must also observe the natural decay and corruption of the human body. In my education my father had taken the greatest precautions that my mind should be impressed with no supernatural horrors. I do not ever remember to have trembled at a tale of superstition or to have feared the apparition of a spirit. Darkness had no effect upon my fancy, and a churchyard was to be merely the receptacle of bodies deprived of life, which, from being the seat of beauty and strength, had become food for the worm. Now I was led to examine the cause and progress of this decay and forced to spend days and nights in vaults and charnel-houses. My attention was fixed upon every object the most insupportable to the delicacy of the human feelings. I saw how the fine form of man was degraded and wasted; I beheld the corruption of death succeed to the blooming cheek of life; I saw how the worm inherited the wonders of the eye and brain. I paused, examining and analysing all the minutiae of causation, as exemplified in the change from life to death, and death to life, until from the midst of this darkness a sudden light broke in upon me—a light so brilliant and wondrous, yet so simple, that while I became dizzy with the immensity of the prospect which it illustrated, I was surprized that among so many men of genius who had directed their enquiries towards the same science, that

I alone should be reserved to discover so astonishing a secret.

Remember, I am not recording the vision of a madman. The sun does not more certainly shine in the heavens than that which I now affirm is true. Some miracle might have produced it, yet the stages of the discovery were distinct and probable. After days and nights of incredible labour and fatigue, I succeeded in discovering the cause of generation and life; nay, more, I became myself capable of bestowing animation upon lifeless matter.

The astonishment which I had at first experienced on this discovery soon gave place to delight and rapture. After so much time spent in painful labour, to arrive at once at the summit of my desires was the most gratifying consummation of my toils. But this discovery was so great and overwhelming that all the steps by which I had been progressively led to it were obliterated, and I beheld only the result. What had been the study and desire of the wisest men since the creation of the world was now within my grasp. . . .

. . . Learn from me, if not by my precepts, at least by my example, how dangerous is the acquirement of knowledge and how much happier that man is who believes his native town to be the world, than he who aspires to become greater than his nature will allow.

When I found so astonishing a power placed within my hands, I hesitated a long time concerning the manner in which I should employ it. Although I possessed the capacity of bestowing animation, yet to prepare a frame for the reception of it, with all its intricacies of fibres, muscles, and veins, still remained a work of inconceivable difficulty and labour. I doubted at first whether I should attempt the creation of a being like myself, or one of simpler organization; but my imagination was too much exalted by my first success to permit me to doubt of my ability to give life to an animal as complex and wonderful as man. The materials at present within my command hardly appeared adequate to so arduous an undertaking, but I doubted not that I should ultimately succeed. I prepared myself for a multitude of reverses; my operations might be incessantly baffled, and at last my work be imperfect; yet when I considered the improvement which every day takes place in science and mechanics, I was encouraged to hope my present attempts would at least lay the foundations of future success. Nor could I consider the magnitude and complexity of my plan as any argument of its impracticability. It was with these feelings that I began the creation of a human being. As the minuteness of the parts formed a great hindrance to my speed, I resolved, contrary to my first intention, to make the being of a gigantic stature; that is to say, about eight feet in height, and proportionably large. After having formed this determination and having spent some months in successfully collecting and arranging my materials, I began.

No one can conceive the variety of feelings which bore me onwards, like a hurricane, in the first enthusiasm of success. Life and death appeared to be ideal bounds, which I should first break through, and pour a torrent of light into our dark world. A new species would bless me as its creator and source; many happy and excellent natures would owe their being to me. No father could claim the gratitude of his child so completely as I should deserve theirs. Pursuing these reflections, I thought that if I could bestow animation upon lifeless matter, I might in process of time (although I now found it impossible) renew life where death had apparently devoted the body to corruption.

These thoughts supported my spirits, while I pursued my undertaking with unremitting ardour. My cheek had grown pale with study, and my person had become emaciated with confinement. Sometimes, on the very brink of certainty, I failed; yet still I clung to the hope which the next day or the next hour might realize. One secret which I alone possessed was the hope to which I had dedicated myself; and the moon gazed on my midnight labours, while, with unrelaxed and breathless eagerness, I pursued nature to her hiding-places. Who shall conceive the horrors of my secret toil as I dabbled among the unhallowed damps of the grave or tortured the living animal to animate the lifeless clay? My limbs now tremble, and my eyes swim with the remembrance; but then a resistless and almost frantic impulse urged me forward; I seemed to have lost all soul or sensation but for this one pursuit. It was indeed but a passing trance, that only made me feel with renewed acuteness so soon as, the unnatural stimulus ceasing to operate, I had returned to my old habits. I collected bones from charnel-houses and disturbed, with profane fingers, the tremendous secrets of the human frame. In a solitary chamber, or rather cell, at the top of the house, and separated from all the other apartments by a gallery and staircase, I kept my workshop of filthy creation: my eyeballs were starting from their sockets in attending to the details of my employment. The dissecting room and the slaughter-house furnished many of my materials; and often did my human nature turn with loathing from my occupation, whilst, still urged on by an eagerness which perpetually increased, I brought my work near to a conclusion. . . .

It was on a dreary night of November that I beheld the accomplishment of my toils. With an anxiety that almost amounted to agony, I collected the instruments of life around me, that I might infuse a spark of being into the lifeless thing that lay at my feet. It was already one in the morning; the rain pattered dismally against the panes, and my candle was nearly burnt out, when, by the glimmer of the half-extinguished light, I saw the dull yellow eye of the creation open; it breathed hard, and a convulsive motion agitated its limbs.

How can I describe my emotions at this catastrophe, or how delineate the wretch whom with such infinite pains and care I had endeavoured to form? His limbs were in proportion, and I had selected his features as beautiful. Beautiful! Great God! His yellow skin scarcely covered the work of muscles and arteries beneath; his hair was of a lustrous black, and flowing; his teeth of pearly whiteness; but these luxuriances only formed a more horrid contrast with his watery eyes, that seemed almost of the same colour as the dun-white sockets in which they were set, his shrivelled complexion and straight black lips.

The different accidents of life are not so changeable as the feelings of human nature. I had worked hard for nearly two years, for the sole purpose of infusing life into an inanimate body. For this I had deprived myself of rest and health. I had desired it with an ardour that far exceeded moderation; but now that I had finished, the beauty of the dream vanished, and breathless horror and disgust filled my heart. Unable to endure the aspect of the being I had created, I rushed out of the room and continued a long time traversing my bedchamber, unable to

compose my mind to sleep. At length lassitude succeeded to the tumult I had before endured, and I threw myself on the bed in my clothes, endeavouring to seek a few moments of forgetfulness. But it was in vain; I slept, indeed, but I was disturbed by the wildest dreams. I thought I saw Elizabeth, in the bloom of health, walking in the streets of Ingolstadt. Delighted and surprized, I embraced her, but as I imprinted the first kiss on her lips, they became livid with the hue of death; her features appeared to change, and I thought that I held the corpse of my dead mother in my arms; a shroud enveloped her form, and I saw the grave-worms crawling in the folds of the flannel. I started from my sleep with horror; a cold dew covered my forehead, my teeth chattered, and every limb became convulsed; when, by the dim and yellow light of the moon, as it forced its way through the window shutters, I beheld the wretch—the miserable monster whom I had created. He held up the curtain of the bed; and his eyes, if eyes they may be called, were fixed on me. His jaws opened, and he muttered some inarticulate sounds, while a grin wrinkled his cheeks. He might have spoken, but I did not hear; one hand was stretched out, seemingly to detain me, but I escaped and rushed downstairs. I took refuge in the courtyard belonging to the house which I inhabited, where I remained during the rest of the night, walking up and down in the greatest agitation, listening attentively, catching and fearing each sound as if it were to announce the approach of the daemoniacal corpse to which I had so miserably given life.

Byron and the Promethean Myth

The Promethean myth found its most passionate champion in the life and works of the British poet George Gordon, Lord Byron (1788–1824). Byron was one of the most flamboyant personalities of the age (Figure **28.3**). Dedicated to the pleasures of the senses, he was equally impassioned by the ideals of liberty and brotherhood. In his brief, mercurial life, he established the prototype of the romantic hero, often called the Byronic hero. As a young man, Byron (much like Turner) traveled restlessly throughout Europe and the Mediterranean, devouring the landscape and the major sites. A physically attractive man (despite the handicap of a club foot) with dark, brooding eyes, he engaged in numerous love affairs, including one with his half-sister. In 1816, Byron abandoned an unsuccessful marriage and left England for good. He lived in Italy for a time with the Shelleys and a string of mistresses. By this time, Byron had earned the reputation of dangerous nonconformity that led an English woman, catching sight of the poet in Rome, to warn her daughter: "Do not look at him! He is dangerous to look at." In 1824, Byron sailed to Greece to aid the Greeks in their war of independence against the Turks—one of the many episodes in the turbulent history of nineteenth-century nationalism. There, in his last heroic role, he died of a fever.

Throughout his life, Byron was given to periodic bouts of creativity and dissipation. A man of violent passions, he harbored a desperate need to unbosom his innermost thoughts and feelings. In Italy, where he composed two of his greatest poems, *Childe Harold's Pilgrimage* (1813–1814)

Figure 28.3 THOMAS PHILLIPS, *Lord Byron Sixth Baron in Albanian Costume*, 1813. Oil on canvas, 29½ × 24½ in. National Portrait Gallery, London.

and *Don Juan* (1819–1824), he described his frenzied spirit thus: "half mad . . . between metaphysics, mountains, lakes, love unextinguishable, thoughts unutterable, and the nightmare of my own delinquencies." The heroes of Byron's poems were surely autobiographical: Childe Harold, the wanderer who, alienated from society, seeks companionship in nature; Don Juan, the libertine who cannot satiate his sexual desires; and Prometheus, the god who "stole from Heaven the flame, for which he fell." Prometheus preoccupied Byron as a symbol of triumphant individualism. For Byron, capturing the imagination in art or in life was comparable to stealing the sacred fire. In a number of his poems, Byron compares the fallen Napoleon to the mythic Prometheus—symbol of heroic ambition and ungovernable passions. And, in the stirring ode called simply "Prometheus," Byron makes of the Promethean myth a parable for the romantic imagination. He begins by recalling the traditional story of the hero whose "Godlike crime was to be kind." He goes on to identify Prometheus as "a symbol and a sign" to mortals who, although "part divine," are doomed to "funereal destiny." Like Prometheus, says Byron, we must strive to defy that destiny by pursuing the creative projects that will outlive us. Byron's verses mingle defiance and hope with melancholy and despair.

READING 5.10   Byron's "Prometheus" (1816)

Titan! to whose immortal eyes   1
  The sufferings of mortality,
  Seen in their sad reality,
Were not as things that gods despise;
What was thy pity's recompense?   5
A silent suffering, and intense;
The rock, the vulture,[1] and the chain,
All that the proud can feel of pain,
The agony they do not show,
The suffocating sense of woe,   10
  Which speaks but in its loneliness,
And then is jealous lest the sky
Should have a listener, nor will sigh
  Until its voice is echoless.
Titan! to thee the strife was given   15
  Between the suffering and the will,
  Which torture where they cannot kill;
And the inexorable Heaven,
And the deaf tyranny of Fate,

The ruling principle of Hate,   20
Which for its pleasure doth create
The things it may annihilate,
Refused thee even the boon to die:
The wretched gift eternity
Was thine—and thou hast borne it well.   25
All that the Thunderer[2] wrung from thee
Was but the menace which flung back
On him the torments of thy rack;
The fate thou didst so well foresee,
But would not to appease him tell;   30
And in thy Silence was his Sentence,
And in his Soul a vain repentance,
And evil dread so ill dissembled,
That in his hand the lightnings trembled.

Thy Godlike crime was to be kind,   35
  To render with thy precepts less
  The sum of human wretchedness,
And strengthen Man with his own mind;
But baffled as thou wert from high,
Still in thy patient energy,   40
In the endurance, and repulse
  Of thine impenetrable Spirit,
Which Earth and Heaven could not convulse,
  A mighty lesson we inherit:
Thou art symbol and a sign   45

---

[1]Byron replaces the mythological eagle with a vulture.

[2]Zeus, the supreme god of the Greeks.

To Mortals of their fate and force;
Like thee, Man is in part divine,
    A troubled stream from a pure source;
And Man in portions can foresee
His own funereal destiny,   **50**
His wretchedness, and his resistance,
And his sad unallied existence:
To which his Spirit may oppose
Itself—and equal to all woes,
    And a firm will, and a deep sense,   **55**
Which even in torture can descry
    Its own concenter'd recompense,[3]
Triumphant where it dares defy,
And making Death a Victory.

Pushkin: The Byron of Russia

Napoleon's invasion of Russia in 1812 was one of the most dramatic events in nineteenth-century history. Sorely outnumbered by the Grand Army of Napoleon, Russian troops resorted to a "scorched earth" policy that produced severe shortages of food for French and Russians alike. As Napoleon advanced on Moscow, leaving a trail of bloody battles, the Russians burned their own capital city. Napoleon ultimately captured Moscow, but within a few months he and his badly diminished army retreated from Russia, never to return. Deeply moved by Napoleon's role in stirring Russian nationalism, Alexander Pushkin (1799–1837)—Russia's leading lyric poet and dramatist—eulogized the hero who, as he explains in the poem "Napoleon," had "launched the Russian nation/Upon its lofty destinies."

Pushkin, whose maternal great-grandfather was a black African general, came from an old aristocratic family. Nevertheless, he claimed comradery with Russia's humble commoners and, taking pride in his African ancestry, he boasted "I am a versewright and a bookman, . . ./No financier, no titled footman,/A commoner: great on his own." Like Byron, Pushkin championed political freedom; he defended liberal causes that resulted in his banishment to South Russia and ultimately to his dismissal from the foreign service. His agonizing death, at the age of thirty-seven, was the result of wounds suffered in a duel with his wife's alleged lover. Pushkin's romantic tragedies and long narrative poems reveal his great admiration for Shakespeare and for Pushkin's British contemporary, Byron, and earned him a reputation as "the Byron of Russia." Some of Pushkin's works, such as *Boris Godunov* (1825) and *Eugene Onegin* (1833)—modeled in part on Byron's *Don Juan*—would inspire operas by composers Modest Mussorgsky (1839–1881) and Peter Ilyich Tchaikovsky (see chapter 29) respectively. The lyric poem "Napoleon," part of which follows, conveys Pushkin's gift for buoyant, energetic language and his profound respect for the figure whom he viewed as both the oppressor and the liberator of Russia.

[3]Catch a glimpse of the Spirit's own sufficient reward.

A wondrous fate is now fulfilled,   **1**
Extinguished a majestic man.
In somber prison night was stilled
Napoleon's grim, tumultuous span.
The outlawed potentate has vanished,   **5**
Bright Nike's mighty, pampered son;
For him, from all Creation banished,
Posterity has now begun.

O hero, with whose bloodied story
Long, long the earth will still resound,   **10**
Sleep in the shadow of your glory,
The desert ocean all around . . .
A tomb of rock, in splendor riding!
The urn that holds your mortal clay,
As tribal hatreds are subsiding,   **15**
Now sends aloft a deathless ray.

How recently your eagles glowered
Atop a disenfranchised world,
And fallen sovereignties cowered
Beneath the thunderbolts you hurled!   **20**
Your banners at a word would shower
Destruction from their folds and dearth,
Yoke after yoke of ruthless power
You fitted on the tribes of earth.

. . . .

Vainglorious man! Where were you faring,   **25**
Who blinded that astounding mind?
How came it in designs of daring
The Russian's heart was not divined?
At fiery sacrifice not guessing,
You idly fancied, tempting fate,   **30**
We would seek peace and count it blessing;
You came to fathom us too late . . .

Fight on, embattled Russia mine,
Recall the rights of ancient days!
The sun of Austerlitz,[1] decline!   **35**
And Moscow, mighty city, blaze!
Brief be the time of our dishonor,
The auspices are turning now;
Hail Moscow—Russia's blessings on her!
War to extinction, thus our vow!   **40**

The diadem of iron[2] shaking
In stiffened fingers' feeble clasp,
He stares into a chasm, quaking,
And is undone, undone at last.
Behold all Europe's legions sprawling . . .   **45**

[1]The site of Napoleon's greatest victory where, on December 2, 1805, he defeated the combined Austrian and Russian forces, acquiring control of European lands north of Rome and making him King of Italy.
[2]The iron crown of Lombardy, dating back to the fifth century, which Napoleon had assumed some time after the Italian campaigns.

The wintry fields' encrimsoned glow
Bore testimony to their falling
Till blood-prints melted with the snow.

. . . .

Let us hold up to reprobation
Such petty-minded men as chose   50
With unappeasable damnation
To stir his laurel-dark repose!
Hail him! He launched the Russian nation
Upon its lofty destinies
And augured ultimate salvation   55
For man's long-exiled liberties.

The Abolitionists: American Prometheans

Among the most fervent champions of liberty in
nineteenth-century America were those who crusaded
against the institution of slavery. Indeed, their efforts initiated a movement for black nationalism that would continue well into the twentieth century (see chapter 36). It
is unlikely that the leaders of the abolitionist crusade
against slavery regarded themselves in the image of a
Napoleon or the fictional Prometheus but, as historical
figures, the abolitionists were the heroes of their time.
They fought against the enslavement of Africans (and
their descendants), a practice that had prevailed in
America since the sixteenth century.[3] Although the abolitionists constituted only a small minority of America's
population, their arguments were emotionally charged and
their protests were often dramatic and telling. Anti-
slavery novels, the most famous of which was *Uncle Tom's
Cabin* (1852) by Harriet Beecher Stowe (1811–1896),
stirred up public sentiment against the brutality and injustice of the system. Originally serialized in an anti-slavery
newspaper, Stowe's novel sold over one million copies
within a year of its publication. But the most direct
challenge to slavery came from the slaves themselves,
and none more so than the slave rebels who—like
Prometheus—mounted outright attacks against their owners and masters in their efforts to gain a prized privilege:
freedom. While slave rebellions were rare in nineteenth-
century America—between 1800 and 1860 only two
reached the level of overt insurrection—the threat or
rumor of rebellion was terrifying to slaveowners.

One of the most notable insurrections of the century
took place in Southampton County, Virginia, in 1831: Nat
Turner (1800–1831), a slave preacher and mystic, believed
that he was divinely appointed to lead the slaves to freedom. The Turner rebellion resulted in the deaths of at
least fifty-seven whites (and many more blacks, killed
when the rebellion was suppressed) and the destruction of
several area plantations. Following the defeat of the rebel
slaves, the captive Turner explained his motives to a local
attorney, who prepared a published version of his account
in the so-called "Confessions of Nat Turner."

---

[3]The origins and history of the transatlantic slave trade are discussed in
chapters 18 and 25.

Frederick Douglass A longer, more vividly detailed
autobiography, the *Narrative of the Life of Frederick
Douglass: An American Slave* (1845), came from the pen
of the nineteenth century's leading African-American
crusader for black freedom (Figure **28.4**). Born a slave on
the east coast of Maryland, Douglass (1817–1883) had
taught himself how to read and write at an early age; he
escaped bondage in Baltimore in 1838 and eventually
found his way to New England, where he joined the
Massachusetts Antislavery Society. A powerful public
speaker, who captivated his audiences with the account
of his life in bondage and in freedom, Douglass served as
living proof of the potential of black slaves to achieve
brilliantly as free persons. He wrote extensively and
eloquently in support of abolition, describing the
"dehumanizing character of slavery" for both blacks and
whites, and defending the idea that, by abandoning
slavelike behavior, even slaves could determine their
own lives. On occasion, he employed high irony—
contradiction between literal and intended meanings—as
is the case with his justification of theft as a moral act if
perpetrated by a slave against his master. Though it is
unlikely that Douglass had in mind any reference to the
Promethean motif of heroic defiance, the parallel is not
without significance. "A Slave's Right to Steal" comes
from *My Bondage and My Freedom*, the revised and
enlarged version of Douglass' autobiography.

READING 5.12   From Douglass' *My Bondage and My Freedom* (1855)

. . . There were four slaves of us in the kitchen, and four whites   1
in the great house—Thomas Auld, Mrs. Auld, Hadaway Auld
(brother of Thomas Auld), and little Amanda. The names of the
slaves in the kitchen, were Eliza, my sister; Priscilla, my aunt;
Henry, my cousin; and myself. There were eight persons in the
family. There was, each week, one half bushel of corn-meal
brought from the mill; and in the kitchen, corn-meal was
almost our exclusive food, for very little else was allowed us.
Out of this half bushel of corn-meal, the family in the great
house had a small loaf every morning; thus leaving us, in the   10
kitchen, with not quite a half a peck of meal per week, apiece.
This allowance was less than half the allowance of food on
Lloyd's plantation. It was not enough to subsist upon; and we
were, therefore, reduced to the wretched necessity of living at
the expense of our neighbors. We were compelled either to
beg, or to steal, and we did both. I frankly confess, that while I
hated everything like stealing, *as such,* I nevertheless did not
hesitate to take food, when I was hungry, wherever I could find
it. Nor was this practice the mere result of an unreasoning
instinct; it was, in my case, the result of a clear apprehension   20
of the claims of morality. I weighed and considered the matter
closely, before I ventured to satisfy my hunger by such means.
Considering that my labor and person were the property of
Master Thomas, and that I was by him deprived of the
necessaries of life—necessaries obtained by my own labor—
it was easy to deduce the right to supply myself with what was
my own. It was simply appropriating what was my own to the

Figure 28.4 *Portrait of Frederick Douglass*, 1847. Daguerreotype. National Portrait Gallery, Smithsonian Institution, Washington, D.C. Collection William Rubel.

use of my master, since the health and strength derived from such food were exerted in *his* service. To be sure, this was stealing, according to the law and gospel I heard from St. Michael's pulpit; but I had already begun to attach less importance to what dropped from that quarter, on that point, while, as yet, I retained my reverence for religion. It was not always convenient to steal from master, and the same reason why I might, innocently, steal from him, did not seem to justify me in stealing from others. In the case of my master, it was only a question of *removal*—the taking his meat out of the tub, and putting it into another; the ownership of the meat was not affected by the transaction. At first, he owned it in the *tub*, and last, he owned it in *me*. His meat house was not always open. There was a strict watch kept on that point, and the key was on a large bunch in Rowena's pocket. A great many times have we, poor creatures, been severely pinched with hunger, when meat and bread have been moulding under the lock, while the key was in the pocket of our mistress. This had been so when she *knew* we were nearly half starved; and yet, that mistress, with saintly air, would kneel with her husband, and pray each morning that a merciful God would bless them in basket and in store, and save them, at last, in his kingdom. But I proceed with the argument.

It was necessary that the right to steal from *others* should be established; and this could only rest upon a wider range of generalization than that which supposed the right to steal from my master.

It was sometime before I arrived at this clear right. The reader will get some idea of my train of reasoning, by a brief statement of the case. "I am," thought I, "not only the slave of Master Thomas, but I am the slave of society at large. Society at large has bound itself, in form and in fact, to assist Master Thomas in robbing me of my rightful liberty, and of the just reward of my labor; therefore, whatever rights I have against Master Thomas, I have, equally, against those confederated with him in robbing me of liberty. As society has marked me out as privileged plunder, on the principle of self-preservation I am justified in plundering in turn. Since each slave belongs to all; all must, therefore, belong to each."

I shall here make a profession of faith which may shock some, offend others, and be dissented from by all. It is this: Within the bounds of his just earnings, I hold that the slave is fully justified in helping himself to the *gold and silver, and the best apparel of his master, or that of any other slaveholder; and that such taking is not stealing in any just sense of that word.*

The morality of *free* society can have no application to *slave* society. Slaveholders have made it almost impossible for the slave to commit any crime, known either to the laws of God or to the laws of man. If he steals, he takes his own; if he kills his master, he imitates only the heroes of the revolution. Slaveholders I hold to be individually and collectively responsible for all the evils which grow out of the horrid relation, and I believe they will be so held at the judgment, in the sight of a just God. Make a man a slave, and you rob him of moral responsibility. . . .

Sojourner Truth While Frederick Douglass was among the first African-Americans to win international attention through his skills at public speaking, his female contemporary, Sojourner Truth (ca. 1797–1883), brought wit and a woman's passion to the fight against slavery. Born to slave parents in Ulster County, New York, Isabella Bomefree was sold four times before the age of thirty, an inauspicious beginning for a woman who would become one of America's most vocal abolitionists, an evangelist, and a champion of women's rights. After being emancipated in 1828, Bomefree traveled widely in the United States, changing her name to Sojourner Truth in 1843, as she committed her life to "sharing the truth" in matters of human dignity. Although she never learned to read or write, she was determined to have her voice heard across the nation and for future generations. To accomplish the latter, she dictated her story to a friend, Olive Gilbert. The narrative, which was published in 1850, recounts the major events of her life, including the tale of how Isabella, the mother of five children, engaged in an heroic legal battle to win back her fiveyear-old son, who was illegally sold into slavery in New York State. Sojourner Truth used her talents as an orator to communicate Christian religious visions, as well as to voice her opposition to slavery, capital punishment, and the kidnapping and sale of black children (a common practice in some parts of the country). She also supported prison reform, helped to relocate former slaves, and defended the rights of women. Sharp-tongued and outspoken (and a lifelong pipe-smoker), Sojourner Truth won popular notoriety for the short, impromptu speech, *Ain't I a Woman?*, delivered in 1851 to the Woman's Convention at Akron, Ohio. While scholars question the authenticity of various versions of the speech (which was published by abolitionists some twelve years later), no such debate clouds Sojourner's narrative, which, even in this short excerpt, conveys a sense of her straightforward rhetoric.

READING 5.13 From *The Narrative of Sojourner Truth* (1850)

Isabella's marriage

Subsequently, Isabella was married to a fellow-slave, named Thomas, who had previously had two wives, one of whom, if not both, had been torn from him and sold far away. And it is more than probable, that he was not only allowed but encouraged to take another at each successive sale. I say it is probable, because the writer of this knows from personal observation, that such is the custom among slaveholders at the present day; and that in a twenty months' residence among them, we never knew any one to open the lip against the practice; and when we severely censured it, the slaveholder had nothing to say; and the slave pleaded that, under existing circumstances, he could do no better.   10

Such an abominable state of things is silently tolerated, to say the least, by slaveholders—deny it who may. And what is that religion that sanctions, even by its silence, all that is embraced in the *"Peculiar Institution"*? If there *can* be any thing more diametrically opposed to the religion of Jesus, than the working of this soul-killing system—which is as truly sanctioned by the religion of America as are her ministers and churches—we wish to be shown where it can be found.   20

We have said, Isabella was married to Thomas—she was, after the fashion of slavery, one of the slaves performing the ceremony for them; as no true minister of Christ *can* perform, as in the presence of God, what he knows to be a mere *farce*, a *mock* marriage, unrecognised by any civil law, and liable to be annulled at any moment, when the interest or caprice of the master should dictate.

With what feelings must slaveholders expect us to listen to their horror of amalgamation in prospect, while they are well aware that we know how calmly and quietly they contemplate   30 the present state of licentiousness their own wicked laws have created, not only as it regards the slave, but as it regards the more privileged portion of the population of the South?

Slaveholders appear to me to take the same notice of the vices of the slave, as one does of the vicious disposition of his horse. They are often an inconvenience; further than that, they care not to trouble themselves about the matter.

Slave Songs and Spirituals

The nineteenth century witnessed the flowering of a unique type of folk song that expressed the heroic grief and hopes of the American slave community. Slave songs, sometimes termed "sorrow songs," formed the basis of what later became known as "spirituals." These songs, the most significant musical creation of America's antebellum slave population, were a distinctive cultural form that blended the Methodist and Baptist evangelical church music of the eighteenth century with musical traditions brought from Africa to the Americas in the course of two hundred years. A communal vehicle that conveyed the fervent longing for freedom, slave songs and spirituals based their content in Bible stories, usually focused on deliverance—the passage of the "Hebrew children" out of Egyptian bondage, for instance—and the promise of ultimate, triumphant liberation. A typical spiritual, such as *Sometimes I Feel Like a Motherless Child*, tempers despair with enduring faith. In form, spirituals embellished typically Protestant melodies and antiphonal structures with the complex, percussive rhythms (such as polymeter and syncopation), overlapping call and response patterns, and improvisational techniques of traditional African music (see chapter 18).

This powerful form of religious music came to public attention only after 1871, when a white instructor of vocal music at Fisk University in Tennessee took nine black students on a university fund-raising tour. A similar group was established by Hampton Institute (now Hampton University in Virginia) in 1873. Beyond the commercial popularity of this song form, spirituals have come to influence the development of numerous musical genres, including jazz, gospel, and blues (see chapter 36).

Goethe's Faust: The Quintessential Romantic Hero

Of all literary heroes of the nineteenth century, perhaps the most compelling is Goethe's Faust. The story of Faust is based on a sixteenth-century German legend of a historical figure named Johann or Georg Faust. A traveling physician and a practitioner of black magic, he is reputed to have sold his soul to the devil in exchange for infinite knowledge and personal experience. The Faust legend became the subject of numerous dramas, the first of which was written by the English playwright Christopher Marlowe (1564–1593), who turned the story into a tragedy in which Faust loses his soul. Faust was the favorite Renaissance symbol of the lust for knowledge and experience balanced against the perils of eternal damnation—a motif that figured largely in literary characterizations of Don Juan as well. In the hands of the German poet Johann Wolfgang von Goethe (1749–1832), Faust became the paradigm of Western man and—more broadly—of the human quest for knowledge, experience, and power. He was the quintessential romantic hero, the epitome of the human desire to transcend physical limitations and to master all realms of knowledge. The Faustian hero, like Prometheus or the apotheosized Napoleon, sought power that might permit him to control the world.

Goethe's *Faust* is one of the most monumental literary works of its time. Goethe conceived the piece during the 1770s, published Part I in 1808, but did not complete it until 1832; hence, *Faust* was the product of Goethe's entire career. Although ostensibly a drama, *Faust* more closely resembles an epic poem. It is written in a lyric German, with a richness of verse forms that is typical of romantic poetry.

As a play, it deliberately ignores the classical unities of time and place—indeed, its shifting "cinematic" qualities make it more adaptable to modern film than to the traditional stage. Despite a cosmic breadth, which compares with Milton's *Paradise Lost* or Dante's *Divine Comedy*, Goethe's *Faust* focuses more narrowly on the human condition. Goethe neither seeks to justify God's ways to humanity nor to allegorize the Christian ascent to salvation; rather, he uncovers the tragic tension between heroic aspirations and human limitations. Goethe, a student of law, medicine, theology, theater, biology, optics, and alchemy, seems to have modeled Faust after himself. Faust is a man of deep learning, a Christian, and a scientist. He is, moreover, a creative genius, whose desire to know and achieve has dominated his life, but he feels stale, bored, and deeply dissatisfied with all theoretical modes of understanding. He is driven to exhaust other kinds of experience—not only intellectual but sensual, erotic, aesthetic, and, finally, spiritual.

The Prologue of *Faust* is set in Heaven, where (in a manner reminiscent of the Book of Job) a wager is made between Mephistopheles (Satan) and God. Mephistopheles bets God that he can divert Faust from "the path that is true and fit." God contends that, though "men make mistakes as long as they strive," Faust will never relinquish his soul to Satan. In the first part of the tragedy, Mephistopheles proceeds to make a second pact, this one

Figure 28.5
EUGÈNE DELACROIX,
Mephistopheles Appearing to Faust in His Study, illustration for Goethe's *Faust*, 1828. Lithograph, 10¾ × 9 in. The Metropolitan Museum of Art, New York. Rogers Fund, 1917 (17.12).

with Faust himself: If he can satisfy Faust's deepest desires and ambitions to the hero's ultimate satisfaction, then Mephistopheles will win Faust's soul. Mephistopheles lures the despairing Faust out of the study that Faust calls "This God-damned dreary hole in the wall"—away from the life of the mind and into the larger world of experience (Figure **28.5**). The newly liberated hero then engages in a passionate love affair with a young maiden named Gretchen. Discovering the joys of the sensual life, Faust proclaims the priority of the heart ("Feeling is all!") over the mind. Faust's romance, however, has tragic consequences, including the deaths of Gretchen's mother, illegitimate child, brother, and, ultimately, Gretchen herself. Nevertheless, at the close of Part One, Gretchen's pure and selfless love wins her salvation.

In the second part of Goethe's *Faust*—and symbolically in the life of Faust's imagination—the hero travels with Mephistopheles through a netherworld in which he meets an array of witches, sirens, and other fantastic creatures. He also encounters the ravishing Helen of Troy. Helen, the symbol of ideal beauty, acquaints Faust with the entire history and culture of humankind; but Faust remains unsated. His unquenched thirst for experience now leads him to pursue a life of action for the public good. He undertakes a vast land-reclamation project, which provides habitation for millions of people, and in this endeavor—so different, it might be observed, from Candide's reclusive "garden" (see chapter 25)—the aged and near-blind Faust begins to find personal fulfillment. He dies, however, before fully realizing his dream; hence he never actually avows the satisfaction that would damn his soul to Hell. And although Mephistopheles gathers a hellish host to apprehend Faust's soul when it leaves his body, God's angels spirit his soul to Heaven.

The heroic Faust is a timeless symbol of the Western drive for consummate knowledge, experience, and the will to exert power over nature. Though it is possible to reproduce here only a small portion of Goethe's 12,000-line poem, the following excerpt conveys the powerful lyricism, the verbal subtleties, and the shifts between high seriousness and comedy that make Goethe's *Faust* a literary masterpiece.

READING 5.14   From Goethe's *Faust* (1808)

Prologue in Heaven

The Lord. The Heavenly Hosts. Mephistopheles following (the Three Archangels step forward).

Raphael: The chanting sun, as ever, rivals   1
The chanting of his brother spheres
And marches round his destined circuit—[1]
A march that thunders in our ears.
His aspect cheers the Hosts of Heaven
Though what his essence none can say;

These inconceivable creations
Keep the high state of their first day.
Gabriel: And swift, with inconceivable swiftness,
The earth's full splendor rolls around,   10
Celestial radiance alternating
With a dread night too deep to sound;
The sea against the rocks' deep bases
Comes foaming up in far-flung force,
And rock and sea go whirling onward
In the swift spheres' eternal course.
Michael: And storms in rivalry are raging
From sea to land, from land to sea,
In frenzy forge the world a girdle
From which no inmost part is free   20
The blight of lightning flaming yonder
Marks where the thunder-bolt will play;
And yet Thine envoys, Lord, revere
The gentle movement of Thy day.
Choir of Angels: Thine aspect cheers the Hosts of Heaven
Though what Thine essence none can say,
And all Thy loftiest creations
Keep the high state of their first day.
(Enter Mephistopheles)[2]
Mephistopheles: Since you, O Lord, once more approach and ask
If business down with us be light or heavy—   30
And in the past you've usually welcomed me—
That's why you see me also at your levee.
Excuse me, I can't manage lofty words—
Not though your whole court jeer and find me low;
My pathos certainly would make you laugh
Had you not left off laughing long ago.
Your suns and worlds mean nothing much to me;
How men torment themselves, that's all I see.
The little god of the world, one can't reshape, reshade him;
He is as strange to-day as that first day you made him.   40
His life would be not so bad, not quite,
Had you not granted him a gleam of Heaven's light;
He calls it Reason, uses it not the least
Except to be more beastly than any beast.
He seems to me—if your Honor does not mind—
Like a grasshopper—the long-legged kind—
That's always in flight and leaps as it flies along
And then in the grass strikes up its same old song.
I could only wish he confined himself to the grass!
He thrusts his nose into every filth, alas.   50
Lord: Mephistopheles, have you no other news?
Do you always come here to accuse?
Is nothing ever right in your eyes on earth?
Mephistopheles: No, Lord! I find things there as downright
bad as ever.
I am sorry for men's days of dread and dearth;
Poor things, *my* wish to plague 'em isn't fervent.
Lord: Do you know Faust?

---

[1] The sun is treated here as one of the planets, all of which, according to Pythagoras, moved harmoniously in crystalline spheres.

---

[2] The name possibly derives from the Hebrew "Mephistoph," meaning "destroyer of the gods."

[3] Compare the exchange between God and Satan at the beginning of the Book of Job (see chapter 2).

Mephistopheles: The Doctor?

Lord: Aye, my servant.[3]

Mephistopheles: Indeed! He serves you oddly enough,
I think.   60
The fool has no earthly habits in meat and drink.
The ferment in him drives him wide and far,
That he is mad he too has almost guessed;
He demands of heaven each fairest star
And of earth each highest joy and best,
And all that is new and all that is far
Can bring no calm to the deep-sea swell of his breast.

Lord: Now he may serve me only gropingly,
Soon I shall lead him into the light.
The gardener knows when the sapling first turns green   70
That flowers and fruit will make the future bright.

Mephistopheles: What do you wager? You will lose him yet,
Provided *you* give *me* permission
To steer him gently the course I set.

Lord: So long as he walks the earth alive,
So long you may try what enters your head;
Men make mistakes as long as they strive.

Mephistopheles: I thank you for that; as regards the dead,
The dead have never taken my fancy.
I favor cheeks that are full and rosy-red;   80
No corpse is welcome to my house;
I work as the cat does with the mouse.

Lord: Very well; you have my full permission.
Divert this soul from its primal source
And carry it, if you can seize it,
Down with you upon your course—
And stand ashamed when you must needs admit:
A good man with his groping intuitions
Still knows the path that's true and fit.

Mephistopheles: All right—but it won't last for long.   90
I'm not afraid my bet will turn out wrong.
And, if my aim prove true and strong,
Allow me to triumph wholeheartedly.
Dust shall he eat—and greedily—
Like my cousin the Snake renowned in tale and song.[4]

Lord: That too you are free to give a trial;
I have never hated the likes of you.
Of all the spirits of denial
The joker is the last that I eschew.
Man finds relaxation too attractive—   100
Too fond too soon of unconditional rest;
Which is why I am pleased to give him a companion
Who lures and thrusts and must, as devil, be active.
But ye, true sons of Heaven,[5] it is your duty
To take your joy in the living wealth of beauty.
The changing Essence which ever works and lives
Wall you around with love, serene, secure!
And that which floats in flickering appearance
Fix ye it firm in thoughts that must endure.

Choir of Angels: Thine aspect cheers the Hosts of
Heaven   110
Though what Thine essence none can say,
And all Thy loftiest creations
Keep the high state of their first day.
(Heaven closes)

Mephistopheles *(Alone)*: I like to see the Old One now and then
And try to keep relations on the level
It's really decent of so great a person
To talk so humanely even to the Devil.

The First Part of the Tragedy Night

(In a high-vaulted narrow Gothic room Faust, restless, in a chair at his desk)

Faust: Here stand I, ach, Philosophy
Behind me and Law and Medicine too
And, to my cost, Theology—[6]   120
All these I have sweated through and through
And now you see me a poor fool
As wise as when I entered school!
They call me Master, they call me Doctor,[7]
Ten years now I have dragged my college
Along by the nose through zig and zag
Through up and down and round and round
And this is all that I have found—
The impossibility of knowledge!
It is this that burns away my heart;   130
Of course I am cleverer than the quacks,
Than master and doctor, than clerk and priest,
I suffer no scruple or doubt in the least,
I have no qualms about devil or burning,
Which is just why all joy is torn from me,
I cannot presume to make use of my learning,
I cannot presume I could open my mind
To proselytize and improve mankind.

Besides, I have neither goods nor gold,
Neither reputation nor rank in the world;   140
No dog would choose to continue so!
Which is why I have given myself to Magic
To see if the Spirit may grant me to know
Through its force and its voice full many a secret,
May spare the sour sweat that I used to pour out
In talking of what I know nothing about,
May grant me to learn what it is that girds
The world together in its inmost being,
That the seeing its whole germination, the seeing
Its workings, may end my traffic in words.   150

O couldst thou, light of the full moon,
Look now thy last upon my pain,
Thou for whom I have sat belated
So many midnights here and waited
Till, over books and papers, thou
Didst shine, sad friend, upon my brow!
O could I but walk to and fro

---

[4]In Genesis 3:14, God condemns the serpent to go on its belly and eat dust for the rest of its days.
[5]The archangels.

[6]Philosophy, law, medicine, and theology were the four programs of study in medieval universities.
[7]The two advanced degrees beyond the baccalaureate.

On mountain heights in thy dear glow
Or float with spirits round mountain eyries
Or weave through fields thy glances glean   160
And freed from all miasmal theories
Bathe in thy dew and wash me clean![8]
Oh! Am I still stuck in this jail?
This God-damned dreary hole in the wall
Where even the lovely light of heaven
Breaks wanly through the painted panes!
Cooped up among these heaps of books
Gnawed by worms, coated with dust,
Round which to the top of the Gothic vault
A smoke-stained paper forms a crust.   170
Retorts and canisters lie pell-mell
And pyramids of instruments,
The junk of centuries, dense and mat—
Your world, man! World? They call it that!

And yet you ask why your poor heart
Cramped in your breast should feel such fear,
Why an unspecified misery
Should throw your life so out of gear?
Instead of the living natural world
For which God made all men his sons   180
You hold a reeking mouldering court
Among assorted skeletons.
Away! There is a world outside!
And this one book of mystic art
Which Nostradamus[9] wrote himself,
Is this not adequate guard and guide?
By this you can tell the course of the stars,
By this, once Nature gives the word,
The soul begins to stir and dawn,
A spirit by a spirit heard,   190
In vain your barren studies here
Construe the signs of sanctity.
You Spirits, you are hovering near;
If you can hear me, answer me!
(He opens the book and perceives the sign of the Macrocosm)[10]
Ha! What a river of wonder at this vision
Bursts upon all my senses in one flood!
And I feel young, the holy joy of life
Glows new, flows fresh, through nerve and blood!
Was it a god designed this hieroglyph to calm
The storm which but now raged inside me,   200
To pour upon my heart such balm,
And by some secret urge to guide me
Where all the powers of Nature stand unveiled around me?
Am I a God? It grows so light!
And through the clear-cut symbol on this page
My soul comes face to face with all creating Nature.

At last I understand the dictum of the sage:
"The spiritual world is always open,
Your mind is closed, your heart is dead;
Rise, young man, and plunge undaunted   210
Your earthly breast in the mourning red."
(He contemplates the sign)
Into one Whole how all things blend,
Function and live within each other!
Passing gold buckets to each other
How heavenly powers ascend, descend!
The odor of grace upon their wings,
They thrust from heaven through earthly things
And as all sing so *the* All sings!
What a fine show! Aye, but only a show!
Infinite Nature, where can I tap thy veins?   220

Where are thy breasts, those well-springs of all life
On which hang heaven and earth,
Towards which my dry breast strains?
They well up, they give drink, but I feel drought and dearth.
(He turns the pages and perceives the sign of the Earth Spirit)[11]
How differently this new sign works upon me!
Thy sign, thou Spirit of the Earth, 'tis thine
And thou art nearer to me.
At once I feel my powers unfurled,
At once I grow as from new wine
And feel inspired to venture into the world,   230
To cope with the fortunes of earth benign or malign,
To enter the ring with the storm, to grapple and clinch,
To enter the jaws of the shipwreck and never flinch.
Over me comes a mist,
The moon muffles her light,
The lamp goes dark.
The air goes damp. Red beams flash
Around my head. There blows
A kind of a shudder down from the vault
And seizes on me.   240
It is thou must be hovering round me, come at my prayers!
Spirit, unveil thyself!
My heart, oh my heart, how it tears!
And how each and all of my senses
Seem burrowing upwards towards new light, new breath!
I feel my heart has surrendered, I have no more defences.
Come then! Come! Even if it prove my death!
*(He seizes the book and solemnly pronounces the sign of the Earth
Spirit. There is a flash of red flame and the Spirit appears in it)*
    Spirit: Who calls upon me?
    Faust: Appalling vision!
    Spirit: You have long been sucking at my sphere,   250
Now by main force you have drawn me here
And now—

---

[8]Goethe's conception of nature as a source of sublime purification may
be compared with similar ideas held by the nature poets and the
transcendentalists discussed in chapter 27.
[9]Michel de Notredame or Nostradamus (1503–1566) was a French
astrologer famous for his prophecies of future events.
[10]Signs of the universe, such as the pentagram, were especially popular
among those who practiced magic and the occult arts.

---

[11]The Earth Spirit, here used to represent the active, sensual side of
Faust's nature as opposed to the contemplative, spiritual side
represented by the Macrocosm. Goethe suggested representing the
Erdgeist on the stage by means of a magic lantern device that would
magnify and project the head of Apollo or Zeus at giant proportions.

Faust: No! Not to be endured!

Spirit: With prayers and with paintings you have procured
The sight of my face and the sound of my voice—
Now I am here. What a pitiable shivering
Seizes the Superman. Where is the call of your soul?
Where the breast which created a world in itself
And carried and fostered it, swelling up, joyfully quivering,
Raising itself to a level with Us, the Spirits? 260
Where are you, Faust, whose voice rang out to me,
Who with every nerve so thrust yourself upon me?
Are you the thing that at a whiff of my breath
Trembles throughout its living frame,
A poor worm crawling off, askance, askew?

Faust: Shall I yield to Thee, Thou shape of flame?
I am Faust, I can hold my own with Thee.

Spirit: In the floods of life, in the storm of work,
In ebb and flow,
In warp and weft, 270
Cradle and grave,
An eternal sea,
A changing patchwork,
A glowing life,
At the whirring loom of Time I weave
The living clothes of the Deity.

Faust: Thou who dost rove the wide world round,
Busy Spirit, how near I feel to Thee!

Spirit: You are like that Spirit which you can grasp,
Not me! 280

(The Spirit vanishes)

Faust: Not Thee!
Whom then?
I who am Godhead's image,
Am I not even like Thee!

(A knocking on the door)

Death! I know who that is. My assistant!
So ends my happiest, fairest hour.
The crawling pedant must interrupt
My visions at their fullest flower!

[Faust converses with his assistant Wagner on the fruitlessness of a life of study. When Wagner leaves, Faust prepares to commit suicide; but he is interrupted by the sounds of churchbells and choral music. Still brooding, he joins Wagner and the townspeople as they celebrate Easter Sunday. At the city gate, Faust encounters a black poodle, which he takes back with him to his studio. The dog is actually Mephistopheles, who soon makes his real self known to Faust.]

(The same room. Later)

Faust: Who's knocking? Come in! *Now* who wants to annoy me?

Mephistopheles *(outside door)*: It's I. 290

Faust: Come in!

Mephistopheles *(outside door)*: You must say "Come in" three times.

Faust: Come in then!

Mephistopheles *(entering)*: Thank you; you overjoy me.

---

¹²Low or morbid spirits.

We two, I hope, we shall be good friends;
To chase those megrims¹² of yours away
I am here like a fine young squire to-day,
In a suit of scarlet trimmed with gold
And a little cape of stiff brocade,
With a cock's feather in my hat 300
And at my side a long sharp blade,
And the most succinct advice I can give
Is that you dress up just like me,
So that uninhibited and free
You may find out what it means to live.

Faust: The pain of earth's constricted life, I fancy,
Will pierce me still, whatever my attire;
I am too old for mere amusement,
Too young to be without desire.
How can the world dispel my doubt? 310
You must do without, you must do without!
That is the everlasting song
Which rings in every ear, which rings,
And which to us our whole life long
Every hour hoarsely sings.
I wake in the morning only to feel appalled,
My eyes with bitter tears could run
To see the day which in its course
Will not fulfil a wish for me, not one;
The day which whittles away with obstinate carping 320
All pleasures—even those of anticipation,
Which makes a thousand grimaces to obstruct
My heart when it is stirring in creation.
And again, when night comes down, in anguish
I must stretch out upon my bed
And again no rest is granted me,
For wild dreams fill my mind with dread.
The God who dwells within my bosom
Can make my inmost soul react;
The God who sways my every power 330
Is powerless with external fact.
And so existence weighs upon my breast
And I long for death and life—life I detest.

Mephistopheles: Yet death is never a wholly welcome guest.

Faust: O happy is he whom death in the dazzle of victory
Crowns with the bloody laurel in the battling swirl!
Or he whom after the mad and breakneck dance
He comes upon in the arms of a girl!
O to have sunk away, delighted, deleted,
Before the Spirit of the Earth,¹³ before his might! 340

Mephistopheles: Yet I know someone who failed to drink
A brown juice on a certain night.¹⁴

Faust: Your hobby is espionage—is it not?

Mephistopheles: Oh I'm not omniscient—but I know a lot.

Faust: Whereas that tumult in my soul
Was stilled by sweet familiar chimes
Which cozened the child that yet was in me
With echoes of more happy times,
I now curse all things that encompass

---

¹³The Earth Spirit of the previous passage.
¹⁴Mephistopheles alludes to Faust's contemplation of suicide by poison earlier in the drama.

The soul with lures and jugglery   350
And bind it in this dungeon of grief
With trickery and flattery.
Cursed in advance be the high opinion
That serves our spirit for a cloak!
Cursed be the dazzle of appearance
Which bows our senses to its yoke!
Cursed be the lying dreams of glory,
The illusion that our name survives!
Cursed be the flattering things we own,
Servants and ploughs, children and wives!   360
Cursed be Mammon[15] when with his treasures
He makes us play the adventurous man
Or when for our luxurious pleasures
He duly spreads the soft divan!
A curse on the balsam of the grape!
A curse on the love that rides for a fall!
A curse on hope! A curse on faith!
And a curse on patience most of all!
(The invisible Spirits sing again)
    Spirits: Woe! Woe!
You have destroyed it,   370
The beautiful world;
By your violent hand
'Tis downward hurled!
A half-god has dashed it asunder!
From under
We bear off the rubble to nowhere
And ponder
Sadly the beauty departed.
Magnipotent
One among men,   380
Magnificent
Build it again,
Build it again in your breast!
Let a new course of life
Begin
With vision abounding
And new songs resounding
To welcome it in!
    Mephistopheles: These are the juniors
Of my faction.   390
Hear how precociously they counsel
Pleasure and action.
Out and away
From your lonely day
Which dries your senses and your juices
Their melody seduces.
Stop playing with your grief which battens
Like a vulture on your life, your mind!
The worst of company would make you feel
That you are a man among mankind.   400
Not that it's really my proposition
To shove you among the common men;
Though I'm not one of the Upper Ten.
If you would like a coalition

With me for your career through life,
I am quite ready to fit in,
I'm yours before you can say knife.
I am your comrade;
If you so crave,
I am your servant, I am your slave.   410
    Faust: And what have I to undertake in return?
    Mephistopheles: Oh it's early days to discuss what that is.
    Faust: No, no, the devil is an egoist
And ready to do nothing gratis
Which is to benefit a stranger.
Tell me your terms and don't prevaricate!
A servant like you in the house is a danger.
    Mephistopheles: I will bind myself to your service in this world,
To be at your beck and never rest nor slack;
When we meet again on the other side,   420
In the same coin you shall pay me back.
    Faust: The other side gives me little trouble;
First batter this present world to rubble,
Then the other may rise—if that's the plan.
This earth is where my springs of joy have started.
And this sun shines on me when broken-hearted;
If I can first from them be parted,
Then let happen what will and can!
I wish to hear no more about it—
Whether there too men hate and love   430
Or whether in those spheres too, in the future,
There is a Below or an Above.
    Mephistopheles: With such an outlook you can risk it.
Sign on the line! In these next days you will get
Ravishing samples of my arts;
I am giving you what never man saw yet.
    Faust: Poor devil, can *you* give anything ever?
Was a human spirit in its high endeavor
Even once understood by one of your breed?
Have you got food which fails to feed?   440
Or red gold which, never at rest,
Like mercury runs away through the hand?
A game at which one never wins?
A girl who, even when on my breast,
Pledges herself to my neighbor with her eyes?
The divine and lovely delight of honor
Which falls like a falling star and dies?
Show me the fruits which, before they are plucked, decay
And the trees which day after day renew their green!
    Mephistopheles: Such a commission doesn't alarm me,   450
I have such treasures to purvey.
But, my good friend, the time draws on when we
Should be glad to feast at our ease on something good.
    Faust: If ever I stretch myself on a bed of ease,
Then I am finished! Is that understood?
If ever your flatteries can coax me
To be pleased with myself, if ever you cast
A spell of pleasure that can hoax me—
Then let *that* day be my last!
That's my wager![16]   460

---

[15]Riches or material wealth.

---

[16]The wager between Faust and Mephistopheles recalls that between
God and Mephistopheles in the Prologue.

Mephistopheles: Done!

Faust: Let's shake!
If ever I say to the passing moment
"Linger for a while! Thou art so fair!"
Then you may cast me into fetters,
I will gladly perish then and there!
Then you may set the death-bell tolling,
Then from my service you are free,
The clock may stop, its hand may fall,
And that be the end of time for me! 470

Mephistopheles: Think what you're saying, we shall not forget it.

Faust: And you are fully within your rights;
I have made no mad or outrageous claim.
If I stay as I am, I am a slave—
Whether yours or another's, it's all the same.

Mephistopheles: I shall this very day at the College Banquet
Enter your service with no more ado,
But just one point—As a life-and-death insurance
I must trouble you for a line or two.

Faust: So you, you pedant, you too like things in writing? 480
Have you never known a man? Or a man's word?
Never?
Is it not enough that my word of mouth
Puts all my days in bond for ever?
Does not the world rage on in all its streams
And shall a promise hamper *me*?
Yet this illusion reigns within our hearts
And from it who would be gladly free?
Happy the man who can inwardly keep his word;
Whatever the cost, he will not be loath to pay! 490
But a parchment, duly inscribed and sealed,
Is a bogey from which all wince away.
The word dies on the tip of the pen
And wax and leather lord it then.
What do you, evil spirit, require?
Bronze, marble, parchment, paper?
Quill or chisel or pencil of slate?
You may choose whichever you desire.

Mephistopheles: How can you so exaggerate
With such a hectic rhetoric? 500
Any little snippet is quite good—
And you sign it with one little drop of blood.

Faust: If that is enough and is some use,
One may as well pander to your fad.

Mephistopheles: Blood is a very special juice.

Faust: Only do not fear that I shall break this contract.
What I promise is nothing more
Than what all my powers are striving for.
I have puffed myself up too much, it is only
Your sort that really fits my case. 510
The great Earth Spirit has despised me
And Nature shuts the door in my face.
The thread of thought is snapped asunder.
I have long loathed knowledge in all its fashions.
In the depths of sensuality
Let us now quench our glowing passions!
And at once make ready every wonder
Of unpenetrated sorcery!

Let us cast ourselves into the torrent of time,
Into the whirl of eventfulness, 520
Where disappointment and success,
Pleasure and pain may chop and change
As chop and change they will and can;
It is restless action makes the man.

Mephistopheles: No limit is fixed for you, no bound;
If you'd like to nibble at everything
Or to seize upon something flying round—
Well, may you have a run for your money!
But seize your chance and don't be funny!

Faust: I've told you, it is no question of happiness. 530
The most painful joy, enamored hate, enlivening
Disgust—I devote myself to all excess.
My breast, now cured of its appetite for knowledge,
From now is open to all and every smart,
And what is allotted to the whole of mankind
That will I sample in my inmost heart,
Grasping the highest and lowest with my spirit,
Piling men's weal and woe upon my neck,
To extend myself to embrace all human selves
And to founder in the end, like them, a wreck. 540

Mephistopheles: O believe me, who have been chewing
These iron rations many a thousand year,
No human being can digest
This stuff, from the cradle to the bier.
This universe—believe a devil—
Was made for no one but a god!
He exists in eternal light
But *us* he has brought into the darkness
While *your* sole portion is day and night.

Faust: I will all the same! 550
Mephistopheles: That's very nice.
There's only one thing I find wrong;
Time is short, art is long.[17]
You could do with a little artistic advice.
Confederate with one of the poets
And let him flog his imagination
To heap all virtues on your head,
A head with such a reputation:
Lion's bravery,
Stag's velocity, 560
Fire of Italy,
Northern tenacity.
Let *him* find out the secret art
Of combining craft with a noble heart
And of being in love like a young man,
Hotly, but working to a plan.
Such a person—*I'd* like to meet him;
"Mr. Microcosm" is how I'd greet him.

Faust: What am I then if fate must bar
My efforts to reach that crown of humanity 570
After which all my senses strive?

Mephistopheles: You are in the end . . . what you are.
You can put on full-bottomed wigs with a million locks,

---

[17]An adaptation of the famous Latin aphorism "Ars longa, vita brevis" ("Art is long-lasting, but life is short").

You can put on stilts instead of your socks,
You remain for ever what you are.
  Faust: I feel my endeavours have not been worth a pin
When I raked together the treasures of the human mind,
If at the end I but sit down to find
No new force welling up within.
I have not a hair's breadth more of height,
I am no nearer the Infinite.
  Mephistopheles: My very good sir, you look at things
Just in the way that people do;
We must be cleverer than that
Or the joys of life will escape from you.
Hell! You have surely hands and feet,
Also a head and you-know-what;
The pleasures I gather on the wing,
Are they less mine? Of course they're not!
Suppose I can afford six stallions,
I can add that horse-power to my score
And dash along and be a proper man
As if my legs were twenty-four.
So good-bye to thinking! On your toes!
The world's before us. Quick! Here goes!
I tell you, a chap who's intellectual
Is like a beast on a blasted heath
Driven in circles by a demon
While a fine green meadow lies round beneath.
  Faust: How do we start?
  Mephistopheles: We just say go—and skip.
But please get ready for this pleasure trip.
(Exit Faust)
  Only look down on knowledge and reason,
The highest gifts that men can prize,
Only allow the spirit of lies
To confirm you in magic and illusion,
And then I have you body and soul.
Fate has given this man a spirit
Which is always pressing onwards, beyond control,
And whose mad striving overleaps
All joys of the earth between pole and pole.
Him shall I drag through the wilds of life
And through the flats of meaninglessness,
I shall make him flounder and gape and stick
And to tease his insatiableness
Hang meat and drink in the air before his watering lips;
In vain he will pray to slake his inner thirst,
And even had he not sold himself to the devil
He would be equally accursed.
(Re-enter Faust)
  Faust: And now, where are we going?
  Mephistopheles: Wherever you please.
The small world, then the great for us.
With what pleasure and what profit
You will roister through the syllabus!
  Faust: But I, with this long beard of mine,
I lack the easy social touch,
I know the experiment is doomed;
Out in the world I never could fit in much.
I feel so small in company

580

590

600

610

620

I'll be embarrassed constantly.
  Mephistopheles: My friend, it will solve itself, any such
misgiving;
Just trust yourself and you'll learn the art of living.
  Faust: Well, then, how do we leave home?
Where are your grooms? Your coach and horses?
  Mephistopheles: We merely spread this mantle wide,
It will bear us off on airy courses.
But do not on this noble voyage
Cumber yourself with heavy baggage.
A little inflammable gas which I'll prepare
Will lift us quickly into the air.
If we travel light we shall cleave the sky like a knife.
Congratulations on your new course of life!

630

640

Romantic Love and Romantic Stereotypes

Romantic love, the sentimental and all-consuming passion for spiritual as well as sexual union with the opposite sex, was a favorite theme of nineteenth-century writers, painters, and composers. Many artists perceived friendship, religious love, and sexual love—both heterosexual and homosexual—as closely related expressions of an ecstatic harmony of souls. Passionate love, and especially unrequited or unfulfilled love, was the subject of numerous romantic literary works. To name but three: Goethe's *Sorrows of Young Werther* (1774) told the story of a lovesick hero whose passion for a married woman leads him to commit suicide—the book was so popular that it made suicide something of a nineteenth-century vogue; Hector Berlioz's *Symphonie fantastique* (1830–1831) described the composer's obsessive infatuation with a flamboyant actress (see chapter 29); and Richard Wagner's opera *Tristan and Isolde* (1859) dramatized the tragic fate of two legendary medieval lovers.

While male romantics generated an image of masculinity that emphasized self-invention, courage, and the quest for knowledge and power, they persisted in glorifying the female as chaste, passive, and submissive, or, on the other hand, characterizing her as dangerous and threatening. Romantic writers inherited the dual view of womankind that had prevailed since the Middle Ages: Like Eve, woman was the *femme fatale*, the seducer and destroyer of mankind; like Mary, however, woman was the source of salvation and the symbol of all that was pure and true. The Eve stereotype is readily apparent in such works as Prosper Mérimée's novel *Carmen*, on which the opera by Georges Bizet (1835–1875) was based, while the Mary stereotype is present in countless nineteenth-century stories, including *Faust* itself, where Gretchen is cast as the Eternal Female, the source of procreation and personal salvation. The following lines by the German poet Heinrich Heine (1797–1856), which were set to music by his contemporary Robert Schumann (1810–1856), typify the female as angelic, ethereal, and chaste—an object that thrilled and inspired the imaginations of many European romantics.

CHAPTER TWENTY-NINE

The romantic style in art and music

"Success is impossible for me if I cannot write as my heart dictates."
Verdi

As with literature, so it was in the visual arts and in music: Nineteenth-century artists favored subjects that allowed them to explore their personal feelings and give free rein to the imagination. Nature and the natural landscape, the hero and heroism, and nationalist struggles for political independence—the very themes that captured the imagi-nation of romantic writers—also inspired much of the art and music of the nineteenth century. Romantic artists abandoned the cool serenity and rationality of the neoclassical style in favor of emotion and spontaneity. While neoclassicists sought symmetry and order, romantics favored irregularity and even irrationality. While neoclassical

Figure 29.1 ANTOINE-JEAN GROS, *Napoleon Visiting the Plague Victims at Jaffa*, 1804. Oil on canvas, 17 ft. 5 in. × 23 ft. 7 in. Louvre, Paris. Photo: © R.M.N., Paris.

painters defined form by means of line (an artificial or "intellectual" boundary between the object and the space it occupied), romantics preferred to model form by way of color. While neoclassicists generally used shades of a single color for each individual object (coloring the red object red, for example), romantics might use touches of complementary colors to heighten the intensity of the painted object. And while neoclassical painters smoothed out brushstrokes to leave an even and polished surface finish, romantics often left their brushstrokes visible, as if to underline the immediacy of the creative act. Romantic artists often deliberately blurred details and exaggerated the sensuous aspects of texture and tone. Rejecting neoclassical propriety and decorum, they produced a style that made room for temperament, accident, and individual genius.

Heroic Themes in Art

Gros and the Glorification of the Hero

Among the principal themes of romantic art were those that glorified creative individualism, patriotism, and nationalism. Napoleon Bonaparte, the foremost living hero of the age and the symbol of French nationalism, was the favorite subject of many early nineteenth-century French painters. Napoleon's imperial status was celebrated in the official portraits executed by his "first painter," Jacques-Louis David (see Figure 28.1); but the heroic dimension of Napoleon's career was publicized by yet another member of his staff, Antoine-Jean Gros (1775–1835). Gros' representations of Napoleon's military campaigns became powerful vehicles of political propaganda.

Gros was a pupil of David, but, unlike David, Gros rejected the formal austerity of neoclassicism. In his monumental canvas, *Napoleon Visiting the Plague Victims at Jaffa* (Figure 29.1), Gros converted a minor historical event—Napoleon's tour of his plague-ridden troops in Jaffa (in Palestine)—into an allegorical drama. Gros cast Napoleon in the guise of Christ healing the wounds of his followers. He enhanced the drama of the composition by means of atmospheric contrasts of light and dark and by vivid details that draw the eye from the foreground, filled with the bodies of the diseased and dying, into the background with its distant cityscape. Gros' composition and painterly technique anticipated the romantic style. In its

content, the painting manifested the romantic taste for themes of personal heroism, suffering, and death. When it was first exhibited in Paris, an awed public adorned it with palm branches and wreaths. But the inspiration for Gros' success was also the source of his undoing: After Napoleon was sent into exile, Gros' career declined, and he committed suicide by throwing himself into the River Seine.

Romantic Heroism in Goya and Géricault

Throughout most of Western history, the heroic image in art was bound up with either classical lore or Christian legend. But with Gros, we see one of the first distinctive images of heroism based on contemporary events. The Spanish master Francisco Goya (1746–1828) helped to pioneer this phenomenon in nineteenth-century art. Having begun his career as a rococo-style tapestry designer, Goya came into prominence as court painter to the Spanish king Charles IV in Madrid. As court painter, Goya followed in the footsteps of Velázquez, although he often brought unflattering realism to his portrait likenesses. During the latter half of his lifetime, and especially after the invasion of Spain by Napoleon's armies in 1808, Goya's art took a new turn. Horrified by the guerrilla violence of the Spanish occupation, he became a bitter social critic, producing some of the most memorable records of human warfare and savagery in the history of Western art.

The Third of May, 1808: The Execution of the Defenders of Madrid (Figure **29.2**) was Goya's nationalistic response to the events following an uprising of Spanish citizens against the French army of occupation. In a punitive measure, the French troops rounded up Spanish suspects in the streets of Madrid, and brutally executed them in the city outskirts. Goya recorded the episode against a dark sky

Figure 29.2 FRANCISCO GOYA, *The Third of May, 1808: The Execution of the Defenders of Madrid*, 1814. Oil on canvas, 8 ft. 6 in. × 10 ft. 4 in. Prado, Madrid.

Figure 29.3 (left) **FRANCISCO GOYA**, *Brave Deeds Against the Dead*, from the "Disasters of War" series, ca. 1814. Etching.

in the shadows, the hulking executioners are lined up as anonymously as pieces of artillery. Goya composed the scene with an imaginative force. His emphatic contrasts of light and dark, theatrical use of color, and graphic details heighten the intensity of a contemporary political event.

An indictment of butchery in the name of war, *The Third of May, 1808* is itself restrained compared to "The Disasters of War," a series of etchings and **aquatints** that Goya produced in the years of the French occupation of Spain. The gruesome prints that make up "The Disasters of War" have their source in historical fact as well as in Goya's imagination. *Brave Deeds Against the Dead* (Figure **29.3**) is a shocking record of the inhuman cruelty of Napoleon's troops, as well as a reminder that the heroes of modern warfare are often its innocent victims.

Goya's contemporary, the French painter Théodore Géricault (1791–1824), broadened the range of romantic subjects. Géricault found inspiration in the restless vitality of untamed horses and the ravaged faces of the clinically

and an ominous urban skyline. In the foreground, an off-center lantern emits a triangular prism of light that illuminates the fate of the Spanish rebels: Some lie dead in pools of blood, others cover their faces in fear and horror. Among the victims is a young man whose arms are flung upward in a final gesture of terror and defiance. Goya deliberately spotlights this wide-eyed and bewildered figure as he confronts imminent death. On the right,

Figure 29.4 (below) **THÉODORE GÉRICAULT**, *The Raft of the "Medusa,"* 1818. Oil on canvas, 16 ft. 1 in. × 23 ft. 6 in. Louvre, Paris. Photo: © R.M.N., Paris.

insane, subjects uncommon in academic art, but which reflect the romantic fascination with the life that lay beyond the bounds of reason. The painting that brought Géricault instant fame, *The Raft of the "Medusa,"* immortalized a dramatic event that made headlines in Géricault's own time: the wreck of a government frigate called the "Medusa" and the ghastly fate of its survivors (Figure **29.4**). When the ship hit a reef 50 miles off the coast of West Africa, the inexperienced captain, a political appointee, tried ignobly to save himself and his crew, who filled the few available lifeboats. Over a hundred passengers piled onto a makeshift raft, which was to be towed by the lifeboats. Cruelly, the crew set the raft adrift. With almost no food and supplies, chances of survival were scant; after almost two weeks, in which most died and several resorted to cannibalism, the raft was sighted and fifteen survivors were rescued.

Géricault (a staunch opponent of the regime that appointed the captain of the "Medusa") was so fired by newspaper reports of the tragedy that he resolved to immortalize it in paint. He interviewed the few survivors, made drawings of the mutilated corpses in the Paris morgue, and even had a model of the raft constructed in his studio. The result was enormous, both in size (the canvas measures 16 feet 1 inch × 23 feet 6 inches) and in dramatic impact. In the decade immediately preceding the invention of photography, Géricault provided the public with a powerful visual record of a sensational contemporary event. He organized his composition on the basis of a double triangle: One triangle is formed by the two lines that stay the mast and bisected by the mast itself, the other by the mass of agitated figures culminating in the magnificently painted torso of a black man who signals the distant vessel that will make the rescue. Sharp diagonals, vivid contrasts of light and dark (reminiscent of Caravaggio), and muscular nudes (inspired by Michelangelo and Rubens) heighten the emotional impact of the piece. Géricault's *Raft* elevates ordinary men to the position of heroic combatants in the eternal struggle against the forces of nature. It eulogizes, moreover, the collective heroism of humble human beings confronting deadly danger, a motif equally popular in romantic literature—witness, for instance, Victor Hugo's *Les Misérables* (1862). Finally, as with Turner's *Slave Ship* and Goya's *Third of May*, it publicly protests an aspect of contemporary political injustice.

Delacroix and the Imagery of Heroism

While Goya and Géricault democratized the image of the hero, Géricault's pupil and follower Eugène Delacroix (1798–1863) raised that image to Byronic proportions. A melancholic intellectual, Delacroix shared Byron's intense hatred of tyranny, his sense of alienation, his self-glorifying egotism, and his faith in the role of the imagination—features all readily discernible in the pages of his diary. Much like Byron, Wordsworth, and Goethe, Delacroix called the imagination "paramount" in the life of the artist. "Strange as it may seem," he observed in his diary, "the great majority of people are devoid of imagination. Not only do they lack the keen, penetrating imagination which would allow them to see objects in a vivid way—which would lead them, as it were, to the very root of things—but they are equally incapable of any clear understanding of works in which imagination predominates."*

Delacroix loved dramatic narrative; he favored sensuous and violent subjects drawn from contemporary life, popular literature, and ancient and medieval history. A six-month visit in 1832 to Morocco, neighbor of France's newly conquered colony of Algeria, was to have a lifelong impact on his interest in exotic subjects and his love of light and color. He depicted the harem women of Islamic Africa, recorded the poignant and shocking results of the Turkish massacres in Greece, brought to life Dante's *Inferno*, and made memorable illustrations for Goethe's *Faust* (see Figure 28.5). His paintings of human and animal combat, such as *Arabs Skirmishing in the Mountains* (Figure **29.5**), are filled with fierce vitality. Such works are faithful to his declaration, "I have no love for reasonable painting."

---

* The Journal of Eugène Delacroix, translated by Lucy Norton. London: Phaidon Press, 1951, 137, 348–349).

Figure 29.5 EUGÈNE DELACROIX, *Arabs Skirmishing in the Mountains*, 1863. Oil on linen, 36⅜ × 29⅜ in. © 1998 Board of Trustees, National Gallery of Art, Washington, D.C. Chester Dale Fund, 1966.

Figure 29.6 (above) **EUGÈNE DELACROIX**, *Liberty Leading the People*, 1830. Oil on canvas, 8 ft. 6 in. × 10 ft. 7 in. Louvre, Paris. Photo: © R.M.N., Paris.

Figure 29.7 (left) **JACQUES-LOUIS DAVID**, *The Oath of the Horatii*, 1785. Oil on canvas, 10 ft. 10 in. × 14 ft. Louvre, Paris. Photo: © R.M.N., Paris.

strewn with corpses. A bayonet in one hand and the tricolor flag of France in the other, Liberty presses forward to challenge the forces of tyranny. She is champion of "the people": the middle class, as represented by the gentleman in a frock coat; the lower class, as symbolized by the scruffy youth carrying pistols; and racial minorities, as conceived in the black saber-bearer at the left. She is, moreover, France itself, the banner-bearer of the spirit of nationalism that infused nineteenth-century European history.

Delacroix's painting *Liberty Leading the People* is often compared with David's *Oath of the Horatii* (Figure **29.7**) because both paintings are clear calls to heroic action. But in conception and in style, the two paintings are totally different. While David looked to the Roman past for his theme, Delacroix drew on the issues of his time, allegorizing *real* events in order to increase their dramatic impact. And whereas David's appeal was essentially elitist, Delacroix celebrated the collective heroism of ordinary people. Yet Delacroix was never a slave to the facts: Although, for instance, the nudity of the fallen rebel in the left foreground (clearly related to the nudes of Géricault's *Raft*) had no basis in fact—it is uncommon to lose one's trousers in combat—the detail served to emphasize vulnerability and the imminence of death in battle. In his diary, Delacroix defended the artist's freedom to take liberties with form and content: "The most sublime effects of every master," he wrote, "are often the result of *pictorial licence*; for example, the lack of finish in Rembrandt's work, the exaggeration in Rubens. Mediocre painters never have sufficient daring, they never get beyond themselves." Stylistically, Delacroix's *Liberty* explodes with romantic passion. Surging rhythms link the smoke-filled background with the figures of the advancing rebels and the bodies of the fallen heroes heaped in the foreground. Gone are the cool restraints, the linear clarity, and the gridlike regularity of David's *Oath*. Gone also are the slick, finished surfaces. Delacroix's canvas resonates with dense textures and loose, rich brushstrokes. Color charges through the painting in a manner that recalls Rubens (see chapter 21), whose style Delacroix deeply admired.

Delacroix's *Liberty* instantly became a symbol of democratic aspirations. In 1884 France sent as a gift of friendship to the young American nation a monumental copper and cast-iron statue of an idealized female bearing a tablet and a flaming torch (Figure **29.8**). Designed by Frédéric-Auguste Bartholdi (1834–1904), the Statue of Liberty (Liberty Enlightening the World) is the "sister" of Delacroix's painted heroine; it has become a classic image of freedom for homeless and oppressed people everywhere.

Figure 29.8 FRÉDÉRIC-AUGUSTE BARTHOLDI, Statue of Liberty (Liberty Enlightening the World), Liberty Island (Bedloe's Island), New York, 1871–1884. Framework constructed by A. G. Eiffel. Copper sheets mounted on steel frame, height 152 ft. Photo: Mike Newton/Robert Harding Picture Library, London.

In his politically charged *Liberty Leading the People* (Figure **29.6**), Delacroix transformed a contemporary event (the Revolution of 1830) into a heroic allegory of the struggle for human freedom. When King Charles X dissolved the French legislature and took measures to repress voting rights and freedom of the press, liberal leaders, radicals, and journalists rose in rebellion. Delacroix translated this rebellion into a monumental painting that showed a handsome, bare-breasted female—the personification of Liberty—leading a group of French rebels through the narrow streets of Paris and over barricades

1836 Samuel Colt produces a six-cylinder revolver

1841 the breech-loading rifle known as the "needlegun" is introduced

1847 an Italian chemist develops explosive nitroglycerin

The Heroic Theme in Sculpture

In sculpture as in painting, heroic subjects served the cause of nationalism. *The Departure of the Volunteers of 1792* (Figure **29.9**) by François Rude (1784–1855) embodied the dynamic heroism of the Napoleonic Era. Installed at the foot of the Arch of Triumph (see chapter 26), which stands at the end of the Champs Elysées in Paris, the 42-foot-high stone sculpture commemorates the patriotism of a band of French volunteers—presumably the battalion of Marseilles, who marched to Paris in 1792 to defend the Republic. Young or old, nude or clothed in ancient or medieval garb (a device that augmented dramatic effect while universalizing the heroic theme), the spirited members of this small citizen army are led by the

Figure 29.9 FRANÇOIS RUDE, *La Marseillaise (The Departure of the Volunteers of 1792)*, 1833–1836. Stone, approx. 42 ft. × 26 ft. Arch of Triumph, Paris. Paul M.R. Maeyaert, Mont de l'Enclos (Orroir), Belgium.

way to Europe for academic training. She remained in Rome to pursue her career and gained great notoriety for her skillfully carved portrait busts and allegorical statues, some of which exalted the heroic roles of women in biblical and ancient history. Many of her works are now lost and almost nothing is known of her life after 1885.

Nineteenth-century nationalism stimulated passionate curiosity about other nations and ethnic groups. Just as Catlin looked to Native Americans as a source of colorful imagery (see chapter 27), so European artists turned to the East and to Africa for exotic subjects. Napoleon's invasion of Egypt (1798–1801) had started a virtual craze for things North African, and these interests were further stimulated by the French presence in Algeria beginning in the 1830s. Charles-Henri-Joseph Cordier (1827–1905), a member of Rude's studio and a favorite exhibitor in the academic Salon of Paris, requested a governmental assignment in Africa in order to make a record of its peoples. The result of Cordier's ethnological studies was a series of twelve busts of Africans and Asians, executed by means of innovative polychrome techniques that combined bronze or colored marble with porphyry, jasper, and onyx from Algerian quarries (Figure 29.11). Cordier's portrait heads reveal a sensitivity to individual personality and a commitment to capturing the dignity of his models. Rather than perceiving his subjects as exotic "others," he regarded them as racial types "at the point," as he explained, "of merging into one and the same people."

Figure 29.10 EDMONIA LEWIS (above) *Forever Free*, 1867. Marble, height 40½ in. Howard University Art Gallery, Washington, D.C.

Figure 29.11 CHARLES-HENRI-JOSEPH CORDIER (below) *African in Algerian Costume*, ca. 1856–1857. Bronze and onyx, 37¾ × 26 × 14 in. Musée d'Orsay, Paris. Photo: © R.M.N., Paris.

allegorical figure of Bellona, the Roman goddess of war. Like Delacroix's Liberty, Rude's classical goddess urges the patriots onward. The vitality of the piece is enhanced by deep undercutting, which results in dramatic contrasts of light and dark. In this richly textured work, Rude captured the revolutionary spirit and emotional fervor of the marching song of this battalion, *La Marseillaise*, which the French later adopted as their national anthem.

In America, the passage of the Thirteenth Amendment to the Constitution, which outlawed the practice of slavery in the United States, was met with a similar outburst of heroic celebration. In the commemorative marble sculpture, *Forever Free* (1867), a young slave who has broken his chains raises his arm in victory, while his female companion kneels in grateful prayer (Figure 29.10). The artist who conceived this remarkable work of art, Edmonia Lewis (1845–?) was the daughter of an African-American father and a Chippawa mother. Like most talented young American artists of this era, Lewis made her

Figure 29.12 **CHARLES BARRY** and **A. W. N. PUGIN**, Houses of Parliament, London, 1840–1860. Length 940 ft. Photo: © Peter Ashworth, London.

Trends in Mid-Nineteenth-Century Architecture

Neomedievalism in the West

Architects of the early to mid-nineteenth century regarded the past as a source of inspiration and moral instruction. Classical Greek and republican Roman buildings embodied the political and aesthetic ideals of nation-builders like Napoleon and Jefferson (see chapter 26); but the austere dignity of neoclassicism did not appeal to all tastes, nor did the romantic embrace of the past confine itself to Greco-Roman culture. More typical of the romantic imagination was a deep affection for the medieval world with its brooding castles and towering cathedrals. No less than neoclassicism, neomedievalism was the product of an energetic effort to revive the distinctive features of a nation's historical and cultural past, hence an expression of nationalism. In England, where the Christian heritage of the Middle Ages was closely associated with national identity, writers embraced the medieval past: Alfred Lord Tennyson (1802–1892), poet laureate of Great Britain, for instance, fused early British legend with the Christian mission in a cycle of Arthurian poems entitled *Idylls of the King*; while Sir Walter Scott immortalized medieval heroes and heroines in avidly read historical novels and romantic poems.

Figure 29.13 (right) **JAMES RENWICK** and **WILLIAM BODRIGUE**, Saint Patrick's Cathedral, Fifth Avenue and 50th Street, New York, 1853–1858. World Wide Photo. © Museum of the City of New York.

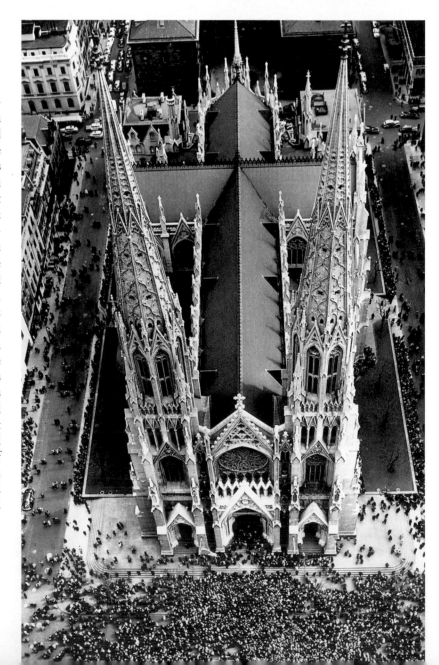

In architecture, the revival of the Gothic style was equally distinctive. The British Houses of Parliament, conceived by Charles Barry (1795–1860) and Augustus Welby Northmore Pugin (1812–1852) and begun in 1836, are among the most aesthetically successful large-scale neo-Gothic public buildings. The picturesque combination of spires and towers fronting on the River Thames in London was the product of Pugin's conviction that the Gothic style best expressed the dignity befitting the official architecture of a Christian nation (Figure **29.12**). Moreover, the Gothic style was symbolically appropriate for the building that epitomized the principles of parliamentary rule, pioneered in England with the signing of the Magna Carta in 1215. Pugin's affection for the neo-Gothic also reflected his own personal experience: His architectural conversion to the Gothic occurred almost simultaneously with his religious conversion to Roman Catholicism. For Pugin, Christian architecture, characterized by purity of structure and the meaningful application of details, was the visual correlative of the Catholic faith. The Houses of Parliament might be said to reflect the importance of medieval historical tradition—both religious and political—in shaping England's self-image.

Neomedievalism gave rise to a movement for the archeological restoration of churches and castles throughout Europe; but it also inspired some extraordinary new architectural activity in North America. College and university buildings (such as those at Harvard and Yale), museums (such as the Smithsonian in Washington, D.C.), and numerous churches and cathedrals became candidates for construction in the Romanesque or the Gothic style.

One of the most elegant examples of the Gothic revival in the United States is Saint Patrick's Cathedral in New York City (Figure **29.13**), which (along with Grace Church in Manhattan and the Smithsonian) was designed by James Renwick (1818–1895).

Exoticism in Western Architecture

While nineteenth-century architects embraced both the classical and medieval past, they also found inspiration in the "exotic" architecture of the East, and especially those parts of the world in which the European powers were building colonial empires. The most intriguing Western pastiche of non-Western styles is the Royal Pavilion at Brighton, which combines a fanciful assortment of Chinese, Indian, and Islamic motifs (Figure **29.14**). Designed by the English architect John Nash (1752–1835) between 1815 and 1821 as a seaside resort for the Prince Regent, Nash raised bulbous domes and slender minarets over a hidden frame of cast iron, the structural medium that would soon come to dominate modern architecture (see chapter 30). The bizarre fantasy of the interior decor, which includes water lily chandeliers and cast-iron palm trees with copper leaves, produced an eclectic style that was called in its own time "Indian Gothic."

The Romantic Style in Music

"Music is the most romantic of all the arts—one might almost say, the only genuine romantic one—for its sole subject is the infinite." Thus wrote the German novelist and musician, E. T. A. Hoffmann (1776–1822). Like many

Figure 29.14 JOHN NASH, The Royal Pavilion, Brighton, from the northeast, 1815–1821. Photo: © Angelo Hornak, London.

romantic composers, Hoffmann believed that music held a privileged position in its capacity to express what he called "an inexpressible longing." For the romantics, music—the most abstract and elusive of the arts—was capable of freeing the intellect and speaking directly to the heart.

The nineteenth century produced an enormous amount of fine music in all genres—a phenomenon that is reflected in the fact that audiences today listen to more nineteenth-century music than to music of any other time period. The hallmark of romantic music is personalized expression, and this feature is as apparent in large orchestral works as it is in small, intimate pieces. Like romantic poets and painters, romantic composers modified classical "rules" in order to increase expressive effects. They abandoned the precise forms and clear contours of classical music in favor of expanded or loosened forms, singable melodies, and lively shifts in meter and tempo. Just as romantic painters exploited color to heighten emotional impact, so composers elevated tone color (the distinctive quality of musical sound made by a voice, a musical instrument, or a combination of instruments) to a status equal to melody, harmony, and rhythm.

During the romantic era the orchestra grew to grand proportions. Mid-nineteenth-century orchestras were often five times larger than those used by Haydn and Mozart. While the volume of sound expanded, the varieties of instrumental possibilities also grew larger, in part because of technical improvements made in the instruments themselves. For instance, brass instruments (such as the trumpet and the tuba) gained new pitches and a wider range with the addition of valves; and woodwind instruments (such as the flute and the clarinet) underwent structural changes that greatly facilitated fingering and tuning. Such mechanical improvements expanded the tonal potential of musical instruments and produced a virtual revolution in orchestral textures.

In terms of musical composition, the symphony and the concerto were the most important of the large forms; equally popular, however, were song forms, especially songs that dealt with themes of love and death or nature and nature's moods. Composers found inspiration in heroic subjects, in contemporary events, and in the legends and histories of their native lands. Like the romantic painters and writers, they favored exotic, faraway themes. Both in small musical forms and in large operatic compositions, they made every effort to achieve an ideal union of poetry and music. As in the eighteenth century, in the nineteenth century composers were often also performers—no distinction was made between the two. They drew attention to their own technical abilities by writing music (usually for piano or violin) that only highly accomplished musicians like themselves could perform with facility. No longer completely at the mercy of the patronage system, they indulged, often publicly, in bouts of euphoria, melancholy, and petty jealousy. The talented Genoese composer and violinist, Niccolò Paganini (1782–1840), for instance, refused to publish his own pieces, which he performed with such astounding technical agility that rumor had it he had come by his virtuosity through a pact with the devil.

The Genius of Beethoven

The leading composer of the early nineteenth century and one of the greatest musicians of all time was the German-born Ludwig van Beethoven (1770–1827). Beethoven's lifelong residency in Vienna brought him in contact with the music of Mozart and Haydn, with whom he studied briefly. It also provided the composer with the fundamentals of the classical style (see chapter 26) from which he would stray. A skillful pianist, organist, and violinist, Beethoven composed works in almost every medium and form. His thirty-two piano sonatas tested the expressive potential of an instrument that—having acquired in the early nineteenth century an iron frame, two or three pedals, and thicker strings—was capable of extraordinary brilliance in tone and greater degrees of expressiveness, features that made the piano the most popular musical instrument of the nineteenth century.

Beethoven's greatest enterprise was his nine symphonies. These remarkable compositions generally adhered to the format of the classical symphony, but they moved beyond the boundaries of classical structure and were longer and more complex than any instrumental compositions written by Mozart or Haydn. Nevertheless, his indebtedness to classical composition makes him something of a bridge between the classical and romantic eras. Beethoven expanded the dimensions of the classical form and enriched its instrumental textures. By adding trombones and bass clarinets to the symphony orchestra and doubling the number of flutes, oboes, clarinets, and bassoons in his scoring, he vastly broadened the expressive range and dramatic power of orchestral sound. The expanded tone color and rich sonorities of Beethoven's symphonies are in part the product of such instruments as the piccolo, bass drum, and cymbals, all of which Beethoven added to the symphony orchestra.

Beethoven's genius lay in his introduction of a new rhythmic vitality that governed shifting patterns of grandeur and intimacy. In his use of musical **dynamics** (gradations of loudness and softness), Beethoven was more explicit and varied than his classical predecessors. Prior to 1812 Beethoven made use of only five terms to indicate the softness or loudness of piano performance; increasingly, however, he expanded the classical vocabulary with such words as *dolente* ("sorrowful") and *teneramente* ("tenderly") to indicate nuances. Like other romantic artists—Delacroix, in particular, comes to mind—Beethoven blurred the divisions between the structural units of a composition, exploiting textural contrasts for expressive effect. He often broke with classical form, adding, for example, a fifth movement to his Sixth (or "Pastoral") Symphony and embellishing the finale of his Ninth Symphony with a chorus and solo voices. Beethoven's daring use of dissonances, his sudden pauses and silences, and his brilliance of thematic and rhythmic invention reflect his preference for dramatic spontaneity over measured regularity. The powerful opening notes of the Fifth Symphony—a motif that Beethoven is said to have called "fate knocking at the door"—exemplify his affection for inventive repetitions and surging rhythms that propel the music toward a powerful climax.

Figure 29.15 *Beethoven Composing the "Pastoral" by a Brook*, from the Twenty-Second Almanac of the Zürich Musikgesellschaft for 1834: Biography of Ludwig van Beethoven. Colored lithograph, 6½ × 5⅝ in. By permission of the Beethoven Haus, Bonn. H. C. Bodmer Collection.

hammer strikes of sound and follows with a series of themes that feature the French horn, the symbol of the hero throughout the entire piece. The second movement is a somber and solemn funeral march. For the third movement, instead of the traditional minuet, Beethoven penned a vigorous **scherzo** (in Italian, "joke"), which replaced the elegance of a courtly dance with a melody that was fast and vigorous—a joke in that it was undanceable! The last movement, a victory finale, brings the themes of the first movement together with a long coda that again features the horn. It is worth noting that for the triumphant last movement of this stirring symphony, Beethoven included musical passages originally written for a ballet on the theme of Prometheus.

Difficult as it is to imagine, Beethoven wrote much of his greatest music when he was functionally deaf. From the age of twenty-nine, when he became aware of a progressive degeneration of his hearing, he labored against depression and despair. Temperamental and defiant, Beethoven scorned the patronage system that had weighed heavily upon both Mozart and Haydn, and sold his musical compositions as an independent artist. Unlike Haydn and Mozart, he declared contempt for the nobility and ignored their demands. In 1802 he confided to his family, "I am bound to be misunderstood; for me there can be no relaxation with my fellow men, no refined conversations, no mutual exchange of ideas. I must live alone like one who has been banished." In retreat from society, the alienated composer turned to nature (Figure **29.15**). In the woods outside of Vienna, Beethoven roamed with his musical sketchbook under one arm, often singing to himself in a loud voice. "Woods, trees and rock," he wrote in his diary, "give the response that man requires." Beethoven's discovery that

Like Byron and Gros, Beethoven admired Napoleon as a popular hero and a champion of liberty. In 1799, he dedicated his Third Symphony to Napoleon, adding to the title page the subtitle "Eroica" ("Heroic"). When Napoleon crowned himself emperor in 1804, however, Beethoven angrily scratched out Napoleon's name, so that when the piece was published, it bore only a generalized dedication: "to the memory of a great man." Beethoven's Third Symphony is colossal in size and complexity. It follows the standard number and order of movements found in the classical symphony, but it is almost twice as long as a typical classical symphony of some twenty to twenty-five minutes. The first movement, ♪ which one French critic called "the Grand Army of the soul," engages six rather than the traditional two themes dictated by sonata form. The movement begins with two commanding

♪ See Music Listening Selections at end of chapter.

nature mirrored his deepest emotions inspired his programmatic Sixth (or "Pastoral") Symphony of 1808, which he subtitled "A recollection of country life." Each of the five movements of the "Pastoral" is labeled with a specific reference to nature: "Awakening of happy feelings on arriving in the country"; "By the brook"; "Joyous gatherings of country folk"; "Storm"; and "Shepherd's Song, happy and thankful feelings after the storm." In the tradition of Vivaldi's *Four Seasons* (see chapter 23), Beethoven occasionally imitated the sounds of nature. For example, at the end of the second movement, flute, oboe, and clarinet join to create bird calls; and a quavering *tremolo* (the rapid repetition of a tone to produce a trembling effect) on the lower strings suggests the sounds of a murmuring brook.

German Art Songs

The art songs of Beethoven's Austrian contemporary Franz Schubert (1797–1828) aptly reflect the nineteenth-century composer's ambition to unite poetry and music. Schubert is credited with originating the **lied** (German for "song," pl. *lieder*), an independent song for solo voice and piano. The *lied* is not a song in the traditional sense but, rather, a poem recreated in musical terms. Its lyric qualities, like those of simple folk songs, are generated by the poem itself. The *lieder* of Schubert, Robert Schumann (1810–1856), and Johannes Brahms (1833–1897), which set to music the poetry of Heine and Goethe, among others, are intimate evocations of personal feelings and moods. Such pieces recount tales of love and longing, describe nature and its moods (some forty songs are related to water or to fish), or lament the transience of human happiness.

Among Schubert's 1,000 or so works (which include nine symphonies and numerous chamber pieces) are 600 *lieder*. Of these, Schubert's musical settings for Goethe's ballads rank as some of the best expressions of musical romanticism. "*Gretchen am Spinnrade*" ("Gretchen at the Spinning Wheel"), written when the composer was only seventeen years old, is based on a poem by Goethe which occurs near the end of Part I of *Faust*. In the piece, Gretchen laments the absence of her lover Faust and anticipates the sorrows that their love will bring. Repeated three times are the poignant lines with which the song opens: "My peace is gone, my heart is sore:/I shall find it never and never more." While the melody and tone color of the voice line convey the sadness expressed in the words of the poem, the propelling piano line captures the rhythms of the spinning wheel. Yet another of Schubert's finest art songs is "*Erlkönig*" ("The Erlking"), ♪ which combines elements of the natural (a raging storm), the supernatural (the figure of death in the person of the legendary king of the elves), and the heroic (a father's desperate effort to save the life of his ailing son). Here, Schubert's music mingles the rhythms of the stormy ride on horseback, the struggle for survival, and the threatening lure of death. Schubert himself died of syphilis at the age of thirty-one.

The Programmatic Symphonies of Berlioz

The French composer Hector Berlioz (1803–1869) began his first symphony in 1830. An imaginative combination of the story of Faust and Berlioz's own life, the *Symphonie fantastique* tells the dramatic tale of Berlioz's "interminable and inextinguishable passion"—as he described it—for the captivating Irish actress Harriet Smithson. Berlioz wrote the symphony in the first flush of his passion, when he was only twenty-seven years old. Following an intense courtship, he married Harriet, only to discover that he and the woman he idolized were dreadfully mismatched—the marriage turned Smithson into an alcoholic and Berlioz into an adulterer.

The *Symphonie fantastique* belongs to the genre known as **program music**, that is, instrumental music endowed with a specific literary or pictorial content indicated by the composer. Berlioz was not the first to write music that was programmatic: In *The Four Seasons*, Vivaldi had linked music to poetic phrases, as had Beethoven in his "Pastoral" Symphony. But Berlioz was the first to build an entire ymphony around a set of musical motifs that told a story. The popularity of program music during the nineteenth century testifies to the powerful influence of literature upon the other arts. Berlioz, whose second symphony, *Harold in Italy*, was inspired by Byron's *Childe Harold* (see chapter 28), was not alone in his attraction to literary subjects. The Hungarian composer Franz Liszt (1811–1886) wrote symphonic poems based on the myth of Prometheus and Shakespeare's *Hamlet*. He also composed the *Faust Symphony*, which he dedicated to Berlioz. And the Russian composer Peter Ilyich Tchaikovsky (1840–1893) wrote many programmatic pieces, including the tone poem *Romeo and Juliet*. Finally, landmark political events inspired the composition of nationalistic program music, such as Beethoven's *Battle Symphony* of 1813 (also known as "Wellington's Victory") and Tchaikovsky's colorful *1812 Overture* (1880), which, commemorating Napoleon's retreat from Moscow, incorporated portions of the national anthems of both France and Tsarist Russia.

In the *Symphonie fantastique*, Berlioz links a specific mood or event to a musical phrase, or **idée fixe** ("fixed idea"). This recurring musical motif, which Berlioz introduces within the first five minutes of the opening movement, becomes the means by which the composer binds together the individual parts of his dramatic narrative. Subtitled "Episode in the Life of an Artist," the *Symphonie fantastique* is an account of the young musician's opium-induced dream, in which, according to Berlioz's program notes, "the Beloved One takes the form of a melody in his mind, like a fixed idea which is ever returning and which he hears everywhere." Unified by the *idée fixe*, the symphony consists of a sequence of five parts, each distinguished by a particular mood: the lover's "reveries and passions"; a ball at which the hero meets his beloved; a stormy scene in the country; a "March to the Scaffold" ♪ (marking the hero's dream of murdering his lover and his subsequent execution); and a final and feverishly orchestrated "Dream of a Witches' Sabbath" inspired by Goethe's *Faust*. (Berlioz's *Damnation of Faust*, a piece for soloists, chorus, and orchestra, likewise drew on Goethe's great drama.) The "plot" of the *Symphonie fantastique*, published along with the musical score, was (and usually still is) printed in program notes available to listeners. But the written narrative is *not* essential to the enjoyment of the music, for, as Berlioz himself explained, the music holds authority as absolute sound, above and beyond its programmatic associations.

Berlioz, the spiritual heir to Beethoven, took liberties with traditional symphonic form. He composed the *Symphonie fantastique* in five movements instead of the usual four and combined instruments inventively so as to create unusual sets of sound. In the third movement, for example, a solo English horn and four kettledrums produce the effect of "distant thunder." He also expanded tone color, stretching the register of clarinets to screeching highs, for instance, and playing the strings of the violin with the wood of the bow instead of with the hair. Berlioz's

favorite medium was the full symphony orchestra, which he enlarged to include 150 musicians. Called "the apostle of bigness," Berlioz conceived an *ideal* orchestra that consisted of over 400 musicians, including 242 string instruments, 30 pianos, 30 harps, and a chorus of 360 voices. The monumental proportions of Berlioz's orchestras drew spoofs in contemporary cartoons, such as that by the French illustrator Gustave Doré (Figure **29.16**). But Berlioz, who was also a talented writer and a music critic for Parisian newspapers, thumbed his nose at the critics in lively essays that defended his own musical philosophy.

The Piano Music of Chopin

If the nineteenth century was the age of romantic individualism, it was also the age of the **virtuoso**: composers wrote music that might be performed gracefully and accurately only by individuals with extraordinary technical skills. The quintessential example is the Polish-born composer Frédéric Chopin (1810–1849). At the age of seven, Chopin gave his first piano concert in Warsaw. Slight in build even as an adult, Chopin had small hands that nevertheless could reach like "the jaws of a snake" (as one of his peers observed) across the keys of the piano. After leaving Warsaw, Chopin became the acclaimed pianist of the Paris *salons* and a close friend of Delacroix (who painted the portrait in Figure **29.17**), Berlioz, and many of the leading novelists of his age, including George Sand (see chapter 28), with whom he had a stormy seven-year love affair.

In his brief lifetime—he died of tuberculosis at the age of thirty-nine—Chopin created an entirely personal musical idiom linked to the expressive potential of the modern piano. For the piano, Chopin wrote over two hundred pieces, most of which were small, intimate works, such as dances, *préludes* (short keyboard pieces in one movement), **nocturnes** (slow, songlike pieces), **impromptus** (short keyboard compositions that sound improvised), and *études* (instrumental studies designed to improve a player's technique). Chopin's Etude in G-flat Major, **Opus** 10, No. 5, ♪ is a breathtaking piece that challenges the performer to play very rapidly on the black keys, which are less than half the width of the white keys.

Much like Delacroix, Chopin was given to violent mood swings. And, as with Delacroix's paintings, which though carefully contrived give the

Figure 29.16 GUSTAVE DORÉ, Berlioz Conducting Massed Choirs, nineteenth-century caricature. © Corbis/Bettmann, London.

♪ See Music Listening Selections at end of chapter.

bold contrasts of calm meditation and bravura, while his nocturnes—like the romantic landscapes of Friedrich and Corot (see Figures 27.9 and 27.10)—are often dreamy and wistful. Of his dance forms, the polonaise and the mazurka preserve the robustness of the folk tunes of his native Poland, while the waltz mirrors the romantic taste for a new type of dance, more sensuous and physically expressive than the courtly and formal minuet. Considered vulgar and lewd when it was introduced in the late eighteenth century, the waltz, with its freedom of movement and intoxicating rhythms, became the most popular of all nineteenth-century dances.

The Romantic Ballet

The theatrical art form known as "ballet" reached immense popularity in the Age of Romanticism. While the great ballets of Tchaikovsky—*Swan Lake*, *The Nutcracker*, and *Sleeping Beauty*—brought fame to Russia at the end of the century, it was in nineteenth-century Paris that romantic ballet was born. By the year 1800, ballet had moved from the court to the theater, where it was enjoyed as a middle-class entertainment. Magnificent theaters, such as the Paris Opéra (Figure **29.18**), completed in 1875 by J. L. Charles Garnier (1825–1878), became showplaces for public entertainment. The neo-baroque facade of the opera house reflects Garnier's awareness that Greek architects had painted parts of their buildings; but the glory of the structure is its interior, which takes as its focus a sumptuous grand staircase (Figure **29.19**). Luxuriously appointed, and illuminated by means of the latest technological

impression of spontaneity, so Chopin's music seems improvised—the impetuous record of fleeting feeling, rather than the studied product of diligent construction. The most engaging of his compositions are marked by fresh turns of harmony and free tempos and rhythms. Chopin might embellish a melodic line with unusual and flamboyant devices, such as a rolling **arpeggio** (the sounding of the notes of a chord in rapid succession). His *préludes* provide

Figure 29.18 J. L. CHARLES GARNIER, the facade of the Opéra, Paris, 1860–1875. Giraudon, Paris.

Figure 29.19 J. L. CHARLES GARNIER, the Grand Staircase in the Opéra, Paris, 1862–1875.
Engraving from Charles Garnier, *Le Nouvel Opéra de Paris*, 1880, Vol. 2, plate 8.

invention, gaslight, the Paris Opéra became the model for public theaters throughout Europe. For the facade, Jean-Baptiste Carpeaux (1827–1875) created a 15-foot-high sculpture whose exuberant rhythms capture the spirit of the dance as the physical expression of human joy (Figure **29.20**).

The ballets performed on the stage of the Paris Opéra launched a Golden Age in European dance. In Paris in 1832, the Italian-born **prima ballerina** (the first, or leading, female dancer in a ballet company) Maria Taglioni (1804–1884) perfected the art of dancing *sur les points* ("on the toes") (Figure **29.21**). Taglioni's performance in the ballet *La Sylphide* (choreographed by her father) was hailed as nothing less than virtuoso. Clothed in a diaphanous dress with a fitted bodice and a bell-shaped skirt (the prototype of the tutu), Taglioni performed perfect **arabesques**—a ballet position in which the dancer stands on one leg with the other extended in back and one or both arms held to create the longest line possible from one extremity to the other. She also astonished audiences by crossing the stage in three magnificent, floating leaps. While faithful to the exact steps of the classical ballet, Taglioni brought to formal dance the new, more sensuous spirit of nineteenth-century romanticism.

Popular legends and fairy tales inspired many of the ballets of the romantic era, including *La Sylphide*, *Giselle*, and the more widely known *Swan Lake* and *Sleeping Beauty*, composed by Tchaikovsky. The central figure of each ballet is usually some version of the angelic female—a fictional creature drawn from fable, fairy tale, and fantasy. The sylph in *La Sylphide* was a mythical nature deity who was thought to inhabit the air, as, for instance, nymphs were thought to inhabit the woodlands. In *La Sylphide*, a sylph enchants the hero and lures him away from his bride-to-be. Pursued by the hero, she nevertheless evades his grasp and dies—the victim of a witch's malevolence—before their love is consummated. The heroine of *La Sylphide* (and other romantic ballets) along with the prima ballerina who assumed that role were symbols of the elusive ideals of love and beauty eulogized by such romantic poets as Byron and Keats (see chapters 27 and 28). She conformed as well to the stereotype of the pure and virtuous female found in the pages of Sand's romantic novels. The traditional equation of beauty and innocence in the person of the idealized female is well illustrated in the comments of one French critic, who described "the aerial and virginal grace of Taglioni," and exulted, "She flies like a spirit in the midst of transparent clouds of white muslin—she resembles a happy angel." Clearly, the nineteenth-century ballerina was the romantic realization of the Eternal Female, a figure that fits the stereotype of the angelic woman.

Figure 29.20 JEAN-BAPTISTE CARPEAUX, *The Dance*, 1868. Stone. Created for the facade of the Opéra, Paris, now in Musée d'Orsay, Paris. Photo: © R.M.N., Paris.

Figure 29.21 Maria Taglioni in her London debut of 1830. Bibliothèque Nationale, Paris.

Romantic Opera

Verdi and Italian Grand Opera

Romantic opera, designed to appeal to a growing middle-class audience, came into existence after 1820. The culmination of baroque theatricality, romantic opera was grand both in size and in spirit. It was a flamboyant spectacle that united all aspects of theatrical production—music, dance, stage sets, and costumes. While Paris was the operatic capital of Europe in the first half of the nineteenth century, Italy ultimately took the lead in seducing the public with hundreds of wonderfully tuneful and melodramatic romantic operas.

The leading Italian composer of the romantic era was Giuseppe Verdi (1813–1901). In Verdi's twenty-six operas, including *Rigoletto* (1851), *La Traviata* (1853), and *Otello* (1887), the long, unbroken Italian operatic tradition that began with Monteverdi (see chapter 20) came to its peak. Reflecting on his gift for capturing high drama in music, Verdi exclaimed, "Success is impossible for me if I cannot write as my heart dictates." The heroines of Verdi's operas, also creatures of the heart, usually die for love. Perhaps the

most famous of Verdi's operas is *Aïda*, which was commissioned in 1870 by the Turkish viceroy of Egypt to mark the opening of the Suez Canal. *Aïda* made a nationalistic plea for unity against foreign domination—one critic called the opera "agitator's music." Indeed, the aria "O patria mia" ("O my country") is an expression of Verdi's ardent love for the newly unified Italy. But *Aïda* is also the passionate love story of an Egyptian prince and an Ethiopian princess held as a captive slave. Verdi's stirring arias, vigorous choruses, and richly colored orchestral passages can be enjoyed by listening alone, but the dramatic force of this opera can only be appreciated by witnessing first-hand a theatrical performance—especially one that engages such traditional paraphernalia as horses, chariots, and, of course, elephants.

Wagner and the Birth of Music-Drama

In Germany, the master of grand opera and one of the most formidable composers of the century was Richard Wagner (1813–1883). The stepson of a gifted actor, Wagner spent much of his childhood composing poems and plays and setting them to music. This union of music and literature culminated in the birth of what Wagner called **music-drama**, a unique synthesis of sound and story. Passionately nationalistic, Wagner drew almost exclusively on heroic themes from Germany's medieval past. He wrote his own librettos and composed scores that brought to life the fabulous events and personalities featured in German folk tales and legends. His aim, as he himself explained, was "to force the listener, for the first time in the history of opera, to take an interest in a poetic idea, by making him follow all its developments" as dramatized simultaneously in sound and story.

Of Wagner's nine principal operas, his greatest is a monumental, fifteen-hour cycle of four music-dramas collectively titled *Der Ring des Nibelungen* (*The Ring of the Nibelung*). Based on Norse and Germanic mythology, *The Ring* involves the quest for a magical but accursed golden ring, the power of which would provide its possessor with the potential to control the universe. Out of a struggle between the gods of Valhalla and an assortment of giants, dragons, and dwarfs emerges the hero, Siegfried, whose valorous deeds secure the ring for his lover Brünnhilde. In the end Siegfried loses both his love and his life, and Valhalla crumbles in flames, destroying the gods and eliciting the birth of a new order. Like Goethe, whose *Faust* was a lifetime effort and a tribute to his nation's past, Wagner toiled on the monumental *Ring* for over twenty-five years, from 1848 to 1874.

Awesome in imaginative scope, *The Ring* brings to life some of the hero myths that shaped the Western, and especially Germanic, literary tradition. Equally imaginative is the music, which matches its poetry in scope and drama.

lar person, thing, or idea in the story. *The Ring*, which features a total of twenty *leitmotifs*, is a complex web of dramatic and musical themes. "Every bar of dramatic music," Wagner proclaimed, "is justified only by the fact that it explains something in the action or in the character of the actor." The artist's mission, insisted Wagner, is to communicate "the necessary spontaneous emotional mood"; and in his expressive union of poetry and music, Wagner fulfilled that mission.

SUMMARY

In both form and content, romantic art ignited the imagination. Romantic artists generally elevated the heart over the mind and the emotions over the intellect. They favored subjects that gave free rein to the imagination, to the mysteries of the spirit, and to the cult of the ego. Increasingly independent of the official sources of patronage, they regarded themselves as the heroes of their age.

Romantic artists favored heroic themes and personalities, especially those that illustrated the struggle for political independence. Gros, Géricault, Goya, and Delacroix stretched the bounds of traditional subject matter to include controversial contemporary events, exotic subjects, and medieval legends. Their artworks gave substance to the spirit of nationalism that swept through nineteenth-century Europe. The search for national identity is also evident in the Gothic revival in Western architecture. Neomedievalism challenged neoclassicism in paying homage to Europe's historic past. As the romantics preferred themes exalting spontaneous emotion over poised objectivity, they launched a new freedom in composition and technique. Romantic painters rejected neoclassical rules of pictorial balance and clarity and tended to model forms by means of bold color and vigorous brushwork.

Romantic music found inspiration in heroic and nationalistic themes, as well as in nature's moods and the vagaries of human love. In their desire to express strong personal emotions, composers often abandoned classical models and stretched musical forms to fit their feelings. The enlargement of the symphony orchestra in size and expressive range is apparent in the works of Beethoven, Berlioz, and Wagner. Berlioz's *idée fixe* and Wagner's *leitmotif* tied sound to story, evidence of the romantic search for an ideal union of poetry and music. Lyrical melodies and tone color became as important to romantic music as the free use of form and color were to romantic painters. Schubert united poetry and music in the intimate form of

Figure 29.22 Welsh National Opera production of Wagner's *The Rhinegold* from *The Ring of the Nibelung.* Performing Arts Library, London.

According to Wagner, heroic music was made possible only by a heroic orchestra—his totaled 115 pieces, including 64 strings. Unlike Verdi, whose operas generally reflect nineteenth-century musical practice, Wagner's music-dramas anticipate some of the more radical experiments of the twentieth century, including the dissolution of classical tonality (see chapter 32). In fact, Wagner's music-dramas shattered traditional Western operatic techniques. Whereas composers normally divided the dramatic action into recitatives, arias, choruses, and instrumental passages, with the vocal line predominating, the mature Wagner gives the entire dramatic action to the orchestra, which engulfs the listener in a maelstrom of uninterrupted melody. In Wagner's operas, the vocal line is blended with a continuous orchestral line. Character and events emerge with clarity, however, owing to Wagner's use of **leitmotifs** (an anglicized German word for "leading motifs"), short musical phrases that—like Berlioz's *idées fixes*—designate a particu-

the *lied*, while Chopin captured a vast range of moods and emotions in virtuoso piano pieces.

Two of the most popular forms of musical expression in the nineteenth century were ballet and opera. Romantic ballet, which featured themes drawn from fantasy and legend, flowered in France and, later, in Russia. Grand opera was brought to its peak in Italy by Verdi and in Germany by Wagner, both of whom exploited nationalistic themes. The fact that so much nineteenth-century art, music, and dance is still enjoyed today reflects the strength of romanticism both as a style and as an attitude of mind.

SUGGESTIONS FOR READING

Bernier, Olivier. *The World in 1800*, New York: John Wiley & Sons, 2000.

Boime, Albert. *Hollow Icons: The Politics of Sculpture in Nineteenth-Century France*. Kent, Ohio: Kent State University Press, 1987.

Clark, Kenneth. *The Romantic Rebellion: Romantic Versus Classic Art*. New York: Harper, 1986.

Conrad, Peter. *Romantic Opera and Literary Form*. Berkeley, Calif.: University of California Press, 1977.

Friedlander, Walter. *David to Delacroix*, translated by Robert Goldwater. Cambridge, Mass.: Harvard University Press, 1974.

Gerhard, Anselm. *The Urbanization of Opera: Music Theater in Paris in the Nineteenth Century*, translated by Mary Whittall. Chicago: University of Chicago Press, 1998.

Hannoosh, Michele. *Painting and the Journal of Eugène Delacroix*. Princeton, N.J.: Princeton University Press, 1996.

Migel, Parmenia. *The Ballerinas: From the Court of Louis XIV to Pavlova*. New York: Macmillan, 1972.

Plantinga, Leon. *Romantic Music*. New York: Norton, 1982.

Rosen, Charles. *The Romantic Generation*. Cambridge, Mass.: Harvard University Press, 1995.

Vaughan, William. *Romantic Art*. London: Thames and Hudson, 1978.

Weber, William. *Music and the Middle Classes: The Social Structure of Concert Life in London, Paris and Vienna*. New York: Holmes Meier, 1975.

MUSIC LISTENING SELECTIONS

CD Two Selection 12 Beethoven, Symphony No. 3 in E-flat Major, "The Eroica," first movement, excerpt, 1803–1804.

CD Two Selection 13 Schubert, "Erlkönig," 1815.

CD Two Selection 14 Berlioz, *Symphonie fantastique*, Op. 14, "March to the Scaffold," fourth movement, excerpt, 1830.

CD Two Selection 15 Chopin, Etude in G-flat Major, Op. 10, No. 5, 1833.

GLOSSARY

aquatint a type of print produced by an engraving method similar to etching but involving finely granulated tonal areas rather than line alone

arabesque in ballet, a position in which the dancer stands on one leg with the other extended behind and one or both arms held to create the longest line possible from one extremity of the body to the other

arpeggio the sounding of the notes of a chord in rapid succession

dynamics the gradations of loudness or softness with which music is performed

étude (French, "study") an instrumental study designed to improve a player's performance technique

idée fixe (French, "fixed idea") a term used by Berlioz for a recurring theme in his symphonic works

impromptu (French, "improvised") a short keyboard composition that sounds as if it were improvised

leitmotif (German, "leading motif") a short musical theme that designates a person, object, place, or idea and that reappears throughout a musical composition

lied (German, "song," pl. *lieder*) an independent song for solo voice and piano; also known as "art song"

music-drama a unique synthesis of sound and story in which both are developed simultaneously and continuously; a term used to describe Wagner's later operas

nocturne a slow, songlike piece, usually written for piano; the melody is played by the right hand, and a steady, soft accompaniment is played by the left

opus (Latin, "work") a musical composition; followed by a number, it designates either the chronological place of a musical composition in the composer's total musical output or the order of its publication; often abbreviated "op."

prima ballerina the first, or leading, female dancer in a ballet company

program music instrumental music endowed with specific literary or pictorial content that is indicated by the composer

scherzo (Italian, "joke") in Beethoven's music, a sprightly, lively movement

tremolo in music, the rapid repetition of a single pitch or two pitches alternately, producing a trembling effect

virtuoso one who exhibits great technical ability, especially in musical performance; also used to describe a musical composition demanding (or a performance demonstrating) great technical skill

PART TWO

Realism and the modernist turn

While romanticism dominated the art and culture of the West until almost the last decade of the nineteenth century, the *realist* point of view began to take shape as early as the 1850s. As a style, *realism* called for an objective and unidealized assessment of everyday life. The new style emerged partly in response to the social and economic consequences of industrialism and partly as an expression of discontent with the contemporary political and economic climate. As a cultural movement, realism reflected popular demands for greater access to material wealth and a denunciation of the sentimental and nostalgic view of the past. Reformers weighed the benefits of industrialization against the human costs of modern technology. Realist artists exhibited a profound sense of social consciousness and a commitment to contemporary problems of class and gender. Unlike the romantics, who felt alienated from society and often sought to escape the oppressive materialism of the modern world, realists saw themselves as men and women "of their time."

The second half of the nineteenth century saw the modernization of Russia, the unification of both Italy and Germany, and the extension of Western economic control and political authority in Africa, Latin America, and Asia. The rush for territory and empire brought the West into a position of dominion over most of the less industrialized parts of the world. As Western nations scrambled for colonial influence, they assumed an ever-growing lead in technology and the arts. In the last quarter of the century, France emerged as the center of Western artistic productivity. Paris became a melting pot for artists and writers, many of whom turned their backs on both romanticism and realism. London and Paris hosted World's Fairs that brought the cultures of the non-Western world to the eyes of astonished Westerners. On the eve of the modern era, European culture experienced what Friedrich Nietzsche called "a chaos, a nihilistic sigh, an utter bewilderment, an instinct of weariness." Philosophers, poets, artists, and composers became preoccupied with the world of fleeting sensations and intuitive reality. Japanese, African, and Oceanic art, which flourished in the precolonial decades of the nineteenth century, had a visible impact on the work of Western artists, inspiring inquiry into art as a language of form and feeling, rather than as a vehicle for moral or religious truths. As the technologies of electric light, steel construction, synthetic paints, and stop-action photography emerged, new ways of viewing the world were matched by new methods of recording experience. The city, with its monumental skyscrapers and its bustling mix of people, became the site of the modernist turn.

(opposite) **CAMILLE PISSARRO**, detail of *Le Boulevard Montmartre: Rainy Weather, Afternoon*, 1897. Oil on canvas, 20⅝ × 26 in. Private Collection. Bridgeman Art Library, London.

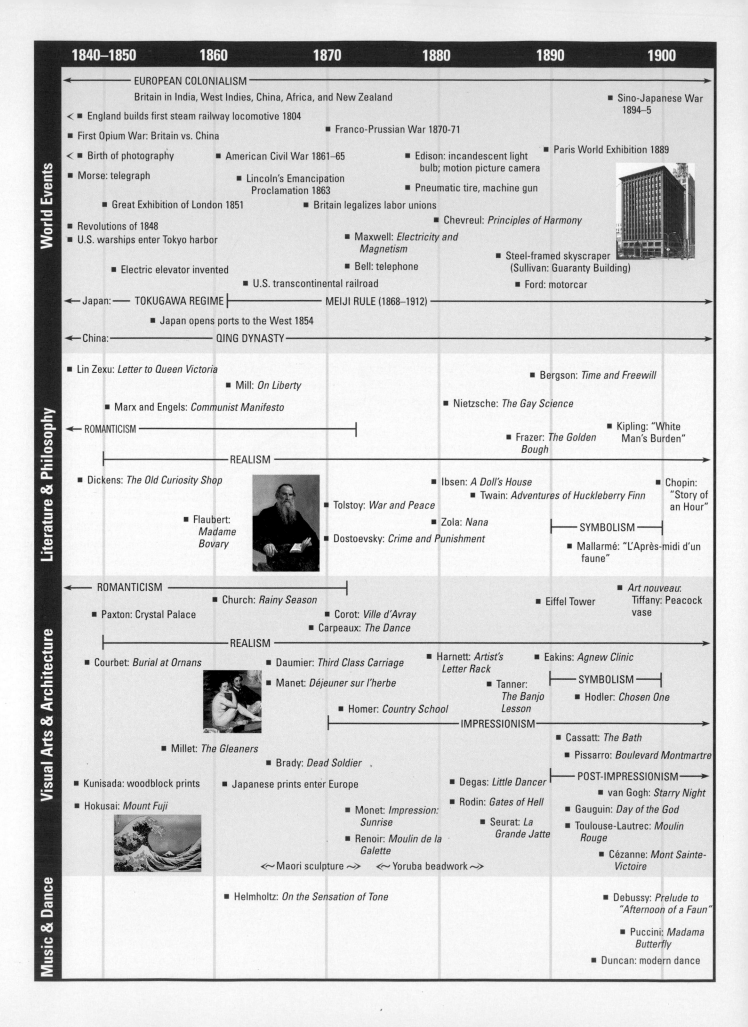

1840–1850   1860   1870   1880   1890   1900

World Events

EUROPEAN COLONIALISM
Britain in India, West Indies, China, Africa, and New Zealand

- Sino-Japanese War 1894–5
- England builds first steam railway locomotive 1804
- Franco-Prussian War 1870–71
- First Opium War: Britain vs. China
- Birth of photography
- American Civil War 1861–65
- Edison: incandescent light bulb; motion picture camera
- Paris World Exhibition 1889
- Morse: telegraph
- Lincoln's Emancipation Proclamation 1863
- Pneumatic tire, machine gun
- Great Exhibition of London 1851
- Britain legalizes labor unions
- Chevreul: *Principles of Harmony*
- Revolutions of 1848
- Maxwell: *Electricity and Magnetism*
- U.S. warships enter Tokyo harbor
- Steel-framed skyscraper (Sullivan: Guaranty Building)
- Electric elevator invented
- Bell: telephone
- U.S. transcontinental railroad
- Ford: motorcar

Japan: TOKUGAWA REGIME | MEIJI RULE (1868–1912)
- Japan opens ports to the West 1854

China: QING DYNASTY

Literature & Philosophy

- Lin Zexu: *Letter to Queen Victoria*
- Bergson: *Time and Freewill*
- Mill: *On Liberty*
- Nietzsche: *The Gay Science*
- Marx and Engels: *Communist Manifesto*

ROMANTICISM
- Kipling: "White Man's Burden"
- Frazer: *The Golden Bough*

REALISM
- Dickens: *The Old Curiosity Shop*
- Ibsen: *A Doll's House*
- Chopin: "Story of an Hour"
- Tolstoy: *War and Peace*
- Twain: *Adventures of Huckleberry Finn*
- Flaubert: *Madame Bovary*
- Zola: *Nana*
- Dostoevsky: *Crime and Punishment*

SYMBOLISM
- Mallarmé: "L'Après-midi d'un faune"

Visual Arts & Architecture

ROMANTICISM
- Church: *Rainy Season*
- Art nouveau: Tiffany: Peacock vase
- Paxton: Crystal Palace
- Corot: *Ville d'Avray*
- Eiffel Tower
- Carpeaux: *The Dance*

REALISM
- Courbet: *Burial at Ornans*
- Daumier: *Third Class Carriage*
- Harnett: *Artist's Letter Rack*
- Eakins: *Agnew Clinic*
- Manet: *Déjeuner sur l'herbe*
- Tanner: *The Banjo Lesson*

SYMBOLISM
- Hodler: *Chosen One*
- Homer: *Country School*

IMPRESSIONISM
- Millet: *The Gleaners*
- Cassatt: *The Bath*
- Pissarro: *Boulevard Montmartre*
- Brady: *Dead Soldier*

POST-IMPRESSIONISM
- Kunisada: woodblock prints
- Japanese prints enter Europe
- Degas: *Little Dancer*
- van Gogh: *Starry Night*
- Hokusai: *Mount Fuji*
- Rodin: *Gates of Hell*
- Gauguin: *Day of the God*
- Monet: *Impression: Sunrise*
- Seurat: *La Grande Jatte*
- Toulouse-Lautrec: *Moulin Rouge*
- Renoir: *Moulin de la Galette*
- Cézanne: *Mont Sainte-Victoire*

<— Maori sculpture ~>   <— Yoruba beadwork ~>

Music & Dance

- Helmholtz: *On the Sensation of Tone*
- Debussy: *Prelude to "Afternoon of a Faun"*
- Puccini: *Madama Butterfly*
- Duncan: modern dance

CHAPTER THIRTY

Industry, empire, and the realist style

"Show me an angel and I'll paint one"
Courbet

Nations have long drawn their strength and identity from their economic and military superiority over other nations. In the decades following the American and French revolutions, nationalism and the quest for national identity spurred movements for popular sovereignty in the West. But a more aggressive form of nationalism marked the late nineteenth century. Fueled by advancing industrialism, Western nations not only continued to compete among themselves for economic and political preeminence, but they also sought control of markets throughout the world. The combined effects of nationalism, industrialism, and the consequent phenomena of imperialism and colonialism influenced the direction of modern Western history and that of the world beyond the West as well.

It was in this climate that the realist style emerged. Realists challenged the acute subjectivity, exoticism, and escapism that typified romanticism. In the spirit of science and technology—enterprises that placed great value on the physical world—realists called for fidelity to nature and an unidealized assessment of contemporary life. Finally, they insisted on a clear-eyed attention to social problems, especially those related to the advance of nationalism and industrial progress.

The Global Dominion of the West

Advancing Industrialism

Industrialism provided the economic and military basis for the West's rise to a position of dominance over the rest of the world. This process is well illustrated in the history of the railroad, the most important technological phenomenon of the early nineteenth century and one made possible by the combined technologies of steam power, coal, and iron. The first all-iron rails were forged in Britain in 1789, but it was not until 1804 that the British built their first steam railway locomotive, and several more decades until "iron horses" became a major mode of transportation. The drive to build national railways spread throughout much of Europe and North America. By 1850, 23,000 miles of railway track crisscrossed Europe, linking the sources of raw materials to factories and markets. In the coal-mining region of the Ruhr Valley in Northern Germany and across the vast continent of North America, railroads facilitated economic and political expansion. As Western nations colonized other parts of the globe, they took with them the railroad and other agents of industrialism.

By 1880, Western technology included the internal combustion engine, the telegraph, the telephone, the camera, and—perhaps most significant for the everyday life of human beings—electricity. Processed steel, aluminum, the steam turbine, and the pneumatic tire—all products of the 1880s—further altered the texture of life in the industrialized world. These devices, along with more lethal instruments of war such as the fully automatic "machine gun," gave Europe clear advantages over other parts of the globe and facilitated Western imperialism in less industrially developed areas. In the enterprise of empire-building, the industrialized nations of Britain, France, Belgium, Germany, Italy, and the United States took the lead.

Colonialism and the New Imperialism

The history of European expansion into Asia, Africa, and other parts of the globe dates back at least to the Age of the Renaissance. Between approximately 1500 and 1800, Europeans established trading outposts in Africa, China, and India. But not until after 1800, in the wake of the Industrial Revolution, did European imperialism transform the territories of foreign powers into outright colonial possessions. Driven by the need for raw materials and markets for their manufactured goods, and aided immeasurably by their advanced military technology, the industrial nations quickly colonized vast parts of Asia, Africa, and Latin America. So massive was this effort that, by the end of the nineteenth century, the West had established economic, political, and cultural dominance over much of the world.

European imperialists defended the economic exploitation of weaker countries with the view, inspired by social Darwinism, that in politics, as in nature, the strongest or

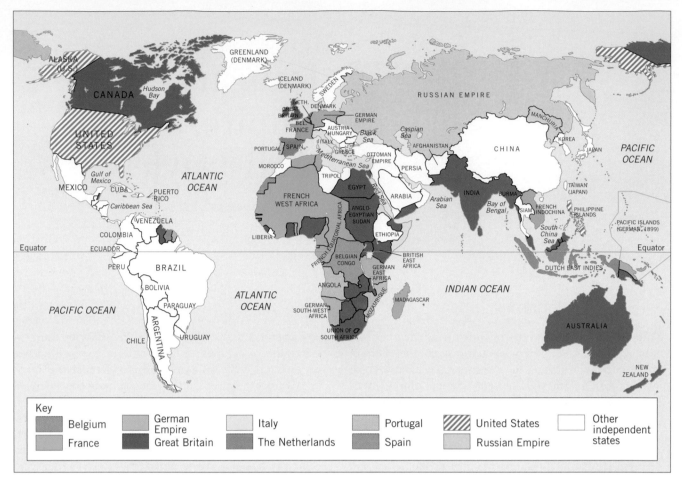

Map 30.1 European Colonies and Independent Nations in 1900.

"most fit" prevailed in the "struggle for survival." Since Caucasians had proved themselves the "most fit," they argued, it was the white population's "burden" to care for, protect, and rule over the "less fit" nonwhite peoples of the earth. Britain, the leader in European industrialization, spearheaded the thrust of colonization. The self-appointed mission of Western rule in less technologically developed countries was best expressed in a poem by one of the most popular British writers of his time, Rudyard Kipling (1864–1936). Three verses of his poem "The White Man's Burden" sum up two of the key imperialist notions: racial superiority and the spirit of paternal and heroic deliverance.

READING 5.16   From Kipling's "The White Man's Burden" (1899)

Take up the White Man's burden—   1
    Send forth the best ye breed—
Go bind your sons to exile
    To serve your captive's need;
To wait in heavy harness,   5
    On fluttered folk and wide—
Your new-caught, sullen peoples,
    Half-devil and half-child.

. . . .

Take up the White Man's Burden—
    Ye dare not stoop to less—   10
Nor call too loud on Freedom
    To cloak your weariness;
By all ye cry or whisper,
    By all ye leave to do,
The silent, sullen peoples   15
    Shall weigh your Gods and you.

Take up the White Man's burden—
    Have done with childish days—
The lightly proffered laurel,
    The easy, ungrudged praise.   20
Comes now, to search your manhood
    Through all the thankless years,
Cold, edged with dear-bought wisdom,
    The judgment of your peers!

Kipling dedicated "The White Man's Burden" to the United States to commemorate the American annexation of the Philippines in 1899, but the pattern for colonialism had been cut many decades earlier by his native Britain. The first major landmass to be subjugated by Britain was India, where commercial imperialism led to conquest, and finally, to British rule in 1858. In less than a century, the nation had established control over so much territory across the globe that they could legitimately claim that "the sun never set" on the British Empire (Map **30.1**).

The most dramatic example of the new imperialism took place in Africa. In 1880, European nations controlled only ten percent of the continent; but by 1900 all of Africa, save Ethiopia and Liberia, had been carved up by European powers, which introduced new models of political and economic authority, often with little regard for native populations. The partitioning of Africa began in 1830 with the French conquest of Algeria (in the north). In the decades thereafter, Belgium laid claim to the Congo, and the Dutch and the British fought each other for control of South Africa—both nations savagely wresting land from the Zulu and other African peoples. A century-long series of brutal wars with the Asante Empire in West Africa left the British in control of the Gold Coast, while the conquest of the Sudan in 1898 saw 11,000 Muslims killed by British machine guns (the British themselves lost twenty-eight men). Profit-seeking European companies leased large tracts of African land from which native goods such as rubber, diamonds, and gold might be extracted; and increasingly Africans were forced to work on white-owned plantations and mines. The seeds of racism and mutual contempt were sown in this troubled era, an era that predictably spawned modern liberation movements, such as those calling for Pan-Islamic opposition to colonialism (see chapter 36).

By the mid-nineteenth century, the United States (itself a colony of Britain until 1776) joined the scramble for economic control. America forced Japan to open its doors to Western trade in 1853. This event, which marked the end of Japan's seclusion, ushered in the overthrow of the Tokugawa regime (see chapter 21) and marked the beginning of Japanese modernization under Meiji rule (1858–1912). In the Western hemisphere, the United States established its own overseas empire. North Americans used the phrase "manifest destiny" to describe and justify a policy of unlimited expansion into the American West, Mexico, and elsewhere. The end result was the United States' acquisition of more than half of Mexico, the control of the Philippines and Cuba, and a dominant position in the economies of the politically unstable nations of Latin America. Although Westerners rationalized their militant expansionism by contending that they were "civilizing" the backward peoples of the globe, in fact their diplomatic policies contributed to undermining cultural traditions, to humiliating and often enfeebling the civilizations they dominated, and to creating conditions of economic dependency that would last well into the twentieth century (see chapter 36).

1844	Samuel Morse (American) transmits the first telegraph message
1866	the first successful transatlantic telegraph cable is laid
1869	the first American transcontinental railroad is completed
1875	Alexander Graham Bell (Scottish) produces the first functional telephone in America

China and the West

The nineteenth century marked the end of China's long history as an independent civilization. The European powers, along with Russia and Japan, carved out trade concessions in China. Subsequent trade policies, which took advantage of China's traditionally negative view of profit-taking, delayed any potential Chinese initiative toward industrialization. More devastating still was the triangular trade pattern in opium and tea between India, China, and Britain. Established by Britain in the early nineteenth century, the policy was based on the need to stem the tide of British gold and silver that flowed to China to buy tea, a favorite British beverage. The Chinese had used narcotic opium for centuries, but as a result of Britain's new trade policies, large quantities of the drug—harvested in India—were exported directly to China. In exchange, the Chinese shipped tea to Britain. As opium addiction became an increasingly severe social problem (and following the opium-related death of the Chinese emperor's son), the Chinese made every effort to restrict the importation of the drug and to stem the activities of opium smugglers (Figure 30.1). British merchants refused to cooperate. The result was a series of wars between Britain and China (the Opium Wars, 1839–1850) that brought China to its knees. In 1839, just prior to the first of these wars, the Chinese Commissioner Lin Zexu (1785–1850) sent a detailed communication to the British queen pleading for Britain's assistance in ending opium smuggling and trade. Whether or not Queen Victoria ever read Lin's letter is unknown, but the document remains a literary monument to the futile efforts of a great Asian civilization to achieve peace through diplomacy in the age of imperialism.

READING 5.17   From Lin Zexu's *Letter of Advice to Queen Victoria* (1839)

A communication: magnificently our great Emperor soothes and pacifies China and the foreign countries, regarding all with the same kindness. If there is profit, then he shares it with the peoples of the world; if there is harm, then he removes it on behalf of the world. This is because he takes the mind of heaven and earth as his mind. **1**

The kings of your honorable country by a tradition handed down from generation to generation have always been noted for their politeness and submissiveness. We have read your successive tributary memorials saying, "In general our **10** countrymen who go to trade in China have always received His Majesty the Emperor's gracious treatment and equal justice," and so on. Privately we are delighted with the way in which the honorable rulers of your country deeply understand the grand principles and are grateful for the Celestial grace. For this reason the Celestial Court in soothing those from afar has redoubled its polite and kind treatment. The profit from trade has been enjoyed by them continuously for two hundred years.

Figure 30.1 *Westerners Through Chinese Eyes.* Sketch from a Shanghai picture magazine, *Dian-shi-zhai-hua-bao*, founded in 1884. The inscription reads: "Opium coming to China has become an evil beyond control. If it is not Heaven's will to stop it, there is no other way to save the situation. Heretofore it has been said that only we Chinese are opium smokers. Not so. A French addict in the prime of life, traveling with his wife, an English friend, and a French servant, lay down to smoke in a Singapore hotel but next morning became ill and died—the doctor said from smoking too much. How can one not be afraid!"

This is the source from which your country has become known for its wealth.

But after a long period of commercial intercourse, there appear among the crowd of barbarians both good persons and bad, unevenly. Consequently there are those who smuggle opium to seduce the Chinese people and so cause the spread of the poison to all provinces. Such persons who only care to profit themselves, and disregard their harm to others, are not tolerated by the laws of heaven and are unanimously hated by human beings. His Majesty the Emperor, upon hearing of this, is in a towering rage. He has especially sent me, his commissioner, to come to Kwangtung, and together with the governor-general and governor jointly to investigate and settle this matter. . . .

We find that your country is [some 20,000 miles] from China.

Yet there are barbarian ships that strive to come here for trade for the purpose of making a great profit. The wealth of China is used to profit the barbarians. That is to say, the great profit made by barbarians is all taken from the rightful share of China. By what right do they then in return use the poisonous drug to injure the Chinese people? Even though the barbarians may not necessarily intend to do us harm, yet in coveting profit to an extreme, they have no regard for injuring others. Let us ask, where is your conscience? I have heard that the smoking of opium is very strictly forbidden by your country; that is because the harm caused by opium is clearly understood. Since it is not permitted to do harm to your own country, then even less should you let it be passed on to the harm of other countries—how much less to China! Of all that China exports to foreign countries, there is not a single thing which is not beneficial to people: they are of benefit when eaten, or of benefit when used, or of benefit when resold: all are beneficial. Is there a single article from China which has done any harm to foreign countries? Take tea and rhubarb, for example; the foreign countries cannot get along for a single day without them. If China cuts off these benefits with no sympathy for those who are to suffer, then what can the barbarians rely upon to keep themselves alive? Moreover the [textiles] of foreign countries cannot be woven unless they obtain Chinese silk. If China, again, cuts off this beneficial export, what profit can the barbarians expect to make? As for other foodstuffs, beginning with candy, ginger, cinnamon, and so forth, and articles for use, beginning with silk, satin, chinaware, and so on, all the things that must be had by foreign countries are innumerable. On the other hand, articles coming from the outside to China can only be used as toys. We can take them or get along without them. Since they are not needed by China, what difficulty would there be if we closed the frontier and stopped the trade? Nevertheless our Celestial Court lets tea, silk, and other goods be shipped without limit and circulated everywhere without begrudging it in the slightest. This is for no other reason but to share the benefit with the people of the whole world.

The goods from China carried away by your country not only supply your own consumption and use, but also can be divided up and sold to other countries, producing a triple profit. Even if you do not sell opium, you still have this threefold profit. How can you bear to go further, selling products injurious to others in order to fulfil your insatiable desire?

Suppose there were people from another country who carried opium for sale to England and seduced your people into buying and smoking it; certainly your honorable ruler would deeply hate it and be bitterly aroused. We have heard heretofore that your honorable ruler is kind and benevolent. Naturally you would not wish to give unto others what you yourself do not want. We have also heard that the ships coming to Canton have all had regulations promulgated and given to them in which it is stated that it is not permitted to carry contraband goods. This indicates that the administrative orders of your honorable rule have been originally strict and clear. Only because the trading ships are numerous, heretofore perhaps they have not been examined with care. Now after this communication has been dispatched and you have clearly understood the strictness of the prohibitory laws of the

Celestial Court, certainly you will not let your subjects dare again to violate the law. . . .

Now we have set up regulations governing the Chinese people. He who sells opium shall receive the death penalty and he who smokes it also the death penalty. Now consider this: if the barbarians do not bring opium, then how can the Chinese people resell it, and how can they smoke it? The fact is that the wicked barbarians beguile the Chinese people into a death **100** trap. How then can we grant life only to these barbarians? He who takes the life of even one person still has to atone for it with his own life; yet is the harm done by opium limited to the taking of one life only? Therefore in the new regulations, in regard to those barbarians who bring opium to China, the penalty is fixed at decapitation or strangulation. This is what is called getting rid of a harmful thing on behalf of mankind. . . .

To the European mind, the benefits of Western science, technology, and religion far outweighed the negative impact of colonialism. But the "gift" of progress was received in China with extreme caution and increasing isolationism. No dramatically new developments took place in the arts of China (nor, for that matter, in India) during the nineteenth century; in general, there was a marked decline in productivity and originality. The full consequences of Western colonialism in Asia and elsewhere, however, would not become clear until the twentieth century (see chapter 34).

Social and Economic Realities

In global terms, advancing industrialization polarized the nations of the world into the technologically advanced—the "haves"—and the technologically backward—the "have-nots." But industrialization had an equally profound impact within the industrialized nations themselves: It changed the nature and character of human work, altered relationships between human beings, and affected the natural environment. Prior to 1800 the practice of accumulating capital for industrial production and commercial profit played only a limited role in European societies. But after 1800, industrial production, enhanced by advances in machine technology, came to be controlled by a relatively small group of middle-class **entrepreneurs** (those who organize, manage, and assume the risks of a business) and by an even smaller number of **capitalists** (those who provide investment capital). Industrialization created wealth, but that wealth was concentrated in the hands of a small minority of the population. The vast majority of men and women lived hard lives supported by meager wages—the only thing they had to sell was their labor. Factory laborers, including women and children, worked under dirty and dangerous conditions for long hours—sometimes up to sixteen hours per day (Figure **30.2**). In the 1830s almost half of London's funerals were for children under ten years old. Mass production brought more (and cheaper) goods to more people more rapidly, ultimately raising the standard of living for industrialized nations. But European industrialism and the unequal distribution of wealth contributed to a dramatic

Figure 30.2 ADOLPH FRIEDRICH ERDMANN VON MENZEL, *Iron Mill (Das Eisenwalzwerk—Moderne Zyklopen)*, 1875. Oil on canvas, 5 ft. ¼ in. × 8 ft. 3⅝ in. Nationalgalerie, Stäatliche Museen Preussischer Kulturbesitz, Berlin. Photo: Klaus Göken.

gap between capitalist entrepreneurs—the "haves" of society—and the working classes—the "have-nots." In 1846, the British statesman Benjamin Disraeli (1804–1881) described Britain under the rule of Queen Victoria (1819–1901) as two nations: the nation of the poor and the nation of the rich.

Beginning in 1848, the lower classes protested against these conditions with sporadic urban revolts. Economic unrest prevailed not only in the cities but in rural areas as well, where agricultural laborers were often treated like slaves—in America, until after the Civil War (1861–1865), most of those who worked the great Southern plantations were, in fact, African-American slaves. Between 1855 and 1861, there were almost five hundred peasant uprisings across Europe (Figure 30.3). Reform, however, was slow in coming. Outside of

Figure 30.3 KÄTHE KOLLWITZ, *March of the Weavers*, from "The Weavers Cycle," 1897. Etching, 8⅜ × 11⅝ in. The University of Michigan Museum of Art, 1956/1.21.

England—in Germany, for instance—trade unions and social legislation to benefit the working classes did not appear until 1880 or later, while in Russia economic reform would require nothing less than a full-scale revolution.

Nineteenth-Century Social Theory

Among nineteenth-century European intellectuals there developed a serious debate over how to address the social results of industrial capitalism. Matters of social reform were central to the development of nineteenth-century ideologies, or doctrines, that dictated specific policies of political and economic action. Traditional *conservatives* stressed the importance of maintaining order and perpetuating conventional power structures and religious authority. *Liberals*, on the other hand, whose ideas were rooted in Enlightenment theories of human progress and perfectibility (see chapter 24), supported gradual reform through enlightened legal systems, constitutional guarantees, and a generally equitable distribution of material benefits. The British liberal Jeremy Bentham (1748–1832) advanced the doctrine of *utilitarianism*, which held that governments should work to secure "the greatest happiness for the greatest number of people"; while Bentham's student, John Stuart Mill (1806–1873), expounded the ideology of social liberalism. Mill emphasized freedom of thought over equality and personal happiness. He held that individuals must be free to direct their own lives, but, recognizing the disadvantages that might result from free competition, he argued that the state must protect its weaker members by acting to regulate the economy where private initiative failed to do so. Mill feared that the general will—the will of unenlightened, propertyless masses—might itself prove tyrannical and oppressive. He concluded, therefore, in his classic statement of the liberal creed, *On Liberty* (1859), that "as soon as any part of a person's conduct affects prejudicially the interests of others, society has jurisdiction over it." For Mill, as for most nineteenth-century liberals, governments had to intervene to safeguard and protect the wider interests of society.

Such theories met with strenuous opposition from European *socialists*. For the latter, neither conservatism nor liberalism responded adequately to current social and economic inequities. Socialists attacked capitalism as unjust; they called for the common ownership and administration of the means of production and distribution in the interest of a public good. Society, according to the socialists, should operate entirely in the interest of the needs of the people, communally and cooperatively, rather than competitively. Such utopian socialists as Pierre Joseph Proudhon (1809–1865) envisioned a society free of state control, while the more extreme *anarchists* favored the complete dissolution of the state and the elimination of the force of law.

1839	Charles Goodyear (American) produces industrial-strength rubber
1846	Elias Howe (American) patents an interlocking-stitch sewing machine
1866	the first dynamo, capable of generating massive quantities of electricity, is produced
1876	Nikolaus Otto (German) produces a workable internal-combustion engine

The Radical Views of Marx and Engels

The German theorist Karl Marx (1818–1883) agreed with the socialists that bourgeois capitalism corrupted humanity, but his theory of social reform was an even more radical version of socialism, for it preached violent revolution that would both destroy the old order and usher in a new society. Marx began his career by studying law and philosophy at the University of Berlin. Moving to Paris, he became a lifelong friend of the social scientist and journalist Friedrich Engels (1820–1895). Marx and Engels shared a similar critical attitude toward the effects of European industrial capitalism. By 1848 they completed the *Communist Manifesto*, a short treatise published as the platform of a workers' association called the Communist League. The *Manifesto*, which still remains the "guidebook" of Marxist socialism, demanded the "forcible overthrow of all existing social conditions" and the liberation of the **proletariat**, or working class. Marx offered an even more detailed criticism of the free enterprise system in *Das Kapital*, a work on which he toiled for thirty years.

The *Communist Manifesto* is a sweeping condemnation of the effects of capitalism on the individual and society at large. The first section of the treatise (part of which is included in Reading 5.18) defends the claim that "the history of all hitherto existing society is the history of class struggles." The authors argue that capitalism concentrates wealth in the hands of the few, providing great luxuries for some, while creating an oppressed and impoverished proletariat. The psychological effects of such circumstances, they contend, are devastating: Bourgeois capitalism alienates workers from their own productive efforts and robs individuals of their basic humanity. Finally, the authors call for revolution by which workers will seize the instruments of capitalistic production and abolish private ownership.

The social theories of Marx and Engels had enormous practical and theoretical influence. They not only supplied a justification for lower-class revolt, but they brought attention to the role of economics in the larger life of a society. Marx described human behavior and human history in exclusively materialistic terms, arguing that the conditions under which one earned a living determined all other aspects of life: social, political, and cultural. A student of the Hegelian dialectic (see chapter 27), Marx viewed history as a struggle between "haves" (thesis) and "have-nots" (antithesis) that would resolve in the synthesis of a classless society. From Hegel, Marx derived the utopian idea of the perfectibility of the state. The end product of dialectical change, argued Marx, was a society free of class antagonisms and the ultimate dissolution of the state itself.

Although Marx and Engels failed to anticipate capitalism's potential to spread rather than to limit wealth, their manifesto gave sharp focus to prevailing class differences and to the actual condition of the European economy of their time. And despite the fact that Marx and Engels did not provide any explanation of *how* their classless society might function, their apocalyptic call to revolution would be heeded in the decades to come. Oddly enough, Communist revolutions would occur in some of the least industrialized countries of the world, such as Russia and China, rather than in the most industrialized countries, as Marx and Engels expected. Elsewhere, Communists would operate largely through *nonrevolutionary* vehicles, such as labor unions and political organizations, to initiate better working conditions, higher wages, and greater social equality. But the anti-Communist revolutions and the collapse of the Communist government in the Soviet Union in the late twentieth century reveal mounting frustration with the failure of most Communist regimes to raise economic standards among the masses. Although the *Manifesto* did not accurately predict the economic destiny of the modern world, the treatise remains a classic expression of nineteenth-century social consciousness.

READING 5.18 From Marx's and Engels' *Communist Manifesto* (1848)

I Bourgeois and Proletarians[1]

The history of all hitherto existing society is the history of class struggles. **1**

Freeman and slave, patrician and plebeian, lord and serf, guild-master[2] and journeyman, in a word, oppressor and oppressed, stood in constant opposition to one another, carried on an uninterrupted, now hidden, now open fight, a fight that each time ended either in a revolutionary reconstitution of society at large or in the common ruin of the contending classes.

In the earlier epochs of history we find almost everywhere a complicated arrangement of society into various orders, a **10** manifold gradation of social rank. In ancient Rome we have patricians, knights, plebeians, slaves; in the Middle Ages, feudal lords, vassals, guild-masters, journeymen, apprentices, serfs; in almost all of these classes, again, subordinate gradations.

The modern bourgeois society that has sprouted from the ruins of feudal society has not done away with class antagonisms. It has but established new classes, new conditions of oppression, new forms of struggle in place of the old ones. **20**

Our epoch, the epoch of the bourgeoisie, possesses, however, this distinctive feature: it has simplified the class antagonisms. Society as a whole is splitting up more and more into two great hostile camps, into two great classes directly facing each other: Bourgeoisie and Proletariat.

From the serfs of the Middle Ages sprang the chartered burghers of the earliest towns. From these burgesses the first elements of the bourgeoisie were developed.

The discovery of America, the rounding of the Cape, opened up fresh ground for the rising bourgeoisie. The East Indian and **30** Chinese markets, the colonization of America, trade with the colonies, the increase in the means of exchange and in

---

[1] By bourgeoisie is meant the class of modern capitalists, owners of the means of social production and employers of wage labor. By proletariat, the class of modern wage-laborers who, having no means of production of their own, are reduced to selling their labor power in order to live. [1888.]

[2] Guild-master, that is, a full member of a guild, a master within, not a head of a guild. [1888.]

commodities generally, gave to commerce, to navigation, to industry, an impulse never before known, and thereby, to the revolutionary element in the tottering feudal society, a rapid development.

The feudal system of industry, under which industrial production was monopolized by closed guilds, now no longer sufficed for the growing wants of the new markets. The manufacturing system took its place. The guild-masters were **40** pushed on one side by the manufacturing middle class; division of labor between the different corporate guilds vanished in the face of division of labor in each single workshop.

Meantime the markets kept ever growing, the demand ever rising. Even manufacture no longer sufficed. Thereupon, steam and machinery revolutionized industrial production. The place of manufacture was taken by the giant, Modern Industry, the place of the industrial middle class by industrial millionaires—the leaders of whole industrial armies, the modern bourgeois.

Modern industry has established the world market, for which **50** the discovery of America paved the way. This market has given an immense development to commerce, to navigation, to communication by land. This development has, in its turn, reacted on the extension of industry; and in proportion as industry, commerce, navigation, railways extended, in the same proportion the bourgeoisie developed, increased its capital, and pushed into the background every class handed down from the Middle Ages.

We see, therefore, how the modern bourgeoisie is itself the product of a long course of development, of a series of **60** revolutions in the modes of production and of exchange.

Each step in the development of the bourgeoisie was accompanied by a corresponding political advance of that class. An oppressed class under the sway of the feudal nobility, an armed and self-governing association in the medieval commune,[3] here independent urban republic (as in Italy and Germany), there taxable "third estate" of the monarchy (as in France), afterward, in the period of manufacture proper, serving either the semi-feudal or the absolute monarchy as a counterpoise against the nobility, and, in fact, cornerstone of **70** the great monarchies in general, the bourgeoisie has at last, since the establishment of Modern Industry and of the world market, conquered for itself, in the modern representative State, exclusive political sway. The executive of the modern State is but a committee for managing the common affairs of the whole bourgeoisie.

The bourgeoisie, historically, has played a most revolutionary part.

The bourgeoisie, wherever it has got the upper hand, has put an end to all feudal, patriarchal, idyllic relations. It has **80** pitilessly torn asunder the motley feudal ties that bound man to his "natural superiors," and has left remaining no other nexus between man and man than naked self-interest, than callous "cash payment." It has drowned the most heavenly

---

[3]"Commune" was the name taken in France by the nascent towns even before they had conquered from their feudal lords and masters local self-government and political rights as the "Third Estate." Generally speaking, for the economic development of the bourgeoisie, England is here taken as the typical country; for its political development, France. [1888.]

ecstasies of religious fervor, of chivalrous enthusiasm, of philistine sentimentalism, in the icy water of egotistical calculation. It has resolved personal worth into exchange value, and in place of the numberless indefeasible chartered freedoms has set up that single, unconscionable freedom— Free Trade. In one word, for exploitation, veiled by religious **90** and political illusions, it has substituted naked, shameless, direct, brutal exploitation.

The bourgeoisie has stripped of its halo every occupation hitherto honored and looked up to with reverent awe. It has converted the physician, the lawyer, the priest, the poet, the man of science, into its paid wage-laborers.

The bourgeoisie has torn away from the family its sentimental veil, and has reduced the family relation to a mere money relation. . . .

The bourgeoisie, by the rapid improvement of all instruments **100** of production, by the immensely facilitated means of communication, draws all, even the most barbarian, nations into civilization. The cheap prices of its commodities are the heavy artillery with which it batters down all Chinese walls, with which it forces the barbarians' intensely obstinate hatred of foreigners to capitulate. It compels all nations, on pain of extinction, to adopt the bourgeois mode of production; it compels them to introduce what it calls civilization into their midst, i.e., to become bourgeois themselves. In a word, it creates a world after its own image. **110**

The bourgeoisie has subjected the country to the rule of the towns. It has created enormous cities, has greatly increased the urban population as compared with the rural, and has thus rescued a considerable part of the population from the idiocy of rural life. Just as it has made the country dependent on the towns, so it has made barbarian and semi-barbarian countries dependent on the civilized ones, nations of peasants on nations of bourgeois, the East on the West.

The bourgeoisie keeps doing away more and more with the scattered state of the population, of the means of production, **120** and of property. It has agglomerated population, centralized means of production, and has concentrated property in a few hands. The necessary consequence of this was political centralization. Independent or but loosely connected provinces with separate interests, laws, governments and systems of taxation became lumped together into one nation, with one government, one code of laws, one national class interest, one frontier and one customs tariff.

The bourgeoisie during its rule of scarce one hundred years has created more massive and more colossal productive forces **130** than have all preceding generations together. Subjection of nature's forces to man, machinery, application of chemistry to industry and agriculture, steam navigation, railways, electric telegraphs, clearing of whole continents for cultivation, canalization of rivers, whole populations conjured out of the ground—what earlier century had even a presentiment that such productive forces slumbered in the lap of social labor? . . .

But not only has the bourgeoisie forged the weapons that bring death to itself; it has also called into existence the men who are to wield those weapons—the modern working class, **140** the proletarians.

In proportion as the bourgeoisie, i.e., capital, is developed, in the same proportion is the proletariat, the modern working class, developed—a class of laborers who live only as long as they find work, and who find work only as long as their labor increases capital. These laborers, who must sell themselves piecemeal, are a commodity like every other article of commerce, and are consequently exposed to all the vicissitudes of competition, to all the fluctuations of the market.

Owing to the extensive use of machinery and to division of labor, the work of the proletarians has lost all individual character and, consequently, all charm for the workman. He becomes an appendage of the machine, and it is only the most simple, most monotonous, and most easily acquired knack that is required of him. . . .

Modern industry has converted the little workshop of the patriarchal master into the great factory of the industrial capitalist. Masses of laborers, crowded into the factory, are organized like soldiers. As privates of the industrial army they are placed under the command of a perfect hierarchy of officers and sergeants. Not only are they slaves of the bourgeois class and of the bourgeois State; they are daily and hourly enslaved by the machine, by the overseer and, above all, by the individual bourgeois manufacturer himself. The more openly this despotism proclaims gain to be its end and aim, the more petty, the more hateful and the more embittering it is.

The less the skill and exertion of strength implied in manual labor, in other words, the more modern industry becomes developed, the more is the labor of men superseded by that of women. Differences of age and sex no longer have any distinctive social validity for the working class. All are instruments of labor, more or less expensive to use, according to their age and sex.

No sooner is the exploitation of the laborer by the manufacturer so far at an end that he receives his wages in cash, than he is set upon by the other portions of the bourgeoisie, the landlord, and shopkeeper, the pawnkeeper, etc. . .

II Proletarians and Communists

. . . The Communist revolution is the most radical rupture with traditional property relations; no wonder that its development involves the most radical rupture with traditional ideas.

But let us have done with the bourgeois objections to Communism.

We have seen above that the first step in the revolution by the working class is to raise the proletariat to the position of ruling class, to win the battle of democracy.

The proletariat will use its political supremacy to wrest, by degrees, all capital from the bourgeoisie, to centralize all instruments of production in the hands of the State, i.e., of the proletariat organized as the ruling class; and to increase the total of productive forces as rapidly as possible. . . .

III Position of the Communists

. . . The Communists disdain to conceal their views and aims. They openly declare that their ends can be attained only by the forcible overthrow of all existing social conditions. Let the ruling classes tremble at a Communistic revolution. The proletarians have nothing to lose but their chains. They have a world to win.

WORKING MEN OF ALL COUNTRIES, UNITE!

Mill and Women's Rights

While Marx and Engels criticized a society that made middle-class women "mere instrument[s] of production," Mill described women of all classes as the unwilling subjects of more powerful males. In the eloquent treatise entitled *The Subjection of Women*, Mill condemned the legal subordination of one sex to the other as objectively "wrong in itself, and . . . one of the chief hindrances to human improvement." Mill's optimism concerning the unbounded potential for social change—a hallmark of liberalism—may have been shortsighted, for all women would not obtain voting rights in Britain until 1928. Nevertheless, the first women's college—Mount Holyoke—was founded at South Hadley, Massachusetts, in 1836; and in 1848, at Seneca Falls in upstate New York, American feminists, led by Elizabeth Cady Stanton (1815–1902) and Susan B. Anthony (1820–1906), issued the first of many declarations that demanded female equality in all areas of life. The rights of women had been an issue addressed in the literature of feminists from Christine de Pisan to Condorcet and Mary Wollstonecraft (see chapter 24), but nowhere was the plight of women more eloquently treated than in Mill's essay. Mill compared the subjection of women to that of other subject classes in the history of culture. But his most original contribution was his analysis of the male/female relationship and his explanation of how that relationship differed from that of master and slave.

> ## READING 5.19 From Mill's *The Subjection of Women* (1869)

All causes, social and natural, combine to make it unlikely that women should be collectively rebellious to the power of men. They are so far in a position different from all other subject classes that their masters require something more from them than actual service. Men do not want solely the obedience of women, they want their sentiments. All men, except the most brutish, desire to have, in the woman most nearly connected with them, not a forced slave but a willing one, not a slave merely, but a favorite. They have therefore put everything in practice to enslave their minds. The masters of all other slaves rely, for maintaining obedience, on fear, either fear of themselves, or religious fears. The masters of women wanted more than simple obedience, and they turned the whole force of education to effect their purpose. All women are brought up from the very earliest years in the belief that their ideal of character is the very opposite to that of men; not self-will and government by self-control, but submission and yielding to the control of others. All the moralities tell them that it is the duty of women and all the current sentimentalities that it is their nature to live for others, to make complete abnegation of themselves, and to have no life but in their affections. And by their affections are meant the only ones they are allowed to have—those to the men with whom they are connected, or to the children who constitute an additional and indefeasible tie between them and a man. When we put together three things—first, the natural attraction between opposite sexes; secondly, the wife's entire dependence on the husband, every privilege or pleasure she has being either his gift, or depending entirely on his will; and lastly, that the principal object of human pursuit, consideration, and all objects of social ambition can in general be sought or obtained by her only through him, it would be a miracle if the object of being attractive to men had not become the polar star of feminine education and formation of character. And this great means of influence over the minds of women having been acquired, an instinct of selfishness made men avail themselves of it to the utmost as a means of holding women in subjection, by representing to them meekness, submissiveness, and resignation of all individual will into the hands of a man, as an essential part of sexual attractiveness. . . .

The preceding considerations are amply sufficient to show that custom, however universal it may be, affords in this case no presumption and ought not to create any prejudice in favor of the arrangements which place women in social and political subjection to men. But I may go further, and maintain that the course of history, and the tendencies of progressive human society afford not only no presumption in favor of this system of inequality of rights, but a strong one against it; and that, so far as the whole course of human improvement up to this time, the whole stream of modern tendencies warrants any inference on the subject, it is that this relic of the past is discordant with the future and must necessarily disappear.

For, what is the peculiar character of the modern world—the difference which chiefly distinguishes modern institutions, modern social ideas, modern life itself, from those of times long past? It is, that human beings are no longer born to their place in life and chained down by an inexorable bond to the place they are born to, but are free to employ their faculties and such favorable chances as offer, to achieve the lot which may appear to them most desirable. Human society of old was constituted on a very different principle. All were born to a fixed social position and were mostly kept in it by law or interdicted from any means by which they could emerge from it. As some men are born white and others black, so some were born slaves and others freemen and citizens; some were born patricians, others plebeians; some were born feudal nobles, others commoners. . . .

The old theory was that the least possible should be left to the choice of the individual agent; that all he had to do should, as far as practicable, be laid down for him by superior wisdom. Left to himself he was sure to go wrong. The modern conviction, the fruit of a thousand years of experience, is that things in which the individual is the person directly interested never go right but as they are left to his own discretion; and that any regulation of them by authority, except to protect the rights of others, is sure to be mischievous. . . .

The New Historicism

While issues of class and gender preoccupied some of the finest minds of the nineteenth century, so too did matters surrounding the interpretation of the historical past. For many centuries, history was regarded as a branch of literature rather than a social science. The romantic histories, such as those of Thomas Carlyle (see chapter 25), served to emphasize the role of great men in shaping the destinies of nations. At the same time, the spirit of high patriotism inspired nineteenth-century historians such as Thomas Babington Macaulay in Britain and Fustel de Coulanges in France to write nationalistic histories that brought attention to the greatness of their own people and culture.

Patriotism, however, also led historians to renew their efforts to retrieve the evidence of the past. Scholars compiled vast collections of primary source materials; and, enamoured of the new, positivist zeal for objective measurement and recording, they tried to apply scientific methods to the writing of history. The result was an effort to recreate history "as it actually was," a movement later called *historicism*. Led by the German historian Leopold von Ranke (1795–1886), historians made every attempt to produce historical works that depended on the objective interpretation of eyewitness reports and authentic documents. Von Ranke himself produced sixty volumes on modern European history which rested on the critical study of sources that he had gleaned from various archives. This method of writing history still dominates modern-day historiography.

The new historicism that scholars brought to the critical study of religious history stirred great controversy and challenged the compatibility of science and religion. Rejecting all forms of supernaturalism, some nineteenth-century scholars disputed the literal interpretation of the Bible, especially where its contents conflicted with scientific evidence (as in the case of the Virgin Birth). Since the facts of Jesus' life were so few, some also questioned the historicity of Jesus (whether or not he had ever actually lived), while still others—such as the eminent French scholar Ernest Renan, author of the *Life of Jesus* (1863)—questioned his divinity. Renan and his followers offered a rationalist reconstruction of religious history which worked to separate personal belief and moral conduct from conventional religious history and dogma. At the same time, as universal education spread throughout the literate world and Church and state moved further apart, education and teaching became increasingly secularized.

Realism in Literature

The Novels of Dickens and Twain

Inequities of class and gender had existed throughout the course of history, but in an age that pitted the progressive effects of industrial capitalism against the realities of poverty and inequality, social criticism was inevitable. Nineteenth-century writers pointed to these conditions and described them with unembellished objectivity. This unblinking attention to contemporary life and experience was the basis for the style known as *literary realism*.

More than any other genre, the nineteenth-century novel—through its capacity to detail characters and conditions—best fulfilled the realist credo of depicting life with complete candor. In contrast with romanticism, which embraced heroic and exotic subjects, realism portrayed men and women in actual, everyday, and often demoralizing situations. It examined the social consequences of middle-class materialism, the plight of the working class, and the subjugation of women, among other matters. While realism did not totally displace romanticism as the dominant literary mode of the nineteenth century, it often appeared alongside the romantic—indeed, romantic and sentimental elements might be found in generally realistic narratives. Such was the case in the novels of Charles Dickens (1812–1870) in England and Mark Twain, the pseudonym of Samuel Langhorne Clemens (1835–1910), in America. Twain's writings, including his greatest achievement, *The Adventures of Huckleberry Finn*, reveal a blend of humor and irony that is not generally characteristic of Dickens. But both writers employ a masterful use of dialect, sensitivity to pictorial detail, and a humanitarian sympathy in their descriptions of nineteenth-century life in specific locales—for Twain, the rural farmlands along the Mississippi River, and for Dickens, the streets of England's industrial cities.

Dickens, the most popular English novelist of his time, came from a poor family who provided him with little formal education. His early experiences supplied some of the themes for his most famous novels: *Oliver Twist* (1838) vividly portrays the slums, orphanages, and boarding schools of London; *Nicholas Nickleby* (1839) is a bitter indictment of England's brutal rural schools; and *David Copperfield* (1850) condemns debtors' prisons and the conditions that produced them. Dickens' novels are frequently theatrical, his characters may be drawn to the point of caricature, and his themes often suggest a sentimental faith in kindness and good cheer as the best antidotes to the bitterness of contemporary life. But, as the following excerpt illustrates, Dickens' grasp of realistic detail was acute, and his portrayal of physical ugliness was unflinching. In this passage from *The Old Curiosity Shop*, Dickens painted an unforgettable picture of the horrifying urban conditions that gave rise to the despair of the laboring classes and inspired their cries for social reform. Dickens' description of the English milltown of Birmingham, as first viewed by the novel's heroine, little Nell, and her grandfather, finds striking parallels in nineteenth-century visual representations of Europe's laboring poor; it also calls to mind the popular conceptions of Hell found in medieval art and literature (see chapter 12).

READING 5.20   From Dickens' *The Old Curiosity Shop* (1841)

. . . A long suburb of red-brick houses—some with patches of garden-ground, where coal-dust and factory smoke darkened the shrinking leaves and coarse, rank flowers; and where the struggling vegetation sickened and sank under the hot breath of kiln and furnace, making them by its presence seem yet more blighting and unwholesome than in the town itself—a long, flat, straggling suburb passed, they came by slow degrees upon a cheerless region, where not a blade of grass was seen to grow; where not a bud put forth its promise in the spring; where nothing green could live but on the surface of the stagnant pools, which here and there lay idly sweltering by the black roadside. [10]

Advancing more and more into the shadow of this mournful place, its dark depressing influence stole upon their spirits, and filled them with a dismal gloom. On every side, as far as the eye could see into the heavy distance, tall chimneys, crowding on each other, and presenting that endless repetition of the same dull, ugly form, which is the horror of oppressive dreams, poured out their plague of smoke, obscured the light, and made foul the melancholy air. On mounds of ashes by the wayside, [20] sheltered only by a few rough boards, or rotten pent-house roofs, strange engines spun and writhed like tortured creatures; clanking their iron chains, shrieking in their rapid whirl from time to time as though in torment unendurable, and making the ground tremble with their agonies. Dismantled houses here and there appeared, tottering to the earth, propped up by fragments of others that had fallen down, unroofed, windowless, blackened, desolate, but yet inhabited. Men, women, children, wan in their looks and ragged in attire, tended the engines, fed their tributary fires, begged upon the road, or scowled half [30] naked from the doorless houses. Then came more of the wrathful monsters, whose like they almost seemed to be in their wildness and their untamed air, screeching and turning round and round again; and still, before, behind, and to the right and left, was the same interminable perspective of brick towers, never ceasing in their black vomit, blasting all things living or inanimate, shutting out the face of day, and closing in on all these horrors with a dense dark cloud.

But night-time in this dreadful spot!—night, when the smoke was changed to fire; when every chimney spirited up its flame; [40] and places, that had been dark vaults all day, now shone red-hot, with figures moving to and fro within their blazing jaws, and calling to one another with hoarse cries—night, when the noise of every strange machine was aggravated by the darkness; when the people near them looked wilder and more savage; when bands of unemployed laborers paraded in the roads, or clustered by torch-light round their leaders, who told them in stern language of their wrongs, and urged them on to frightful cries and threats; when maddened men, armed with sword and firebrand, spurning the tears and prayers of women [50] who would restrain them, rushed forth on errands of terror and destruction, to work no ruin half so surely as their own—night, when carts came rumbling by, filled with rude coffins (for contagious disease and death had been busy with the living crops); when orphans cried, and distracted women shrieked and followed in their wake—night, when some called for bread, and some for drink to drown their cares; and some with tears, and some with staggering feet, and some with bloodshot eyes, went brooding home—night, which, unlike the night that Heaven sends on earth, brought with it no peace, nor quiet, nor signs of [60] blessed sleep—who shall tell the terrors of the night to that young wandering child! . . .

Mark Twain's literary classic, *The Adventures of Huckleberry Finn*, is the most widely taught book in American literature. Published as a sequel to the popular "boys' book," *The Adventures of Tom Sawyer* (1876), which, like Dickens' novels, appeared in serial format, the novel recounts the adventures of the young narrator, Huck Finn, and the runaway slave, Jim, as the two make their way down the Mississippi River on a ramshackle raft. As humorist, journalist, and social critic, Twain offered his contemporaries a blend of entertainment and vivid insight into the dynamics of a unique time and place: the American South just prior to the Civil War. More universally, he conveys the innocence of youthful boyhood as it wrestles with the realities of greed, hypocrisy, and the moral issues arising from the troubled relations between mid-nineteenth century American blacks and whites. These he captures in an exotic blend of dialects, the vernacular rhythms and idioms of local, untutored speech.

In the excerpt that follows, Huck, a poor, ignorant, but good-hearted southern boy, experiences a crisis of conscience when he must choose between aiding and abetting a fugitive slave—a felony offense in the slave states of the south—and obeying the law, by turning over his older companion and friend to the local authorities. Huck's moral dilemma, the theme of this excerpt, was central to the whole system of chattel slavery. Historically, slaves were considered property (chattel), that is, goods that could be bought, sold, or stolen. Clearly, however, they were also human beings. In opting to help Jim escape, Huck is, in effect, an accomplice to a crime. Nevertheless, Huck chooses to aid Jim the *man*, even as he violates the law in harboring Jim the *slave*.

READING 5.21 From Twain's *The Adventures of Huckleberry Finn* (1884)

Chapter 16

We slept most all day, and started out at night, a little ways behind a monstrous long raft that was as long going by as a procession. She had four long sweeps[1] at each end, so we judged she carried as many as thirty men, likely. She had five big wigwams aboard, wide apart, and an open camp fire in the middle, and a tall flag-pole at each end. There was a power of style about her. It *amounted* to something being a raftsman on such a craft as that.

We went drifting down into a big bend, and the night clouded up and got hot. The river was very wide, and was walled with solid timber on both sides; you couldn't see a break in it hardly ever, or a light. We talked about Cairo,[2] and wondered whether we would know it when we got to it. I said likely we wouldn't, because I had heard say there warn't but about a dozen houses there, and if they didn't happen to have them lit up, how was we going to know we was passing a town? Jim said if the two big rivers joined together there, that would show. But I said maybe we might think we was passing the foot of an island and coming into the same old river again. That disturbed Jim—and me too. So the question was, what to do? I said, paddle ashore the first time a light showed, and tell them pap was behind, coming along with a trading-scow, and was a green hand at the business, and wanted to know how far it was to Cairo. Jim thought it was a good idea, so we took a smoke on it and waited.

1

10

20

There warn't nothing to do, now, but to look out sharp for the town, and not pass it without seeing it. He said he'd be mighty sure to see it, because he'd be a free man the minute he seen it, but if he missed it he'd be in the slave country again and no more show for freedom. Every little while he jumps up and says:

"Dah she is!"

But it warn't. It was Jack-o-lanterns, or lightning-bugs;[3] so he set down again, and went to watching, same as before. Jim said it made him all over trembly and feverish to be so close to freedom. Well, I can tell you it made me all over trembly and feverish, too, to hear him, because I begun to get it through my head that he *was* most free—and who was to blame for it? Why, *me*. I couldn't get that out of my conscience, no how nor no way. It got to troubling me so I couldn't rest; I couldn't stay still in one place. It hadn't ever come home to me before, what this thing was that I was doing. But now it did; and it staid with me, and scorched me more and more. I tried to make out to myself that I warn't to blame, because I didn't run Jim off from his rightful owner; but it warn't no use, conscience up and says, every time, "But you knowed he was running for his freedom, and you could a paddled ashore and told somebody." That was so—I couldn't get around that, noway. That was where it pinched. Conscience says to me, "What had poor Miss Watson done to you, that you could see her nigger go off right under your eyes and never say one single word? What did that poor old woman do to you, that you could treat her so mean? Why, she tried to learn you your book, she tried to learn you your manners, she tried to be good to you every way she knowed how. *That's* what she done."

I got to feeling so mean and so miserable I most wished I was dead. I fidgeted up and down the raft, abusing myself to myself, and Jim was fidgeting up and down past me. We neither of us could keep still. Every time he danced around and says, "Dah's Cairo!" it went through me like a shot, and I thought if it *was* Cairo I reckoned I would die of miserableness.

Jim talked out loud all the time while I was talking to myself. He was saying how the first thing he would do when he got to a free State he would go to saving up money and never spend a single cent, and when he got enough he would buy his wife, which was owned on a farm close to where Miss Watson lived; and then they would both work to buy the two children, and if their master wouldn't sell them, they'd get an Ab'litionist to go and steal them.

It most froze me to hear such talk. He wouldn't ever dared to talk such talk in his life before. Just see what a difference it made in him the minute he judged he was about free. It was according to the old saying, "give a nigger and inch and he'll take an ell." Thinks I, this is what comes of my not thinking. Here was this nigger which I had as good as helped to run away, coming right out flat-footed and saying he would steal his children—children that belonged to a man I didn't even know; a man that hadn't ever done me no harm.

I was sorry to hear Jim say that, it was such a lowering of him. My conscience got to stirring me up hotter than ever, until at last I says to it, "Let up on me—it ain't too late, yet—I'll paddle ashore at the first light, and tell." I felt easy, and happy,

30

40

50

60

70

80

---

[1] Long oars.
[2] A city in Illinois.

---

[3] Fireflies.

and light as a feather, right off. All my troubles was gone. I went to looking out sharp for a light, and sort of singing to myself. By-and-by one showed. Jim sings out:

"We's safe, Huck, we's safe! Jump up and crack yo' heels, dat's de good ole Cairo at las', I jis knows it!"

I says:

"I'll take the canoe and go see, Jim. It mightn't be, you know."

He jumped and got the canoe ready, and put his old coat in the bottom for me to set on, and give me the paddle; and as I shoved off, he says: **90**

"Pooty soon I'll be a-shout'n for joy, en I'll say, it's all on accounts o' Huck; I's a free man, en I couldn't ever ben free ef it hadn' ben for Huck; Huck done it. Jim won't ever forgit you, Huck; you's de bes' fren' Jim's ever had; en you's de *only* fren' ole Jim's got now."

I was paddling off, all in a sweat to tell on him; but when he says this, it seemed to kind of take the tuck all out of me. I went along slow then, and I warn't right down certain whether **100** I was glad I started or whether I warn't. When I was fifty yards off, Jim says:

"Dah you goes, de ole true Huck; de on'y white genlman dat ever kep' his promise to old Jim."

Well, I just felt sick. But I says, I *got* to do it—I can't get *out* of it. Right then, along comes a skiff with two men in it, with guns, and they stopped and I stopped. One of them says:

"What's that, yonder?"

"A piece of a raft," I says.

"Do you belong on it?" **110**

"Yes, sir."

"Any men on it?"

"Only one, sir."

"Well, there's five niggers run off to-night, up yonder above the head of the bend. Is you man white or black?"

I didn't answer up prompt. I tried to, but the words wouldn't come. I tried, for a second or two, to brace up and out with it, but I warn't man enough—hadn't the spunk of a rabbit. I see I was weakening; so I just give up trying, and up and says—

"He's white." **120**

"I reckon we'll go and see for ourselves."

"I wish you would," says I, "because it's pap that's there, and maybe you'd help me tow the raft ashore where the light is. He's sick—and so is mam and Mary Ann."

"Oh, the devil! we're in a hurry, boy. But I s'pose we've got to. Come—buckle to your paddle, and let's get along."

I buckled to my paddle and they laid to their oars. When we had made a stroke or two, I says:

"Pap'll be mighty much obleeged to you, I can tell you. Everybody goes away when I want them to help me tow the **130** raft ashore, and I can't do it by myself."

"Well, that's infernal mean. Odd, too. Say, boy, what's the matter with your father?"

"It's the—a—the—well, it ain't anything, much."

They stopped pulling. It warn't but a mighty little ways to the raft, now. One says:

"Boy, that's a lie. What *is* the matter with your pap? Answer up square, now, and it'll be the better for you."

"I will, sir, I will, honest—but don't leave us, please. It's the—the—gentlemen, if you'll only pull ahead, and let me **140**

heave you the head-line, you won't have to come a-near the raft—please do."

"Set her back, John, set her back!" says one. They backed water. "Keep away, boy—keep to looard.[4] Confound it, I just expect the wind has blowed it to us. Your pap's got the smallpox, and you know it precious well. Why didn't you come out and say so? Do you want to spread it all over?"

"Well," says I, a-blubbering, "I've told everybody before, and then they just went away and left us."

"Poor devil, there's something in that. We are right down **150** sorry for you, but we—well, hang it, we don't want the smallpox, you see. Look here, I'll tell you what to do. Don't you try to land by yourself, or you'll smash everything to pieces. You float along down about twenty miles and you'll come to a town on the left-hand side of the river. It will be long after sun-up, then, and when you ask for help, you tell them your folks are all down with chills and fever. Don't be a fool again, and let people guess what is the matter. Now we're trying to do you a kindness; so you just put twenty miles between us, that's a good boy. It wouldn't do any good to land yonder where the **160** light is—it's only a wood-yard. Say—I reckon your father's poor, and I'm bound to say he's in pretty hard luck. Here—I'll put a twenty dollar gold piece on this board, and you get it when it floats by. I feel mighty mean to leave you, but my kingdom! it won't do to fool with small-pox, don't you see?"

"Hold on, Parker," says the other man, "here's a twenty to put on the board for me. Good-bye, boy, you do as Mr. Parker told you, and you'll be all right."

"That's so, my boy—good-bye, good-bye. If you see any runaway niggers, you get help and nab them, and you can **170** make some money by it."

"Good-bye, sir," says I, "I won't let no runaway niggers get by me if I can help it."

They went off, and I got aboard the raft, feeling bad and low, because I knowed very well I had done wrong, and I see it warn't no use for me to try to learn to do right; a body that don't get *started* right when he's little, ain't got no show[5]—when the pinch comes there ain't nothing to back him up and keep him to his work, and so he gets beat. Then I thought a minute, and says to myself, hold on,—s'pose you'd a done right and give **180** Jim up; would you felt better than what you do now? No, says I, I'd feel bad—I'd feel just the same way I do now. Well, then, says I, what's the use you learning to do right, when it's troublesome to do right and ain't no trouble to do wrong, and the wages is just the same? I was stuck. I couldn't answer that. So I reckoned I wouldn't bother no more about it, but after this always do whichever come handiest at the time. . . .

Russian Realism: Dostoevsky and Tolstoy

More pessimistic than Dickens or Twain, and more profoundly analytic of the universal human condition, were the Russian novelists Fyodor Dostoevsky (1821–1881) and Leo Tolstoy (1828–1910). Both men were born and bred in wealth, but both turned against upper-class Russian society and sympathized with the plight of the lower

---

[4]Leeward; away from the wind.
[5]Has no chance.

Figure 30.4 ILYA REPIN, *Portrait of Leo Tolstoy*, 1887. Oil on canvas, Tretyakov Gallery, Moscow. Novosti, London.

classes. Tolstoy ultimately renounced his wealth and property and went to live and work among the peasants. Tolstoy's historical novel *War and Peace* (1869), often hailed as the greatest example of realistic Russian fiction, traces the progress of five families whose destinies unroll against the background of Napoleon's invasion of Russia in 1812. In this sprawling narrative, as in many of his other novels, Tolstoy exposes the privileged position of the nobility and the cruel exploitation of the great masses of Russian people. This task, along with sympathy for the cause of Russian nationalism in general, was shared by Tolstoy's friend and admirer, Ilya Repin (1844–1930), whose portrait of Tolstoy brings the writer to life with skillful candor (Figure **30.4**). Russia's preeminent realist painter, Repin rendered with detailed accuracy the miserable lives of ordinary Russians—peasants, laborers, and beggars—in genre paintings that might well serve as illustrations for the novels of Tolstoy and Dostoevsky.

In contrast with Tolstoy, Dostoevsky pays greater attention to philosophical and psychological issues. The characters in Dostoevsky's novels are often victims of a dual plight: poverty and conscience. Their energies are foiled by the struggle to resolve their own contradictory passions.

The novels *Crime and Punishment* (1866), *The Possessed* (1871), and *The Brothers Karamazov* (1880) feature protagonists whose irrational behavior and its psychological consequences form the central theme of the novel. In *Crime and Punishment*, Raskolnikov, a young, poor student, murders an old woman and her younger sister; his crime goes undetected. Thereafter, he struggles with guilt—the self-punishment for his criminal act. He also struggles with the problems arising from one's freedom to commit evil. In the following excerpt, the protagonist addresses the moral question of whether extraordinary individuals, by dint of their uniqueness, have the right to commit immoral acts. The conversation, which takes place between Raskolnikov and his friends, is spurred by an article on crime that Raskolnikov had published in a journal shortly after dropping out of university. This excerpt is typical of Dostoevsky's fondness for developing character through monologue and dialogue, rather than through descriptive detail. Dostoevsky's realism (and his genius) lies in the way in which he forces the reader to understand the character as that character tries to understand himself.

READING 5.22 From Dostoevsky's *Crime and Punishment* (1866)

"... the 'extraordinary' man has the right ... I don't mean a [1]
formal, official right, but he has the right in himself, to permit
his conscience to overstep ... certain obstacles, but only in the
event that his ideas (which may sometimes be salutary for all
mankind) require it for their fulfilment. You are pleased to say
that my article is not clear; I am ready to elucidate it for you, as
far as possible. Perhaps I am not mistaken in supposing that is
what you want. Well, then. In my opinion, if the discoveries of
Kepler and Newton, by some combination of circumstances,
could not have become known to the world in any other way [10]
than by sacrificing the lives of one, or ten, or a hundred or more
people, who might have hampered or in some way been
obstacles in the path of those discoveries, then Newton would
have had the right, or might even have been under an obligation
... to *remove* those ten or a hundred people, so that his
discoveries might be revealed to all mankind. It does not follow
from this, of course, that Newton had the right to kill any Tom,
Dick, or Harry he fancied, or go out stealing from market-stalls
every day. I remember further that in my article I developed the
idea that all the ... well, for example, the law-givers and [20]
regulators of human society, beginning with the most ancient,
and going on to Lycurgus, Solon, Mahomet, Napoleon and so

¹Raskolnikov's views are similar to those expressed by Napoleon III in his book *Life of Julius Caesar*. The newspaper *Golos* (*Voice*) had recently summarized the English *Saturday Review*'s analysis of Napoleon's ideas about the right of exceptional individuals (such as Lycurgus, Mahomet, and Napoleon I) to transgress laws and even to shed blood. The book appeared in Paris in March 1865; the Russian translation in April! [Lycurgus: the founder of the military regime of ancient Sparta; Mahomet: Muhammad, the prophet of Allah and founder of the religion Islam; Solon: statesman and reformer in sixth-century-B.C.E. Athens.]

on, were without exception transgressors,[1] by the very fact that in making a new law they *ipso facto* broke an old one, handed down from their fathers and held sacred by society; and, of course, they did not stop short of shedding blood, provided only that the blood (however innocent and however heroically shed in defence of the ancient law) was shed to their advantage. It is remarkable that the greater part of these benefactors and law-givers of humanity were particularly blood-thirsty. In a word, I deduce that all of them, not only the great ones, but also those who diverge ever so slightly from the beaten track, those, that is, who are just barely capable of saying something new, must, by their nature, inevitably be criminals—in a greater or less degree, naturally. Otherwise they would find it too hard to leave their rut, and they cannot, of course, consent to remain in the rut, again by the very fact of their nature; and in my opinion they ought not to consent. In short, you see that up to this point there is nothing specially new here. It has all been printed, and read, a thousand times before. As for my division of people into ordinary and extraordinary, that I agree was a little arbitrary, but I do not insist on exact figures. Only I do believe in the main principle of my idea. That consists in people being, by the law of nature, divided *in general* into two categories: into a lower (of ordinary people), that is, into material serving only for the reproduction of its own kind, and into people properly speaking, that is, those who have the gift or talent of saying *something new* in their sphere. There are endless subdivisions, of course, but the distinctive characteristics of the two categories are fairly well marked: the first group, that is the material, are, generally speaking, by nature staid and conservative, they live in obedience and like it. In my opinion they ought to obey because that is their destiny, and there is nothing at all degrading to them in it. The second group are all law-breakers and transgressors, or are inclined that way, in the measure of their capacities. The aims of these people are, of course, relative and very diverse; for the most part they require, in widely different contexts, the destruction of what exists in the name of better things. But if it is necessary for one of them, for the fulfilment of his ideas, to march over corpses, or wade through blood, then in my opinion he may in all conscience authorize himself to wade through blood—in proportion, however, to his idea and the degree of its importance—mark that. It is in that sense only that I speak in my article of their right to commit crime. (You will remember that we really began with the question of legality.) There is, however, not much cause for alarm: the masses hardly ever recognize this right of theirs, and behead or hang them (more or less), and in this way, quite properly, fulfil their conservative function, although in following generations these same masses put their former victims on a pedestal and worship them (more or less). The first category are always the masters of the present, but the second are the lords of the future. The first preserve the world and increase and multiply; the second move the world and guide it to its goal. Both have an absolutely equal right to exist. In short, for me all men have completely equivalent rights, and—*vive la guerre éternelle*—until we have built the New Jerusalem, of course!"[2]

"You do believe in the New Jerusalem, then?"

"Yes, I do," answered Raskolnikov firmly; he said this with his eyes fixed on one spot on the carpet, as they had been all through his long tirade.

"A-and you believe in God? Forgive me for being so inquisitive."

"Yes, I do," repeated Raskolnikov, raising his eyes to Porfiry.

"A-a-and do you believe in the raising of Lazarus?"

"Y-yes. Why are you asking all this?"

"You believe in it literally?"

"Yes."

"Ah . . . I was curious to know. Forgive me. But, returning to the previous subject—they are not always put to death. Some, on the contrary . . ."

"Triumph during their lifetime? Oh, yes, some achieve their ends while they still live, and then . . ."

"They begin to mete out capital punishment themselves?"

"If necessary, and, you know, it is most usually so. Your observation is very keen-witted."

"Thank you. But tell me: how do you distinguish these extraordinary people from the ordinary? Do signs and portents appear when they are born? I mean to say that we could do with rather greater accuracy here, with, so to speak, rather more outward signs: please excuse the natural anxiety of a practical and well-meaning man, but couldn't there be, for example, some special clothing, couldn't they carry some kind of brand or something? . . . Because, you will agree, if there should be some sort of mix-up, and somebody from one category imagined that he belonged to the other and began 'to remove all obstacles,' as you so happily put it, then really . . ."

"Oh, that very frequently happens! This observation of yours is even more penetrating than the last."

"Thank you."

"Not at all. But you must please realize that the mistake is possible only among the first group, that is, the 'ordinary' people (as I have called them, perhaps not altogether happily). In spite of their inborn inclination to obey, quite a number of them, by some freak of nature such as is not impossible even among cows, like to fancy that they are progressives, 'destroyers,' and propagators of the 'new world,' and all this quite sincerely. At the same time, they really take no heed of *new people*; they even despise them, as reactionary and incapable of elevated thinking. But, in my opinion, they cannot constitute a real danger, and you really have nothing to worry about, because they never go far. They might sometimes be scourged for their zealotry, to remind them of their place; there is no need even for anyone to carry out the punishment: they will do it themselves, because they are very well conducted: some of them do one another this service, and others do it for themselves with their own hands . . . And they impose on themselves various public penances besides—the result is beautifully edifying, and in short, you have nothing to worry about . . . This is a law of nature."

"Well, at least you have allayed my anxieties on that score a little; but here is another worry: please tell me, are there many of these people who have the right to destroy others, of these 'extraordinary' people? I am, of course, prepared to bow down

[2]New Jerusalem, symbolic of the ideal order, after the end of time, is a Heaven on Earth, a new paradise. See the description in Revelation 21 (the Apocalypse). The French phrase means, "Long live perpetual war."

before them, but all the same you will agree that it would be terrible if there were very many of them, eh?"

"Oh, don't let that trouble you either," went on Raskolnikov in the same tone. "Generally speaking, there are extremely few people, strangely few, born, who have a new idea, or are even **140** capable of saying anything at all *new*. One thing only is clear, that the ordering of human births, all these categories and subdivisions, must be very carefully and exactly regulated by some law of nature. This law is, of course, unknown at present, but I believe that it exists, and consequently that it may be known. The great mass of men, the common stuff of humanity, exist on the earth only in order that at last, by some endeavour, some process, that remains as yet mysterious, some happy conjunction of race and breeding, there should struggle into life a being, one in a thousand, capable, in **150** however small a degree, of standing on his own feet. Perhaps one in ten thousand (I am speaking approximately, by way of illustration) is born with a slightly greater degree of independence, and one in a hundred thousand with even more. One genius may emerge among millions, and a really great genius, perhaps, as the crowning point of many thousands of millions of men. In short, I have not been able to look into the retort whence all this proceeds. But a definite law there must be, and is; it cannot be a matter of chance. . . ."

The Literary Heroines of Flaubert and Chopin

Nineteenth-century novelists shared a special interest in examining conflicts between social conventions and personal values, especially as they affected the everyday lives of women. Gustave Flaubert's *Madame Bovary* (1857), Tolstoy's *Anna Karenina* (1877), and Kate Chopin's *The Awakening* (1899) are representative of the nineteenth-century writer's concern with the tragic consequences following from the defiance of established social and moral codes by passionate female figures. The heroines in these novels do not create the world in their own image; rather, the world—or more specifically, the social and economic environment—molds them and governs their destinies. Flaubert (1821–1880), whom critics have called "the inventor of the modern novel," stripped his novels of sentimentality and of all preconceived notions of behavior. He aimed at a precise description of not only the stuff of the physical world but also the motivations of his characters.

In *Madame Bovary*, his most famous novel, Flaubert tells the story of a middle-class woman who desperately seeks to escape the boredom of her mundane existence. Educated in a convent and married to a dull, small-town physician, Emma Bovary tries to live out the fantasies that fill the pages of her favorite romance novels, but her efforts to do so prove disastrous and lead to her ultimate destruction. Flaubert reconstructs with a minimum of interpretation the details of Emma's provincial surroundings and her bleak marriage. A meticulous observer, he sought *le mot juste* ("the exact word") to describe each concrete object and each psychological state—a practice that often prevented him from writing more than one or two pages of prose per week. Since the novel achieves its full effect through the gradual development of plot and character, no brief excerpt can possibly do it justice. Nevertheless, the following excerpt, which describes the deterioration of the adulterous affair between Emma Bovary and the young clerk Léon, illustrates Flaubert's ability to characterize places and persons by means of the fastidious selection and accumulation of descriptive details.

READING 5.23 From Flaubert's *Madame Bovary* (1857)

In the end Léon had promised never to see Emma again; and he **1** reproached himself for not having kept his word, especially considering all the trouble and reproaches she still probably held in store for him—not to mention the jokes his fellow clerks cracked every morning around the stove. Besides, he was about to be promoted to head clerk: this was the time to turn over a new leaf. So he gave up playing the flute and said good-bye to exalted sentiments and romantic dreams. There isn't a bourgeois alive who in the ferment of his youth, if only for a day or for a minute, hasn't thought himself capable of **10** boundless passions and noble exploits. The sorriest little woman-chaser has dreamed of Oriental queens; in a corner of every notary's heart lie the moldy remains of a poet.

These days it only bored him when Emma suddenly burst out sobbing on his breast: like people who can stand only a certain amount of music, he was drowsy and apathetic amidst the shrillness of her love; his heart had grown deaf to its subtler overtones.

By now they knew each other too well: no longer did they experience, in their mutual possession, that wonder that **20** multiplies the joy a hundredfold. She was as surfeited with him as he was tired of her. Adultery, Emma was discovering, could be as banal as marriage.

But what way out was there? She felt humiliated by the degradation of such pleasures; but to no avail: she continued to cling to them, out of habit or out of depravity; and every day she pursued them more desperately, destroying all possible happiness by her excessive demands. She blamed Léon for her disappointed hopes, as though he had betrayed her; and she even longed for a catastrophe that would bring about their **30** separation, since she hadn't the courage to bring it about herself.

Still, she continued to write him loving letters, faithful to the idea that a woman must always write to her lover.

But as her pen flew over the paper she was aware of the presence of another man, a phantom embodying her most ardent memories, the most beautiful things she had read and her strongest desires. In the end he became so real and accessible that she tingled with excitement, unable though she was to picture him clearly, so hidden was he, godlike, under his **40** manifold attributes. He dwelt in that enchanted realm where silken ladders swing from balconies moon-bright and flower-scented. She felt him near her: he was coming—coming to ravish her entirely in a kiss. And the next moment she would drop back to earth, shattered; for these rapturous love-dreams drained her more than the greatest orgies.

Almost immediately after *Madame Bovary* appeared (in the form of six installments in the *Revue de Paris*), the novel was denounced as an offense against public and religious morals, and Flaubert, as well as the publisher and the printer of the *Revue*, was brought to trial before a criminal court. All three men were ultimately acquitted, but not before an eloquent lawyer had defended all the passages (including those in Reading 5.23) that had been condemned as wanton and immoral.

A similar situation befell the American writer Kate Chopin (1851–1904), whose novel *The Awakening* was banned in her native city of St. Louis shortly after its publication in 1899. The novel, a frank examination of female sexual passion and marital infidelity, violated the tastes of the society in which Chopin had been reared and to which she returned in 1883. Unlike Flaubert, whose novels convey the staleness and inescapability of French provincial life, many of Chopin's stories deliberately ignore the specifics of time and place. Others are set in Louisiana, where Chopin lived for twelve years with her husband and six children. Chopin was successful in selling her Louisiana dialect stories, many of which explore matters of class, race, and gender within the world of Creole society, but her novels fell into obscurity soon after her death: *The Awakening*, whose heroine defies convention by committing adultery, did not receive positive critical attention until the 1950s.

While Chopin absorbed the realist strategies and social concerns of Flaubert, she brought to her prose a unique sensitivity to the nuances of human (and especially female) behavior—a challenge to popular romantic female stereotypes (see chapter 28). Her work also reveals a remarkable talent for narrating a story with jewel-like precision. Chopin's taut descriptive style reaches unparalleled heights in the short prose piece known as "The Story of an Hour." Here, the protagonist's brief taste of liberation takes on an ironic fatal turn.

READING 5.24   Kate Chopin's "The Story of an Hour" ("The Dream of an Hour") (1894)

Knowing that Mrs. Mallard was afflicted with a heart trouble, great care was taken to break to her as gently as possible the news of her husband's death.   1

It was her sister Josephine who told her, in broken sentences: veiled hints that revealed in half concealing. Her husband's friend Richards was there, too, near her. It was he who had been in the newspaper office when intelligence of the railroad disaster was received, with Brently Mallard's name leading the list of "killed." He had only taken time to assure himself of its truth by a second telegram, and had hastened   10 to forestall any less careful, less tender friend in bearing the sad message.

She did not hear the story as many women have heard the same, with a paralysed inability to accept its significance. She wept at once, with a sudden, wild abandonment, in her sister's arms. When the storm of grief had spent itself she went away to her room alone. She would have no one follow her.

There stood, facing the open window, a comfortable, roomy armchair. Into this she sank, pressed down by a physical exhaustion that haunted her body and seemed to reach into   20 her soul.

She could see in the open square before her house the tops of trees that were all aquiver with the new spring life. The delicious breath of rain was in the air. In the street below a peddler was crying his wares. The notes of a distant song which some one was singing reached her faintly, and countless sparrows were twittering in the eaves.

There were patches of blue sky showing here and there through the clouds that had met and piled one above the other in the west facing her window.   30

She sat with her head thrown back upon the cushion of the chair, quite motionless, except when a sob came into her throat and shook her, as a child who has cried itself to sleep continues to sob in its dreams.

She was young, with a fair, calm face, whose lines bespoke repression and even a certain strength. But now there was a dull stare in her eyes, whose gaze was fixed away off yonder on one of those patches of blue sky. It was not a glance of reflection, but rather a suspension of intelligent thought.

There was something coming to her and she was waiting for   40 it, fearfully. What was it? She did not know; it was too subtle and elusive to name. But she felt it, creeping out of the sky, reaching toward her through the sounds, the scents, the color that filled the air.

Now her bosom rose and fell tumultuously. She was beginning to recognize this thing that was approaching to possess her, and she was striving to beat it back with her will—as powerless as her white slender hands would have been.

When she abandoned herself a little whispered word   50 escaped her slight parted lips. She said it over and over under her breath: "free, free, free!" The vacant stare and the look of terror that had followed it went from her eyes. They stayed keen and bright. Her pulses beat fast, and the coursing blood warmed and relaxed every inch of her body.

She did not stop to ask if it were not a monstrous joy that held her. A clear and exalted perception enabled her to dismiss the suggestion as trivial.

She knew that she would weep again when she saw the kind, tender hands folded in death: fixed and grey and dead.   60 But she saw beyond that bitter moment a long procession of years to come that would belong to her absolutely. And she opened and spread her arms out to them in welcome.

There would be no one to live for her during those coming years; she would live for herself. There would be no powerful will bending hers in that blind persistence with which men and women believe they have a right to impose a private will upon a fellow-creature. A kind intention or a cruel intention made the act seem no less a crime as she looked upon it in that brief moment of illumination.   70

And yet she loved him—sometimes. Often she had not. What did it matter! What could love, the unsolved mystery, count for in the face of this possession of self-assertion which she suddenly recognized as the strongest impulse of her being!

"Free! Body and soul free!" she kept whispering.

Josephine was kneeling before the keyhole, imploring for admission. "Louise, open the door! I beg; open the door—you will make yourself ill. What are you doing, Louise? For heaven's sake open the door."

"Go away. I'm not making myself ill." No: she was drinking 80 in a very elixir of life through that open window.

Her fancy was running riot along those days ahead of her. Spring days, and summer days, and all sorts of days that would be her own. She breathed a quick prayer that life might be long. It was only yesterday she had thought with a shudder that life might be long.

She arose at length and opened the door to her sister's importunities. There was a feverish triumph in her eyes, and she carried herself unwittingly like a goddess of Victory. She clasped her sister's wrist, and together they descended the 90 stairs. Richards stood waiting for them at the bottom.

Some one was opening the front door with a latchkey. It was Brently Mallard who entered, a little travel-stained, composedly carrying his grip-sack and umbrella. He had been far from the scene of accident, and did not even know there had been one. He stood amazed at Josephine's piercing cry; at Richards' quick motion to screen him from the view of his wife.

But Richards was too late.

When the doctors came they said she had died of heart 100 disease—of joy that kills.

Zola and the Naturalistic Novel

Kate Chopin's contemporary Emile Zola (1840–1902) initiated a variant form of literary realism known as *naturalism*. Somewhat like realism, naturalist fiction was based on the premise that life should be represented objectively and without embellishment or idealization. But naturalists differed from realists in taking a deterministic approach that showed human beings as products of environmental or hereditary factors over which they had little or no control. Just as Marx held that economic life shaped all aspects of culture, so naturalists believed that material and social elements determined human conduct. In his passion to describe the world with absolute fidelity, Zola amassed notebooks of information on a wide variety of subjects, including coal mining, the railroads, the stock market, and the science of surgery. Zola treated the novel as an exact study of commonplace, material existence. He presented a slice of life that showed how social and material circumstances influenced human behavior. Zola's subjects were as brutally uncompromising as his style. *The Grog Shop* (1877) offered a terrifying picture of the effects of alcoholism on industrial workers; *Germinal* (1885) exposed the bitter lives of French coal miners; and his most scandalous novel, *Nana* (1880), was a scathing portrayal of a beautiful but unscrupulous prostitute.

Strong elements of naturalism are found in the novels of many late nineteenth-century writers in both Europe and America. Thomas Hardy (1840–1928) in England, and Stephen Crane (1871–1900), Jack London (1876–1916), and Theodore Dreiser (1871–1945) in America are the most notable of the English-language literary naturalists.

The Plays of Ibsen

The Norwegian dramatist Henrik Ibsen (1828–1906) brought to the late nineteenth-century stage concerns similar to those that appeared in the novels of the European and American realists. A moralist and a student of human behavior, Ibsen rebelled against the artificial social conventions that led people to pursue self-deluding and hypocritical lives. Ibsen was deeply concerned with contemporary issues and social problems. He shocked the public by writing prose dramas that addressed such controversial subjects as insanity, incest, and venereal disease. At the same time, he explored universal themes of conflict between the individual and society, between love and duty, and between husband and wife.

In 1879, Ibsen wrote the classic drama of female liberation, *A Doll's House*. The play traces the awakening of a middle-class woman to the meaninglessness of her role as "a doll-wife" living in "a doll's house." Threatened with blackmail over a debt she had incurred years earlier, Nora Helmer looks to her priggish, egotistical husband Torvald for protection. But Torvald too is a victim of the small-mindedness and social restraints of his time and place. When he fails to rally to his wife's defense, Nora realizes the frailty of her dependent lifestyle. She comes to recognize that her first obligation is to herself and to her dignity as a reasonable human being. Nora's revelation brings to life, in the forceful language of everyday speech, the psychological tension between male and female that Mill had analyzed only ten years earlier in his treatise on the subjection of women. Ibsen does not resolve the question of whether a woman's duties to husband and children come before her duty to herself; yet, as is suggested in the following exchange between Nora and Torvald (excerpted from the last scene of *A Doll's House*), Nora's self-discovery precipitates the end of her marriage. Nora shuts the door on the illusions of the past as emphatically as Ibsen—a half-century after Goethe's *Faust*—may be said to have turned his back on the world of romantic idealism.

READING 5.25 From Ibsen's *A Doll's House* (1879)

Act III, Final Scene

[Late at night in the Helmers' living room. Instead of retiring, Nora suddenly appears in street clothes.]

Helmer: . . . What's all this? I thought you were going to 1 bed. You've changed your dress?

Nora: Yes, Torvald; I've changed my dress.

Helmer: But what for? At this hour?

Nora: I shan't sleep tonight.

Helmer: But, Nora dear—

Nora *[looking at her watch]:* It's not so very late—Sit down, Torvald; we have a lot to talk about.

[She sits at one side of the table.]

Helmer: Nora—what does this mean? Why that stern 10 expression?

Nora: Sit down. It'll take some time. I have a lot to say to you.

[Helmer sits at the other side of the table.]

Helmer: You frighten me, Nora. I don't understand you.

Nora: No, that's just it. You don't understand me; and I have never understood you either—until tonight. No, don't interrupt me. Just listen to what I have to say. This is to be a final settlement, Torvald.

Helmer: How do you mean?

Nora *[after a short silence]*: Doesn't anything special strike you as we sit here like this?

Helmer: I don't think so—why?

Nora: It doesn't occur to you, does it, that though we've been married for eight years, this is the first time that we two—man and wife—have sat down for a serious talk?

Helmer: What do you mean by serious?

Nora: During eight whole years, no—more than that—ever since the first day we met—we have never exchanged so much as one serious word about serious things.

Helmer: Why should I perpetually burden you with all my cares and problems? How could you possibly help me to solve them?

Nora: I'm not talking about cares and problems. I'm simply saying we've never once sat down seriously and tried to get to the bottom of anything.

Helmer: But, Nora, darling—why should you be concerned with serious thoughts?

Nora: That's the whole point! You've never understood me—A great injustice has been done me, Torvald; first by Father, and then by you.

Helmer: What a thing to say! No two people on earth could ever have loved you more than we have!

Nora *[shaking her head]*: You never loved me. You just thought it was fun to be in love with me.

Helmer: This is fantastic!

Nora: Perhaps. But it's true all the same. While I was still at home I used to hear Father airing his opinions and they became my opinions; or if I didn't happen to agree, I kept it to myself—he would have been displeased otherwise. He used to call me his doll-baby, and played with me as I played with my dolls. Then I came to live in your house—

Helmer: What an expression to use about our marriage!

Nora *[undisturbed]*: I mean—from Father's hands I passed into yours. You arranged everything according to your tastes, and I acquired the same tastes, or I pretended to—I'm not sure which—a little of both, perhaps. Looking back on it all, it seems to me I've lived here like a beggar, from hand to mouth. I've lived by performing tricks for you, Torvald. But that's the way you wanted it. You and Father have done me a great wrong. You've prevented me from becoming a real person.

Helmer: Nora, how can you be so ungrateful and unreasonable! Haven't you been happy here?

Nora: No, never. I thought I was; but I wasn't really.

Helmer: Not—not happy!

Nora: No, only merry. You've always been so kind to me. But our home has never been anything but a play-room. I've been your doll-wife, just as at home I was Papa's doll-child. And the children, in turn, have been my dolls. I thought it fun when you played games with me, just as they thought it fun when I played games with them. And that's been our marriage, Torvald.

Helmer: There may be a grain of truth in what you say, even though it is distorted and exaggerated. From now on things will be different. Play-time is over now; tomorrow lessons begin!

Nora: Whose lessons? Mine, or the children's?

Helmer: Both, if you wish it, Nora, dear.

Nora: Torvald, I'm afraid you're not the man to teach me to be a real wife to you.

Helmer: How can you say that?

Nora: And I'm certainly not fit to teach the children.

Helmer: Nora!

Nora: Didn't you just say, a moment ago, you didn't dare trust them to me?

Helmer: That was in the excitement of the moment! You mustn't take it so seriously!

Nora: But you were quite right, Torvald. That job is beyond me; there's another job I must do first: I must try and educate myself. You could never help me to do that; I must do it quite alone. So, you see—that's why I'm going to leave you.

Helmer: *[jumping up]*. What did you say—?

Nora: I shall never get to know myself—I shall never learn to face reality—unless I stand alone. So I can't stay with you any longer.

Helmer: Nora! Nora!

Nora: I am going at once. I'm sure Kristine will let me stay with her tonight—

Helmer: But, Nora—this is madness! I shan't allow you to do this. I shall forbid it!

Nora: You no longer have the power to forbid me anything. I'll only take a few things with me—those that belong to me. I shall never again accept anything from you.

Helmer: Have you lost your senses?

Nora: Tomorrow I'll go home—to what was my home, I mean. It might be easier for me there, to find something to do.

Helmer: You talk like an ignorant child, Nora—!

Nora: Yes. That's just why I must educate myself.

Helmer: To leave your home—to leave your husband, and your children! What do you suppose people would say to that?

Nora: It makes no difference. This is something I must do.

Helmer: It's inconceivable! Don't you realize you'd be betraying your most sacred duty?

Nora: What do you consider that to be?

Helmer: Your duty towards your husband and your children—I surely don't have to tell you that!

Nora: I've another duty just as sacred.

Helmer: Nonsense! What duty do you mean?

Nora: My duty towards myself.

Helmer: Remember—before all else you are a wife and mother.

Nora: I don't believe that any more. I believe that before all else I am a human being, just as you are—or at least that I should try and become one. I know that most people would agree with you, Torvald—and that's what they say in books. But I can no longer be satisfied with what most people say—or what they write in books. I must think things out for myself—get clear about them.

Helmer: Surely your position in your home is clear enough? Have you no sense of religion? Isn't that an infallible guide to you?

Nora: But don't you see, Torvald—I don't really know what religion is.

Helmer: Nora! How *can* you!

Nora: All I know about it is what Pastor Hansen told me when I was confirmed. He taught me what he thought religion was—said it was this and that. As soon as I get away by myself, I shall have to look into that matter too, try and decide whether what he taught me was right—or whether it's right for me, at least. 140

Helmer: A nice way for a young woman to talk! It's unheard of! If religion means nothing to you, I'll appeal to your conscience; you must have some sense of ethics, I suppose? Answer me! Or have you none?

Nora: It's hard for me to answer you, Torvald. I don't think I know—all these things bewilder me. But I do know that I think quite differently from you about them. I've discovered that the law, for instance, is quite different from what I had imagined; but I find it hard to believe it can be right. It seems it's criminal for a woman to try and spare her old, sick, father, or save her 150 husband's life! I can't agree with that.

Helmer: You talk like a child. You have no understanding of the society we live in.

Nora: No, I haven't. But I'm going to try and learn. I want to find out which of us is right—society or I.

Helmer: You are ill, Nora; you have a touch of fever; you're quite beside yourself.

Nora: I've never felt so sure—so clear-headed—as I do tonight.

Helmer: "Sure and clear-headed" enough to leave your 160 husband and your children?

Nora: Yes.

Helmer: Then there is only one explanation possible.

Nora: What?

Helmer: You don't love me any more.

Nora: No; that is just it.

Helmer: Nora!—What are you saying!

Nora: It makes me so unhappy, Torvald; for you've always been so kind to me. But I can't help it. I don't love you any more. 170

Helmer *[mastering himself with difficulty]*: You feel "sure and clear-headed" about this too?

Nora: Yes, utterly sure. That's why I can't stay here any longer. . . .

1835 William H. F. Talbot (English) invents the negative–positive photographic process

1837 Louis J. M. Daguerre (French) uses a copper plate coated with silver to produce the first daguerreotype

1860 production begins on the first Winchester repeating rifle (in America)

1866 explosive dynamite is first produced in Sweden

1888 George Eastman (American) perfects the "Kodak" box camera

Realism in the Visual Arts
The Birth of Photography

One of the most significant factors in the development of the realist mentality was the birth of photography. While a painting or an engraving might bring to life the content of the artist's imagination, a photograph offered an authentic record of a moment vanished in time. Photography, literally "writing with light," had its beginnings in 1835, when William Henry Fox Talbot (1800–1877) invented the fundamental negative–positive process that allowed multiple prints to be produced from a single exposure. Talbot's French contemporary, Louis J. M. Daguerre (1787–1851), developed a different process which used a light-sensitive metal plate and fixed the image with common chemicals. Unlike Talbot's images, Daguerre's could not be reproduced—each image was unique. Nevertheless, in the next decades, the more widely publicized and technically improved product, known as a *daguerreotype*, came into popularity throughout Europe and America, where it fulfilled a growing demand for portraits. Gradual improvements in camera lenses and in the chemicals used to develop the visible image hastened the rise of photography as a popular device for recording the physical world with unprecedented accuracy.

Photography presented an obvious challenge to the authority of the artist, who, throughout history, had assumed the role of nature's imitator. But artists were slow

Figure 30.5 JULIA MARGARET CAMERON, *Whisper of the Muse (G. F. Watts and Children)*, ca. 1865. Photograph. The Royal Photographic Society, Bath.

nesses. Photographs were used as calling cards and to record the faces of notable individuals (see Figure 28.4), as well as those of criminals, whose "mug shots" became a useful tool for the young science of criminology. Some photographers, such as the British pioneer Julia Margaret Cameron (1815–1879), used the camera to recreate the style of romantic painting. Imitating the effects of the artist's paintbrush, Cameron's soft-focus portraits are romantic in spirit and sentiment (Figure **30.5**). Others used the camera to establish themselves as masters of unvarnished realism. The French master Gaspart-Félix Tournachon, known as Nadar (1820–1910), made vivid portrait studies of such celebrities as George Sand, Berlioz, and Sarah Bernhardt. Nadar was the first to experiment with aerial photography (see Figure 30.12). He also introduced the use of electric light in a series of extraordinary photographs documenting the sewers and catacombs beneath the city of Paris.

Inevitably, nineteenth-century photographs served as social documents: The black-and-white images of poverty-stricken families and ram-shackle tenements produced by Thomas Annan (1829–1887), for instance, record with gritty realism the notorious slums of nineteenth-century Glasgow, Scotland (Figure **30.6**). Such photographs could easily illustrate the novels of Charles Dickens. In a similar vein, the documentary photographs of the American Civil War (1861–1865) produced by Mathew B. Brady (1823–1896) and his staff testify to the importance of the photographer as a chronicler of human life. Brady's 3,500 Civil War photographs include mundane scenes of barracks and munitions as well as unflinching views of human carnage (Figure **30.7**). By the end of the century, the Kodak "point and shoot" handheld camera gave vast numbers of people the freedom to take their own photographic images.

to realize the long-range impact of photography—that is, the camera's potential to liberate artists from reproducing the physical "look" of nature. Critics proclaimed that photographs, as authentic facsimiles of the physical world, should serve artists as aids to achieving greater realism in canvas painting; and many artists did indeed use photographs as factual resources for their compositions. Nevertheless, by mid-century, both Europeans and Americans were using the camera for a wide variety of purposes: They made topographical studies of exotic geographic sites, recorded architectural monuments, and produced thousands of portraits. Photography provided ordinary people with portrait images that had previously only been available to those who could afford painted like-

Figure 30.7 MATHEW B. BRADY or staff, *Dead Confederate Soldier with Gun, Petersburg, Virginia*, 1865. Photograph. The Library of Congress, Washington, D.C.

Courbet and French Realist Painting

In painting no less than in literature and photography, realism came to challenge the romantic style. The realist preference for concrete, matter-of-fact depictions of everyday life provided a sober alternative to both the remote, exotic, and heroic imagery of the romantics and the noble and elevated themes of the neoclassicists. Obedient to the credo that artists must confront the experiences and appearances of their own time, realist painters abandoned the nostalgic landscapes and heroic themes of romantic art in favor of compositions depicting the consequences of industrialism (see Figure 30.2) and the lives of ordinary men and women.

The leading realist of nineteenth-century French painting was Gustave Courbet (1819–1877). A farmer's son, Courbet was a self-taught artist, an outspoken socialist, and a staunch defender of the realist cause. "A painter," he protested, "should paint only what he can see." Indeed, most of Courbet's works—portraits, landscapes, and contemporary scenes—remain true to the tangible facts of his immediate vision. With the challenge "Show me an angel and I'll paint one," he taunted both the romantics and the neoclassicists. Not angels but ordinary individuals in their actual settings and circumstances interested Courbet.

In *The Stone-Breakers*, Courbet depicted two rural laborers performing the most menial of physical tasks (Figure **30.8**). The painting, which Courbet's friend Proudhon called "the first socialist picture," outraged the critics because its subject matter was mundane and its figures were crude, ragged, and totally unidealized. Moreover, the figures were positioned with their backs turned toward the viewer, thus violating, by nineteenth-century standards, the rules of propriety and decorum enshrined in French academic art (see chapter 21). But despite such "violations" Courbet's painting appealed to the masses. In a country whose population was still two-thirds rural and largely poor, the stolid dignity of hard labor was a popular subject—so popular, in fact, that it was often

Figure 30.8 GUSTAVE COURBET, *The Stone-Breakers*, 1849. Oil on canvas, 5 ft. 3 in. × 8 ft. 6 in. Formerly Gemäldegalerie, Dresden (destroyed 1945).

romanticized. A comparison of *The Stone-Breakers* with a study by Jean-François Millet (1814–1875) for his painting *The Gleaners* (Figure **30.9**) illustrates the difference between Courbet's undiluted realism and Millet's romanticized realism. Millet's workers are as ordinary and anony-mous as Courbet's, but they are also dignified and graceful, betraying a distant kinship with Raphael's heroic figures (see chapter 17). Whereas Courbet's workers seem trapped behind the narrow roadside bank, Millet's dominate a broad and ennobling vista. And while Courbet's scene has

Figure 30.9 JEAN-FRANÇOIS MILLET, *The Gleaners*, ca. 1857. Black conté crayon on paper, approx. 6⅞ × 10⅜ in. The Baltimore Museum of Art. The George A. Lucas Collection (BMA 1996.53.18686).

Figure 30.10 GUSTAVE COURBET, *Burial at Ornans*, 1849–1850. Oil on canvas, 10 ft. 3 in. × 21 ft. 9 in. Musée d'Orsay, Paris. Photo: © R.M.N., Paris.

the "random" and accidental look of a snapshot, Millet's composition—in which the contours of haystacks and wagon subtly echo the curved backs of the laborers—observes the traditional academic precepts of balance and formal design. Millet removed nature's "flaws" and imposed the imagination upon the immediate evidence of the senses. His romanticized views of the laboring classes became some of the best-loved images of the nineteenth century (and were later sold in popular engraved versions). Particularly favored were Millet's portrayals of rural women at work—spinning, sewing, tending sheep, and

feeding children—which worked to idealize the female as selfless and saintly. Courbet, however, remained brutally loyal to nature and the mundane world; he knew that the carefree peasant was an idyllic stereotype that existed not in real life, but rather in the urban imagination. He surely would have agreed with his British contemporary, the novelist George Eliot (Mary Ann Evans), that "no one who is well acquainted with the English peasantry can pronounce them merry."

Courbet's most daring effort to record ordinary life in an unembellished manner was his monumental *Burial at*

Ornans (Figure **30.10**). The huge canvas (over 10 × 21 feet) consists of fifty-two life-sized figures disposed around the edges of a freshly-dug grave. Western representations of Christian burial traditionally emphasized the ritual or theatrical aspects of death and disposal, but in this painting Courbet minimizes any display of pomp and ceremony. The kneeling gravedigger and the attendant dog are as important to the pictorial statement as are the priest and his retinue. And the mourners, including some of Courbet's most homely subjects, play a more prominent role in the composition than the deceased, whose body is nowhere in view. With the objectivity of a camera eye, Courbet banished from his canvas all sentimentality and artifice.

1798	Aloys Senefelder (Bavarian) develops lithography
1822	William Church (American) patents an automatic typesetting machine
1844	wood-pulp production provides cheap paper for newspapers and periodicals

Social Realism in the Art of Daumier

The French artist Honoré Daumier (1808–1879) left the world a detailed record of the social life of his time. He had no formal academic education, but his earliest training was in **lithography**—a printmaking process created by drawing on a stone plate (Figure 30.11). Lithography, a product of nineteenth-century print technology, was a cheap and popular means of providing illustrations for newspapers, magazines, and books. Daumier produced over four thousand lithographs, often turning out two to three per week for distribution by various Paris newspapers and journals. For his subject matter, Daumier turned directly to the world around him: the streets of Paris, the theater, the law courts. The advancing (and often jarring) technology of modern life attracted Daumier's interest: pioneer experiments in aerial photography (Figure 30.12), the telegraph, the sewing machine, the repeating rifle, the railroad, and urban renewal projects that included widening the streets of Paris. But Daumier did not simply depict the facts of modern life; he frequently ridiculed them. Skeptical as to whether new technology and social progress could radically alter the human condition, he drew attention to characteristic human weaknesses, from the hypocrisy of lawyers and the pretensions of the *nouveaux riches* to the pompous and all too familiar complacency of self-serving officials (Figure 30.13). The ancestors of modern-day political cartoons, Daumier's lithographs often depend on gesture and caricature to convey his bitter opposition to the monarchy, political corruption, and profiteering. Such criticism courted danger, especially since in mid-nineteenth-century France, it was illegal to caricature individuals publicly without first obtaining their permission. Following the

Figure 30.12 HONORÉ DAUMIER, *Nadar Raising Photography to the Heights of Art*, 1862. Lithograph. The balloonist, photographer, draftsman, and journalist Gaspard-Félix Tournachon, called Nadar, took his first photograph from a balloon. Historical Pictures Service, Chicago.

Figure 30.11 Lithography is a method of making prints from a flat surface; it is also called planography. An image is first drawn or painted with an oil-based lithographic crayon or pencil on a smooth limestone surface. The surface is wiped with water, which will not stick to the applied areas of greasy lithographic ink because oil and water do not mix. The greasy areas resist the water and are thus exposed. The surface is then rolled with printing ink, which adheres only to the parts drawn in the oil-based medium. Dampened paper is placed over the stone, and a special flatbed press rubs the back of the paper, transferring the work from the stone to the covering sheet.

publication of his 1831 lithograph, which depicted the French king Louis Philippe as an obese Gargantua atop a commode/throne from which he defecated bags of gold, Daumier spent six months in jail.

Primarily a graphic artist, Daumier completed fewer than three hundred paintings. In *The Third-Class Carriage*, he captured on canvas the shabby monotony of nineteenth-century lower-class railway travel (Figure 30.14). The part of the European train in which tickets were the least expensive was also, of course, the least comfortable: It lacked glass windows (hence was subject to more than average amounts of smoke, cinders, and clatter) and was equipped with hard wooden benches rather than cushioned seats. Three generations of poor folk—an elderly woman, a younger woman, and her children—occupy the foreground of Daumier's painting. Their lumpish bodies suggest weariness and futility, yet they convey a humble dignity reminiscent of Rembrandt's figures (see chapter 22). Dark and loosely sketched oil glazes underscore the mood of cheerless resignation. Daumier produced a forthright image of common humanity in a contemporary urban setting.

Figure 30.13 HONORÉ DAUMIER, *Le Ventre Législatif* (*The Legislative Belly*), 1834. Lithograph, 11 × 17 in. Arizona State University Art Collections, Arizona State University, Tempe, Arizona. Gift of Oliver B. James.

Figure 30.14 HONORÉ DAUMIER, *The Third-Class Carriage*, ca. 1862. Oil on canvas, 25¾ × 35½ in. The Metropolitan Museum of Art, New York. H. O. Havemeyer Collection. Bequest of Mrs. H. O. Havemeyer, 1929 (29.100.129). Photograph by Malcolm Varon. © 1986 The Metropolitan Museum of Art.

The Scandalous Realism of Manet

Realism in the paintings of Edouard Manet (1832–1883) presented an unsettling challenge to tradition. Manet was an admirer of the art of the old masters, especially Velázquez, but he was equally enthralled by the life of his own time—by Parisians and their middle-class pleasures. No less than Flaubert or Ibsen, Manet shocked the public by recasting traditional subjects in modern guise. In a large canvas of 1863 entitled *Déjeuner sur l'herbe (Luncheon on the Grass)*, he depicted a nude woman calmly enjoying a picnic lunch with two fully clothed men, while a second, partially clothed, woman bathes in a nearby stream Figure **30.15**).

When submitted to the Paris Salon of 1863, *Déjeuner* was rejected by the jury of the Royal Academy. Nevertheless, that same year it was displayed at the Salon des Refusés ("the Salon of the Rejected Painters"), a landmark exhibition authorized by the French head of state in response to public agitation against the tyranny of the

Academy. No sooner was Manet's painting hung, however, than visitors tried to poke holes in the canvas and critics began to attack its coarse "improprieties"; *Déjeuner sur l'herbe* was pronounced scandalous.

While Manet's subject matter—the nude in a landscape—was quite traditional (see, for instance, *Pastoral Concert*, Figure **30.16**) and some of his motifs were borrowed from a sixteenth-century engraving of a Raphael tapestry (Figure **30.17**), the figures in *Déjeuner* were neither classical nor historical. They represent neither woodland nymphs nor Olympian gods and goddesses, but blatantly contemporary people—specifically, Manet's favorite female model, Victorine Meurent (in the nude), and his future brother-in-law (the reclining male figure).

Female nudity had been acceptable in European art since the early Renaissance, as long as it was cast in terms of myth or allegory, but in a contemporary setting—one that eliminated the barrier between fantasy and ordinary life—such nudity was considered indecent. By denying his

Figure 30.15 EDOUARD MANET, *Déjeuner sur l'herbe*, 1863. Oil on canvas, 7 ft. × 8 ft. 10 in. Musée d'Orsay, Paris. Photo: © R.M.N., Paris.

audience the traditional conventions by which to view the painting, Manet created a work of art that—as with *Madame Bovary*—implied the degeneracy of French society. Like Flaubert, who cultivated authenticity of detail and an impersonal narrative style, Manet took a neutral stance, one that presented the facts with cool objectivity. Critics also attacked Manet's inelegant style: One wrote, "The nude does not have a good figure, and one cannot imagine anything uglier than the man stretched out beside her, who has not even thought of removing, out of doors, his horrible padded cap."

In a second painting completed in 1863, *Olympia*, Manet again "debased" a traditional subject—the reclining nude (Figure **30.18**). The short, stocky Olympia (Victorine again) stares at the viewer boldly and with none of the subtle allure of a Titian Venus or an Ingres Odalisque. Her satin slippers, the enticing black ribbon at her throat, and other details in the painting distinguish her as a courtesan—a high-class prostitute. Manet's urban contemporaries were not blind to this fact, but the critics were unsparingly brutal. One journalist called Olympia "a sort of female gorilla" and warned, "Truly, young girls and women about to become mothers would do well, if they are wise, to run away from this spectacle." Like Flaubert's *Madame Bovary* or Zola's *Nana*, Manet's *Olympia* desentimentalized the image of the female. By deflating the ideal and rendering reality in commonplace terms, Manet not only offended public taste, he implicitly challenged the traditional view of art as the bearer of noble themes.

Manet further defied tradition by employing new painting techniques. Imitating current photographic practice, he bathed his figures in bright light and, using a minimum of shading, flattened them so that they resembled the figures in Japanese prints (see Figure 31.11). Even Manet's friends were critical: Courbet mockingly compared

Figure **30.17** MARCANTONIO RAIMONDI, detail from *The Judgment of Paris*, ca. 1520. Engraving after Raphael tapestry. Giraudon.

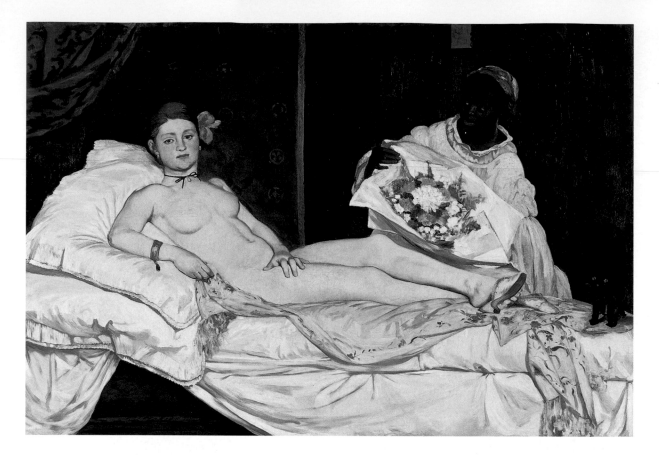

Olympia to the Queen of Spades in a deck of playing cards. Manet's practice of eliminating halftones and laying on fresh, opaque colors (instead of building up form by means of thin, transparent glazes) anticipated impressionism, a style he embraced later in his career.

Realism in American Painting

Although most American artists received their training in European art schools, their taste for realism seems to have sprung from a native affection for the factual and the material aspects of their immediate surroundings. In the late nineteenth century, an era of gross materialism known as the Gilded Age, America produced an extraordinary number of first-rate realist painters. These individuals explored a wide variety of subjects, from still life and portraiture to landscape and genre painting. Like such literary giants as Mark Twain, American realist painters fused keen observation with remarkable descriptive skills. One of the most talented of the American realists was William M. Harnett (1848–1892), a still-life painter and a master of *trompe l'oeil* ("fools the eye") illusionism. Working in the tradition of

Figure 30.18 (above) **EDOUARD MANET**, *Olympia*, 1863. Oil on canvas, 4 ft. 3¼ in. × 6 ft. 2¾ in. Musée d'Orsay, Paris. Photo: © R.M.N., Paris.

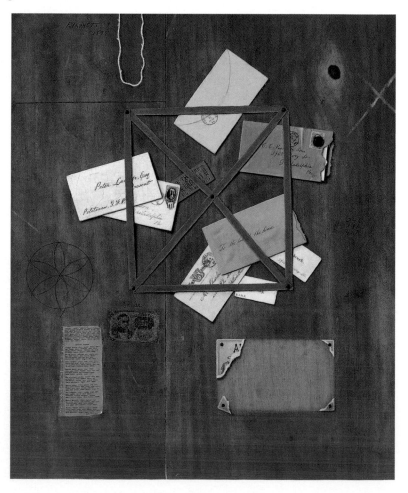

Figure 30.19 (right) **WILLIAM MICHAEL HARNETT**, *The Artist's Letter Rack*, 1879. Oil on canvas, 30 × 25 in. The Metropolitan Museum of Art, New York. Morris K. Jesup Fund, 1966 (66.13). © 1981 The Metropolitan Museum of Art.

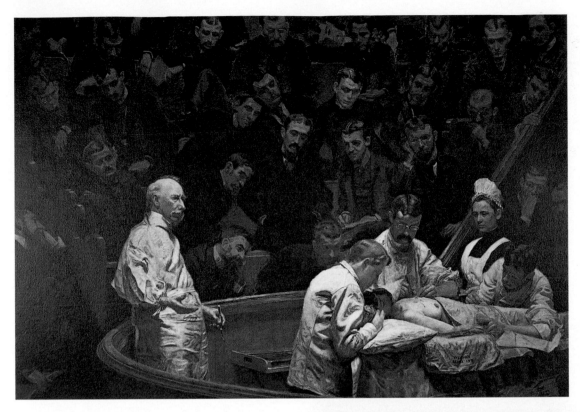

Figure 30.20 (left)
THOMAS EAKINS,
The Agnew Clinic, 1889.
Oil on canvas, 6 ft. 2½ in.
× 10 ft. 10½ in.
University of Pennsylvania
School of Medicine.

Figure 30.21 (below)
**REMBRANDT VAN
RIJN**, *The Anatomy
Lesson of Dr. Nicolaes
Tulp*, 1632. Oil on canvas,
5 ft. 3⅜ in. × 7 ft. 1¼ in.
Mauritshuis,
The Hague.

seventeenth-century Dutch still-life masters, Harnett recorded mundane objects with such hair-fine precision that some of them—letters, newspaper clippings, and calling cards—seem to be pasted on the canvas (Figure **30.19**).

In the genre of portraiture, the Philadelphia artist Thomas Eakins (1844–1916) mastered the art of producing uncompromising likenesses such as that of the poet Walt Whitman (see Figure 27.11). Like most nineteenth-century American artists, Eakins received his training in European art schools, but he ultimately emerged as a painter of the American scene and as an influential art instructor. At the Pennsylvania Academy of Fine Arts, he received criticism for his insistence on working from nude models and was forced to resign for removing the loincloth of a male model in a class that included female students. Eakins was among the first artists to choose subjects from the world of sports, such as boxing and boating, while his fascination with scientific anatomy—he dissected cadavers at Jefferson Medical College in Philadelphia—led him to produce some unorthodox representations of medical training and practice. One of his most notable canvases, *The Agnew Clinic* (Figure **30.20**), is a dispassionate view of a hospital amphitheater in which a doctor lectures to students on the subject of a surgical procedure. Eakins, a photographer of some note, often used the camera to collect visual data for his compositions. He never romanticized his subjects, and while he owed much to Rembrandt and Velázquez—*The Agnew Clinic* surely looks back to Rembrandt's *The Anatomy Lesson of Dr. Nicolaes Tulp* (Figure 30.21)—his works communicate a fresh and stubbornly precise record of the natural world.

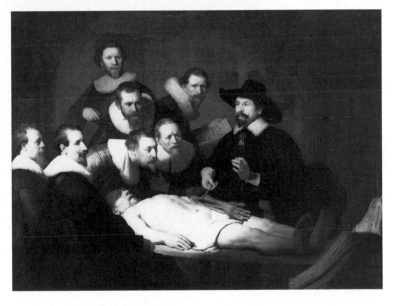

Eakins' student, Henry Ossawa Tanner (1859–1937)—like Edmonia Lewis and other African-American artists—found Paris more receptive than America. A talented genre painter, landscape artist, and photographer, the deeply religious Tanner brought to his work a concern for simple, everyday events as practiced by working-class people. In *The Banjo Lesson*, Tanner depicts an intimate domestic scene in which an African-American boy receives musical instruction from his grandfather (Figure **30.22**). A fine technician and a fluent colorist, Tanner showed regularly in Paris; in 1909, he was elected to the National Academy of Design, New York.

American realists were keenly aware of the new art of photography; some, like Tanner and Eakins, were themselves photographers. But realists were also indebted

to the world of journalism, which assumed increasing importance in transmitting literate culture. Winslow Homer (1836–1910) began his career as a newspaper illustrator and a reporter for the New York magazine *Harper's Weekly*. The first professional artist to serve as a war correspondent, Homer produced on-the-scene documentary paintings and drawings of the American Civil War, which *Harper's* converted to wood-engraved illustrations (Figure **30.23**). Although Homer often generalized the facts of the events he actually witnessed, he never moralized on or allegorized his subjects (as did, for instance, Goya or Delacroix). His talent for graphic selectivity and dramatic concentration rivaled that of America's first war photographer, Mathew B. Brady (see Figure 30.7).

Apart from two trips to Europe, Homer spent most of his life in New England, where he painted subjects that were both ordinary and typically American. Scenes of hunting and fishing reveal Homer's deep affection for nature, while his many genre paintings reflect a fascination with the activities of American women and children. In *The Country School* (Figure **30.24**), Homer combined crisply articulated details and stark patterns of light and shadow to convey the controlled atmosphere of the rural American schoolhouse, a subject dominated by the authoritative figure of the female teacher.

Homer was also interested in the role of African-Americans in contemporary culture, but he was somewhat critical of visual representations that portrayed America's slaves as

Figure 30.22 (above) **HENRY OSSAWA TANNER**, *The Banjo Lesson*, c.1893. Oil on canvas, 48 × 35 in. Hampton University Museum, Hampton, Virginia.

Figure 30.23 (right) **WINSLOW HOMER**, *The War for the Union: A Bayonet Charge*, published in *Harper's Weekly*, July 12, 1862. Wood engraving, 13⅝ × 20⅝ in. The Metropolitan Museum of Art, New York, Harris Brisbane Fund, 1929 (29.88.3 [3]).

Figure 30.24 **WINSLOW HOMER**, *The Country School*, 1871. Oil on canvas, 21⅜ × 38⅜ in. The Saint Louis Art Museum. Museum Purchase.

merry and content. One of his most enigmatic paintings, *The Gulf Stream*, shows a black man adrift in a rudderless boat surrounded by shark-filled waters which are whipped by the winds of an impending tornado (Figure **30.25**). While realistic in execution, the painting may be interpreted as a romantic metaphor for the isolation and plight of black Americans in the decades following the Civil War. Homer shared with earlier nineteenth-century artists, including Turner, Melville, and Géricault, an almost obsessive interest in the individual's life and death

struggle with the sea. However, compared (for instance) with Géricault's more theatrical rendering of man against nature in *The Raft of the "Medusa"* (see Figure 29.4), Homer's painting is a matter-of-fact study of human resignation in the face of deadly peril.

Figure **30.25** **WINSLOW HOMER**, *The Gulf Stream*, 1899. Oil on canvas, 28⅛ × 49⅛ in. The Metropolitan Museum of Art, New York. Catharine Lorillard Wolfe Collection. Catharine Lorillard Wolfe Fund, 1906 (06.1234). © 1984 The Metropolitan Museum of Art.

American audiences loved their realist painters, but, occasionally, critics voiced mixed feelings. The American novelist Henry James (1843–1916), whose novels probed the differences between European and American character, assessed what he called Homer's "perfect realism," with these words:

> He is almost barbarously simple, and, to our eye, he is horribly ugly; but there is nevertheless something one likes about him. What is it? For ourselves, it is not his subjects. We frankly confess that we detest his subjects—his barren plank fences, his glaring, bald, blue skies, his big, dreary, vacant lots of meadows, his freckled, straight-haired Yankee urchins, his flat-breasted maidens, suggestive of a dish of rural doughnuts and pie, his calico sun-bonnets, his flannel shirts, his cowhide boots. He has chosen the least pictorial features of the least pictorial range of scenery and civilization; he has resolutely treated them as if they were pictorial, as if they were every inch as good as Capri or Tangiers; and, to reward his audacity, he has incontestably succeeded. It . . . is a proof that if you will only be doggedly literal, though you may often be unpleasing, you will at least have a stamp of your own.*

---

*Quoted in John W. McCoubrey, *American Art 1700–1960. Sources and Documents.* Englewood Cliffs, N.J.: Prentice-Hall, 1965, 165.

Late Nineteenth-Century Architecture

While many nineteenth-century European architects pursued neo-classical and neomedieval revivalism, others were experimenting with the possibilities of an exciting new structural medium: cast iron. The new medium, which provided strength without bulk, allowed architects to span broader widths and raise structures to greater heights than those achieved by traditional stone masonry. Although iron would change the history of architecture more dramatically than any advance in technology since the Roman invention of concrete, European architects were slow to realize its potential. In England, where John Nash had used cast iron in 1815 as the structural frame for the Brighton Pavilion (see chapter 29), engineers did not begin construction on the first cast-iron suspension bridge until 1836 and not until mid-century was iron used as skeletal support for mills, warehouses, and railroad stations.

Figure 30.26 JOSEPH PAXTON, interior of Crystal Palace, 1851. Cast and wrought iron and glass, length 1,851 ft. Institut für Geschichte und Theorie der Architektur an der ETH, Zürich.

Figure 30.27 **GUSTAVE EIFFEL**, Eiffel Tower, Paris, 1889. Wrought iron on a reinforced concrete base, original height 984 ft. Photo: Roger-Viollet, Paris.

The innovator in the use of iron for public buildings was, in fact, not an architect but a distinguished horticulturalist and greenhouse designer, Joseph Paxton (1801–1865). Paxton's Crystal Palace (Figure **30.26**), erected for the Great Exhibition of London in 1851, was the world's first prefabricated building and the forerunner of the "functional" steel and glass architecture of the twentieth century. Consisting entirely of cast- and wrought-iron girders and 18,000 panes of glass and erected in only nine months, the 1,851-foot-long structure—its length a symbolic reference to the year of the Exhibition—resembled a gigantic greenhouse. Light entered through its transparent walls and air filtered in through louvered windows. Thousands flocked to see the Crystal Palace; yet most European architects found the glass and iron structure bizarre. Although heroic in both size and conception, the Crystal Palace had almost no immediate impact on European architecture. Dismantled after the exhibition and moved to a new site, however, it was hailed as a masterpiece of prefabrication and portability decades before it burned to the ground in 1930.

Like the Crystal Palace, the Eiffel Tower (Figure **30.27**) originated as a novelty, but it soon became emblematic of early modernism. The viewing tower constructed by the engineer Gustave Eiffel (1832–1923) for the Paris World Exhibition of 1889 is, in essence, a tall (1,064-foot-high) cast-iron skeleton equipped with elevators that offer the visitor magnificent aerial views of Paris. Aesthetically, the tower linked the architectural traditions of the past with those of the future: Its sweeping curves, delicate tracery, and dramatic verticality recall the glories of the Gothic cathedral, while its majestic ironwork anticipated the austere abstractions of international-style architecture (see chapter 32). Condemned as a visual monstrosity when it was first erected, the Eiffel Tower emerged as a positive symbol of the soaring confidence of the industrial age. This landmark of heroic materialism remained for four decades (until the advent of the American skyscraper) the tallest structure in the world.

In an age of advancing industrialism, ornamental structures such as the Eiffel Tower and the Crystal Palace gave way to functional ones. Inevitably, the skyscraper was to become the prime architectural expression of modern corporate power and the urban scene. By 1850, there were seven American cities with more than 100,000

1773 the first cast-iron bridge is built in England

1851 the first international industrial exposition opens in London

1856 Henry Bessemer (British) perfects the process for producing inexpensive steel

1857 E. G. Otis (American) installs the first safety elevator

1863 the first "subway" (the London Underground) begins operation

inhabitants, and before 1900, the populations of at least three of these—New York, Philadelphia, and Chicago—swelled as a result of the millions of immigrants who came to live and work in the metropolitan community. The physical character of the premodern city, whose buildings were no more than four stories high, changed enormously with the construction of skyscrapers. Multistoried vertical giants were made possible by the advancing technology of steel, a medium that was perfected in 1856. Lighter, stronger, and more resilient than cast iron, steel used as a frame could carry the entire weight of a structure, thus eliminating the need for solid weight-bearing masonry walls. Steel made possible a whole new concept of building design characterized by lighter materials, flat roofs, and large windows. In 1868, the six-story Equitable Life Insurance building in New York City was the first office structure to install an electric elevator. By the 1880s, architects and engineers in Chicago combined the new steel frame with the elevator to raise structures of more than ten stories in height. William Le Baron Jenney (1832–1907) built a definitive steel-frame skyscraper, the Home Insurance Building in Chicago, which, ironically, hides its metal skeleton beneath a traditional-looking brick and masonry facade. It fell to his successor, Louis Henry Sullivan (1856–1924), to create multistory buildings, such as the Guaranty Building in Buffalo (Figure 30.28), whose exteriors

Figure 30.28 LOUIS HENRY SULLIVAN and **DANKMAR ADLER**, Guaranty Building, Buffalo, New York, 1894–1895. Steel frame. Collection, David R. Phillips, Chicago Architectural Photographing Company.

proudly reflect the structural simplicity of their steel frames. Within decades, the American skyscraper became an icon of modern urban culture.

Realism in Music

In Italian opera of the late nineteenth century, a movement called **verismo** (literally, "truth-ism," but more generally "realism" or "naturalism") paralleled the emphasis on reality in literature and art. Realist composers rejected the heroic characters of romantic grand opera and presented the problems and conflicts of people in familiar and everyday—if occasionally somewhat melodramatic—situations. The foremost "verist" in music was the Italian composer Giacomo Puccini (1858–1924). Puccini's *La Bohème*, the tragic love story of young artists (called

"bohemians" for their unconventional lifestyles) in the Latin Quarter of Paris, was based on a nineteenth-century novel called *Scenes of Bohemian Life*. The colorful orchestration and powerfully melodic arias of *La Bohème* evoke the joys and sorrows of true-to-life characters. While this poignant musical drama was received coldly at its premiere in 1897, *La Bohème* has become one of the best loved of nineteenth-century grand operas.

Another of Puccini's operas, *Madame Butterfly*, offered European audiences a timely, if moralizing, view of the Western presence in Asia and one that personalized the clash of opposing cultures. The story, which takes place in Nagasaki in the years following the reopening of Japanese ports to the West, begins with the wedding of a young United States Navy lieutenant to a fifteen-year-old *geisha* (a Japanese girl trained as a social companion to men) known as "Butterfly." The American is soon forced to leave with his fleet, while for three years Butterfly, now the mother of his son, faithfully awaits his return. When, finally, he arrives (accompanied by his new American bride) only to claim the child, the griefstricken Butterfly takes the only honorable path available to her: She commits suicide. This tragic tale, which had appeared as a novel, a play, and a magazine story, was based on a true incident. Set to some of Puccini's most lyrical music for voice and orchestra, *Madame Butterfly* reflects the composer's fascination with Japanese culture, a fascination most evident in Puccini's poetic characterization of the delicate Butterfly. And while neither the story nor the music of the opera is authentically Japanese, its *verismo* lies in its frank (if melodramatic) account of the traumas consequent to the meeting of East and West.

SUMMARY

During the second half of the nineteenth century, as the social consequences of Western industrialism became increasingly visible, realism came to rival romanticism both as a style and as an attitude of mind. Western industrialism, imperialism, and colonialism had a shaping influence on the non-Western world. While the ideologies of liberalism, conservatism, utilitarianism, and socialism offered varying solutions to contemporary problems of social injustice, Marx and Engels called for action in the form of violent proletarian revolution that would end private ownership of the means of economic production. The leading proponent of liberalism, John Stuart Mill, defended the exercise of individual liberty as protected by the state. Mill's opposition to the subjection of women gave strong support to nineteenth-century movements for women's rights.

In the arts, realism emerged as a style concerned with recording contemporary subject matter in true-to-life terms. Such novelists as Dickens in England, Dostoevsky and Tolstoy in Russia, Flaubert and Zola in France, and Twain and Chopin in America described contemporary social conditions sympathetically and with fidelity to detail. Flaubert and Chopin provided alternatives to romantic idealism in their realistic characterizations of female figures. Zola's novels introduced a naturalistic perception of human beings as determined by hereditary and sociological factors. Ibsen pioneered modern drama in his fearless portrayal of class and gender conflicts.

Photography and lithography were invented during the nineteenth century; both media encouraged artists to produce objective records of their surroundings. By the mid-nineteenth century the camera was used to document all aspects of contemporary life as well as to provide artists with detailed visual data for their compositions. In painting, Courbet led the realist movement with canvases depicting the activities of humble and commonplace men and women. Daumier employed the new technique of lithography to show his deep concern for political and social conditions in rapidly modernizing France. Manet shocked art critics by recasting traditional subjects in contemporary terms. In America, realist painters, including Eakins,

Tanner, and Homer, recorded typically American pastimes in an unembellished, forthright manner. Paxton's Crystal Palace, the world's first prefabricated cast-iron structure, offered a prophetic glimpse into the decades that would produce steel-framed skyscrapers. Though realism did not adapt itself to music in any specific manner, the Italian "verist" Puccini wrote operas that captured the lives of nineteenth-century Europeans with a truth to nature comparable to that in realist novels and paintings. On the whole, the varieties of realism in nineteenth-century cultural expression reflect a profound concern for social and economic inequities and a critical reassessment of traditional Western values.

GLOSSARY

capitalist one who provides investment capital in economic ventures

entrepreneur one who organizes, manages, and assumes the risks of a business

lithography a printmaking process created by drawing on a stone plate; see Figure 30.11

proletariat a collective term describing industrial workers who lack their own means of production and hence sell their labor to live

verismo (Italian, "realism") a type of late nineteenth-century opera that presents a realistic picture of life, instead of a story based in myth, legend, or ancient history

SUGGESTIONS FOR READING

Berlin, Isaiah. *Karl Marx: His Life and Environment.* New York: Oxford University Press, 1978.

Clark, T. J. *The Painting of Modern Life: Paris in the Art of Manet and His Followers.* New York: Knopf, 1984.

Cachin, Françoise. *Manet: The Influence of the Modern,* translated by Rachel Kaplan. New York: Abrams, 1995.

Duncan, Graeme C. *Marx and Mill: Two Views of Social Conflict and Social Harmony.* Cambridge: Cambridge University Press, 1973.

Friedrich, Otto. *Olympia: Paris in the Age of Manet.* New York: Harper, 1992.

Hamilton, G. H. *Manet and His Critics.* New Haven: Yale University Press, 1986.

Johns, Elizabeth. *American Genre Painting: The Politics of Everyday Life.* New Haven: Yale University Press, 1994.

Kearns, Katherine. *Nineteenth-Century Literary Realism: Through the Looking Glass.* Cambridge: Cambridge University Press, 1996.

Larkin, Maurice. *Man and Society in Nineteenth-Century Realism, Determinism and Literature.* Totowa, N.J.: Rowman and Littlefield, 1977.

Nochlin, Linda. *Realism.* New York: Viking Press, 1993.

Rosen, Charles, and Henri Zerner. *Romanticism and Realism: The Mythology of Nineteenth-Century Art.* New York: Viking, 1984.

Shi, David E. *Realism in American Thought and Culture, 1850–1920.* New York: Oxford University Press, 1993.

Smart, Paul. *Mill and Marx: Individual Liberty and the Roads to Freedom.* New York: St. Martin's, 1991.

CHAPTER THIRTY-ONE

The move toward modernism

"Is not the nineteenth century ... a century of decadence?"
Nietzsche

During the last quarter of the nineteenth century, France was the center of most of the important developments in the arts of Western Europe. Especially in Paris, poets, painters, and composers turned their backs on both romanticism and realism. They pursued styles that neither idealized the world nor described it with reforming zeal. Their art was more concerned with sensory experience than with moral purpose, with feeling than with teaching. Unlike their predecessors, these artists had little interest in exalting the noble, the sacred, or the factual; instead, they made art that obeyed purely aesthetic impulses, that—like music—communicated meaning through shape or sound, pattern or color. Their principle was coined by Walter Pater in 1868 in the slogan *l'art pour l'art* or "art for art's sake."

Late nineteenth-century science and technology helped to shape this new approach in the arts. In 1873, the British physicist James Clerk Maxwell (1831–1879) published his *Treatise on Electricity and Magnetism*, which explained that light waves consisting of electromagnetic particles produced radiant energy. In 1879, after numerous failures, the American inventor Thomas Edison (1847–1931) moved beyond scientific theory to create the first efficient incandescent light bulb. Incandescent electric light provided a sharper perception of reality that—along with the camera—helped to shatter the world of romantic illusion. By the year 1880, the telephone transported the human voice over thousands of miles. In the late 1880s Edison developed the technique of moving pictures. The invention of the internal combustion engine led to

the production of modern motorcars in the 1890s, a decade that also witnessed the invention of the x-ray and the development of radiotelegraphy. Such developments accelerated the tempo of life and drew attention to the role of the senses in defining experience.

Late Nineteenth-Century Thought

Nietzsche's New Morality

The most provocative thinker of the late nineteenth century was the German philosopher and poet Friedrich Wilhelm Nietzsche (1844–1900). Nietzsche was a classical philologist, a professor of Greek at the University of Basle, and the author of such notable works as *The Birth of Tragedy* (1872), *Thus Spoke Zarathustra* (1883–1892), and *The Genealogy of Morals* (1887). In these, as in his shorter pieces, Nietzsche voiced the sentiments of the radical moralist. Deeply critical of his own time, he called for a revision of all values. He rejected organized religion, attacking Christianity and other institutionalized religions as contributors to the formation of a "slave morality." He was equally critical of democratic institutions, which he saw as rule by mass mediocrity; instead he lauded the "superman" or superior individual (German, *Übermensch*), whose singular vision and courage would, in his view, produce a "master" morality. Nietzsche did not launch his ideas in the form of a well-reasoned philosophic system, but rather as aphorisms, maxims, and expostulations whose brilliance and visceral force bear out his claim that he wrote "with his blood." Reflecting the cynicism of the late nineteenth century, he asked, "Is man merely a mistake of God's? Or God merely a mistake of man's?"

Nietzsche shared with Dostoevsky the view that European materialism had led inevitably to decadence and decline. In *The Antichrist*, published in 1888, shortly before Nietzsche became insane (possibly a result of syphilis), he wrote:

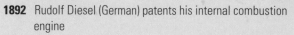

1877 Thomas Edison (American) invents the phonograph

1892 Rudolf Diesel (German) patents his internal combustion engine

1893 Henry Ford (American) test-drives the "gasoline-buggy"

Mankind does not represent a development toward something better or stronger or higher in the sense accepted today. "Progress" is merely a modern idea, that is, a false ideal. The European of today is vastly inferior in value to the European of the Renaissance: further development is altogether not according to any necessity in the direction of elevation, enhancement, or strength.*

The following readings demonstrate Nietzsche's incisive imagination and caustic wit. The first, taken from *The Gay Science* (1882) and entitled "The Madman," is a parable that harnesses Nietzsche's iconoclasm to his gift for prophecy. The others, excerpted from *Twilight of the Idols* (or *How One Philosophizes with a Hammer*, 1888), address the art for art's sake spirit of the late nineteenth century and the fragile relationship between art and morality.

READING 5.26   From the Works of Nietzsche

The Gay Science (1882)

The Madman. Have you not heard of that madman who lit a   1
lantern in the bright morning hours, ran to the market place,
and cried incessantly, "I seek God! I seek God!" As many of
those who do not believe in God were standing around just
then, he provoked much laughter. Why, did he get lost? said
one. Did he lose his way like a child? said another. Or is he
hiding? Is he afraid of us? Has he gone on a voyage? or
emigrated? Thus they yelled and laughed. The madman jumped
into their midst and pierced them with his glances.

"Whither is God" he cried. "I shall tell you. *We have killed*   10
him—you and I. All of us are his murderers. But how have we
done this? How were we able to drink up the sea? Who gave
us the sponge to wipe away the entire horizon? What did we
do when we unchained this earth from its sun? Whither is it
moving now? Whither are we moving now? Away from all
suns? Are we not plunging continually? Backward, sideward,
forward, in all directions? Is there any up or down left? Are we
not straying as through an infinite nothing? Do we not feel the
breath of empty space? Has it not become colder? Is not night
and more night coming on all the while? Must not lanterns be   20
lit in the morning? Do we not hear anything yet of the noise of
the gravediggers who are burying God? Do we not smell
anything yet of God's decomposition? Gods too decompose.
God is dead. God remains dead. And we have killed him. How
shall we, the murderers of all murderers, comfort ourselves?
What was holiest and most powerful of all that the world has
yet owned has bled to death under our knives. Who will wipe
this blood off us? What water is there for us to clean
ourselves? What festivals of atonement, what sacred games
shall we have to invent? Is not the greatness of this deed too   30
great for us? Must not we ourselves become gods simply to
seem worthy of it? There has never been a greater deed; and
whoever will be born after us—for the sake of this deed he
will be part of a higher history than all history hitherto."

Here the madman fell silent and looked again at his
listeners; and they too were silent and stared at him in
astonishment. At last he threw his lantern on the ground, and
it broke and went out. "I come too early," he said then; "my
time has not come yet. This tremendous event is still on its
way, still wandering—it has not yet reached the ears of man.   40
Lightning and thunder require time, the light of the stars
requires time, deeds require time even after they are done,
before they can be seen and heard. This deed is still more
distant from them than the most distant stars—*and yet they*
have done it themselves."

It has been related further that on that same day the
madman entered divers churches and there sang his *requiem*
aeternam deo. Led out and called to account, he is said to have
replied each time, "What are these churches now if they are
not the tombs and sepulchers of God?"   50

Twilight of the Idols (1888)

L'art pour l'art. The fight against purpose in art is always a fight   1
against the moralizing tendency in art, against its subordination
to morality. *L'art pour l'art* means, "The devil take morality!" But
even this hostility still betrays the overpowering force of the
prejudice. When the purpose of moral preaching and of
improving man has been excluded from art, it still does not
follow by any means that art is altogether purposeless, aimless,
senseless—in short, *l'art pour l'art*, a worm chewing its own
tail. "Rather no purpose at all than a moral purpose!"—that is
the talk of mere passion. A psychologist, on the other hand,   10
asks: what does all art do? does it not praise? glorify? choose?
prefer? With all this it strengthens or weakens certain
valuations. Is this merely a "moreover"? an accident? something
in which the artist's instinct had no share? Or is it not the very
presupposition of the artist's ability? Does his basic instinct aim
at art, or rather at the sense of art, at life? at a desirability of
life? Art is the great stimulus to life: how could one understand
it as purposeless, as aimless, as *l'art pour l'art*?

One question remains: art also makes apparent much that is
ugly, hard, and questionable in life; does it not thereby spoil   20
life for us? And indeed there have been philosophers who
attributed this sense to it: "liberation from the will" was what
Schopenhauer taught as the over-all end of art; and with
admiration he found the great utility of tragedy in its "evoking
resignation." But this, as I have already suggested, is the
pessimist's perspective and "evil eye." We must appeal to the
artists themselves. What does the tragic artist communicate of
himself? Is it not precisely the state *without* fear in the face of
the fearful and questionable that he is showing? This state
itself is a great desideratum;[1] whoever knows it, honors it with   30
the greatest honors. He communicates it—*must* communicate
it, provided he is an artist, a genius of communication. Courage
and freedom of feeling before a powerful enemy, before a
sublime calamity, before a problem that arouses dread—this
triumphant state is what the tragic artist chooses, what he
glorifies. Before tragedy, what is warlike in our soul celebrates
its Saturnalia;[2] whoever is used to suffering, whoever seeks

---

*The Antichrist, in Walter Kaufmann, ed. The Portable Nietzsche. New
York: Viking Press, 1965, 571.

---

[1]Something desired as essential.
[2]An orgy, or unrestrained celebration.

out suffering, the heroic man praises his own being through tragedy—to him alone the tragedian presents this drink of sweetest cruelty. **40**

. . . .

One might say that in a certain sense the nineteenth century *also* strove for all that which Goethe as a person had striven for: universality in understanding and in welcoming, letting everything come close to oneself, an audacious realism, a reverence for everything factual. How is it that the over-all result is no Goethe, but chaos, a nihilistic sigh, an utter bewilderment, an instinct of weariness which in practice continually drives toward a recourse to the eighteenth century? (For example, as a romanticism of feeling, as altruism and hypersentimentality, as feminism in taste, as socialism in **50** politics.) Is not the nineteenth century, especially at its close, merely an intensified, *brutalized* eighteenth century, that is, a century of *decadence*? So that Goethe would have been—not merely for Germany, but for all of Europe—a mere interlude, a beautiful "in vain"? But one misunderstands great human beings if one views them from the miserable perspective of some public use. That one cannot put them to any use, that in itself may belong to greatness. . . .

While Nietzsche anticipated the darker side of modernism, the theories of Henri Bergson (1859–1941) presented a more positive point of view. Bergson, the most important French philosopher of his time, offered a picture of the world that paralleled key developments in the arts and sciences of the late nineteenth century and anticipated modern notions of time and space. Bergson viewed life as a vital impulse that evolved creatively, much like a work of art. According to Bergson, two primary powers, intellect and intuition, governed the lives of human beings. While intellect perceives experience in individual and discrete terms, or as a series of separate and solid entities, intuition grasps experience as it really is: a perpetual stream of sensations. Intellect isolates and categorizes experience according to logic and geometry; intuition, on the other hand, fuses past and present into one organic whole. For Bergson, instinct, or intuition, is humankind's noblest faculty, and *duration*, or "perpetual becoming," is the very stuff of reality—the essence of life. In 1889, Bergson published his treatise *Time and Freewill*, in which he explained that true experience is durational, a constant unfolding in time, and that reality, which can only be apprehended intuitively, is a series of qualitative changes that merge into one another without precise outlines.

Poetry in the Late Nineteenth Century: The Symbolists

Bergson's poetical view of nature had much in common with the aesthetics of the movement known as *symbolism*, which flourished from roughly 1885 to 1910. The symbolists held that the visible world did not constitute a true or universal reality. They therefore rejected realistic, objec-

tive representation in favor of subjective expression that drew on sensory experience, dreams, and myth. By means of ambiguous but powerful images, the symbolists strived to *suggest* ideas and feelings that might evoke an ideal rather than a real world. Religious mysticism, the erotic, and the supernatural were favorite themes of symbolist artists. In literature, the French poets Charles Baudelaire (1821–1867), Paul Verlaine (1844–1896), Arthur Rimbaud (1854–1891), and Stéphane Mallarmé (1842–1898), and the Belgian playwright Maurice Maeterlinck (1862–1949), tried to capture in language the ineffable dimension of intuitive experience. Rejecting both the romanticism and the realism/naturalism of nineteenth-century writers, they aimed to free language of its traditional descriptive and expressive functions. For the symbolists, reality was a swarm of sensations that could never be described but only translated via poetic symbols—verbal images that, through the power of suggestion, elicited moods and feelings beyond the literal meanings of words. In one of the prose poems from his *Illuminations*, for example, Rimbaud describes flowers as "Bits of yellow gold seeded in agate, pillars of mahogany supporting a dome of emeralds, bouquets of white satin and fine rods of ruby surround the water rose."* The symbolists tried to represent nature without effusive commentary, to "take eloquence and wring its neck," as Verlaine put it. In order to imitate the indefiniteness of experience itself, they might string words together without logical connections. Hence, in symbolist poetry, images seem to flow into one another, and "meaning" often lies between the lines.

For Stéphane Mallarmé, the "new art" of poetry was a religion, and the poet-artist was its oracle. Unlike realist writers, who stressed social interaction and reform, Mallarmé inclined to melancholy and to the cultivation of an intimate literary style based on the "music" of words. He held that art was "accessible only to the few" who nurtured "the inner life." Mallarmé's poems are tapestries of sensuous, dreamlike motifs that resist definition and analysis. To name a thing, Mallarmé insisted, was to destroy it, while to suggest experience was to create it. Such were the principles that inspired his pastoral poem, "L'Après-midi d'un faune" ("The Afternoon of a Faun"). The poem is a reverie of an erotic encounter between two mythological woodland creatures, a faun (part man, part beast) and a nymph (a beautiful forest maiden). As the faun awakens, he tries to recapture the experiences of the previous afternoon. Whether his elusive memories belong to the world of dreams or to reality is uncertain; but, true to Bergson's theory of duration, experience becomes a stream of sensations in which past and present merge. As the following excerpt illustrates, Mallarmé's verbal rhythms are free and hypnotic, and his images, which follow one another with few logical transitions, are intimately linked to the world of the senses.

---

* *The Norton Anthology of World Literature*, 4th ed. New York: Norton, 1980, 1188.

READING 5.27 From Mallarmé's "The Afternoon of a Faun" (1876)

I would immortalize these nymphs: so bright   1
Their sunlit coloring, so airy light,
It floats like drowsing down. Loved I a dream?
My doubts, born of oblivious darkness, seem
A subtle tracery of branches grown   5
The tree's true self—proving that I have known,
Thinking it love, the blushing of a rose.
But think. These nymphs, their loveliness . . . suppose
They bodied forth your senses' fabulous thirst?
Illusion! which the blue eyes of the first,   10
As cold and chaste as is the weeping spring,
Beget: the other, sighing, passioning,
Is she the wind, warm in your fleece at noon?
No; through this quiet, when a weary swoon
Crushes and chokes the latest faint essay   15
Of morning, cool against the encroaching day,
There is no murmuring water, save the gush
Of my clear fluted notes; and in the hush
Blows never a wind, save that which through my reed[1]
Puffs out before the rain of notes can speed   20
Upon the air, with that calm breath of art
That mounts the unwrinkled zenith visibly,
Where inspiration seeks its native sky.
You fringes of a calm Sicilian lake,
The sun's own mirror which I love to take,   25
Silent beneath your starry flowers, tell
How here I cut the hollow rushes, well
Tamed by my skill, when on the glaucous gold
Of distant lawns about their fountain cold
A living whiteness stirs like a lazy wave;   30
And at the first slow notes my panpipes gave
These flocking swans, these naiads, rather, fly
Or dive.

                    . . . .

See how the ripe pomegranates bursting red
To quench the thirst of the mumbling bees have bled;   35
So too our blood, kindled by some chance fire,
Flows for the swarming legions of desire.
At evening, when the woodland green turns gold
And ashen grey, 'mid the quenched leaves, behold!
Red Etna[2] glows, by Venus visited,   40
Walking the lava with her snowy tread
Whene'er the flames in thunderous slumber die.
I hold the goddess!
                        Ah, sure penalty!
But the unthinking soul and body swoon
At last beneath the heavy hush of noon.   45
Forgetful let me lie where summer's drouth
Sifts fine the sand and then with gaping mouth
Dream planet-struck by the grape's round wine-red star.
Nymphs, I shall see the shade that now you are.

---

[1] A pipe or flute.
[2] A volcanic mountain in Sicily.

Music in the Late Nineteenth Century: Debussy

It is no surprise that symbolist poetry, itself a kind of music, found its counterpart in music. Like the poetry of Mallarmé, the music of Claude Debussy (1862–1918) engages the listener through nuance and atmosphere. Debussy's compositions consist of broken fragments of melody, the outlines of which are blurred and indistinct. "I would like to see the creation . . . of a kind of music without themes and motives," wrote Debussy, "formed on a single continuous theme, which is uninterrupted and which never returns on itself."

Debussy owed much to Richard Wagner and the romantic composers who had abandoned the formal clarity of classical composition (see chapter 29). He was also indebted to the exotic music of Bali in Indonesia, which he had heard performed at the Paris Exposition of 1889. Debussy experimented with the five-tone scale found in East Asian music and with nontraditional kinds of harmony. He deviated from the traditional Western practice of returning harmonies to the tonic, or "home tone," introducing shifting harmonies with no clearly defined tonal center. His rich harmonic palette, characterized by unusually constructed chords, reflects a fascination with tone color that may have been inspired by the writings of the German physiologist Hermann von Helmholtz (1821–1894)—especially his treatise *On the Sensations of Tone as a Physiological Basis for the Theory of Music* (1863). But Debussy found his greatest inspiration in contemporary poetry and painting. He was a close friend of many of the symbolist poets, whose texts he often set to music. His first orchestral composition, *Prelude to "The Afternoon of a Faun"* (1894), ♪ was (in his words) a "very free illustration of Mallarmé's beautiful poem," which had been published eighteen years earlier. Debussy originally intended to write a dramatic piece based on the poem, but instead produced a ten-minute orchestral prelude which shares the dreamlike quality of the poem. (In 1912, his score became the basis for a twelve-minute ballet choreographed by the Russian dancer Nijinsky, shown in Figure 32.28; see chapter 32.)

Debussy had little use for the ponderous orchestras of the French and German romantics. He scored the *Prelude* for a small orchestra whose unusual combination of wind and brass instruments might recreate Mallarmé's delicate mood of reverie. A sensuous melody for unaccompanied flute provides the composition's opening theme, which is then developed by flutes, oboes, and clarinets. Harp, triangle, muted horns, and lightly brushed cymbals contribute luminous tonal textures that—like the images of the poem itself—seem based in pure sensation. Transitions are subtle rather than focused, and melodies seem to drift without resolution. Imprecise tone clusters and shifting harmonies create fluid, nebulous effects that call to mind the shimmering effects of light on water and the ebb and flow of ocean waves. Indeed, water—a favorite motif of impressionist art—is the subject of many of Debussy's orchestral sketches, such as *Gardens in the Rain* (1903), *Image: Reflections in the Water* (1905), and *The Sea* (1905).

♪ See Music Listening Selection at end of chapter.

Painting in the Late Nineteenth Century

Symbolism

In the visual arts, symbolism, which flourished throughout Europe, featured a new emphasis on the simplification of line, arbitrary color, and expressive, flattened form. *The Chosen One* (Figure **31.1**) by the Swiss artist Ferdinand Hodler (1853–1918) employs these techniques to depict a young male child surrounded by a circle of angelic figures. The painting does not represent a specific event; rather, it suggests a mysterious and unnamed rite of passage. Symbolist emphasis on suggestion rather than depiction constituted a move in the direction of modernist abstraction and expressionism (see chapter 32).

Impressionism

The nineteenth-century art style that captured most fully the intuitive realm of experience, and thus, closely paralleled the aesthetic ideals of Bergson, Mallarmé, and Debussy, was *impressionism*. Luminosity, the interaction of light and form, subtlety of tone, and a preoccupation with sensation itself were the major features of impressionist art. Impressionist subject matter preserved the romantic fasci-nation with nature and the realist preoccupation with late nineteenth-century French society. But impressionism departed from both the romantic effort to idealize nature and the realist will to record nature with unbiased objectivity. An art of pure sensation, impressionism was, in part, a response to nineteenth-century research into the physics of light, the chemistry of paint, and the laws of optics. Such publications as *Principles of Harmony and the Contrast of Colors* by the nineteenth-century French chemist Michel Chevreul (1786–1889), along with treatises on the physical properties of color and musical tone by Hermann von Helmholtz mentioned above, offered new insights into the psychology of perception. At the same time, late nineteenth-century chemists produced the first synthetic pigments, which replaced traditional earth pigments with brilliant new colors. Such developments in science and technology contributed to the birth of the new art of light and color.

Monet: Pioneer of Impressionism

In 1874 the French artist Claude Monet (1840–1926) exhibited a work of art that some critics consider the first modern painting. *Impression: Sunrise* (Figure **31.2**) is patently a seascape; but the painting says more about *how* one sees than about *what* one sees. It transcribes the fleeting effects of light and the changing atmosphere of water

Figure 31.1 FERDINAND HODLER, *The Chosen One*, 1893–1894. Tempera and oil on canvas, 7 ft. 3½ in. × 9 ft. 10½ in. Kunstmuseum, Berne.

Figure 31.2 CLAUDE MONET, *Impression: Sunrise*, 1873. Oil on canvas, 19⅝ × 25½ in. Musée Marmottan, Paris. Photo: © R.M.N., Paris.

and air into a tissue of small dots and streaks of color—the elements of pure perception. To achieve luminosity, Monet coated the raw canvas with gesso, a chalklike medium. Then, working in the open air and using the new chemical paints (available in the form of portable metallic tubes), he applied brushstrokes of pure, occasionally unmixed, color. Monet ignored the brown underglazes artists traditionally used to build up form. And, arguing that there were no "lines" in nature, he refused to delineate forms with fixed contours; rather, he evoked form by means of color. Instead of blending his colors to create a finished effect, he placed them side by side, rapidly building up a radiant impasto. In order to intensify visual effect, he juxtaposed complementary colors, putting touches of orange (red and yellow) next to blue and adding bright tints of rose, pink, and vermilion. Monet rejected the use of browns and blacks to create shadows; instead, he applied colors complementary to the hue of the object casting the shadow, thus more closely approximating the prismatic effects of light on the human eye. Monet's canvases captured the external envelope: the instantaneous visual sensations of light itself.

Monet was by no means the first painter to deviate from academic techniques. In defining form, Constable had applied color in rough dots and dabs, Delacroix had occasionally juxtaposed complementary colors to increase brilliance, and Manet had often omitted halftones. But Monet went further by interpreting form as color itself, which, rapidly applied, conveyed a sense of immediacy. Consequently, *Impression: Sunrise* struck the critics as a radically new approach in art. One critic dismissed the painting as "only an impression," no better than "wallpaper in its embryonic state," thus unwittingly giving the name "impressionism" to the movement that would dominate French art of the 1870s and 1880s.

Monet's early subjects include street scenes, picnics, café life, and boating parties at the fashionable tourist resorts that dotted the banks of the Seine near Paris. However, as Monet found light and color more compelling than Parisian society, his paintings became more impersonal and formless. Wishing to fix sensation, or as he put it, to "seize the intangible," he painted the changing

1879	Edison produces the incandescent light bulb	
1889	Edison invents equipment to take and show moving pictures	
1898	Wilhelm C. Röntgen (German) discovers x-rays	

Figure 31.3 CLAUDE MONET, *Rouen Cathedral, West Facade, Sunlight*, 1894. Oil on canvas, 39½ × 26 in. © 1998 Board of Trustees, National Gallery of Art, Washington, D.C. Chester Dale Collection, 1962.

effects of light on such mundane objects as poplar trees and haystacks. Often working on a number of canvases at once, he might generate a series of paintings that showed his subject in morning light, under the noon sun, and at sunset. Between 1892 and 1894, after a trip to England during which he became familiar with the colorist seascapes of Turner (see Figures 27.7, 27.8), Monet produced no less than thirty different versions of the west facade of Rouen Cathedral (Figure 31.3). As with the other subjects he painted—including the water gardens that he himself created at his summer home in Giverny—Monet seized the thirteenth-century cathedral with his eye rather than with his intellect. This great monument of medieval Christendom, whose surface more resembles a wedding cake than a Gothic church, is rendered not as a sacred symbol but as the site of physical sensation.

Monet may be considered an ultrarealist in his effort to reproduce with absolute fidelity the ever-changing effects of light. His freedom from preconceived ideas of nature prompted his contemporary Paul Cézanne to exclaim that he was "only an eye," but, he added admiringly, "what an eye!" Ironically, Monet's devotion to the physical truth of nature paved the way for modern abstraction—the concern with the intrinsic qualities of the subject, rather than with its literal appearance. Indeed, the panoramic water-garden paintings of Monet's last decades are visionary meditations on light and space.

Renoir, Pissarro, and Degas

Impressionism was never a single, uniform style; rather, the designation embraced the individual approaches of many different artists throughout Europe and America. Nevertheless, the group of artists who met regularly in the 1870s and 1880s at the Café Guerbois in Paris had much in common. To a greater or lesser extent, their paintings reflected Monet's stylistic manner of rendering nature in short strokes of brilliant color. Above all, impressionism brought painterly spontaneity to a celebration of the leisure activities and diversions of urban life: dining, dancing, theater-going, boating, and socializing. In this sense, the most typical impressionist painter might be Pierre-Auguste Renoir (1841–1919). Le Moulin de la Galette, an outdoor café and dance hall located in Montmartre (the bohemian section of nineteenth-century Paris), provided the setting for one of Renoir's most ravishing tributes to youth and informal pleasure (Figure 31.4). In the painting, elegantly dressed young men and women—artists, students, and working-class members of Parisian society—dance, drink, and flirt with one another in the flickering golden light of the late afternoon sun.

Renoir's colleague, Camille Pissarro (1830–1903), was born in the West Indies but settled in Paris in 1855. The

Figure 31.4 PIERRE-AUGUSTE RENOIR, *Le Moulin de la Galette*, 1876. Oil on canvas, 4 ft. 3½ in. × 5 ft. 9 in. Musée d'Orsay, Paris. Photo: © R.M.N., Paris.

oldest and one of the most prolific of the impressionists, he exhibited in all eight of the impressionist group shows. Like Monet and Renoir, Pissarro loved outdoor subjects: peasants working in the fields, the magical effects of freshly fallen snow, and sunlit rural landscapes. Late in his career, however, as his eyesight began to fail, he gave up painting out-of-doors. Renting hotel rooms that looked out upon the streets of Paris, Pissarro produced engaging cityscapes (Figure **31.5**)—sixteen of Paris boulevards in 1897 alone. Strikingly similar to popular panoramic pho-

tographs of turn-of-the-century Paris, Pissarro's urban scenes capture the rhythms of urban life; throngs of horse-drawn carriages and pedestrians are bathed in the misty atmosphere that envelops Paris after the rain. Asked by a young artist for advice on "how to paint," Pissarro suggested that one record visual perceptions with immediacy, avoid defining the outlines of things, observe reflections of color and light, and honor only one teacher: nature.

Edgar Degas (1834–1917) regularly exhibited with the impressionists; but his style remained unique, for he never

Figure 31.6 **EDGAR DEGAS**, *Before the Ballet*, 1890–1892. Oil on canvas, 15¾ × 35 in. © 1998 Board of Trustees, National Gallery of Art, Washington, D.C. Widener Collection.

Figure 31.7 EDGAR DEGAS, *The False Start*, ca. 1870. Oil on canvas, 12⅝ × 15¾ in. Yale University Art Gallery, New Haven. John Hay Whitney, B.A., 1926 Collection.

sacrificed line and form to the beguiling qualities of color and light. Whether depicting the urban world of cafés, racecourses, theaters, and shops, or the demimonde of laundresses and prostitutes, Degas concentrated his attention on the fleeting and intimate moment (Figure **31.6**). He rejected the traditional "posed" model as a subject, seeking instead to capture momentary and even awkward gestures such as stretching and yawning. Degas' untiring attention to racehorses and ballet dancers mirrored his lifelong fascination with matters of balance and motion (Figure **31.7**). In his efforts to recreate the appearance of physical movement in space, he learned much from the British artist, photographer, and inventor Eadweard Muybridge (1830–1904), whose stop-action photographs of the 1870s and 1880s were revolutionary in their time (Figure **31.8**).

Degas was a consummate draftsman and a master designer. He used innovative compositional techniques which balance a sense of spontaneity and improvisation with a mood of reverie. For instance, in *Before the Ballet*, he presents the subject as if seen from below and at an angle that boldly leaves "empty" the lower left half of the composition. He also experimented with asymmetrical compositions in which figures and objects (or fragments of either) might disappear off the edge of the canvas, as if the

image were caught at random. Such innovations testify to the influence of photography, with its accidental "slice of life" potential, as well as that of Japanese woodcuts, which began to enter Europe in the 1860s.

Figure 31.8 EADWEARD MUYBRIDGE, *Photo Sequence of Racehorse*, 1884–1885. Photograph. Library of Congress, Washington, D.C.

Figure 31.9 (above and opposite) **KUNISADA**, triptych showing the different processes of printmaking, early nineteenth century. Japanese woodblock color print.

Right: a woman with an original drawing pasted onto a block conversing with another who is sharpening blades on a whetstone.

Center: a woman (in the foreground) sizing paper sheets which are then hung up to dry; another is removing areas with no design from the block with a chisel.

Left: the printer has just finished taking an impression by rubbing the *baren* (a round pad made of a coil of cord covered by a bamboo sheath) over the paper on the colored block; numerous brushes and bowls of color are visible. Kunisada has made the design more interesting by using women, though the craftsmen were invariably men (information from Julia Hutt, *Understanding Far Eastern Art.* New York: Dutton, 1987, 53). Courtesy of the Trustees of the Victoria and Albert Museum, London.

Japanese Woodblock Prints and Western Art

The Japanese woodblock prints that were entering Europe (along with other Asian goods) in the late nineteenth century were produced in great numbers in the period between roughly 1660 and 1860. Though the prints were a new commodity for Europeans, they represented the end of a long tradition in Japanese art—one that began declining after Japan was forced to open its doors to the West in the 1860s. Japan's decorative tradition, which looked back to the Heian period (784–1185), came to flower in the magnificent folding screens commissioned by wealthy patrons of the sixteenth and seventeenth centuries. Usually executed on a ground of gold leaf, such screens featured flat, unmodulated colors, undulating lines, and a daring use of "empty" space (see chapter 21). Japanese woodblock prints, the execution of which is depicted in some detail in a set of three prints by Kunisada (1786–1864; Figure **31.9**), shared many of the stylistic attributes seen in such earlier aristocratic artforms. They also often incorporated startling perspective vantage-points, such as the bird's-eye view seen in Kunisada's compositions. Woodblock prints, however, were often more rapidly produced (most frequently by men, despite Kunisada's rendering). Their subject matter usually came from the everyday life of bustling, urban Edo (now Tokyo) —especially from the *ukiyo*, "the floating (or fleeting) world" of courtesans, actors, and dancers (Figure **31.11**).

During the mid-nineteenth century, Japanese woodblock artists added landscapes to their print repertory. The landscape prints, often produced as a series of views of local Japanese sites, resemble the topographical studies of Turner and Cole (see chapter 27). But they operated out of entirely different stylistic imperatives: Unlike the European romantics, the Japanese had little interest in the picturesque; rather, they gave attention to bold contrasts and dramatic arrangements of abstract shapes and colors. They also explored unusual ways of layering planes that reduced the sense of continuity between near and far objects. All of these features are evident in one of the most popular mid-nineteenth-century Japanese landscape

prints: *Mount Fuji Seen Below a Wave at Kanagawa* (Figure **31.10**), from the series "Thirty-six Views of Mount Fuji" by Katsushika Hokusai (1760–1849).

When Japanese prints arrived in the West, they exercised an immediate impact on fine and commercial art, including the art of the lithographic poster (Figure **31.12**). Monet and Degas bought them (along with Chinese porcelains) in great numbers, and van Gogh, a great admirer of Hokusai, insisted that his own work was "founded on Japanese art."

Théodore Duret, a French art critic of the time and an enthusiast of impressionist painting, was one of the first writers to observe the impact of Japanese prints on nineteenth-century artists. In a pamphlet called "The Impressionist Painters" (1878), Duret explained:

> We had to wait until the arrival of Japanese albums before anyone dared to sit down on the bank of a river to juxtapose on canvas a boldly red roof, a white wall, a green poplar, a yellow road, and blue water. Before Japan it was impossible; the painter always lied. Nature with its frank colors was in plain sight, yet no one ever saw anything on canvas but attenuated colors, drowning in a general halftone.
>
> As soon as people looked at Japanese pictures, where the most glaring, piercing colors were placed

Figure 31.10 (below) **KATSUSHIKA HOKUSAI**, *Mount Fuji Seen Below a Wave at Kanagawa*, from "Thirty-six Views of Mount Fuji," Tokugawa Period. Full-color woodblock print, width 14¾ in. Courtesy, Museum of Fine Arts, Boston. Spaulding Collection.

side by side, they finally understood that there were new methods for reproducing certain effects of nature.*

Japonisme, the influence of Japan on European art, proved to be multifaceted: The prints sparked the impressionist interest in casual urban subjects (especially those involving women) and inspired fresh approaches to composition and color. At the same time, the elegant naturalism and refined workmanship of Asian cloisonné enamels, ceramics, lacquerwares, ivories, silks, and other collectibles were widely imitated in the Arts and Crafts movements that flourished at the end of the century.

*Quoted in Linda Nochlin, *Impressionism and Post-Impressionism 1874–1904.* Englewood Cliffs, N.J.: Prentice-Hall (1966), 8–9.

Figure 31.12 (below) **HENRI DE TOULOUSE-LAUTREC**, *Jane Avril*, 1899. Lithograph, printed in color, 22 × 14 in. The Museum of Modern Art, New York. Gift of Abby Aldrich Rockefeller. Photograph © 1997 The Museum of Modern Art, New York.

JANE Avril

H.Stern, Paris.

1899

Figure 31.11 (above) **TORII KIYONOBU**, *Actor as a Monkey Showman.* Woodblock print, 13¼ × 6¼ in. The Metropolitan Museum of Art, New York. Rogers Fund, 1936 (JP 2623).© 1994 The Metropolitan Museum of Art.

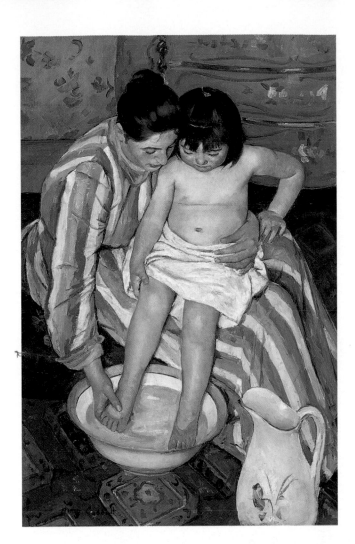

Cassatt and Toulouse-Lautrec

One of the most notable artists to come under the influence of Japanese prints was the American painter Mary Cassatt (1844–1926). Cassatt spent most of her life in Paris, where she became a friend and colleague of Degas, Renoir, and other impressionists, with whom she exhibited regularly. Like Degas, she painted mainly indoors, cultivating a style that combined forceful calligraphy, large areas of unmodulated color, and unusual perspectives—the major features of the Japanese woodcuts—with a taste for female subjects. Cassatt brought a unique sensitivity to domestic themes that featured mothers and children enjoying everyday tasks and diversions (Figure 31.13). Thus, like Manet, Cassatt secularized and updated an age-old, popular theme: that of mother and child. These gentle and optimistic images appealed to American collectors and did much to increase the popularity of impressionist art in the United States. Yet the so-called "Madonna of American art" preferred life in Paris to that in prefeminist America.

Cassatt's gentle visions of domestic life stand in strong contrast to the paintings of Henri de Toulouse-Lautrec (1864–1901). Toulouse-Lautrec, the descendant of an aristocratic French family, practiced many of the stylistic principles of impressionism, but his choice of subject matter was often so intimate that members of his own family condemned his work as unacceptable to "well-bred people." The art of Toulouse-Lautrec shows a more seamy side of Parisian life— the life of cabaret dancers and prostitutes who, like Zola's Nana, lived on the margins of middle-class society (Figure 31.14). Toulouse-Lautrec self-consciously mocked traditional ideas of beauty and propriety. He stylized figures—almost to the point of caricature—in bold and forceful silhouettes.

Figure 31.13 (above) **MARY CASSATT**, *The Bath*, 1891–1892. Oil on canvas, 39½ × 26 in. Photograph © 1998, The Art Institute of Chicago. All Rights Reserved. Robert A. Waller Fund (1910.2).

Figure 31.14 (right) **HENRI DE TOULOUSE-LAUTREC**, *At The Moulin-Rouge*, 1893–1895. Oil on canvas, 4 ft. ⅜ in. × 4 ft. 7¼ in. Photograph © 1993, The Art Institute of Chicago. All Rights Reserved. Helen Birch Bartlett Memorial Collection (1928.610).

Fleshtones might be distorted by artificial light or altered by the stark white makeup (borrowed from Japanese theater) that was current in European fashion.

Toulouse-Lautrec pioneered the art of poster design. In his color lithographs of the voluptuous pleasures of Parisian nightlife, he used bright, flat colors, sinuous lines, and startling juxtapositions of positive and negative space (see Figure 31.12)—stylistic features that reflect the direct influence of eighteenth-century Japanese kabuki prints (see Figure 31.11).

Art Nouveau

The posters of Toulouse-Lautrec bear the seductive stamp of *art nouveau* (French for "new art"), an ornamental style that became enormously popular in the late nineteenth century. *Art nouveau* artists shared with members of the English Arts and Crafts movement a high regard for the fine artisanship of the preindustrial Middle Ages, an era that achieved an ideal synthesis of the functional and the decorative in daily life. The proponents of the new style

Figure 31.15 VICTOR HORTA, Tassel House, Brussels, 1892–1893. © Bastin & Evrard Photodesigners.

also prized the arts of Asia and Islam, which tended to favor bold, flat, organic patterns and semi-abstract linear designs. Acknowledging the impact of the Japanese woodcut style, one French critic insisted that Japanese blood had mixed with the blood of *art nouveau* artists.

Art nouveau originated in Belgium among architects working in the medium of cast iron, but it quickly took on an international reach that affected painting, as well as the design of furniture, textiles, glass, ceramics, and jewelry. The Belgian founder of *art nouveau*, Victor Horta (1861–1947), brought to his work the Arts and Crafts veneration for fine craftsmanship and the symbolist glorification of the sensuous and fleeting forms in nature. A distinguished architect and a great admirer of Eiffel's 1,064-foot-high tower (see Figure 30.27), Horta translated the serpentine lines and organic rhythms of flowers and plants into magnificent glass and cast-iron designs for public buildings and private residences (Figure **31.15**).

"Art in nature, nature in art" was the motto of *art nouveau*. The sinuous curves of blossoms, leaves, and tendrils, conceived in iron and immortalized in such notable monuments as the Paris Métro (the subway), also showed up in wallpaper, poster design, book illustration, tableware, and jewelry. In *art nouveau*, as in late nineteenth-century literature and in impressionist painting,

Figure 31.17 TIFFANY GLASS AND DECORATING CO., peacock vase, 1892–1902. Iridescent "favrile" glass, blues and greens with feather and eye decorations, height 14⅛ in. The Metropolitan Museum of Art, New York. Gift of H. O. Havemeyer, 1896 (96.17.10). © 1987 The Metropolitan Museum of Art.

Figure 31.16 EUGÈNE GRASSET, Comb. ca. 1900. ¼ × 2¾ in. Musée Galliera, Paris. Photo: R.M N./Bulloz, Paris.

women were a favorite subject. The female, often shown with long, luxuriant hair, might be pictured as seductress or enchantress. She might appear as a fairy or water nymph (Figure **31.16**), a poetic, sylphlike creature. In *art nouveau* pins, bracelets, and combs, she is the living counterpart of vines and flowers fashioned in delicately crafted metal armatures and semi-precious stones. Such images suggest that *art nouveau*, although modern in its effort to communicate meaning by way of shapes, patterns, and decoration, was actually the final expression of a century-long romantic infatuation with nature.

In America, *art nouveau* briefly attracted the attention of such architects as Louis Sullivan (see chapter 30), who embellished parts of his otherwise austere office buildings and department stores with floral cast-iron ornamentation. It also inspired the magnificent glass designs of Louis Comfort Tiffany (Figure **31.17**). The son of Charles L. Tiffany, founder of the famed New York jewelry house, Louis was a great admirer of Chinese *cloisonnés* and ancient glass techniques. His innovative studio methods included assembly-line production, the use of templates, and the employment of female artisans who received the same wages as males—a policy that caused great controversy in Tiffany's time. Tiffany's inventive glass designs, which featured floral arabesques and graceful geometric patterns, made him one of the masters of the international *art nouveau* style.

Sculpture in the Late Nineteenth Century

Degas and Rodin

While *art nouveau* artists brought organic naturalism to decorative design, the two greatest European sculptors of the late nineteenth century, Edgar Degas and Auguste Rodin (1840–1917), captured a similar vitality in three-dimensional, figural form. Like the impressionists, Degas and Rodin were interested in lifelike movement and the sensory effects of light. To catch these fleeting qualities, they modeled their figures rapidly in wet clay or wax. The numerous bronze casts made from these originals after the artists' deaths preserve the spontaneity of the additive process. Indeed, Degas' sculptures bear the imprints of his fingers and fingernails.

Degas executed all of his seventy-four sculptures as exercises preliminary to his paintings. Throughout his life, but especially as his vision began to decline, the artist increasingly turned to making wax and clay "sketches" of racehorses, bathers, and ballerinas—his favorite subjects. Only one of these sculptures, the *Little Fourteen-Year-Old Dancer*, was exhibited as a finished artwork during Degas' lifetime. The reddish-brown wax original, made eerily lifelike by the artist's addition of a tutu, stockings, bodice, ballet shoes, a green satin ribbon, and hair from a horsehair wig (embedded strand by strand into the figure's head), was the subject of some controversy in the Parisian art world of 1881 (a world that would not see such mixed-media innovations for another half-century). The bronze cast of Degas' *Dancer* (Figure **31.18**), whose dark

Figure 31.18 (above) **EDGAR DEGAS**, *Little Fourteen-Year-Old Dancer*, 1880–1881. Probably cast in bronze, tulle skirt and satin hair ribbon, height 3 ft. 3 in. The Metropolitan Museum of Art, New York. H. O. Havemeyer Collection. Bequest of Mrs. H. O. Havemeyer, 1929. (29.100.370 View #2). © 1981 The Metropolitan Museum of Art.

Figure 31.19 (right) **AUGUSTE RODIN**, *Dancing Figure*, 1905. Graphite with orange wash, 12⅞ × 9⅜ in. © 1998 Board of Trustees, National Gallery of Art, Washington, D.C. Gift of Mrs. John W. Simpson.

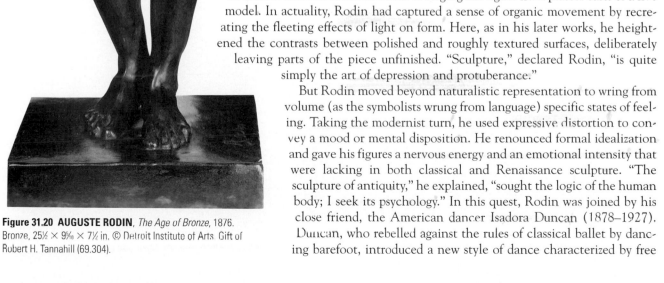

Figure 31.21 Isadora Duncan in *La Marseillaise*. Collection of the Library of Congress, Washington, D.C.

Figure 31.20 AUGUSTE RODIN, *The Age of Bronze*, 1876. Bronze, 25½ × 9⅝ × 7½ in. © Detroit Institute of Arts. Gift of Robert H. Tannahill (69.304).

surfaces contrast sensuously with the fabric additions, retains the supple grace of the artist's finest drawings and paintings.

Like Degas, Rodin was keenly interested in movement and gesture. In hundreds of drawings, he recorded the dancelike rhythms of studio models whom he bid to move about freely rather than assume traditional, fixed poses (Figure **31.19**). But it was in the three-dimensional media that Rodin made his greatest contribution. One of his earliest sculptures, *The Age of Bronze* (Figure **31.20**), was so lifelike that critics accused him of forging the figure from plaster casts of a live model. In actuality, Rodin had captured a sense of organic movement by recreating the fleeting effects of light on form. Here, as in his later works, he heightened the contrasts between polished and roughly textured surfaces, deliberately leaving parts of the piece unfinished. "Sculpture," declared Rodin, "is quite simply the art of depression and protuberance."

But Rodin moved beyond naturalistic representation to wring from volume (as the symbolists wrung from language) specific states of feeling. Taking the modernist turn, he used expressive distortion to convey a mood or mental disposition. He renounced formal idealization and gave his figures a nervous energy and an emotional intensity that were lacking in both classical and Renaissance sculpture. "The sculpture of antiquity," he explained, "sought the logic of the human body; I seek its psychology." In this quest, Rodin was joined by his close friend, the American dancer Isadora Duncan (1878–1927). Duncan, who rebelled against the rules of classical ballet by dancing barefoot, introduced a new style of dance characterized by free

Figure 31.22 AUGUSTE RODIN, *The Gates of Hell*, 1880–1917. Bronze, 20 ft. 8 in. × 13 ft. 1 in. Philadelphia Museum of Art. Gift of Jules E. Mastbaum.

Figure 31.23 AUGUSTE RODIN, *The Kiss*, 1886–1898. Marble, over life-size. Musée Rodin, Paris. Photo: © R.M.N., Paris.

form, personalized gestures, and movements that were often fierce, earthy, and passionate (Figure **31.21**). "I have discovered the art that has been lost for two thousand years," claimed Duncan.

As in Duncan's choreography, so in Rodin's greatest pieces, a particular psychological condition might inspire sculptural form. Such is the case with Rodin's *The Gates of Hell* (Figure **31.22**), a set of doors designed for the projected Paris Museum of Decorative Arts. Loosely modeled after Ghiberti's *Gates of Paradise* (see chapter 17), the portal consists of a swarm of powerful images that represent the tortured souls of Dante's *Inferno* (see chapter 12).

These images, which melt into each other without logical connection, operate by intuition and suggestion, like the imagery in a Mallarmé poem or a Monet landscape. For eight years Rodin added and deleted figures, modeling the Gates section by section. Although he never completed the commission, he remained compelled by its contents, recasting many of the figures individually in bronze and in marble. The two most famous of these individual sculptures are *The Kiss* (Figure **31.23**) and *The Thinker*. The latter—one of the best known of Rodin's works— originally represented Dante contemplating his creation of the underworld from atop its portals.

The Arts of Africa and Oceania

While Degas and Rodin brought a new expressiveness to Western sculptural tradition, their representations of the human body adhered to a perceptual—rather than a conceptual or symbolic—language of form. During the late nineteenth century, an alternate formal vocabulary inspired by European contact with Africa and Oceania (the islands of the South and Central Pacific, Map **31.1**) would come to influence Western art. At the same time, the native cultures of Africa and Oceania absorbed various aspects of Western culture. Nineteenth-century Africa and Oceania were essentially preindustrial and preliterate. Their social organization was tribal, their economies were agricultural, and their gods and spirits were closely associated with nature and natural forces that were the object of communal and individual worship (see chapter 18). In some parts of Africa, kingdoms with longstanding traditions of royal authority flourished until colonial intrusion brought them to an end. The oral traditions of African literature and music, however, came to be recorded during the nineteenth century in written languages based on Arabic and Western forms.

Africa and Oceania consisted of thousands of tightly knit communities in which reverence for deceased ancestors and for the gods was expressed by means of elaborate systems of worship. Reliquaries, masks, and cult figures were among the many power objects created by local artists to harness the spirits of ancestors, for use in rites of passage, and in rituals that ensured the continuity and well-being of the community. These magico-religious figures did not serve a merely decorative role, nor did they carry the narrative and representational authority of most Western art. Rather, as vessels for powerful spirits, their value lay in their ability to channel or transmit spiritual energy. Unlike nineteenth-century Western art, the arts of Africa and Oceania rarely emerged as the personal vision of a single artistic personality. While sharing with Western symbolist art (for instance) a disregard for objective representation and a dependence on symbolic imagery, often expressively simplified or distorted, the arts of these cultures—in both function and form—lay outside of nineteenth-century Western academic tradition.

The visual arts of nineteenth-century Africa and Oceania reflect long-established cultural styles and traditions, many of which extend back over a thousand years. Indeed, much of the art created in these regions during the nineteenth century has its stylistic and functional origins in conventional forms handed down from generation to generation within tribes, regional groups, and kingdoms. So, for example, nineteenth-century Bambara masks from Mali preserve the techniques and styles practiced almost without interruption since the founding of Mali's first empire in the thirteenth century (see chapter 18, Figures

Map 31.1 The Islands of the South Pacific.

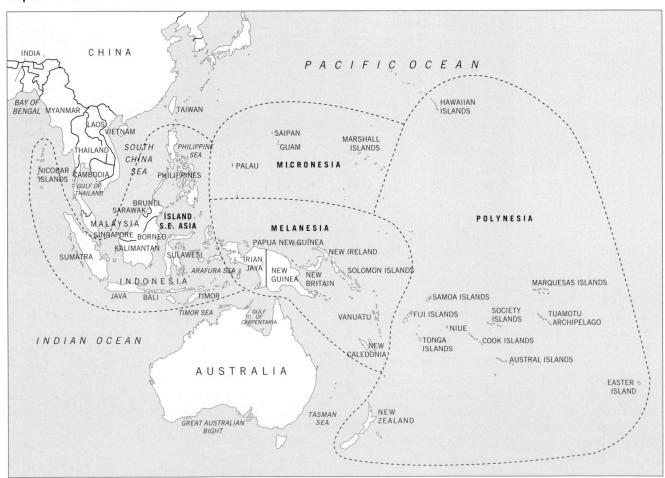

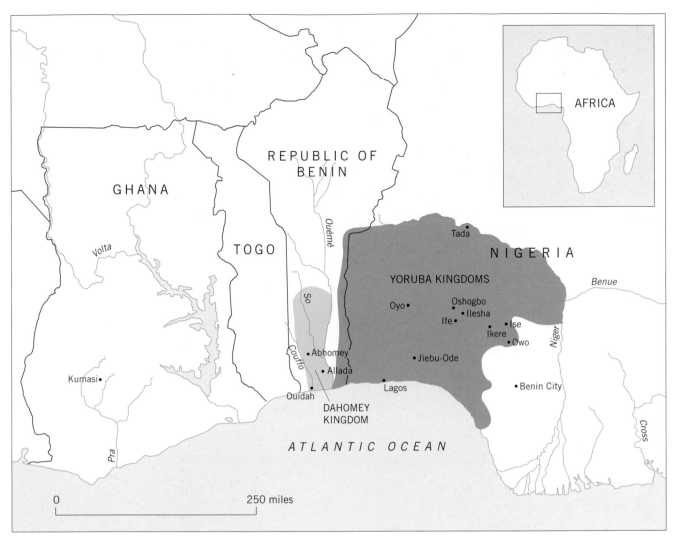

Map 31.2 The Kingdoms of Yoruba and Dahomey.

18.5 and 18.8). Reliable dating of African and Oceanic artworks is difficult to achieve, and items are often mis-dated in the historical literature. It is clear, however, that most extant works now preserved in European museums date from the late nineteenth and early twentieth centuries, though they were probably preceded by similar works that no longer exist. And although productivity from region to region in Africa and from island to island in Oceania varies dramatically, some parts of Africa and Oceania produced their most significant artwork during that time. The classic period in Kenya-Kayan art, from the island of Borneo, for instance, dates from the mid-nineteenth to early twentieth century. And among the Maori peoples of New Zealand, the art of woodcarving, usually employed in the construction of elaborate wooden meetinghouses, flourished during the 1900s. Teams of woodcarvers using European tools produced expressive totemic images embellished with elaborate patterns of tattoos that—similar to African scarification—were popular throughout the South Pacific (see Figure 31.28).

In Africa, even as the incursions of the French disrupt-ed the Yoruba kingdoms of Nigeria (Map **31.2**), royal authority asserted itself in the increased production of magnificent beaded objects, some of which served to iden-tify and embellish the power and authority of the king. The beaded conical crown that belonged to King Glele (1858–1889) of Dahomey (the modern Republic of Benin), for instance, is surmounted by a bird that symbol-izes potent supernatural powers and the all-surpassing majesty of the ruler (Figure **31.24**). Beadwork had been practiced in West Africa since the sixteenth century, when the Portuguese introduced the first Venetian glass beads to that continent. However the "golden age" of beadwork occurred in the late nineteenth century, when uniformly sized European "seed beads" in a wide variety of colors first became available. It is noteworthy that in West Africa beading was an activity reserved exclusively for men.

A second example of high artistic productivity in nineteenth-century Africa comes from the genre of free-standing sculpture: The image of the war god, Gu (Figure **31.25**), commissioned by King Glele as a symbol of his own military might, was carved from wood and covered with hammered brass (said to have come from spent bullet shells). Brandishing two scimitars, the figure served to guard the gate that led into the city of Abhomey. Its fierce, scarified face with its jutting jaw, the wide flat feet, and taut, stylized physique reflect a powerful synthesis of naturalism and abstraction that typifies nineteenth-century African art, but, at the same time, belongs to a long tradition of West African sculpture. The image failed, however, in its protective mission: shortly after the death of King Glele in 1889, his kingdom fell to French colonial forces.

African and Oceanic cultures came into the Western purview with the onset of European imperialism and subsequent colonialism. Ironically, while the colonialists described the highly stylized and generally abstract art forms of these regions as "primitive" (implying simplicity and a lack of sophistication by Western academic standards), Western artists and intellectuals came to appreciate the powerful originality of non-Western art, whose vision of nature and the universe seemed at once direct and more profound than the art of the West. Already in the eighteenth century, the French philosopher Jean Jacques Rousseau (see chapter 25) had glorified "exotic" cultures for their freedom from

Figure 31.24 (below) Yoruba-style beaded crown, nineteenth century. Beads and mixed media, height 17¾ in. Musée de l'Homme, Paris. MA.36.21.62.

Figure 31.25 (above) **GANHU HUNTONDJI** (attributed), The war god Gu, nineteenth century. Brass and wood, height 41½ in. Musée Dapper, Paris.

the taint of civilization. Nineteenth-century romantics and world-weary industrialized Europeans followed suit by exalting "the primitive." The *Exposition Universelle* (World's Fair), held in Paris in 1889, contributed to the interest in foreign cultures by bringing to public view, along with the arts of Asia, the native arts of Africa and Oceania. Reconstructions of villages from the Congo and Senegal, Japan and China, Polynesia and other South Sea islands introduced the non-Western world to astonished Europeans. Remote societies and their artistic achievements quickly became objects of research for the new disciplines of anthropology (the science of humankind and its culture) and ethnography, the branch of anthropology that studies preliterate peoples or groups. In 1890, the Scottish anthropologist Sir James Frazer (1854–1941) published *The Golden Bough*, a pioneer study of magic and religion as reflected in ancient and traditional folk customs. Tragically, however, it was often the case that even as these cultures were coming to be known by ethnographers and their art collected and installed in Western museums, their brilliance, originality, and output began to wane. The French painter Paul Gauguin (1848–1903), who recorded his impressions of Tahiti in his romanticized journal *Noa Noa*, observed:

> The European invasion and monotheism have destroyed the vestiges of a civilization which had its own grandeur. . . . [The Tahitians] had been richly endowed with an instinctive feeling for the harmony necessary between human creations and the animal and plant life that formed the setting and decoration of their existence, but this has now been lost. In contact with us, with our school, they have truly become "savages" . . .*

The appeal of the primitive among late nineteenth-century figures such as Gauguin reflected a more than casual interest in the world beyond the West. It constituted a rebellion against Western sexual and societal taboos—a rebellion that would become full-blown in the primitivism of early modern art (see chapter 32).

Postimpressionism

The group of Western artists who followed the impressionists—loosely designated as "postimpressionists"—are linked by their modernist direction: Pursuing an art-for-art's-sake aestheticism, they prized pictorial invention over and above pictorial illusion. The postimpressionists were largely uninterested in satisfying the demands of public and private patrons; they made only sporadic efforts to sell what they produced. Although strongly individualistic, they were all profoundly concerned with the formal language of art and its capacity to capture sensory experience. Like impressionism, postimpressionism can be seen as an intensification of romantic artists' efforts to share their subjective responses to the real world. But unlike the

*From Paul Gauguin, *Noa Noa*, translated by O. F. Theis. New York: Noonday Press, 1964, 106.

romantics (and the impressionists), the postimpressionists made a conscious effort to bring order to the world of pure sensation. These pioneers of modern art put into practice the point of view of the French artist and theorist Maurice Denis (1870–1943): Denis believed that a painting was not first and foremost a pictorial reproduction of reality but was essentially "a flat surface covered with shapes, lines, and colors assembled in a particular order." This credo, as realized in postimpressionist painting, would drive most of the major modern art movements of the early twentieth century (see chapter 32).

Van Gogh and Gauguin

The Dutch artist Vincent van Gogh (1853–1890) was a passionate idealist whose life was marred by loneliness, poverty, depression, and a hereditary mental illness which ultimately drove him to suicide. During his career he produced over seven hundred paintings and thousands of drawings, of which he sold less than a half-dozen in his lifetime. Influenced by Japanese prints, van Gogh painted landscapes, still lifes, and portraits in a style that featured flat, bright colors, a throbbing, sinuous line, and short, choppy brushstrokes. His heavily pigmented surfaces were often manipulated with a palette knife or built up by applying paint directly from the tube. Deeply moved by music (especially the work of Wagner), van Gogh shared with the romantics an attitude toward nature that was both inspired and ecstatic. His emotional response to an object, rather than its physical appearance, often deter-

Figure 31.26 VINCENT VAN GOGH, *Self-Portrait*, 1889. Oil on canvas, 25½ × 21¼ in. Musée d'Orsay, Paris. Photo: © R.M.N., Paris.

Figure 31.27 VINCENT VAN GOGH, *The Starry Night*, 1889. Oil on canvas, 29 × 36¼ in. The Museum of Modern Art, New York. Acquired through the Lillie P. Bliss Bequest. Photograph © 1997 The Museum of Modern Art, New York.

mined his choice of colors, which he likened to orchestrated sound. As he explained to his brother Theo, "I use color more arbitrarily so as to express myself more forcefully." Van Gogh's painting *The Starry Night* (Figure **31.27**), a view of the small French town of Saint-Rémy, is electrified by thickly painted strokes of white, yellow, orange, and blue. Cypresses writhe like flames, stars explode, the moon seems to burn like the sun, and the heavens heave and roll like ocean waves. Here, van Gogh's expressive use of color invests nature with visionary frenzy.

In his letters to Theo (an art dealer by profession), van Gogh pledged his undying faith in the power of artistic creativity. In 1888, just two years before he committed suicide, he wrote: "I can do without God both in my life and in my painting, but I cannot, ill as I am, do without something which is greater than I, which is my life—the power to create. And if, defrauded of the power to create physically, a man tries to create thoughts in place of children, he is still part of humanity." Assessing his own creativity,

van Gogh claimed that making portraits allowed him to cultivate what was "best and deepest." "Altogether," he explained, "it is the only thing in painting which moves me to the depths, and which more than anything else makes me feel the infinite."* For van Gogh, the challenge of portraiture lay in capturing the heart and soul of the model. In his many portraits of friends and neighbors, and in the twenty-four self-portraits painted between 1886 and 1889, van Gogh raised the mood of romantic subjectivity to new levels of confessional intensity. In the *Self-Portrait* of 1889 (Figure **31.26**), for instance, where the pale flesh-tones of the head are set against an almost monochromatic blue field, the skull takes on a forbidding, even spectral presence—an effect enhanced by the lurid green facial shadows and the blue-green eyes, slanted (as he related to Theo) so as to make himself look Japanese. His brushstrokes, similar to those that evoke the coiling heavens in

*In Irving Stone, ed., *Dear Theo: The Autobiography of Vincent van Gogh*. New York: New American Library, 1937, 382, 370.

Figure 31.28 Fragment of a Maori doorpost, from New Zealand. University of Pennsylvania Museum, Philadelphia (neg. S4134161).

The Starry Night, charge the surface with undulating rhythms that sharply contrast with the immobile human figure. This visual strategy underscores the artist's alienation from his surroundings; it becomes more meaningful in light of van Gogh's confession (to his friend and colleague Gauguin) that he saw himself in this portrait as a simple Buddhist monk.

If van Gogh may be said to have apprehended an inner vision of nature, Paul Gauguin tried to recast nature in its unblemished state. Abandoning his wife, his children, and his job as a Paris stockbroker, this prototype of the modern bohemian traveled to Martinique in the West Indies, to Brittany in Northwest France, and to Southern France before finally settling on the island of Tahiti in the South Seas. Gauguin, in his self-conscious effort to assume the role of "the civilized savage," shared the fascination with unspoiled nature that characterized the writings of Rousseau and Thoreau. Indeed, his bohemianism may be said to represent the "last gasp" of romanticism. But Gauguin's flight to the South Seas was also typical of the search for a lost Eden and the fascination with non-Western cultures that swept through the intellectual community of late nineteenth-century Europe.

Gauguin took artistic inspiration from the folk culture of Brittany, from the native arts of the South Sea islands, and from dozens of other nonacademic sources. What impressed him was the self-taught immediacy and authenticity of folk and tribal artforms, especially those that made use of powerful, totemic abstraction (Figure 31.28). His own

Figure 31.29 (below) **PAUL GAUGUIN**, *The Day of the God (Mahana no Atua)*, 1894. Oil on canvas, 27⅜ ×35⅝ in. Photograph © 1998, The Art Institute of Chicago. All Rights Reserved. Helen Birch Bartlett Memorial Collection (1926.198).

style, nurtured in the symbolist precepts (discussed earlier in this chapter) and influenced by Japanese woodcuts and photographs of Japanese temple reliefs on view at the Paris Exposition, featured flat, often distorted and brightly colored shapes that seem to float on the surface of the canvas. In *The Day of the God* (Figure **31.29**), bright blues, yellows, and pinks form rhythmic tapestry-like patterns reminiscent of Japanese prints and *art nouveau* posters. Like the verbal images of the symbolist poets, Gauguin's colored shapes evoke a mood and imply ideas that lie beyond literal description. For example, the languid, organic shapes in the foreground pool of water and the fetal positions of the figures lying on the shore are suggestive of birth and regeneration—motifs appropriate to the totemic guardian figure (pictured at top center of the canvas), who resembles the creator god and supreme deity of Maori culture (compare Figure 31.28).

Gauguin's figures cast no shadows, and his bold, unmodeled colors, like those of van Gogh, often bear little relationship to visual appearance. (The blues in the background of *The Day of the God*, for instance, are of the same intensity as those in the foreground.) Gauguin joined van Gogh at Arles in the fall of 1888, and for a brief time the two artists lived and worked side by side. Volatile and temperamental, they often engaged in violent quarrels, and during one of van Gogh's psychotic episodes (which ended in his cutting off part of his own ear), he even attempted

to kill Gauguin. But despite their intense personal differences, van Gogh and Gauguin were fraternal pioneers in the search for a provocative language of form and color.

Seurat and Cézanne

Extending the techniques of the impressionists in a different direction, the postimpressionist French painter Georges Seurat (1859–1891) treated color as analytically as a modern laboratory technician. Seurat was trained academically and, like the academicians Poussin and David, he brought balance and order to his style. The forms in his compositions, for instance, seem plotted along an invisible graph of vertical and horizontal lines that run parallel to the picture plane. A similar fervor for order may have inspired Seurat's novel use of tiny dots of color (in French, *points*), which he applied side by side (and sometimes one inside another) to build up dense clusters that give the impression of solid form—a style known as *pointillism*. Seurat arrived at the technique of dividing color into component parts after studying the writings of Chevreul and other pioneers in color theory. Leaving nothing to chance (Gauguin called him "the little green chemist"), Seurat analyzed color into its component tints. He applied each tint so that its juxtaposition with the next would produce the desired degree of vibration to the eye of the beholder. Although Seurat shared the impressionists' fascination with light and color, he shunned spontaneity, and though he

Figure 31.30 GEORGES SEURAT, *Sunday Afternoon on the Island of La Grande Jatte*, 1884–1886. Oil on canvas, 6 ft. 9½ in. × 10 ft. ⅜ in. Photograph © 1998, The Art Institute of Chicago. All Rights Reserved. Helen Birch Bartlett Memorial Collection (1926.224).

Figure 31.31 PAUL CÉZANNE, *The Basket of Apples*, ca. 1895. Oil on canvas, 25¾ × 32 in. Photograph © 1998, The Art Institute of Chicago. All Rights Reserved. Helen Birch Bartlett Memorial Collection (1926.252).

made his sketches out-of-doors, he executed his paintings inside his studio, usually at night and under artificial light.

Seurat's monumental *Sunday Afternoon on the Island of La Grande Jatte* shows a holiday crowd of Parisians relaxing on a sunlit island in the River Seine (Figure **31.30**). Although typically impressionistic in its subject matter—urban society at leisure—the painting (along with the twenty-seven preparatory panels on the same theme) harbors little of the impressionist's love for intimacy and fleeting sensation. Every figure is isolated from the next as if each were frozen in space and unaware of another's existence. One critic railed, "Strip his figures of the colored fleas that cover them; underneath you will find nothing, no thought, no soul." Seurat's universe, with its atomized particles of color and its self-contained figures, may seem devoid of human feeling, but, at the same time, its exquisite regularity provides a comforting alternative to the chaos of experience. Indeed, the lasting appeal of *La Grande Jatte* lies in its effectiveness as a symbolic retreat from the tumult of everyday life and the accidents of nature.

More so than Seurat, Paul Cézanne (1839–1906) served as a bridge between the art of the nineteenth century and that of the twentieth. Cézanne began his career as an impressionist but his traditional subjects—such as landscapes, portraits, and still lifes—show a greater concern for the formal aspects of the painting than for its subject matter. His effort to "redo nature after Poussin," that is, to find the enduring forms of nature that were basic to all great art, made Cézanne the first modernist artist.

Cézanne's determination to invest his pictures with a strong sense of three-dimensional form (a feature often neglected by the impressionists) led to a method of building up form by means of small, flat planes of color, larger than (but not entirely unlike) Seurat's colored dots. Abandoning the intuitive and loosely organized compositions of the impressionists, Cézanne also sought to restore to painting the sturdy, formal structure of academic composition. His concern for pictorial unity inspired him to take bold liberties with form and perspective, and, ultimately, to modify traditional methods of reproducing the appearance of physical objects in space: He might, for instance, tilt and flatten surfaces; reduce (or abstract) familiar objects to such basic geometric shapes as cylinders, cones, and spheres; or depict various objects in a single composition from different points of view. Cézanne's still lifes are not so much likenesses of tempting apples,

Figure 31.32 PAUL CÉZANNE, *Mont Sainte-Victoire*, 1902–1904. Oil on canvas, 27½ × 35¼ in. Philadelphia Museum of Art. George W. Elkins Collection (Acces. E′36–1–1).

peaches, or pears as they are architectural arrangements of colored forms (Figure **31.31**). In short, where narrative content often seems neglected, form itself has meaning.

Cézanne's mature style developed when he left Paris and returned to live in his native area of Southern France. Here he tirelessly painted the local landscape: Dozens of times he painted the rugged, stony peak of Mont Sainte-Victoire near his hometown of Aix-en-Provence. Among Cézanne's last versions of the subject is a landscape in which trees and houses have become an abstract network of colored facets of paint (Figure **31.32**). By applying colors of the same intensity to different parts of the canvas—note the bright green and rich violet brushstrokes in both sky and landscape—Cézanne challenged traditional distinctions between foreground and background. In Cézanne's canvases, all parts of the composition, like the flat shapes of a Japanese print, become equal in value. Cézanne's methods, which transformed an ordinary mountain into an icon of stability, led the way to modern abstraction.

SUMMARY

Art for art's sake was neither a movement nor a style but rather a prevailing spirit in European and especially French culture of the last quarter of the nineteenth century. In all of the arts, there was a new attention to sensory experience rather than to moral and didactic purpose. At the same time, advances in optics, electricity, and other areas of science and technology brought attention to matters of motion and light. Paralleling the radical changes in technology and art, the German iconoclast Nietzsche questioned the moral value of art and rallied superior individuals to topple old gods—that is, to reject whatever was sentimental and stale in Western tradition. Amidst new theories of sensation and perception, the French philosopher Bergson stressed the role of intuition in grasping the true nature of durational reality. The symbolists devised a language of sensation that evoked feeling rather than described experience. In Mallarmé's "L'Après-midi d'un faune," images unfold as sensuous, discontinuous fragments. Similar effects occur in the music of Debussy, where delicately shaded harmonies gently drift without resolution.

The French impressionists, led by Monet, were equally representative of the late nineteenth-century interest in sensation and sensory experience. These artists tried to record an instantaneous vision of their world, sacrificing the details of perceived objects in order to capture the effects of light and atmosphere. Renoir, Degas, Cassatt, and Toulouse-Lautrec produced informal and painterly canvases that offer a glimpse into the pleasures of nineteenth-century European urban life. Stop-action photographs and the flat, linear designs of Japanese prints influenced the style of the impressionists. Japanese woodcuts also anticipated the decorative style known as *art nouveau*, which dominated architecture, poster design, and Western arts and crafts in the last decades of the century. In sculpture, the works of Degas and Rodin reflect a common concern for figural gesture and movement. Rodin's efforts to translate inner states of feeling into expressive physical form were mirrored by Isadora Duncan's innovations in modern dance.

The visual intensity of such Western artforms seemed dim, however, in the light of those artifacts newly arrived in the West from the cultures of Africa and Oceania. Nonwestern art would come to play a major part in the move to modernism that occurred in the last decade of the nineteenth century. The postimpressionists van Gogh, Gauguin, Seurat, and Cézanne renounced the impressionist infatuation with the fleeting effects of light to devise new pictorial strategies. Van Gogh and Gauguin used color not as an atmospheric envelope but as a tool for personal and visionary expression. Seurat and Cézanne reacted against the formlessness of impressionism by creating styles that featured architectural stability and solid, simplified forms. On the threshold of the twentieth century,

artists would escape the naturalistic bias of both romanticism and realism by boldly shedding their former roles as idealizers and imitators of nature.

SUGGESTIONS FOR READING

Berger, Klaus. *Japonisme in Western Painting from Whistler to Matisse*, translated by David Britt. New York: Cambridge University Press, 1992.

Blier, Suzanne Preston. *The Royal Arts of Africa: The Majesty of Form*. New York: Abrams, 1998.

Gogh, Vincent van. *Van Gogh's Diary: The Artist's Life in His Own Words and Art*. New York: Morrow, 1971.

Goldwater, Robert. *Symbolism*. London: Allen Lane, 1979.

Herbert, Robert L. *Impressionism: Art, Leisure and Parisian Society*. New Haven: Yale University Press, 1988.

Kroegger, M. E. *Literary Impressionism*. New Haven: Yale University Press, 1973.

Nord, Philip. *Impressionism and Politics: Art and Democracy in the Nineteenth Century*. New York: Routledge, 2000.

Rewald, John. *The History of Impressionism*. New York: New York Graphic Society, 1980.

Schmutzler, Robert. *Art Nouveau*. New York: Abrams, 1962.

Silverman, Deborah. *Art Nouveau in Fin-de-Siècle France: Politics, Psychology, and Style*. Berkeley, Calif.: University of California Press, 1989.

Solomon, Robert. *Reading Nietzsche*. New York: Oxford University Press, 1988.

Thomas, Nicholas. *Oceanic Art*. London: Thames and Hudson, 1995.

Whitford, Frank. *Japanese Prints and Western Painting*. New York: Macmillan, 1977.

MUSIC LISTENING SELECTION

CD Two Selection 16   Debussy, *Prélude à "L'après-midi d'un faune,"* 1894.

The triumph of modernism

Since the birth of civilization, no age has broken with tradition more radically or more self-consciously than the twentieth century. In part, the modernist break with the past represents the willful rejection of former values, but it also registers the revolutionary effects of science and technology on all aspects of life. Among the swelling populations of modern cities, the pace of living became faster and more chaotic than ever before. At the same time, electronic technology began to transform the planet earth into what Canadian sociologist Marshall McLuhan called a "global village." In the global village of the twentieth century, communication between geographically remote parts of the world was almost instantaneous, and every new development—technological, ecological, political, and intellectual—potentially affected every villager. Social and geographic mobility, receptivity to change, and a self-conscious quest for the new, the different, and even the outrageous were the hallmarks of this largely secular and materialistic world community.

The metaphoric "shrinking" of the planet actually began at the end of the nineteenth century, with the invention of the telephone (1876), wireless telegraphy (1891), and the internal combustion engine (1897), which made possible the first automobiles. By 1903, the airplane joined the string of enterprises that ushered in an era of rapid travel and communication. Such technology was as revolutionary for the twentieth century as metallurgy was

for the fourth millennium B.C.E. However, while metallurgy ushered in the birth of civilization, modern technology (machine guns, poison gas, and nuclear power) gave civilization the tools for self-destruction.

The end of the nineteenth century was a time of relative peace and optimistic faith in technological progress and human productivity. Throughout the world, however, sharp contrasts existed between rich and poor, between democratic and totalitarian ideologies, and between technologically backward and technologically advanced nations. As the powerful nations jockeyed for political and economic primacy, and as Europe and the United States continued to build their industrial and military might, few anticipated the possibility of armed conflict. In 1914, that possibility became a reality in the outbreak of the first of two world wars. The "Great War," the first total war in European history, ended forever the so-called age of innocence. And by the end of World War II, in 1945, nothing would ever seem certain again.

The modern era—roughly the first half of the twentieth century—has yielded a rich diversity of ideas and art styles. These are addressed thematically: in chapters that treat the modernist assault on tradition, Sigmund Freud's influential role in the culture of the twentieth century, the brutal impact of totalitarianism and two world wars, and finally, the arts at mid-century, as they reflect the alienation and anxiety that dominated the postwar era.

(opposite) **MARCEL DUCHAMP**, detail of *Nude Descending a Staircase, #2*, 1912. Oil on canvas, 58 × 35 in. Philadelphia Museum of Art. Louise and Walter Arensberg Collection. © Succession Marcel Duchamp. ADAGP, Paris and DACS, London 2000.

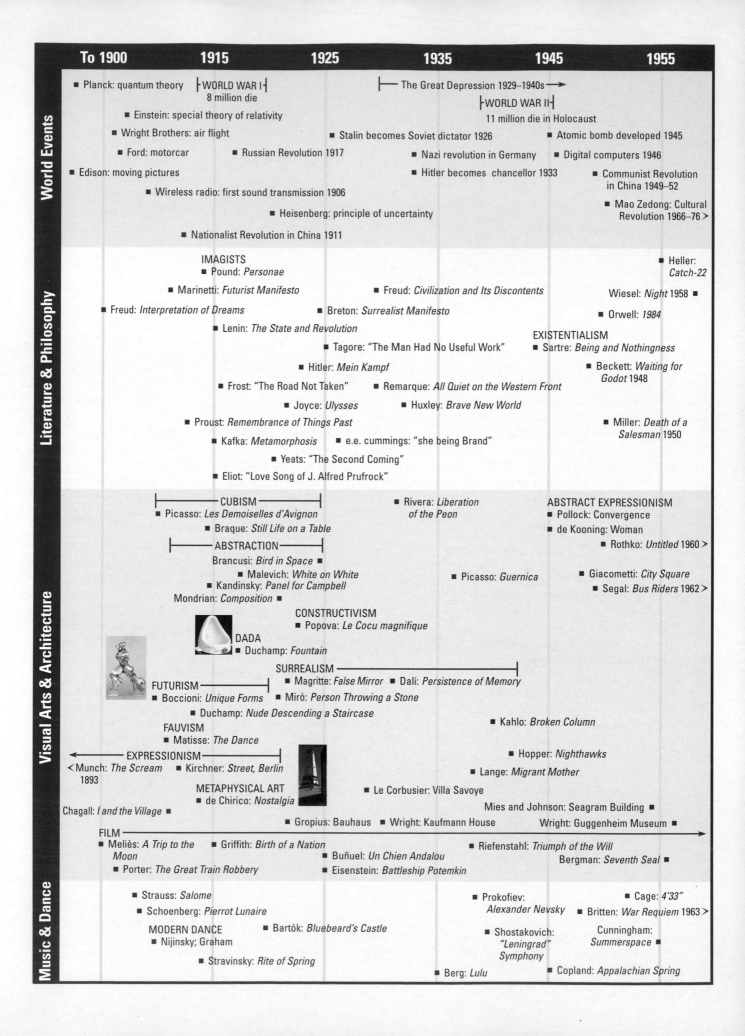

	To 1900	1915	1925	1935	1945	1955

World Events

- Planck: quantum theory
- ⊢WORLD WAR I⊣ 8 million die
- ⊢ The Great Depression 1929–1940s →
- Einstein: special theory of relativity
- ⊢WORLD WAR II⊣ 11 million die in Holocaust
- Wright Brothers: air flight
- Stalin becomes Soviet dictator 1926
- Atomic bomb developed 1945
- Ford: motorcar
- Russian Revolution 1917
- Nazi revolution in Germany
- Digital computers 1946
- Edison: moving pictures
- Hitler becomes chancellor 1933
- Communist Revolution in China 1949–52
- Wireless radio: first sound transmission 1906
- Heisenberg: principle of uncertainty
- Mao Zedong: Cultural Revolution 1966–76 ⟩
- Nationalist Revolution in China 1911

Literature & Philosophy

- IMAGISTS
  - Pound: *Personae*
- Heller: *Catch-22*
- Marinetti: *Futurist Manifesto*
- Freud: *Civilization and Its Discontents*
- Wiesel: *Night* 1958
- Freud: *Interpretation of Dreams*
- Breton: *Surrealist Manifesto*
- Orwell: *1984*
- Lenin: *The State and Revolution*
- EXISTENTIALISM
  - Sartre: *Being and Nothingness*
- Tagore: "The Man Had No Useful Work"
- Hitler: *Mein Kampf*
- Beckett: *Waiting for Godot* 1948
- Frost: "The Road Not Taken"
- Remarque: *All Quiet on the Western Front*
- Joyce: *Ulysses*
- Huxley: *Brave New World*
- Proust: *Remembrance of Things Past*
- Miller: *Death of a Salesman* 1950
- Kafka: *Metamorphosis*
- e.e. cummings: "she being Brand"
- Yeats: "The Second Coming"
- Eliot: "Love Song of J. Alfred Prufrock"

Visual Arts & Architecture

- ⊢CUBISM⊣
  - Picasso: *Les Demoiselles d'Avignon*
- Rivera: *Liberation of the Peon*
- ABSTRACT EXPRESSIONISM
  - Pollock: Convergence
- Braque: *Still Life on a Table*
- de Kooning: Woman
- ⊢ABSTRACTION⊣
- Rothko: *Untitled* 1960 ⟩
- Brancusi: *Bird in Space*
- Malevich: *White on White*
- Picasso: *Guernica*
- Giacometti: *City Square*
- Kandinsky: *Panel for Campbell*
- Segal: *Bus Riders* 1962 ⟩
- Mondrian: *Composition*
- CONSTRUCTIVISM
  - Popova: *Le Cocu magnifique*
- DADA
  - Duchamp: *Fountain*
- SURREALISM
  - Magritte: *False Mirror*
  - Dalí: *Persistence of Memory*
- FUTURISM
  - Boccioni: *Unique Forms*
  - Miró: *Person Throwing a Stone*
- Duchamp: *Nude Descending a Staircase*
- FAUVISM
  - Matisse: *The Dance*
- Kahlo: *Broken Column*
- ← EXPRESSIONISM ⊣
  - ⟨ Munch: *The Scream* 1893
  - Kirchner: *Street, Berlin*
- Hopper: *Nighthawks*
- Lange: *Migrant Mother*
- METAPHYSICAL ART
  - de Chirico: *Nostalgia*
- Le Corbusier: Villa Savoye
- Chagall: *I and the Village*
- Mies and Johnson: Seagram Building
- Gropius: Bauhaus
- Wright: Kaufmann House
- Wright: Guggenheim Museum
- FILM →
  - Meliès: *A Trip to the Moon*
  - Griffith: *Birth of a Nation*
  - Riefenstahl: *Triumph of the Will*
  - Porter: *The Great Train Robbery*
  - Buñuel: *Un Chien Andalou*
  - Bergman: *Seventh Seal*
  - Eisenstein: *Battleship Potemkin*

Music & Dance

- Strauss: *Salome*
- Prokofiev: *Alexander Nevsky*
- Cage: *4'33"*
- Schoenberg: *Pierrot Lunaire*
- Britten: *War Requiem* 1963 ⟩
- MODERN DANCE
  - Nijinsky; Graham
- Bartók: *Bluebeard's Castle*
- Shostakovich: "Leningrad" Symphony
- Cunningham: *Summerspace*
- Stravinsky: *Rite of Spring*
- Berg: *Lulu*
- Copland: *Appalachian Spring*

CHAPTER THIRTY-TWO

The modernist assault

"What is real is not the external form, but the essence of things."
Constantin Brancusi

The New Physics

At the turn of the nineteenth century, atomic physicists advanced a model of the universe that altered the one that Isaac Newton had provided two centuries earlier. Newton's universe had operated according to smoothly functioning mechanical laws that generally corresponded with the world of sense perception. Modern physicists, however, discovered that at the physical extremities of nature—in the microcosmic realm of atomic particles and in the macrocosmic world of outer space—Newton's laws did not apply. The laws that, in fact, governed these systems only became clear when physicists succeeded in measuring the speed of light as it moved through space. In 1900, the German physicist Max Planck (1858–1947) discovered that light was a form of radiant energy that traveled through space in *quanta*, that is, separate and discontinuous bundles of atomic particles—the fundamental units of matter. Following this and other groundbreaking discoveries in quantum physics (as the field came to be called), another German physicist, Albert Einstein (1879–1955), explained the intrinsic relationship between matter and energy. Energy, argued Einstein, is itself matter multiplied by the speed of light squared, a relationship expressed by the formula $E = mc^2$.

In 1905, Einstein also produced his *special theory of relativity*, a radically new approach to the concepts of time, space, and motion. While Newton had held that an object preserved the same properties whether at rest or in motion, Einstein theorized that as an object approached the speed of light, its mass increased and its motion slowed. Time and space, according to Einstein, were not separate coordinates (as physicists had heretofore conceived) but, rather, indivisible and reciprocal entities. Einstein's discoveries indicated that the universe was shapeless and subject to constant change and, further, that the positions of atomic particles and their velocity might not be calculable with any certainty. In 1920 the research of the German physicist Werner Heisenberg (1901–1976)

confirmed Einstein's theory: Heisenberg's *principle of uncertainty* stated that since the very act of measuring subatomic phenomena would alter those phenomena, the position and the velocity of a particle could not be measured simultaneously with any accuracy. Thus, at the onset of the twentieth century, modern physics had replaced the absolute and rationalist model of the universe with one whose operations seemed disjunctive and uncertain.

The practical and the theoretical implications of quantum physics and relativity were immense. Jet propulsion, radar technology, and computer electronics were only three of the numerous long-range consequences of atomic physics. The new science gave humankind greater insight into the operations of nature, but it also provided a gloomier view of the cosmos. In contrast with the optimistic (if mechanical) view of nature provided by Enlightenment cosmology and nineteenth-century technology, modern physics described a universe whose operations violated the inexorable sequence of cause and effect. While Newtonian physics encouraged human control of nature, modern science pictured an indifferent cosmos whose basic components—atomic particles—were inaccessible to both the human eye and the camera (and hence beyond the realm of the senses). Moreover, the operations of that cosmos seemed to lie beyond predictability or control.

The new physics, dependent mainly on mathematical theory, became increasingly remote from the average person's understanding. Atomic fission, the splitting of atomic particles (accomplished only after 1920), and the atomic bomb itself (first tested in 1945) confirmed the validity of Einstein's formula, $E = mc^2$. But it also paved the way for the atomic age, an age that carried with it the possibility of total annihilation. And even if the planet did escape atomic destruction, its demise, in the long run, was inevitable; for, according to the new physics, substance and energy were diffusing inexorably into darkness. As one writer explained, "The sun is slowly but surely burning out, the stars are dying embers, and everywhere in the cosmos heat is turning to cold, matter is dissolving into radiation,

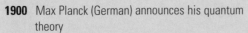

1900 Max Planck (German) announces his quantum theory

1903 Henry Ford (American) introduces the Model A automobile

1905 Albert Einstein (German) announces his special theory of relativity

1910 Bertrand Russell and Alfred North Whitehead (British) publish their *Principia Mathematica*, a systematic effort to base mathematics in logic

1913 Niels Bohr (Danish) applies quantum theory to atomic structure

1916 Einstein announces his general theory of relativity

and energy is being dissipated into empty space."* Though the final curtain was not predicted to fall for billions of years, the portents were ominous.

As Einstein challenged the established way of viewing the external world, the Austrian physician Sigmund Freud was proposing a new and equally revolutionary way of perceiving the internal, or subconscious, world of the human being (see chapter 33). And, as if to confirm Freud's darkest insights, in 1914 Europe embarked on the first of two wars, both of which used the potentially liberating tools of the new science to annihilate human life. World War I, more devastating than any previously fought on this planet, compounded the prevailing mood of insecurity and convinced many that the death of culture was at hand.

Early Twentieth-Century Poetry

The literature of the early twentieth century mirrored the somber mood of uncertainty. Unlike the romantics of the nineteenth century, early modern poets found in nature neither a source of ecstasy nor a means of personal redemption. Their poetry did not characterize human beings as heroic or inspired; rather, it described an indifferent cosmos, whose inhabitants might be insecure, questioning, and even perverse. While early twentieth-century poetry was less optimistic than romantic poetry, it was also less effusive and self-indulgent. Indeed, its lyric strains were frequently as discordant as those of early modern music and modern art.

The Imagists

Poets of the early twentieth century cultivated a language of expression that was as conceptual and abstract as that of modern physics. Like the nineteenth-century symbolist poets (see chapter 31), early twentieth-century poets rejected self-indulgent sentiment and sought a more concentrated style that involved paring down the subject in order to capture its intrinsic or essential qualities—a process called **abstraction**. They rejected fixed meter and rhyme and wrote instead in a style of free verse that became

*Lincoln Barnett, *The Universe and Dr. Einstein*. New York: The New American Library, 1948, 102.

notorious for its abrupt and discontinuous juxtaposition of lean and sparse images. Appropriately, these poets called themselves *imagists*. Led by the Americans Ezra Pound (1885–1972), Amy Lowell (1874–1925), and Hilda Doolittle (1886–1961), who signed her poems simply "H.D.," the imagists took as their goal the search for verbal compression, concentration, and economy of expression.

The American expatriate Ezra Pound was one of the most influential of the imagist poets. By the age of twenty-three, Pound had abandoned his study of language and literature at American universities for a career in writing that led him to Europe, where he wandered from England to France and Italy. A poet, critic, and translator, Pound was thoroughly familiar with the literature of his contemporaries. But he cast his net wide: He studied the prose and poetry of ancient Greece and Rome, China and Japan, medieval France and Renaissance Italy—often reading the work of literature in its original language. As a student of Oriental calligraphy, he drew inspiration from the sparseness and immediacy of Chinese characters. He was particularly fascinated by the fact that the Chinese poetic line, which presented images without grammar or syntax, operated in the same intuitive manner that nature worked upon the human mind. It was this vitality that Pound wished to bring to poetry.

In Chinese and Japanese verse—especially in the Japanese poetic genre known as **haiku**—Pound found the key to his search for concentrated expression. Two *haiku*-like poems are to be found in the collection called *Personae*.

READING 6.1 From Pound's *Personae* (1926)

"In a Station of the Metro"

The apparition of these faces in the crowd;
Petals on a wet, black bough.

"The Bathtub"

As a bathtub lined with white porcelain,
When the hot water gives out or goes tepid,
So is the slow cooling of our chivalrous passion,
O my much praised but-not-altogether-satisfactory lady.

Pound imitated the *haiku*-style succession of images to evoke subtle, metaphoric relationships between things. He conceived what he called the "rhythmical arrangement of words" to produce an emotional "shape." In the *Imagist Manifesto* (1913) and in various interviews, Pound outlined the cardinal points of the imagist doctrine: Poets should use "absolutely no word that does not contribute to the presentation"; they should employ free verse rhythms "in sequence of the musical phrase." Ultimately, Pound summoned his contemporaries to cast aside traditional modes of Western versemaking and to "make it new"—a dictum allegedly scrawled on the bathtub of an ancient Chinese emperor. "Day by day," wrote Pound, "make it new/cut underbrush/pile the logs/keep it growing." The injunction to "make it new" became the rallying cry of modernism.

The imagist search for an abstract language of expression, which, as we shall see, loosely paralleled the visual artist's quest for absolute form, stood at the beginning of the modernist revolution in poetry. It also opened the door to a more concealed and elusive style of poetry, one that drew freely on the cornucopia of world literature and history. The poems that Pound wrote after 1920, particularly the *Cantos* (the unfinished opus on which Pound labored for fifty-five years), challenge the reader with foreign language phrases, obscene jokes, and arcane literary and historical allusions. These poems contrast sharply with the terse precision and eloquent purity of Pound's early imagist efforts.

Frost and Lyric Poetry

Not all of Pound's contemporaries heeded the imagist doctrine. Robert Frost (1874–1963), the best known and one of the most popular of American poets, offered an alternative to the highly abstract style of the modernists. While Frost rejected the romantic sentimentality of much nineteenth-century verse, he embraced the older tradition of lyric poetry. He wrote in metered verse and jokingly compared the modernist use of free verse to playing tennis without a net. Frost avoided dense allusions and learned references. In plain speech he expressed deep affection for the natural landscape and an abiding sympathy with the frailties of the human condition. He described American rural life as uncertain and enigmatic—at times, notably dark. "My poems," explained Frost, "are all set to trip the reader head foremost into the boundless." Frost's "The Road Not Taken" is written in the rugged and direct language that became the hallmark of his mature style. The poem exalts a profound individualism as well as a sparseness of expression in line with the modernist injunction to "make it new."

READING 6.2 Frost's "The Road Not Taken" (1916)

Two roads diverged in a yellow wood,   1
And sorry I could not travel both
And be one traveler, long I stood
And looked down one as far as I could
To where it bent in the undergrowth;   5

Then took the other, as just as fair,
And having perhaps the better claim,
Because it was grassy and wanted wear,
Though as for that the passing there
Had worn them really about the same,   10

And both that morning equally lay
In leaves no step had trodden black.
Oh, I kept the first for another day!
Yet knowing how way leads on to way,
I doubted if I should ever come back.   15

I shall be telling this with a sigh
Somewhere ages and ages hence:
Two roads diverged in a wood, and I—
I took the one less traveled by,
And that has made all the difference.   20

Early Twentieth-Century Art

As with modernist poetry, the art of the first decades of the twentieth century came to challenge all that preceded it. Liberated by the camera from the necessity of imitating nature, **avant-garde** painters and sculptors turned their backs on academic standards and the tyranny of representation. They pioneered an authentic, "stripped down" style that, much like imagist poetry, evoked rather than described experience. Like the imagists, visual artists tried to abstract the intrinsic qualities and essential meanings of their subject matter to arrive at a concentrated emotional experience. The language of pure form did not, however, rob art of its humanistic dimension; rather, it provided artists with a means by which to move beyond traditional ways of representing nature and to interpret the visual world in daring new ways.

Early modern artists probed the tools and techniques of formal expression more fully than any artists since the Renaissance. They challenged the role of art as illusion and broadened Western conceptions of the meaning and value of art. Exploring unconventional media, they created art that blurred the boundaries between painting and sculpture. And, like the imagists, they found inspiration in the arts of non-Western cultures; primitivism, abstraction, and experimentation were hallmarks of the modernist revolt against convention and tradition.

Picasso and the Birth of Cubism

The giant of twentieth-century art was the Spanish-born Pablo Picasso (1881–1973). During his ninety-two-year life, Picasso worked in almost every major art style of the century, some of which he himself inaugurated. He produced thousands of paintings, drawings, sculptures, and prints—a body of work that in its size, inventiveness, and influence, is nothing short of phenomenal. As a child, he showed an extraordinary gift for drawing, and by the age of twenty his precise and lyrical line style rivaled that of Raphael and Ingres. In 1903, the young painter left his native Spain to settle in Paris. There, in the bustling capital of the Western art world, he came under the influence of impressionist and postimpressionist painting, and took as his subjects café life, beggars, prostitutes, and circus folk. Much like the imagists, Picasso worked to refine form and color in the direction of concentrated expression, reducing the colors of his palette first to various shades of blue and then, after 1904, to tones of rose. By 1906, the artist began to abandon traditional Western modes of pictorial representation. Adopting the credo that art must be subversive—that it must defy all that is conventional, literal, and trite—he initiated a bold new style. That style was shaped by two major forces: Cézanne's paintings, which had been the focus of two major Paris exhibitions; and the arts of Africa, Iberia, and Oceania, examples of which were appearing regularly in Paris galleries and museums (see chapters 18 and 31). In Cézanne's canvases, with their

Figure 32.1 PAUL CÉZANNE, *The Large Bathers*, 1906. Oil on canvas, 6 ft. 10⅞ in. × 8 ft. 2¾ in. Philadelphia Museum of Art. Purchased with the W. P. Wilstach Fund. Photo: Graydon Wood, 1988 (W'37–1–1).

flattened planes and arbitrary colors (Figure **32.1**), Picasso recognized a rigorous new language of form that worked to define nature's underlying structure. And in African and Oceanic sculpture, he discovered the significance of art as fetish, that is, as the palpable embodiment of potent magical forces. As he later explained, "For me the masks were not just sculptures; they were magical objects . . . intercessors against unknown, threatening spirits."

Picasso's foremost assault on tradition was *Les Demoiselles d'Avignon*, a large painting of five nude women—the "ladies" of a bordello—in a curtained interior (Figure **32.3**). The subject matter of the painting originated in the long, respectable tradition of the female nude group, usually set in a landscape (see Figure 32.1). In the early sketches for *Les Demoiselles*, originally called *The Philosophical Brothel* (a reference to a house of prostitution in Barcelona), Picasso included two male figures, one of whom resembled the artist himself. In the summer of 1907, however, after visiting the Musée d'Ethnographie du Trocadéro in Paris, Picasso fell deeply under the spell of tribal art. He reworked the canvas, transforming the narrative content—five self-advertising prostitutes—into a fierce iconic image that he later called his "first exorcism picture." *Les Demoiselles* came to violate every shred of tradition; indeed it made Manet's *Olympia* (see chapter 30) look comfortably old fashioned. The manner in which Picasso "made new" a traditional subject in Western art is worth examining: The figures in *Les Demoiselles* seem to have been taken apart and reassembled as if the artist were testing the physics of disjunction and discontinuity. At

Figure 32.2 Kota reliquary figure from the People's Republic of the Congo. Wood, copper, and brass, height 30¼ in. Völkerkunde Museum der Universität, Zurich.

Figure 32.3 PABLO PICASSO, *Les Demoiselles d'Avignon*, Paris, 1907. Oil on canvas, 8 ft. × 7 ft. 8 in. The Museum of Modern Art, New York. Acquired through the Lillie P. Bliss Bequest. Photograph © 2000 The Museum of Modern Art, New York. © Succession Picasso/DACS 2000.

least three of the figures are rendered not from a single vantage point but from multiple viewpoints, as if one's eye could travel freely in time and space. The body of the crouching female on the far right is seen from the back, while her face, savagely striated like the scarified surface of an African sculpture (Figure **32.2**), is seen from the front.[1] The noses of the two central females appear in profile,

while their eyes are frontal—a convention Picasso may have borrowed from ancient Egyptian frescoes. The relationship between the figures and the shallow space they occupy is equally disjunctive, a condition compounded by brutally fractured planes of color—brick reds and vivid blues—that resemble shards of glass. Picasso stripped his female subjects of all sensuous appeal and made them as forbidding as tribal fetish figures. In one disquieting stroke, he banished the image of the alluring female nude from the domain of Western art.

Les Demoiselles was the precursor of an audacious new style known as *cubism*, a style that came to challenge the

[1]While scholars debate the question of exactly which tribal artworks Picasso might have seen at the Musée d'Ethnographie, all concur that copper-clad Kota reliquary guardians like that pictured in Figure 32.2 were among the African objects on display in 1907.

Figure 32.4 PABLO PICASSO, *Man with a Violin*, 1911. Oil on canvas, 39½ × 29⅛ in. Philadelphia Museum of Art. Louise and Walter Arensberg Collection.

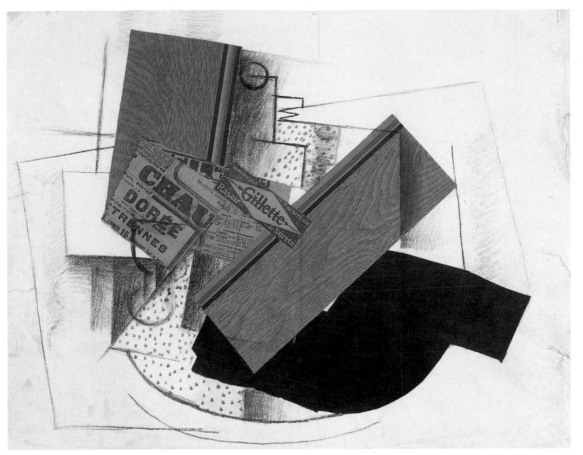

Figure 32.5 GEORGES BRAQUE, *Still Life on a Table*, ca. 1914. Collage on paper, 18⅜ × 24⅜ in. Collection of Mr. and Mrs. Claude Lauren, Paris. Photo: Musée national d'art moderne, Centre Georges Pompidou, Paris. © ADAGP, Paris and DACS, London 2000.

principles of Renaissance painting as dramatically as Einstein's theory of relativity had challenged Newtonian physics. In the decade that followed *Les Demoiselles*, the comfortable, recognizable world of the senses disappeared beneath a scaffold of semitransparent planes and short, angular lines; ordinary objects were made to look as if they had exploded and been reassembled somewhat arbitrarily in bits and pieces (Figure **32.4**). With *analytic cubism*, as the style came to be called, a multiplicity of viewpoints replaced one-point perspective. The cubist image, conceived as if one were moving around, above, and below the subject and even perceiving it from within, appropriated the fourth dimension—time itself. As Picasso and his French colleague Georges Braque (1882–1963) collaborated in a search for an ever more pared down language of form, compositions became increasingly abstract and colors became cool and controlled: Cubism came to offer a new formal language, one wholly unconcerned with narrative content. Years later, Picasso defended the viability of this new language: "The fact that for a long time cubism has not been understood . . . means nothing. I do not read English, an English book is a blank book to me. This does not mean that the English language does not exist."

Around 1912, a second phase of cubism, namely *synthetic cubism*, emerged, when Braque first included three pieces of wallpaper in a still-life composition. Picasso and Braque, who thought of themselves as space pioneers (much like the Wright brothers), pasted mundane objects such as wine labels, playing cards, and scraps of newspaper onto the surface of the canvas—a technique known as **collage** (from the French *coller*, "to paste"). The result was a kind of art that was neither a painting nor a sculpture, but both at the same time. The two artists filled their canvases with puns, hidden messages, and subtle references to contemporary events; but the prevailing strategy in all of these artworks was to test the notion of art as illusion. In Braque's *Still Life on a Table* (Figure **32.5**), strips of imitation wood graining, a razor blade wrapper, and newspaper clippings serve the double function of "presenting" and "representing." Words and images wrenched out of context here play off one another like some cryptographic bill-board. Prophetic of twentieth-century art in general, Braque would proclaim, "The subject is not the object of the painting, but a new unity, the lyricism that results from method."

1901	the first international radio broadcast is made by Guglielmo Marconi (Italian)
1903	Orville and Wilbur Wright (American) make the first successful airplane flight
1927	the first motion picture with synchronized sound (*The Jazz Singer*) is released
1927	Werner Heisenberg (German) announces his "uncertainty principle"

Figure 32.6 (left) Ceremonial mask, from Wobé or Grebo, Ivory Coast, late nineteenth century. Painted wood, feathers, and fibers, height 11 in. Musée de l'Homme, Paris. Photo: © R.M.N., Paris.

Figure 32.7 (below) **PABLO PICASSO**, *Guitar*, 1912–1913. Construction of sheet metal and wire, 30½ × 13¾ × 7⅝ in. The Museum of Modern Art, New York. Gift of the artist. Photograph © 2000 The Museum of Modern Art, New York. © Succession Picasso/DACS 2000.

In these same years, Picasso created the first assemblages —artworks that were built up, or pieced together, from miscellaneous three-dimensional objects. Like the collage, the assemblage depended on the imaginative combination of found objects and materials, but the new procedure constituted a radical alternative to traditional techniques of carving in stone and modeling in clay or plaster. The art of assemblage drew inspiration from African and Oceanic traditions of combining natural materials (such as cowrie beads and raffia) for masks and costumes; it also took heed of the expressive simplifications that typify fetish figures, reliquaries, and other tribal artforms (Figure **32.6**). Thus, Picasso's *Guitar* of 1912–1913 achieved its powerful effect by means of fragmented planes, deliberate spatial inversions (note the projecting soundhole), and the wedding of commonplace materials such as sheet metal and wire (Figure **32.7**).

Within a decade, Western sculptors were employing the strategies of synthetic cubism in ways that reflected modern models of time and space. The Russian-born cubist Alexander Archipenko (1887–1964) fashioned the female form so that an area of negative space actually constitutes the head (Figure **32.8**). Similar efforts at integrating space and mass characterize the monumental bronze sculptures of the British artist Henry Moore (1898–1986).

Figure 32.8 (right) **ALEXANDER ARCHIPENKO**, *Woman Combing Her Hair*, 1915. Bronze, 13¾ × 3¼ × 3⅛ in. (including base). The Museum of Modern Art, New York. Acquired through the Lillie P. Bliss Bequest. Photograph © 2000 The Museum of Modern Art, New York. © ARS, NY and DACS, London 2000.

Futurism

Technology and art, linked by the modernist mandate to "make it new," sparked the Italian movement known as *futurism*. The Italian poet and iconoclast Filippo Tommaso Marinetti (1876–1944) issued a series of manifestoes that attacked museum art (and all forms of academic culture) and linked contemporary artistic expression to industry, technology, and urban life. Marinetti, who held that "war was the only healthgiver of the world," demanded an art of "burning violence" that would free Italy from its "fetid gangrene of professors, archeologists, antiquarians, and rhetoricians." "We declare," he wrote in his *Futurist Manifesto* of 1909, "that there can be no modern painting except from the starting

point of an absolutely modern sensation. . . . A roaring motorcar is more beautiful than the winged *Victory of Samothrace*" (the famous Hellenistic sculpture illustrated in chapter 5). "The gesture that we would reproduce on canvas shall no longer be a fixed moment in universal dynamism. It shall simply be the dynamic sensation itself."

The futuristic alternative to static academicism was produced by Umberto Boccioni (1882–1916), whose near life-size bronze figure captures the sensation of motion as it pushes forward like a automated robot (Figure **32.9**). The striding male, which consists of an aggressive series of dynamic, jagged lines, is clearly human in form, despite Boccioni's assertion (in his 1912 *Technical Manifesto of Futurist Sculpture*) that artists should "abolish .. the traditionally exalted place of subject matter."

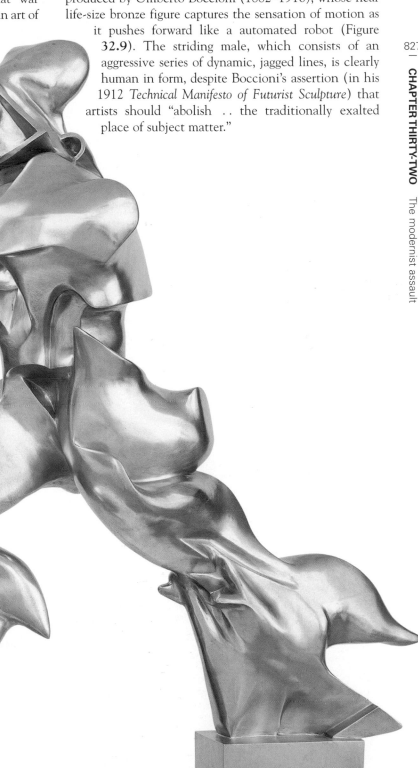

Figure 32.9 UMBERTO BOCCIONI, *Unique Forms of Continuity in Space*, 1913. Bronze (cast 1931), 43⅞ × 34⅞ × 15¾ in. The Museum of Modern Art, New York. Acquired through the Lillie P. Bliss Bequest. Photograph © 2000 The Museum of Modern Art, New York.

The futurists were enthralled by the speed and dynamism of automobiles, trains, and airplanes, and enchanted by new forms of technology, including the machine gun, Rome's newly installed electric Brunt Arc street lamps, and—naturally enough—the new industry of motion pictures. Inspired by the time-lapse photography of Eadweard Muybridge (see chapter 31) and by pioneer efforts in film, they painted images whose "multiple profiles" gave the appearance of movement in time and space. One such example, by the Italian futurist Giacomo Balla (1871–1958), captures the image of a lively dachshund and his female owner (Figure **32.10**). Though more playful than violent in spirit, the painting exemplifies the futurist infatuation with dynamic flux. Rapid-action photography and the futurist celebration of objects in motion—along with the "magic" of the x-ray (not in wide use until 1910)—also shaped the early career of Marcel Duchamp (1887–1968). When Duchamp's *Nude Descending a Staircase #2* (Figure **32.11**) was exhibited at the International Exhibition of Modern Art (known as the Armory Show) in New York City, one critic mocking-

ly called the painting "an explosion in a shingle factory." Yet, from the time of its first showing in 1913, the painting (and much of the art in the Armory exhibition) had a formative influence in the rise of American modernism. Futurism did not last beyond the end of World War I, but its impact was felt in both the United States and Russia, where futurist efforts to capture the sense of form in motion would coincide with the first developments in the technology of cinematography (discussed later in this chapter).

Matisse and Fauvism

While cubists and futurists were principally concerned with matters of space and motion, another group of modernists, led by the French artist Henri Matisse (1869–1954), made *color* the principal feature of their canvases. This group, named "fauves" (from the French *fauve*, "wild beast") by a critic who saw their work at the 1905 exhibition in Paris, employed flat, bright colors in the arbitrary manner of van Gogh and Gauguin. But whereas the latter had used color to evoke a mood or a decorative

Figure 32.10 GIACOMO BALLA, *Dynamism of a Dog on a Leash (Leash in Motion)*, 1912. Oil on canvas 2 ft. 11 3/4 in. x 3 ft. 7 3/8 in. Albright-Knox Art Gallery, Buffalo, New York. George F. Goodyear Bequest.

Figure 32.11 MARCEL DUCHAMP, *Nude Descending a Staircase, #2*, 1912. Oil on canvas, 58 × 35 in. Philadelphia Museum of Art. Louise and Walter Arensberg Collection. © Succession Marcel Duchamp. ADAGP, Paris and DACS, London 2000.

THE BIRTH OF MOTION PICTURES

It is no coincidence that the art of motion pictures was born at a time when artists and scientists were obsessed with matters of space and time. Indeed, as an art that captures rapidly changing experience, cinema may be *the* quintessentially modern medium. The earliest public film presentations took place in Europe and the United States in the mid-1890s: In 1895, Thomas Edison was the first American to publicly project moving images on a screen, while in France, the brothers Auguste and Louis Lumière perfected the process by which cellulose film ran smoothly in a commercial projector. These first experiments delighted audiences with recreations of everyday reality. It was not until 1902, however, that film was used to create a reality all its own: In that year the French filmmaker Georges Méliès (1861–1938) completed a theatrical sequence called *A Trip to the Moon*, a fantastic reconstruction of reality based on a Jules Verne novel. One year later, the American director Edwin S. Porter (1869–1941) produced the twelve-minute silent film *The Great Train Robbery*, which treated the myth of American frontier life in the story of a sensational holdup, followed by the pursuit and capture of the bandits. These pioneer narrative films established the idiom for two of the most popular genres in cinematic history: the science fiction film and the "western."

Between 1908 and 1912, Hollywood became the center of American cinema. D. W. Griffith (1875–1948), the leading director of his time, made major innovations in cinematic technique. He introduced the use of multiple cameras and camera angles, as well as such new techniques as close-ups, fade-outs, and flashbacks, which, when joined together in an edited sequence, greatly expanded the potential of film narrative. Griffith's three-hour-long silent film, *The Birth of a Nation* (1915), was an epic account of the American Civil War and the Reconstruction Era that followed in the South. Unfortunately, despite the film's technical excellence, its negative portrayal of African-Americans contributed to creating a stereotype of blacks as violent and ignorant savages. Until the late 1920s, all movies were silent—filmmakers used captions to designate the spoken word wherever appropriate and live musical accompaniment was often provided in the theater. Well before the era of the "talkies," cinematographers used the camera not simply as a disinterested observer, but as a medium for conveying the emotional states of the characters. Indeed, in the absence of sound, filmmakers were forced to develop the affective structure of the film by essentially visual means. According to some film critics, the aesthetics of film as a medium were compromised when sound was added. Nevertheless, by 1925 it was apparent that film was destined to become one of the major artforms of the twentieth century.

effect, the younger artists were concerned with color only as it served pictorial structure; their style featured bold spontaneity and the direct and instinctive application of pigment. Critics who called these artists "wild beasts" were in fact responding to the use of color in ways that seemed both crude and savage. They attacked the art of the fauves as "color madness" and "the sport of a child." For Matisse, however, color was the font of pure and sensuous pleasure. In his portrait of Madame Matisse (which he subtitled *The Green Line*), broad flat swaths of paint give definition to a visage that is bisected vertically by an acrid green stripe (Figure **32.12**). Matisse brought new daring to Cézanne's flat color patches, using them to stylize form in the manner of the tribal artworks that he collected. At the same time, he invested the canvas with a thrilling color radiance, that, like smell (as Matisse himself observed), suffuses our senses subtly but directly. In contrast with Picasso, who held that art was a weapon with which to jar the

senses, Matisse sought "an art of balance, of purity and serenity, devoid of troubling or depressing subject matter ... something like a good armchair in which to rest from physical fatigue."

Matisse was among the first to articulate the modernist scorn for representational art: "Exactitude is not truth," he insisted. In *Notes of a Painter*, published in 1908, he explained that colors and shapes were the equivalents of feelings rather than the counterparts of forms in nature. Gradually, as he came to be influenced by Islamic miniatures and Russian icons, Matisse moved in the direction of schematic simplicity and extraordinary color sensuousness. A quintessential example of his facility for color abstraction is *Dance I* (Figure **32.13**). The painting's lyrical arabesques and unmodeled fields of color call to mind ancient Greek vase paintings. At the same time, Matisse captures the exhilaration of the primordial round—the traditional dance of almost all Mediterranean cultures.

Figure 32.12 (left) **HENRI MATISSE**, *Madame Matisse (The Green Line)*, 1905. Oil on canvas, 16 x 12 ¾ in. Statens Museum for Kunst, Copenhagen. Photo: Hans Petersen/© Succession H. Matisse/DACS 2000.

Figure 32.13 (below) **HENRI MATISSE**, *Dance 1*, 1909. Oil on canvas, 8 ft. 6½ in. × 12 ft. 9½ in. The Museum of Modern Art, New York (Gift of Nelson A. Rockefeller in honor of Alfred H. Barr, Jr.). Photo: © 2000 The Museum of Modern Art, New York/ © Succession H. Matisse/DACS 2000.

Brancusi and Abstraction

Although cubists, futurists, and fauves pursued their individual directions, they all shared the credo of abstract art: the belief that the artist must evoke the essential and intrinsic qualities of the subject rather than describe its physical properties. In early modern sculpture, the guardian of this credo was Constantin Brancusi (1876–1957). Born in Romania and trained in Bucharest, Vienna, and Munich, Brancusi came to Paris in 1904. There, after a brief stay in Rodin's studio, he fell under the spell of ancient fertility figures and the tribal sculpture of Africa and Polynesia. Inspired by these objects, whose spiritual power lay in their visual immediacy and their truth to materials, Brancusi proceeded to create an art of radically simple, organic forms. While he began by closely observing the living object—whether human or animal—he progressively eliminated all naturalistic details until he arrived at a form that captured the essence of the subject. Like his good friend Ezra Pound, Brancusi achieved a concentrated expression in forms so elemental that they seem to speak a universal language. A case in point is *Bird in Space* (Figure **32.14**), of which Brancusi made over thirty versions in various sizes and materials. The sculpture is of no particular species of feathered creature, but it captures perfectly the concept of "birdness." It is, as Brancusi explained, "the essence of flight." "What is real," he insisted, "is not the external form, but the essence of things." The slender form, curved like a feather, unites birdlike qualities of grace and poise with the dynamic sense of soaring levitation characteristic of mechanical flying machines, such as rockets and airplanes. Indeed, when Brancusi's bronze *Bird* first arrived in America, United States customs officials mistook it for a piece of industrial machinery.

Abstraction and Photography

Photography enthusiastically embraced the modernist aesthetic. The American photographer Edward Weston (1886–1953) was among the pioneers of photographic abstraction. His close-up photograph of two nautilus shells evokes the twin ideas of flower (a magnolia blossom, according to Weston himself) and female (Figure **32.15**). Weston took photography beyond the realm of the representational: He used the camera not simply to record the natural world, but to explore new avenues of visual experience.

Figure 32.14 (left) **CONSTANTIN BRANCUSI**, *Bird in Space*, 1928. Polished bronze, height 4 ft. 6 in. Museum of Modern Art, New York. Given anonymously. Photo: © 2000 The Museum of Modern Art, New York/ © ADAGP, Paris and DACS, London 2000.

Figure 32.15 (right) **EDWARD WESTON**, *Two Shells*, 1927. Photograph. Print by Cole Weston. Reproduced by permission of the Center for Creative Photography, University of Tucson Arizona.

Nonobjective Art

Between 1909 and 1914, three artists working independent of one another in different parts of Europe moved to purge art of all recognizable subject matter. The Russians Wassily Kandinsky (1866–1944) and Kasimir Malevich (1878–1935) and the Dutchman Piet Mondrian (1872–1944), pioneers of **nonobjective art**, had all come into contact with the principal art movements of the early twentieth century: cubism, futurism, and fauvism. They were also familiar with the postimpressionist premise that a painting was, first and foremost, a flat surface covered with colors assembled in a particular order. But their research into subjectless form had yet another goal: that of achieving an art whose purity would offer a spiritual remedy for the soullessness of modern life.

Kandinsky, whose career in art only began at the age of forty, was deeply influenced by the fauves, the symbolists (see chapter 31), and by Russian folk art. (He confessed a debt as well to atomic theory and urged young artists to study the new physics.) While he filled his early paintings with intense and vibrant colors, he observed with some dismay that the subject matter in his canvases tended to "dissolve" into his colors. One evening, upon returning to his studio in Munich, Kandinsky experienced a "revelation" that led him to abandon pictorial subject matter. The incident is described in his *Reminiscences* of 1913:

> I saw an indescribably beautiful picture drenched with an inner glowing. At first I hesitated, then I rushed toward this mysterious picture, of which I saw nothing but forms and colors, and whose content was incomprehensible. Immediately I found the key to the puzzle: it was a picture I had painted, leaning against the wall, standing on its side. . . . Now I knew for certain that the [pictorial] object harmed my paintings.*

From this point on, Kandinsky began to assemble colors, lines, and shapes without regard to recognizable objects (Figure **32.16**). He called his absolute paintings "improvisations" or "abstract compositions" and numbered them in series. In his engaging treatise *Concerning the Spiritual in Art* (1910), he described colors as potent forces for evoking mood and insisted that "color can exercise enormous influence upon the body."

Figure 32.16 WASSILY KANDINSKY, *Panel for Edwin Campbell No. 1*, 1914. Oil on canvas, 5 ft. 4 in. × 3 ft. ¼ in. The Museum of Modern Art, New York. Mrs. Simon Guggenheim Fund. Photograph © 2000 The Museum of Modern Art, New York. © ADAGP, Paris and DACS, London 2000.

*"Reminiscences," in *Modern Artists on Art*, ed. Robert L. Herbert. Englewood Cliffs, N.J.: Prentice Hall, 1964, 32.

Figure 32.17 KASIMIR MALEVICH, *Suprematist Composition: White on White*, 1918. Oil on canvas, 31¼ × 31¼ in. The Museum of Modern Art, New York. Photograph © 2000 The Museum of Modern Art, New York.

Figure 32.18 PIET MONDRIAN, *Horizontal Tree*, 1911. Oil on canvas, 29⅝ × 43⅞ in. Munson-Williams-Proctor Institute, New York. © 2000 Mondrian/HolzmanTrust c/o Beeldrecht, Amsterdam, Holland & DACS, London.

Such insights anticipated modern research in chromotherapy, that is, the use of colors and colored light to affect body states. According to Kandinsky, painting was a spiritually liberating force akin to music—he himself was an amateur cellist and friend of many avant-garde composers. "Painting," he proclaimed, "is a thundering collision of different worlds, intended to create a new world."

Kandinsky's Russian contemporary Kasimir Malevich arrived at nonrepresentational art not by way of fauvism but through the influence of analytic cubism, a style that asserted the value of line over color. Seeking to "free art from the burden of the object" and to rediscover "pure feeling in creative art," Malevich created an austere style limited to the strict geometry of the square, the circle, and the rectangle (Figure **32.17**). Malevich called these shapes "suprematist elements" and his style *suprematism*. "To the suprematist," wrote Malevich, "the visual phenomena of the objective world are, in themselves, meaningless; the significant thing is feeling . . . quite apart from the environment in which it is called forth."* By restricting his art to the arrangement of ideal geometric shapes on the two-dimensional picture plane, Malevich replaced the world of appearance with a language of form as precise and exacting as that of modern physics.

The early works of the third pioneer of nonobjective art, Piet Mondrian, reveal this Dutch artist's keen sensitivity to his native countryside as well as his inclination to discover geometric order in nature (Figure **32.18**). Mondrian's

---

*"Suprematism," in *Modern Artists on Art*, 93.

Figure 32.19 (right) **PIET MONDRIAN**, *Composition in Red, Yellow, Blue, and Black*, 1921. Oil on canvas, 23¼ × 23¼ in. Collection, Haags Gemeentemuseum, The Hague. © 2000 Mondrian/HolzmanTrust c/o Beeldrecht, Amsterdam, Holland & DACS, London.

Figure 32.20 (below) **GERRIT RIETVELD**, *Red Blue Chair*, 1923. Painted wood, 34⅛ × 26 × 33 in; seat height 13 in.. The Museum of Modern Art, New York. Gift of Philip Johnson. Photograph © The Museum of Modern Art, New York. © DACS 2000.

landscapes reflect his distant kinship to Jan Vermeer (see chapter 23), as well as his admiration for another of his countrymen, Vincent van Gogh (see chapter 31). As early as 1910, however, Mondrian began to strip his canvases of references to recognizable subject matter. He limited his visual vocabulary to "pure" forms: rectangles laid out on a grid of horizontal and vertical lines, the three primary colors (red, yellow, and blue), and three values—white, gray, and black (Figure **32.19**). The paring-down process achieved a compositional balance of geometric elements, an "equivalence of opposites" similar to the satisfying equilibrium of an algebraic equation. Although Mondrian would eventually migrate to America, in the Netherlands the movement he initiated was called simply *De Stijl* (The Style). Despite differences of opinion among its members—Mondrian resigned in 1925 in opposition to a colleague's use of diagonals—De Stijl was to have worldwide impact, especially in the areas of architecture and furniture design (Figure **32.20**).

The disappearance of the object in early twentieth-century art is often mistakenly associated with the dehumanization of modern life. However, one of the great ironies of the birth of nonobjective art is its indebtedness to the mystical and transcendental philosophies that were current in the early modern era. One of the most influential of these was *theosophy*, a blend of Eastern and Western religions that emphasizes communion with nature by purely spiritual means. Mondrian, a member of the Dutch Theosophical Society, equated spiritual progress with geometric clarity. In his view, the law of equivalence reflected "the true content of reality." "Not only science," wrote Mondrian, "but art also, shows us that reality, at first incomprehensible, gradually reveals itself by the mutual relations that are inherent in things. Pure science and pure art, disinterested and free, can lead the advance in the recognition of the laws which are based on these relationships."* The commitment to pure abstraction as the language of spirituality—a commitment central to the careers of Kandinsky, Malevich, and Mondrian—reflects the idealized humanism of modernists who perceived their art as a wellspring of harmony and order.

---

*"Plastic Art and Pure Plastic Art," in *Modern Artists on Art*, 119.

Russian Constructivism

While De Stijl had a formative influence on modern architecture, furniture design, and commercial advertising, the most utilitarian and (at the same time) utopian of the movements for "pure art" flourished in prerevolutionary Russia. *Constructivism*, which had its roots in both futurism and the purist teachings of Malevich, advocated the application of geometric abstraction to all forms of social enterprise. Russian constructivists, who called themselves "artist-engineers," worked to improve the everyday lives of the masses by applying the new abstraction to the industrial arts, theater, film, typography, textile design, and architecture. Liubov Popova (1889–1924), one of the many talented female members of this movement, designed stage sets and costumes for the Russian theater (Figure **32.21**), thus putting into practice the constructivist motto "Art into production." Like other modernists, the constructivists worked to break down the barriers between fine and applied art, but unlike any other modern art movement, constructivism received official state sanction. Following the Russian Revolution, however, the Soviet Union would bring about the demise of one of the most innovative episodes in modern art (see chapter 34).

Figure 32.21 (below) **LIUBOV POPOVA**, Set design for Fernand Crommelynk, *Le Cocu magnifique*, State Institute of Theatrical Art, Moscow, 1922. Gouache on paper, 19½ × 27 in. State Trekiov Gallery, Moscow. Gift of George Custakis.

Early Twentieth-Century Architecture

While modern concepts of simultaneity and motion were realized in the technology of motion pictures, the revolution in visual abstraction found monumental expression in architecture. Early modern architects made energetic use of two new materials—structural steel and **ferroconcrete**—in combination with the cantilever principle of construction. The cantilever, a horizontal beam supported at only one end and projecting well beyond the point of support, had first appeared in the timber buildings of China (see chapter 14); but the manufacture of the structural steel cantilever ushered in a style whose austere simplicity had no precedents. That style was inaugurated by Frank Lloyd Wright (1869–1959), the leading figure in the history of early modern architecture.

The Architecture of Wright

Frank Lloyd Wright, the first American architect of world significance, was the foremost student of the Chicago architect Louis Sullivan (see chapter 30). Wright's style combined the new technology of steel and glass with the aesthetic principles of Oriental architecture. Wright visited Japan when he was in his thirties and was impressed by the grace and purity of Japanese art. He especially admired the respect for natural materials and the sensitivity to the relationship between setting and structure that characterized traditional Japanese architecture (see chapter 14). In his earliest domestic commissions, Wright embraced the East Asian principle of horizontality, by which the building might hug the earth. He imitated the low, sweeping ceilings and roofs of Chinese and Japanese pavilions and pagodas. From the Japanese, whose interior walls often consist of movable screens, Wright also borrowed the idea of interconnecting interior and exterior space. At the same time, he used the structural steel frame and the cantilever technique to open up large areas of uninterrupted space; and he insisted that the exterior appearance of the structure clearly mirror all major divisions of interior space. Wright refined this formula in a series of innovative domestic homes in the American Midwest, pioneering the so-called Prairie School of architecture that lasted from roughly 1900 until World War I.

The classic creation of Wright's early career was the Robie House in Chicago, completed in 1909 (Figure **32.22**). Here, Wright made the fireplace the center of the residential interior. He crossed the long main axis of the house with counteraxes of low, cantilevered roofs that push out into space over terraces and verandas. He subordinated decorative details to the overall design of the house, allowing his materials—brick, glass, and natural rock—to assume major roles in establishing the unique character of the structure. As Wright insisted, "To use any material wrongly is to abuse the integrity of the whole

Figure 32.22 FRANK LLOYD WRIGHT, Robie House, Chicago, Illinois, 1909. Brick, glass, natural rock. Photo: Wayne Andrews/Esto. © ARS, NY and DACS, London 2000.

Figure 32.23 FRANK LLOYD WRIGHT, Fallingwater, Kaufmann House, Bear Run, Pennsylvania, 1936–1939. Reinforced concrete, stone, masonry, steel-framed doors and windows, enclosed area 5,800 sq. ft. Photo: Hedrich-Blessing, courtesy Chicago Historical Society. © ARS, NY and DACS, London 2000.

design." The result was a style consisting of crisp, interlocking planes, contrasting textures, and interpenetrating solids and voids—a domestic home that was as abstract and dynamic as an analytic cubist painting. Wright's use of the cantilever and his integration of landscape and house reached new imaginative heights in Fallingwater, the extraordinary residence he designed in 1936 for the American businessman Edgar J. Kaufmann at Bear Run, Pennsylvania (Figure **32.23**). Embracing a natural waterfall, the ferroconcrete and stone structure seems to grow organically out of the natural wooded setting, yet dominate that setting by its pristine equilibrium.

The Bauhaus and the International Style

Wright's brilliant synthesis of art and technology melded with the utopian vision of Russian constructivism to pave the way for the establishment of the *Bauhaus*, modernism's most influential school of architecture and applied art. Founded in 1919 by the German architect and visionary Walter Gropius (1883–1969), the Bauhaus pioneered an instructional program that reformed modern industrial society by fusing the technology of the machine age with the purest principles of functional design. Throughout its brief history (1919–1933), and despite its frequent relocation (from Weimar to Dessau, and finally Berlin), the Bauhaus advocated a close relationship between function and formal design, whether in furniture, lighting fixtures,

typography, photography, industrial products, or architecture. Bauhaus instructors had little regard for traditional academic styles; they eagerly endorsed the new synthetic materials of modern technology, a stark simplicity of design, and the standardization of parts for affordable, mass-produced merchandise, as well as for large-scale housing. Some of Europe's leading artists, including Kandinsky and Mondrian, taught at the Bauhaus. Like Gropius, these artists envisioned a new industrial society liberated by the principles of abstract design. When the Nazis closed down the school in 1933, many of its finest instructors, such as the photographer László Moholy-Nagy, architect and designer Marcel Breuer, and artist Josef Albers, went to the United States, where they exercised tremendous influence on the development of modern American architecture and industrial art. (In 1929, a group of wealthy Americans had already established the first international collection of modern art: New York City's Museum of Modern Art.)

Under the direction of Gropius, the Bauhaus launched the *international style* in architecture, which brought to the marriage of structural steel, ferroconcrete, and sheet glass a formal precision and geometric austerity that resembled a Mondrian painting (see Figure 32.18). In the four-story glass building Gropius designed to serve as the Bauhaus craft shops in Dessau, unadorned curtain walls of glass (which meet uninterrupted at the corners of the structure)

Figure 32.24 WALTER GROPIUS, Workshop wing, Bauhaus Building, Dessau, Germany, 1925–1926. Steel and glass. Photograph courtesy The Museum of Modern Art, New York.

were freely suspended on structural steel cantilevers (Figure **32.24**). This fusion of functional space and minimal structure produced a purist style that paralleled the abstract trends in poetry, painting, and sculpture discussed earlier in this chapter.

The revolutionary Swiss architect and town planner Charles-Edouard Jeanneret (1887–1965), who called himself Le Corbusier (a pun on the word "raven"), was not directly affiliated with the Bauhaus, but he shared Gropius' fundamental concern for efficiency of design, standardization of building techniques, and promotion of low-cost housing. In 1923, Le Corbusier wrote the treatise *Towards a New Architecture*, in which he proposed that modern architectural principles should imitate the efficiency of the machine. "Machines," he predicted, "will lead to a new order both of work and of leisure." Just as form follows function in the design of airplanes, automobiles, and machinery in general, so it must in modern

Figure 32.25 LE CORBUSIER, Villa Savoye, Poissy, France, 1928–1929. Ferroconcrete and glass. © FLC/ADAGP, Paris and DACS, London 2000.

Figure 32.26 LE CORBUSIER, Unité d'Habitation apartment block, Marseilles, France, 1946–1952. Photo: Lucien Hervé, Paris.

domestic architecture. Le Corbusier was fond of insisting that "the house is a machine for living." With apocalyptic fervor he urged,

> We must create the mass-production spirit.
> The spirit of constructing mass-production houses.
> The spirit of living in mass-production houses.
> The spirit of conceiving mass-production houses.
>
> If we eliminate from our hearts and minds all dead concepts in regard to the house, and look at the question from a critical and objective point of view, we shall arrive at the "House-Machine," the mass-production house, healthy (and morally so too) and beautiful in the same way that the working tools and instruments that accompany our existence are beautiful.*

In the Villa Savoye, a residence located outside of Paris at Poissy, Le Corbusier put these revolutionary concepts to work (Figure **32.25**). The residence, now considered a "classic" of the international style, consists of simple and unadorned masses of ferroconcrete punctured by ribbon windows. It is raised above the ground on *pilotis*, pillars that free the ground area of the site. (Some modern architects have abused the *pilotis* principle to create parking space for automobiles.) The Villa Savoye features a number of favorite Le Corbusier devices, such as the roof garden, the open spatial plan that allows one to close off or open up space according to varying needs, and the free facade that consists of large areas of glass—so-called "curtain walls." Le Corbusier's genius for fitting form to function led, during the 1930s, to his creation of the first high-rise urban apartment buildings—structures that housed over a thousand people and consolidated facilities for

shopping, recreation, and child care under a single roof (Figure **32.26**). These "vertical cities," as stripped of decorative details as the sculptures of Brancusi, have become hallmarks of urban modernism.

Early Twentieth-Century Music

As with poetry, painting, and architecture, musical composition underwent dramatic changes in the first decades of the last century. The assaults on traditional verse rhythms in poetry and on representational forms in painting and sculpture were paralleled in music by radical experiments in tonality and meter. Until the late nineteenth century, most music was tonal, that is, structured on a single key or tonal center; but by the second decade of the twentieth century, musical compositions might be **polytonal** (having several tonal centers) or **atonal** (without a tonal center). Further, instead of following a single meter, a composition might be **polyrhythmic** (having two or more different meters at the same time), or (as with imagist poems) it might obey no fixed or regular metrical pattern.

Modern composers rejected conventional modes of expression, including traditional harmonies and instrumentation. Melody—like recognizable subject matter in painting—became of secondary importance to formal considerations of composition. Modern composers invented no new forms comparable to the fugue or the sonata; rather, they explored innovative effects based on dissonance, the free use of meter, and the unorthodox combination of musical instruments, some of which they borrowed from non-Western cultures. They employed unorthodox sources of sound, such as sirens, bullhorns, and doorbells; and they began to incorporate silence in their compositions, much as cubist sculptors introduced negative space into mass. The results were as startling to the ear as cubism was to the eye.

*Le Corbusier, *Towards a New Architecture*, translated by Frederick Etchells. New York: Praeger, 1970, 12–13.

SUMMARY

During the first decade of the twentieth century, atomic physicists provided a model of the universe that was both more dynamic and more complex than any previously conceived. Matter, they explained, is a form of energy; time and space are relative to the position of the individual observer; and the universe itself is subject to changes that occur abruptly and without transition. Writers, painters, and composers of the first decades of the twentieth century challenged the established way of viewing the indifferent cosmos that they occupied. The fragmentation of form and the disjunctive juxtaposition of motifs in the poetry, art, music, and dance of this period seem to mirror the modern physicist's image of an atomic universe, whose laws are relative and whose operations lack smooth and predictable transitions.

Abstraction and formalism characterize the modernist aesthetic. In the poems of the imagists, as in the cubist paintings of Picasso and the sculpture of Brancusi, a concentrated reduction of form overtook naturalism and representation. With Kandinsky, Malevich, and Mondrian, painting freed itself entirely of recognizable objects. In architecture, Frank Lloyd Wright combined the tools of glass and steel technology with the aesthetics of Asian art to invent a style of unprecedented simplicity. Gropius, founder of the Bauhaus, and Le Corbusier, pioneer of the vertical city, developed the international style, which proclaimed the credo of functional design. The austere formalism of the international style would come to dominate much of the urban architecture of the twentieth century. In music and dance, the modernist assault was equally evident. Arnold Schoenberg and Igor Stravinsky introduced atonality, polytonality, and polyrhythm as formal alternatives to the time-honored Western traditions of pleasing harmonies and uniform meter. Vaslav Nijinsky and Martha Graham liberated dance from academic strictures.

Armed with up-to-date concepts of time and space, modernists rallied to "make it new." Pound's poems, Picasso's cubist compositions, and Stravinsky's early scores remain exemplary of the modernist search for powerful new kinds of expression. And while such works may have seemed as strange and forbidding as modern physics, they were equally effective in shattering the time-honored principles and values of the humanistic tradition.

GLOSSARY

abstraction the process by which subject matter is pared down or simplified in order to capture intrinsic or essential qualities; also, any work of art that reflects this process

atonality in music, the absence of a tonal center or definite key

avant-garde (French, "vanguard") those who create or produce styles and ideas ahead of their time; also, an unconventional movement or style

collage (French, *coller*, "to paste") a composition created by pasting materials such as newspaper, wallpaper, photographs, or cloth on a flat surface or canvas

ferroconcrete a cement building material reinforced by embedding wire or iron rods; also called "reinforced concrete"

haiku a Japanese light verse form consisting of seventeen syllables (three lines of five, seven, and five)

nonobjective art art that lacks recognizable subject matter; also called "nonrepresentational art"

polyrhythm in music, the device of using two or more different rhythms at the same time; also known as "polymeter"

polytonality in music, the simultaneous use of multiple tonal centers or keys; for compositions using only two tonal centers, the word "bitonality" applies

serial technique in music, a technique that involves the use of a particular series of notes, rhythms, and other elements that are repeated over and over throughout the piece

twelve-tone system a kind of serial music that demands the use of all twelve notes of the chromatic scale (all twelve half-tones in an octave) in a particular order or series; no one note can be used again until all eleven have appeared

SUGGESTIONS FOR READING

Calder, Nigel. *Einstein's Universe*. New York: Greenwich House, 1988.

Giedion, Siegfried. *Space, Time and Architecture: The Growth of a New Tradition*. Cambridge, Mass.: Harvard University Press, 1967.

Hertz, Richard, and Norman M. Klein, eds. *Twentieth-Century Art Theory: Urbanism, Politics, and Mass Culture*. Englewood Cliffs, N.J.: Prentice Hall, 1990.

Hughes, Robert. *The Shock of the New: Art and the Century of Change*. New York: Knopf, 1993.

Kern, Stephen. *The Culture of Time and Space, 1880–1918*. Cambridge, Mass.: Harvard University Press, 1986.

Nute, Kevin. *Frank Lloyd Wright and Japan: The Role of Traditional Japanese Art and Architecture in the Work of Frank Lloyd Wright*. New York: Van Nostrand Reinhold, 1994.

Perkins, David. *A History of Modern Poetry: Modernism and After*. New York: Belknap Press, 1987.

Peyser, Joan. *Twentieth-Century Music: The Sense Behind the Sound*. New York: Schirmer, 1980.

Torgovnick, Marianna. *Gone Primitive: Savage Intellects, Modern Lives*. Chicago: University of Chicago Press, 1995.

Taruskin, Richard. *Stravinsky and the Russian Traditions*. 2 vols. Berkeley, Calif.: University of California Press, 1996.

Yablonskaya, M.N. *Women Artists of Russia's New Age*. New York: Rizzoli, 1990.

MUSIC LISTENING SELECTIONS

CD Two Selection 17 Schoenberg, *Pierrot Lunaire*, Op. 21, Part 3, No. 15, "Heimweh," 1912.

CD Two Selection 18 Stravinsky, *The Rite of Spring*, "Sacrificial Dance," 1913, excerpt.

CHAPTER THIRTY-THREE

The Freudian revolution

"Only children, madmen, and savages truly understand the 'in-between' world of spiritual truth."
Paul Klee

Freud and the Psyche

No figure in modern Western history has had more influence on our perception of ourselves than Sigmund Freud (1856–1939). Freud, a Jewish intellectual who graduated in medicine from the University of Vienna, Austria, in 1880, was the first to map the subconscious geography of the human psyche (or mind). His early work with severely disturbed patients, followed by a period of intensive self-analysis, led him to develop a systematic procedure for treating emotional illnesses. Freud was the founder of *psychoanalysis*, a therapeutic method by which repressed desires are brought to the conscious level to reveal the sources of emotional disturbance. Freud pioneered the principal tools of this method—dream analysis and "free association" (the spontaneous verbalization of thoughts)—and favored these techniques over hypnosis, the procedure preferred by notable physicians with whom he had studied.

Freud theorized that instinctual drives, especially the libido, or sex drive, governed human behavior. According to Freud, guilt from the repression of instinctual urges dominates the subconscious life of human beings and manifests itself in emotional illness. Most psychic disorders, he argued, were the result of sexual traumas stemming from the child's subconscious attachment to the parent of the opposite sex and jealousy of the parent of the same sex, a phenomenon Freud called the Oedipus complex (in reference to the ancient Greek legend in which Oedipus, king of Thebes, unwittingly kills his father and marries his mother). Freud shocked the world with his analysis of infant sexuality and, more generally, with his proclamation that the psychic lives of human beings were formed by the time they were five years old.

Of all his discoveries, Freud considered his research on dream analysis most important. In 1900 he published *The Interpretation of Dreams*, in which he defended the significance of dreams in deciphering the unconscious life of the individual. In *Totem and Taboo* (1913), he examined the function of the subconscious in the evolution of the earliest forms of religion and morality. And in "The Sexual Life of Human Beings," a lecture presented to medical students at the University of Vienna in 1916, he examined the psychological roots of sadism, homosexuality, fetishism, and voyeurism—subjects still considered taboo in some social circles. Freud's theories opened the door to the clinical appraisal of previously guarded types of human behavior; and, by bringing attention to the central place of sexuality in human life, they irrevocably altered popular attitudes toward human sexuality. His controversial writings also had a major impact on the treatment of the mentally ill. Until at least the eighteenth century, people generally regarded psychotic behavior as evidence of possession by demonic or evil spirits, and the mentally ill were often locked up like animals. Freud's studies argued that neuroses and psychoses were illnesses that required medical treatment.

In describing the activities of the human psyche, Freud proposed a theoretical model, the terms of which (though often oversimplified and misunderstood) have become basic to *psychology* (the study of mind and behavior) and fundamental to our everyday vocabulary. This model pictures the psyche as consisting of three parts: the *id*, the *ego*, and the *superego*. The id, according to Freud, is the seat of human instincts and the source of all physical desires, including nourishment and sexual satisfaction. Seeking fulfillment in accordance with the pleasure principle, the id is the driving force of the subconscious realm. Freud perceived the second part of the psyche, the ego, as the administrator of the id: The ego is the "manager" that attempts to adapt the needs of the id to the real world. Whether by dreams or by **sublimation** (the positive modification and redirection of primal urges), the ego mediates between potentially destructive desires and social necessities. In Freud's view, civilization was the product of the ego's effort to modify the primal urges of the id. The third agent in the psychic life of the human being, the superego, is the moral monitor commonly called the "conscience." The superego monitors human behavior according to principles inculcated by parents, teachers, and other authority figures.

Freud's tripartite psyche constituted a radical model of human behavior. Copernicus had dislodged human beings from their central location in the cosmos, and Darwin had deposed *Homo sapiens* from a special place over and above other living creatures; now Freud dealt the final blow: He attacked the traditional notion that human reason and rational thought governed human actions. Indeed, while Freud himself believed as firmly as any Enlightenment rationalist in the reforming power of science, his theories challenged the centuries-old belief in the supremacy of human reason.

As is the case with many great thinkers, Freud made some questionable judgments and was likely wrong in some of his formulations. Recent revisionists have criticized Freud's theories on repression (arguing that they are inherently untestable), his analysis of female sexuality (especially the sexist notion of "penis envy" as a female affliction), and the methodology of psychoanalysis itself (the effectiveness of which has been challenged by proponents of biomedical psychiatry and behavioral psychology). Indeed, a hotly debated question—yet to be resolved—is whether mental illnesses are biological dysfunctions (best treated pharmacologically) or psychosocial dysfunctions related to infant trauma, early childhood problems, and the like (best treated by some form of psychoanalysis), or both. While Freud may be valued today less as a scientist than as an artist, philosopher, and theorist, it is noteworthy that Freud himself anticipated many late twentieth-century developments in neuropsychiatry, the branch of medicine that deals with diseases of the mind and nervous system. In the long run, however, Freud's most significant contributions were to the development of modern intellectual history, specifically in his insistence that the inner recesses of the mind were valid and meaningful parts of the personality, and that dreams and fantasies were as vital to human life as reason itself.

In challenging reason as the governor of human action, Freud questioned the very nature of human morality. He described benevolent action and altruistic conduct as mere masks for self-gratification, and religion as a form of mass delusion. Such views were central to the essay *Civilization and Its Discontents*, in which Freud explored at length the relationship between psychic activity and human society. Enumerating the various ways in which all human beings attempt to escape the "pain and unpleasure" of life, Freud argued that civilization itself was the collective product of sublimated instincts. The greatest impediment to civilization, he claimed, was human aggression, which he defined as "an original, self-subsisting instinctual disposition in man." The following excerpts offer some idea of Freud's incisive analysis of the psychic life of human beings.

READING 6.3   From Freud's *Civilization and its Discontents* (1930)

We will . . . turn to the less ambitious question of what men themselves show by their behavior to be the purpose and intention of their lives. What do they demand of life and wish **1**

to achieve in it? The answer to this can hardly be in doubt. They strive after happiness; they want to become happy and to remain so. This endeavor has two sides, a positive and a negative aim. It aims, on the one hand, at an absence of pain and unpleasure, and, on the other, at the experiencing of strong feelings of pleasure. In its narrower sense the word "happiness" only relates to the last. In conformity with this **10** dichotomy in his aims, man's activity develops in two directions, according as it seeks to realize—in the main, or even exclusively—the one or the other of these aims.

As we see, what decides the purpose of life is simply the programme of the pleasure principle. This principle dominates the operation of the mental apparatus from the start. There can be no doubt about its efficacy, and yet its programme is at loggerheads with the whole world, with the macrocosm as much as with the microcosm. There is no possibility at all of its being carried through; all the regulations of the universe **20** run counter to it. One feels inclined to say that the intention that man should be "happy" is not included in the plan of "Creation." What we call happiness in the strictest sense comes from the (preferably sudden) satisfaction of needs which have been dammed up to a high degree, and it is from its nature only possible as an episodic phenomenon. When any situation that is desired by the pleasure principle is prolonged, it only produces a feeling of mild contentment. We are so made that we can derive intense enjoyment only from a contrast and very little from a state of things. Thus our **30** possibilities of happiness are already restricted by our constitution. Unhappiness is much less difficult to experience. We are threatened with suffering from three directions: from our own body, which is doomed to decay and dissolution and which cannot even do without pain and anxiety as warning signals; from the external world, which may rage against us with overwhelming and merciless forces of destruction; and finally from our relations to other men. The suffering which comes from this last source is perhaps more painful to us than any other. We tend to regard it as a kind of gratuitous **40** addition, although it cannot be any less fatefully inevitable than the suffering which comes from elsewhere. . . .

An unrestricted satisfaction of every need presents itself as the most enticing method of conducting one's life, but it means putting enjoyment before caution, and soon brings its own punishment. The other methods in which avoidance of unpleasure is the main purpose, are differentiated according to the source of unpleasure to which their attention is chiefly turned. Some of these methods are extreme and some moderate; some are one-sided and some attack the problem **50** simultaneously at several points. Against the suffering which may come upon one from human relationships the readiest safeguard is voluntary isolation, keeping oneself aloof from other people. The happiness which can be achieved along this path is, as we see, the happiness of quietness. Against the dreaded external world one can only defend oneself by some kind of turning away from it, if one intends to solve the task by oneself. There is, indeed, another and better path: that of becoming a member of the human community, and, with the help of a technique guided by science, going over to the attack **60** against nature and subjecting her to the human will. Then one is working with all for the good of all. But the most interesting methods of averting suffering are those which seek to influence our own organism. In the last analysis, all suffering is nothing else than sensation; it only exists in so far as we feel it, and we only feel it in consequence of certain ways in which our organism is regulated.

The crudest, but also the most effective among these methods of influence is the chemical one—intoxication. I do not think that anyone completely understands its mechanism, but it is a fact that there are foreign substances which, when present in the blood or tissues, directly cause us pleasurable sensations; and they also so alter the conditions governing our sensibility that we become incapable of receiving unpleasurable impulses. The two effects not only occur simultaneously, but seem to be intimately bound up with each other. But there must be substances in the chemistry of our own bodies which have similar effects, for we know at least one pathological state, mania, in which a condition similar to intoxication arises without the administration of any intoxicating drug. Besides this, our normal mental life exhibits oscillations between a comparatively easy liberation of pleasure and a comparatively difficult one, parallel with which there goes a diminished or an increased receptivity to unpleasure. It is greatly to be regretted that this toxic side of mental processes has so far escaped scientific examination. The service rendered by intoxicating media in the struggle for happiness and in keeping misery at a distance is so highly prized as a benefit that individuals and people alike have given them an established place in the economics of their libido.[1] We owe to such media not merely the immediate yield of pleasure, but also a greatly desired degree of independence from the external world. For one knows that, with the help of this "drowner of cares," one can at any time withdraw from the pressure of reality and find refuge in a world of one's own with better conditions of sensibility. As is well known, it is precisely this property of intoxicants which also determines their danger and their injuriousness. They are responsible, in certain circumstances, for the useless waste of a large quota of energy which might have been employed for the improvement of the human lot. . . .

Another technique for fending off suffering is the employment of the displacements of libido which our mental apparatus permits of and through which its function gains so much in flexibility. The task here is that of shifting the instinctual aims in such a way that they cannot come up against frustration from the external world. In this, sublimation of the instincts lends its assistance. One gains the most if one can sufficiently heighten the yield of pleasure from the sources of psychical and intellectual work. When that is so, fate can do little against one. A satisfaction of this kind, such as an artist's joy in creating, in giving his phantasies body, or a scientist's in solving problems or discovering truths, has a special quality which we shall certainly one day be able to characterize in metapsychological terms. At present we can only say figuratively that such satisfactions seem "finer and higher." But their intensity is mild as compared with that derived from the sating of crude and primary instinctual impulses; it does not convulse our physical being. And the

weak point of this method is that it is not applicable generally: it is accessible to only a few people. It presupposes the possession of special dispositions and gifts which are far from being common to any practical degree. And even to the few who do possess them, this method cannot give complete protection from suffering. It creates no impenetrable armor against the arrows of fortune, and it habitually fails when the source of suffering is a person's own body. . . .

Another procedure operates more energetically and more thoroughly. It regards reality as the sole enemy and as the source of all suffering, with which it is impossible to live, so that one must break off all relations with it if one is to be in any way happy. The hermit turns his back on the world and will have no truck with it. But one can do more than that; one can try to re-create the world, to build up in its stead another world in which its most unbearable features are eliminated and replaced by others that are in conformity with one's own wishes. But whoever, in desperate defiance, sets out upon this path to happiness will as a rule attain nothing. Reality is too strong for him. He becomes a madman, who for the most part finds no one to help him in carrying through his delusion. It is asserted, however, that each one of us behaves in some one respect like a paranoiac, corrects some aspect of the world which is unbearable to him by the construction of a wish and introduces this delusion into reality. A special importance attaches to the case in which this attempt to procure a certainty of happiness and a protection against suffering through a delusional remoulding of reality is made by a considerable number of people in common. The religions of mankind must be classed among the mass-delusions of this kind. No one, needless to say, who shares a delusion ever recognizes it as such. . . .

Religion restricts this play of choice and adaptation, since it imposes equally on everyone its own path to the acquisition of happiness and protection from suffering. Its technique consists in depressing the value of life and distorting the picture of the real world in a delusional manner—which presupposes an intimidation of the intelligence. At this price, by forcibly fixing them in a state of psychical infantilism and by drawing them into a mass-delusion, religion succeeds in sparing many people an individual neurosis. But hardly anything more. . . . During the last few generations mankind has made an extraordinary advance in the natural sciences and in their technical application and has established his control over nature in a way never before imagined. The single steps of this advance are common knowledge and it is unnecessary to enumerate them. Men are proud of those achievements, and have a right to be. But they seem to have observed that this newly-won power over space and time, this subjugation of the forces of nature, which is the fulfillment of a longing that goes back thousands of years, has not increased the amount of pleasurable satisfaction which they may expect from life and has not made them feel happier. From the recognition of this fact we ought to be content to conclude that power over nature is not the *only* precondition of human happiness, just as it is not the *only* goal of cultural endeavor; we ought not to infer from it that technical progress is without value for the economics of our happiness. One would like to ask: is there, then, no positive gain in pleasure, no unequivocal increase in

[1] The instinctual desires of the id, most specifically, the sexual urge.

my feeling of happiness, if I can, as often as I please, hear the voice of a child of mine who is living hundreds of miles away or if I can learn in the shortest possible time after a friend has reached his destination that he has come through the long and difficult voyage unharmed? Does it mean nothing that medicine has succeeded in enormously reducing infant mortality and the danger of infection for women in childbirth and, indeed, in considerably lengthening the average life of a civilized man? And there is a long list that might be added to benefits of this kind which we owe to the much-despised era of scientific and technical advances. But here the voice of pessimistic criticism makes itself heard and warns us that most of these satisfactions follow the model of the "cheap enjoyment" extolled in the anecdote—the enjoyment obtained by putting a bare leg from under the bedclothes on a cold winter night and drawing it in again. If there had been no railway to conquer distances, my child would never have left his native town and I should need no telephone to hear his voice; if travelling across the ocean by ship had not been introduced, my friend would not have embarked on his sea-voyage and I should not need a cable to relieve my anxiety about him. What is the use of reducing infantile mortality when it is precisely that reduction which imposes the greatest restraint on us in the begetting of children, so that, taken all round, we nevertheless rear no more children than in the days before the reign of hygiene, while at the same time we have created difficult conditions for our sexual life in marriage, and have probably worked against the beneficial effects of natural selection? And, finally, what good to us is a long life if it is difficult and barren of joys, and if it is so full of misery that we can only welcome death as a deliverer? . . .

. . . men are not gentle creatures who want to be loved, and who at the most can defend themselves if they are attacked; they are, on the contrary, creatures among whose instinctual endowments is to be reckoned a powerful share of aggressiveness. As a result, their neighbor is for them not only a potential helper or sexual object, but also someone who tempts them to satisfy their aggressiveness on him, to exploit his capacity for work without compensation, to use him sexually without his consent, to seize his possessions, to humiliate him, to cause him pain, to torture and to kill him. . . .

The existence of this inclination to aggression, which we can detect in ourselves and justly assume to be present in others, is the factor which disturbs our relations with our neighbor and which forces civilization into such a high expenditure [of energy]. In consequence of this primary mutual hostility of human beings, civilized society is perpetually threatened with disintegration. The interest of work in common would not hold it together; instinctual passions are stronger than reasonable interests. Civilization has to use its utmost efforts in order to set limits to man's aggressive instincts and to hold the manifestations of them in check by psychical reaction-formations. Hence, therefore, the use of methods intended to incite people into identifications and aim-inhibited relationships of love, hence the restriction upon sexual life, and hence too the [idealist] commandment to love one's neighbor as oneself—a commandment which is really justified by the fact that nothing else runs so strongly counter to the original nature of man. In spite of every effort, these endeavors of civilization have not so far achieved very much. It hopes to prevent the crudest excesses of brutal violence by itself assuming the right to use violence against criminals, but the law is not able to lay hold of the more cautious and refined manifestations of human aggressiveness. The time comes when each one of us has to give up as illusions the expectations which, in his youth, he pinned upon his fellowmen, and when he may learn how much difficulty and pain has been added to his life by their ill-will. . . .

Freud's Followers

Freud's writings explored so many aspects of human experience that, inevitably, his theories would be tested and laid open to assault. In the second half of the twentieth century, for instance, some physicians questioned the scientific validity of psychoanalysis and its usefulness as a form of treatment. At the same time, feminists, whose movement for women's liberation (see chapter 36) clearly owes much to Freud's critique of sexual morality, have attacked Freud's patriarchal image of the female as passive, weak, and dependent. Nevertheless, Freud's immediate followers recognized that they stood in the shadow of an intellectual giant. Although some psychoanalysts disagreed with Freud's dogmatic theory that all neuroses stemmed from the traumas of the id, most took his discoveries as the starting point for their own inquiries into human behavior. For instance, Freud's Viennese associate Alfred Adler (1870–1937), who pioneered the field of individual psychology, sought to explain the ego's efforts to adapt to its environment. Coining the term "inferiority complex," Adler concentrated on analyzing problems related to the ego's failure to achieve its operational goals in everyday life.

Another of Freud's colleagues, the Swiss physician Carl Gustav Jung (1875–1961), found Freud's view of the psyche too narrow and overly deterministic. Jung argued that the personal, unconscious life of the individual rested on a deeper and more universal layer of the human psyche, which he called the **collective unconscious**. According to Jung, the collective unconscious belongs to humankind at large, that is, to the human family. It manifests itself throughout history in the form of dreams, myths, and fairy tales. The **archetypes** of that realm—primal patterns that reflect the deep psychic needs of humankind as a species—reveal themselves as familiar motifs and characters, such as "the child-god," "the hero," and "the wise old man." Jung's investigations into the cultural history of humankind disclosed endless similarities among the symbols and myths of different religions and bodies of folklore. These he took to support his theory that the archetypes were the innate, inherited contents of the human mind.

Some of Jung's most convincing observations concerning the life of the collective unconscious appear in his essay "Psychological Aspects of the Mother Archetype" (1938). In this essay, Jung discusses the manifestations of the female archetype in personal life, as mother, grandmother, stepmother, nurse, or governess; in religion, as the redemptive Mother of God, the Virgin, Holy Wisdom, and the various nature deities of ancient myth and religion;

and in the universal symbolism of things and places associated with fertility and fruitfulness, such as the cornucopia, the garden, the fountain, the cave, the rose, the lotus, the magic circle, and the uterus. The negative aspect of the female archetype, observed Jung, usually manifests itself as the witch in traditional fairy tales and legends. Jung emphasized the role of the collective unconscious in reflecting the "psychic unity" of all cultures. He treated the personal psyche as part of the larger human family, and, unlike Freud, he insisted on the positive value of religion in satisfying humankind's deepest psychic desires.

The New Psychology and Literature

The impact of the new psychology was felt throughout Europe. Freud's theories, and particularly his pessimistic view of human nature, intensified the mood of uncertainty produced by the startling revelations of atomic physics and the outbreak of World War I. The Freudian revolution affected all aspects of artistic expression, not the least of which was literature. A great many figures in early twentieth-century fiction were profoundly influenced by Freud; three of the most famous of these are Marcel Proust, Franz Kafka, and James Joyce. In the works of these novelists the most significant events are those that take place in the psychic life of dreams and memory. The narrative line of the story may be interrupted by unexpected leaps of thought, intrusive recollections, self-reflections, and sudden dead ends. Fantasy may alternate freely with rational thought. The lives of the heroes—or, more exactly, antiheroes—in these stories are often inconsequential, while their concerns, though commonplace or trivial, may be obsessive, bizarre, and charged with passion.

Proust's Quest for Lost Time

Born in Paris, Marcel Proust (1871–1922) spent his youth troubled by severe attacks of asthma and recurring insecurities over his sexual orientation. Devastated by the death of his mother in 1905, Proust withdrew completely from Parisian society. He retreated into the semidarkness of a cork-lined room, where, shielded from noise, light, and frivolous society, he pursued a life of introspection and literary endeavor. Between 1913 and 1927 Proust produced a sixteen-volume novel entitled *A la recherche du temps perdu* (literally, "In Search of Lost Time," but usually translated as *Remembrance of Things Past*). This lengthy masterpiece provides a reflection of the society of turn-of-the-century France, but its perception of reality is wholly internal. Its central theme is the role of memory in retrieving past experience and in shaping the private life of the individual. Proust's mission was to rediscover a sense of the past by reviving sensory experiences buried deep within his psyche, that is, to bring the unconscious life to the conscious level. "For me," explained Proust, "the novel is . . . psychology in space and time."

In the first volume of *A la recherche du temps perdu*, entitled *Swann's Way*, Proust employs the Freudian technique of "free association" to recapture from the recesses of memory the intense moment of pleasure occasioned by the taste of a piece of cake soaked in tea. The following excerpt illustrates Proust's ability to free experience from the rigid order of mechanical time and invade the richly textured storehouse of the psyche. It also illustrates the modern notion of the mental process as a "stream of thought," a concept that had appeared as early as 1884 in the writings of the American psychologist William James (1842–1910) and in the works of Henri Bergson (1859–1941), who argued that reality is best understood as a perpetual flux in which past and present are inseparable (see chapter 31).

READING 6.4   From Proust's *Swann's Way* (1913)

The past is hidden somewhere outside the realm, beyond the reach of intellect, in some material object (in the sensation which that material object will give us) which we do not suspect. And as for that object, it depends on chance whether we come upon it or not before we ourselves must die.

Many years had elapsed during which nothing of Combray, save what was comprised in the theatre and the drama of my going to bed there, had any existence for me, when one day in winter, as I came home, my mother, seeing that I was cold, offered me some tea, a thing I did not ordinarily take. I declined at first, and then, for no particular reason, changed my mind. She sent out for one of those short, plump little cakes called "petites madeleines," which look as though they had been moulded in the fluted scallop of a pilgrim's shell. And soon, mechanically, weary after a dull day with the prospect of a depressing morrow, I raised to my lips a spoonful of the tea in which I had soaked a morsel of the cake. No sooner had the warm liquid, and the crumbs with it, touched my palate than a shudder ran through my whole body, and I stopped, intent upon the extraordinary changes that were taking place. An exquisite pleasure had invaded my senses, but individual, detached, with no suggestion of its origin. And at once the vicissitudes of life had become indifferent to me, its disasters innocuous, its brevity illusory—this new sensation having had on me the effect which love has of filling me with a precious essence; or rather this essence was not in me, it was myself. I had ceased now to feel mediocre, accidental, mortal. Whence could it have come to me, this all-powerful joy? I was conscious that it was connected with the taste of tea and cake, but that it infinitely transcended those savours, could not, indeed, be of the same nature as theirs. Whence did it come? What did it signify? How could I seize upon and define it?

I drink a second mouthful, in which I find nothing more than in the first, a third, which gives me rather less than the second. It is time to stop; the potion is losing its magic. It is plain that the object of my quest, the truth, lies not in the cup but in myself. The tea has called up in me, but does not itself understand, and can only repeat indefinitely with a gradual loss of strength, the same testimony; which I, too, cannot interpret, though I hope at least to be able to call upon the tea for it again and to find it there presently, intact and at my disposal, for my final enlightenment. I put down my cup and

1

10

20

30

40

examine my own mind. It is for it to discover the truth. But how? What an abyss of uncertainty whenever the mind feels that some part of it has strayed beyond its own borders; when it, the seeker, is at once the dark region through which it must go seeking, where all its equipment will avail it nothing. Seek? More than that: create. It is face to face with something which does not so far exist, to which it alone can give reality and substance, which it alone can bring into the light of day. 50

And I begin again to ask myself what it could have been, this unremembered state which brought with it no logical proof of its existence, but only the sense that it was a happy, that it was a real state in whose presence other states of consciousness melted and vanished. I decide to attempt to make it reappear. I retrace my thoughts to the moment at which I drank the first spoonful of tea. I find again the same state, illumined by no fresh light. I compel my mind to make one further effort, to follow and recapture once again the 60 fleeting sensation. And that nothing may interrupt it in its course I shut out every obstacle, every extraneous idea, I stop my ears and inhibit all attention to the sounds which come from the next room. And then, feeling that my mind is growing fatigued without having any success to report, I compel it for a change to enjoy that distraction which I have just denied it, to think of other things, to rest and refresh itself before the supreme attempt. And then for the second time I clear an empty space in front of it. I place in position before my mind's eye the still recent taste of that first mouthful, and I feel 70 something start within me, something that leaves its resting-place and attempts to rise, something that has been embedded like an anchor at a great depth; I do not know yet what it is, but I can feel it mounting slowly; I can measure the resistance, I can hear the echo of great spaces traversed.

Undoubtedly what is thus palpitating in the depths of my being must be the image, the visual memory which, being linked to that taste, has tried to follow it into my conscious mind. But its struggles are too far off, too much confused; scarcely can I perceive the colorless reflection in which are 80 blended the uncapturable whirling medley of radiant hues, and I cannot distinguish its form, cannot invite it, as the one possible interpreter, to translate to me the evidence of its contemporary, its inseparable paramour, the taste of cake soaked in tea; cannot ask it to inform me what special circumstance is in question, of what period in my past life.

Will it ultimately reach the clear surface of my consciousness, this memory, this old, dead moment which the magnetism of an identical moment has travelled so far to importune, to disturb, to raise up out of the very depths of my being? I cannot tell. 90 Now that I feel nothing, it has stopped, has perhaps gone down again into its darkness, from which who can say whether it will ever rise? Ten times over I must essay the task, must lean down over the abyss. And each time the natural laziness which deters us from every difficult enterprise, every work of importance, has urged me to leave the thing alone, to drink my tea and to think merely of the worries of to-day and of my hopes for tomorrow, which let themselves be pondered over without effort or distress of mind.

And suddenly the memory returns. The taste was that of 100 the little crumb of madeleine which on Sunday mornings at Combray (because on those mornings I did not go out before church-time), when I went to say good day to her in her bedroom, my aunt Léonie used to give me, dipping it first in her own cup of real or of lime-flower tea. The sight of the little madeleine had recalled nothing to my mind before I tasted it; perhaps because I had so often seen such things in the interval, without tasting them, on the trays in pastry-cooks' windows, that their image had dissociated itself from those Combray days to take its place among others more recent; 110 perhaps because of those memories, so long abandoned and put out of mind, nothing now survived, everything was scattered; the forms of things, including that of the little scallop-shell of pastry, so richly sensual under its severe, religious folds, were either obliterated or had been so long dormant as to have lost the power of expansion which would have allowed them to resume their place in my consciousness. But when from a long-distant past nothing subsists, after the people are dead, after the things are broken and scattered, still, alone, more fragile, but with more vitality, more 120 unsubstantial, more persistent, more faithful, the smell and taste of things remain poised a long time, like souls, ready to remind us, waiting and hoping for their moment, amid the ruins of all the rest; and bear unfaltering, in the tiny and almost impalpable drop of their essence, the vast structure of recollection.

And once I had recognized the taste of the crumb of madeleine soaked in her decoction of lime-flowers which my aunt used to give me (although I did not yet know and must long postpone the discovery of why this memory made me so 130 happy) immediately the old grey house upon the street, where her room was, rose up like the scenery of a theatre to attach itself to the little pavilion, opening on to the garden, which had been built out behind it for my parents (the isolated panel which until that moment had been all that I could see); and with the house the town, from morning to night and in all weathers, the Square where I was sent before luncheon, the streets along which I used to run errands, the country roads we took when it was fine. And just as the Japanese amuse themselves by filling a porcelain bowl with water and steeping 140 in it little crumbs of paper which until then are without character or form, but, the moment they become wet, stretch themselves and bend, take on color and distinctive shape, become flowers or houses or people, permanent and recognisable, so in that moment all the flowers in our garden and in M. Swann's park, and the water-lilies on the Vivonne and the good folk of the village and their little dwellings and the parish church and the whole of Combray and of its surroundings, taking their proper shapes and growing solid, sprang into being, towns and gardens alike, from my cup of tea. . . . 150

The Nightmare Reality of Kafka

For Proust, memory was a life-enriching phenomenon, but for the German-Jewish novelist Franz Kafka (1883–1924), the subconscious life gave conscious experience bizarre and threatening gravity. Written in German, Kafka's novels and short stories take on the reality of dreams in which characters are nameless, details are precise but grotesque, and events lack logical consistency. Kafka's novels create a nightmarish world in which the central characters become victims of unknown or imprecisely understood forces. They may be caught in absurd but commonplace circumstances involving guilt and frustration, or they may be threatened by menacing events that appear to have neither meaning nor purpose. In Kafka's novel *The Trial* (1925), for instance, the protagonist is arrested, convicted, and executed, without ever knowing the nature of his crime. In "The Metamorphosis," one of the most disquieting short stories of the twentieth century, the central character, Gregor Samsa, wakes one morning to discover that he has turned into a large insect. The themes of insecurity and vulnerability that recur in Kafka's novels reflect the mood that prevailed during the early decades of the century. Kafka himself was afflicted with this insecurity: Shortly before he died in 1924, he asked a close friend to burn all of his manuscripts; the friend disregarded the request and saw to it that Kafka's works, even some that were unfinished, were published. Consequently, Kafka's style, which builds on deliberate ambiguity and fearful contradiction, has had a major influence on modern fiction. Although "The Metamorphosis" is too long to reproduce here in full, the excerpt that follows conveys some idea of Kafka's surreal narrative style.

READING 6.5 From Kafka's "The Metamorphosis" (1915)

As Gregor Samsa awoke one morning from uneasy dreams he found himself transformed in his bed into a gigantic insect. He was lying on his hard, as it were armor-plated, back and when he lifted his head a little he could see his dome-like brown belly divided into stiff arched segments on top of which the bed quilt could hardly keep in position and was about to slide off completely. His numerous legs, which were pitifully thin compared to the rest of his bulk, waved helplessly before his eyes. 1

What has happened to me? he thought. It was no dream. His room, a regular human bedroom, only rather too small, lay quiet between the four familiar walls. Above the table on which a collection of cloth samples was unpacked and spread out—Samsa was a commercial traveler—hung the picture, which he had recently cut out of an illustrated magazine and put into a pretty gilt frame. It showed a lady, with a fur cap on and a fur stole, sitting upright and holding out to the spectator a huge fur muff into which the whole of her forearm had vanished! 10

Gregor's eyes turned next to the window, and the overcast sky—one could hear raindrops beating on the window gutter—made him quite melancholy. What about sleeping a little longer and forgetting all this nonsense, he thought, but it could not be done, for he was accustomed to sleep on his right side and in his present condition he could not turn himself over. However violently he forced himself towards his right side he always rolled on to his back again. He tried it at least a hundred times, shutting his eyes to keep from seeing his struggling legs, and only desisted when he began to feel in his side a faint dull ache he had never experienced before. 20

Oh God, he thought, what an exhausting job I've picked on! 30

Traveling about day in, day out. It's much more irritating work than doing the actual business in the office, and on top of that there's the trouble of constant traveling, of worrying about train connections, the bed and irregular meals, casual acquaintances that are always new and never become intimate friends. The devil take it all! He felt a slight itching upon his belly; slowly pushed himself on his back nearer to the top of the bed so that he could lift his head more easily; identified the itching place which was surrounded by many small white spots the nature of which he could not understand and made to touch it with a leg, but drew the leg back immediately, for the contact made a cold shiver run through him. . . . 40

He looked at the alarm clock ticking on the chest. Heavenly Father! he thought. It was half-past six o'clock and the hands were quietly moving on, it was even past the half-hour, it was getting on toward a quarter to seven. Had the alarm clock not gone off? From the bed one could see that it had been properly set for four o'clock; of course it must have gone off. Yes, but was it possible to sleep quietly through that ear-splitting noise? Well, he had not slept quietly, yet apparently all the more soundly for that. But what was he to do now? The next train went at seven o'clock; to catch that he would need to hurry like mad and his samples weren't even packed up, and he himself wasn't feeling particularly fresh and active. And even if he did catch the train he wouldn't avoid a row with the chief, since the firm's porter would have been waiting for the five o'clock train and would have long since reported his failure to turn up. . . . 50 60

As all this was running through his mind at top speed without his being able to decide to leave his bed—the alarm clock had just struck a quarter to seven—there came a cautious tap at the door behind the head of his bed. "Gregor," said a voice—it was his mother's—"it's a quarter to seven. Hadn't you a train to catch?" That gentle voice! Gregor had a shock as he heard his own voice answering hers, unmistakably his own voice, it was true, but with a persistent horrible twittering squeak behind it like an undertone, that left the words in their clear shape only for the first moment and then rose up reverberating round them to destroy their sense, so that one could not be sure one had heard them rightly. Gregor wanted to answer at length and explain everything, but in the circumstances he confined himself to saying: "Yes, yes, thank you, Mother, I'm getting up now." The wooden door between them must have kept the change in his voice from being noticeable outside, for his mother contented herself with this statement and shuffled away. Yet this brief exchange of words had made the other members of the family aware that Gregor was still in the house, as they had not expected, and at one of the side doors his father was already knocking, gently, yet with his fist. "Gregor, Gregor," he called, "what's the matter with you?" And after a little while he called again in a deeper voice: "Gregor! Gregor!" At the other side door his sister was saying in a low, plaintive tone: "Gregor? Aren't you well? Are you needing anything?" He answered them both at once: "I'm just ready," and did his best to make his voice sound as normal as possible by enunciating the words very clearly and leaving long pauses between them. So his father went back to his breakfast, but his sister whispered: "Gregor, open the door, do." . . . 70 80 90

[Unexpectedly, the chief clerk arrives to find out why Gregor is not at work. He demands to see him.]

Slowly Gregor pushed the chair towards the door, then let go of it, caught hold of the door for support—the soles at the end of his little legs were somewhat sticky—and rested against it for a moment after his efforts. Then he set himself to turning the key in the lock with his mouth. It seemed, unhappily, that he hadn't really any teeth—what could he grip the key with?—but on the other hand his jaws were certainly very strong; with their help he did manage to set the key in motion, heedless of the fact that he was undoubtedly damaging them somewhere, since a brown fluid issued from his mouth, flowed over the key and dripped on the floor. "Just listen to that," said the chief clerk next door; "he's turning the key." That was a great encouragement to Gregor; but they should all have shouted encouragement to him, his father and mother too: "Go on Gregor," they should have called out, "keep going, hold on to that key!" And in the belief that they were all following his efforts intently, he clenched his jaws recklessly on the key with all the force at his command. As the turning of the key progressed he circled round the lock, holding on now only with his mouth, pushing on the key, as required, or pulling it down again with all the weight of his body. The louder click of the finally yielding lock literally quickened Gregor. With a deep breath of relief he said to himself: "So I didn't need the locksmith," and laid his head on the handle to open the door wide.

Since he had to pull the door towards him, he was still invisible when it was really wide open. He had to edge himself slowly round the near half of the double door, and to do it very carefully if he was not to fall plump upon his back just on the threshold. He was still carrying out this difficult manoeuvre, with no time to observe anything else, when he heard the chief clerk utter a loud "Oh!"—it sounded like a gust of wind—and now he could see the man, standing as he was nearest to the door, clapping one hand before his open mouth and slowly backing away as if driven by some invisible steady pressure. His mother—in spite of the chief clerk's directions—first clasped her hands and looked at his father, then took two steps towards Gregor and fell on the floor among her outspread skirts, her face quite hidden on her breast. His father knotted his fist with a fierce expression on his face as if he meant to knock Gregor back into his room, then looked uncertainly round the living room, covered his eyes with his hands and wept till his great chest heaved. . . .

Joyce and Stream of Consciousness Prose

One of the most influential writers of the early twentieth century, and also one of the most challenging, was the Irish expatriate James Joyce (1882–1941). Born in Dublin and educated in Jesuit schools, Joyce abandoned Ireland in 1905 to live abroad. In Paris, he studied medicine and music but made his livelihood there and elsewhere by teaching foreign languages and writing short stories. Joyce's style reflects his genius as a linguist and his keen sensitivity to the musical potential of words. His treatment of plot and character is deeply indebted to Freud, whose earliest publications Joyce had consumed with interest.

Joyce was the master of the **interior monologue**, a literary device consisting of the private musings of a character in the form of a "stream of consciousness"—a succession of images and ideas connected by free association rather than by logical argument or narrative sequence. The stream of consciousness device resembles the free association technique used by Freud in psychotherapy; it also recalls the discontinuous verse style of the imagist poets (see chapter 32). In a stream of consciousness novel, the action is developed through the mind of the principal character as he or she responds to the dual play of conscious and subconscious stimuli. The following passage from Joyce's 600-page novel *Ulysses* (1922) provides a brief example:

> He crossed to the bright side, avoiding the loose cellarflap of number seventy-five. The sun was nearing the steeple of George's church. Be a warm day I fancy, Specially in these black clothes feel it more. Black conducts, reflects (refracts is it?), the heat. But I couldn't go in that light suit. Make a picnic of it. His Boland's breadvan delivering with trays our daily but she prefers yesterday's loaves turnovers crisp crowns hot. Makes you feel young. Somewhere in the east: early morning: set off at dawn, travel round in front of the sun, steal a day's march on him. Keep it up for ever never grow a day older technically. . . . Wander along all day. Meet a robber or two. Well, meet him. Getting on to sundown. The shadows of the mosques along the pillars: priest with a scroll rolled up. A shiver of the trees, signal, the evening wind. I pass on. Fading gold sky. A mother watches from her doorway. She calls her children home in their dark language. High wall: beyond strings twanged. Night sky moon, violet, colour of Molly's new garters. Strings. Listen. A girl playing one of these instruments what do you call them: dulcimers. I pass. . . .*

Joyce modeled his sprawling novel on the Homeric epic, the *Odyssey*. But Joyce's modern version differs profoundly from Homer's. Leopold Bloom, the main character of *Ulysses*, is as ordinary as Homer's Odysseus was heroic; his adventures seem trivial and insignificant by comparison with those of his classical counterpart. Bloom's commonplace experiences, as he wanders from home to office, pub, and brothel, and then home again—a one-day "voyage" through the streets of Dublin—constitute the plot of the novel. The real "action" of *Ulysses* takes place in the minds of its principal characters: Bloom, his acquaintances, and his wife Molly. Their collective ruminations produce an overwhelming sense of desolation and a startling awareness that the human psyche can never extricate itself from the timeless blur of experience. Joyce's stream of consciousness technique and his dense accumulation of unfamiliar and oddly compounded words make this monumental novel difficult to grasp—yet it remains more accessible than his experimental, baffling prose work, *Finnegans*

---

*James Joyce, *Ulysses*. New York: Vintage Books edition, Knopf, 1966, 57.

Wake (1939). Initially, however, it was censorship that made *Ulysses* inaccessible to the public: Since Joyce treated sexual matters as freely as all other aspects of human experience, critics judged his language obscene. The novel was banned in the United States until 1933.

The combined influence of Freud and Joyce was visible in much of the first-ranking literature of the twentieth century. Writers such as Gertrude Stein (1874–1946) and the Nobel laureates Thomas Mann (1875–1955) and William Faulkner (1897–1962) extended the use of the stream of consciousness technique. In theater the American playwright Eugene O'Neill (1888–1953) fused Greek myth with Freudian concepts of guilt and repression in the dramatic trilogy *Mourning Becomes Electra* (1931). He devised dramatic techniques that revealed the characters' buried emotions, such as two actors playing different aspects of a single individual, the use of masks, and the embellishment of dialogue with accompanying asides. The new psychology extended its influence to performance style as well: Freud's emphasis on the interior life inspired the development of **method acting**, a style of modern theatrical performance that tried to harness "true emotion" and "affective memory" from childhood experience in the interpretation of dramatic roles. The pioneer in method acting was the Russian director and actor Konstantin Stanislavsky (1863–1938), whose innovative techniques as head of the Moscow Art Theater spread to the United States in the early 1930s. There, his method inspired some of America's finest screen and stage actors, such as James Dean (1931–1955) and Marlon Brando (b.1924).

The New Freedom in Poetry

Modern poets avidly seized upon stream of consciousness techniques to emancipate poetry from syntactical and grammatical bonds—a mission that had been initiated by the symbolists and refined by the imagists. The French writer Guillaume Apollinaire (1880–1918), a close friend of Picasso and an admirer of cubism, wrote poems that not only liberated words from their traditional placement in the sentence but also freed sentences from their traditional arrangement on the page. Inspired by the designs of ordinary handbills, billboards, and signs, Apollinaire created **concrete poems**, that is, poems produced in the shape of external objects, such as watches, neckties, and pigeons. He arranged the words in the poem "Il Pleut" ("It Rains"), for instance, as if they had fallen onto the page like raindrops from the heavens. Such word-pictures, which Apollinaire called "lyrical ideograms," inspired the poet to exult, "I too am a painter!"

The American poet e.e.cummings (1894–1962) arrived in France in 1917 as a volunteer ambulance driver for the Red Cross. Like Apollinaire, cummings wrote poems that violated the traditional rules of verse composition. To sharpen the focus of a poem, he subjected typography and syntax to acrobatic distortions that challenged the eye as well as the ear. cummings poked fun at modern society by packing his verse with slang, jargon, and sexual innuendo. As the following poem suggests, his lyrics are often infused with large doses of playful humor.

READING 6.6 cummings' [she being Brand]
(1926)

she being Brand   1

-new;and you
know consequently a
little stiff i was
careful of her and(having   5
thoroughly oiled the universal
joint tested my gas felt of
her radiator made sure her springs were O.

K.)i went right to it flooded-the-carburetor cranked her

up, slipped the   10
clutch(and then somehow got into reverse she
kicked what
the hell)next
minute i was back in neutral tried and

again slo-wly;bare,ly nudg.   ing(my   15

lev-er Right-
oh and her gears being in
A 1 shape passed
from low through
second-in-to-high like   20
greasedlightning) just as we turned the corner of Divinity

avenue i touched the accelerator and give

her the juice,good

                        (it

was the first ride and believe i we was   25
happy to see how nice she acted right up to
the last minute coming back down by the Public
Gardens i slammed on

the
internalexpanding   30
&
externalcontracting
brakes Bothatonce and

brought allofher tremB
-ling   35
to a: dead.

stand-
;Still)

The New Psychology and the Visual Arts

It was in the visual arts that the new psychology made its most dramatic and long-lasting impact. As artists brought to their work their hidden emotions, repressed desires, and their dreams and fantasies, art became the pursuit of the subconscious. The irrational and antirational forces of the id became the subject and the inspiration for an assortment

Figure 33.1 EDVARD MUNCH, *The Scream*, 1893. Oil, pastel, and casein on cardboard, 35¾ × 29 in. National Gallery, Oslo.
© The Munch-Museum/The Munch-Ellingsen-Group. BONO, Oslo, DACS, London 2000.

of styles. These include expressionism, metaphysical art, dada, and surrealism. Expressionism and surrealism had particularly important effects on photography and film, as well as on the fields of commercial and applied arts that flourished in the second half of the century. Indeed, in every aspect of our daily experience, from fashion designs to magazine and television advertisements, the evidence of the Freudian revolution is still visible.

Expressionism

The pioneer expressionist painter of the twentieth century was the Norwegian Edvard Munch (1863–1944). Munch was a great admirer of Henrik Ibsen, his contemporary, whose plays (see chapter 30) examine the inner conflicts and repressed desires of their characters. Obsessed with the traumas of puberty and frustrated sexuality, Munch was also deeply troubled by personal associations with illness and death—tuberculosis had killed both his mother and sister. Such subjects provided the imagery for his paintings and woodcuts; but it was in his style—a haunting synthesis of violently distorted forms and savage colors—that Munch captured the anguished intensity of the neurosis that caused his own mental collapse in 1908. *The Scream* (Figure **33.1**), a painting that has become a universal symbol of the modern condition, takes its mood of urgency and alarm from the combined effects of sinuous clouds, writhing blue-black waters, and a dramatically receding pier (a popular meeting spot near Munch's summer cottage). These visual rhythms suggest the resonating sound of the voiceless cry described by Munch in the notes to a preliminary drawing for the painting: "I walked with two friends. Then the sun sank. Suddenly the sky turned red as blood . . . My friends walked on, and I was left alone, trembling with fear. I felt as if all nature were filled with one mighty unending shriek." The ghostly foreground figure—Munch himself—may have been inspired by an Inka mummy the artist had seen in the Paris Exhibition of 1889.

Munch's impassioned style foreshadowed *German expressionism*. Like the cubists and fauves in France and the futurists in Italy, young artists in Germany rebelled against the "old-established forces" of academic art. Influenced by Freud and by the arts of Africa and Oceania, two modernist groups emerged: in Dresden, *Die Brücke* (The Bridge) was founded in 1905; the second, established in Munich in 1911, called itself *Der Blaue Reiter* (The Blue Rider). Though marked by strong personal differences, the artists of these two groups pursued a style that has come to be known as German expressionism. This style, marked by free distortions of form and color that evoke pathos, violence, and emotional intensity,

flourished until the beginning of World War I. The expressionists inherited the brooding, romantic sensibility of Goethe, Nietzsche, Wagner, and van Gogh. They favored macabre and intimate subjects, which they rendered by means of distorted forms, harsh colors, and the bold and haunting use of black.

Led by Ernst Ludwig Kirchner (1880–1938), members of *Die Brücke* included Erich Heckel (1883–1970), Karl Schmidt-Rottluff (1884–1976), and Emil Nolde (1867–1956). These artists, who envisioned their movement as a "bridge" to modernism, embraced art as an outpouring of "inner necessity," emotion, and ecstasy. Seized by the prewar tensions of urban Germany, they produced probing self-portraits, tempestuous landscapes, and ominous cityscapes. In the painting *Street, Berlin* (Figure **33.2**), Kirchner's jagged lines and dissonant colors, accented by aggressive areas of black, evoke the image of urban life as crowded, impersonal, and threatening. His convulsive distortions of figural form reveal the influence of African sculpture, while the nervous intensity of his line style reflects his indebtedness to the German graphic tradition

Figure 33.2 ERNST LUDWIG KIRCHNER, *Street, Berlin*, 1913. Oil on canvas, 47½ × 35⅞ in. The Museum of Modern Art, New York. Purchase. Photograph © 2000 The Museum of Modern Art, New York.

Figure 33.3 GIORGIO DE CHIRICO, *The Nostalgia of the Infinite*, 1914; dated on painting 1911. Oil on canvas, 53¼ × 25½ in. The Museum of Modern Art, New York. Purchase. Photograph © 2000 The Museum of Modern Art, New York. © DACS 2000.

pioneered by Albrecht Dürer in the sixteenth century (see chapter 19). Like Dürer, Kirchner rendered many of his subjects (including portraits and cityscapes) in woodcut—the favorite medium of the German expressionists.

Metaphysical Art and Fantasy

While the German expressionists brought a new degree of subjective intensity to depicting the visible world, other artists explored the life that lay beyond sensory experience. One of these artists was Giorgio de Chirico (1888–1978). Born in Greece, de Chirico moved to Italy in 1909, where he rejected the tenets of Italian futurism (see chapter 32) and pioneered instead a style that he called "metaphysical," that is, "beyond physical reality." In canvases executed between 1910 and 1920, de Chirico brought the world of the subconscious into the realm of art. Combining sharply conceived images, contradictory perspectives, unnatural colors, and illogically cast shadows, de Chirico produced disturbing, dreamlike effects similar to those achieved by Kafka in prose. In his painting *The Nostalgia of the Infinite* (Figure **33.3**), two figures, dwarfed by eerie shadows, stand in the empty courtyard; five flags flutter mysteriously in an airless, acid green sky. The vanishing point established by the orthogonal lines of the portico on the right contradicts the low placement of the distant horizon. Of his disquieting cityscapes, de Chirico explained, "There are more enigmas in the shadow of a man who walks in the sun than in all the religions of past, present, and future." De Chirico anticipated a mode of representation known as *magic realism*, in which commonplace objects and events are exaggerated or juxtaposed in unexpected ways to evoke a mood of mystery or fantasy.

Equally fantastic in spirit but more indebted in style to the lessons of cubism and fauvism were the paintings of the Russian-born Marc Chagall (1887–1985). Chagall arrived in Paris in 1910 and, like his countryman and fellow expatriate Igor Stravinsky, he infused his first compositions with the folk tales and customs of his native land. In Chagall's nostalgic recollection of rural Russia called *I and the Village* (Figure **33.4**), the disjunctive sizes and positions of the figures and the fantastic colors obey the logic of the subconscious world rather than the laws of physical reality. Chagall freely superimposed images upon one another or showed them floating in space, defying the laws of gravity. Autobiographical motifs, such as the fiddle player and the levitating lovers, became Chagall's hallmarks in the richly colored canvases, murals, and stained glass windows of his long and productive career.

Figure 33.4 MARC CHAGALL, *I and the Village,* 1911. Oil on canvas, 6 ft. 3⅝ in. × 4 ft. 11⅝ in. The Museum of Modern Art, New York. Mrs. Simon Guggenheim Fund. Photograph © 2000 The Museum of Modern Art, New York. © ADAGP, Paris and DACS, London 2000.

The Dada Movement

Although expressionism and fantasy played major roles in modern art, neither broke with tradition as aggressively as the movement known as *dada*, whose proponents would undertake to challenge the very nature of art. Founded in 1916 in Zürich, Switzerland, the dada movement consisted of a loosely knit group of European painters and poets who, perceiving World War I as evidence of a world gone mad, dedicated themselves to spreading the gospel of irrationality. The nonsensical name of the movement, "dada" (French for "hobbyhorse"), which was chosen by inserting a penknife at random into the pages of a dictionary, symbolized their irreverent stance. If the world had gone mad, should not its art be equally mad? Dada answered with art that was the product of chance, accident, or outrageous behavior. Deliberately violating "good taste," dada constituted an assault on middle-class values and artistic convention. The dadaists met frequently at the Café Voltaire in Zürich, where they orchestrated "noise concerts" and recited poetry informed by **improvisation** and free association. The Romanian poet Tristan Tzara (1896–1963) produced poems from words cut out of newspapers and randomly scattered on a table, while the French sculptor and poet Jean Arp (1887–1966) constructed collages and relief sculptures from shapes arranged "according to the laws of chance." Such attacks on rationalist tradition and on modern technocracy in general reflected the spirit of **nihilism** (the denial of traditional and religious and moral principles) that flowered in the ashes of the war. In his "Lecture on Dada" in 1922, Tzara declared, "The acts of life have no beginning or end. Everything happens in a completely idiotic way. Simplicity is called dada. . . . Like everything in life, dada is useless."

As with poetry and painting, dada theater paid homage to Freud by liberating "everything obscure in the mind, buried deep, unrevealed," as one French playwright explained. Narrative realism and traditional characterization gave way to improvisation and the performance of

Figure 33.6 MARCEL DUCHAMP, *L.H.O.O.Q.*, 1919. Rectified ready-made, pencil on a reproduction of the *Mona Lisa*, 7¾ × 4⅞ in. Collection of Mrs. Mary Sisler. © Succession Marcel Duchamp. ADAGP, and DACS, London 2000.

random and bizarre incidents. One form of dada theater, the *theater of cruelty*, known for its violent and scatological themes, anticipated theater of the absurd plays written during the 1950s and 1960s (see chapter 35).

The spirit of the dadaists was most vividly realized in the work of the French artist Marcel Duchamp (1887–1968). Early in his career, Duchamp had flirted with cubism and futurism, producing the influential *Nude Descending a Staircase #2* (see Figure 32.11); but after 1912, Duchamp abandoned professional painting and turned to making—or remaking—art objects. In 1913 he mounted a bicycle wheel atop a barstool, thus producing the first "ready-made," as well as the first **mobile** (a sculpture with moving parts). Four years later, Duchamp would launch the landmark ready-made of the century: he placed a common urinal on a pedestal, signed the piece with the fictitious name, "R. Mutt," and submitted it for an exhibition held by the American Society of Independent Artists (Figure **33.5**). The piece, which he called *Fountain*, was rejected; but its long-term impact was enormous. By designating the "found object" a work of art, Duchamp mocked conventional techniques of making art. Further, by wrenching the object out of its preordained context, Duchamp suggested

Figure 33.5 MARCEL DUCHAMP, *Fountain (Urinal)*, 1917. Ready-made, height 24 in. Photo courtesy of Sidney Janis Gallery, New York. © Succession Marcel Duchamp. ADAGP, Paris and DACS, London 2000.

that the image obeyed a logic of its own, a logic whose "rules" flouted traditional aesthetic norms. Thus, *Fountain* not only attacked the barriers between art and life, but called forth art that exalted the nonsensical, the accidental, and the absurd. Perhaps most important, however, *Fountain* introduced to modern art the revolutionary notion that a work of art was first and foremost about an artist's *idea*. *Fountain* was not art because Duchamp had "made" it, but because he had removed it from the context of everyday life and had given it a whole new identity (as art). Pursuing this logic, the artist might also alter (or "remake") existing art, as for example, when Duchamp drew a mustache on a reproduction of Leonardo da Vinci's venerable *Mona Lisa* (see chapter 17), adding at the bottom a series of letters that, when recited rapidly (in French) describe the sitter in lusty street slang (Figure **33.6**). This "corrected ready-made," as Duchamp called the piece, expressed the artist's disdain for Western high art. It established the modern artist as maverick—the self-appointed prophet and defiler of tradition.

Moving to New York City in 1918, Duchamp labored for ten years on his *magnum opus*, a large glass and wire assemblage filled with esoteric sexual symbolism. He called it *The Bride Stripped Bare by Her Bachelors, Even*. After 1920, Duchamp went "underground," spending as much time perfecting his chess game (his favorite pastime) as making art. Nevertheless, his small, pioneering body of work and his irreverent view that art "has absolutely no existence as . . . truth" have had a powerful influence on scores of poets, painters, and composers even into the twenty-first century.

Surrealism and Abstract Surrealists: Picasso, Miró, and Klee

The word *surrealism*, coined by Guillaume Apollinaire in 1917, came to describe one of the century's most intriguing literary and artistic movements—a movement devoted to expressing in conscious life the workings of the subconscious mind. The French critic André Breton (1896–1966) inaugurated surrealism in the first "Surrealist Manifesto" (1924), in which he proclaimed the artist's liberation from reason and the demands of conventional society. The surrealists paid explicit homage to Freud and his writings, especially those on free association and dream analysis. Indeed, Breton himself visited Freud in Vienna in 1921. In describing the surrealist's commitment to glorifying the irrational aspect of the human psyche, Breton proclaimed,

> We are still living under the reign of logic. . . . But in this day and age logical methods are applicable only to solving problems of secondary interest. The absolute rationalism that is still in vogue allows us to consider only facts relating directly to our experience. . . .

[Experience] is protected by the sentinels of common sense. Under the pretense of civilization and progress, we have managed to banish from the mind everything that may rightly or wrongly be termed superstition, or fancy; forbidden is any kind of search for truth which is not in conformance with accepted practices. It was, apparently, by pure chance, that a part of our mental world which we pretended not to be concerned with any longer—and, in my opinion, by far the most important part—has been brought back to light. For this we must give thanks to the discoveries of Sigmund Freud. . . . The imagination is perhaps on the point of reasserting itself, of reclaiming its rights.*

Breton defined surrealism as "psychic automatism, in its pure state," that is, creative effort guided by thought functions

*André Breton, "Manifesto of Surrealism" (1924). From *Manifestoes of Surrealism* by André Breton, translated by Richard Seaver and Helen R. Lane. Ann Arbor, Mich.: University of Michigan Press, 1969, 9.

Figure 33.7 PABLO PICASSO, *Seated Woman*, Paris, 1927. Oil on wood, 4 ft. 3⅛ in. × 3 ft. 2¼ in. The Museum of Modern Art, New York. Gift of James Thrall Soby. Photograph © 2000 The Museum of Modern Art, New York. © Succession Picasso/DACS 2000.

free of rational control and "exempt from any aesthetic or moral concern." He emphasized the omnipotence of the dream state in guiding the surrealist enterprise.

Just as writers developed literary techniques such as stream of consciousness to achieve a new freedom from rational control, so visual artists devised a variety of liberating methods and processes. Some juxtaposed realistically painted objects in ways that produce a visionary reality approximating the reality of dreams. Others explored psychic automatism, allowing the hand to move spontaneously and at random, as if casually doodling or improvising. Still others tried to recover a sense of childlike spontaneity by filling their paintings with free-spirited, biomorphic shapes. The latter two groups produced various kinds of abstract surrealism, while the former pioneered visionary surrealism. Fundamentally, however, the paradox of surrealist art rested on the artist's *conscious* effort to capture *subconscious* experience.

Breton recognized Picasso as one of the pioneers of surrealist art. As early as 1907, in *Les Demoiselles d'Avignon* (see Figure 32.3), Picasso had begun to radicalize the image of the human figure; by the mid-1920s, brutal dissection and savage distortion dominated his art. In 1927, Picasso painted the *Seated Woman* (Figure **33.7**), the image of a "split personality" that seemed to symbolize Freud's three-part psyche. The head of the female consists of a frontal view, as well as at least two profile views, each of which reveals a different aspect of her personality. In scores of paintings and sculptures, as well as in the stream of consciousness prose he wrote during the 1930s, Picasso introduced double meanings and visual puns, thus securing his reputation as the master of metamorphosis in twentieth-century art. Indeed, the "split personality" motif continued to preoccupy Picasso throughout his long artistic career.

In the paintings of the Spanish artist Joan Miró (1893–1983), the surrealist's search for subconscious experience kindled the artist's personal mythology. Employing a style that suggests a child's representation, Miró made biomorphic creatures and spiny, abstract organisms the denizens of a fantastic universe. The "person" in Miró's *Person Throwing a Stone at a Bird* (Figure **33.8**) resembles a large, white, one-footed ameba; the bird is a stick figure with a flaming cockscomb; and the stone is an egglike object whose trajectory is traced by means of a dotted line.

Figure 33.8 JOAN MIRÓ, *Person Throwing a Stone at a Bird*, 1926. Oil on canvas, 29 × 36¼ in. The Museum of Modern Art, New York. Purchase. Photograph © 2000 The Museum of Modern Art, New York. © ADAGP, Paris and DACS, London 2000.

Figure 33.9 PAUL KLEE, *Fish Magic*, 1925. Oil on canvas, mounted on board, 30⅜ × 38½ in. Philadelphia Museum of Art. The Louise and Walter Arensberg Collection ('50–134–112). © DACS 2000.

Superficially the depiction of a playful act, the painting conjures up a dreamlike ritual that unfolds ominously against a darkened sea and sky.

The Swiss-born painter Paul Klee (1879–1940) stood on the fringes of surrealism. One of the most sophisticated artists of the century, Klee was a brilliant draftsman who created physically small artworks that resemble hieroglyphic puzzles. His abstractions, like the entries in his personal diaries, are characterized by gentle humor and exquisite finesse; they belong to the substratum of the mind—the subconscious repository of mysterious symbols. "Art does not represent the visible," Klee insisted, "rather, it renders visible [the invisible]." Klee's *Fish Magic* (Figure **33.9**), painted during his tenure as a teacher at the Bauhaus, consists of a group of carefully arranged organic motifs that resemble sacred signs. Flowers, fish, and human figure, all executed with pictographic simplicity, share the ambient space of planets whose rhythms are measured by a mysteriously suspended clock. The painting validates Klee's claim that art is "a parable of Creation," the product of imagination guided by instinctual stimuli. Klee was among the first artists to recognize the art of the untutored and the mentally ill. "Only children, madmen, and savages," he wrote, "truly understand the 'in-between' world of spiritual truth."

Visionary Surrealists: Magritte and Dali

While Picasso, Miró, and Klee favored abstract, organic images, other surrealists combined meticulously painted objects in ways that were often shocking or unexpected. The most notable of the European visionary surrealists were René Magritte and Salvador Dali. Both were superb draftsmen whose *trompe l'oeil* skills elicited a disquieting dream reality. Profoundly influenced by de Chirico, the Belgian artist Magritte (1898–1967) juxtaposed realistically detailed objects in startling and irrational ways. In one of Magritte's paintings, a coffin takes the place of a reclining figure; in another, a birdcage is substituted for the head of the sitter; and in still another, human toes appear on a pair of leather shoes. In a small piece entitled *The Treachery (or Perfidy) of Images* (1928), Magritte portrays with crisp and faultless accuracy a briar pipe, beneath which appears the legend "This is not a pipe." The painting addresses the age-old distinction between the real world—the world of the *actual* pipe—and the painted image, whose reality is the virtual *illusion* of a pipe. At the

Figure 33.10 (above) **RENÉ MAGRITTE**, *The False Mirror* (*Le Faux Miroir*), 1928. Oil on canvas, 21¼ × 31⅞ in. The Museum of Modern Art, New York. Purchase. Photograph © 2000 The Museum of Modern Art, New York. © ADAGP, Paris and DACS, London 2000.

Figure 33.11 (right) **SALVADOR DALI**, *The Persistence of Memory* (*Persistance de la Mémoire*), 1931. Oil on canvas, 9½ × 13 in. The Museum of Modern Art, New York. Given anonymously. Photograph © 2000 The Museum of Modern Art, New York. © Kingdom of Spain, universal heir of Salvador Dali/DACS 2000.

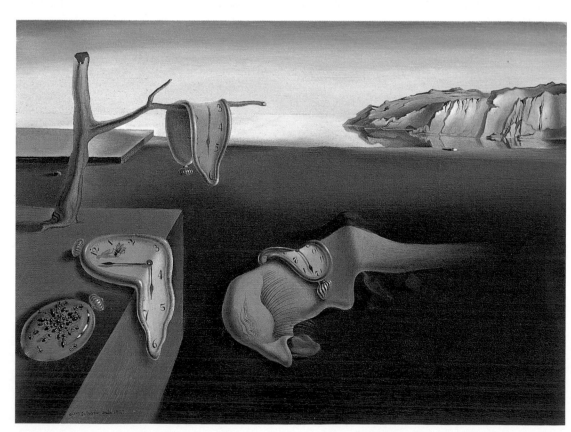

same time, it anticipates modern efforts to determine how words and images differ in conveying information. Questions of reality versus illusion are also brought to bear in Magritte's *The False Mirror*, which consists of a single large eye whose iris is the very cloud-filled sky that it perceives (Figure **33.10**). Magritte's magic realism tests assumptions about the real world, while it asserts with deadpan humor its own bizarre laws. Modern advertising, which owes much to Magritte, has transformed some of his images into contemporary icons—the "false mirror" serves, ironically enough, as a trademark of CBS television.

The Spanish painter and impresario Salvador Dali (1904–1989) was as much a showman as an artist. Cultivating the bizarre as a lifestyle, Dali exhibited a perverse desire to shock his audiences. Drawing motifs from his own erotic dreams and fantasies, he executed both natural and unnatural images with meticulous precision, combining them in unusual settings or giving them grotesque attributes. Dali's infamous *The Persistence of Memory* (Figure **33.11**) consists of a broad and barren landscape occupied by a leafless tree, three limp watches, and a watchcase crawling with ants. One of the timepieces plays host to a fly, while another rests upon a mass of brain matter resembling a profiled self-portrait—a motif that the artist frequently featured in his works. To seek an explicit message in this painting—even one addressing modern notions of time—would be to miss the point, for, as Dali himself observed, his "hand-painted dream photographs" were designed to "stamp themselves indelibly upon the mind."

The Women of Surrealism

Perhaps more than any other movement in the history of early modernism, surrealism—which encouraged the free and uninhibited exploration of the interior life—attracted women artists. Arguably the most celebrated female painter of the early twentieth century is Mexico's Frida Kahlo (1907–1954). Kahlo's paintings, of which more than one third are self-portraits, reflect the determined effort (shared by many modern feminists) to present the female image as something other than the object of male desire. "I am the subject I know best," explained Kahlo, whose art bears testimony to what she called the "two great accidents" of her life: a bus crash that at the age of eighteen left her disabled, and her stormy marriage to the notorious Mexican mural painter Diego Rivera (see chapter 34). Like Rivera, Kahlo was a fer-

vent Marxist and a nationalist who supported the revolutionary government that took control of Mexico in 1921. But the subject matter of Kahlo's art is Frida herself: her paintings record the experience of chronic pain, both physical (her accident required some thirty surgeries and ultimately involved the amputation of her right leg) and psychic (repeated miscarriages, for example, left her incapable of bearing a child). Kahlo's canvases betray her close identification with Mexican folk culture and folk art, which traditionally features visceral and diabolical details. At the same time, her taste for realistically conceived but shockingly juxtaposed images reflects her debt to de Chirico and the magic realist style. In *The Broken Column* (Figure **33.12**), Kahlo pictures herself as sufferer and savior, an emblematic figure that recalls the devotional icons of Mexico's religious shrines.

A pioneer modernist on the American scene, Georgia O'Keeffe (1887–1986) is often classified with America's regional painters. However, her treatment of haunting, biomorphic shapes abstracted from greatly enlarged

Figure 33.12 FRIDA KAHLO, *The Broken Column*, 1944. Oil on canvas, 15¾ × 12¼ in. Museo Frida Kahlo, Mexico City. Collection Lola Olmedo.

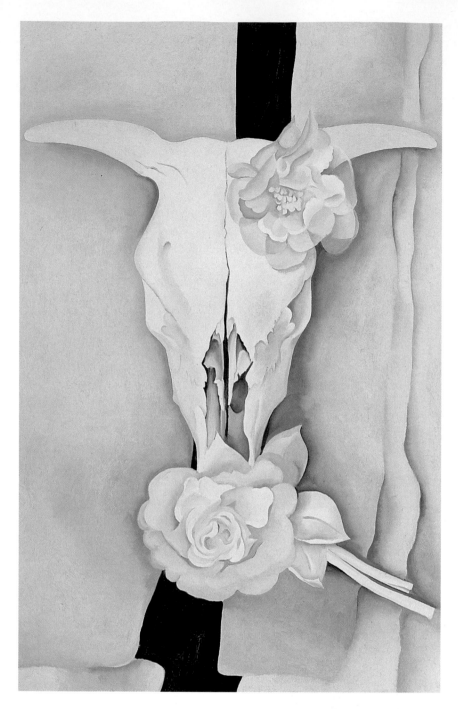

flowers and bleached animal bones gives her early paintings a menacing presence (Figure 33.13). In a fluid line style that distills the essence of the subject, the so-called "high priestess" of early modernism brought a visionary clarity to the most ordinary ingredients of the American landscape.

Enlarging or combining commonplace objects in ways that were unexpected and shocking—the hallmark of the visionary surrealists—was a particularly effective strategy for surrealist sculptors; and in this domain as well, women made notable contributions. The furlined cup and saucer (Figure 33.14) conceived by the Swiss-German sculptor Meret Oppenheim (1913–1985) is shocking in its irreverent combination of familiar but disparate elements. Conceived in the irreverent spirit of Duchamp's modified ready-mades, Oppenheim's *Object: Breakfast in Fur* provokes a sequence of discomfiting and threatening narrative associations.

Dada and Surrealist Photography

Photography was an ideal medium with which to explore the layers of the human subconscious. Photographers experimented with double exposure and unorthodox darkroom techniques to create unusual new effects similar to those of visionary surrealist painters and sculptors. Liberating photography from traditional pictorialism, a group of Berlin Dadaists invented a new kind of collage consisting of "found" images—usually printed materials taken from books, magazines, and newspapers—pasted on a flat surface, a

Figure 33.13 (above) **GEORGIA O'KEEFFE**, *Cow's Skull: with Calico Roses*, 1931. Oil on canvas, 36⁵⁄₁₆ × 24⅛ in. Art Institute of Chicago (Gift of Georgia O'Keefe, 1947.712). © ARS, New York and DACS, London 2000. Photo © 2000, The Art Institute of Chicago.

Figure 33.14 (right) **MERET OPPENHEIM**, *Object (Le Déjeuner en fourrure)*, 1936. Fur-covered cup, saucer, and spoon; cup 4⅜ in. diameter; saucer 9⅜ in. diameter; spoon 8 in. long; overall height 2⅞ in. The Museum of Modern Art, New York. Purchase. Photograph © 2000 The Museum of Modern Art, New York. © DACS 2000.

technique called **photomontage**. One champion of the technique, Raoul Hausmann (1886–1971), called photomontage "the 'alienation' of photography" and defined its importance as "a visually and conceptually new image of the chaos of an age of war and revolution." The only female member of the group, Hannah Höch (1889–1979), who had prepared advertising brochures for a Berlin newspaper, redirected her skills (and feminist concerns) to the creation of intriguing, disorienting compositions such as *Cut with the Kitchen Knife* (Figure **33.15**). Bits and pieces of images, some human, others mechanical, are punctuated with the word "dada," inviting interpretation and, at the same time, subverting viewers' visual and conceptual expectations. The series of "quick cuts" between the images anticipated experiments in cinematic photomontage that were to transform the history of film (see chapter 34).

Figure 33.15 HANNAH HÖCH, *Cut with the Kitchen Knife,* 1919. Collage of pasted papers, 44⅞ × 35½ in. Nationalgalerie, Staatliche Museen Preussischer Kulturbesitz, Berlin. © DACS 2000. Photo: © Bildarchiv Preussischer Kulturbesitz, Berlin.

helmet, but has travelled so far that it does not go through. I wipe the mud out of my eyes. A hole is torn up in front of me. Shells hardly ever land in the same hole twice, I'll get into it. With one bound I fling myself down and lie on the earth as flat as a fish; there it whistles again, quickly I crouch together, claw for cover, feel something on the left, shove in beside it, it gives way, I groan, the earth leaps, the blast thunders in my ears, I creep under the yielding thing, cover myself with it, draw it over me, it is wood, cloth, cover, cover, miserable cover against the whizzing splinters.

I open my eyes—my fingers grasp a sleeve, an arm. A wounded man? I yell to him—no answer—a dead man. My hand gropes farther, splinters of wood—now I remember again that we are lying in the graveyard.

But the shelling is stronger than everything. It wipes out the sensibilities, I merely crawl still deeper into the coffin, it should protect me, and especially as Death himself lies in it too.

Before me gapes the shell-hole. I grasp it with my eyes as with fists. With one leap I must be in it. There, I get a smack in the face, a hand clamps on to my shoulder—has the dead man waked up?—The hand shakes me, I turn my head, in the second of light I stare into the face of Katczinsky, he has his mouth wide open and is yelling. I hear nothing, he rattles me, comes nearer, in a momentary lull his voice reaches me: "Gas—Gaas—Gaaas—Pass it on."

I grab for my gas-mask. Some distance from me there lies someone. I think of nothing but this: That fellow there must know: Gaaas—Gaaas— — —

I call, I lean toward him, I swipe at him with the satchel, he doesn't see—once again, again—he merely ducks—it's a recruit—I look at Kat desperately, he has his mask ready—I pull out mine too, my helmet falls to one side, it slips over my face, I reach the man, his satchel is on the side nearest me, I seize the mask, pull it over his head, he understands, I let go and with a jump drop back into the shell-hole.

The dull thud of the gas-shells mingles with the crashes of the high explosives. A bell sounds between the explosions, gongs, and metal clappers warning everyone—Gas—Gas—Gaas.

Someone plumps down behind me, another. I wipe the goggles of my mask clear of the moist breath. It is Kat, Kropp, and someone else. All four of us lie there in heavy, watchful suspense and breathe as lightly as possible.

These first minutes with the mask decide between life and death: is it tightly woven? I remember the awful sights in the hospital: the gas patients who in day-long suffocation cough their burnt lungs up in clots.

Cautiously, the mouth applied to the valve, I breathe. The gas still creeps over the ground and sinks into all hollows. Like a big, soft jelly-fish it floats into our shell-hole and lolls there obscenely. I nudge Kat, it is better to crawl out and lie on top than to stay here where the gas collects most. But we don't get as far as that; a second bombardment begins. It is no longer as though the shells roared; it is the earth itself raging.

With a crash something black bears down on us. It lands close beside us; a coffin thrown up.

I see Kat move and crawl across. The coffin has hit the fourth man in our hole on his outstretched arm. He tries to tear off his gas-mask with the other hand. Kropp seizes him just in time, twists the hand sharply behind his back and holds it fast.

Kat and I proceed to free the wounded arm. The coffin lid is loose and bursts open, we are easily able to pull it off, we toss the corpse out, it slides to the bottom of the shell-hole, then we try to loosen the under-part.

Fortunately the man swoons and Kropp is able to help us. We no longer have to be careful, but work away till the coffin gives with a sigh before the spade that we have dug in under it.

It has grown lighter. Kat takes a piece of the lid, places it under the shattered arm, and we wrap all our bandages round it. For the moment we can do no more.

Inside the gas-mask my head booms and roars—it is nigh bursting. My lungs are tight, they breathe always the same hot, used-up air, the veins on my temples are swollen, I feel I am suffocating.

A grey light filters through to us. I climb out over the edge of the shell-hole. In the dirty twilight lies a leg torn clean off; the boot is quite whole, I take that all in at a glance. Now someone stands up a few yards distant. I polish the windows, in my excitement they are immediately dimmed again, I peer through them, the man there no longer wears his mask.

I wait some seconds—he has not collapsed—he looks around and makes a few paces—rattling in my throat I tear my mask off too and fall down, the air streams into me like cold water, my eyes are bursting, the wave sweeps over me and extinguishes me. . . .

Figure 34.1 MAX ERNST, *Two Ambiguous Figures*, 1919. Collage with gouache and pencil, 9½ × 6½ in. © ADAGP, Paris and DACS, London 2000.

World War I Art

In Germany, World War I brought protests from many visual artists. One of the most outspoken was Max Ernst (1891–1976), whose career flowered in the dada and surrealist movements. Shortly after the war, Ernst began to create unsettling visual fantasies assembled from bits of photographs and prints that he cut from magazines, books, and newspapers. In the collage-painting *Two Ambiguous Figures* (Figure **34.1**), he combined the paraphernalia of modern warfare with the equipment of the scientist's laboratory. Ernst's machinelike monsters are suspiciously reminiscent of the gas-masked soldiers that he encountered during his four-year stint in the German infantry. Sadly enough, Ernst's demons have become prophetic icons of modern warfare. Poison gas, used by the Iraqis in the 1980s war with Iran, received renewed international attention during the widely televised Gulf War of 1991, when images of both soldiers and civilians donning gas masks were a common, if appalling, sight.

The art of George Grosz (1893–1959) was unique in its imaginative blend of social criticism and biting satire. Discharged from the army in 1916 after a brief experience at the front, Grosz mocked the German military and its corrupt and mindless bureaucracy in sketchy, brittle compositions filled with pungent caricatures. For example, the wartime pen and ink drawing, *Fit for Active Service* (Figure **34.2**), shows a fat German army doctor pronouncing a skeletal cadaver "O.K.," hence, fit to serve in combat. Here, Grosz makes pointed reference to the prevailing military practice of drafting old (and even ill) men. In a trenchant line style, he evokes a sense of the macabre similar to that captured by Remarque in the novel *All Quiet on the Western Front*. Like Remarque (and hundreds of other European artists and writers), Grosz fled Nazi Germany for the United States in the 1930s, where he eventually became an American citizen.

Fernand Léger's art (1881–1955) is usually classed with that of the cubists, but it was Léger's wartime

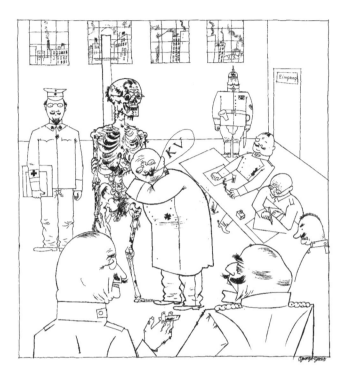

Figure 34.2 (above) **GEORGE GROSZ**, *Fit for Active Service*, 1916–1917. Pen and brush and ink on paper, 20 × 14⅜ in. The Museum of Modern Art, New York. A. Conger Goodyear Fund. Photograph © 2000 The Museum of Modern Art, New York. © DACS 2000.

Figure 34.3 (right) **FERNAND LÉGER**, *Three Women*, 1921, Oil on canvas, 6 ft. ½in. × 8 ft. 3 in. The Museum of Modern Art, New York. Mrs Simon Guggenheim Fund. © ADAGP, Paris and DACS, London 2000.

Figure 34.4 A.I. STRAKHOV, *Emancipated Women Build Socialism! 8th March, Day of the Liberation of Women*, 1920. Colored lithograph, 42½ × 26¾ in.

experience that actually shaped the artist's long and productive career. During his four years on the front, Léger came to appreciate both the visual eloquence of modern machinery and the common humanity of the working-class soldiers with whom he shared the trenches. "Dazzled" (as he put it) by the breech of a 75-millimetre gun as it stood in the sunlight, Léger discovered similar kinds of beauty in ordinary human beings and in everyday objects—"the pots and pans on the white wall of your kitchen." "I invent images from machines," he claimed. The anonymity of urban life and the cold monumentality of the city—gray, hard, and sleek—became major themes for Léger in the postwar years. This "mechanical" aesthetic is visible in his painting, *Three Women* (Figure **34.3**). Robust and robotic, the near-identical nudes (and their cat) share a common, austere geometry.

The Russian Revolution

One of the last of the European powers to become industrialized, Russia entered World War I in 1914 under the leadership of Tzar Nicholas II. Within a single year, the Russian army lost over one million men and a million more soldiers deserted. Russian involvement in the war, compounded by problems of government corruption and a weak and essentially agrarian economy, reduced the nation to desperate straits. Food and fuel shortages threatened the entire civilian population. By 1917, a full-scale revolution was under way: Strikes and riots broke out in the cities, while in the countryside peasants seized the

EXPERIMENTAL FILM

Léger produced one of the earliest and most influential abstract films in the history of motion pictures. Developed in collaboration with the American journalist Dudley Murphy, *Ballet mécanique* (*Mechanical Ballet*, 1923–1924) puts into motion a series of abstract shapes and mundane objects (such as bottles and kitchen utensils), which, interspersed with human elements, convey a playful but dehumanized sense of everyday experience. The rhythms and juxtapositions of the images suggest—without any narrative—the notion of modern life as mechanized, routine, standardized, and impersonal. The repeated image of a laundry woman, for instance, alternating with that of a rotating machine part, plays on the associative qualities of visual motifs in ways that would influence filmmakers for decades.

land of their aristocratic landlords. The Revolution of 1917 forced the abdication of the Tzar and ushered in a new regime, which, in turn, was seized by members of the Russian Socialist party under the leadership of the Marxist revolutionary Vladimir Ilyich Lenin (1870–1924). Between 1917 and 1921, by means of shrewd political manipulation and a reign of terror conducted by the Red Army and the secret police, Lenin installed the left-wing faction of the Marxist Socialists—the Bolsheviks—as the party that would govern a nation of more than 150 million people. By tailoring Marxist ideas to the needs of revolutionary Russia, Lenin became the architect of Soviet communism.

In his treatise *Imperialism, the Highest Stage of Capitalism* (1916), Lenin followed Marx in describing imperialism as an expression of the capitalist effort to monopolize raw materials and markets throughout the world. Lenin agreed with Marx that a "dictatorship of the proletariat" was the first step in liberating the workers from bourgeois suppression. While condemning the state as "the organ of class domination," he projected the transition to a classless society in a series of phases, which he outlined in the influential pamphlet "The State and Revolution" (1917). According to Lenin, in the first phase of communist society (generally called socialism), private property would be converted into property held in common and the means of production and distribution would belong to the whole of society. Every member of society would perform a type of labor and would be entitled to a "quantity of products" (drawn from public warehouses) that corresponded to his or her "quantity of work." (A favorite Lenin slogan ran, "He who does not work does not eat.") Accordingly, as Lenin explained, "a form of state is still necessary, which, while maintaining public ownership of the means of production, would preserve the equality of labor and equality in the distribution of products." In the first phase of communism, then, the socialist state prevailed.

In the second phase of communism, however, the state would disappear altogether. As Lenin explained,

> The state will be able to wither away completely when society has realized the rule: "From each according to his ability; to each according to his needs," *i.e.*, when people have become accustomed to observe the fundamental rules of social life, and their labor is so productive that they voluntarily work *according to their ability*. . . . There will then be no need for any exact calculation by society of the quantity of products to be distributed to each of its members; each will take freely according to his needs.*

Lenin was aware that such a social order might be deemed "a pure Utopia"; yet, idealistically, he anticipated the victory of communist ideals throughout the world. The reality was otherwise. In early twentieth-century Russia, the Bolsheviks created a dictatorship *over* rather than *of* the proletariat. In 1918, when the Constituent Assembly refused to approve Bolshevik power, Lenin dissolved the Assembly. (In free elections Lenin's party received less than a quarter of one percent of the vote.) He then eliminated all other parties and consolidated the Communist Party in the hands of five men—an elite committee called the Politburo, which Lenin himself chaired. In 1922, Russia was renamed the Union of Soviet Socialist Republics (U.S.S.R.), and in 1924 the constitution established a sovereign Congress of Soviets. But this body was actually governed by the leadership of the Communist Party, which maintained absolute authority well after Lenin's death.[1]

The Communist Party established the first **totalitarian** regime of the twentieth century. This totalitarian regime subordinated the life of the individual to that of the state. Through strict government control of political, economic, and cultural life, and by means of coercive measures such as censorship and terrorism, the state imposed its will upon the conduct of the society. Soviet communists persecuted all individuals and religious groups whose activities they deemed threatening to the state. Using educational propaganda and the state-run media, they worked tirelessly to indoctrinate Soviet citizens to the virtues of communism. Under the rule of Joseph Stalin (1879–1953), who took control of the communist bureaucracy in 1926, the Soviets launched vast programs of industrialization and agricultural collectivization (the transformation of private farms into government-run units) that demanded heroic sacrifice among the Soviet people. Peasants worked long hours on state-controlled farms, earning a bare subsistence wage. Stalin crushed all opposition: His secret police "purged" the state of dissidents, who were either imprisoned, exiled to *gulags* (labor camps), or executed. Between 1928 and 1938, the combination of severe famine and Stalin's inhuman policies (later known as "the great terror") took the lives of 15 to 20 million Russians.

Communism enforced totalitarian control over all aspects of cultural expression. In 1934, the First All-Union Congress of Soviet Writers officially approved the style of *socialist realism* in the arts. At the same time, it condemned all expressions of "modernism" (from cubist painting to hot jazz) as "bourgeois decadence." The congress called upon Soviet artists to create "a true, historically concrete portrayal of reality in its revolutionary development." Artists—including Malevich and the pioneer Russian constructivists—were instructed to communicate simply and directly, to shun all forms of decadent (that is, modern) Western art, and to describe only the positive aspects of socialist society. In realistically conceived posters, the new Soviet man and woman were portrayed earnestly operating tractors or running factory machinery (Figure **34.4**). Thus the arts served to reinforce in the public mind the ideological benefits of communism. Socialist realism and the philosophy of art as mass propaganda lent support to almost every totalitarian regime of the twentieth century.

---

* *The State and Revolution.* New York: International Publishers, 1932, 1943, 71–80

[1] The Communist Party ceased to rule upon the collapse of the Soviet Union in 1991.

The Great Depression and the American Scene

World War I left Europe devastated, and massive economic problems burdened both the Central Powers and the Allied nations. In the three years following the war, world industrial production declined by more than a third, prices dropped sharply, and over 30 million people lost their jobs. The United States emerged from the war as the great creditor nation, but its economy was inextricably tied to world conditions. Following the inevitable crash of inflated stock prices in 1929, a growing paralysis swept through the American economy which developed into the Great Depression, a world crisis that lasted until the 1940s.

The Great Depression inspired literary descriptions of economic oppression and misery that were often as much social documents as fictional narratives. The most memorable of these is the American novel *The Grapes of Wrath*, written in 1939 by John Steinbeck (1902–1968). The story recounts the odyssey of a family of Oklahoma migrant farmers who make their way to California in search of a living. In straightforward and photographically detailed prose, Steinbeck describes courageous encounters with starvation, injustice, and sheer evil. Like the soldiers in Remarque's regiment, the members of the Joad family (and especially the matriarch, Ma Joad) display heroism in sheer survival. *The Grapes of Wrath* is an example of *social realism*, a style that presents socially significant subject matter in an objective and lifelike manner. Not to be confused with socialist realism, which operated to glorify the socialist state, social realism was often the vehicle of social criticism and political protest. A writer, declared Steinbeck, is "the watchdog of society"; he must "set down his time as nearly as he can understand it."

During the depression, social realism also dominated the visual arts in America. In opposition to modernists who sacrificed subject matter to formal abstraction (Picasso, Kandinsky, and Mondrian, for instance), American social realists painted recognizable imagery that communicated the concerns of the masses. The Missouri-born Thomas Hart Benton (1889–1975) devoted his

Figure 34.5 THOMAS HART BENTON, *City Activities with Dance Hall*, from the mural series "America Today," 1930. Distemper and egg tempera on gessoed linen with oil glaze, 7 ft. 8 in. × 11 ft. 2½ in. Collection, A×A Financial Inc. through its subsidiary The Equitable Life Assurance Society of the U.S., New York. Photo: Dorothy Zeidman 2000. © T. H. Benton and R. P. Benton Testamentary Trusts/VAGA, New York/DACS, London 2000.

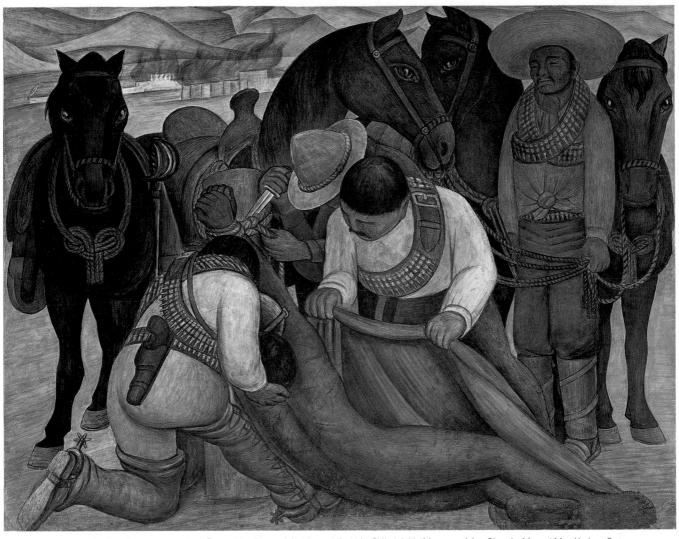

Figure 34.6 DIEGO RIVERA, *Liberation of the Peon*, 1931. Fresco, 6 ft. 2 in. × 7 ft. 11 in. Philadelphia Museum of Art. Given by Mr. and Mrs. Herbert Cameron Morris ('43–46–1).

career to the depiction of American scenes that often called into question political and economic policies leading to the Great Depression. Benton aimed to commemorate "true" American values by immortalizing the lives of common men and women, whom he pictured as rugged and energetic. In three sets of public murals completed between 1930 and 1933, Benton created an extraordinary pictorial history of the United States. He portrayed steelworking, mining, farming, and other working-class activities, as well as bootlegging, gospel singing, crapshooting, and a wide variety of essentially common pastimes. Benton's *City Activities*, one section from a set of murals depicting American life during the Prohibition era, is a montage of "clips" from such popular urban entertainments as the circus, the movie theater, and the dancehall (Figure **34.5**). A ticker-tape machine—the symbol of Wall Street commercialism and American greed—appears in the upper part of the mural; it is balanced in the lower foreground by another instrument of commercialism—bootlegging equipment. Benton, who appears with paintbrush in hand in the lower-right of the painting, admired the purity of Midwestern rural life. His assessment of America's urban centers as "nothing but coffins for living

and thinking" is powerfully conveyed in *City Activities*.

In Benton's hands the mural was not mere decoration. It was a major form of public art, one that revealed ordinary American life as vividly as Renaissance murals mirrored the elitist world of sixteenth-century Italy. Benton drew inspiration from two great Mexican muralists: José Clemente Orozco (1883–1949) and Diego Rivera (1886–1957). Their paintings, characterized by simple yet powerful forms and bold colors, capture the vitality and the futility of the Mexican Revolution—one of many militant efforts at reforming economic and social conditions in Central and South America during the first half of the twentieth century (Figure **34.6**). The Mexican revolution, however, was particularly significant as the first social revolution of the century to engage the active participation of great masses of peasants and urban workers. Rivera championed their cause by featuring (in his richly populated murals) sympathetic depictions of peasants, often intermingled with the imagery of their Mayan and Aztec forebears. By emphasizing the Amerindian aspect of Mexico's history, Rivera's art—like the revolution itself—helped to effect a change in Mexico's self-image.

During the Great Depression photography was pressed

Figure 34.7 DOROTHEA LANGE, *Migrant Mother, Nipomo, California,* 1936. Gelatin-silver print. Library of Congress, Washington, D.C.

into political service. United States federal agencies sponsored a program to provide a permanent record of economic and social conditions in rural America. Migration and rural poverty—bread-lines, beggars, and the shanty-towns of America's impoverished classes—became part of the straightforward style of *documentary photography*. The New York photographer Dorothea Lange (1895–1965) traveled across the country to record the conditions of destitute farmers who had fled the Midwestern Dust Bowl for the fields of California. *Migrant Mother* (Figure **34.7**), which Lange photographed at a farm camp in Nipomo, California, is the portrait of a gaunt thirty-two-year-old woman who had become the sole supporter of her six children. Forced to sell her last possessions for food, the anxious but unconquerable heroine in this photograph might have stepped out of the pages of Steinbeck's *Grapes of Wrath*. Lange's moving image reaches beyond a specific time and place to universalize the twin evils of poverty and oppression.

1927	the first television transmission is viewed in America
1930	the British invent a workable jet engine
1938	the Germans split the atom to achieve nuclear fission
1939	British scientists produce pure penicillin
1945	the first experimental atomic bomb is exploded at Alamogordo, New Mexico

Totalitarianism and World War II

In Germany, widespread discontent and turmoil followed the combined effects of the Great Depression and the humiliating peace terms dictated by the victorious Allies. Crippling debts forced German banks to close in 1931, and at the height of the depression only one-third of all Germany's workers were fully employed. In the wake of these conditions, the young ideologue Adolf Hitler (1889–1945) rose to power. By 1933, Hitler was chancellor of Germany and the leader (in German, *Führer*) of the National Socialist German Workers' party (the *Nazi* party), which would lead Germany again into world war.

A fanatic racist, Hitler shaped the Nazi platform. He blamed Germany's ills on the nation's internal "enemies," whom he identified as Jews, Marxists, bourgeois liberals, and "social deviates." Hitler promised to "purify" the German state of its "threatening" minorities and rebuild the country into a mighty empire. He manipulated public opinion by using all available means of propaganda—especially the radio, which brought his voice into every German home. In his autobiographical work *Mein Kampf* (*My Struggle*), published in 1925, Hitler set forth a fanatical theory of "Aryan racial superiority" that would inspire some of the most malevolent episodes in the history of humankind, including genocide: the systematic extermination of millions of Jews, along with thousands of Roman Catholics, gypsies, homosexuals, and other minorities. Justifying his racist ideology, he wrote:

> What we must fight for is to safeguard the existence and reproduction of our race and our people, the sustenance of our children and the purity of our blood, the freedom and independence of the fatherland so that our people may mature for the fulfillment of the mission allotted to it by the creator of the universe.*

Mein Kampf exalted the totalitarian state as "the guardian of a millennial future in the face of which the wishes and the selfishness of the individual must appear as nothing and submit." "The state is a means to an end," insisted Hitler. "Its end lies in the preservation and advancement of physically and psychically homogeneous creatures."

Less than twenty years after the close of World War I the second, even more devastating, world war threatened. The conditions that contributed to the outbreak of World War II included the failure of the peace settlement that had ended World War I and the undiminished growth of nationalism and militarism. But the specific event that initiated a renewal of hostilities was Hitler's military advance into Poland in 1939.

Once again, two opposing alliances were formed: Germany, Italy, Bulgaria, and Hungary comprised the Axis powers (the term describing the imaginary line between Rome and Berlin), while France and Britain and, in 1941,

Mein Kampf, translated by Ralph Manheim. Boston: Houghton Mifflin, 1943, 324.

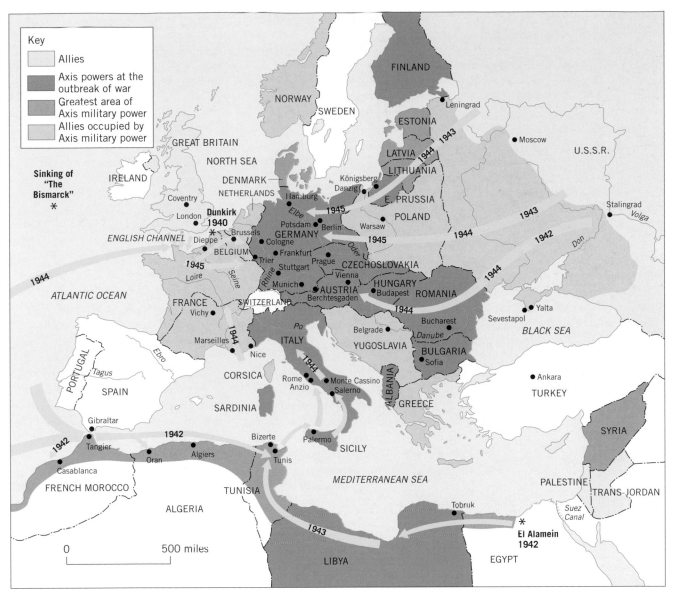

Map 34.2 World War II: The Defeat of the Axis, 1942–1945.

the United States and the Soviet Union, constituted the major Allied forces. Germany joined forces with totalitarian regimes in Italy (under Benito Mussolini) and in Spain (under General Francisco Franco), and the hostilities quickly spread into North Africa, the Balkans, and elsewhere (Map **34.2**). The fighting that took place during the three-year civil war in Spain (1936–1939) and in the German attack on the Netherlands in 1940 anticipated the merciless aspects of total war. In Spain, Nazi dive-bombers destroyed whole cities, while in the Netherlands, German tanks, parachute troops, and artillery overran the country in less than a week. The tempo of death was quickened as German air power attacked both military and civilian targets. France fell to Germany in 1940, and Britain became the target of systematic German bombing raids. At the same time, violating a Nazi-Soviet pact of 1939, Hitler invaded the Soviet Union, only to suffer massive defeat in the Battle of Stalingrad in 1942.

The United States, though supportive of the Allies, again tried to hold fast to its policy of "benevolent neutrality." It was brought into the war nevertheless by Japan,

which had risen rapidly to power in the late nineteenth century. Japan had defeated the Russians in the Russo-Japanese War of 1904. The small nation had successfully invaded Manchuria in 1931 and established a foothold in China and Southeast Asia. In December 1941, in opposition to United States efforts at restricting Japanese trade, the Japanese naval air service dropped bombs on the American air base at Pearl Harbor in Hawaii. The United States, declaring war on Japan, joined the twenty-five other nations that opposed the Axis powers and sent combat forces to fight in both Europe and the Pacific. The war against Japan was essentially a naval war, but it involved land and air attacks as well. Its climax was America's attack on two Japanese cities, Hiroshima and Nagasaki, in August of 1945. The bombing, which annihilated over 120,000 people (mostly civilians) and forced the Japanese to surrender within a matter of days, ushered in the atomic age. Just months before the bombing of Hiroshima, as German forces gave way to Allied assaults on all fronts, Hitler committed suicide. World War II came to a close with the surrender of both Germany and Japan in 1945.

World War II Poetry

World War II poetry around the globe carried to new extremes the sentiments of despair and futility. The American poet and critic Randall Jarrell (1914–1965), who served in the army air force from 1942 to 1946, described military combat as dehumanizing and degrading. In the short poem "The Death of the Ball Turret Gunner," a World War II airman, speaking from beyond the grave, recounts his fatal experience as an air force gunner. Encased in the Plexiglas bubble dome of an airplane ball turret—like an infant in his mother's womb—he "wakes" to "black flak" and dies; the startling image of birth in death fuses the states of dreaming and waking. Jarrell observed that modern combat, fueled by sophisticated technical instruments, neither fostered pride nor affirmed human nobility. Rather, such combat turned the soldier into a technician and an instrument of war. It robbed him of personal identity and reduced him to the level of an object—a thing to be washed out by a high-pressure steam hose. The note to the title of the poem was provided by the poet himself. In Japan, lamentation preceded rage. The *haiku*, the light verse form that had traditionally enshrined such images as cherry blossoms and spring rain, now became the instrument by which Japanese poets evoked the presence of death. Kato Shuson (1905–1993) introduced the three *haikus* reproduced below with the following words: "In the middle of the night there was a heavy air raid. Carrying my sick brother on my back I wandered in the flames with my wife in search of our children."

READING 6.9   Poems Of World War II

Jarrell's "The Death of the Ball Turret Gunner"[1] (1945)

From my mother's sleep I fell into the State,
And I hunched in its belly till my wet fur froze.[2]
Six miles from earth, loosed from its dream of life,
I woke to black flak and the nightmare fighters.
When I died they washed me out of the turret with a hose.

Shuson's *haikus* (ca. 1945)

Hi no oku ni	In the depths of the flames
Botan kuzururu	I saw how a peony
Sama wo mitsu	Crumbles to pieces.
Kogarashi ya	Cold winter storm—
Shōdo no kinko	A safe-door in a burnt-out site
Fukinarasu	Creaking in the wind.
Fuyu kamome	The winter sea gulls—
Sei no ie nashi	In life without a house,
Shi no haka nashi	In death without a grave.

---

[1]"A ball turret was a Plexiglas sphere set into the belly of a B-17 or B-24 and inhabited by two .50 caliber machine-guns and one man, a short, small man. When this gunner traced with his machine-guns a fighter attacking his bomber from below, he revolved with the turret; hunched upside-down in his little sphere, he looked like the fetus in the womb. The fighters which attacked him were armed with cannon firing explosive shells. The hose was a steam hose."
[2]The airman's fur-lined flight jacket.

World War II Fiction

As in the poetry of Jarrell, the novels of World War II were characterized by nihilism and resignation, their heroes robbed of reason and innocence. In such novels as *From Here to Eternity* (1951) by James Jones (1921–1977) and *The Naked and the Dead* (1948) by Norman Mailer (b. 1923), war makes men and machines interchangeable—the very brutality of total war dehumanizes its heroes. Mailer's raw, naturalistic novels, which are peppered with the four-letter words that characterize so much modern fiction, portray a culture dominated by violence and sexuality. Stylistically, Mailer often deviated from the traditional beginning-middle-and-end narrative format, using instead such cinematic techniques as flashback.

This episodic technique also prevails in the novels of Joseph Heller (1923–1999), Kurt Vonnegut (b. 1922), and other **gallows humor** writers. "Gallows" (or "black") humor is a form of literary satire that mocks modern life by calling attention to situations that seem too ghastly or too absurd to be true. Such fiction often describes the grotesque and the macabre in the passionless and nonchalant manner of a contemporary newspaper account. Like an elaborate hate joke, the gallows humor novel provokes helpless laughter at what is hideous and awful. Modern war, according to these humorists, is the greatest of all hate jokes: Dominated by bureaucratic capriciousness and mechanized destruction, it is an enterprise that has no victors, only victims.

Heller's *Catch-22* (1955), one of the most popular gallows humor novels to emerge from World War II, marks the shift from the realistic description of modern warfare (characteristic of the novels of Remarque, Jones, and Mailer) to its savage satirization. Heller based the events of *Catch-22* on his own experiences as an air force bombardier in World War II. The novel takes place on an air base off the coast of Italy, but its plot is less concerned with the events of the war than with the dehumanizing operations of the vast military bureaucracy that runs the war. Heller describes this bureaucracy as symbolic of "the humbug, hypocrisy, cruelty and sheer stupidity of our mass society." Heller's rendering of the classic armed forces condolence form-letter satirizes the impersonal character of modern war and provides a brief example of his biting style:

> Dear Mrs.,/Mr.,/Miss,/or Mr. and Mrs.— — —:
> Words cannot express the deep personal grief I experienced when your husband,/son,/father,/or brother was killed,/wounded,/or reported missing in action.

Catch-22 is a caustic blend of nihilism and forced cheerfulness. The characters in the novel—including a navigator who has no sense of direction and an aviator who bombs his own air base for commercial advantage—operate at the mercy of a depersonalizing system. As they try their best to preserve their identity and their sanity, they become the enemies of the very authorities that sent them to war.

Responses to Totalitarianism

While total war became a compelling theme in twentieth-century fiction, so too did totalitarianism, especially as it was described by those who had experienced it firsthand. Until Stalin's death in 1953, a reign of terror prevailed in the Soviet Union. As many found out, the slightest deviation from orthodox Marxist-Stalinist decorum resulted in imprisonment, slave labor, or execution. Aleksandr Solzhenitsyn (b. 1918) served in the Russian army during World War II, and although he had twice received recognition for bravery in combat, Solzhenitsyn was arrested in 1945 for veiled anti-Stalinist comments he had made in a letter to a friend. He was sentenced to eight years of imprisonment, spending half the term in a *gulag* in Siberia and the other half teaching mathematics in a Moscow prison. His Siberian experience provided the eyewitness material for his first novel, *One Day in the Life of Ivan Denisovich* (1962), which was followed in 1973–1976 by *The Gulag Archipelago*, a documentary description of Soviet prison life. These dispassionate accounts of the grim conditions of totalitarianism are searing indictments of savage inhumanity, and testaments to the heroism of the victims of Soviet political oppression.

Like Stalin, Hitler wielded unlimited and often ruthless authority. He destroyed democratic institutions in Germany, condemned avant-garde art, modern architecture, atonal music, and jazz as "degenerate," attacked Einstein's theories as "Jewish physics," and proceeded to eliminate—by means of the *Gestapo* (the Nazi secret police)—all opposition to his program of mass conformity. In 1933, over 35,000 Germans died either by suicide or from "unexplained causes." Over the next ten years, concentration camps arose in Austria, Poland, and Germany to house Hitler's "impure" minorities. It is estimated that 6 million Jews and 5 million non-Jews were put to death in Nazi gas chambers—a hideous episode in European history known as the Holocaust.

In Germany, the voices of actual witnesses to the atrocities of the Holocaust were for the most part silenced by death, but drawings by camp inmates and documentary photographs taken just after the war (see Figure 34.10) provide shocking visual evidence of modern barbarism. One of the most eloquent survivors of the Holocaust is the writer Elie Wiesel (b. 1928), recipient of the Nobel Peace Prize in 1986. At the age of fifteen, Wiesel, a Romanian Jew, was shipped with his entire family to the concentration camp at Auschwitz, Poland. From there the family was split up, and Wiesel and his father were sent to a labor camp in Buchenwald, Germany, where the youth saw his father and hundreds of others killed by the Nazis. Liberated in 1945, Wiesel transmuted the traumatic experiences of his childhood into prose. "Auschwitz," wrote Wiesel, "represents the negation and failure of human progress: it negates the human design and casts doubts on its validity." *Night*, Wiesel's autobiographical record of the Nazi terrors, is a graphic account of Hitler's barbarism. The brief excerpt that follows reveals the anguish Wiesel and other Jews experienced in confronting what appeared to be "God's silence" in the face of brutal injustice.

READING 6.10   From Wiesel's *Night* (1958)

One day, the electric power station at Buna was blown up. The Gestapo, summoned to the spot, suspected sabotage. They found a trail. It eventually led to the Dutch Oberkapo.[1] And there, after a search, they found an important stock of arms. 1

The Oberkapo was arrested immediately. He was tortured for a period of weeks, but in vain. He would not give a single name. He was transferred to Auschwitz. We never heard of him again.

But his little servant had been left behind in the camp in prison. Also put to torture, he too would not speak. Then the SS[2] sentenced him to death, with two other prisoners who had been discovered with arms. 10

One day when we came back from work, we saw three gallows rearing up in the assembly place, three black crows. Roll call. SS all round us, machine guns trained: the traditional ceremony. Three victims in chains—and one of them, the little servant, the sad-eyed angel.

The SS seemed more preoccupied, more disturbed than usual. To hang a young boy in front of thousands of spectators was no light matter. The head of the camp read the verdict. All eyes were on the child. He was lividly pale, almost calm, biting his lips. The gallows threw its shadow over him. 20

This time the Lagerkapo[3] refused to act as executioner. Three SS replaced him.

The three victims mounted together onto the chairs.

The three necks were placed at the same moment within the nooses.

"Long live liberty!" cried the two adults.

But the child was silent.

"Where is God? Where is He?" someone behind me asked.

At a sign from the head of the camp, the three chairs tipped over. 30

Total silence throughout the camp. On the horizon, the sun was setting.

"Bare your heads!" yelled the head of the camp. His voice was raucous. We were weeping.

"Cover your heads!"

Then the march past began. The two adults were no longer alive. Their tongues hung swollen, blue-tinged. But the third rope was still moving; being so light, the child was still alive. . . .

For more than half an hour he stayed there, struggling between life and death, dying in slow agony under our eyes. And we had to look him full in the face. He was still alive when I passed in front of him. His tongue was still red, his eyes were not yet glazed. 40

Behind me, I heard the same man asking:

"Where is God now?"

And I heard a voice within me answer him:

"Where is He? Here He is—He is hanging here on this gallows. . . ."

That night the soup tasted of corpses. . . . 50

---

[1] The foreman of the prisoners, selected from among them by the Nazis.
[2] A special police force that operated the camps.
[3] The prisoner who acted as foreman of the warehouse.

FILM IN THE WAR ERA

Film provided a permanent historical record of the turbulent military and political events of the early twentieth century. It also became an effective medium of political propaganda. In Russia, Lenin envisioned film as an invaluable means of spreading the ideals of communism. Following the Russian Revolution, he nationalized the fledgling motion-picture industry. At the hand of the Russian filmmaker Sergei Eisenstein (1898–1948), film operated both as a vehicle for political persuasion and as a fine art. Eisenstein shaped the social and artistic potential of cinema by combining realistic narrative with symbolic imagery. In *The Battleship Potemkin* (1925), his silent film masterpiece, Eisenstein staged the 1905 mutiny of the Tzar's soldiers to resemble an on-the-spot documentary. He used to brilliant effect the technique of **montage**, the assembling of cinematic shots in rapid succession. In the final sequence of the film, the events of a riot in the city of Odessa are captured with graphic force. Eisenstein interposed images of the advancing Tzarist police with a series of alternating close-ups and long shots of civilian victims, including those of a mother who is killed trying to save her infant in a baby carriage that careens down a broad flight of stairs (Figure **34.8**). The so-called "Odessa Steps sequence," whose rapidly increasing tempo works to evoke apprehension and terror, is an ingenious piece of editing that has been imitated with great frequency by modern filmmakers. Two years later, in 1927, Eisenstein made the Russian Revolution itself the subject of the film *Ten Days That Shook the World*. Both in his silent movies and in those he made later with sound, Eisenstein developed techniques that drew the viewer into the space of the film. He deliberately cut off parts of faces to bring attention to the eyes, played one shot off the next to build a conflicting and often discontinuous sequence, and devised visual angles that, in true constructivist fashion, produced startling asymmetrical abstractions. The masterpiece of Eisenstein's post-silent film career was *Alexander Nevsky* (1938), a film that exalted the thirteenth-century Russian prince who defended the motherland against the onslaught of the Teutonic knights. Here Eisenstein linked the musical score (composed by Sergei Prokofiev) to the pacing of the cinematic action: specifically, to the compositional flow of individual shots in the visual sequence—a technique known as "vertical montage." In place of the operatic crowd scenes of his earlier films, Eisenstein framed the protagonist within landscapes and battle scenes that were as gloriously stylized as monumental paintings. *Alexander Nevsky* earned the approval of Joseph Stalin and the acclaim of the Russian people. It survives as a landmark in the history of inventive film-making.

While Eisenstein used film to glorify the collective and individual heroism of the Soviet people, German filmmakers working for Hitler turned motion pictures into outright vehicles of state propaganda. The filmmaker and former actress Leni Riefenstahl (b. 1902) received unlimited state subsidies to produce the most famous propaganda film of all time, *The Triumph of the Will* (1934). Riefenstahl engaged a crew of 135 people to film the huge rallies and ceremonies

Figure 34.8 SERGEI M. EISENSTEIN, *The Battleship Potemkin*, 1925. Film stills from Act IV, "The Odessa Steps Massacre." Courtesy, The Museum of Modern Art/Film Stills Library.

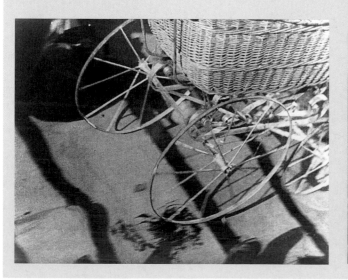

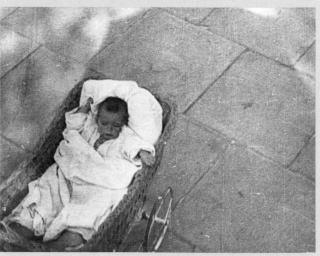

Figure 34.9 LENI RIEFENSTAHL, *The Triumph of the Will*, 1934. Film still showing Himmler, Hitler, and Lutze framed by columns of people as they approach the memorial monument in Nuremberg, Germany. Courtesy, The Museum of Modern Art/Film Stills Library.

staged by Hitler and the Nazi party, including their first meeting in Nuremberg. *The Triumph of the Will* is a synthesis of documentary fact and sheer artifice. Its bold camera angles and stark compositions seem in themselves totalitarian—witness the absolute symmetry and exacting conformity of the masses of troops that frame the tiny figures of Hitler and his compatriots at the Nuremberg rally (Figure **34.9**).

In America, film served to inform, to boost morale, and to propagandize for the Allied cause; but it also served

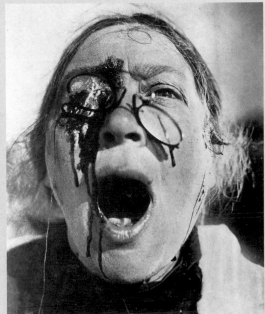

as entertainment and escape. At the height of the Depression as well as during the war era millions of Americans flocked to movie-theaters each week. While such prize-winning movies as *All Quiet on the Western Front* (1930) and *From Here to Eternity* (1953) were painfully realistic, numerous other films romanticized and glamorized the war. An exception to the standard war-movie fare was *The Great Dictator* (1940), which was directed by the multitalented British-born actor and filmmaker Charlie Chaplin (1889–1977). In this hilarious satire of Fascist dictatorship, Adolf Hitler (known in the film as Adenoid Hynkel and played by Chaplin) rises to power as head of the "Double Cross Party," only to be arrested by his own troops, who mistake him for a Jewish barber.

The Visual Arts in the War Era

Photojournalism

The realities of World War II were recorded by an international array of photojournalists. One of the most gifted was Lee Miller (1907–1977), an American debutante who became the first female wartime photojournalist and an early witness to the horrors of the German concentration camps (Figure **34.10**). The American photographer Robert Capa (1897–1954) produced notable pictures of World War II paratroopers, and the French photographer Henri Cartier-Bresson (b. 1908) immortalized the plight of war-torn Europe in hundreds of aesthetically compelling social realist photographs.

In the Soviet Union, photography came under the totalitarian knife, as Stalin's propagandists carefully excised from official photographs unseemly images of political brutality. The "remaking" of history via photomanipulation—a technique that would become popular among American filmmakers at the end of the century—had its ignoble beginnings in the war era.

Picasso's *Guernica*

On the afternoon of April 26, 1937, in the midst of the Spanish Civil War (1936–1939) that pitted republican forces against the Fascist dictatorship of General Francisco Franco, the German air force (in league with the Spanish Fascists) dropped incendiary bombs on Guernica, a small Basque market town in Northeast Spain. News of the event—the first aerial bombardment of a civilian target—reached Paris, where, as the death toll mounted, Pablo Picasso read with horror the illustrated newspaper accounts of the attack. Earlier in the year, the artist had been invited to contribute a painting for the Spanish Pavilion of the Paris World's Fair. The bombing of Guernica provided him with inspiration for the 26- by 12-foot mural that would become this century's most memorable antiwar image (Figure **34.11**).

More powerful than any literary description, *Guernica* captures the grim brutality and suffering of the wartime era. Picasso used monochromatic tones—the ashen grays of incineration—which also call to mind the documentary media of mass communication: newspapers, photographs, and film. However, *Guernica* is far from documentary. Indeed, its abstract treatment of flattened, distorted forms contrasts sharply with the social realist truth-to-nature style that dominated much of the art produced in Europe and America between the wars. Picasso's style combines the cubist affection for strong, angular motifs with an expressionistic treatment of form. The bull and horse of the Spanish bullfight, Picasso's lifelong metaphor for savage discord, share the shallow stage with a broken statue of a warrior and four women, one of whom holds a dead infant. This figure, her upturned head issuing a voiceless scream, is the physical embodiment of human grief. At the center of the painting, the horse, whose body bears the gaping wound of a spear, rears its head as if to echo the woman's anguished cry. The shattered statue of a warrior at the bottom of the composition symbolizes war's corrupting effect on the artifacts of high culture, just as it mocks the militant idealism represented by traditional war monuments. Sharp contrasts of light and dark establish the geometric structure that gives drama to the composition in a manner that recalls Goya's *The Third of May, 1808* (see chapter 29). Like Goya's powerful painting, but phrased in the vocabulary of modern abstraction, *Guernica* is a universal symbol of protest. It illustrates Picasso's insistent argument for art as a "weapon against the enemy."

Music in the War Era

Every totalitarian government in history has feared the power of music and condemned those musical styles that threatened mass conformity. In Nazi Germany, jazz was forbidden on the basis of its free and improvised style and its association with black musicians; in communist China, Beethoven's music was banned as the sound of the independent spirit. In Soviet Russia, Lenin's regime laid down the specific rule that composers write only music that "communicated" to the people; since atonality was associated with elitism and inscrutability, it was to be avoided, along with other expressions of Western "decadence." "Music," observed Lenin, "is a means of unifying great masses of people."

Music, however, also allows for ambiguity of meaning, as the career of the eminent Russian

Figure 34.10 LEE MILLER, *Buchenwald, Germany*, 30 April 1945. Photograph. Photo: © Lee Miller Archive, Penrose Film Productions, Chiddingly, East Sussex.

Figure 34.11 PABLO PICASSO, *Guernica*, 1937. Oil on canvas, 11 ft. 5½ in. × 25 ft. 5¾ in. Museo Nacional Centro de Arte Reina Sofía, Madrid.
© Succession Picasso/DACS 2000.

composer, Dmitri Shostakovich (1906–1975), illustrates. Enrolled at thirteen in the Leningrad Conservatory, Shostakovich was the product of rigorous classical training. His compositions, including fifteen symphonies, fifteen string quartets, and numerous scores for ballet, opera, plays, and motion pictures, incorporate songlike melodies and insistent rhythmic repetition. They are essentially tonal, but they make dramatic use of dissonance and frequently evoke a reflective, melancholic mood. Although Shostakovich appeared to be a loyal adherent to Russian communism, his music received constant criticism for its "bourgeois formalism." Finally, upon the performance of his Seventh ("Leningrad") Symphony in 1941, Soviet leaders hailed the work as a celebration of the Soviet triumph against the Nazi invasion of Leningrad. Only in 1979, when Shostakovich's memoirs were smuggled out of the Soviet Union, did it become apparent that the composer intended the piece as an attack on Stalin's inhumanity toward his own people.

The aesthetic philosophy of the Russian composer Sergei Prokofiev (1891–1953) also seemed to defend Soviet principles. "In my view," he wrote, "the composer . . . is in duty bound to serve man, the people. He must be a citizen first and foremost, so that his art may consciously extol human life and lead man to a radiant future." In 1948, the Soviets nevertheless denounced Prokofiev's music as "too modern." Prokofiev's compositions, most of which reveal his preference for classical form, are tonal and melodic, but they are boldly inventive in modulation and harmonic dissonance. In his scores for the ballets *Romeo and Juliet* (1935) and *Cinderella* (1944), in his cantata for the Eisenstein film *Alexander Nevsky* (1938), and in such shorter, modern-day classics as the witty *Lieutenant Kije Suite* (1934) and the orchestral fairy tale *Peter and the Wolf* (1936), Prokofiev demonstrated a talent for driving rhythms, sprightly marches, and unexpected, often whimsical shifts of tempo and melody.

Twentieth-century composers were frequently moved to commemorate the horrors of war in music. The most monumental example of such music is the *War Requiem* (1963) written by the British composer Benjamin Britten (1913–1976) to accompany the opening of England's renovated Coventry Cathedral, which had been partially destroyed by German bombs. Britten was a master at setting text to music. In the *War Requiem* he juxtaposed the Roman Catholic Mass for the Dead (the Latin Requiem Mass) with the war poems of Wilfred Owen in such a way that Owen's lines offer ironic commentary on traditional religious thought. Britten's imaginative union of sacred ritual and secular song calls for orchestra, chorus, boys' chorus, and three soloists. Poignant in spirit and dramatic in effect, Britten's oratorio may be seen as the musical analogue of Picasso's *Guernica*.

If it were possible to capture in music the agony of war, the Polish composer Krzystof Penderecki (b. 1933) has come closest to doing so. His *Threnody in Memory of the Victims of Hiroshima* (1960) consists of violent torrents of dissonant, percussive sound, some of which is produced by beating on the bodies of the fifty-two stringed instruments for which the piece is scored. The ten-minute song of lamentation for the dead begins with a long, screaming tone produced by playing the highest pitches possible on the violins; it is followed by passages punctuated by **tone clusters** (groups of adjacent dissonant notes). The rapid shifts in densities, timbres, rhythms, and dynamics are jarring and disquieting—effects consistent with the subject matter of the piece. *Threnody* was said to be the "anguished cry" that proclaimed the birth of the musical avant-garde behind the Iron Curtain. Penderecki's angry blurring of tones also characterizes his *Dies Irae* (1967), subtitled *Oratorio Dedicated to the Memory of those Murdered at Auschwitz*. Like Britten's *War Requiem*,

Penderecki's composition draws on Christian liturgy—here the traditional hymn of Last Judgment (the "Day of Wrath")—to convey a mood of darkness and despair. The *Dies Irae*—first performed on the grounds of a former concentration camp—is punctuated by clanking chains and piercing sirens. Painfully harsh and abrasive, it remains a symbol of the Holocaust's haunting impact.

Copland and the American Sound

One of America's finest twentieth-century composers, Aaron Copland (1900–1990) turned away from the horrors of war; however, just as the music of Shostakovich and Prokofiev was rooted in Russian soil, so that of Copland drew nourishment from native American idioms. The New York composer spiced his largely tonal compositions with the simple harmonies of American folk songs, the clarity of Puritan hymns, and the lively and often syncopated rhythms of jazz and Mexican dance. In 1941, Copland advised American composers to find alternatives to the harsh and demanding serialism of their European colleagues: "The new musical audiences will have to have music they can comprehend," he insisted. "It must therefore be simple and direct . . . Above all, it must be fresh in feeling." Copland achieved these goals in all his compositions, especially in the ballet scores *Billy the Kid* (1938), *Rodeo* (1940), and *Appalachian Spring* (1944). *Appalachian Spring*, commissioned by the Martha Graham Dance Company, features five variations on the familiar Shaker song, "'Tis the Gift to Be Simple." 🎵 In directing an orchestral rehearsal for the piece in 1974, Copland urged, "Make it more American in spirit, in that the sentiment isn't shown on the face." Copland also composed for film, winning an Oscar in 1949 for his score for *The Heiress*. Like the murals of Thomas Hart Benton, Copland's music wedded American themes to a vigorous and readily accessible language of form.

The Communist Revolution in China

The history of totalitarianism was not confined to the West. In the course of the twentieth century, modern tyrants wiped out whole populations in parts of Cambodia, Vietnam, Iraq, Africa, and elsewhere. Of all the Asian countries, however, China experienced the most dramatic changes. In 1900, less than ten percent of the Chinese population owned almost eighty percent of the land. Clamoring for reform, as well as for independence from foreign domination, nationalist forces moved to redistribute land among an enormous peasant population dominated by a small number of wealthy landowners. By 1911, the National People's Party had overthrown the Manchu leaders (see chapter 21) and established a republican government. But the Nationalists failed to provide an efficient land redistribution program

and, after 1937, they lost much of their popular support. Following World War II, the communist forces under the leadership of Mao Zedong (1893–1976) rose to power, and in 1949 they formed the People's Republic of China.

In China as in Russia, the Communist Party gained exclusive control of the government, with Mao serving as both chairman of the party and head of state. Mao called upon the great masses of citizens to work toward radical reform. "The theory of Marx, Engels, Lenin and Stalin is universally applicable," wrote Mao; but, he added, "We should regard it not as a dogma, but as a guide to action." A competent poet and scholar, Mao drew up the guidelines for the new society of China, a society that practiced cooperative endeavor and self-discipline. These guidelines were published in 1963 as the *Quotations from Chairman Mao* which became the "bible" of the Chinese Revolution. On youth, Mao wrote, "The world is yours, as well as ours, but in the last analysis, it is yours. You young people, full of vigor and vitality, are in the bloom of life, like the sun at eight or nine in the morning. Our hope is placed in you." On women: "In order to build a great socialist society, it is of the utmost importance to arouse the broad masses of women to join in productive activity. Men and women must receive equal pay for equal work in production." On the masses: "The masses have boundless creative power . . . the revolutionary war is a war of the masses; it can be waged only by mobilizing the masses and relying on them."*

Mao's ambitious reforms earned the support of the landless masses, but his methods for achieving his goals struck at the foundations of traditional Chinese culture. He tried to replace the old order, and especially the Confucian veneration of the family, with new socialist values that demanded devotion to the local economic unit—and ultimately to the state. Between 1949 and 1952, in an effort to make his reforms effective, Mao authorized the execution of some 2 to 5 million people, including the wealthy landowners themselves. To carry out his series of five-year plans for economic development in industry and agriculture, Mao also instituted totalitarian practices, such as indoctrination, exile, and repeated purges of the voices of opposition.

Like the century's other totalitarian leaders, Mao directed artists to infuse literature with an ideological content that celebrated the creative powers of the masses. To some extent, however, the movement for a "people's literature" furthered reforms that had been launched during the political revolution of 1911: At that time, traditional styles of writing, including the "book language" of the classics, gave way to the language of common, vernacular speech. The new naturalistic style was strongly influenced by Western literature and journalism. Chinese writers responded enthusiastically to modern European novels, surrealistic short stories, and psychological dramas—poets even imitated such Western forms as the sonnet. In the visual arts, the influence of late nineteenth-century Western printmakers such as Käthe Kollwitz (see chapter

Mao Tse-Tung's Quotations: The Red Guard's Handbook, introduction by Stewart Fraser. Nashville, Tenn.: Peabody International Center, 1967, 118, 256, 288, 297.

Figure 34.12 LI HUA, *Roar!* 1936. Woodcut, 8 x 6 in. Lu Xun Memorial, Shanghai.

30), helped to shape the powerful social realism of many Chinese artists, including Li Hua (1907–1994). Li's stark and searing woodcut of a bound man (Figure **34.12**)—a metaphor for modern China—reiterates the silent scream of Munch (see Figure 33.1) and Eisenstein (see Figure 34.8). During the Cultural Revolution (1966–1976) China's communist regime reinstated the official policy of socialist realism as it had been defined by the First All-Union Congress of Soviet Writers in 1934. The consequences of this policy would work to foment the liberation movements of the last decades of the century.

SUMMARY

The twentieth century was molded in the crucible of total war and totalitarianism. World Wars I and II were more devastating in nature and effect than any previous wars in world history. The Russian Revolution of 1917 marked the beginnings of Soviet communism and ushered in decades of totalitarian rule. Revolutions in China and Mexico were equally traumatic in destroying agelong traditions. In Europe, the Nazi policy of militant racism under Adolf Hitler brought about the brutal deaths of millions.

Artists responded to these events with rage, disbelief, and compassion. Searing indictments of World War I are found in literature and the visual arts. World War II literature emphasized the dehumanizing effects of war. In the poems of Jarrell, as in the novels of gallows humor fiction writers, war became a metaphor for all modern-day varieties of cruelty and perversion; the firsthand experiences of Solzhenitsyn in the Russian *gulags* and Wiesel in Nazi concentration camps are no less poignant and shocking.

In America, during the period between the wars, the effects of the Great Depression encouraged the rise of social realism, a style that dominates the novels of

Steinbeck and the paintings of Benton. Throughout the world, photographs and film documented twentieth-century warfare, even as they served ideological ends. Working in Paris, Picasso produced the quintessential antiwar painting, *Guernica*.

Composers of the wartime era also felt the effects of current political events. Living under the critical eye of the communist regime, Shostakovich and Prokofiev composed in distinctly different, but memorable, musical styles. In England, Benjamin Britten commemorated World War II in his *War Requiem*, while in Poland Penderecki immortalized the harsh realities of twentieth-century genocide. Total war and totalitarianism touched all of the arts of the twentieth century and left upon them the indelible imprint of despair.

GLOSSARY

gallows humor (or "black humor") the use of morbid and absurd situations for comic and satirical purposes in modern fiction and drama

montage in art, music, or literature, a composite made by freely juxtaposing usually heterogeneous images; in cinema, the production of a rapid succession of images to present a stream of interconnected ideas (see also Glossary, chapter 33 "photomontage")

tone cluster a group of adjacent dissonant notes, such as the notes of a scale, sounded together

totalitarian a political regime that imposes the will of the state upon the life and conduct of the individual

SUGGESTIONS FOR READING

Andrews, Julia A. *Painters and Politics in the People's Republic of China, 1949–1979*. Berkeley, Calif.: University of California Press, 1994.

Arnold, Ben. *Music and War*. New York: Garland Publishing, 1993.

Braham, Randolph, L., ed. *Reflections of the Holocaust in Art and Literature*. Irvington, N.Y.: Columbia University Press, 1990.

Cork, Richard. *A Bitter Truth: Avant-Garde Art and the Great War*. New Haven: Yale University Press, 1994.

Eksteins, Modris. *Rites of Spring: The Great War and the Birth of the Modern Age*. Boston: Houghton Mifflin, 1989.

Langer, Lawrence L. *Holocaust Testimonies: The Ruins of Memory*. New Haven: Yale University Press, 1993.

Mosse, George L., ed. *Nazi Culture: Intellectual, Cultural, and Social Life in the Third Reich*, translated by Salvator Attanasio, et al. New York: Schocken Books, 1981.

Rothstein, Arthur. *Documentary Photography*. Boston: Focal Press, 1986.

Walsh, Jeffrey. *American War Literature 1914 to Vietnam*. New York: St. Martin's Press, 1982.

Zeman, Zbynek. *Selling the War: Art and Propaganda in World War II*. New York: Bookthrift, 1982.

MUSIC LISTENING SELECTION

CD Two Selection 19 Copland, *Appalachian Spring*, excerpt 1944.

CHAPTER THIRTY-FIVE

The quest for meaning

"Man is nothing else but what he makes of himself."
Jean-Paul Sartre

The nightmare of World War II left the world's population in a state of shock and disillusion. The Western democracies had held back the forces of totalitarian aggression, but the future seemed as threatening as ever. Communism and capitalist democracy now confronted one another in hostile distrust. And both possessed atomic weapons with the potential to extinguish the human race. The pessimism that accompanied the two world wars was compounded by a loss of faith in the bedrock beliefs of former centuries. The realities of trench warfare, the concentration camps, and Hiroshima made it difficult to maintain that human beings were rational by nature, that technology would work to advance human happiness, and that the universe was governed by a benevolent God. There is little wonder that the events of the first half of the twentieth century caused a loss of confidence in the eternal truths, including faith in a Supreme Being. The sense of estrangement from God and reason produced a condition of anxious withdrawal that has been called "alienation." Like a visitor to a foreign country, the modern individual felt estranged from all that was comforting and certain.

The condition of alienation was further aggravated by the depersonalizing influence of modern science and technology. In the mid-twentieth century, the breach between humanism and science seemed wider than ever; increasingly intellectuals questioned the social value of scientific technology to human progress. Optimists still envisioned modern technology as a liberating force for humankind. The American behavioral psychologist B. F. Skinner (1904–1990), for instance, anticipated a society in which the behavior of human beings might be scientifically engineered for the benefit of both the individual and the community. In the futuristic novel *Walden Two* (1948), Skinner created a fictional society in which the "technology of behavior" replaced traditional "prescientific" views of freedom and dignity. *Walden Two* is typical of a large body of utopian literature that exalted science as a positive force in shaping the future.

Pessimists, on the other hand, feared—and still fear—that modern technology might produce catastrophes ranging from a nuclear holocaust to the absolute loss of personal freedom. Dystopian novels, that is, novels that picture societies in which conditions are dreadful and bleak, reflect this negative outlook. *Brave New World* (1932) by the British writer Aldous Huxley (1894–1963), *1984* (1949) by England's George Orwell (the pen name of Eric Arthur Blair, 1903–1950), and *Fahrenheit 451* (1953) by the American Ray Bradbury (b. 1920) all present fictional totalitarian societies in which modern technology and the techniques of human engineering operate to destroy human freedom. *Brave New World* describes an imaginary society of the seventh century "A.F." ("after Henry Ford," the early twentieth-century American automobile manufacturer). In Huxley's futuristic society, babies are conceived in test tubes and, following the assembly line methods invented by Henry Ford for the manufacture of cars, individuals are behaviorally conditioned to perform socially beneficial tasks. From this "brave new world," the concept and practice of family life have been eradicated; human anxieties are quelled by means of *soma* (a mood-altering drug); and art, literature, and religion—all of which, according to the custodians of technology, threaten communal order and stability—have been ruthlessly purged.

Existentialism and Freedom

While *utopians* envisioned science and technology as potentially liberating and *dystopians* saw them as potentially threatening, both schools implicitly acknowledged that environment determined human behavior. "We are what we are conditioned to be," held the futurists. But partisans of the new humanist philosophy called *existentialism* argued otherwise. "We are what we choose to be," insisted the existentialists; "we create both ourselves and our freedom by our every choice." Existentialism, the most influential philosophic movement of the twentieth century, had its roots in the late nineteenth century, most notably in the writings of the Danish philosopher Søren Kierkegaard (1813–1855). But it rose to prominence through the efforts of the French left-wing intellectual, Jean-Paul Sartre.

The Philosophy of Sartre

Jean-Paul Sartre (1905–1980), the leading existentialist philosopher of the twentieth century, also made significant contributions as a playwright, novelist, journalist, and literary critic. Sartre had fought in World War II and been active in the French resistance to the German occupation of France. These experiences influenced his personal quest for meaning and identity in a universe that he perceived as devoid of moral absolutes.

Sartre's philosophy, as expounded in his classic work *Being and Nothingness* (1943), took as its basic premise the idea that existence precedes essence, that is, that one's material being exists prior to and independent of any intrinsic factors. Sartre's premise challenged the fundamentals of traditional philosophy: Plato had identified "essence" as Forms (or Ideas) that were eternal and unchanging. For Aristotle, reason—humankind's capacity for rational thought—was the "essence" that separated human beings from the lower animals. Philosophers from Descartes through Kant followed the ancients by defending the notion that primary internal principles of being preceded being itself—a view that was metaphysically compatible with Christian theology. Sartre proposed, however, that human beings have no fixed nature. They are not imbued, by a Supreme Being, with any special divinity, nor are they (by nature) rational. They are neither imprisoned by subconscious forces (as Freud had held) nor are they determined by specific economic conditions (as Marx had maintained). Born into the world as body/matter, they proceed to make the choices by which they form their own natures. In Sartre's analysis, each individual is the sum of his or her actions. In that human beings must choose at every turn between a variety of possibilities, they are (in Sartre's words) "condemned to be free." Moreover, since every choice implies a choice for all humankind, each individual bears the overwhelming burden of total responsibility—a condition that Sartre called "anguish."

Sartre's viewpoint struck a balance between optimism and despair. While freedom and meaning depend on human action, said Sartre, all human actions, by necessity, are played out within a moral void—that is, within a universe lacking divine guidance and absolute values. To our profound despair, we seek meaning in a meaningless world. Yet, because human life is all there is, it must be cherished. According to Sartre, the human condition is one of anxiety experienced in the face of nothingness and the inevitability of death. Such anxiety is compounded because we alone are responsible for our actions. To disclaim responsibility for those actions by blaming external causes—"the Devil made me do it," "The ghetto turned me into a criminal," or "My parents were too lenient"—or to deny the possibility of alternative actions is to act in "bad faith." For Sartre, no forms of human engineering, technocratic or otherwise, can usurp the human potential

for free action. To fly from freedom and responsibility is a form of self-deception and inauthenticity. "We are alone, with no excuses," according to Sartre.

In addition to his major philosophic work, Sartre wrote a number of significant novels, short stories, and plays. The most gripping of his plays, *No Exit* (1945), features three characters trapped in a "hell" they have created by their efforts to justify the acts of bad faith that have shaped their lives. The principal ideas set forth in these most famous of Sartre's writings are summarized in the lecture entitled "Existentialism," which Sartre presented in Paris in 1945. In the following excerpt from this essay, Sartre discusses existentialism as "an ethics of action and involvement" and explores the meaning of existential anguish.

READING 6.11 From Sartre's "Existentialism" (1945)

. . . Atheistic existentialism . . . states that if God does not exist, there is at least one being in whom existence precedes essence, a being who exists before he can be defined by any concept, and that this being is man, or, as Heidegger[1] says, human reality. What is meant here by saying that existence precedes essence? It means that, first of all, man exists, turns up, appears on the scene, and, only afterwards, defines himself. If man, as the existentialist conceives him, is indefinable, it is because at first he is nothing. Only afterward will he be something, and he himself will have made what he [10] will be. Thus, there is no human nature, since there is no God to conceive it. Not only is man what he conceives himself to be, but he is also only what he wills himself to be after this thrust toward existence.

Man is nothing else but what he makes of himself. Such is the first principle of existentialism. It is also what is called subjectivity, the name we are labeled with when charges are brought against us. But what do we mean by this, if not that man has a greater dignity than a stone or table? For we mean that man first exists, that is, that man first of all is the being [20] who hurls himself toward a future and who is conscious of imagining himself as being in the future. Man is at the start a plan which is aware of itself, rather than a patch of moss, a piece of garbage, or a cauliflower; nothing exists prior to this plan; there is nothing in heaven; man will be what he will have planned to be. Not what he will want to be. Because by the word "will" we generally mean a conscious decision, which is subsequent to what we have already made of ourselves. I may want to belong to a political party, write a book, get married; but all that is only a manifestation of an [30] earlier, more spontaneous choice that is called "will." But if existence really does precede essence, man is responsible for what he is. Thus, existentialism's first move is to make every man aware of what he is and to make the full responsibility of his existence rest on him. And when we say that a man is responsible for himself, we do not only mean that he is responsible for his own individuality, but that he is responsible

---

[1] A German philosopher (1889–1976) whose writings had a major influence on Sartre and other existentialists.

for all men.

The word subjectivism has two meanings, and our opponents play on the two. Subjectivism means, on the one hand, that an individual chooses and makes himself; and, on the other, that it is impossible for man to transcend human subjectivity. The second of these is the essential meaning of existentialism. When we say that man chooses his own self, we mean that every one of us does likewise; but we also mean by that that in making this choice he also chooses all men. In fact, in creating the man that we want to be, there is not a single one of our acts which does not at the same time create an image of man as we think he ought to be. To choose to be this or that is to affirm at the same time the value of what we choose, because we can never choose evil. We always choose the good, and nothing can be good for us without being good for all.

If, on the other hand, existence precedes essence, and if we grant that we exist and fashion our image at one and the same time, the image is valid for everybody and for our whole age. Thus, our responsibility is much greater than we might have supposed, because it involves all mankind. If I am a workingman and choose to join a Christian trade-union rather than be a communist, and if by being a member I want to show that the best thing for man is resignation, that the kingdom of man is not of this world, I am not only involving my own case—I want to be resigned for everyone. As a result, my action has involved all humanity. To take a more individual matter, if I want to marry, to have children; even if this marriage depends solely on my own circumstances or passion or wish, I am involving all humanity in monogamy and not merely myself. Therefore, I am responsible for myself and for everyone else. I am creating a certain image of man of my own choosing. In choosing myself, I choose man.

This helps us understand what the actual content is of such rather grandiloquent words as anguish, forlornness, despair. As you will see, it's all quite simple.

First, what is meant by anguish? The existentialists say at once that man is anguish. What that means is this: the man who involves himself and who realizes that he is not only the person he chooses to be, but also a lawmaker who is, at the same time, choosing all mankind as well as himself, cannot escape the feeling of his total and deep responsibility. Of course, there are many people who are not anxious; but we claim that they are hiding their anxiety, that they are fleeing from it. Certainly, many people believe that when they do something, they themselves are the only ones involved, and when someone says to them, "What if everyone acted that way?" they shrug their shoulders and answer, "Everyone doesn't act that way." But really, one should always ask himself, "What would happen if everybody looked at things that way?" There is no escaping this disturbing thought except by a kind of double-dealing. A man who lies and makes excuses for himself by saying "not everybody does that," is someone with an uneasy conscience, because the act of lying implies that a universal value is conferred upon the lie. . . .

The existentialist . . . thinks it very distressing that God does not exist, because all possibility of finding values in a heaven of ideas disappears along with Him; there can no longer be an *a priori* Good, since there is no infinite and perfect

consciousness to think it. Nowhere is it written that the Good exists, that we must be honest, that we must not lie; because the fact is we are on a plane where there are only men. Dostoevsky said, "If God didn't exist, everything would be possible." That is the very starting point of existentialism. Indeed, everything is permissible if God does not exist, and as a result man is forlorn, because neither within him nor without does he find anything to cling to. He can't start making excuses for himself.

If existence really does precede essence, there is no explaining things away by reference to a fixed and given human nature. In other words, there is no determinism, man is free, man is freedom. On the other hand, if God does not exist, we find no values or commands to turn to which legitimize our conduct. So, in the bright realm of values, we have no excuse behind us, nor justification before us. We are alone, with no excuses.

That is the idea I shall try to convey when I say that man is condemned to be free. Condemned, because he did not create himself, yet, in other respects is free; because, once thrown into the world, he is responsible for everything he does. The existentialist does not believe in the power of passion. He will never agree that a sweeping passion is a ravaging torrent which fatally leads a man to certain acts and is therefore an excuse. He thinks that man is responsible for his passion.

The existentialist does not think that man is going to help himself by finding in the world some omen by which to orient himself. Because he thinks that man will interpret the omen to suit himself. Therefore, he thinks that man, with no support and no aid, is condemned every moment to invent man. Ponge,[2] in a very fine article, has said, "Man is the future of man." That's exactly it. But if it is taken to mean that this future is recorded in heaven, that God sees it, then it is false, because it would really no longer be a future. If it is taken to mean that whatever a man may be, there is a future to be forged, a virgin future before him, then this remark is sound. But then we are forlorn. . . .

Now, for the existentialist there is really no love other than one which manifests itself in a person's being in love. There is no genius other than one which is expressed in works of art; the genius of Proust is the sum of Proust's works; the genius of Racine is his series of tragedies. Outside of that, there is nothing. Why say that Racine could have written another tragedy, when he didn't write it? A man is involved in life, leaves his impress on it, and outside of that there is nothing. To be sure, this may seem a harsh thought to someone whose life hasn't been a success. But, on the other hand, it prompts people to understand that reality alone is what counts, that dreams, expectations, and hopes warrant no more than to define a man as a disappointed dream, as miscarried hopes, as vain expectations. In other words, to define him negatively and not positively. However, when we say, "You are nothing else than your life," that does not imply that the artist will be judged solely on the basis of his works of art; a thousand other things will contribute toward summing him up. What we mean is that a man is nothing else than a series of undertakings, that he is the sum, the organization, the

_____

[2]Francis Ponge (1899–1987) was a French poet and critic.

ensemble of the relationships which make up these undertakings. . . .

If it is impossible to find in every man some universal essence which would be human nature, yet there does exist a universal human condition. It's not by chance that today's thinkers speak more readily of man's condition than of his nature. By condition they mean, more or less definitely, the *a priori* limits which outline man's fundamental situation in the universe. Historical situations vary; a man may be born a slave in a pagan society or a feudal lord or a proletarian. What does not vary is the necessity for him to exist in the world, to be at work there, to be there in the midst of other people, and to be mortal there. . . .

But there is another meaning of humanism. Fundamentally it is this: man is constantly outside of himself; in projecting himself, in losing himself outside of himself, he makes for man's existing; and, on the other hand, it is by pursuing transcendent goals that he is able to exist; man, being this state of passing-beyond, and seizing upon things only as they bear upon this passing-beyond, is at the heart, at the center of this passing-beyond. There is no universe other than a human universe, the universe of human subjectivity. This connection between transcendency, as a constituent element of man— not in the sense that God is transcendent, but in the sense of passing beyond—and subjectivity, in the sense that man is not closed in on himself but is always present in a human universe, is what we call existentialist humanism. Humanism, because we remind man that there is no lawmaker other than himself, and that in his forlornness he will decide by himself; because we point out that man will fulfill himself as man, not in turning toward himself, but in seeking outside of himself a goal which is just this liberation, just this particular fulfillment.

From these few reflections it is evident that nothing is more unjust than the objections that have been raised against us. Existentialism is nothing else than an attempt to draw all the consequences of a coherent atheistic position. It isn't trying to plunge man into despair at all. But if one calls every attitude of unbelief despair, like the Christians, then the word is not being used in its original sense. Existentialism isn't so atheistic that it wears itself out showing that God doesn't exist. Rather, it declares that even if God did exist, that would change nothing. There you've got our point of view. Not that we believe that God exists, but we think that the problem of His existence is not the issue. In this sense existentialism is optimistic, a doctrine of action, and it is plain dishonesty for Christians to make no distinction between their own despair and ours and then to call us despairing.

160

170

180

190

200

Christian Existentialism

While Sartre excluded the question of God's existence from his speculations, Christian existentialists saw little contradiction between the belief in a Supreme Being and the ethics of human freedom and responsibility. They held that religious philosophy need not concern itself with the proof or disproof of God's existence; rather, it should focus on the moral life of the individual. Beyond what Kierkegaard had called the "leap of faith" from which all religious belief proceeded, there lay a continuing moral responsibility for one's own life. According to the philosophers Karl Jaspers (1883–1969) and Gabriel Marcel (1889–1973), God had challenged human beings to act as free and responsible creatures.

Among Christian theologians, a similar concern for the moral life of the individual moved religion out of the seminaries and into the streets. The Protestant theologian Reinhold Niebuhr (1892–1971) criticized doctrinaire theology and called for the revival of moral conduct in an immoral society. Convinced that human participation was essential to social redemption, Niebuhr urged Christians to cultivate the roles of humility and justice in modern life. Niebuhr's contemporary and fellow Lutheran Paul Tillich (1886–1965) boldly rejected the concept of a personal god. For Tillich, anxiety and alienation were conditions preliminary to the mystical apprehension of a "God above the God of theism."

Literature at Mid-Century

Sartre's secular philosophy inspired a new kind of literary hero: a hero who, deprived of traditional values and religious beliefs, bears the burden of freedom and the total responsibility for his actions. The existential hero—or, more exactly, antihero—took up the quest for meaning: Alienated by nature and circumstance, this hero makes choices in a world lacking moral absolutes, a world in which no act might be called "good" unless it is chosen in conscious preference to its alternatives. Unlike the heroes of old, the modern antihero is neither noble nor sure of purpose. He might act decisively, but with full recognition of the absence of shared cultural values and moral absolutes. Trapped rather than liberated by freedom, the antihero might have trouble getting along with others or simply making it through the day—"Hell," says one of Sartre's characters in *No Exit*, "is other people." Encountering the frustrating conditions of meaninglessness and irrationality, the antihero might achieve nothing other than the awful recognition of the absurdity of the life experience.

Twentieth-century literature is filled with antiheroes— characters whose lives illustrate the absurdity of the human condition. Sartre's compatriot Albert Camus (1913 –1960) defined the absurd as the "divorce between man and life, actor and setting." In Camus' short stories and novels, including his classic work, *The Stranger* (1942), the antihero inevitably confronts the basic existential

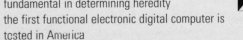

1944	a Canadian bacteriologist proves DNA is fundamental in determining heredity
1946	the first functional electronic digital computer is tested in America
1947	quantum electrodynamics (QED) studies "irregular" behavior of subatomic particles
1948	Bell Laboratories develop the transistor
1951	nuclear reactors are utilized successfully to produce electricity
1951	color television first appears in the U.S.A.

imperatives: "Recognize your dignity as a human being"; "Choose and commit yourself to action." The central character of Camus' *The Stranger* is the quintessential alienated man: He is estranged from traditional social values and unable to establish his sense of being except through continual rebellion. Camus' view of human nature was less cynical than Sartre's and more concerned with the value of benevolent reconciliation between human beings. At the same time, the situations described by Camus in his novels—and his own death in an automobile crash—seem inescapably arbitrary and absurd.

Although existentialism was an essentially European phenomenon, the existential hero appears in the literature of twentieth-century writers throughout the world, most notably in the novels of Argentina's Jorge Luis Borges and Japan's Oē Kenzaburo. In postwar America, the existential perspective cut across regional lines, from the deep South of William Faulkner and Walker Percy to John Cheever's New England and Bernard Malamud's New York: and from the urban Midwest of Saul Bellow to California's Beat Generation writers. The antihero assumes a quintessentially American flavor in the Pulitzer prize-winning drama *Death of a Salesman* (1949) by Arthur Miller (b. 1915). Miller's salesman, Willy Loman, is a "little man" who has met failure at every turn, but cannot recognize the inauthenticity of his false claims to material success and the futility of his self-deception. An American classic, *Salesman* depends on traditional dramatic structure in bringing to life a complex, but ultimately sympathetic existential figure. An entirely different type of theater, however, would come to dominate the postwar era.

Theater of the Absurd

The international movement known as *theater of the absurd* so vividly captured the anguish of modern society that some critics called it "the true theater of our time." Abandoning classical theater from Sophocles and Shakespeare through Ibsen and Miller, absurdist playwrights rejected traditional dramatic structure (in which action moves from conflict to resolution), along with traditional modes of character development. The absurdist play, which drew stylistic inspiration from dada performance art and surrealist film, usually lacks dramatic progression, direction, and resolution. Its characters undergo little or no change, dialogue contradicts actions, and events follow no logical order. Dramatic action, leavened with gallows humor, may consist of irrational and grotesque situations that remain unresolved at the end of the performance—as is often the case with real life.

The principal figures of absurdist theater reflect the international character of the movement: They include Samuel Beckett (Irish), Eugène Ionesco (Romanian), Harold Pinter (British), Fernando Arrabal (Spanish), Jean Genet (French), and Edward Albee (American). Of these, Samuel Beckett (1906–1989), recipient of the Nobel Prize in 1969, earned the greatest distinction. Early in his career, Beckett came under the influence of James Joyce, parts of whose novel *Finnegans Wake* he recorded from dictation, as the aging Joyce was losing his eyesight. Beckett admired Joyce's experimental use of language. He also shared the views of the Austrian linguistic philosopher Ludwig Wittgenstein (see chapter 37), who held that human beings were imprisoned by language and consequently cut off from the possibility of true understanding. The concept of language as the prisonhouse of the mind— a point of view that had far-reaching consequences in postmodern philosophy—was fundamental to Beckett's dramatic style. It is particularly apparent in his most notable work, *Waiting for Godot*, written in 1948 and first staged in 1952. The main "action" of the play consists of a running dialogue—terse, repetitive, and often comical— between two tramps as they await the mysterious "Godot" (who, despite their anxious expectations, never arrives). Critics find in Godot a symbol of salvation, revelation, or, most commonly, God—an interpretation that Beckett himself rejected. Nevertheless, the absent "deliverer" (perhaps by his very absence) gives a modicum of meaning to the lives of the central characters. Their longings and delusions, their paralysis and ignorance, are anticipated in the opening line, "Nothing to be done." The progress of the play, animated by an extraordinary blend of biblical references, broad slapstick, comic wordplay, Zenlike propositions, and crude jokes, gives life to Sartre's observation that "man first of all is the being who hurls himself toward a future" (see Reading 6.11). A parable of the existential condition, *Waiting for Godot* dwells on the divorce between expectation and event. At the same time (and as the brief excerpt from the end of Act Two illustrates), the play underscores the futility of communication between frail creatures who cling (and wait) together.

READING 6.12 From Beckett's *Waiting for Godot* (1948)

Estragon: Where shall we go?   1
Vladimir: Not far.
Estragon: Oh yes, let's go far away from here.
Vladimir: We can't.
Estragon: Why not?
Vladimir: We have to come back to-morrow.
Estragon: What for?
Vladimir: To wait for Godot.
Estragon: Ah! (*Silence.*) He didn't come?
Vladimir: No.   10
Estragon: And now it's too late.
Vladimir: Yes, now it's night.
Estragon: And if we dropped him. (*Pause.*) If we dropped him?
Vladimir: He'd punish us. (*Silence. He looks at the tree.*) Everything's dead but the tree.
Estragon (*Looking at the tree*): What is it?
Vladimir: It's the tree.
Estragon: Yes, but what kind?
Vladimir: I don't know. A willow.   20
(*Estragon draws Vladimir towards the tree. They stand motionless before it. Silence.*)
Estragon: Why don't we hang ourselves?

Vladimir: With what?

Estragon: You haven't got a bit of rope?

Vladimir: No.

Estragon: Then we can't.

(Silence.)

Vladimir: Let's go.

Estragon: Wait, there's my belt.

Vladimir: It's too short.

Estragon: You could hang on to my legs.

Vladimir: And who'd hang on to mine?   30

Estragon: True.

Vladimir: Show all the same. *(Estragon loosens the cord that holds up his trousers which, much too big for him, fall about his ankles. They look at the cord.)* It might do at a pinch. But is it strong enough?

Estragon: We'll soon see. Here.

(They each take an end of the cord and pull. It breaks. They almost fall.)

Vladimir: Not worth a curse.

(Silence.)

Estragon: You say we have to come back to-morrow?

Vladimir: Yes.

Estragon: Then we can bring a good bit of rope.   40

Vladimir: Yes.

(Silence.)

Estragon: Didi.

Vladimir: Yes.

Estragon: I can't go on like this.

Vladimir: That's what you think.

Estragon: If we parted? That might be better for us.

Vladimir: We'll hang ourselves tomorrow. *(Pause.)* Unless Godot comes.

Estragon: And if he comes?

Vladimir: We'll be saved.   50

(Vladimir takes off his hat (Lucky's), peers inside it, feels about inside it, shakes it, knocks on the crown, puts it on again.)

Estragon: Well? Shall we go?

Vladimir: Pull on your trousers.

Estragon: What?

Vladimir: Pull on your trousers.

Estragon: You want me to pull off my trousers?

Vladimir: Pull ON your trousers.

Estragon *(Realizing his trousers are down)*: True. *(He pulls up his trousers.)*

Vladimir: Well? Shall we go?

Estragon: Yes, let's go.   60

(They do not move.)

(Curtain.)

Poetry at Mid-Century

T. S. Eliot

The theme of alienation permeates the poetry of the twentieth century; however, no English-speaking poet captured the mood of anxiety and the modern quest for meaning more powerfully than the American-born writer T. S. (Thomas Stearns) Eliot (1888–1965). In the verse drama *The Rock*, written in 1934, Eliot summed up the crisis that threatened to engulf the modern world:

> All our knowledge brings us nearer to our ignorance,
> All our ignorance brings us nearer to death,
> But nearness to death no nearer to God.
> Where is the wisdom we have lost in knowledge?
> Where is the knowledge we have lost in
>   information?
> The cycles of Heaven in twenty centuries
> Bring us farther from God and nearer to the Dust.*

Educated at Harvard University in philosophy and the classics, Eliot was studying at Oxford when World War I broke out. He remained in England after the war, becoming a British citizen in 1927 and converting to the Anglican church in the same year. Eliot's grasp of modern philosophy, world religions, anthropology, and the classical literature of Asia and the West made him the most esteemed literary critic of his time. His erudition also informed his poetic style. Like his colleague Ezra Pound, whom he met in 1914, Eliot tried to rid modern poetry of romantic sentiment. He insisted that the poet must seek the verbal formula or "objective correlative" (as he called it) that gives precise shape to feeling. Eliot's poetry features inventive rhythms, irregular cadences, and startling images that appear pieced together like fragments of a jigsaw puzzle. Many of his poems are densely packed with personal reminiscences and intriguing literary allusions. His poem *The Waste Land* (1922), which takes as its theme the aridity of modern life, had the effect—as one of his contemporaries remarked—of an atom bomb. While it did not wipe away all earlier poetic styles, it established the idiom of modern poetry as compressed, complex, demanding, and serious.

The poem "The Love Song of J. Alfred Prufrock," though written before World War II, belongs in this chapter because it so perfectly captures the condition of the existential antihero. The "love song" is actually the dramatic monologue of a timid and neurotic middle-aged man who has little faith in himself or his capacity for effective action. Prufrock's cynicism and despair presage the failure of nerve and the sense of impotence that marked the postwar generation. At the same time, his sense of powerlessness and moral inertia have made Prufrock an archetype of the spiritual loss that some critics associate with the modern condition in general.

Eliot sets the tone of Prufrock's monologue with a montage of powerfully compressed and gloomy images: "one-night cheap hotels," "sawdust restaurants," "soot that falls from chimneys," "narrow streets," "lonely men in shirtsleeves." Throughout the poem, he interweaves literary vignettes that illuminate Prufrock's bankrupt idealism. Prufrock's lack of heroic vision is underscored, for instance, by allusions to the biblical prophets and to the heroes of history and art, such as Michelangelo and Hamlet. Repeatedly, Prufrock laments his self-conscious retreat from action. Finally, in the last lines of the poem,

---

*T. S. Eliot, choruses from *The Rock* in *The Complete Poems and Plays 1909–1950*. New York: Harcourt, Brace and Company, 1952, 96.

he reflects on his loss of faith in the conventional sources of wisdom. He observes that the voices of inspiration have been submerged by all-too-human voices, including his own. The despairing final lines of the poem are Eliot's epitaph for the modern antihero.

READING 6.13 Eliot's "The Love Song of J. Alfred Prufrock" (1915)

S'io credesse che mia risposta fosse
A persona che mai tornasse al mondo,
Questa fiamma staria senza piu scosse.
Ma perciocche giammai di questo fondo
Non torno vivo alcun s'i'odo il vero,
Senza tema d'infamia ti rispondo.[1]

Let us go then, you and I,   1
When the evening is spread out against the sky
Like a patient etherised upon a table;
Let us go, through certain half-deserted streets,
The muttering retreats   5
Of restless nights in one-night cheap hotels
And sawdust restaurants with oyster-shells:
Streets that follow like a tedious argument
Of insidious intent
To lead you to an overwhelming question . . .   10
Oh, do not ask, "What is it?"
Let us go and make our visit.

In the room the women come and go
Talking of Michelangelo.

The yellow fog that rubs its back upon the window-panes,   15
The yellow smoke that rubs its muzzle on the window-panes
Licked its tongue into the corners of the evening,
Lingered upon the pools that stand in drains,
Let fall upon its back the soot that falls from chimneys,
Slipped by the terrace, made a sudden leap,   20
And seeing that it was a soft October night,
Curled once about the house, and fell asleep.

And indeed there will be time
For the yellow smoke that slides along the street,
Rubbing its back upon the window-panes;   25
There will be time, there will be time
To prepare a face to meet the faces that you meet;
There will be time to murder and create,
And time for all the works and days of hands[2]
That lift and drop a question on your plate;   30
Time for you and time for me,
And time yet for a hundred indecisions,
And for a hundred visions and revisions,
Before the taking of a toast and tea.

In the room the women come and go   35
Talking of Michelangelo.

And indeed there will be time
To wonder, "Do I dare?" and, "Do I dare?"
Time to turn back and descend the stair,
With a bald spot in the middle of my hair—   40
(They will say: "How his hair is growing thin!")
My morning coat, my collar mounting firmly to the chin,
My necktie rich and modest, but asserted by a simple pin—
(They will say: "But how his arms and legs are thin!")
Do I dare   45
Disturb the universe?
In a minute there is time
For decisions and revisions which a minute will reverse.

For I have known them all already, known them all—
Have known the evenings, mornings, afternoons,   50
I have measured out my life with coffee spoons;
I know the voices dying with a dying fall
Beneath the music from a farther room.
    So how should I presume?

And I have known the eyes already, known them all—   55
The eyes that fix you in a formulated phrase,
And when I am formulated, sprawling on a pin,
When I am pinned and wriggling on the wall,
Then how should I begin
To spit out all the butt-ends of my days and ways?   60
    And how should I presume?

And I have known the arms already, known them all—
Arms that are braceleted and white and bare
(But in the lamplight, downed with light brown hair!)
Is it perfume from a dress   65
That makes me so digress?
Arms that lie along a table, or wrap about a shawl.
    And should I then presume?
    And how should I begin?

. . . .

Shall I say, I have gone at dusk through narrow streets   70
And watched the smoke that rises from the pipes
Of lonely men in shirt-sleeves, leaning out of windows? . . .

I should have been a pair of ragged claws
Scuttling across the floors of silent seas.

. . . .

And the afternoon, the evening, sleeps so peacefully!   75
Smoothed by long fingers,
Asleep . . . tired . . . or it malingers,
Stretched on the floor, here beside you and me.
Should I, after tea and cakes and ices,
Have the strength to force the moment to its crisis?   80
But though I have wept and fasted, wept and prayed,
Though I have seen my head (grown slightly bald)
    brought in upon a platter,[3]

---

[1]Lines from Dante's "Inferno," Canto 27, 61–66, spoken by Guido da Montefeltro, who was condemned to Hell for the sin of false counseling. In explaining his punishment to Dante, Guido is still apprehensive of the judgment of society.

[2]An ironic allusion to the poem "Works and Days" by the eighth-century B.C.E. poet Hesiod, which celebrates the virtues of hard labor on the land.

[3]A reference to John the Baptist, who was beheaded by Herod (Matthew 14.3–11). Prufrock perceives himself as victim but as neither saint nor martyr.

I am no prophet—and here's no great matter;[3]
I have seen the moment of my greatness flicker,
And I have seen the eternal Footman hold my coat, and
  snicker,   85
And in short, I was afraid.

  And would it have been worth it, after all,
After the cups, the marmalade, the tea,
Among the porcelain, among some talk of you and me,
Would it have been worth while,   90
To have bitten off the matter with a smile,
To have squeezed the universe into a ball[4]
To roll it toward some overwhelming question,
To say: "I am Lazarus, come from the dead,[5]
Come back to tell you all, I shall tell you all"—   95
If one, settling a pillow by her head,
    Should say: "That is not what I meant at all,
    That is not it, at all."

              . . . .

  And would it have been worth it, after all,
Would it have been worth while,   100
After the sunsets and the dooryards and the sprinkled streets,
After the novels, after the teacups, after the skirts that
  trail along the floor—
And this, and so much more?—
It is impossible to say just what I mean!
But as if a magic lantern threw the nerves in patterns on
  a screen: 105
Would it have been worth while
If one, settling a pillow or throwing off a shawl,
And turning towards the window, should say:
    "That is not it at all,
    That is not what I meant, at all."   110

              . . . .

  No! I am not Prince Hamlet, nor was meant to be;
Am an attendant lord, one that will do
To swell a progress, start a scene or two,
Advise the prince; no doubt, an easy tool,[6]
Deferential, glad to be of use,   115
Politic, cautious, and meticulous;
Full of high sentence, but a bit obtuse;
At times, indeed, almost ridiculous—
Almost, at times, the Fool.

    I grow old . . . I grow old . . .   120
I shall wear the bottoms of my trousers rolled.[7]

    Shall I part my hair behind? Do I dare to eat a peach?
I shall wear white flannel trousers, and walk upon the beach.
I have heard the mermaids singing, each to each.

---

[4]A reference to the line "Let us roll all our strength and all our
sweetness up into one ball," from the poem "To his Coy Mistress," by
the seventeenth-century English poet Andrew Marvell, in which
Marvell presses his lover to "seize the day."
[5]According to the Gospel of John (11.1–44), Jesus raised Lazarus from
the grave.
[6]A reference to Polonius, the king's adviser in Shakespeare's *Hamlet*, as
well as to Guido da Montefeltro—both of them false counselors.
[7]In Eliot's time, rolled or cuffed trousers were considered fashionable.

I do not think that they will sing to me.   125
I have seen them riding seaward on the waves
Combing the white hair of the waves blown back
When the wind blows the water white and black.

We have lingered in the chambers of the sea
By sea-girls wreathed with seaweed red and brown   130
Till human voices wake us, and we drown.

Dylan Thomas

The moral inertia that afflicted Eliot's Prufrock was not
shared by the poet Dylan Thomas (1914–1953), who proclaimed himself a Welshman first and a drunkard second.
One of the twentieth century's most powerful wordsmiths,
Thomas took an exuberant approach to the modern condition. His poem "Do Not Go Gentle Into That Good
Night," published just after the death of his father in 1951,
makes a plea for life-affirming action even in the face of
death. Thomas creates a musical litany with the phrases
"wise men," "good men," "wild men," "grave men"—
resolving four of the six stanzas with the imperative: "rage
against the dying of the light." The reference to those
"who see with blinding sight" was probably inspired by the
loss of vision that the poet's schoolteacher father suffered
during his last years of life, but it also may be taken as an
allusion to his father's agnosticism, that is, to his spiritual
blindness—and, more generally, to the mood of alienation
afflicting a generation of modern disbelievers. In 1954,
Igor Stravinsky used this poem as the basis for *In
Memoriam Dylan Thomas*, a piece written for tenor, string
orchestra, and two trombones.

READING 6.14 Thomas' "Do Not Go Gentle Into That Good Night" (1951)

Do not go gentle into that good night,   1
Old age should burn and rave at close of day;
Rage, rage against the dying of the light.

Though wise men at their end know dark is right,
Because their words had forked no lightning they   5
Do not go gentle into that good night.

Good men, the last wave by, crying how bright
Their frail deeds might have danced in a green bay,
Rage, rage against the dying of the light.

Wild men who caught and sang the sun in flight,   10
And learn, too late, they grieved it on its way,
Do not go gentle into that good night.

Grave men, near death, who see with blinding sight
Blind eyes could blaze like meteors and be gay,
Rage, rage against the dying of the light.   15

And you, my father, there on the sad height,
Curse, bless, me now with your fierce tears, I pray.
Do not go gentle into that good night.
Rage, rage against the dying of the light.

Rabindranath Tagore

T. S. Eliot's Asian contemporary Rabindranath Tagore (1861–1941) shared Eliot's perception of a world in spiritual deterioration. For Tagore, the crisis of modern society lay in a set of misplaced values that prized the rush of business and the acquisition of material comforts at the expense of beauty, creativity, and spiritual harmony. Born in Bengal (while the province was still under British control), Tagore was raised in a family of artists, musicians, and social reformers. After a brief stay in England, he returned to India, where he became a prolific writer, publishing some sixty volumes of poetry, plays, stories, and novels. In India, Tagore pursued his ambition to foster a "spiritual unity of all races" by founding an international educational institute for the exchange of ideas between Western scholars and Indian students. Awarded the Nobel Prize for literature in 1913, Tagore left a body of writings that offers an Eastern, and specifically Hindu, approach to the modern quest for meaning. In his provocative allegory, "The Man Had No Useful Work," Tagore deals gently with the existential responsibility for individual choice. The narrative poem questions the value of the practical, goal-oriented pursuits that drive most modern societies. It also plays on the ironic truth that works of art may be both meaningless and essential.

READING 6.15   Tagore's "The Man Had No Useful Work" (1921)

The man had no useful work, only vagaries of various kinds.   1
Therefore it surprised him to find himself in Paradise after a
   life spent perfecting trifles.
Now the guide had taken him by mistake to the wrong
   Paradise—one meant only for good, busy souls.

In this Paradise, our man saunters along the road only to
   obstruct the rush of business.
He stands aside from the path and is warned that he tramples
   on sown seed. Pushed, he starts up: hustled, he moves on.   5
A very busy girl comes to fetch water from the well. Her feet
   run on the pavement like rapid fingers over harp-strings.
   Hastily she ties a negligent knot with her hair, and loose
   locks on her forehead pry into the dark of her eyes.
The man says to her, "Would you lend me your pitcher?"
"My pitcher?" she asks, "to draw water?"
"No, to paint patterns on."
"I have no time to waste," the girl retorts in contempt.   10

Now a busy soul has no chance against one who is supremely
   idle.
Every day she meets him at the well, and every day he repeats
   the same request, till at last she yields.
Our man paints the pitcher with curious colors in a mysterious
   maze of lines.
The girl takes it up, turns it round and asks, "What does it
   mean?"
"It has no meaning," he answers.   15

The girl carries the pitcher home. She holds it up in different
   lights and tries to con its mystery.

At night she leaves her bed, lights a lamp, and gazes at it from
   all points of view.
This is the first time she has met with something without
   meaning.

On the next day the man is again near the well.
The girl asks, "What do you want?"   20
"To do more work for you!"
"What work?" she enquires.
"Allow me to weave colored strands into a ribbon to bind your
   hair."
"Is there any need?" she asks.
"None whatever," he allows.   25
The ribbon is made, and thenceforward she spends a great
   deal of time over her hair.

The even stretch of well-employed time in that Paradise
   begins to show irregular rents.
The elders are troubled; they meet in council.
The guide confesses his blunder, saying that he has brought
   the wrong man to the wrong place.
The wrong man is called. His turban, flaming with color,
   shows plainly how great that blunder has been.   30
The chief of the elders says, "You must go back to the earth."
The man heaves a sigh of relief: "I am ready."
The girl with the ribbon round her hair chimes in: "I also!"
For the first time the chief of the elders is faced with a
   situation which has no sense in it.

Islamic Poetry

In the Muslim world, where Western technology and Western imperialism have weighed heavily in the transition from ancient to modern ways, Islamic culture and religious devotion have not only endured, but flourished. In spite of political and social challenges to traditional belief and practice, Islam has become the world's fastest growing faith, a response perhaps to the vigorous pan-Islamic movement that began in the late nineteenth century. Postwar Islamic literature (written in Arabic, Persian, English, and other languages) tends to be inspired by spiritual rather than nationalist ideals. Modern Islamic poetry, much of which remains untranslated, departs considerably from its ancient forms; but the rich harvest of twentieth-century Islamic poets suggests the beginnings of a new literary golden age.

Muhammad Iqbal (1875–1938), who died before the outbreak of World War II, is regarded as the most eminent writer of Muslim India. Like Tagore, Iqbal studied law and philosophy in Europe, then returned to his native India to make a lasting mark in literature. His prose and poetry are written in Urdu (the language of present-day Pakistan), Persian, and English. In tracts that reflect his close study of both Muslim and European thought, Iqbal championed the civilizing role of Islam in modern life. He urged the formation of an independent Muslim state in Hindu India, but emphasized the importance of achieving brotherhood among India's Muslim, Christian, and Hindu populations. While he defended the centrality of Islamic law in the Muslim community, he envisioned an ideal community that transcended ethnic, racial, and national loyalties. The poet-philosopher urged his readers to replace the mystical ideals of passive contemplation and withdrawal with a modern doctrine of choice and action that might make Islam the leading moral force in South Asia. Deeply critical of injustice, godlessness, and false ideals—all of which he equated with a failing Western morality—he infused the pan-Islamic ideals of early modernism with new fervor. In the two poems represented below, Iqbal gives voice to the despair felt by Muslims worldwide, who view nationalism and modernism as twin threats to spirituality and holy law.

Indonesia, whose majority population is Muslim, produced its greatest poet, Chairil Anwar (1922–1949), in the first half of the twentieth century. Anwar was greatly influenced by Western literature and the modern taste for colloquial verse. "At the Mosque," one of seventy poems written during the course of his twenty-six years, reflects his personal struggle to maintain an intimate relationship with God in the face of doubt and despair.

READING 6.16   Islamic Poems

Iqbal's "Revolution" (1938)

Death to man's soul is Europe, death is Asia
To man's will: neither feels the vital current.
In man's hearts stirs a revolution's torrent;
Maybe our old world too is nearing death.

Iqbal's "Europe and Syria" (1936)

This land of Syria gave the West a Prophet
Of purity and pity and innocence;
And Syria from the West as recompense
Gets dice and drink and troops of prostitutes.

Anwar's "At the Mosque" (1943)

I shouted at Him   1
Until He came.

We met face to face.

Afterwards He burned in my breast.
All my strength struggles to extinguish Him.   5
My body, which won't be driven, is soaked with sweat.

This room
Is the arena where we fight,

Destroying each other,
One hurling insults, the other gone mad.   10

FILM AT MID-CENTURY

In the postwar era, filmmakers took a number of new directions. In Italy, the *neorealism* of Roberto Rossellini (1906–1977) probed the bitter consequences of fascism. With the film *Open City* (1945), Rossellini replaced the cinema of entertainment with a brutal new genre that chronicled human tragedies as if they were natural disasters. Exploiting the commonplace in both style and substance, Rossellini employed non-professional actors and filmed entirely on location. Neorealist cinema self-consciously rejected the artifice of cinematic moralizing and Hollywood "staging," seeking instead to depict the harsh realities of commonplace existence.

A second direction in postwar film appeared in the form of *film noir*, a cinematic style (especially popular in Germany, France, and America) that dealt with the dark world of crime and intrigue. Unlike the gangster movies of the 1930s, *film noir* conveyed a mood of disillusion and resignation proceeding from moral ambiguities between good and evil. In the American film *Double Indemnity* (1944), the *femme fatale* (the dangerous, seductive woman) made one of her earliest cinematic appearances. And in the *film noir* classic, *A Touch of Evil* (1958), the multitalented director and actor Orson Welles (1915–1985) used long takes (shots of twenty or more seconds), high and low camera positions, and off-center compositions that worked to create sinister characters and ominous settings.

A third film genre, the *thriller*, dominated by the impresario Alfred Hitchcock (1899–1980), depended on suspense rather than graphic violence for its impact. Hitchcock's unique combination of story and style—quick shots that alternate between the character and the (often fearful) object of their gaze—were particularly successful in such films as *Rear Window* (1954) and *Psycho* (1960).

Postwar cinema took up the quest for meaning by way of films that questioned traditional, moral values. The pioneer Japanese filmmaker Akira Kurosawa (1910–1998) explored the complexities of modern life by way of traditional *samurai* legends. A highly skilled director, Kurosawa used unusual camera angles, flashbacks, and a stringent economy of expression in the classic films *Rashō mon* (1950) and *The Seven Samurai* (1954). These films convey Kurosawa's view that positive social action can redeem the world's evils. Less optimistic are the films of the Swedish cinematic giant Ingmar Bergman (b. 1918). In his almost four dozen films, Bergman probed the troubled lives of modern men and women. The loss of God, the acknowledgment of spiritual and emotional alienation, and the anxieties that accompany self-understanding are the principal themes of his films, the most notable of which are *The Seventh Seal* (1956), *Wild Strawberries* (1957), and *Persona* (1966). Bergman's cinematic triumph *The Seventh Seal* is an allegorical tale of despair in the face of impending death. Set in medieval Europe (and inspired by the Revelation of Saint John), it is the story of a medieval knight who returns from the Crusades, only to confront widespread plague and human suffering at home. The disillusioned knight ultimately challenges Death to a game of chess, the stakes of which are life itself. Bergman compared filmmaking to composing music: a non-narrative and largely intuitive enterprise. His apocalyptic visions, translated to film, proceeded from what he called "the administration of the unspeakable."

The Visual Arts at Mid-Century

Painting

During the first half of the century, almost all important new styles in painting had originated in Paris or other European cities. After 1945, however, the United States, and New York City in particular, took the lead in the production of a radical new art style called *abstract expressionism*. Abstract expressionism had its roots in the modern artist's assault on traditional, representational art. It took inspiration from the reductionist abstractions of Picasso and Matisse, the colorist experiments of Wassily Kandinsky, the random performances of dada, and the "automatic" art of the surrealists. At the same time, it reflected new evidence concerning the role of choice and chance in the operation of the physical universe: By mid-century, research in particle physics confirmed the theory that quantum reality consists of random patterns that evolve in a process of continuous change. Whether or not such theories directly influenced the visual arts, they paralleled the experiments in random art that occurred at this time in more than one part of the world. In postwar

Figure 35.1 WILLEM DE KOONING, *Woman and Bicycle*, 1952–1953. Oil on canvas, 6 ft. 4½ in. × 4 ft. 1 in. Whitney Museum of American Art, New York. Purchase 55.35. Photograph: Geoffrey Clements © 1998 Whitney Museum of American Art, New York. © Willem de Kooning Revocable Trust/ARS, New York and DACS, London 2000.

Figure 35.2 TOREI ENJI, *Calligraphic Talisman*, late eighteenth century. Sumi on paper, 50¾ × 10⅞ in. Gitter-Yelen Collection, New Orleans.

Japan, members of the radical group known as the Gutai Bijutsu Kyokai (Concrete Art Association) harnessed physical action to chance in dynamic performance-centered works. Gutai "action events," which featured the energetic and sometimes outrageous manipulation of paint (flung or hurled at the canvas), allied the random techniques of surrealism to native Japanese traditions in spontaneous, gestural Zen painting (see Figure 35.2).

In America, abstract expressionism ushered in the so-called "heroic age of American painting." The pioneers of the movement were a group of talented immigrants who had escaped Nazi oppression and the perils of war-torn Europe. These artists included Arshile Gorky (1905–1948), Hans Hofmann (1880–1966), and Willem de Kooning (1904–1997), all of whom migrated to New York between 1920 and 1930. Working on large canvases and using oversized brushes, Gorky, Hofmann, and de Kooning applied paint in a loose, free, and instinctive manner that emphasized the physical gesture—the *act* of painting. Abstract expressionist paintings were usually nonrepresen-

tational, but where recognizable subject matter appeared, as in de Kooning's series of fierce, totemic women—one of his favorite subjects—it was rendered with frenzied, subjective urgency (Figure **35.1**). De Kooning's wide-eyed females, taken by some to suggest the artist's negative view of women, were actually inspired by Sumerian votive sculptures and Earth Mother fetishes (see chapter 2). By contrast, the huge black-and-white canvases of Franz Kline (1910–1962) consist entirely of imposing, abstract shapes. Though wholly nonrepresentational, they call to mind the powerful angularity of bridges, steel mills, and other monuments of postwar urban expansion (Figure **35.3**). Kline, who used housepainters' brushes on canvases that often measured over 10 feet square, achieved a sense of rugged immediacy (which he called "snap") and a balance between improvisation and control similar to that found in the calligraphy of Zen masters (Figure **35.2**).

The best known of the abstract expressionists was Wyoming-born Jackson Pollock (1912–1956). His early paintings reveal a coarse figural style and brutal brushwork similar to de Kooning's, but, by 1945, Pollock had devised a technique that made action itself the subject of the painting. Instead of mounting the canvas on an easel, he strapped it on the floor of his studio and proceeded to drip, splash, pour, and spread oil, enamel, and commercial

Figure 35.3 FRANZ KLINE, *Mahoning*, 1956. Oil and paper collage on canvas, 6 ft. 8 in. × 8 ft. 4 in. Collection of Whitney Museum of American Art, New York. Purchase, with funds from the Friends of the Whitney Museum of American Art. Photograph © 1994 Geoffrey Clements, New York. © ARS, NY and DACS, London 2000.

aluminum paints across its surface (Figure **35.4**). Layered filaments of paint—the artist's seductive "handwriting"—mingled with sand, nails, matches, bottle shards, and occasional cigarette butts. This daring, allover technique enabled Pollock (as he explained) "to walk around [the canvas], work from the four sides and literally be *in* the painting," a method inspired by the healing rituals of Navaho sand painting whose union of intuition, improvisation, and rigorous control he admired. "It seems to me," observed Pollock, "that the modern painter cannot express his age, the airplane, the atom bomb, the radio, in the old forms of the Renaissance or of any other past culture. Each age finds its own technique." Pollock's *action paintings* may strike us as baffling studies in sensation, density, and rhythm (Figure **35.5**), but they are apt metaphors for an age that defined physical reality in terms of process, uncertainty, and molecular energy. Like the currents in some cosmic whirlpool, Pollock's galactic threads seem to expand beyond the limits of the canvas, as if to mirror postwar theories of quantum forces in an expanding universe. In fact, Pollock's compositions anticipated the photographs of outer space taken in 1995 by the Hubble Space Telescope. Pollock viewed each of his works of art as having "a life of its own," but he insisted that *he* controlled its direction: "There is no accident, just as there is no beginning and no end."

While Pollock pioneered action painting, other mid-century artists explored *color field painting*, a type of total abstraction that involved the application of large, often transparent layers of paint to the surface of the canvas.

Figure 35.4 Jackson Pollock at work in his Long Island studio, 1950. Photo: © Hans Namuth, New York, 1983.

Figure 35.5 JACKSON POLLOCK, *Convergence*, 1952. Oil on canvas, 8 × 13 ft. Albright-Knox Art Gallery, Buffalo, New York. Gift of Seymour H. Knox, 1956. © ARS, New York and DACS, London 2000.

compositions, often heroic in scale, capture the transparent freshness of watercolors.

In a culture increasingly dominated by mass mechanization, abstract expressionists asserted their preference for an art of spontaneous action. They sought a balance between choice and chance that obeyed the existential credo of self-actualization. They elevated the *process* of making art to a status that was almost as important as the *product*. As the movement developed, the size of the canvas expanded as if to accommodate the heroic ambitions of the artists themselves. Abstract expressionists seemed to turn their backs on bourgeois taste by creating artworks that were simply too large to hang in the average living room. Ironically, however, this style, which opposed the depersonalizing effects of capitalist technology, came to be prized by the guardians of that technology. Abstract expressionist paintings, which now hang in large numbers of corporate offices and banks, have become hallmarks of modern sophistication.

The abstract expressionists represented a decisive break with the realist tradition in American painting and with social realism in particular. Nevertheless, throughout the century, representational art continued to flourish, especially among the regionalists, that is, artists associated

Figure 35.6 (left) **MARK ROTHKO**, *Untitled*, 1960. Oil on canvas, 5 ft. 9 in. × 4 ft. 2⅛ in. San Francisco Museum of Modern Art. Acquired through a gift of Peggy Guggenheim. © Kate Rothko Prizel and Christopher Rothko/DACS 2000.

Figure 35.7 (below) **HELEN FRANKENTHALER**, *Before the Canes*, 1958. Oil on canvas, 8 ft. 6 ⅛ in. x 8 ft. 8 ⅜ in. University Art Museum, University of California, Berkeley, California.

The canvases of Mark Rothko (1903–1970) consist of translucent, soft-edged blocks of color that float mysteriously on the surfaces of yet other fields of color (Figure **35.6**). Rothko's huge, sensuous compositions derive their power from the subtle interaction of rich colors, which seem to glow from within; but they are not mere studies in color relationships. Rothko himself insisted that his subject matter was "tragedy, ecstasy, and doom," states of mind that are best appreciated by close—18 inches, advised the artist—contemplation of the luminous originals, whose subtlety is lost in photographic reproduction. "The people who weep before my pictures are having the same religious experience I had when I painted them," he contended; "and if you . . . are moved only by their color relationships, then you miss the point." Rothko took his own life in 1970.

While Rothko's abstract shapes are usually self-contained, those of Helen Frankenthaler (b. 1928) tend to swell and expand like exotic blooms (Figure **35.7**). Frankenthaler cultivated the practice of pouring thin washes of paint directly from coffee tins onto raw or **unprimed** (without gesso undercoat) canvas. Her lyrical

Figure 35.8 **EDWARD HOPPER**, *Nighthawks*, 1942. Oil on canvas, 33⅛ × 60⅛ in. Art Institute of Chicago. Chicago Friends of American Art Collection, 1942.51.

Figure 35.9 **FRANCIS BACON**, *Study after Velázquez's Portrait of Pope Innocent X*, 1953. Oil on canvas, 5 ft. ¼ in. x 3 ft. 10 ½ in. Des Moines Art Center (Nathan Emory Coffin Collection, purchased with funds from the Coffin Fine Arts Trust). Photo: © Michael Tropea, Chicago. © Estate of Francis Bacon/ARS, NY and DACS, London 2000.

with specific geographic locations. The paintings of the New York artist Edward Hopper (1882–1967), for instance, present a figurative view of an urban America that is bleak and empty of meaningful relationships. Hopper's fondness for American cinema and theater is reflected in his oddly cropped, artificially lit compositions that often resemble film stills. Like the film still, Hopper's frozen moments seems to belong to a larger narrative. In *Nighthawks* (Figure **35.8**), Hopper depicts a harshly lit all-night diner, whose occupants share a small space but little intimacy. His characters, estranged and isolated in the mundane interiors of "one-night cheap hotels" and "saw-dust restaurants," call to mind Eliot's Prufrock.

Across the Atlantic, the major figure in postwar European art was the Dublin-born painter Francis Bacon (1909–1992). Self-trained, Bacon infused European expressionism with an eccentric approach to form that turned human and animal figures into flayed carcasses and mangled skeletons. Like a sorcerer, he transformed his favorite images from film, magazine illustrations, and the history of art into grotesque and deformed (but sensuously painted) icons. Bacon's resurrection of Diego Velázquez's famous *Portrait of Pope Innocent X* (1650), for example, stands as a visceral statement of alienation and anguish (Figure **35.9**). Here, as in many of Bacon's compositions, the figure is imprisoned in a transparent cage and immobilized by ambiguous lines of force—an effect that may have been inspired by Bacon's fascination with x-ray imagery. The venerable pope's raging, silent scream, a logo for despiritualized modernism, looks back to Munch, Eisenstein, and Picasso, all of whom Bacon admired.

Figure 35.10 ALBERTO GIACOMETTI, *City Square (La Place)*, 1948. Bronze, 8½ × 25⅜ × 17¼ in. The Museum of Modern Art, New York. Purchase. Photograph © 2000 The Museum of Modern Art, New York. © ADAGP, Paris and DACS, London 2000.

Sculpture

The mood of existential anxiety also dominated international sculpture. What the art critic Herbert Read called a "geometry of fear" was evident in both the figurative and the nonfigurative sculpture of the Swiss artist Alberto Giacometti (1901–1966). In 1930 Giacometti came under the influence of surrealism, but in the postwar era he devised a new language with which to describe the human figure and the human condition. In both small and large clay works, thereafter cast in bronze, he transformed his subjects into haunting, spindly creatures that seem to symbolize the existential solitude of the individual amidst the modern metropolis (Figure **35.10**). Giacometti's disengaged and ravaged figures were greatly admired by Sartre, who wrote the introduction to the catalogue for the artist's one-man exhibition in New York City in 1948. The artist's ties to existentialist writers secured his commission to design the set for the original production of Beckett's *Waiting for Godot*.

In America, the haunting works of George Segal (1924–2000) captured the modern mood of alienation. Segal devised a unique method of constructing life-sized figures from plaster casts of live models, often members of his own family and friends. He installed these ghostly replicas in ordinary settings staged with uncast props: bar stools, streetlights, beds, bus seats (Figure **35.11**). These "assembled environments," as he called them, allowed Segal to comment—in the course of his career—on matters of alienation, social injustice, and the failure of communication in modern life. Stylistically, Segal's tableaux linked the tradition of realist sculpture to the pop and performance art movements of the later twentieth century (see chapter 38).

Figure 35.11 GEORGE SEGAL, *Bus Riders*, 1962. Plaster, cottongauze, steel, wood, and vinyl, 5 ft. 10 in. × 3 ft. 6⅜ in. × 7 ft. 6¾ in. Hirshhorn Museum and Sculpture Garden, Smithsonian Institution, Washington, D.C. Gift of Joseph H. Hirshhorn, 1966. Photo: Lee Stalsworth. © George Segal/DACS, London/VAGA, New York 2000.

The nonfigurative sculpture of the postwar era shared the vitality and subjectivity of abstract expressionist painting. American sculptors, exploiting such industrial materials as welded iron and steel, constructed abstract objects that were monumental in size and dynamic in spirit. Among the pioneers in the domain of *constructed sculpture* was the American artist David Smith (1906–1965). Smith learned to weld in an automobile plant and became familiar with a variety of other industrial processes while working in a wartime locomotive factory. His early pieces were large, welded iron forms sprayed with multiple layers of automobile enamel. During the 1950s, he began to construct box-like stainless steel forms whose surfaces he burnished and scraped with motorized tools so that they reflected the colors of their surroundings (Figure **35.12**). Smith forged a new structural language based on industrial techniques. His heroic forms share the calligraphic energy of Franz Kline's gestural abstractions: They capture a sense of aggressive movement, even as they animate the space around them. While the art of Giacometti and Segal evokes a mood of existential despair, Smith's style symbolizes the optimistic spirit of postwar America.

The American sculptor Alexander Calder (1898–1976) was a contemporary of the surrealists, whom he met in Paris in 1926. Influenced by the work of Duchamp and Miró, Calder created whimsical wire constructions, which he motorized or hung from ceilings so that they floated freely in the air. Calder's wind-driven mobiles, which range from a few feet in size to enormous proportions, take advantage of the "chance" effects of air currents to create constantly changing relationships between volumes and voids, that is, between brightly colored, biomorphic aluminum shapes and the surrounding space (Figure **35.13**).

Figure 35.12 (labove) **DAVID SMITH**, *Cubi XIX*, 1964. Stainless steel, 113⅛ × 21¾ × 20¾ in. Krauss #667. Collection, The Tate Gallery, London. Photo: David Smith. © Estate of David Smith/DACS, London/ VAGA, New York 2000.

Figure 35.13 (right) **ALEXANDER CALDER**, *Big Red*, 1959. Sheet metal and steel wire, 6 ft. 2 in. × 9 ft. 6 in. Collection of Whitney Museum of American Art, New York. Purchase, with funds from the Friends of the Whitney Museum of American Art, and exchange. 61.46. Photograph copyright © 2000 Whitney Museum of American Art. Photograph by Geoffrey Clements, New York. © ADAGP, Paris and DACS, London 2000.

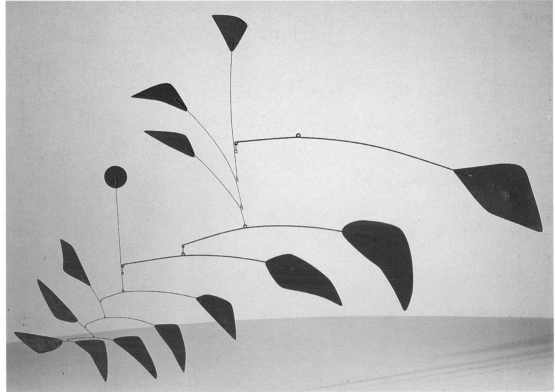

Figure 35.14 **IRWIN CHANIN** and **GILMORE CLARKE**, Stuyvesant Town and Peter Cooper Village, New York, 1947. Photo: © The Bettmann Archive, New York.

Architecture at Mid-Century

By the middle of the twentieth century public architecture assumed a distinctly international character. The principles of international style architecture, based on the use of structural steel, ferroconcrete, and glass, had gained popularity through the influence of Bauhaus-trained architects and Le Corbusier (see chapter 32). Standardization and machinelike efficiency became the hallmarks of high-rise urban apartment buildings, constructed in their thousands to provide low-rent housing in the decades after 1930 (Figure **35.14**). In the building of schools, factories, and offices, the simplicity and austerity of the international style echoed the mood of depersonalization that prevailed in the arts. International style skyscrapers became symbols of corporate wealth and modern technocracy. They reflected the ideals of the twentieth century as powerfully as the Gothic cathedral summed up the spirit of the High Middle Ages. Among the most daring of the international style proponents was the Dutch architect (and the last director of the Bauhaus) Ludwig Mies van der Rohe (1886–1969). Mies' credo "less is more" inspired austere structures such as the Seagram Building in New York City, designed in partnership with Philip Johnson (b. 1906) in 1958 (Figure **35.15**). This sleek, unadorned slab of metallic bronze and amber glass was "the last word" in sophisticated machine engineering and a monument to the "form follows function" mandate of the international style. The

Figure 35.15 (right) **LUDWIG MIES VAN DER ROHE**, Seagram Building, New York, 1954–1958. Metallic bronze and amber glass. Photo: Ezra Stoller/ © Esto. Courtesy Joseph E. Seagram & Sons, Inc. © DACS 2000.

Figure 35.16 EERO SAARINEN, Trans World Airlines Terminal, Kennedy Airport, New York, 1962. Photo: Balthazar Korab, Troy, Michigan.

proportions of the building are as impeccable as those of any classical structure: The raised level at the bottom is balanced at the top by a four-story band of darker glass. For decades, the Seagram Building influenced glass-and-steel-box architecture; unfortunately, in many of its imitators, it was the cool, impersonal quality of the building and not its poetic simplicity that prevailed.

At mid-century, some of the world's leading architects (including Le Corbusier, Frank Lloyd Wright, and the Finnish architect Eero Saarinen) reacted against the strict geometry and functional purism of international style architecture. Instead, they provided subjective, personal, and even romantic alternatives to the cool rationalism of the international style. Using the medium of cast concrete, they created organically shaped structures that were as gestural as the sculptures of Smith and as lyrical as the paintings of Frankenthaler. The Trans World Airlines Terminal at New York's Kennedy Airport (Figure **35.16**), for example, designed by Saarinen (1910–1961), is a metaphor for flight: Its cross-vaulted roof—a steel structure surfaced with concrete—flares upward like a gigantic bird. The interior of the terminal unfolds gradually and mysteriously to embrace fluid, uninterrupted space. Equally inventive in both design and function is Frank Lloyd Wright's Guggenheim Museum in Manhattan. Its interior, which resembles the inside of a huge snail shell, consists of a continuous spiral ramp fixed around an open, central well (Figure **35.17**). A clear glass dome at the top allows natural light to bathe interior space, whose breath-

taking enclosure competes seductively with almost any artwork exhibited therein. A ten-story limestone extension added in 1992 reduces the dramatic contrast between the rotunda and its urban setting, but it does not destroy the eloquence of the original design (Figure **35.18**). The Guggenheim remains the definitive example of the modern architectural imagination.

Music and Dance at Mid-Century

Many of the artworks discussed in this chapter reflect the modern artist's quest for a balance between freedom and control, and between meaninglessness and purposeful action. In the domain of music, the American writer/composer John Cage (1912–1992) epitomized that quest. Cage styled himself a student of architecture and gardening, and a devotee of Zen Buddhism; he was also a concert pianist and one of the most influential avant-garde composers of the twentieth century. A leading spokesperson for inventive creativity in modern music, Cage embraced chance and experimentation as fundamental to artistic expression. "Everything we do is music," argued Cage, whose dadaesque definition exalted music as a combination of sounds (specific pitches), noise (non-pitched sounds), and silence, with rhythm as the common denominator.

Cage's approach to music—like Pollock's to painting—made process and accident central to the work. In 1938 Cage invented the prepared piano, a traditional Steinway piano "prepared" by attaching to its strings

Figure 35.17 FRANK LLOYD WRIGHT, The Solomon R. Guggenheim Museum interior, 1957–1959.
Photo: Robert E. Mates/Courtesy of the Solomon R. Guggenheim Museum. © ARS, NY and DACS, London 2000.

Figure 35.18 FRANK LLOYD WRIGHT, The Solomon R. Guggenheim Museum, New York, 1957–1959.
Photo: David Heald/Courtesy of the Solomon R. Guggenheim Museum © ARS, NY and DACS, London 2000.

Figure 35.19 MERCE CUNNINGHAM, Set and costumes by Robert Rauschenberg, *Summerspace*, 1958. © Robert Rauschenberg/DACS, London and VAGA, New York 2000.

pieces of rubber, bamboo slats, bolts, and other objects. When played, the prepared piano becomes something like a percussion instrument, the sounds of which resemble those of a Balinese orchestra; as Cage observed, "a percussive orchestra under the control of a single player." Influenced by Schoenberg as well as by Asian music, Cage's early compositions—including his *Sonata V* ♪ (1948)—are delicate in timbre and texture and elegant in percussive rhythms. However, his later works were radically experimental, especially in their effort to accommodate silence and non-pitched sound. In 1953, Cage composed *4' 33"*, a piece in which a performer sits motionless before the piano for four minutes and thirty-three seconds. The "music" of *4' 33"* consists of the fleeting sounds that occur during the designated time period—the breathing of the pianist, the shuffling of the audience's feet, or, perhaps, the distant hum of traffic outside of the concert hall.

Like *4' 33"*, much of Cage's music is **aleatory**, that is, based on chance or random procedures. To determine the placement of notes in a musical composition, Cage might apply the numbers dictated in a throw of the dice or incorporate the surface stains and imperfections on an otherwise blank piece of sheet music. Cage found inspiration for random techniques in the *I Ching*, the ancient oracular Chinese *Book of Changes*, and in the psychic automatism of dada and surrealist art. These techniques are basic to Cage's *Music of Changes* (1951), written for piano, and to his *Imaginary Landscape No. 4* (1951), a composition that calls for twelve radios playing simultaneously with twenty-

four performers (two at each radio) randomly turning the volume and selector controls. Such antimusical music celebrates the absurd and random nature of the modern experience. At the same time, it tests the traditional relationship between composers and performers, and between artistic conception and execution. For despite the chance methods by which Cage arrives at making music, each of his compositions is fully scored; that is even the most unconventional passages follow Cage's explicit directions. Ultimately, Cage's "scored improvisations" embrace the existential notion that every creative act, and even the decision *not* to act, requires choice. The very decision in favor of chance engages the act of choosing and, further, of deciding whether to roll dice, toss coins, or employ some other random method.

Cage's ideas, as publicized in his numerous essays and lectures, had an enormous influence on younger artists. Indeed, his "chance" aesthetic inspired the international neo-dada movement known as *Fluxus*. Fluxus artists, writers, filmmakers, and musicians experimented with minimal, performance-oriented works that left the viewer to complete the work of art (see chapter 38). In the mid-1940s, Cage met the American choreographer Merce Cunningham (b. 1922) and the young painter Robert Rauschenberg (b. 1925). At Black Mountain College in North Carolina, they collaborated in staging performances that employed improvisational techniques. As the director of Cunningham's dance company (founded in 1953), Cage combined dance, mime, poetry, music, slide projections, and moving pictures in some of the first and most innovative mixed media performances of the century.

♪ See Music Listening Selection at end of chapter.

Cunningham's contribution to modern choreography was revolutionary. Rejecting the representational, story-telling dance style of his teacher, Martha Graham (see chapter 32), along with her use of the body to express psychological states, he concentrated exclusively on movement and form. Cunningham's choreography disavowed the traditional association between music and dance. In a Cunningham piece, music may coexist with dance, but its rhythms do not necessarily determine those of the dancers. Cunningham treats all body movements, even such ordinary ones as running, jumping, and falling, as equally important to dance. He may combine physical forces in ways that are unexpected or determined by chance. His technically rigorous choreography calls for clean, expansive body gestures that unfold in large, lateral spatial fields. Thus his compositions share the raw energy and spontaneity that characterize the canvases of the abstract expressionists. Just as Cunningham disclaims traditional dance positions, so he ignores traditional staging (whereby dancers are assigned to specific spaces). He creates a spatial continuum, which—like a Pollock painting or a Cage composition—lacks a fixed center. In *Summerspace* (1958), for instance, for which Rauschenberg designed the sets and costumes, dancers travel confidently in different directions, often overlapping in space (Figure **35.19**). Cunningham explores the tensions between chance and choice and between freedom and control that lie at the heart of existential expression.

SUMMARY

Alienation and anxiety were the two principal conditions of the postwar mentality. Pessimists feared the destructive potential of modern technology and anticipated the demise of human freedom. Philosophers and poets lamented the death of God. Existentialism, a humanistic philosophy formulated by Jean-Paul Sartre, emphasized the role of individual choice in a world that lacked moral absolutes. Both secular and Christian existentialism charged human beings with full responsibility for their freely chosen actions.

Twentieth-century writers gave serious attention to the existential condition and to the anguish produced by the freedom to choose. Modern antiheroes—Eliot's Prufrock and the burlesque tramps in Beckett's *Waiting for Godot*—all contend with the despair of making choices in an essentially meaningless universe. Their survival seems to depend only upon an authentic commitment to action. The voices of Asian writers such as Tagore, Iqbal, and Anwar pursue the quest for meaning in parts of the world where modernism does as much to threaten as to reshape tradition.

In the visual arts, the movement known as abstract expressionism reflects an heroic effort at self-actualization through the gestural and often brutal application of paint to canvas. The action paintings of Pollock, the color field paintings of Frankenthaler, and the constructions of David Smith and Alexander Calder explore the dynamic balance between chance and choice. While these artists work in an abstract mode, others, such as Hopper, Giacometti, Segal, and Bacon, employ representational means of exploring the modern condition of alienation. At mid-century, the international style culminated in classic glass-box skyscrapers and spawned thousands of soulless imitations that reinforced the cold, impersonal nature of the modern urban community. However, a new wave of ferroconcrete architecture, as exemplified in Wright's Guggenheim Museum, challenged the austerity of the international style.

In the domains of music and dance, as in the visual arts, the postwar generation took the absence of absolutes as the starting point for free experimentation. John Cage, the foremost member of the musical avant-garde, explored the possibilities of silence, noise, and chance operations. Merce Cunningham redefined modern dance as movement stripped of thematic and musical associations. While the mood of alienation and anxiety pervaded the postwar decades, artists struggled to sustain their faith in the human capacity for choice, and their hope that, as William Faulkner asserted in his Nobel Prize Address of 1950, "[Man] is immortal, not because he alone among creatures has an inexhaustible voice, but because he has a soul, a spirit of compassion and sacrifice and endurance."

GLOSSARY

aleatory (Latin, *alea,* "dice") any kind of music composed according to chance or random procedures

unprimed lacking the gesso undercoat normally applied to the surface of the canvas

SUGGESTIONS FOR READING

Belgrad, Daniel. *The Culture of Spontaneity: Improvisation and the Arts in Postwar America.* Chicago: University of Chicago Press, 1998.

Doss, Erika. *Benton, Pollock, and the Politics of Modernism: From Regionalism to Abstract Expressionism.* Chicago: University of Chicago Press, 1991.

Jowett, Deborah. *Time and the Dancing Image.* New York: William Morrow, 1990.

Marcuse, Herbert. *One Dimensional Man: Studies in the Ideology of Advanced Industrial Society.* Boston: Beacon Press, 1964.

Policari, Stephen. *Abstract Expressionism and the Modern Experience.* New York: Cambridge University Press, 1991.

Roose-Evans, James. *Experimental Theatre: From Stanislavsky to Peter Brook.* New York: Routledge1996.

Rosenthal, Mark. *Abstraction in the Twentieth Century: Total Risk, Freedom, Discipline.* New York: Abrams, 1996.

Stromberg, Roland N. *After Everything: Western Intellectual History Since 1945.* New York: St. Martin's Press, 1975.

Tomkins, Calvin. *The Bride and the Bachelors: Five Masters of the Avant-Garde.* New York: Viking, 1968.

MUSIC LISTENING SELECTION

CD Two Selection 20   Cage, *Sonata V,* 1948, excerpt.

PART TWO

The postmodern turn

The "postmodern turn" describes a constellation of significant changes in all aspects of the global community. During the postwar era, the nations of the world came to be classified according to their level of economic prosperity: The industrialized capitalistic nations, including the United States, most of Western Europe, Japan, and Canada, constituted the "First World." The less industrialized socialist states of the Soviet Union and Eastern Europe made up the "Second World"; the rest—over one hundred nations located primarily in Africa, Asia, and Latin America—were the poor or emerging nations of the "Third World." At mid-century, nations were polarized ideologically between the forces of democratic capitalism and Soviet-style communism. Intense competition for world supremacy in political and military affairs marked the Cold War, a rivalry dominated by the two superpowers, the United States and the Soviet Union. Although internal strife, civil wars within colonial territories, and changing political and economic relationships between and within nations prompted the intervention of First World powers, total war gave way to local and regional conflicts.

Since mid-century, colonial states throughout the world have claimed independence from imperial control; ethnic and racial minorities, and other disenfranchised or oppressed groups, have launched impassioned quests for equality and identity. Ongoing rivalries between religious groups in the Middle East (and elsewhere) and Third World poverty and instability continue to threaten world peace. Nevertheless, the late twentieth century was an era of population growth, urbanization, expanding materialism, and progress toward political, economic, and social equality. At the close of the century, a higher quality of life and a more egalitarian social structure prevailed in more parts of the global village than ever before in history. The dismantling of the Berlin Wall (1989) and the collapse of Soviet communism (1991)—events that marked the end of the Cold War—fed rising expectations for the future of democracy worldwide and for a new spirit of cooperation between the superpowers.

With regard to the arts and ideas, the postmodern turn involved a shift away from modernism, or what the critic Robert Hughes has called "the Messianic era of modernism," and modernism's faith in a new world order. Modernist utopianism, the existential ideal of responsible action, and the heroic celebration of freedom that infused the arts at mid-century have largely disappeared. They have given way to more skeptical claims for human progress—claims shaped by a knowing and often cynical view of the historical past. Some theorists date the end of modernism from the decade of the Holocaust—an episode they perceive as the crime that refuted modernism's utopian agenda. Others identify the new age with a shift in modern morality (linked to the discovery of effective birth control); while still others perceive postmodernism as a product of the information age, an age of high-speed developments in mass communication (television and computers), molecular physics, space exploration, and biotechnology, all of which have extended human knowledge and power beyond that of any previous era. At the onset of a new millennium, globalism—an outlook that is worldwide in scope—reflects the increasing interdependence between all parts of the earth. An integrating force, globalism inspires the arts of a media-shaped world culture.

(opposite) **FRANK GEHRY**, Guggenheim Museum, Bilbao. 1997. Commissioned by the Solomon R.Guggenheim Foundation

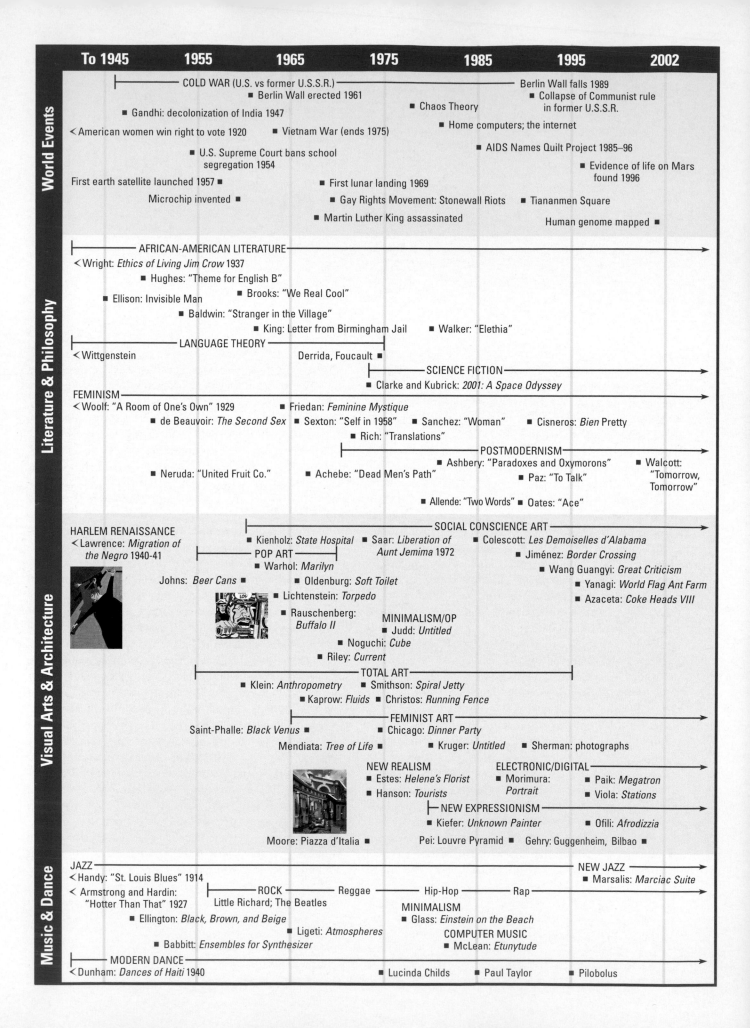

To 1945	1955	1965	1975	1985	1995	2002

World Events

- COLD WAR (U.S. vs former U.S.S.R.)
- Berlin Wall erected 1961
- Berlin Wall falls 1989
- Collapse of Communist rule in former U.S.S.R.
- Gandhi: decolonization of India 1947
- Chaos Theory
- Home computers; the internet
- < American women win right to vote 1920
- Vietnam War (ends 1975)
- AIDS Names Quilt Project 1985–96
- U.S. Supreme Court bans school segregation 1954
- Evidence of life on Mars found 1996
- First earth satellite launched 1957 ■
- First lunar landing 1969
- Microchip invented ■
- Gay Rights Movement: Stonewall Riots
- Tiananmen Square
- Martin Luther King assassinated
- Human genome mapped ■

Literature & Philosophy

- AFRICAN-AMERICAN LITERATURE →
- < Wright: *Ethics of Living Jim Crow* 1937
- Hughes: "Theme for English B"
- Brooks: "We Real Cool"
- Ellison: Invisible Man
- Baldwin: "Stranger in the Village"
- King: Letter from Birmingham Jail
- Walker: "Elethia"
- LANGUAGE THEORY
- < Wittgenstein
- Derrida, Foucault ■
- SCIENCE FICTION →
- Clarke and Kubrick: *2001: A Space Odyssey*
- FEMINISM
- < Woolf: "A Room of One's Own" 1929
- Friedan: *Feminine Mystique*
- de Beauvoir: *The Second Sex* ■ Sexton: "Self in 1958" ■ Sanchez: "Woman"
- Cisneros: *Bien* Pretty
- Rich: "Translations"
- POSTMODERNISM
- Ashbery: "Paradoxes and Oxymorons"
- Walcott: "Tomorrow, Tomorrow"
- Neruda: "United Fruit Co." ■ Achebe: "Dead Men's Path"
- Paz: "To Talk"
- Allende: "Two Words" ■ Oates: "Ace"

Visual Arts & Architecture

- HARLEM RENAISSANCE
- < Lawrence: *Migration of the Negro* 1940-41
- SOCIAL CONSCIENCE ART →
- Kienholz: *State Hospital* ■ Saar: *Liberation of Aunt Jemima* 1972
- Colescott: *Les Demoiselles d'Alabama*
- POP ART
- Warhol: *Marilyn*
- Jiménez: *Border Crossing*
- Johns: *Beer Cans* ■
- Oldenburg: *Soft Toilet*
- Wang Guangyi: *Great Criticism*
- Lichtenstein: *Torpedo*
- Yanagi: *World Flag Ant Farm*
- Rauschenberg: *Buffalo II*
- MINIMALISM/OP
- Azaceta: *Coke Heads VIII*
- Judd: *Untitled*
- Noguchi: *Cube*
- Riley: *Current*
- TOTAL ART
- Klein: *Anthropometry* ■ Smithson: *Spiral Jetty*
- Kaprow: *Fluids* ■ Christos: *Running Fence*
- FEMINIST ART →
- Saint-Phalle: *Black Venus* ■
- Chicago: *Dinner Party*
- Mendiata: *Tree of Life* ■ Kruger: *Untitled*
- Sherman: photographs
- NEW REALISM
- Estes: *Helene's Florist*
- ELECTRONIC/DIGITAL →
- Morimura: *Portrait*
- Paik: *Megatron*
- Hanson: *Tourists*
- Viola: *Stations*
- NEW EXPRESSIONISM →
- Kiefer: *Unknown Painter*
- Ofili: *Afrodizzia*
- Moore: Piazza d'Italia ■
- Pei: Louvre Pyramid ■ Gehry: Guggenheim, Bilbao ■

Music & Dance

- JAZZ
- NEW JAZZ →
- < Handy: "St. Louis Blues" 1914
- Marsalis: *Marciac Suite*
- < Armstrong and Hardin: "Hotter Than That" 1927
- ROCK — Reggae — Hip-Hop — Rap →
- Little Richard; The Beatles
- Ellington: *Black, Brown, and Beige*
- MINIMALISM
- Glass: *Einstein on the Beach*
- Ligeti: *Atmospheres*
- COMPUTER MUSIC
- Babbitt: *Ensembles for Synthesizer*
- McLean: *Etunytude*
- MODERN DANCE →
- < Dunham: *Dances of Haiti* 1940
- Lucinda Childs ■ Paul Taylor ■ Pilobolus

CHAPTER THIRTY-SIX

Identity and liberation

"This world is white no longer, and it will never be white again."
James Baldwin

While the mood of despair pervaded much of the postwar era, a second, more positive spirit fueled movements for liberation in many parts of the world. Movements to reform conditions of oppression and inequality ranged from anticolonial drives for independence from foreign control to crusades for ethnic self-identity, and from fierce demands for racial and gender equality to counterculture attacks on prevailing social norms. The drive toward liberation, one of the most potent themes of the twentieth century, inspired many of its most significant works of art. And while the artistic value of all art must, in the long run, be judged without reference to the politics, race, or gender of the artists, such artworks may be better appreciated in the light of the historical circumstances out of which they emerged.

Two major types of liberation movement have marked the second half of the twentieth century: the effort by colonial nations to achieve political, economic, religious, and ethnic independence; and the demand for racial and sexual equality. The first of these—the move toward political and economic independence—resulted from postwar efforts in Third World countries to reduce poverty and raise the standard of living to that of the more highly developed nations. After World War II, the weakened European nations were unable to maintain the military forces necessary to sustain their empires. At the same time, colonial subjects increased their efforts to free themselves of rule by Western nations, which, ironically, had fought for decades to liberate oppressed people from totalitarian dominion.

One of the earliest revolts against colonial rule took place in India. During World War I, the Indian National Congress came under the influence of the Hindu Mohandas Gandhi (1869–1948). Gandhi, whose followers called him "Mahatma," or "great soul," led India's struggle for emancipation from Great Britain. Guided by the precepts of Hinduism, as well as by the Sermon on the Mount and the writings of Thoreau and Tolstoy, Gandhi initiated a policy of peaceful protest against colonial oppression. His program of nonviolent resistance, including fasting and peaceful demonstrations, influenced subsequent liberation movements throughout the world. Gandhi's leadership was crucial to India's emancipation from British control, which occurred in 1947, only one year before he was assassinated by a Hindu fanatic who opposed his conciliatory gestures toward India's Muslim minority. A related movement for liberation was well under way in India and other parts of Asia even before the end of European domination: The pan-Islamic quest for a modern-day Muslim community on the Indian subcontinent resulted, in 1947, in an independent Pakistan. Similar movements to advance Islam as a worldwide moral and religious force continue to flourish into the twenty-first century.

Between 1944 and 1960, many nations, including Jordan, Burma, Palestine, Sri Lanka, Ghana, Malaya, Cyprus, and Nigeria, freed themselves from British rule; Syria, Lebanon, Cambodia, Laos, North and South Vietnam, Morocco, Tunisia, Cameroon, Mali, and other African states won their independence from France; and still other territories claimed independence from the empires of the United States, Japan, the Netherlands, Belgium, and Italy. In Central America, Southeast Asia, and elsewhere, internal conflicts provoked military intervention by First World powers. For instance, between 1964 and 1975, the United States succeeded France in an unsuccessful effort to defend South Vietnam from communist control. The Vietnam War, the longest war in American history, cost the lives of some 50,000 Americans and more than 15 million Vietnamese. More recently, in Eastern Europe the demise of Soviet authority has unleashed age-old ethnic conflicts, producing fragmentation and bloodshed. Sadly, liberation movements often broadcast seeds of tragedy.

Liberation and Literature in Latin America

From the time of Christopher Columbus, the peoples of Latin America have served the political and economic interests of First World countries more powerful than their own. And even after many of the European nations departed from the shores of Argentina, Brazil, Mexico, Peru, and other Latin American states in the early nineteenth century, the conditions that prevailed in the long era of colonialism persisted: The vast majority of Latin Americans, including great masses of peasants of Native American descent, lived in relative poverty, while small, wealthy, landowning elites held power. These elites maintained their power by virtue of their alliance with the financial and industrial interests of First World nations, including (and especially since the 1890s) the United States.

Spanish-speaking and predominantly Catholic, the rapidly growing populations of the more than two dozen nations of Latin America have suffered repeated social upheaval in their attempt to cope with persistent problems of inequality, exploitation, and underdevelopment. The long and bitter history of the Mexican Revolution, commemorated in the murals of Diego Rivera (see Figure 34.6), provides a vivid example. From country to country, political and social reformers have struggled to revolutionize the socioeconomic order, to liberate Latin America from economic colonialism, and to bring about a more equitable distribution of wealth. Support for these essentially socialist movements has come from representatives of the deprived elements of society, including organized labor and, often enough, from the Catholic Church, which has acted on behalf of the masses as an agent of social justice. The "liberation theology" preached by reformist elements in the clergy advanced a powerful new rendering of Christian dogma.

Latin America's artists rallied to support movements for liberation. During the 1960s, the outpouring of exceptionally fine Latin American prose and poetry constituted a literary boom, the influence of which is still being felt worldwide. Among the literary champions of Latin American reform was the Chilean poet Pablo Neruda (1904–1973). Neruda was one of the most prolific and inventive poets in the history of the Spanish language. His poetry, often embellished by violent, surrealist images, endorses a radical, populist ideology. In the poem "The United Fruit Co." he describes the corruption of justice and freedom in the "Banana Republics" of Latin America. The poem, phrased as a mock Last Judgment, smolders with indignation at American policies of commercial exploitation in the nations south of its borders.

READING 6.17 Neruda's "United Fruit Co." (1950)

When the trumpets had sounded and all   1
was in readiness on the face of the earth,
Jehovah divided his universe:
Anaconda, Ford Motors,
Coca-Cola Inc., and similar entities: 5
the most succulent item of all,
The United Fruit Company Incorporated
reserved for itself: the heartland
and coasts of my country,
the delectable waist of America.   10
They rechristened their properties:
the "Banana Republics"—
and over the languishing dead,
the uneasy repose of the heroes
who harried that greatness,   15
their flags and their freedoms,
they established an *opéra bouffe*:
they ravished all enterprise,
awarded the laurels like Caesars,
unleashed all the covetous, and contrived   20
the tyrannical Reign of the Flies—
Trujillo the fly, and Tacho the fly,
the flies called Carias, Martinez,
Ubico[1]—all of them flies, flies
dank with the blood of their marmalade   25
vassalage, flies buzzing drunkenly
on the populous middens:
the fly-circus fly and the scholarly
kind, case-hardened in tyranny.
Then in the bloody domain of the flies   30
The United Fruit Company Incorporated
sailed off with a booty of coffee and fruits
brimming its cargo boats, gliding
like trays with the spoils
of our drowning dominions.   35
And all the while, somewhere in the sugary
hells of our seaports,
smothered by gases, an Indian
fell in the morning:
a body spun off, an anonymous   40
chattel, some numeral tumbling,
a branch with its death running out of it
in the vat of the carrion, fruit laden and foul.

---

[1] The twentieth-century dictators of Latin America: Rafael Molina Trujillo brutally dominated the Dominican Republic from 1930 to 1961; "Tacho" was the nickname for Anastasio Somoza, who controlled Nicaragua from 1937 until his assassination in 1956; Tiburcio Carias, self-styled dictator of Honduras, was supported during the 1930s and 1940s by the United Fruit Company; Maximilian Martinez was the ruthless dictator of El Salvador during the 1930s and 1940s; Jorge Ubico seized power in Guatemala in 1931 and served as a puppet of the United States until 1944.

The Quest for Racial Equality

The most turbulent liberation movement of the twentieth century addressed the issue of racial equality—an issue so dramatically reflected in the African-American* experience that some observers have dubbed this century "The Race Era." Since the days of slavery, millions of black Americans have existed as a Third World minority population living within a First World nation. The Dutch took the first black Africans to America in 1619, and during the late seventeenth and eighteenth centuries, thousands of black slaves were imported to the American colonies, especially those in the South. For 250 years, until the end of the Civil War, slavery was a fact of American life. While the Emancipation Proclamation issued by Abraham Lincoln in 1863 facilitated the liberation of the slaves, it was not until 1865—with the Thirteenth Amendment to the United States Constitution—that all were finally freed. This and other constitutional amendments guaranteed the rights of black people; nevertheless, the lives of African-Americans continued to be harsh and poor by comparison with those of their former white masters. Separation of the races by segregated housing, inferior schools, and exclusion from voting and equal employment were only a few of the inequities suffered by this minority in the post-emancipation United States. It was to these issues and to the more general problem of racism that many African-Americans addressed themselves after World War I.

The Harlem Renaissance

World War I provided African-Americans with new opportunities in education and employment. During and after the war, over 5 million African-Americans migrated from the South to the Northern states. White frustration and fear of black competition for jobs led to race riots in over twenty-five cities during the "bloody summer" of 1919 (Figure **36.1**). New York City became the center of economic opportunity, as well as the melting pot for black people from other parts of the world. Between 1920 and 1940, the quest for racial equality and a search for self-identity among African-Americans inspired an upsurge of creative expression in the arts. Centered in Harlem—a part of New York City occupied largely by African-Americans—poets, painters, musicians, and dancers forged the movement that came to be called the Harlem Renaissance.

One of the most eloquent voices of the Harlem Renaissance was Langston Hughes (1902–1967). Hughes was born in Missouri and moved to New York in 1921, where he became the first African-American to support himself as a professional writer. A musician as well as a journalist and a novelist, Hughes became the rare poet whose powerful phrases ("a dream deferred," "a raisin in

*The current term for an American of African descent, which replaced "Negro," the popular designation of the early twentieth century and, after mid-century, "Black" or "Afro-American."

Figure 36.1 JACOB LAWRENCE, "Race riots were numerous. White workers were hostile toward the migrants who had been hired to break strikes." Panel 50 from "The Migration" series, 1940–1941; text and title revised by the artist, 1993. Tempera on gesso on composition board, 18 × 12 in. The Museum of Modern Art, New York. Gift of Mrs. David M. Levy. Photograph © 2000 The Museum of Modern Art, New York.

the sun," and "black like me") have become enshrined in the canon of American literature. His poems, which capture the musical qualities of the African oral tradition, fuse everyday speech with the rhythms of blues and jazz. Hughes, who regarded poets as "lyric historians," drew deeply on his own experience: His "Theme for English B" records his response to the education of blacks in a dominantly white culture. In "Harlem," a meditation on the "bloody summer" of 1919, Hughes looks to the immediate past to presage the angry riots that have recurred regularly since the 1960s in America's black ghettos.

Like the writers of the Harlem Renaissance, the Chicago-born poet Gwendolyn Brooks (b. 1917 d. 2000) drew upon the idioms of jazz and street slang to produce a vivid picture of Chicago's black ghettos. The first African-American to receive the Pulitzer Prize for poetry (1949), Brooks brought attention to the plight of blacks, especially young black women, in American society. The two poems reproduced below are representative of the early part of her long and productive career.

Hughes' "Theme for English B" (1949)

The instructor said,   1

   Go home and write
   a page tonight.
   And let that page come out of you—
   Then, it will be true.   5

I wonder if it's that simple?

I am twenty-two, colored, born in Winston-Salem.
I went to school there, then Durham, then here
to this college on the hill above Harlem.
I am the only colored student in my class.   10
The steps from the hill lead down into Harlem,
through a park, then I cross St. Nicholas,
Eighth Avenue, Seventh, and I come to the Y,
the Harlem Branch Y, where I take the elevator
up to my room, sit down, and write this page: 15

It's not easy to know what is true for you or me
at twenty-two, my age. But I guess I'm what
I feel and see and hear, Harlem, I hear you:
hear you, hear me—we two—you, me, talk on this page.
(I hear New York, too.) Me—who?   20
Well, I like to eat, sleep, drink, and be in love.
I like to work, read, learn, and understand life.
I like a pipe for a Christmas present,
or records—Bessie, bop, or Bach.
I guess being colored doesn't make me *not* like   25
the same things other folks like who are other races.
So will my page be colored that I write?
Being me, it will not be white.
But it will be
a part of you, instructor.   30
You are white—
yet a part of me, as I am a part of you.
That's American.
Sometimes perhaps you don't want to be a part of me.
Nor do I often want to be a part of you.   35
But we are, that's true!
I guess you learn from me—
although you're older—and white—
and somewhat more free.

This is my page for English B.   40

Hughes' "Harlem" (1951)

What happens to a dream deferred?   1

Does it dry up
like a raisin in the sun?
Or fester like a sore—
And then run?   5
Does it stink like rotten meat?
Or crust and sugar over—
like a syrupy sweet?

Maybe it just sags
like a heavy load.   10

Or does it explode?

Brooks' "The Mother" (1945)

Abortions will not let you forget.   1
You remember the children you got that you did not get,
The damp small pulps with a little or with no hair,
The singers and workers that never handled the air.
You will never neglect or beat   5
Them, or silence or buy with a sweet.
You will never wind up the sucking-thumb
Or scuttle off ghosts that come.
You will never leave them, controlling your luscious sigh,
Return for a snack of them, with gobbling mother-eye.   10

I have heard in the voices of the wind the voices of my
   dim killed children.
I have contracted. I have eased
My dim dears at the breasts they could never suck.
I have said, Sweets, if I sinned, if I seized
Your luck   15
And your lives from your unfinished reach,
If I stole your births and your names,
Your straight baby tears and your games,
Your stilted or lovely loves, your tumults, your marriages,
   aches, and your deaths,

If I poisoned the beginnings of your breaths,   20
Believe that even in my deliberateness I was not deliberate.
Though why should I whine,
Whine that the crime was other than mine?—
Since anyhow you are dead.
Or rather, or instead,   25
You were never made.

But that too, I am afraid,
Is faulty: oh, what shall I say, how is the truth to be said?
You were born, you had body, you died.
It is just that you never giggled or planned or cried. 30

Believe me, I loved you all.
Believe me, I knew you, though faintly, and I loved,
   I loved you
All.

Brooks' "We Real Cool" (1959)

The Pool Players.
Seven at the Golden Shovel.

   We real cool. We
   Left school. We

   Lurk late. We
   Strike straight. We

   Sing sin. We
   Thin gin. We

   Jazz June. We
   Die soon.

Richard Wright and the Realities of Racism

Richard Wright (1908–1960) was born on a cotton plantation in Mississippi and came to New York City in 1937, just after the heyday of the Harlem Renaissance. Wright brought to his writings the anger of a man who had known physical punishment and repeated injustice at the hands of whites. In his novel *Native Son* (1940), the nightmarish story of a poor, young black who kills his white employer's daughter, Wright examined the ways in which the frustrated search for identity led some African-Americans to despair, defiance, and even violent crime. The novel won Wright immediate acclaim and was rewritten for the New York stage in 1941.

In the autobiographical sketch *The Ethics of Living Jim Crow* (1938), Wright records with grim frankness the experience of growing up in a racially segregated community in the American South. "Jim Crow," the stage name of a popular nineteenth-century minstrel performer, Thomas D. Rice, had come to describe anything pertaining to African-Americans, including matters of racial segregation.

READING 6.19 From Wright's *The Ethics of Living Jim Crow* (1938)

I

My first lesson in how to live as a Negro came when I was quite small. We were living in Arkansas. Our house stood behind the railroad tracks. Its skimpy yard was paved with black cinders. Nothing green ever grew in that yard. The only touch of green we could see was far away, beyond the tracks, over where the white folks lived. But cinders were good enough for me and I never missed the green growing things. And anyhow cinders were fine weapons. You could always have a nice hot war with huge black cinders. All you had to do was crouch behind the brick pillars of a house with your hands full of gritty ammunition. And the first woolly black head you saw pop out from behind another row of pillars was your target. You tried your very best to knock it off. It was great fun. I never fully realized the appalling disadvantages of a cinder environment till one day the gang to which I belonged found itself engaged in a war with the white boys who lived beyond the tracks. As usual we laid down our cinder barrage, thinking that this would wipe the white boys out. But they replied with a steady bombardment of broken bottles. We doubled our cinder barrage, but they hid behind trees, hedges, and the sloping embankment of their lawns. Having no such fortifications, we retreated to the brick pillars of our homes. During the retreat a broken milk bottle caught me behind the ear, opening a deep gash which bled profusely. The sight of blood pouring over my face completely demoralized our ranks. My fellow-combatants left me standing paralyzed in the center of the yard, and scurried for their homes. A kind neighbor saw me, and rushed me to a doctor, who took three stitches in my neck.

I sat brooding on my front steps, nursing my wound and waiting for my mother to come from work. I felt that a grave injustice had been done me. It was all right to throw cinders. The greatest harm a cinder could do was leave a bruise. But broken bottles were dangerous; they left you cut, bleeding, and helpless.

When night fell, my mother came from the white folks' kitchen. I raced down the street to meet her. I could just feel in my bones that she would understand. I knew she would tell me exactly what to do next time. I grabbed her hand and babbled out the whole story. She examined my wound, then slapped me.

"How come yuh didn't hide?" she asked me. "How come yuh awways fightin'?"

I was outraged, and bawled. Between sobs I told her that I didn't have any trees or hedges to hide behind. There wasn't a thing I could have used as a trench. And you couldn't throw very far when you were hiding behind the brick pillars of a house. She grabbed a barrel stave, dragged me home, stripped me naked, and beat me till I had a fever of one hundred and two. She would smack my rump with the stave, and, while the skin was still smarting impart to me gems of Jim Crow wisdom. I was never to throw cinders any more. I was never to fight any more wars. I was never, never, under any conditions, to fight *white* folks again. And they were absolutely right in clouting me with the broken milk bottle. Didn't I know she was working hard every day in the hot kitchens of the white folks to make money to take care of me? When was I ever going to learn to be a good boy? She couldn't be bothered with my fights. She finished by telling me that I ought to be thankful to God as long as I lived that they didn't kill me.

All that night I was delirious and could not sleep. Each time I closed my eyes I saw monstrous white faces suspended from the ceiling, leering at me.

From that time on, the charm of my cinder yard was gone. The green trees, the trimmed hedges, the cropped lawns grew very meaningful, became a symbol. Even today when I think of white folks, the hard, sharp outlines of white houses surrounded by trees, lawns, and hedges are present somewhere in the background of my mind. Through the years they grew into an overreaching symbol of fear.

It was a long time before I came in close contact with white folks again. We moved from Arkansas to Mississippi. Here we had the good fortune not to live behind the railroad tracks, or close to white neighborhoods. We lived in the very heart of the local Black Belt. There were black churches and black preachers; there were black schools and black teachers; black groceries and black clerks. In fact, everything was so solidly black that for a long time I did not even think of white folks, save in remote and vague terms. But this could not last forever. As one grows older one eats more. One's clothing costs more. When I finished grammar school I had to go to work. My mother could no longer feed and clothe me on her cooking job.

There is but one place where a black boy who knows no trade can get a job, and that's where the houses and faces are white, where the trees, lawns, and hedges are green. My first job was with an optical company in Jackson, Mississippi. The morning I applied I stood straight and neat before the boss, answering all his questions with sharp yessirs and nosirs. I was very careful to pronounce my *sirs* distinctly, in order that he might know that I was polite, that I knew where I was, and that I knew he was a *white* man. I wanted that job badly.

He looked me over as though he were examining a prize poodle. He questioned me closely about my schooling, being particularly insistent about how much mathematics I had had. He seemed very pleased when I told him I had had two years of algebra.

"Boy, how would you like to try to learn something around here?" he asked me. 100

"I'd like it fine, sir," I said, happy. I had visions of "working my way up." Even Negroes have those visions.

"All right," he said. "Come on."

I followed him to the small factory.

"Pease," he said to a white man of about thirty-five, "this is Richard. He's going to work for us."

Pease looked at me and nodded.

I was then taken to a white boy of about seventeen.

"Morrie, this is Richard, who's going to work for us."

"Whut yuh sayin' there, boy!" Morrie boomed at me. 110

"Fine!" I answered.

The boss instructed these two to help me, teach me, give me jobs to do, and let me learn what I could in my spare time.

My wages were five dollars a week.

I worked hard, trying to please. For the first month I got along O.K. Both Pease and Morrie seemed to like me. But one thing was missing. And I kept thinking about it. I was not learning anything and nobody was volunteering to help me. Thinking they had forgotten that I was to learn something about the mechanics of grinding lenses, I asked Morrie one 120 day to tell me about the work. He grew red.

"Whut yuh tryin' t' do, nigger, get smart?" he asked.

"Naw; I ain' tryin' t' git smart," I said.

"Well, don't, if yuh know whut's good for yuh!"

I was puzzled. Maybe he just doesn't want to help me, I thought. I went to Pease.

"Say, are yuh crazy, you black bastard?" Pease asked me, his gray eyes growing hard.

I spoke out, reminding him that the boss had said I was to be given a chance to learn something. 130

"Nigger, you think you're *white*, don't you?"

"Naw, sir!"

"Well, you're acting mighty like it!"

"But, Mr. Pease, the boss said . . ."

Pease shook his fist in my face.

"This is a *white* man's work around here, and you better watch yourself!"

From then on they changed toward me. They said good-morning no more. When I was just a bit slow in performing some duty, I was called a lazy black son-of-a-bitch. 140

Once I thought of reporting all this to the boss. But the mere idea of what would happen to me if Pease and Morrie should learn that I had "snitched" stopped me. And after all the boss was a white man, too. What was the use?

The climax came at noon one summer day. Pease called me to his workbench. To get to him I had to go between two narrow benches and stand with my back against a wall.

"Yes, sir," I said.

"Richard, I want to ask you something," Pease began pleasantly, not looking up from his work. 150

"Yes, sir," I said again.

Morrie came over, blocking the narrow passage between the benches. He folded his arms, staring at me solemnly.

I looked from one to the other, sensing that something was coming.

"Yes, sir," I said for the third time.

Pease looked up and spoke very slowly.

"Richard, *Mr.* Morrie here tells me you called me *Pease.*"

I stiffened. A void seemed to open up in me. I knew this was the showdown. 160

He meant that I had failed to call him Mr. Pease. I looked at Morrie. He was gripping a steel bar in his hands. I opened my mouth to speak, to protest, to assure Pease that I had never called him simply *Pease,* and that I had never had any intentions of doing so, when Morrie grabbed me by the collar, ramming my head against the wall.

"Now be careful, nigger!" snarled Morrie, baring his teeth. "*I* heard yuh call 'im *Pease*! 'N' if yuh say yuh didn't, yuh're callin' me a *lie*, see?" He waved the steel bar threateningly.

If I had said: No, sir, Mr. Pease, I never called you *Pease* I 170 would have been automatically calling Morrie a liar. And if I said: Yes, sir, Mr. Pease, I called you *Pease*, I would have been pleading guilty to having uttered the worst insult that a Negro can utter to a southern white man. I stood hesitating, trying to frame a neutral reply.

"Richard, I asked you a question!" said Pease. Anger was creeping into his voice.

"I don't remember calling you *Pease*, Mr. Pease," I said cautiously. "And if I did, I sure didn't mean . . ."

"You black son-of-a-bitch! You called me *Pease*, then!" he 180 spat, slapping me till I bent sideways over a bench. Morrie was on top of me, demanding:

"Didn't you call 'im *Pease*? If yuh say yuh didn't, I'll rip yo' gut string loose with this bar, yuh black granny dodger! Yuh can't call a white man a lie 'n' git erway with it, you black son-of-a-bitch!"

I wilted. I begged them not to bother me. I knew what they wanted. They wanted me to leave.

"I'll leave," I promised. "I'll leave right *now*."

They gave me a minute to get out of the factory. I was 190 warned not to show up again, or tell the boss.

I went.

When I told the folks at home what had happened, they called me a fool. They told me that I must never again attempt to exceed my boundaries. When you are working for white folks, they said, you got to "stay in your place" if you want to keep working. . . .

The Civil Rights Movement

Well after World War II, racism remained an undeniable fact of American life. While Americans had fought to oppose Nazi racism in Germany, black Americans endured a system of inferior education, restricted jobs, ghetto housing, and generally low living standards. High crime rates, illiteracy, and drug addiction were evidence of affluent America's awesome failure to assimilate a Third World population that suffered in its midst. The fact that African-Americans had served in great numbers in World War II inspired a redoubled effort to end persistent discrimination and segregation in the United States. During the 1950s and 1960s, that effort came to flower in the civil rights movement. Civil rights leaders of the 1950s demanded enforcement of all the provisions for equality promised in the United States Constitution. Their demands led to a landmark Supreme Court decision in 1954 that banned school segregation; by implication, this decision undermined the entire system of legalized segregation in the United States. Desegregation was met with fierce resistance, especially in the American South. In response to that resistance, the so-called Negro Revolt began in 1955 and continued for over a decade. The revolt took the form of nonviolent, direct action protests, including boycotts of segregated lunch counters, peaceful "sit-ins," and protest marches. Leading the revolt was Dr. Martin Luther King, Jr. (1929–1968), a Protestant pastor and civil rights activist who modeled his campaign of peaceful protest on the example of Gandhi. As president of the Southern Christian Leadership Conference, King served as an inspiration to African-Americans throughout the United States. The urgency of the African-American cause is conveyed in a letter King wrote while confined to jail for marching without a permit in the city of Birmingham, Alabama. The letter addressed a group of local white clergy, who had publicly criticized King for breaking laws that prohibited blacks from using public facilities and for promoting "untimely" demonstrations. After King's letter was published in *The Christian Century* (June 12, 1963), it became (in a shorter version edited by King himself) the key text in a nationwide debate over civil rights: It provided philosophic justification for the practice of civil disobedience as a means of opposing injustice. King's measured eloquence and reasoned restraint stand in ironic contrast to the savagery of the opposition: The Birmingham citizenry used guns, hoses, and attack dogs against the demonstrators, 2,400 of whom were jailed along with King.

READING 6.20   From King's *Letter from Birmingham Jail* (1963)

My dear Fellow Clergymen,
While confined here in the Birmingham City Jail, I came   1
across your recent statement calling our present activities
"unwise and untimely." Seldom, if ever, do I pause to answer
criticism of my work and ideas. But since I feel that you are
men of genuine goodwill and your criticisms are sincerely set
forth, I would like to answer your statement in what I hope
will be patient and reasonable terms.

I think I should give the reason for my being in Birmingham,
since you have been influenced by the argument of "outsiders
coming in." Several months ago our local affiliate here in   10
Birmingham invited us to be on call to engage in a nonviolent
direct action program if such were deemed necessary. We
readily consented and when the hour came we lived up to our
promises. So I am here, along with several members of my
staff, because we were invited here. Beyond this, I am in
Birmingham because injustice is here.

Moreover, I am cognizant of the interrelatedness of all
communities and states. I cannot sit idly by in Atlanta and not
be concerned about what happens in Birmingham. Injustice
anywhere is a threat to justice everywhere. We are caught in   20
an inescapable network of mutuality tied in a single garment
of destiny. Never again can we afford to live with the narrow,
provincial "outsider agitator" idea. Anyone who lives inside
the United States can never be considered an outsider
anywhere in this country.

You deplore the demonstrations that are presently taking
place in Birmingham. But I am sorry that your statement did
not express a similar concern for the conditions that brought
the demonstrations into being. I would not hesitate to say that
it is unfortunate that so-called demonstrations are taking   30
place in Birmingham at this time, but I would say in more
emphatic terms that it is even more unfortunate that the white
power structure of this city left the Negro community with no
other alternative.

In any nonviolent campaign there are four basic steps:
1) collection of the facts to determine whether injustices are
alive; 2) negotiation; 3) self-purification; and 4) direct action.

You may well ask, "Why direct action? Why sit-ins,
marches, etc.? Isn't negotiation a better path?" You are exactly
right in your call for negotiation. Indeed, this is the purpose of   40
direct action. Nonviolent direct action seeks to create such a
crisis and establish such creative tension that a community
that has constantly refused to negotiate is forced to confront
the issue. So the purpose of the direct action is to create a
situation so crisis-packed that it will inevitably open the door
to negotiation.

My friends, I must say to you that we have not made a
single gain in civil rights without determined legal and
nonviolent pressure. History is the long and tragic story of the
fact that privileged groups seldom give up their privileges   50
voluntarily. Individuals may see the moral light and voluntarily
give up their unjust posture; but as Reinhold Niebuhr[1] has
reminded us, groups are more immoral than individuals.

We know through painful experience that freedom is never
voluntarily given by the oppressor; it must be demanded by the
oppressed. For years now I have heard the word "Wait!" It
rings in the ear of every Negro with a piercing familiarity. This
"wait" has almost always meant "never." We must come to
see with the distinguished jurist of yesterday that "justice too
long delayed is justice denied." We have waited for more than   60
three hundred and forty years for our constitutional and God-
given rights.

You express a great deal of anxiety over our willingness to
break laws. This is certainly a legitimate concern. Since we so
diligently urge people to obey the Supreme Court's decision of
1954 outlawing segregation in the public schools, it is rather
strange and paradoxical to find us consciously breaking laws.
One may well ask, "How can you advocate breaking some
laws and obeying others?" The answer is found in the fact
that there are two types of laws. There are *just* laws and   70
there are *unjust* laws. One has not only a legal but a moral
responsibility to obey just laws. Conversely, one has a moral

---

[1] An American Protestant theologian (1892–1971) who urged ethical realism in Christian approaches to political debate (see chapter 35).

responsibility to disobey unjust laws.

Now what is the difference between the two? A just law is a man-made code that squares with the moral law or the law of God. An unjust law is a code that is out of harmony with the moral law. Any law that degrades human personality is unjust. All segregation statutes are unjust because segregation distorts the soul and damages the personality. It gives the segregator a false sense of superiority and the segregated a false sense of inferiority. 80

Let us turn to a more concrete example of just and unjust laws. An unjust law is a code that a majority inflicts on a minority that is not binding on itself. This is *difference* made legal. On the other hand a just law is a code that a majority compels a minority to follow and that it is willing to follow itself. This is *sameness* made legal.

I hope you can see the distinction I am trying to point out. In no sense do I advocate evading or defying the law as the rabid segregationist would do. This would lead to anarchy. One who 100 breaks an unjust law *openly*, *lovingly*, and with a willingness to accept the penalty by staying in jail to arouse the conscience of the community over its injustice, is in reality expressing the very highest respect for law.

Of course there is nothing new about this kind of civil disobedience. It was seen sublimely in the refusal of Shadrach, Meshach, and Abednego to obey the laws of Nebuchadnezzar[2] because a higher moral law was involved. It was practiced superbly by the early Christians.

We can never forget that everything Hitler did in Germany 110 was "legal" and everything the Hungarian freedom fighters did in Hungary was "illegal." It was "illegal" to aid and comfort a Jew in Hitler's Germany.

In your statement you asserted that our actions, even though peaceful, must be condemned because they precipitate violence. But can this assertion be logically made? Isn't this like condemning the robbed man because his possession of money precipitated the evil act of robbery? We must come to see, as federal courts have consistently affirmed, that it is immoral to urge an individual to withdraw his efforts to gain 120 his basic constitutional rights because the quest precipitates violence. Society must protect the robbed and punish the robber.

Over the last few years I have consistently preached that nonviolence demands that the means we use must be as pure as the ends we seek. So I have tried to make it clear that it is wrong to use immoral means to gain moral ends. But now I must affirm that it is just as wrong, or even more so, to use moral means to preserve immoral ends. T. S. Eliot has said that there is no greater treason than to do the right deed for 130 the wrong reason.

I wish you had commended the Negro sit-inners and demonstrators of Birmingham for their sublime courage, their willingness to suffer, and their amazing discipline in the midst of the most inhuman provocation. One day the South will recognize its real heroes. They will include old, oppressed,

battered Negro women, symbolized in a seventy-two-year-old woman of Montgomery, Alabama, who rose up with a sense of dignity and with her people decided not to ride the segregated buses, and responded to one who inquired about 140 her tiredness with ungrammatical profundity: "My feets is tired, but my soul is rested." One day the South will know that when these disinherited children of God sat down at the lunch counters they were in reality standing up for the best in the American dream and the most sacred values in our Judeo-Christian heritage, and thus carrying our whole nation back to great wells of democracy which were dug deep by the founding fathers in the formulation of the Constitution and the Declaration of Independence.

I hope this letter finds you strong in the faith. I also hope 150 that circumstances will soon make it possible for me to meet each of you, not as an integrationist or a civil rights leader, but as a fellow clergyman and a Christian brother. Let us hope that the dark clouds of racial prejudice will soon pass away and the deep fog of misunderstanding will be lifted from our fear-drenched communities and in some not too distant tomorrow the radiant stars of love and brotherhood will shine over our great nation with all of their scintillating beauty.

Yours for the cause of
Peace and Brotherhood 160
Martin Luther King, Jr.

As the Birmingham Letter suggests, Dr. King practiced the tactics of nonviolence to achieve the goals of racial integration and civil rights in America. Another black protest leader of the period took a very different tack: Malcolm Little (1925–1965), who called himself "Malcolm X," experienced firsthand the inequities and degradation of life in white America. For a time he turned to crime and drugs as a means of survival. Arrested and sentenced to prison in 1946, he took the opportunity to study history and religion, and most especially the teachings of Islam. By the time he was released in 1952, he had joined the Nation of Islam and was prepared to launch his career as a Muslim minister. Malcolm and other "Black Muslims" despaired over persistent racism in white America, and determined that blacks should pursue a very different course from that of Dr. King and the Southern Christian Leadership Conference. African-Americans, argued Malcolm, should abandon aspirations for integration. Instead, they should separate from American whites in every feasible way; they should create a black nation in which—through hard work and the pursuit of Muslim morality—they might live equally, in dignity, free of the daily affronts of white racism. These goals should be achieved by all available means, violent if necessary (armed self-defense was a first step). Only by fighting for black nationalism would African-Americans ever gain power and self-respect in racist America. Little wonder that Malcolm was feared and reviled by whites and deemed a dangerous radical by more moderate blacks as well.

In 1963, Malcolm addressed a conference of black leaders in Detroit, Michigan. In this speech, which later came to be called "Message to the Grass Roots," Malcolm

[2]The Chaldean king of the sixth century B.C.E., who, according to the Book of Daniel, demanded that these Hebrew youths worship the Babylonian gods. Nebuchadnezzar cast them into a fiery furnace, but they were delivered unhurt by an angel of God (see Figure 9.7).

addressed a large (almost entirely black) audience representing a cross-section of the African-American community. The power and immediacy of his style is best captured on the tape of the speech published by the African-American Broadcasting and Record Company. Nevertheless, the following brief excerpt provides a glimpse into the ferocious eloquence that Malcolm exhibited throughout his brief career—until his death by assassination in 1965.

READING 6.21 From Malcolm X's *Message to the Grass Roots* (1963)

. . . America has a very serious problem. Not only does [1] America have a very serious problem, but our people have a very serious problem. America's problem is us. We're her problem. The only reason she has a problem is she doesn't want us here. And every time you look at yourself, be you black, brown, red or yellow, a so-called Negro, you represent a person who poses such a serious problem for America because you're not wanted. Once you face this as a fact, then you can start plotting a course that will make you appear intelligent, instead of unintelligent. [10]

What you and I need to do is learn to forget our differences. When we come together, we don't come together as Baptists or Methodists. You don't catch hell because you're a Baptist, and you don't catch hell because you're a Methodist. You don't catch hell because you're a Methodist or Baptist, you don't catch hell because you're a Democrat or a Republican, you don't catch hell because you're a Mason or an Elk, and you sure don't catch hell because you're an American; because if you were an American, you wouldn't catch hell. You catch hell because you're a black man. You catch hell, all of us catch [20] hell, for the same reason.

So we're all black people, so-called Negroes, second-class citizens, ex-slaves. You're nothing but an ex-slave. You don't like to be told that. But what else are you? You are ex-slaves. You didn't come here on the "Mayflower." You came here on a slave ship. In chains, like a horse, or a cow, or a chicken. And you were brought here by the people who came here on the "Mayflower," you were brought here by the so-called Pilgrims, or Founding Fathers. They were the ones who brought you here. [30]

We have a common enemy. We have this in common: We have a common oppressor, a common exploiter, and a common discriminator. But once we all realize that we have a common enemy, then we unite—on the basis of what we have in common. And what we have foremost in common is that enemy—the white man. . . .

As long as the white man sent you to Korea, you bled. He sent you to Germany, you bled. He sent you to the South Pacific to fight the Japanese, you bled. You bleed for white people, but when it comes to seeing your own churches being [40] bombed and little black girls murdered, you haven't got any blood. You bleed when the white man says bleed; you bite when the white man says bite; and you bark when the white man says bark. I hate to say this about us, but it's true. How are you going to be nonviolent in Mississippi, as violent as you were in Korea? How can you justify being nonviolent in Mississippi and Alabama, when your churches are being bombed, and your little girls are being murdered, and at the same time you are going to get violent with Hitler, and Tojo, and somebody else you don't even know? [50]

If violence is wrong in America, violence is wrong abroad. If it is wrong to be violent defending black women and black children and black babies and black men, then it is wrong for America to draft us and make us violent abroad in defense of her. And if it is right for America to draft us, and teach us how to be violent in defense of her, then it is right for you and me to do whatever is necessary to defend our own people right here in this country. . . .

The Literature of the Black Revolution

The passage of the Civil Rights Act in America in 1964 provided an end to official segregation in public places; but continuing discrimination and the growing militancy of some civil rights groups provoked a more violent phase of the protests during the late 1960s and thereafter. Even before the assassination of Martin Luther King, Jr., in 1968, the black revolution had begun to assume a transnational fervor. American voices joined those of their black neighbors in West India, South Africa, and elsewhere in the world. Fired by **apartheid**, the system of strict racial segregation that prevailed legally in the Union of South Africa until 1994, the poet Bloke Modisane (b. 1923) lamented:

> it gets awful lonely,
> lonely;
> like screaming,
> screaming lonely
> screaming down dream alley,
> screaming blues, like none can hear*

In *Black Skin, White Masks* (1958)—the handbook for African revolution—the West Indian essayist and revolutionary Franz Fanon (1925–1961) defended violence as necessary and desirable in overcoming the tyranny of whites over blacks in the colonial world. "At the level of individuals," he wrote, "violence is a cleansing force." In America, where advertising media made clear the disparity between the material comforts of blacks and whites, the black revolution swelled on a tide of rising expectations. LeRoi Jones (b. 1934), who in 1966 adopted the African name Imamu Amiri Baraka, echoed the message of Malcolm X in poems and plays that advocated militant action and pan-Africanism. Attacking the entire white Western literary tradition, Baraka called for "poems that kill"; "Let there be no love poems written," he entreats, "until love can exist freely and cleanly."

Two luminaries of American black protest literature were James Baldwin (1924–1987) and Ralph Ellison (1914–1994). Baldwin, the oldest of nine children raised in Harlem in conditions of poverty, began writing when he was fourteen years old. Encouraged early in his career by

---

*From *Poems from Black Africa*, ed. Langston Hughes. Bloomington: Indiana University Press, 1963, 110.

Richard Wright, Baldwin became a formidable preacher of the gospel of equality. For Baldwin, writing was a subversive act. "You write," he insisted, "in order to change the world, knowing perfectly well that you probably can't, but also knowing that literature is indispensable to the world. In some way, your aspirations and concern for a single man in fact do begin to change the world. The world changes according to the way people see it, and if you alter, even by a millimeter, the way a person looks or people look at reality, then you can change it."

In his novels, short stories, and essays, Baldwin stressed the affinity African-Americans felt with other poverty-stricken populations. Yet, as he tried to define the unique differences between blacks and whites, he observed that black people were strangers in the modern world, a world whose traditions were claimed by whites. As he explained in the essay "Stranger in the Village" (1953):

> [European Whites] cannot be, from the point of view of power, strangers anywhere in the world; they have made the modern world, in effect, even if they do not know it. The most illiterate among them is related, in a way that I am not, to Dante, Shakespeare, Michelangelo, Aeschylus, da Vinci, Rembrandt, and Racine; the cathedral at Chartres says something to them which it cannot say to me. . . . Out of their hymns and dances come Beethoven and Bach. Go back a few centuries and they are in their full glory—but I am in Africa, watching the conquerors arrive.

But Baldwin uncovered a much overlooked truth about the character of the modern world: that black culture has influenced white culture, and especially American culture, in a profound and irreversible manner:

> The time has come to realize that the interracial drama acted out on the American continent has not only created a new black man, it has created a new white man, too. . . . One of the things that distinguishes Americans from other people is that no other people has ever been so deeply involved in the lives of black men, and vice versa. . . . It is precisely this black–white experience which may prove of indispensable value to us in the world we face today. This world is white no longer, and it will never be white again.*

Baldwin's contemporary, Ralph Ellison, a native of Oklahoma and an amateur jazz musician, came to Harlem during the 1930s to study sculpture and musical composition. He was influenced by both Hughes and Wright and soon turned to writing short stories and newspaper reviews. In 1945, he began the novel *Invisible Man*, a fiction masterpiece that probes the black estrangement from white culture. The prologue to the novel, an excerpt of which follows, offers a glimpse into the spiritual odyssey of the "invisible" protagonist. It also broaches, with surrealis-

tic intensity, some of Ellison's most important themes: the nightmarish quality of urban life and the alienation experienced by both blacks and whites in modern American society.

READING 6.22 From Ellison's *Invisible Man* (1952)

I am an invisible man. No, I am not a spook like those who haunted Edgar Allan Poe;[1] nor am I one of your Hollywood-movie ectoplasms. I am a man of substance, of flesh and bone, fiber and liquids—and I might even be said to possess a mind. I am invisible, understand, simply because people refuse to see me. Like the bodiless heads you see sometimes in circus sideshows, it is as though I have been surrounded by mirrors of hard, distorting glass. When they approach me they see only my surroundings, themselves, or figments of their imagination—indeed, everything and anything except me. [10]

Nor is my invisibility exactly a matter of a bio-chemical accident to my epidermis. That invisibility to which I refer occurs because of a peculiar disposition of the eyes of those with whom I come in contact. A matter of the construction of their *inner* eyes, those eyes with which they look through their physical eyes upon reality. I am not complaining, nor am I protesting either. It is sometimes advantageous to be unseen, although it is most often rather wearing on the nerves. Then too, you're constantly being bumped against by those of poor vision. Or again, you often doubt if you really exist. You [20] wonder whether you aren't simply a phantom in other people's minds. Say, a figure in a nightmare which the sleeper tries with all his strength to destroy. It's when you feel like this that, out of resentment, you begin to bump people back. And, let me confess, you feel that way most of the time. You ache with the need to convince yourself that you do exist in the real world, that you're a part of all the sound and anguish, and you strike out with your fists, you curse and you swear to make them recognize you. And, alas, it's seldom successful.

One night I accidentally bumped into a man, and perhaps [30] because of the near darkness he saw me and called me an insulting name. I sprang at him, seized his coat lapels and demanded that he apologize. He was a tall blond man, and as my face came close to his he looked insolently out of his blue eyes and cursed me, his breath hot in my face as he struggled. I pulled his chin down sharp upon the crown of my head, butting him as I had seen the West Indians do, and I felt his flesh tear and the blood gush out, and I yelled, "Apologize! Apologize!" But he continued to curse and struggle, and I butted him again and again until he went down heavily, on his [40] knees, profusely bleeding. I kicked him repeatedly, in a frenzy because he still uttered insults though his lips were frothy with blood. Oh yes, I kicked him! And in my outrage I got out my knife and prepared to slit his throat, right there beneath the lamplight in the deserted street, holding him by the collar with one hand, and opening the knife with my teeth—when it occurred to me that the man had not *seen* me, actually; that

---

*"Stranger in the Village," in James Baldwin, *Notes of a Native Son*. New York: Bantam Press, 1964, 140, 148–149.

[1] A leading American poet, literary critic, and short-story writer (1809–1849), noted for his tales of terror and his clever detective stories.

he, as far as he knew, was in the midst of a walking nightmare! And I stopped the blade, slicing the air as I pushed him away, letting him fall back to the street. I stared at him hard as the lights of a car stabbed through the darkness. He lay there, moaning on the asphalt; a man almost killed by a phantom. It unnerved me. I was both disgusted and ashamed. I was like a drunken man myself, wavering about on weakened legs. Then I was amused. Something in this man's thick head had sprung out and beaten him within an inch of his life. I began to laugh at this crazy discovery. Would he have awakened at the point of Death? Would Death himself have freed him for wakeful living? But I didn't linger. I ran away into the dark, laughing so hard I feared I might rupture myself. The next day I saw his picture in the *Daily News*, beneath a caption stating that he had been "mugged." Poor fool, poor blind fool, I thought with sincere compassion, mugged by an invisible man! . . .

In the literature of the black revolution, especially that of that last three decades of the twentieth century, many of the most powerful voices have been female. Succeeding such notable Harlem Renaissance writers as Zora Neale Hurston (1891–1960) and Dorothy West (b. 1912), two contemporary figures—Toni Morrison (b. 1931) and Alice Walker (b. 1944)—have risen to eminence for their courageous and candid characterizations of black women as they have faced the perils of racism, domestic violence, and sexual abuse. Space permits only a short example of the writings of Alice Walker, whose novel *The Color Purple* won the Pulitzer Prize for literature in 1982. As effective as many of Walker's novels and poems, her short story "Elethia" probes the dual issues of identity and liberation as they come to shape the destiny of a young black female.

READING 6.23 Walker's "Elethia" (1981)

A certain perverse experience shaped Elethia's life, and made it possible for it to be true that she carried with her at all times a small apothecary jar of ashes.

There was in the town where she was born a man whose ancestors had owned a large plantation on which everything under the sun was made or grown. There had been many slaves, and though slavery no longer existed, this grandson of former slaveowners held a quaint proprietary point of view where colored people were concerned. He adored them, of course. Not in the present—it went without saying—but at that time, stopped, just on the outskirts of his memory: his grandfather's time.

This man, whom Elethia never saw, opened a locally famous restaurant on a busy street near the center of town. He called it "Old Uncle Albert's." In the window of the restaurant was a stuffed likeness of Uncle Albert himself, a small brown dummy of waxen skin and glittery black eyes. His lips were intensely smiling and his false teeth shone. He carried a covered tray in one hand, raised level with his shoulder, and over his other arm was draped a white napkin.

Black people could not eat at Uncle Albert's, though they worked, of course, in the kitchen. But on Saturday afternoons a crowd of them would gather to look at "Uncle Albert" and discuss how near to the real person the dummy looked. Only the very old people remembered Albert Porter, and their eyesight was no better than their memory. Still there was a comfort somehow in knowing that Albert's likeness was here before them daily and that if he smiled as a dummy in a fashion he was not known to do as a man, well, perhaps both memory and eyesight were wrong.

The old people appeared grateful to the rich man who owned the restaurant for giving them a taste of vicarious fame. They could pass by the gleaming window where Uncle Albert stood, seemingly in the act of sprinting forward with his tray, and know that though niggers were not allowed in the front door, ole Albert was already inside, and looking mighty pleased about it, too.

For Elethia the fascination was in Uncle Albert's fingernails. She wondered how his creator had got them on. She wondered also about the white hair that shone so brightly under the lights. One summer she worked as a salad girl in the restaurant's kitchen, and it was she who discovered the truth about Uncle Albert. He was not a dummy; he was stuffed. Like a bird, like a moose's head, like a giant bass. He was stuffed.

One night after the restaurant was closed someone broke in and stole nothing but Uncle Albert. It was Elethia and her friends, boys who were in her class and who called her "Thia." Boys who bought Thunderbird and shared it with her. Boys who laughed at her jokes so much they hardly remembered she was also cute. Her tight buddies. They carefully burned Uncle Albert to ashes in the incinerator of their high school, and each of them kept a bottle of his ashes. And for each of them what they knew and their reaction to what they knew was profound.

The experience undercut whatever solid foundation Elethia had assumed she had. She became secretive, wary, looking over her shoulder at the slightest noise. She haunted the museums of any city in which she found herself, looking, usually, at the remains of Indians, for they were plentiful everywhere she went. She discovered some of the Indian warriors and maidens in the museums were also real, stuffed people, painted and wigged and robed, like figures in the Rue Morgue. There were so many, in fact, that she could not possibly steal and burn them all. Besides, she did not know if these figures—with their valiant glass eyes—would wish to be burned.

About Uncle Albert she felt she knew.

What kind of man was Uncle Albert?

Well, the old folks said, he wasn't nobody's uncle and wouldn't sit still for nobody to call him that, either.

Why, said another old-timer, I recalls the time they hung a boy's privates on a post at the end of the street where all the black folks shopped, just to scare us all, you understand, and Albert Porter was the one took 'em down and buried 'em. Us never did find the rest of the boy though. It was just like always—they would throw you in the river with a big old green log tied to you, and down to the bottom you sunk.

He continued.

Albert was born in slavery and he remembered that his

mama and daddy didn't know nothing about slavery'd done ended for near 'bout ten years, the boss man kept them so ignorant of the law, you understand. So he was a mad so-an'-so when he found out. They used to beat him *severe* trying to make him forget the past and grin and act like a nigger. (Whenever you saw somebody acting like a nigger, Albert said, you could be sure he seriously disremembered his past.) But he never would. Never would work in the big house as head servant, neither— always broke up stuff. The master at that time was always going around pinching him too. Looks like he hated Albert more than anything—but he never would let him get a job anywhere else. And Albert never would leave home. Too stubborn.

Stubborn, yes. My land, another one said. That's why it do seem strange to see that dummy that sposed to be old Albert with his mouth open. All them teeth. Hell, all Albert's teeth was knocked out before he was grown.

Elethia went away to college and her friends went into the army because they were poor and that was the way things were. They discovered Uncle Alberts all over the world. Elethia was especially disheartened to find Uncle Alberts in her textbooks, in the newspapers and on t.v.

Everywhere she looked there was an Uncle Albert (and many Aunt Albertas, it goes without saying).

But she had her jar of ashes, the old-timers' memories written down, and her friends who wrote that in the army they were learning skills that would get them through more than a plate glass window.

And she was careful that, no matter how compelling the hype, Uncle Alberts, in her own mind, were not permitted to exist.

African-Americans and the Visual Arts

During the Harlem Renaissance, African-American painters and sculptors made public the social concerns of black poets and writers. In picturing their experience, they drew on African folk idioms and colloquial forms of native expression; but they also absorbed the radically new styles of European modernism. Among these painters, there emerged a "blues aesthetic" that featured bold colors, angular forms, and rhythmic, stylized compositions. One of the most notable artists of the twentieth century, Jacob Lawrence (1917–2000) migrated to Harlem with his family in 1930. Lawrence's powerful style features flat, local colors and angular, abstract forms that owe as much to African art as to synthetic cubism and expressionism. At

Figure 36.2 BETYE SAAR, *The Liberation of Aunt Jemima*, 1972. Mixed media, 11¾ × 8 × 2¾ in. University Art Museum, University of California at Berkeley. Purchased with the aid of funds from the National Endowment for the Arts. Selected by the Committee for the Acquisition of African-American Art.

the same time, Lawrence's lifelong commitment to social and racial issues made him heir to the nineteenth-century artist-critics Goya and Daumier, whom he admired. Painting in tempera on masonite panels, Lawrence won early acclaim for serial paintings that deal with black history and with the lives of black American heroes and heroines. Among the most famous of these is a series of sixty panels known as *The Migration of the Negro* (1940–1941). For *The Migration*—an expressionistic narrative of the great northward movement of African-Americans after World War

AFRICAN AMERICANS AND FILM

The first African-American to establish himself in Hollywood, Spike Lee (b. 1956), has won international acclaim for films that explore race conflicts in the inner city (*Do the Right Thing*, 1989), modern black history (*Malcolm X*, 1992), and the black minstrel tradition (*Bamboozled*, 2000). Lee uses the camera inventively to underline social conflicts, as in his radical close-ups of faces caught in bitter, heated disputes. He favors short, disconnected scenes, the "accidental" effects of the hand-held camera, and editing techniques that often leave the narrative themes of his films unresolved but filled with implications. Lee opened the door to a new wave of black filmmakers that include John Singleton (*Boyz in the Hood*, 1991) and Julie Dash (*Daughters of the Dust*, 1991).

Figure 36.3 ROBERT COLESCOTT, *Les Demoiselles d'Alabama (Vestidas)*, 1985. Acrylic on canvas, 8 ft. × 7 ft. 8 in. Collection of Hanford Yang, New York. Photo courtesy Phyllis Kind Gallery, New York.

I—Lawrence drew on textual sources rather than firsthand visual experience. The drama of each episode (see Figure 36.1) is conveyed by means of powerful, angular rhythms and vigorous, geometric shapes that preserve what Lawrence called "the magic of the picture plane."

Since the mid-twentieth century, African-American artists have taken increasingly bold and ever more cynical approaches to themes of race discrimination and racial stereotyping. The sculptor Betye Saar (b. 1926) abandoned the African-inspired fetishlike sculptures of her early career and turned to fabricating boxed constructions that attacked the icons of commercial white culture. In the mixed media sculpture entitled *The Liberation of Aunt Jemima*, Saar transforms the familiar symbol of American pancakes and cozy kitchens into a gun-toting version of the "mammy" stereotype (Figure **36.2**). The satirist-artist Robert Colescott (b. 1925) creates parodies of famous paintings in which whites are recast as cartoon-style, stereotyped blacks. In doing so, Colescott calls attention to the exclusion of blacks from Western art history. His bitter parody of Delacroix's *Liberty Leading the People* (1976) features a crew of brashly painted African-American rebels commanded by a black-faced Liberty. Colescott's *Les Demoiselles d'Alabama* (Figure **36.3**), an obvious funk-art clone of Picasso's seminal painting (see Figure 32.3), slyly challenges contemporary definitions of primitivism and modernism. Colescott observes, "Picasso started with European art and abstracted through African art, producing 'Africanism' but keeping one foot in European art. I began with Picasso's Africanism and moved toward European art, keeping one foot in Africanism. . . . The irony is what most people (including me) know about African conventions comes from Cubist art. Could a knowledge of European art be so derived as well?"*

African-Americans and Jazz

Possibly the most important contribution made by African-Americans to world culture occurred in the area of music, specifically in the birth and development of that unique form of modern music known as jazz. Jazz is a synthesis of diverse musical elements that came together in the first two decades of the twentieth century, but it was after World War I that jazz came to full fruition as an art form. Although some music historians insist that jazz is the product of place, not race, the primary role of African-Americans in the origins and evolution of jazz is indisputable.

*Lowery S. Sims and M. D. Kahan, *Robert Colescott, A Retrospective, 1975–1986*. San Jose, Calif.: San Jose Museum of Art, 1987, 8.

Jazz is primarily a performer's rather than a composer's art. It is dominated by Afro-Caribbean rhythmic styles combined with a wide range of European and African-American concepts of harmony, melody, and tone color. In its evolution, jazz has incorporated a variety of musical forms, including those of the marching brass band, the minstrel stage, blues, and a piano style known as *ragtime*. Ragtime was essentially a form of piano composition and performance featuring highly syncopated rhythms and simple, straightforward appealing melodies. It apparently originated in the lower Mississippi Valley, but it migrated north after the Civil War and became popular during the 1890s. Its most inspired proponent (if not its inventor) was the black composer and ragtime pianist Scott Joplin (1868–1917). Early jazz performers, like "Jelly Roll" Morton (Ferdinand Joseph LaMonthe, 1885–1941), who claimed to have invented jazz, utilized ragtime rhythms in developing the essential features of the new form.

Blues, a second major contribution to the development of jazz, began as a vocal rather than an instrumental form of music. Native to the United States, but possibly stemming from African song forms and harmonics, blues is an emotive form of individual expression by which one laments one's troubles, loneliness, and despair. A blues song may recall the wailing cries of plantation slaves; it may describe the anguish of separation and loss or the hope for deliverance from oppression. Such blues classics as W. C. Handy's "St. Louis Blues" (1914) ♪ begin with a line that states a simple plaint ("I hate to see the evening sun go down"); the plaint is repeated in a second line, and it is "answered" in a third ("It makes me think I'm on my last go-round")—a pattern derived perhaps from African call and response chants (see chapter 18). Technically, blues makes use of a special scale known as a "blues scale," which features (among other things) the flatted forms of E, G, and B within the standard scale.

♪ See Music Listening Selections at end of chapter.

Figure 36.4 King Oliver's Creole Jazz Band, 1923. Honore Dutrey, Warren "Baby" Dodds, Joe Oliver, Louis Armstrong, Lil Hardin, Bill Johnson, and Johnny Dodds. Courtesy Hogan Jazz Archive, Tulane University.

Both ragtime and blues contributed substantially to the development of jazz as a unique musical idiom. But if jazz manifests any single defining quality, that quality would have to be improvisation—individual and collective. Most jazz performances are based in standard melodies—often familiar popular tunes; the individual performers (and sometimes a group of performers within an ensemble) "improvise" on the base melody. They invent passages while in the process of performing them—a form of "composing as you go"—or they incorporate bits of other (often familiar) melodies into their solos. Most scholars agree that improvisation, either individual or collective, constitutes the single element that most distinguishes jazz from other musical idioms. Finally, jazz employs a unique variation on standard rhythms that performers and afficionados term "**swing**." While it is virtually impossible to define the concept of "swing," it may be described as the practice of playing just off the beat—slightly ahead or behind. "Swinging" normally involves achieving a certain rhythmic "groove"—a combination of rhythm and harmony that vitalizes the ensemble and propels the performance forward. (In the words of a 1940s popular song, "It don't mean a thing if it ain't got that swing!")

Essentially a performance art, jazz depends on improvisation and on the interaction of the ensemble's members as they create an essentially new composition in the very act of performing it. Although syncopated rhythms, the blues motif, a certain harmonic flexibility, and improvisation were not in themselves new, their combination—when vitalized by a "swinging" performance—produced an essentially new art form, one that would have a major impact on Western music for years to come.

The beginnings of American jazz are found in New Orleans, Louisiana, a melting pot for the rich heritage of Spanish, French, African, Caribbean, Indian, and Black Creole musical traditions. Here, black and white musicians drew on the intricate rhythms of African tribal dance and the European harmonies of traditional marching bands. The street musicians who regularly marched behind funeral or wedding processions, many of whom were neither formally trained nor could read music, might play trumpets, trombones, and clarinets; rhythm was provided by tubas as well as snare and bass drums. These musicians made up the "front line" of the parade; the crowd that danced behind them was called the "second line."* Such parade bands performed perhaps the earliest version of what became jazz. Similar bands also played the kinds of music that were popular in nightclubs and dance halls. Louis Armstrong

----

*Not to be confused with a variant usage of the term which distinguishes the rhythm section of a band from the "front line" of reed and brass solo instrumentalists.

(1900–1971), a native of New Orleans who began playing the cornet at the age of twelve, emerged in the 1920s as the foremost jazz musician of the period. Armstrong's innovative solos provided jazz with the breakthrough by which solo improvisation became a central aspect of jazz performance. His ability to re-direct harmonies and to improvise inspired reworkings of standard melodies in his solos—all performed with breathtaking virtuosity—elevated the jazz soloist to a foremost role in ensemble performances. "Satchmo" ("Satchelmouth") Armstrong was also a jazz singer with formidable innovative gifts. He often embellished jazz pieces with **scat singing**—an improvised set of nonsense syllables. His compelling personality and unfailing good spirits brought joy to millions of his fans—thus rendering jazz all the more popular worldwide. Armstrong is widely regarded as having turned jazz into an internationally respected musical form. "Hotter Than That" (1927), ♪ a composition by Lillian Hardin (Armstrong's wife), exemplifies the style termed "hot jazz" (Figure **36.4**); a style that the French in particular elevated to the status of a craze.

In the 1920s jazz spread north to the urban centers of Chicago, Kansas City, and New York. Armstrong moved to Chicago in 1922. In New York, extraordinary jazz and blues singers like Bessie Smith (1898–1937), known by her fans as the "Empress of the Blues," or Billie Holiday (1915–1959)—"Lady Day"—drew worldwide acclaim through the phenomena of radio and phonograph records. In the so-called Jazz Age,

Figure 36.5 **JEAN-MICHEL BASQUIAT**, *Horn Players*, 1983. Acrylic and mixed media on canvas, 8 ft. × 6 ft. 3 in. Courtesy the Eli Broad Family Foundation, Santa Monica, California. © ADAFGP, Paris and DACS, London 2000.

jazz had a major impact on other musical genres. The American composer George Gershwin (1898–1937) incorporated the rhythms of jazz into the mesmerizing *Rhapsody in Blue* (1924), a concert piece for piano and orchestra. Gershwin's *Porgy and Bess* (1935), a fully composed opera dealing with the life of poverty-stricken Charleston African-Americans, combined jazz, blues, and spiritual and folk idioms to produce a fresh, new style of American musical theater. Popular music of the 1930s and 1940s was closely tied to the vogue for big band jazz and the danceable rhythms of swing, a big-band jazz style that fed the dance craze of the 1940s. The white swing bands of Tommy Dorsey, Glenn Miller, and Benny Goodman (who later integrated his band—the first bandleader to do so) played a mix of instrumental swing and popular ballads, while black swing bands like that of William "Count" Basie (1904–1984) leaned more toward blues and a dynamic big-band sound.

In the years following World War II, jazz took on some of the complex and sophisticated characteristics of "art music." The beguiling suite *Black, Brown, and Beige* (1948) composed by Edward Kennedy "Duke" Ellington (1899–

1974) paved the way for concert hall jazz, a form that enjoyed a revival in the 1990s. Ellington was a prolific composer, unquestionably the foremost composer in the jazz idiom (and arguably in *any* idiom) that the United States has produced. On a smaller scale, among groups of five to seven instruments, the jazz of the late 1940s and 1950s engaged the unique improvisational talents of individual performers. New jazz forms included "bebop" (or "bop")—a jazz style characterized by frenzied tempos, complex chord progressions, and dense polyrhythms—and "cool" jazz, a more restrained and gentler style associated with the West Coast. "Ko-Ko," ♪ written by Duke Ellington and performed by the saxophonist Charlie Parker (1920–1955) and the trumpeter John "Dizzy" Gillespie (1917–1993), epitomizes the bop style of the 1940s. Since the jazz renaissance of the 1980s, the New Orleans composer, trumpet prodigy, and teacher Wynton Marsalis (b. 1961) has reconfirmed the role of jazz as America's classical music. ♪ Awarded the Pulitzer Prize in 1995 for his jazz oratorio on slavery, *Blood on the Field*, Marsalis has become the world's most articulate spokesperson for the jazz genre. Likening jazz to the negotiation of ideas, Marsalis holds,

---

♪ See Music Listening Selections at end of chapter.

♪ See Music Listening Selections at end of chapter.

Figure 36.6 Katherine Dunham in the 1945–1946 production of *Tropical Revue*. The Dance Collection, The New York Public Library for the Performing Arts. Astor, Lenox, and Tilden Foundations.

"Jazz is more than the best expression there is of American culture; it is the most democratic of arts." To this day, jazz remains a unique kind of chamber music that combines the best of classical and popular musicianship.

Like the "blues aesthetic" in the poetry and painting of the Harlem Renaissance, a "jazz aesthetic" featuring spontaneity and improvisation infused the 1970s performance phenomenon known as *hip-hop*. A product of the inner-city American subculture, hip-hop brought together loud, percussive music (often electronically "mixed" by disc-jockeys), the spoken word, and street-dance, generating a raw vitality that bordered on the violent (see chapter 38). The paintings of the short-lived Jean-Michel Basquiat (1960–1988) embrace the free improvisations and borrowed "riffs" of modern jazz, even as they infuse the staccato rhythms and jarring lyrics of hip-hop. Basquiat's artworks conflate crude, child-like but familiar images, grim cartoon logos, and scrawled graffiti—an urban folk art style that vents the rage and joy of inner-city youths (like Basquiat himself). *Horn Players*, executed with portable oil sticks on a blackboard-like surface, pays homage to the jazz giants Dizzy Gillespie and Charlie Parker—the word "ornithology" a witty reference to the latter's nickname: "Bird" (Figure **36.5**).

African-Americans and Dance

The African-American impact on twentieth-century dance has rivaled that of music. For centuries, dance served African-Americans as a primary language of religious expression and as a metaphor of physical freedom. By the late nineteenth century, as all-black theatrical companies and minstrel shows toured the United States, black entertainment styles began to reach white audiences. Popular black dances such as the high-kicking cakewalk became the international fad of the early 1900s, and dance techniques—especially tap dancing—influenced both social and theatrical dance.

With the pioneer African-American choreographer Katherine Dunham (b. 1912), black dance moved beyond the level of stage entertainment. An avid student of Caribbean dance, Dunham drew heavily on Afro-Caribbean and African culture in both choreography and the sets and costumes designed by her husband, John Pratt (Figure **36.6**). Dunham's troupe borrowed from Caribbean music the rhythms of the steel band, an instrumental ensemble consisting entirely of steel drums fashioned from oil containers. Originating in Trinidad, steel bands provided percussive accompaniment for calypso and other kinds of improvised dance forms. In her book *Dances of Haiti*, Dunham examines the sociological function of dance—for instance, how communal dance captures the spirit of folk celebrations and how African religious dance interacts with European secular dance. Dunham's work inspired others: Pearl Primus (b. 1919) used her studies in choreography and anthropology (like Dunham, she earned a doctorate in this field) to become the world's foremost authority on African dance. Following a trip to Africa in the 1940s, she brought to modern dance the spirit and substance of native tribal rituals. She also choreographed theatrical versions of African-American spirituals and poems, including those of Langston Hughes. In her book *African Dance*, Primus declared: "The dance is strong magic. The dance is a spirit. It turns the body to liquid steel. It makes it vibrate like a guitar. The body can fly without wings. It can sing without voice."

The achievements of Dunham and Primus gave African-American dance theater international stature. Since 1950, such outstanding choreographers as Alvin Ailey (1931–1989), Donald McKayle (b. 1930), and Arthur Mitchell (b. 1934) have graced the history of American dance. Ailey's *Revelations* (1960), a suite that draws on African-American spirituals, song-sermons, and gospel songs, is an enduring tribute to the cultural history of black Americans. Dance compositions of more recent vintage, often driven by jazz or blues tempos, are filled with explosive excitement. Their choreographic themes continue to make powerful use of the black experience in a predominantly white society.

The Quest for Gender Equality

Throughout history, misogyny (the hatred of women) and the perception of the female sex as inferior in intelligence and strength have enforced conditions of gender inequality. While women make up the majority of the population in many cultures, they have exercised little significant political or economic power. Like many ethnic minorities, women have long been relegated to the position of second-class citizens. In 1900, women were permitted to vote in only one country in the world: New Zealand. By mid-century, women in most First World countries had gained voting rights; nevertheless, their social and economic status has remained far below that of men. As recently as 1985, the World Conference on Women reported that while women represent fifty percent of the world's population and contribute nearly two-thirds of all working hours, they receive only one-tenth of the world's income and own less than one percent of the world's property. Though female inequality has been a fact of history, it was not until the twentieth century that the quest for female liberation took the form of an international movement.

1953	biophysicists determine the molecular structure of DNA	
1953	Jonas Salk (American) tests an effective polio vaccine	
1955	an American endocrinologist produces a successful birth control pill	
1982	the fatal immune system disorder AIDS (Acquired Immune Deficiency Syndrome) is diagnosed	

The Literature of Feminism: Woolf

The history of **feminism** (the principle advocating equal social, political, and economic rights for men and women) reaches back at least to the fourteenth century, when the French poet Christine de Pisan took up the pen in defense of women (see chapter 15). Christine had sporadic followers among Renaissance and Enlightenment humanists. The most notable of these was Mary Wollstonecraft (1759–1797), who published her provocative *Vindication of the Rights of Woman* in London in 1792 (see chapter 24). During the nineteenth century, Condorcet and Mill wrote reasoned pleas for female equality, as did the female novelist George Sand (see chapters 28 and 30). In America, the eloquence of Angelina Grimké (1805–1879) and other suffragettes (women advocating equality for women) was instrumental in winning women the right to vote in 1920.

Among the most impassioned advocates of the feminist movement that flourished in England during the early twentieth century was the novelist Virginia Woolf (1882–1941). Woolf argued that equal opportunity for education and economic advantage were even more important than the right to vote (British women finally gained the vote in 1918). In her novels and essays, Woolf proposed that women might become powerful only by achieving financial and psychological independence from men. Freedom, argued Woolf, is the prerequisite for creativity: For a woman to secure her own creative freedom, she must have money and the privacy provided by "a room of her own." In the feminist essay "A Room of One's Own," Woolf responds to a clergyman's remark that no female could have matched the genius of William Shakespeare. In the excerpt below, Woolf envisions Shakespeare's imaginary sister, Judith, in her sixteenth-century setting. She uses this fictional character to raise some challenging questions concerning the psychological aspects of female creativity.

READING 6.24 From Woolf's "A Room of One's Own" (1929)

. . . Let me imagine, since facts are so hard to come by, what   1
would have happened had Shakespeare had a wonderfully
gifted sister, called Judith, let us say. Shakespeare himself
went, very probably—his mother was an heiress—to the
grammar school, where he may have learnt Latin—Ovid, Virgil
and Horace—and the elements of grammar and logic. He was,
it is well known, a wild boy who poached rabbits, perhaps
shot a deer, and had, rather sooner than he should have done,
to marry a woman in the neighbourhood, who bore him a child
rather quicker than was right. That escapade sent him to seek   10
his fortune in London. He had, it seemed, a taste for the
theatre; he began by holding horses at the stage door. Very
soon he got work in the theatre, became a successful actor,
and lived at the hub of the universe, meeting everybody,
knowing everybody, practising his art on the boards, exercising
his wits in the streets, and even getting access to the palace
of the queen. Meanwhile his extraordinarily gifted sister, let
us suppose, remained at home. She was as adventurous, as

imaginative, as agog to see the world as he was. But she was not sent to school. She had no chance of learning grammar and logic, let alone of reading Horace and Virgil. She picked up a book now and then, one of her brother's perhaps, and read a few pages. But then her parents came in and told her to mend the stockings or mind the stew and not moon about with books and papers. They would have spoken sharply but kindly, for they were substantial people who knew the conditions of life for a woman and loved their daughter— indeed, more likely than not she was the apple of her father's eye. Perhaps she scribbled some pages up in an apple loft on the sly, but was careful to hide them or set fire to them. Soon, however, before she was out of her teens, she was to be betrothed to the son of a neighbouring wool-stapler. She cried out that marriage was hateful to her, and for that she was severely beaten by her father. Then he ceased to scold her. He begged her instead not to hurt him, not to shame him in this matter of her marriage. He would give her a chain of beads or a fine petticoat, he said; and there were tears in his eyes. How could she disobey him? How could she break his heart? The force of her own gift alone drove her to it. She made up a small parcel of her belongings, let herself down by a rope one summer's night and took the road to London. She was not seventeen. The birds that sang in the hedge were not more musical than she was. She had the quickest fancy, a gift like her brother's, for the tune of words. Like him, she had a taste for the theatre. She stood at the stage door; she wanted to act, she said. Men laughed in her face. The manager—a fat, loose-lipped man—guffawed. He bellowed something about poodles dancing and women acting—no woman, he said, could possibly be an actress. He hinted—you can imagine what. She could get no training in her craft. Could she even seek her dinner in a tavern or roam the streets at midnight? Yet her genius was for fiction and lusted to feed abundantly upon the lives of men and women and the study of their ways. At last—for she was very young, oddly like Shakespeare the poet in her face, with the same grey eyes and rounded brows—at last Nick Greene the actor-manager took pity on her; she found herself with child by that gentleman and so— who shall measure the heat and violence of the poet's heart when caught and tangled in a woman's body?—killed herself one winter's night and lies buried at some cross-roads where the omnibuses now stop outside the Elephant and Castle.

. . . any woman born with a great gift in the sixteenth century would certainly have gone crazed, shot herself, or ended her days in some lonely cottage outside the village, half witch, half wizard, feared and mocked at. For it needs little skill in psychology to be sure that a highly gifted girl who had tried to use her gift for poetry would have been so thwarted and hindered by other people, so tortured and pulled asunder by her own contrary instincts, that she must have lost her health and sanity to a certainty. No girl could have walked to London and stood at a stage door and forced her way into the presence of actor-managers without doing herself a violence and suffering an anguish which may have been irrational—for chastity may be a fetish invented by certain societies for unknown reasons—but were none the less inevitable. Chastity had then, it has even now, a religious importance in a woman's life, and has so wrapped itself round with nerves and

instincts that to cut it free and bring it to the light of day demands courage of the rarest. To have lived a free life in London in the sixteenth century would have meant for a woman who was poet and playwright a nervous stress and dilemma which might well have killed her. Had she survived, whatever she had written would have been twisted and deformed, issuing from a strained and morbid imagination. And undoubtedly, I thought, looking at the shelf where there are no plays by women, her work would have gone unsigned. That refuge she would have sought certainly. It was the relic of the sense of chastity that dictated anonymity to women even so late as the nineteenth century. Currer Bell,[1] George Eliot, George Sand, all the victims of inner strife as their writings prove, sought ineffectively to veil themselves by using the name of a man. Thus they did homage to the convention, which if not implanted by the other sex was liberally encouraged by them (the chief glory of a woman is not to be talked of, said Pericles, himself a much- talked-of man), that publicity in women is detestable. Anonymity runs in their blood. . . .

That woman, then, who was born with a gift of poetry in the sixteenth century, was an unhappy woman, a woman at strife against herself. All the conditions of her life, all her all her own instincts, were hostile to the state of mind which is needed to set free whatever is in the brain. But what is the state of mind that is most propitious to the act of creation, I asked. Can one come by any notion of the state that furthers and makes possible that strange activity? Here I opened the volume containing the Tragedies of Shakespeare. What was Shakespeare's state of mind, for instance, when he wrote *Lear* and *Antony and Cleopatra*? It was certainly the state of mind most favourable to poetry that there has ever existed. But Shakespeare himself said nothing about it. We only know casually and by chance that he "never blotted a line." Nothing indeed was ever said by the artist himself about his state of mind until the eighteenth century perhaps. Rousseau perhaps began it. At any rate, by the nineteenth century self-consciousness had developed so far that it was the habit for men of letters to describe their minds in confessions and autobiographies. Their lives also were written, and their letters were printed after their deaths. Thus, though we do not know what Shakespeare went through when he wrote *Lear*, we do know what Carlyle went through when he wrote the *French Revolution*: what Flaubert went through when he wrote *Madame Bovary*: what Keats was going through when he tried to write poetry against the coming of death and the indifference of the world.

And one gathers from this enormous modern literature of confession and self-analysis that to write a work of genius is almost always a feat of prodigious difficulty. Everything is against the likelihood that it will come from the writer's mind whole and entire. Generally material circumstances are against it. Dogs will bark; people will interrupt; money must be made; health will break down. Further, accentuating all these difficulties and making them harder to bear is the world's notorious indifference. It does not ask people to write

---

[1]Currer Bell was the pseudonym for the British novelist Charlotte Brontë (1816–1855); for Eliot and Sand, see chapter 28.

poems and novels and histories; it does not need them. It does not care whether Flaubert finds the right word or whether Carlyle scrupulously verifies this or that fact. Naturally, it will not pay for what it does not want. And so the writer, Keats, Flaubert, Carlyle, suffers, especially in the creative years of youth, every form of distraction and discouragement. A curse, a cry of agony, rises from those books of analysis and confession. "Mighty poets in their misery dead"—that is the burden of their song. If anything comes through in spite of all this, it is a miracle, and probably no book is born entire and uncrippled as it was conceived. 140

But for women, I thought, looking at the empty shelves, these difficulties were infinitely more formidable. In the first place, to have a room of her own, let alone a quiet room or a sound-proof room, was out of the question, unless her parents were exceptionally rich or very noble, even up to the beginning of the nineteenth century. Since her pin money, which 150 depended on the good will of her father, was only enough to keep her clothed, she was debarred from such alleviations as came even to Keats or Tennyson or Carlyle, all poor men; from a walking tour, a little journey to France, from the separate lodging which, even if it were miserable enough, sheltered them from the claims and tyrannies of their families. Such material difficulties were formidable, but much worse were the immaterial. The indifference of the world which Keats and Flaubert and other men of genius have found so hard to bear was in her case not indifference but hostility. The world did 160 not say to her as it said to them, Write if you choose; it makes no difference to me. The world said with a guffaw, Write? What's the good of your writing? . . .

Postwar Feminism: de Beauvoir

In Western Europe and in America, the two world wars had a positive effect on the position of women. In the absence of men during the wars, women assumed many of the jobs in agriculture and in industry. As Woolf predicted, the newly found financial independence of women gave them a sense of freedom and stimulated their demands for legal and social equality. Women's roles in regions beyond the West were also changing. In the Soviet Union, the communist regime put women to work in industry and on the battlefields. In China, where women had been bought and sold for centuries, the People's Republic in 1949 closed all brothels, forbade arranged marriages, and enforced policies of equal pay for equal work. But the feminist movement in postwar Europe and the United States demanded psychological independence as well as job equality; its goals involved raising the consciousness of *both* sexes.

The new woman must shed her passivity and achieve independence through responsible action; this was the charge of the French novelist, social critic, and existentialist Simone de Beauvoir (1908–1986). In the classic feminist text *The Second Sex*, de Beauvoir dethroned the "myth of femininity"—the false and disempowering idea that women possess a unique and preordained "feminine" essence, which condemns them to a role of social and intellectual subordination to men. Reassessing the

biological, psychological, and political reasons for women's dependency, she concluded that while Man defines Woman as "the Other" (or *second* sex), it is women themselves who complacently accept their subordinate position. De Beauvoir called on women everywhere "to renounce all advantages conferred upon them by their alliance" with men. She pursued this goal (unsuccessfully, according to some critics) in her own life: Her fifty-year association with Jean-Paul Sartre constitutes one of the most intriguing partnerships of the century. Although both enjoyed love affairs with other partners, they shared a lifelong marriage of minds.

In the following brief excerpt from *The Second Sex*, de Beauvoir explores the nature of female dependency upon men and the "metaphysical risk" of liberty.

READING 6.25 From de Beauvoir's *The Second Sex* (1949)

If woman seems to be the inessential which never becomes 1 the essential, it is because she herself fails to bring about this change. Proletarians say "We"; Negroes also. Regarding themselves as subjects, they transform the bourgeois, the whites, into "others." But women do not say "We," except at some congress of feminists or similar formal demonstration; men say "women," and women use the same word in referring to themselves. They do not authentically assume a subjective attitude. The proletarians have accomplished the revolution in Russia, the Negroes in Haiti, the Indo-Chinese are battling for 10 it in Indo-China; but the women's effort has never been anything more than a symbolic agitation. They have gained only what men have been willing to grant; they have taken nothing, they have only received.

The reason for this is that women lack concrete means for organizing themselves into a unit which can stand face to face with the correlative unit. They have no past, no history, no religion of their own; and they have no such solidarity of work and interest as that of the proletariat. They are not even promiscuously herded together in the way that creates 20 community feeling among the American Negroes, the ghetto Jews, the workers of Saint-Denis, or the factory hands of Renault. They live dispersed among the males, attached through residence, housework, economic condition, and social standing to certain men— fathers or husbands—more firmly than they are to other women. If they belong to the bourgeoisie, they feel solidarity with men of that class, not with proletarian women; if they are white, their allegiance is to white men, not to Negro women. The proletariat can propose to massacre the ruling class, and a sufficiently 30 fanatical Jew or Negro might dream of getting sole possession of the atomic bomb and making humanity wholly Jewish or black; but woman cannot even dream of exterminating the males. The bond that unites her to her oppressors is not comparable to any other. The division of the sexes is a biological fact, not an event in human history. Male and female stand opposed within a primordial *Mitsein*,[1] and

---
[1]German for "coexistence."

woman has not broken it. The couple is a fundamental unity with two halves riveted together, and the cleavage of society along the line of sex is impossible. Here is to be found the basic trait of woman: she is the *Other* in a totality of which the two components are necessary to one another. . . .

Now, woman has always been man's dependant, if not his slave; the two sexes have never shared the world in equality. And even today woman is heavily handicapped, though her situation is beginning to change. Almost nowhere is her legal status the same as man's, and frequently it is much to her disadvantage. Even when her rights are legally recognized in the abstract, long-standing custom prevents their full expression in the mores. In the economic sphere men and women can almost be said to make up two castes; other things being equal, the former hold the better jobs, get higher wages, and have more opportunity for success than their new competitors. In industry and politics men have a great many more positions and they monopolize the most important posts. In addition to all this, they enjoy a traditional prestige that the education of children tends in every way to support, for the present enshrines the past—and in the past all history has been made by men. At the present time, when women are beginning to take part in the affairs of the world, it is still a world that belongs to men— they have no doubt of it at all and women have scarcely any. To decline to be the Other, to refuse to be a party to the deal—this would be for women to renounce all the advantages conferred upon them by their alliance with the superior caste. Man-the-sovereign will provide woman-the- liege with material protection and will undertake the moral justification of her existence; thus she can evade at once both economic risk and the metaphysical risk of a liberty in which ends and aims must be contrived without assistance. Indeed, along with the ethical urge of each individual to affirm his subjective existence, there is also the temptation to forego liberty and become a thing. This is an inauspicious road, for he who takes it—passive, lost, ruined—becomes henceforth the creature of another's will, frustrated in his transcendence and deprived of every value. But it is an easy road; on it one avoids the strain involved in undertaking an authentic existence. When man makes of woman the *Other*, he may, then, expect her to manifest deep-seated tendencies toward complicity. Thus, woman may fail to lay claim to the status of subject because she lacks definite resources, because she feels the necessary bond that ties her to man regardless of reciprocity, and because she is often very well pleased with her role as the *Other*. . . .

Feminist Poetry

During the 1960s, and especially in the United States, the struggle for equality between the sexes assumed a strident tone. Gender discrimination in both education and employment triggered demands for federal legislation on behalf of women. Even as new types of contraceptives gave women control over their reproductive functions and greater sexual freedoms, the struggle to secure legal and political rights continued, generating protest marches and a spate of consciousness-raising literature. In 1963, Betty Friedan (b. 1921) published *The Feminine Mystique*, which claimed that American society—and commercial advertising in particular—had brainwashed women to prefer the roles of wives and mothers to other positions in life. Friedan was one of the first feminists to attack the theories of Sigmund Freud (see chapter 33), especially Freud's patriarchal view of women as failed men. She challenged women to question the existing order and to seek careers outside the home. With the founding of the National Organization for Women (NOW) in 1966, radical feminists called for a restructuring of all Western institutions.

Since the 1960s, there has been a virtual renaissance of poetry and fiction focused on the twin themes of gender equality and the search for female self-identity. As with the literature of black liberation, feminist writing often seethes with repressed rage and anger. Clearly, not all modern literature written by women addresses exclusively female issues—recent female writers have dealt with subjects as varied as boxing and the plight of the environment. Yet, in postwar literature produced by women, three motifs recur: the victimization of the female, her effort to define her role in a society traditionally dominated by men, and her displacement from her ancient role as goddess and matriarch.

Among the many outstanding feminist poets of the last third of the century are Sylvia Plath (1932–1963), Anne Sexton (1928–1975), Sonia Sanchez (b. 1935), and Adrienne Rich (b. 1929). Anne Sexton probed problems related to the socialization of women and the search for female identity. Deeply confessional, her verse often reflects upon her own troubled life, which (like Plath's) ended in suicide—an ironic fulfillment of Woolf's prophecy concerning the fate of Shakespeare's imaginary sister. In the autobiographical poem "Self in 1958," Sexton explores the images that traditionally have defined women: dolls, apparel, kitchens, and, finally, herself as an extension of her mother. Sexton's poem, which contemplates the female struggle for self-identity in modern society, recalls both Nora's plight in Ibsen's *A Doll's House* (see chapter 30) and Woolf's observation that women "think through their mothers."

The African-American poet Sonia Sanchez deals with the interrelated questions of racism and identity. Sanchez's poetry is more colloquial than Sexton's, and (like Baraka's) it is often fiercely confrontational. In the poem "Woman" Sanchez draws on the literary tradition in which eminent (and usually male) writers call upon the classical gods for inspiration: She invokes the spiritual powers of mother earth to infuse her with courage and creative energy.

The poems of Adrienne Rich are among the most challenging in the feminist canon. They are, to a large extent, impassioned responses to her shifting and often conflicting roles as American, Southerner, Jew, wife, mother, teacher, civil rights activist, feminist, and lesbian. Many of Rich's poems explore the complexities of personal and political relationships, especially as they are affected by gender. In the poem "Translations," she draws attention to the ways in which traditional gender roles polarize the sexes and potentially disempower women.

READING 6.26 The Poems of Sexton, Sanchez, and Rich

Sexton's "Self in 1958" (1966)

What is reality?   1
I am a plaster doll; I pose
with eyes that cut open without landfall or nightfall
upon some shellacked and grinning person,
eyes that open, blue, steel, and close.   5
Am I approximately an I. Magnin[1] transplant?
I have hair, black angel,
black-angel-stuffing to comb,
nylon legs, luminous arms
and some advertised clothes.   10

I live in a doll's house
with four chairs,
a counterfeit table, a flat roof
and a big front door.
Many have come to such a small crossroad.   15
There is an iron bed,
(Life enlarges, life takes aim)
a cardboard floor,
windows that flash open on someone's city,
and little more.   20

Someone plays with me,
plants me in the all-electric kitchen,
Is this what Mrs. Rombauer[2] said?
Someone pretends with me—
I am walled in solid by their noise—   25
or puts me upon their straight bed.
They think I am me!
Their warmth? Their warmth is not a friend!
They pry my mouth for their cups of gin
and their stale bread.   30

What is reality
to this synthetic doll
who should smile, who should shift gears,
should spring the doors open in a wholesome disorder,
and have no evidence of ruin or fears?   35
But I would cry,
rooted into the wall that
was once my mother,
if I could remember how
and if I had the tears.   40

[1] A fashionable department store.
[2] Irma S. Rombauer, author of the popular cookbook, *The Joy of Cooking.*

Sanchez's "Woman" (1978)

Come ride my birth, earth mother   1
tell me how i have become, became
this woman with razor blades between
her teeth.
        sing me my history O earth mother
about tongues multiplying memories   5
about breaths contained in straw.
pull me from the throat of mankind
where worms eat, O earth mother.
come to this Black woman. you.
rider of earth pilgrimages.   10
tell me how i have held five bodies
in one large cocktail of love
and still have the thirst of the beginning sip.
tell me. tellLLLLLL me. earth mother
for i want to rediscover me. the secret of me   15
the river of me. the morning ease of me.
i want my body to carry my words like aqueducts.
i want to make the world my diary
and speak rivers.

rise up earth mother   20
out of rope-strung-trees
dancing a windless dance
come phantom mother
dance me a breakfast of births
let your mouth spill me forth   25
so i creak with your mornings.
come old mother, light up my mind
with a story bright as the sun.

Rich's "Translations" (1972)

You show me the poems of some woman   1
my age, or younger
translated from your language

Certain words occur: *enemy, oven, sorrow*
enough to let me know   5
she's a woman of my time

obsessed

with Love, our subject:
we've trained it like ivy to our walls
baked it like bread in our ovens   10
worn it like lead on our ankles
watched it through binoculars as if
it were a helicopter
bringing food to our famine
or the satellite   15
of a hostile power

I begin so see that woman
doing things: stirring rice
ironing a skirt
typing a manuscript till dawn   20

Figure 36.7 MARISOL ESCOBAR, *Women and Dog*, 1964. Wood, plaster, synthetic polymer, and miscellaneous items, 72¼ × 73 × 30¹⁵⁄₁₆ in. Collection of the Whitney Museum of American Art, New York. Purchase, with funds from the Friends of the Whitney Museum of American Art (64.17 a–g). Photo: Robert E. Mates, N.J. © Marisol Escobar/DACS, London/VAGA, New York 2000.

trying to make a call
from a phonebooth

The phone rings unanswered
in a man's bedroom
she hears him telling someone else   25
Never mind. She'll get tired.
hears him telling her story to her sister

who becomes her enemy
and will in her own time
light her own way to sorrow   30

ignorant of the fact this way of grief
is shared, unnecessary
and political

Feminist Art

The history of world art includes only a small number of female artists. Addressing this fact, the Australian-born feminist Germaine Greer (b. 1939) explained,

> There is . . . no female Leonardo, no female Titian, no female Poussin, but the reason does not lie in the fact that women have wombs, that they can have babies, that their brains are smaller, that they lack vigor, that they are not sensual. The reason is simply that you cannot make great artists out of egos that have been damaged, with wills that are defective, with libidos that have been driven out of reach and energy diverted into neurotic channels.*

The Obstacle Race: The Fortunes of Women Painters and their Work. New York: Farrar, Straus, Giroux, 1979, 327.

A sure indication of change, however, is the fact that, since the middle of the twentieth century, the number of women in the visual arts (and in music as well) has been greater than ever before in history. And, as with feminist poetry, much of the painting and sculpture produced by women artists since the 1960s has been driven by feminist concerns. A few representative examples will suffice to make this point.

Throughout her long and productive career, the Venezuelan artist Marisol Escobar (b. 1930) has used plaster casts, drawings, and prints of her own face, hands, and body to create highly personal life-sized assemblages. Marisol (as she is popularly called) draws inspiration from the folk art of Mexico and pre-Hispanic America, whose brightly painted wooden images of saints and local gods are usually the work of women. She often mixes the traditional media of paint, wood, and plaster with modern synthetics, such as plastic and polyester resin. Marisol's *Women and Dog* (1964) portrays a group of fashionable urban women at leisure (Figure **36.7**). The faces of all the figures are self-portraits of the artist.

The internationally acclaimed French sculptor Niki de Saint Phalle (b. 1930) fabricated gigantic female sculptures that she called "Nanas." In 1963 Saint Phalle exhibited a monumental 80-foot-long, 20-foot-high, and 30-foot-wide Nana that viewers might enter through a doorway between the figure's legs. Inside was a cinema with Greta Garbo movies, a telephone, a refreshment bar, and taped voices of romantic conversations between a man and a woman. Saint Phalle's *Black Venus* (Figure **36.8**), a hugely proportioned polyester "earth mother," wears a heart on her belly and a flower on her breast. This exuberant creature is Saint Phalle's answer to Western stereotypes of female beauty. More closely resembling the ponderous fertility figures of prehistoric cultures (see Introduction) than the refined marble goddesses of classical antiquity (see chapter 5), Saint Phalle's *Venus* celebrates the joys of

sensual freedom. She is the feminist reproof of the idealized and impassive images of womanhood that glut mainstream Western art history.

The militant American feminist Judy Gerowitz (b. 1939), who in 1969 assumed the surname of her native city (hence, Judy Chicago), has been a lifelong advocate of women's art. Chicago pioneered some of the first art communities in which women worked together to produce, exhibit, and sell art. Her efforts ignited the visual arts with the consciousness-raising politics of the feminist movement. Between 1974 and 1979, Chicago directed a project called *The Dinner Party*, a room-size sculpture consisting of a triangular table with thirty-nine place settings, each symbolizing a famous woman in myth or history (Figure **36.9**). The feminist counterpart of the Last Supper, *The Dinner Party* pays homage to such immortals as Nefertiti, Sappho, Queen Elizabeth I, and Virginia Woolf. To carry out this monumental project, Chicago studied the traditionally female arts of embroidery and china painting, inventing at the same time new techniques for combining such dissimilar materials as ceramics and lace. Over three hundred men and women contributed to this cooperative enterprise, which brought international attention to the cultural contributions of women in world history.

In searching for a feminist aesthetic, women artists have brought attention to the female body as representative of nature's procreative forces. The Cuban-born Ana Mendieta (1948–1985) used photography and film to

Figure 36.9 (above) **JUDY CHICAGO**, *The Dinner Party*, 1974–1979. Multimedia, 48 x 48 x 48 ft. © Judy Chicago, 1979. Photo: Donald Woodman.

Figure 36.10 (right) **ANA MENDIETA**, *Untitled* from the *Tree of Life* series, 1977. Color photographs, 20 × 13¼ in. Courtesy Galerie Lelong, New York. © The Estate of Ana Mendieta.

document performances inspired by Afro-Caribbean fertility rituals. For the series known as *Silhouettes*, Mendieta immersed herself in pools of water, sand, and mud, and recorded 200 images of her body or its physical impressions on various earth surfaces. In the photograph *Tree of Life* from this series, the artist, encrusted with mud, appears in the dual guises of dryad (a classical tree nymph) and ancient priestess (Figure **36.10**).

The career of the American photographer Cindy Sherman (b. 1954) addresses one of the more recent concerns of feminist artists: the fact that the *image* of the female in traditional Western art—an image of sweetness, sexiness, and servility—has been shaped by male needs and values. Such images, say contemporary feminists, dominate the world's "great artworks" and reflect the controlling power of the (male) "gaze." Just as Colescott and Saar use art to attack racial stereotypes, so feminists like Sherman make visual assaults on gender stereotypes—those projected by the collective body of "great art" and by the modern-day phenomena of television, "girlie" magazines, and other mass media. Sherman's large, glossy studio photographs of the 1970s feature the artist herself in poses and attire that call attention to the body as political or sexual object. In personalized narratives that resemble

Figure 36.11 CINDY SHERMAN, *Untitled #276*, 1993. Color photograph, edition of six, 6 ft. 8½ in. × 5 ft. 1 in. framed. Courtesy of the artist and Metro Pictures, New York.

Photography is the favorite medium of the Iranian-born Shirin Neshat (b. 1957), who also produces short films. Cast entirely in black and white, Neshat's artworks deal with conflicting values and lifestyles: male and female, Islamic and Western, ancient and modern, rural and urban. Her photographic series, *Women of Allah* (1994), addresses the role of women who fought in the 1979 revolution that overthrew Iran's ruling dynasty. Neshat makes dramatic use of the veil (the large square of black cloth known as the *chador*) to isolate her own face, which—intersected by a rifle—becomes the site of Arabic texts transcribed in Farsi calligraphy (Figure **36.13**). Neshat's controversial photographs (and films) examine the ways in which ideas of spirituality and politics intersect in Islam and how they affect women in the multicultural community.

Sexual Identity

This century's quests for racial and sexual equality have also worked to raise public consciousness in matters of gender,* that is, the way in which sex is used as a structuring principle in human culture and society. Gender, or sexual identity, and sexual freedom are matters that have deeply affected the arts. More so than race, gender determines how people behave and how they are regarded by others. Assumptions concerning gender and, specifically, the sexual and social roles of males and females are rooted

---

*Unlike sex (which designates individuals as either male or female), gender (which distinguishes between masculinity and femininity) is culturally, not biologically, prescribed

Figure 36.12 BARBARA KRUGER, *Untitled ("Your body is a battleground")*, 1989. Photographic silkscreen on vinyl, 9 ft. 4 in. × 9 ft. 4 in. Courtesy Mary Boone Gallery, New York. Photo: Zindman/Freemont, New York.

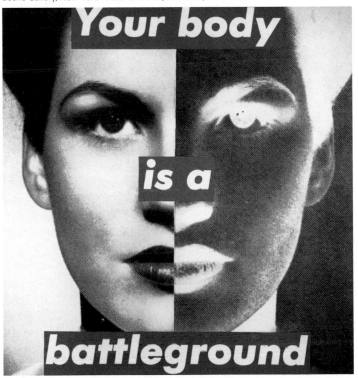

black-and-white movie stills, Sherman recreates commercial stereotypes that mock the subservient roles that women play: the "little woman," the *femme fatale*, the baby doll, the "pinup," and the lovesick teenager. Since the 1980s, Sherman has used the newest techniques in color photography to assault—often in visceral terms—sexual and historical stereotypes of women. She may replace the male image in a world-famous painting with a female image (often Sherman herself), use artificial body parts to "remake" the traditional nude, or flagrantly recast famous females from Western myth, history, and religion. In Figure **36.11**, a flaxen-haired Cinderella, holding the traditional symbol of purity (the lily), assumes the position and apparel of a prostitute. This vulgar figure Sherman "enshrines" in a manner usually reserved in Western art for images of the Virgin.

Well aware of the extent to which commercialism shapes identity, Barbara Kruger (b. 1945) creates photographs that deftly unite word and image to resemble commercial billboards. "Your Body is a Battleground," insists Kruger; by superimposing the message over the divided (positive and negative) image of a female face, the artist calls attention to the controversial issue of abortion in contemporary society (Figure **36.12**).

in traditions as old as Paleolithic culture and as venerated as the Bible. For many, sexual roles are fixed and unchanging. However, these assumptions, like so many others in the cultural history of the twentieth century, have been challenged and reassessed. Gender issues have accompanied a demand for equality on the part of those whose sexual orientation is untraditional: bisexuals, homosexuals (gays and lesbians), and other transgendered individuals. In America homosexuals date the birth of their "liberation" to June 1969, when they openly and violently protested a police raid on the Stonewall Inn, a gay bar in New York's Greenwich Village. Since then, the call for protection against harassment has shifted to litigated demands for social equality. While all societies have included a transgendered subculture, it was not until the last decades of the twentieth century that sexual and public issues intersected to produce some highly controversial questions: Should homosexuals serve in the armed forces? How does homosexuality affect the future of the traditional family? Should sexually explicit art receive public funding? The resolution of these and other gender-related questions continues to play a major role in reshaping the humanistic tradition.

There are a number of reasons why issues of human sexuality became so visible in the culture of the late twentieth century: increasing sexual permissiveness (the

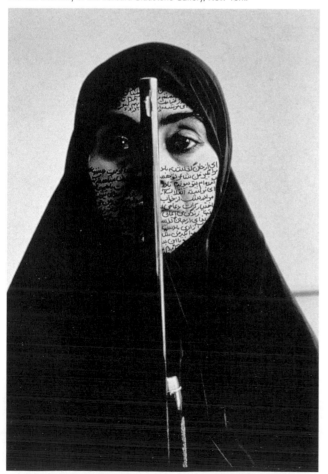

Figure 36.13 SHIRIN NESHAT, *Rebellious Silence*, 1994. Gelatin silver print and ink. Courtesy of the Barbara Gladstone Gallery, New York.

consequence of improved pharmaceutical methods for contra- ception); the activity of the media (especially TV and film) in broadcasting sexually explicit entertainment; and the appearance of the devastating pandemic called AIDS (Acquired Immune Deficiency Syndrome), a life-threatening disease that results from a retrovirus that attacks the blood cells of the body, thus causing a failure of the autoimmune system. Collectively, these phenomena have represented an overwhelming challenge to traditional concepts of sexuality, sexual behavior, and (more generally) to conventional morality. They have also generated a provocative blurring of sex roles (currently exploited in commercial advertising and the popular media). And they have complicated the difficulty of distinguishing between forms of expression that have mere shock value and those that represent a substantial creative achievement. The photographs of Robert Mapplethorpe (1946–1989) are significant in this regard. Mapplethorpe's fine-grained silver gelatin prints display exquisitely composed images ranging from still life subjects to classically posed nudes. Although usually lacking explicit narrative, they reflect the artist's preoccupation with physical and sexual themes: male virility, sado-masochism, androgyny, and sexual identity. A sculptor in his early training, Mapplethorpe presents his subjects as pristine objects, occasionally transforming them into erotic symbols. His photographs depict contemporary sexuality in a manner that is at once detached and impassioned, but they often gain added power as gender-bending parodies of sexual stereotypes—witness the masculinity of Lisa Lyon (herself a weight-lifter) in Figure **36.14** (see also Figure 38.27). Mapplethorpe fulfills the artist's mission to see things (in his words) "like they haven't been seen before."

Themes of human sexuality have also increasingly preoccupied twentieth-century writers. In her science fiction fantasy *The Left Hand of Darkness* (1969), the African-American writer Ursula LeGuin (b. 1929) creates a distant planet, home to creatures with the sexual potential of both males and females. The ambisexuality of the characters in this fictional utopia calls into question human preconceptions about the defined roles of behavior for men and women. Through the device of science fiction, LeGuin suggests a shift in focus from the narrow view of male–female dualities (or opposites) to larger, more urgent matters of interdependence.

While LeGuin examines bisexuality in imaginary settings, others, and in particular gay artists, have dealt with the experience of homosexuality in their day-to-day lives. The past three decades have been especially rich in the production of art that either examines sexual "otherness" or reflects (and celebrates) a "gay sensibility." Since the 1990s, these themes have received unprecedented attention in the popular entertainment media of television and film. They are also the subject of inquiry among scholars of a new discipline known as "queer representation."*

*See Martin Duberman, ed., *Queer Representations: Reading Lives, Reading Cultures*. New York: City University of New York Center for Lesbian and Gay Studies, 1997.

Figure 36.14 ROBERT MAPPLETHORPE, *Lisa Lyon*, 1982. Silver gelatin print. © 1998 Estate of Robert Mapplethorpe. Courtesy Robert Miller Gallery, New York.

By drawing attention to the ways in which matters of sexuality affect society and its institutions, gay art asserts that sexuality and power are as closely related as race and power or gender and power. For example, the Pulitzer Prize-winning play *Angels in America: A Gay Fantasia on National Themes* (written in two parts: *Millennium Approaches*, 1990, and *Perestroika*, 1993) by Tony Kushner (b. 1957) offers a radical vision of American society set against the AIDS epidemic and the politics of conservatism. Kushner urges that the old America—"straight," Protestant, and white—needs to look with greater objectivity at "the fringe" (the variety of ethnic, racial, and sexual minorities) that demands acceptance and its share of power. Kushner's riveting drama represents a movement for body-conscious politics and socially responsible art that animates the last decade of this century (see chapter 37).

Beyond issues of sexual orientation and the struggle against discrimination on the part of the transgendered minority, the more immediate issue of the AIDS pandemic has deeply affected artists of the late twentieth century. Although AIDS has afflicted all segments of the populations throughout the world, the largest group of AIDS victims in the West has been male homosexuals. This group, marginalized by mainstream society, is distinctive, however, in having produced a large number of outstanding artists, many of whom—Mapplethorpe included—have fallen victim to the HIV virus. The loss of so many members of the world arts community motivated artists like Kushner to view contemporary society through the life-death mirror of AIDS, while at the same time emphasizing the need for compassion and justice. Sympathy for AIDS victims of every race, gender, and sexual orientation has called forth an important body of art. Such works range from hand-crafted folk memorials to sophisticated short stories, dance compositions, and symphonies. The *Names Project Quilt*, begun in 1985, engaged twenty thousand ordinary individuals, each of whom created a single 3- by 6-foot fabric panel in memory of someone who died of an HIV-related disease. In 1992, AIDS activists assembled the panels in 16-foot squares and took them to Washington, D.C., to protest governmental inaction with regard to the AIDS crisis. Commemorating the deaths of some 150,000 Americans, the Aids Quilt covered 15 acres of ground between the Washington Monument and Lincoln Memorial. The Names Project continues: In 1996, the quilt panels numbered forty thousand, that is, double the figure of the original.

The AIDS crisis has been the central allegory in the installation project undertaken by the Canadian artists' group, General Idea. *One Day of AZT and One Year of AZT* (1991), a two-part installation featuring some 1,825 plastic pills, refers to typical daily and annual dosages of the AIDS-retardant medication. Circumscribing five coffin-like tablets that occupy the central space, the mock pills line the gallery walls like tiny tombstones. An equally compelling response to the AIDS epidemic is the Symphony No. 1 (1990) by the American composer John Corigliano (b. 1938). Corigliano, whose contribution to postmodern opera is discussed in chapter 38, wrote the so-called *AIDS Symphony* to express his anger and grief at the loss of his many colleagues and friends to this disease. The union of harsh and tender passages that characterizes this musical testament is especially effective in the first movement, appropriately entitled "Apologue:* Rage and Remembrance." One of the most recent monuments to the AIDS crisis is the controversial *Still/Here* (1994), a performance work conceived by the African-American dancer Bill T. Jones (b. 1952). For the piece Jones, who is himself HIV-positive, combined choreography and vocal music with video imagery derived in part from workshops he conducted with AIDS victims. *Still/Here* has provoked heated debate concerning the artistic value of issue-driven art: Does art that showcases sickness and death serve merely to manipulate viewers? This is only one of many questions that probe current efforts to wed art to social action (see chapter 37).

Ethnicity and Identity

"Ethnic identity" refers to the manner in which individuals define themselves as members of a group sharing the same culture and values. Individual identity is a multidimensional phenomenon, a "cluster" of traits that form the totality of one's self-perceived image. Such traits include one's gender, race, language, physical appearance, and personal (including religious) values. The self-affirming significance of ethnic identity is best expressed in the ancient Yoruba proverb that asserts "I am because we are; What I am is what we are." Perceiving oneself as part of an

ethnic group is a major determinant of individual identity, and the freedom to exercise that identity—as it manifests itself in language, music, and other traditional and ritual forms—has become a leading issue in contemporary society.

Ethnic identity has represented a powerful social and political force in the post-colonial, post-Soviet world. Having cast off the rule of colonial powers and totalitarian ideologies, ethnic peoples have sought to reaffirm their primary affiliations—to return to their spiritual roots. Efforts to revive ethnic idenity have coincided frequently with the quest for solidarity and political autonomy. "Identity politics," the exercise of power by means of group solidarity, has—in its most malignant guise—pitted ethnic groups against each other in militant opposition. Such circumstances lie at the base of many (if not most) of the world's current conflagrations in Africa, the Middle East, the Balkans, the Indian subcontinent, and the former Soviet Union.

But ethnicity also underlies many of the creative projects of twentieth-century artists and thinkers. In the United States, the quest for ethnic identity has been a central theme in the arts: Leslie Marmon Silko (b. 1948), for example (of Native American and Mexican ancestry), draws on Pueblo tribal folktales in her poetry and prose; and in the stories of the Chinese-American writer Maxine Hong Kingston (b. 1940), family legends and native Chinese customs become conduits through which the author explores her identity. To these and many more contemporary writers, the oral tradition—stories handed down from generation to generation (often by and through women)—animates autobiographical themes that define a unique ethnic identity in modern society.

Ethnicity has become particularly important among vast numbers of immigrants who have made America their home. Especially in the last half century, dramatic demographic changes (in the form of rising numbers of Latinos and Asian-Americans) have changed the face of the economy, the urban environment, and the culture. By the year 2009, Latinos are expected to surpass African-Americans as the largest ethnic minority in the United States. In all aspects of life, from literature and art to food and dance styles, there has been a flowering of Latino culture. With *The Mambo Kings Play Songs of Love* (1989), the first novel by a Hispanic to win the Pulitzer Prize, the Cuban-American Oscar Hijuelos (b. 1951) brought attention to the impact of Latin American music on American culture, and more generally, to the role of memory in reclaiming one's ethnic roots. Younger writers have given voice to personal problems of adjustment in America's ethnic mosaic and to the ways in which language and customs provide a vital sense of ethnic identity. These are the themes pursued by one of today's leading *Chicana* (Mexican-American female) authors, Sandra Cisneros (b. 1954). Cisneros, who describes the struggle of Chicana women in an alien society, writes in the familiar voice of everyday speech. Of her writing style, she says: "It's very much of an anti-academic voice—a child's voice, a girl's voice, a poor girl's voice, a spoken voice, the voice of an American Mexican. It's in this rebellious realm of

---
*An allegorical narrative usually intended to convey a moral.

antipoetics that I tried to create a poetic text with the most unofficial language I could find." Cisneros dates the birth of her own political consciousness from the moment (in a graduate seminar on Western literature) she recognized her "otherness," that is, her separateness from the dominant culture. An excerpt from her short story *"Bien Pretty"* (*Real Pretty*) illustrates the shaping roles of skin-color, language, and memory in matters of identity.

READING 6.27 From Cisneros' *"Bien* Pretty" (1991)

. . . You have, how do I say it, something. Something I can't [1]
even put my finger on. Some way of moving, of not moving, that belongs to no one but Flavio Munguía. As if your body and bones always remembered you were made by a God who loved you, the one Mama talked about in her stories.

God made men by baking them in an oven, but he forgot about the first batch, and that's how Black people were born. And then he was so anxious about the next batch, he took them out of the oven too soon, so that's how White people were made. But the third batch he let cook until they were [10] golden-golden-golden, and, honey, that's you and me.

God made you from red clay, Flavio, with his hands. This face of yours like the little clay heads they unearth in Teotihuacán. Pinched this cheekbone, then that. Used obsidian flints for the eyes, those eyes dark as the sacrificial wells they cast virgins into. Selected hair thick as cat whiskers. Thought for a long time before deciding on this nose, elegant and wide. And the mouth, ah! Everything silent and powerful and very proud kneaded into the mouth. And then he blessed you, Flavio, with skin sweet as burnt-milk candy, smooth as river water. He made [20] you *bien* pretty even if I didn't always know it. Yes, he did. . . .

Romelia. Forever. That's what his arm said. Forever Romelia in ink once black that had paled to blue. Romelia. Romelia. Seven thin blue letters the color of a vein. "Romelia" said his forearm where the muscle swelled into a flat stone. "Romelia" it trembled when he held me. "Romelia" by the light of the votive lamp above the bed. But when I unbuttoned his shirt a bannered cross above his left nipple murmured "Elsa."

I'd never made love in Spanish before. I mean not with anyone whose *first* language was Spanish. There was crazy [30] Graham, the anarchist labor organizer who'd taught me to eat jalapeños and swear like a truck mechanic, but he was Welsh and had learned his Spanish running guns to Bolivia.

And Eddie, sure. But Eddie and I were products of our American education. Anything tender always came off sounding like the subtitles to a Buñuel film.[1]

But Flavio. When Flavio accidentally hammered his thumb, he never yelled "Ouch!" he said "*¡Ay!*" The true test of a native Spanish speaker.

¡Ay! To make love in Spanish, in a manner as intricate and [40] devout as la Alhambra.[2] To have a lover sigh *mi vida, mi preciosa, mi chiquitita,*[3] and whisper things in that language

---

[1]See chapter 33

[2]A fourteenth-century Islamic palace in Granada, Spain (see Book 2, chapter 10).

[3]"My life, my precious one, my dear little one."

Figure 36.15 LUIS JIMÉNEZ, *Border Crossing* (*Cruzando El Rio Bravo*), 1989. Fiberglass with urethane finish, 10 ft. 7 in. × 4 ft. 6 in. × 4 ft. 6 in. Courtesy the artist. Photo: Kirk Gittings, NM. © ARS, NY and DACS, London 2000.

Figure 36.16 PÉPON OSORIO, *Las Twines*, 1998. Mixed media. Dimensions variable. Courtesy the artist. Photo Frank Gimpaya.

crooned to babies, that language murmured by grandmothers, those words that smelled like your house, like flour tortillas, and the inside of your daddy's hat, like everyone talking in the kitchen at the same time, or sleeping with the windows open, like sneaking cashews from the crumpled quarter-pound bag Mama always hid in her lingerie drawer after she went shopping with Daddy at the Sears.

   That language. That sweep of palm leaves and fringed shawls. That startled fluttering, like the heart of a goldfinch or a fan. Nothing sounded dirty or hurtful or corny. How could I think of making love in English again? English with its starched *r*'s and *g*'s. English with its crisp linen syllables. English crunchy as apples, resilient and stiff as sailcloth.

   But Spanish whirred like silk, rolled and puckered and hissed. . . .

50

In the visual arts, as well, themes of ethnic identity inform all genres of contemporary art. Images from popular Hispanic culture are fundamental to the work of one of America's most celebrated Latino artists, Luis Jiménez (b. 1940). Born to Mexican parents in El Paso, Texas, Jiménez creates life-sized, brightly-colored fiberglass sculptures and lithographic prints. These make reference to Mexican contributions to American culture and to ongoing problems concerning the legal and illegal migration of thousands of Mexicans across the U.S./Mexican border. Dedicated to his father, who entered the United States illegally in 1924, *Border Crossing (Cruzando El Rio Bravo)* pays homage to those who have undertaken this traumatic passage (Figure **36.15**). At once heroic and humble, the 10-foot-high, totem-like sculpture evokes the popular

Mexican view of the border crossing as a spiritual return to native lands and a rite of passage heralding a transformation in status and lifestyle.

Like Jiménez, Pépon Osorio (b. 1955), is troubled by unresolved political issues that have marred the relationship between his homeland and the United States. Born in Puerto Rico but now living in New York, Osorio designs communal performances and mixed media installations (see chapter 38) that deal with matters of race and color. *Las Twines* recreates the tale of a set of twins who are identical in every way, except in skin color (Figure **36.16**). The two girls—one white, the other black—spend their lives in a fruitless search for their parents. The theme underscores the insecurities of mixed race peoples everywhere, but it also illustrates a form of social conflict (based on skin-color) that still prevails in Puerto Rico.

SUMMARY

The quest for liberation from poverty, oppression, and inequality was a prevailing theme in twentieth-century history. In dozens of countries, movements for decolonization followed World War II. At the same time and even into the last decades of the twentieth century, racial and ethnic minorities in various parts of the world fought valiantly to oppose discrimination as practiced by the majority culture. These crusades are yet ongoing among the populations of Eastern Europe, Latin America, and elsewhere.

The struggle of African-Americans to achieve freedom from the evils of racism has a long and dramatic history. From the Harlem Renaissance in the early twentieth century through the civil rights movement of the 1960s, the arts have mirrored that history. In the poems of Langston Hughes and Gwendolyn Brooks, and in the novels of Richard Wright, James Baldwin, Ralph Ellison, and Alice Walker, the plight and the identity of the black in white America have been central themes. The impact of black culture on the visual arts, music, and dance has been equally formidable. Blues and jazz giants from Louis Armstrong to Wynton Marsalis have produced a living body of popular music, while choreographers from Katherine Dunham to Alvin Ailey have inspired generations of dancers to draw on their African heritage.

During the postwar era, women throughout the world worked to gain political, economic, and social equality. The writings of the feminists Virginia Woolf and Simone de Beauvoir influenced women to examine the psychological conditions of their oppression. In America, the feminist movement elicited a virtual golden age in literature. The self-conscious poetry of Anne Sexton, Sonia Sanchez, and Adrienne Rich is representative of this phenomenon. In the visual arts, at least two generations of women have redefined traditional concepts of female identity: first, by celebrating womanhood itself, and, more recently, by attacking outworn stereotypes. One of the most controversial of the twentieth century's liberation movements centered on issues of sexual identity. Amidst the AIDS pandemic, Robert Mapplethorpe and Tony Kushner brought candor and perceptivity to matters of sexuality and sexual behavior. Finally, in the late twentieth century, the quest for ethnic identity—especially among the creolized populations of the Americas—generated a torrent of largely autobiographical artworks. The art inspired by the various liberation movements of the twentieth century is the tangible expression of a global search for personal freedom that continues to shape the humanistic tradition.

GLOSSARY

apartheid a policy of strict racial segregation and political and economic discrimination against the black population in the Union of South Africa

feminism the doctrine advocating equal social, political, and economic rights for women

scat singing a jazz performance style in which nonsense syllables replace the lyrics of a song

swing the jazz performer's practice of varying from the standard rhythms by playing just ahead or just behind the beat; also, a big-band jazz style developed in the 1920s and flourishing in the age of large dance bands (1932–1942)

SUGGESTIONS FOR READING

Broude, Norma, and Mary D. Garrard, eds. *The Power of Feminist Art: The American Movement of the 1970s, History and Impact.* New York: Abrams, 1996.

Cisneros, Sandra. *Woman Hollering Creek and other Stories.* New York: Vintage Books, 1991. pp. 152–154.

Giddens, Gary. *Visions of Jazz: The First Century.* New York: Oxford University Press, 1998.

Gioia, Ted. *The History of Jazz.* New York: Oxford University Press, 1999.

Isaacs, Harold R. *Power and Identity: Tribalism and World Politics.* New York: Harper Collins, 1979.

Lewis, Samella. *Art: African American.* Berkeley: University of California Press, 1994.

Long, Richard A. *The Black Tradition in American Dance.* New York: Rizzoli, 1989.

Lucie-Smith, Edward. *Race, Sex, and Gender: Issues in Contemporary Art.* New York: Abrams, 1994.

Parker, Rozsica, and Griselda Pollock. *Old Mistresses: Women, Art, and Ideology.* New York: Pantheon, 1982.

Powell, Richard J. *Black Art and Culture in the 20th Century.* New York: Thames and Hudson, 1995.

Saslow, James M. *Pictures and Passions: A History of Homosexuality in the Visual Arts.* New York: Viking Press, 1999.

Watson, Steven. *The Harlem Renaissance: Hub of African American Culture, 1920–1930.* New York: Pantheon, 1996.

MUSIC LISTENING SELECTIONS

CD Two Selection 21 Handy, "St. Louis Blues," 1914.
CD Two Selection 22 Hardin/Armstrong, "Hotter than That," 1927.
CD Two Selection 23 Ellington, "Ko-Ko," Gillespie/Parker, 1945.

CHAPTER THIRTY-SEVEN

The information age: message and meaning

"We talk because we are mortal: words are not signs, they are years."
Octavio Paz

We are still too close to the events of the last half century to distinguish the major cultural developments from the minor and ephemeral ones. However, it is clear that the history of the last five decades was altered by two dramatic developments. The first is the shift from an industrial to an information age. In today's First World societies, more than two-thirds of the population is engaged in occupations related to high technology, rather than to farming, manufacturing, and service trades. The agents of high technology, the mass media, and electronic means of communicating, storing, and accessing information have facilitated an information explosion of vast proportions.

The second major development of the last half century follows from scientific advances that have made possible investigations into outer space—the universe at large—and inner space, the province of our own bodies. Science and technology have propelled humankind beyond planet earth and into the cosmos. At the same time, they have provided an unprecedented understanding of the genetic patterns that govern life itself. These phenomena have worked to make the planet smaller, the universe larger, and methods of navigating the two ever more promising.

The tools of electronic technology have shrunk the distances between the inhabitants of the global community.

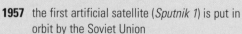

1953 the introduction of the first commercially successful computer

1957 the first artificial satellite (*Sputnik 1*) is put in orbit by the Soviet Union

1959 American engineers produce the first microchip (made from a silicon wafer)

1960 the first lasers are developed in America

1961 a Soviet astronaut becomes the first person to orbit the earth

1969 an American astronaut is the first person to walk on the moon

In the sixteenth century, it was possible to have read every book ever printed, but such a feat would be patently impossible today. The number of books published between 1945 and 1970 alone equaled that issued during the entire 500-year period between the invention of the printing press and the end of World War I. Computer technology has accelerated the process of information production, storage, and retrieval: Computer disks that store whole encyclopedias and on-line electronic books (e-books) are only two of the newest resources of the information age—an age in which all parts of the global village and numberless databases are linked by way of an international network of computers known as the Internet.

Information age culture is dominated by a media-shaped, global model: the *global paradigm* describes the condition of interrelatedness and interdependence among the various parts of the planet. Born in the late twentieth century, this condition of cultural homogeneity is facilitated by a near-global economy, a shared world-ecosystem, and such information age technology as satellite communication and the Internet. Globalism has worked to replace twentieth-century political ideologies with what the Czechoslovakian writer Milan Kundera (b. 1929) calls "imagology." In his novel, *Immortality* (1992), he describes the central place of the image in the global marketplace:

> All ideologies have been defeated: in the end their dogmas were unmasked as illusions and people stopped taking them seriously. For example, communists used to believe that in the course of capitalist development the proletariat would gradually grow poorer and poorer, but when it finally became clear that all over Europe workers were driving to work in their own cars, they felt like shouting that reality was deceiving them. Reality was stronger than ideology. And it is in this sense that imagology surpassed it: imagology is stronger than reality.*

*Milan Kundera, *Immortality*, translated by Peter Kussi. New York: Grove Press, 1992, 114.

Kundera brings attention to the disappearance of a way of life in which ideas depended on direct human experience; but, at the same time, he describes an age in which images, electronically transmitted and globally shared, have come to shape a new reality.

The Information Explosion

Television and computers—the most pervasive forms of high technology—have altered almost every aspect of life in our time (Figure **37.1**). Television, the wonderchild of electronics and the quintessential example of modern mass media, transmits sound and light by electromagnetic waves that carry information instantaneously into homes across the face of the earth. The very name "television" comes from the Greek word *tele*, meaning "far," and the Latin *videre*, meaning "to see"; hence "to see far." Television did not become a common fixture of middle-class life in First World nations until the 1950s, although it had been invented decades before then. By the 1960s the events of a war in the jungles of Vietnam were relayed via electronic communications satellite into American living rooms. In 1969, in a live telecast, the world saw the first astronauts walk on the surface of the moon. And in the early 1990s, during the Middle Eastern conflict triggered by the Iraqi invasion of Kuwait, Americans and Europeans witnessed the first "prime-time war"—a war that was "processed" by censorship and television newscasting.

The second major technological phenomenon of the information age is the computer. Digital computers, machines that process information in the form of numbers, were first used widely in the 1950s. By the 1960s, computers consisting of electronic circuits were able to perform millions of calculations per second. Smaller and more dependable than earlier models, electronic computers facilitated various forms of instantaneous communication. More recently, com-

puters have made possible the science of robotics and the creation of so-called artificial forms of intelligence. As more and more information is electronically stored, processed, and dispersed to ever-increasing numbers of individuals, the possibility of a "computopia," that is, a society run by computers, becomes both a promise and a threat; for, while a computerized society can provide its citizens with more leisure time, it might also work to diminish the human capacity for independent thought and action.

The electronic media bring more information to more people, but they also alter the way in which information is presented. Communication in the information age is

Figure 37.1 NAM JUNE PAIK, *George Boole*, 1995. 1 old Tektronic computer monitor, 1 old Goodyear Atomic metal cabinet, 15 KEC 9-inch television sets, 1 Samsung 13-inch television set, 2 Pioneer laser disk players, 2 original Paik laser disks, abacus, circuit board, aluminium, 90 × 56 × 30 in. Photo: Courtesy Carl Solway Gallery, Cincinnati, Ohio. Photographer: Chris Gomien.

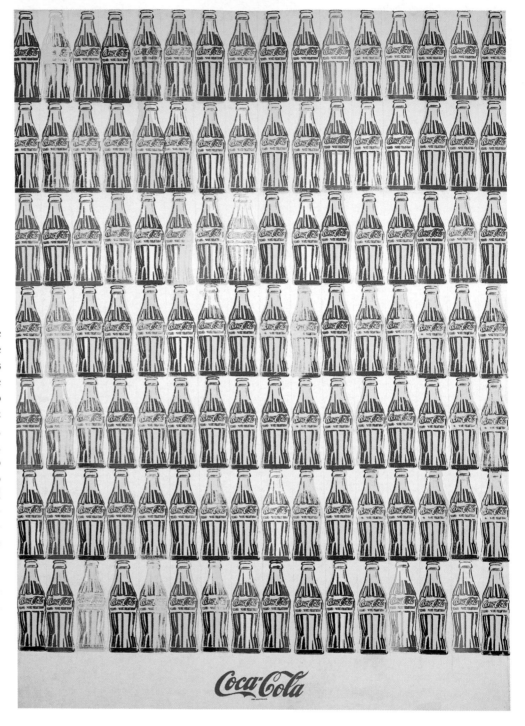

Figure 37.2 ANDY WARHOL, *Green Coca-Cola Bottles*, 1962. Oil on canvas, 6 ft 10½ x 4 ft 9 in. Collection of Whitney Museum of American Art, New York. Purchased with funds from the Friends of the Whitney Museum of American Art. 68.25. Photograph copyright © 2000 Whitney Museum of American Art. © The Andy Warhol Foundation for the Visual Arts, Inc./ARS, New York and DACS, London 2000.

essentially image oriented (Figure **37.2**). Film and television are fundamentally nonverbal modes of communication; they translate words into pictures. In contrast to print, a linear medium, electronic images are generated in diffuse, discontinuous bundles. Moreover, the electronic media tend to homogenize images, that is, to make all images uniform and alike. As information is homogenized, it tends to become devalued; product and message may be sacrificed to process and medium. As the mass media recycle an ill-sorted variety of data, culture itself becomes what one critic has called "a vast garage sale." Indeed, the electronic processing and the rapid diffusion of images via the television screen have worked to blur the differences between the diverse kinds of information that are processed. In contemporary society, commonplace responses to everyday life—the stuff of "popular culture"—are often indistinguishable from forms of elite or "high" culture. Television has turned all information, from protest marches to breakfast cereals, into marketable commodities. However, the electronic media have created a consumer society that often exercises little critical judgment with regard to the information it receives.

Unlike written and spoken modes of communication, which tend to isolate groups of people from one another, electronically processed visual images bring together the world's population. Reared on television, contemporary society is, according to French sociologist Jacques Ellul (b. 1912), the society of "mass man." Modern technology, explains Ellul, has contributed to producing a "psychological collectivism" that has robbed human beings of freedom and self-esteem. Ellul singles out advertising as the most pernicious factor in the evolution of mass man. According to Ellul, advertising is a form of totalitarian control that—like the process of behavioral conditioning in Huxley's *Brave New World*—subordinates the individual to the technostructure, thus destroying the last vestiges of human freedom and dignity. In his perceptive study of twentieth-century Western civilization, *The Technological Society* (1964), Ellul observed,

Advertising [affects] all people; or at least an overwhelming majority. Its goal is to persuade the masses to buy. . . . The inevitable consequence is the creation of the mass man. As advertising of the most varied products is concentrated, a new type of human being, precise and generalized, emerges. We can get a general impression of this new human type by studying America, where human beings tend clearly to become identified with the ideal of advertising. In America, advertising enjoys universal popular adherence and the American way of life is fashioned by it.*

New Directions in Science and Philosophy

String Theory

The two great intellectual achievements of early twentieth-century physics were Einstein's general relativity theory and quantum mechanics. In an effort to reconcile the two, late twentieth-century physicists worked to establish "a theory of everything," one that might explain the "fundamental of fundamentals" that governs the organization and complexity of matter. A new (but yet unproven) theory of everything proposes that all matter—from the page of this book to the skin of a peach—consists of tiny loops of vibrating strings. *String* (or *superstring*) *theory*, most eloquently explained by the American physicist Brian Greene (b. 1962), describes a multi-dimensional universe in which loops of strings and oscillating globules of matter unite all of creation into vibrational patterns.‡ Greene's "elegant universe" constitutes a cosmic model that Pythagoras would have found agreeable (see chapter 5). While the workings of such a universe can be simulated on a computer, human language seems too frail to serve as an explanatory medium. Yet, it is in the arts, and possibly in aesthetic theory that the design of this elegant universe may be best simulated. As the Norwegian physicist Niels Bohr observed, "when it comes to atoms, language can be used only as in poetry."

Chaos Theory

Equally fascinating are the speculations of those who explore the shape and structure of matter itself. The proponents of Chaos Theory find that universal patterns underlie all of nature, and repeat themselves in physical phenomena ranging from the formation of a snowflake to the rhythms of the human heart. Chaos theorists (not only physicists, but also astronomers, mathematicians, biologists, and computer scientists) observe that while these patterns appear random, unstable, and disorderly, they are actually self-similar in scale, like the zigs and zags of a lightning bolt, or oscillating, as in electric currents. To Einstein's famous assertion, "God does not play dice with the universe," these theorists might respond: "Not only does God play dice; but they are loaded."

The Genome and the Body

One of the major projects of the late twentieth century was the successful mapping of the *human genome*. By the year 2000, molecular biologists were able (with the help of computers) to ascertain the order of nearly 3 billion units of DNA, thereby locating genes and determining their functions in the human cellular system. Ultimately, this enterprise is expected to revolutionize the practice of medicine, in both the preventive treatment of gene-related diseases and in the repair and regeneration of tissues. (Already such gene-related research has diminished the number of AIDS deaths internationally.) The tools of genetic engineering give scientists the ability to clone life forms, but also promise the mitigation of what Freud described as one of humankind's greatest threats: the suffering "from our own body, which is doomed to decay and dissolution". From sports medicine to psychoanalysis, society has come to perceive human beings as mechanisms that can be improved, if not perfected, by the right diet, drugs, exercise, and a healthy life-style. The 1990s brought exciting breakthroughs in the area of *cognitive neuroscience*, as new imaging technologies showed how brain waves can influence matter. In recent German experiments in neural consciousness, patients wearing electrodes on their scalp modulate electrical signals to choose letters from a video screen—thus communicating with nothing but one's own brain. These biofeedback experiments are reinforced by neurochemical research: the American biochemist Candace Pert (b. 1946) writes in her groundbreaking book *Molecules of Emotion* (1997), "We know that the immune system, like the central nervous system, has memory and the capacity to learn. Thus, it could be said that intelligence is located not only in the brain but in cells that are distributed throughout the body, and that the traditional separation of mental processes, including emotions, from the body, is no longer valid."* As the gap between mind and body grows narrower, Eastern notions of the symbiosis of matter and spirit have received increased attention in the West. By way of popular literature (such as *Quantum Healing: Exploring the Frontier of Mind/Body Medicine*, 1990), the Indian-born endocrinologist Deepak Chopra (b. 1946) introduced Western audiences to holistic models of meditation and body control that have flourished in India for 2,000 years.

Language Theory

While science moves optimistically to reveal the underlying natural order, philosophy has entered a phase of radical skepticism that denies the existence of any true or uniform system of philosophy. Contemporary philosophers have fastened on the idea, first popularized by the Austrian philosopher Ludwig Wittgenstein (1889–1951), that all forms of expression, and, indeed, all truths, are dominated by the modes of language used to convey ideas.

---

*Jacques Ellul, *The Technological Society*, translated by John Wilkinson. New York: Knopf, 1964, 407–408.
‡Brian Greene, *The Elegant Universe: Superstrings, Hidden Dimensions and the Quest for the Ultimate Theory*. New York, Norton, 1999.

*Candace Pert, *Molecules of Emotion*, (New York: Scribners, 1997), 187.

Wittgenstein, whose life's work was an inquiry into the ways in which language represents the world, argued that sentences (or propositions) were "pictures of reality." Following Wittgenstein, philosophers have tried to unlock the meaning of the *text* (that is, the mode of cultural expression) based on close analysis of its linguistic structure. Language theorists have suggested that one must "deconstruct" or "take apart" discourse in order to "unmask" the many meanings beneath the text. The leaders of *deconstruction*, the French philosophers Jacques Derrida (b. 1930) and Michel Foucault (1926–1984), were influential in arguing that all human beings are prisoners of the very language they use to think and describe the world. People erroneously believe, observed Foucault, that language is their servant; they fail to apprehend that they are forever submitting to its demands. Philosophers, he asserted, should abandon the search for absolute truths and concentrate on the discovery of meaning(s). The American philosopher Richard Rorty (b. 1931) is deeply troubled by the limits of both linguistic inquiry and traditional philosophy. Rorty has argued that the great thinkers of the post-philosophical age are not the metaphysicians or the linguists but, rather, those artists whose works provide others with insights into achieving postmodern self-transformation. What Rorty calls the "linguistic turn" describes the move (among writers and philosophers) to rethink language as verbal coding.

Postmodernism

The term "postmodernism" came into use before World War II to describe the reaction to or against modernism, but by the late 1960s it came to designate the general cultural condition of the late twentieth century. Whether seen as a reaction against modernism or as an entirely new form of modernism, postmodernism is a phenomenon that occurred principally in the West. As a style, it is marked by a bemused awareness of a historical past whose "reality" has been processed by mass communication and information technology. Postmodern artists appropriate (or borrow) pre-existing texts and images from history, advertising, and the media. Their playful amalgam of disparate styles mingles the superficial and the profound and tends to dissolve the boundaries between "high" and "low" art. At the same time, their seemingly incongruous "layering" of images calls to mind the fundamentals of Chaos Theory, which advances a geometry of the universe that is "broken up, twisted, tangled, intertwined."*

In contrast with the elitism of modernism, postmodernism is self-consciously populist, even to the point of inviting the active participation of the beholder. Whereas modern artists (consider Eliot or Kandinsky) exalt the artist as visionary and rebel, postmodern artists bring wry skepticism to the creative act. Less preoccupied than the modernists with formal abstraction and its redeeming power, postmodernists acknowledge art as an information system and a commodity shaped by the electronic media,

its messages, and its modes of communication. The postmodern stance is more disengaged than authorial, its message more enigmatic than absolute. Postmodern writers share the contemporary philosopher's disdain for rational structure and the deconstructionist's fascination with the function of language. They offer alternatives to the high seriousness and introversion of modernist expression, and move instead in the direction of parody (burlesque imitation), whimsy, paradox, and irony.

Literature in the Information Age

Information age writers have explored a wide variety of literary styles and genres, the evidence of which is global in scope. Some have pursued the parodic techniques of *postmodernism*, exposing issues of language and verbal representation. Others probe the rich ambiguities of *magic realism* and the futuristic inventions of *science fiction*. In various styles, but most often in the form of traditional narrative, there has been an uninterrupted outpouring of *social conscience literature*—fiction and non-fiction that addresses such issues as crime, ethnic dislocation, and ecological disaster.

Postmodern Literature

Postmodern writers tend to bypass traditional narrative styles in favor of techniques that test or parody the writer's craft. Prose fiction in this style has been called "metafiction"—fiction about fiction. Such works are filled with fragments of information taken out of their original literary/historical context and juxtaposed with little or no commentary on their meaning. In a single story, a line from a poem by T. S. Eliot or a Shakespeare play may appear alongside a catchy saying or banal slogan from a television commercial, a phrase from a national anthem, or a shopping list, as if the writer were claiming all information as equally valuable. In postmodern fiction, characters undergo little or no development, plots often lack logical direction, and events—whether ordinary, perverse, or fantastic—may be described in the detached tone of a newspaper article. Like the television newscast, the language of postmodern fiction is often diffuse, discontinuous, and filled with innuendo and "commentary." Gallows humor novelist Kurt Vonnegut (b. 1922) uses clipped sentences framed in the present tense. This technique creates a kind of "videofiction" that seems aimed at readers whose attention spans are linked to television programming and instant intellectual gratification. The Italian writer Italo Calvino (1923–1985) engages the reader in a hunt for meanings that lie in the spaces between the act of writing and the events the words describe. Calvino interrupts the story line of his novel *If On a Winter's Night a Traveler* (1979) to confront the reader, thus:

> For a couple of pages now you have been reading
> on, and this would be the time to tell you clearly
> whether this station where I have got off is a station

---

*James Gleick, *Chaos: Making a New Science.* New York: Viking, 1987, 94.

of the past or a station of today; instead the sentences continue to move in vagueness, grayness, in a kind of no man's land of experience reduced to the lowest kind of denominator. Watch out: it is surely a method of involving you gradually, capturing you in the story before you realize it—a trap. Or perhaps the author still has not made up his mind, just as you, reader, for that matter, are not sure what you would most like to read.*

More recently, writers seem to be seeking a universal voice shaped by the vernaculars of the world. Salman Rushdie (b. 1948), who was born in Bombay, India, but lives in New York, writes novels that mingle rock and roll lyrics with Hindu and Greek mythology. A chronicler of the global village, Rushdie joins other writers who reach back to cultural beginnings, yet speak for their own time and place. Don Delillo (b. 1936) captures the cinematic rush of American life in novels that connect major global phenomena—the atomic bomb, the Cold War—to such everyday events as baseball and waste management. Delillo's *Underworld* (1997) is *docufiction*, a genre that fictionalizes historical figures. His style, in which the narrative moves back and forth in time, reflects his (global) credo that "Everything is connected."

As with these prose stylists, so too among postmodern poets, there has been a preference for verse that has as much reference to language as to that which language describes. Postmodern poets convey the idea that language shapes and articulates the self. The Mexican poet and critic Octavio Paz (1914–1999) expresses this idea in the poem "To Talk," in which he defines language as sacred—a human version of divine power. Others, like the American poet John Ashbery (b. 1927), write verse that may be cryptic, wry, and inscrutable. In the poem "Paradoxes and Oxymorons," Ashbery suggests that both language and life are filled with conditions that are incongruous, contradictory, and intrinsically human.

The 1992 Nobel Prize-winner Derek Walcott (b. 1930) writes poetry and plays that reflect his dual Caribbean and European heritage. A native of West India and a world traveler, Walcott considers himself a "mulatto of styles" (biblical, Classical, Shakespearean, and Creole) and a nomad between cultures (Caribbean, European, and African). These themes he develops in the long poem *Omeros* (1990), which places the drama of Homer's epics in a Caribbean setting. In his writings (but also evident in his watercolor studies), allusions to European high culture mingle with intensely visual imagery drawn from his native landscape. Walcott's union of everyday speech, folkloristic dialect, and richly metaphorical English reaches toward a hybridized voice, the multicultural voice of the information age. At the same time, however, Walcott's verse (as reflected, for instance, in the poem "Tomorrow, Tomorrow,") describes his search for personal identity in the polyglot community of the global village.

---

*Italo Calvino, *It Un a Winter's Night a Traveler*, translated by William Weaver. New York: Harcourt Brace Jovanovich, 1981, 12.

READING 6.28 Postmodern Poems

Paz's "To Talk" (1987)

I read in a poem: 1
to talk is divine.
But gods don't speak:
they create and destroy worlds
while men do the talking,   5
Gods, without words,
play terrifying games.

The spirit descends,
untying tongues,
but it doesn't speak words: 10
it speaks flames.
Language, lit by a god
is a prophecy
of flames and a crash
of burnt syllables: 15
meaningless ash.

Man's word
is the daughter of death.
We talk because we are
mortal: words   20
are not signs, they are years.
Saying what they say,
the names we speak
say time: they say us,
we are the names of time.   25
To talk is human.

Ashbery's "Paradoxes and Oxymorons"[1] (1981)

This poem is concerned with language on a very plain level.   1
Look at it talking to you. You look out a window
Or pretend to fidget. You have it but you don't have it.
You miss it, it misses you. You miss each other.

The poem is sad because it wants to be yours, and cannot.   5
What's a plain level? It is that and other things,
Bringing a system of them into play. Play?
Well, actually, yes, but I consider play to be

A deeper outside thing, a dreamed role-pattern,
As in the division of grace these long August days   10
Without proof. Open-ended. And before you know
It gets lost in the steam and chatter of typewriters.

It has been played once more. I think you exist only
To tease me into doing it, on your level, and then you aren't there
Or have adopted a different attitude. And the poem   15
Has set me softly down beside you. The poem is you.

---

[1] A paradox is a statement that seems contradictory or absurd, but may actually be true. An oxymoron is a combination of contradictory terms, such as "wise fool" or "cruel kindness" (see Reading 4.25).

Walcott's "Tomorrow, Tomorrow" (1987)

I remember the cities I have never seen   **1**
exactly. Silver-veined Venice, Leningrad
with its toffee-twisted minarets. Paris. Soon
the Impressionists will be making sunshine out of shade.
Oh! And the uncoiling cobra alleys of Hyderabad.[1]   **5**
To have loved one horizon is insularity;
it blindfolds vision, it narrows experience.
The spirit is willing, but the mind is dirty.
The flesh wastes itself under crumb-sprinkled linens,
widening the Weltanschauung[2] with magazines.   **10**
A world's outside the door, but how upsetting
to stand by your bags on a cold step as dawn
roses the brickwork and before you start regretting,
your taxi's coming with one beep of its horn,
sidling to the curb like a hearse — so you get in.   **15**

Magic Realism

The term "magic realism" originated in the context of the visual arts, where it described a mode of representation (popular among the surrealists) in which realistically depicted objects and events were juxtaposed in unexpected ways that evoked an aura of fantasy (see chapter 33). However, the term has also come to characterize that mixture of fantasy and realism that dominates Latin American literature. Writers of the so-called Latin American "Boom," a literary explosion that began in the late 1960s, employ narrative techniques that evoke a dream-like or mythic reality. Such is evident in the fiction writings of the Colombian novelist Gabriel García Marquéz (b. 1928) and the Chilean writer Isabel Allende (b. 1943). An experienced journalist, Allende is one of the most hypnotic storytellers of our time: Her short stories begin with a single image that unfolds much like a folk or fairy tale. Allende credits the influence of film and television for the modern tendency to "think in images" and to write in short, tightly packed sentences. She claims, however, that the first sentences of her stories are "dictated" to her in a magical manner. In the story "Two Words," Allende combines terse, straightforward narrative and sensuous allegory to interweave universal themes of language, love, and the empowering role of women in Latin American society.

READING 6.29 Allende's "Two Words" (1989)

She went by the name of Belisa Crepusculario, not   **1**
because she had been baptized with that name or given it by her mother, but because she herself had searched until she found the poetry of "beauty" and "twilight" and cloaked herself in it. She made her living selling words. She journeyed through the country from the high cold mountains to the burning coasts, stopping at fairs and in markets where she set

[1] A city in south-central India; also a city in Pakistan on the Indus River.
[2] A German word meaning "world view," one's personal philosophy of the universe.

up four poles covered by a canvas awning under which she took refuge from the sun and rain to minister to her customers. She did not have to peddle her merchandise because from   **10** having wandered far and near, everyone knew who she was. Some people waited for her from one year to the next, and when she appeared in the village with her bundle beneath her arm, they would form a line in front of her stall. Her prices were fair. For five centavos she delivered verses from memory; for seven she improved the quality of dreams; for nine she wrote love letters; for twelve she invented insults for irreconcilable enemies. She also sold stories, not fantasies but long, true stories she recited at one telling, never skipping a word. This is how she carried news from one town to another.   **20** People paid her to add a line or two: our son was born; so-and-so died; our children got married; the crops burned in the field. Wherever she went a small crowd gathered around to listen as she began to speak, and that was how they learned about each other's doings, about distant relatives, about what was going on in the civil war. To anyone who paid her fifty centavos in trade, she gave the gift of a secret word to drive away melancholy. It was not the same word for everyone, naturally, because that would have been collective deceit. Each person received his or her own word, with the assurance   **30** that no one else would use it that way in this universe or the Beyond.

Belisa Crepusculario had been born into a family so poor they did not even have names to give their children. She came into the world and grew up in an inhospitable land where some years the rains became avalanches of water that bore everything away before them and others when not a drop fell from the sky and the sun swelled to fill the horizon and the world became a desert. Until she was twelve, Belisa had no occupation or virtue other than having withstood hunger and   **40** the exhaustion of centuries. During one interminable drought, it fell to her to bury four younger brothers and sisters; when she realized that her turn was next, she decided to set out across the plains in the direction of the sea, in hopes that she might trick death along the way. The land was eroded, split with deep cracks, strewn with rocks, fossils of trees and thorny bushes, and skeletons of animals bleached by the sun. From time to time she ran into families who, like her, were heading south, following the mirage of water. Some had begun the march carrying their belongings on their backs or in   **50** small carts, but they could barely move their own bones, and after a while they had to abandon their possessions. They dragged themselves along painfully, their skin turned to lizard hide and their eyes burned by the reverberating glare. Belisa greeted them with a wave as she passed, but she did not stop, because she had no strength to waste in acts of compassion. Many people fell by the wayside, but she was so stubborn that she survived to cross through that hell and at long last reach the first trickles of water, fine, almost invisible threads that fed spindly vegetation and farther down widened into   **60** small streams and marshes.

Belisa Crepusculario saved her life and in the process accidentally discovered writing. In a village near the coast, the wind blew a page of newspaper at her feet. She picked up the brittle yellow paper and stood a long while looking at it, unable to determine its purpose, until curiosity overcame her shyness. She walked over to a man who was washing his horse in the muddy pool where she had quenched her thirst.

"What is this?" she asked.

"The sports page of the newspaper," the man replied, concealing his surprise at her ignorance.

The answer astounded the girl, but she did not want to seem rude, so she merely inquired about the significance of the fly tracks scattered across the page.

"Those are words, child. Here it says that Fulgencio Barba knocked out El Negro Tiznao in the third round."

That was the day Belisa Crepusculario found out that words make their way in the world without a master, and that anyone with a little cleverness can appropriate them and do business with them. She made a quick assessment of her situation and concluded that aside from becoming a prostitute or working as a servant in the kitchens of the rich there were few occupations she was qualified for. It seemed to her that selling words would be an honorable alternative. From that moment on, she worked at that profession, and was never tempted by any other. At the beginning, she offered her merchandise unaware that words could be written outside of newspapers. When she learned otherwise, she calculated the infinite possibilities of her trade and with her savings paid a priest twenty pesos to teach her to read and write; with her three remaining coins she bought a dictionary. She pored over it from A to Z and then threw it into the sea, because it was not her intention to defraud her customers with packaged words. One August morning several years later, Belisa Crepusculario was sitting in her tent in the middle of a plaza, surrounded by the uproar of market day, selling legal arguments to an old man who had been trying for sixteen years to get his pension. Suddenly she heard yelling and thudding hoofbeats. She looked up from her writing and saw, first, a cloud of dust, and then a band of horsemen come galloping into the plaza. They were the Colonel's men, sent under orders of El Mulato, a giant known throughout the land for the speed of his knife and his loyalty to his chief. Both the Colonel and El Mulato had spent their lives fighting in the civil war, and their names were ineradicably linked to devastation and calamity. The rebels swept into town like a stampeding herd, wrapped in noise, bathed in sweat, and leaving a hurricane of fear in their trail. Chickens took wing, dogs ran for their lives, women and children scurried out of sight, until the only living soul left in the market was Belisa Crepusculario. She had never seen El Mulato and was surprised to see him walking toward her.

"I'm looking for you," he shouted, pointing his coiled whip at her; even before the words were out, two men rushed her—knocking over her canopy and shattering her inkwell—bound her hand and foot, and threw her like a sea bag across the rump of El Mulato's mount. Then they thundered off toward the hills.

Hours later, just as Belisa Crepusculario was near death, her heart ground to sand by the pounding of the horse, they stopped, and four strong hands set her down. She tried to stand on her feet and hold her head high, but her strength failed her and she slumped to the ground, sinking into a confused dream. She awakened several hours later to the murmur of night in the camp, but before she had time to sort

out the sounds, she opened her eyes and found herself staring into the impatient glare of El Mulato, kneeling beside her.

"Well, woman, at last you've come to," he said. To speed her to her senses, he tipped his canteen and offered her a sip of liquor laced with gunpowder.

She demanded to know the reason for such rough treatment, and El Mulato explained that the Colonel needed her services. He allowed her to splash water on her face, and then led her to the far end of the camp where the most feared man in all the land was lazing in a hammock strung between two trees. She could not see his face, because he lay in the deceptive shadow of the leaves and the indelible shadow of all his years as a bandit, but she imagined from the way his gigantic aide addressed him with such humility that he must have a very menacing expression. She was surprised by the Colonel's voice, as soft and well-modulated as a professor's.

"Are you the woman who sells words?" he asked.

"At your service," she stammered, peering into the dark and trying to see him better.

The Colonel stood up, and turned straight toward her. She saw dark skin and the eyes of a ferocious puma, and she knew immediately that she was standing before the loneliest man in the world.

"I want to be President," he announced.

The Colonel was weary of riding across that godforsaken land, waging useless wars and suffering defeats that no subterfuge could transform into victories. For years he had been sleeping in the open air, bitten by mosquitoes, eating iguanas and snake soup, but those minor inconveniences were not why he wanted to change his destiny. What truly troubled him was the terror he saw in people's eyes. He longed to ride into a town beneath a triumphal arch with bright flags and flowers everywhere; he wanted to be cheered, and be given newly laid eggs and freshly baked bread. Men fled at the sight of him, children trembled, and women miscarried from fright; he had had enough, and so he had decided to become President. El Mulato had suggested that they ride to the capital, gallop up to the Palace, and take over the government, the way they had taken so many other things without anyone's permission. The Colonel, however, did not want to be just another tyrant; there had been enough of those before him and, besides, if he did that, he would never win people's hearts. It was his aspiration to win the popular vote in the December elections.

"To do that, I have to talk like a candidate. Can you sell me the words for a speech?" the Colonel asked Belisa Crepusculario. She had accepted many assignments, but none like this. She did not dare refuse, fearing that El Mulato would shoot her between the eyes, or worse still, that the Colonel would burst into tears. There was more to it than that, however; she felt the urge to help him because she felt a throbbing warmth beneath her skin, a powerful desire to touch that man, to fondle him, to clasp him in her arms.

All night and a good part of the following day, Belisa Crepusculario searched her repertory for words adequate for a presidential speech, closely watched by El Mulato, who could not take his eyes from her firm wanderer's legs and virginal breasts. She discarded harsh, cold words, words that were too flowery, words worn from abuse, words that offered improbable promises, untruthful and confusing words, until all she had left were words sure to touch the minds of men and women's intuition. Calling upon the knowledge she had purchased from the priest for twenty pesos, she wrote the speech on a sheet of paper and then signaled El Mulato to untie the rope that bound her ankles to a tree. He led her once more to the Colonel, and again she felt the throbbing anxiety that had seized her when she first saw him. She handed him the paper and waited while he looked at it, holding it gingerly between thumbs and fingertips.

"What the shit does this say?" he asked finally.

"Don't you know how to read?"

"War's what I know," he replied.

She read the speech aloud. She read it three times, so her client could engrave it on his memory. When she finished, she saw the emotion in the faces of the soldier who had gathered round to listen, and saw that the Colonel's eyes glittered with enthusiasm, convinced that with those words the presidential chair would be his.

"If after they've heard it three times, the boys are still standing there with their mouths hanging open, it must mean the thing's damn good, Colonel" was El Mulato's approval.

"All right, woman. How much do I owe you?" the leader asked.

"One peso, Colonel."

"That's not much," he said, opening the pouch he wore at his belt, heavy with proceeds from the last foray.

"The peso entitles you to a bonus. I'm going to give you two secret words," said Belisa Crepusculario.

"What for?"

She explained that for every fifty centavos a client paid, she gave him the gift of a word for his exclusive use. The Colonel shrugged. He had no interest at all in her offer, but he did not want to be impolite to someone who had served him so well. She walked slowly to the leather stool where he was sitting, and bent down to give him her gift. The man smelled the scent of a mountain cat issuing from the woman, a fiery heat radiating from her hips, he heard the terrible whisper of her hair, and a breath of sweetmint murmured into his ear the two secret words that were his alone.

"They are yours, Colonel," she said as she stepped back. "You may use them as much as you please."

El Mulato accompanied Belisa to the roadside, his eyes as entreating as a stray dog's, but when he reached out to touch her, he was stopped by an avalanche of words he had never heard before; believing them to be an irrevocable curse, the flame of his desire was extinguished.

During the months of September, October, and November the Colonel delivered his speech so many times that had it not been crafted from glowing and durable words it would have turned to ash as he spoke. He traveled up and down and across the country, riding into cities with a triumphal air, stopping in even the most forgotten villages where only the dump heap betrayed a human presence, to convince his fellow citizens to vote for him. While he spoke from a platform erected in the middle of the plaza, El Mulato and his men handed out sweets and painted his name on all the walls in gold frost. No one paid the least attention to those advertising ploys; they were dazzled by the clarity of the Colonel's proposals and the poetic lucidity of his arguments, infected by his powerful wish to right the wrongs of history, happy for the first time in their lives. When the Candidate had finished his speech, his soldiers would fire their pistols into the air and set off firecrackers, and when finally they rode off, they left behind a wake of hope that lingered for days on the air, like the splendid memory of a comet's tail. Soon the Colonel was the favorite. No one had ever witnessed such a phenomenon: a man who surfaced from the civil war, covered with scars and speaking like a professor, a man whose fame spread to every corner of the land and captured the nation's heart. The press focused their attention on him. Newspapermen came from far away to interview him and repeat his phrases, and the number of his followers and enemies continued to grow.

"We're doing great, Colonel," said El Mulato, after twelve successful weeks of campaigning.

But the Candidate did not hear. He was repeating his secret words, as he did more and more obsessively. He said them when he was mellow with nostalgia; he murmured them in his sleep; he carried them with him on horseback; he thought them before delivering his famous speech; and he caught himself savoring them in his leisure time. And every time he thought of those two words, he thought of Belisa Crepusculario, and his senses were inflamed with the memory of her feral scent, her fiery heat, the whisper of her hair, and her sweetmint breath in his ear, until he began to go around like a sleepwalker, and his men realized that he might die before he ever sat in the presidential chair.

"What's got hold of you, Colonel?" El Mulato asked so often that finally one day his chief broke down and told him the source of his befuddlement: those two words that were buried like two daggers in his gut.

"Tell me what they are and maybe they'll lose their magic," his faithful aide suggested.

"I can't tell them, they're for me alone," the Colonel replied.

Saddened by watching his chief decline like a man with a death sentence on his head, El Mulato slung his rifle over his shoulder and set out to find Belisa Crepusculario. He followed her trail through all that vast country, until he found her in a village in the far south, sitting under her tent reciting her rosary of news. He planted himself, spraddle-legged, before her, weapon in hand.

"You! You're coming with me," he ordered.

She had been waiting. She picked up her inkwell, folded the canvas of her small stall, arranged her shawl around her shoulders, and without a word took her place behind El Mulato's saddle. They did not exchange so much as a word in all the trip; El Mulato's desire for her had turned into rage, and only his fear of her tongue prevented his cutting her to shreds with his whip. Nor was he inclined to tell her that the Colonel was in a fog, and that a spell whispered into his ear had done what years of battle had not been able to do. Three days later they arrived at the encampment, and immediately, in view of all the troops, El Mulato led his prisoner before the Candidate.

"I brought this witch here so you can give her back her words, Colonel," El Mulato said, pointing the barrel of his rifle at the woman's head. "And then she can give you back your manhood."

The Colonel and Belisa Crepusculario stared at each other, measuring one another from a distance. The men knew then that their leader would never undo the witchcraft of those accursed words, because the whole world could see the voracious-puma eyes soften as the woman walked to him and took his hand in hers.

The Literature of Social Conscience

Urban violence, ethnic and racial division, homelessness, and the search for spiritual renewal in a commodity-driven world were major themes in the literature of the late twentieth century. Writers of that era also responded to the effects of bio-scientific and industrial technology upon the environment and its inhabitants. For example, ecological studies of the interrelationships between organisms and their environments have proved that while modern technology has brought vast benefits to millions of people, it has also worked to violate the global environment. The technology of any one country or region potentially affects the entire global village. For instance, sulphur dioxide and other industrial by-products emitted in one area cause acid rain that damages forests, lakes, and soil in another part of the world. Industrial pollution poisons rivers and oceans. And leaks in nuclear reactors endanger populations thousands of miles from their sites. Such realities, all of which threaten our global environment, have inspired a more holistic regard for the destiny of planet earth.

Contemporary writers have expressed increasing concern over the possibility of ecological disaster. None, however, has spoken for the survival of the planet so passionately as the American poet Gary Snyder (b. 1930). Snyder grew up on a small farm in the Pacific Northwest. His affection for the Native American populations of that region, his travels throughout Asia, and his keen appreciation of Daoism and Zen Buddhism give shape to his pantheistic credo that all creatures (indeed, all living forms) constitute a single whole—the whole of nature. This notion, often associated with the Gaia hypothesis, holds that the earth is a single, purposeful, living whole and the ecosystem a viable model for global integration. In his poetry Snyder tries to achieve a balance between "the world of people and language and society" and "the nonhuman, nonverbal world, which is nature as nature in itself." In "Smokey the Bear Sutra," a poem humorously styled on a Buddhist instructional discourse (see chapter

8), Eastern ritual and Western pop culture combine to warn that the human race is destroying the planet. The American folk hero Smokey the Bear becomes the counterpart of the Great Sun Buddha, who, in the poem, preaches the truth of universal survival.

While ecological disaster still poses a slow, insidious threat to the global community, political terrorism wears the face of immediate, overt violence. Terrorist bombs threaten the safety and freedom of human beings in public places throughout the world, victimizing the innocent and creating a climate of insecurity and fear. The Polish poet and winner of the Nobel Prize for poetry in 1996, Wislawa Szymborska (b. 1923), comments on these aspects of contemporary life in the poem "The Terrorist, He Watches." Like Snyder, Szymborska (pronounced "sheem-BOR-ska") prefers straightforward, conversational speech to the verbal complexities of postmodern poets. Her poems convey a humane and moral urgency that is both universal and personal. In the nervous, yet nonchalant, "voice" of this poet, one detects the gentle apprehension of somebody who has lived most of her life in communist-controlled Poland—a country that lost nearly one-fifth of its population during World War II.

READING 6.30 The Poems of Snyder and Szymborska

Snyder's "Smokey the Bear Sutra"[1] (1969)

Once in the Jurassic, about 150 million years ago,　　　　　1
the Great Sun Buddha in this corner of the Infinite
Void gave a great Discourse to all the assembled elements
and energies: to the standing beings, the walking beings,
the flying beings, and the sitting beings—even grasses,　　5
to the number of thirteen billion, each one born from a
seed, were assembled there: a Discourse concerning
Enlightenment on the planet Earth.

"In some future time, there will be a continent called
America. It will have great centers of power called　　　　10
such as Pyramid Lake, Walden Pond, Mt. Rainier, Big Sur,
Everglades, and so forth; and powerful nerves and channels
such as Columbia River, Mississippi River, and Grand Canyon.
The human race in that era will get into troubles all over
its head, and practically wreck everything in spite of　　15
its own strong intelligent Buddha-nature."

"The twisting strata of the great mountains and the pulsings
of great volcanoes are my love burning deep in the earth.
My obstinate compassion is schist and basalt and
granite, to be mountains, to bring down the rain. In that　20
future American Era I shall enter a new form: to cure
the world of loveless knowledge that seeks with blind hunger;
and mindless rage eating food that will not fill it."

And he showed himself in his true form of
　　　　SMOKEY THE BEAR　　　　　　　　　　　　　　25

---

[1]Gary Snyder, "Smokey the Bear Sutra" (may be reproduced free forever).

A handsome smokey-colored brown bear standing on
his hind legs, showing that he is aroused and watchful.
    Bearing in his right paw the Shovel that digs to the
truth beneath appearances; cuts the roots of useless
attachments, and flings damp sand on the fires of greed
        and war;   **30**
    His left paw in the Mudra[2] of Comradely Display—
        indicating
that all creatures have the full right to live to their limits
and that deer, rabbits, chipmunks, snakes, dandelions,
and lizards all grow in the realm of the Dharma;[3]
    Wearing the blue work overalls symbolic of slaves and   **35**
laborers, the countless men oppressed by a civilization
that claims to save but only destroys;

    Wearing the broad-brimmed hat of the West, symbolic of
the forces that guard the Wilderness, which is the Natural
State of the Dharma and the True Path of man on earth;   **40**
all true paths lead through mountains—

    With a halo of smoke and flame behind, the forest fires
of the kali-yuga,[4] fires caused by the stupidity of those who
think things can be gained and lost whereas in truth all is
contained vast and free in the Blue Sky and Green Earth   **45**
of One Mind;

    Round-bellied to show his kind nature and that the great
earth has food enough for everyone who loves her and
trusts her;

    Trampling underfoot wasteful freeways and needless   **50**
suburbs; smashing the worms of capitalism and
    totalitarianism;

    Indicating the Task: his followers, becoming free of cars,
houses, canned food, universities, and shoes, master the
Three Mysteries of their own Body, Speech, and Mind; and   **55**
fearlessly chop down the rotten trees and prune out the
sick lambs of this country America and then burn the
leftover trash.

Wrathful but Calm, Austere but Comic, Smokey the Bear will
Illuminate those who would help him; but for those who would
hinder or slander him.   **60**
            HE WILL PUT THEM OUT
Thus his great Mantra:[5]
    Namah samanta vajranam chanda maharoshana
    Sphataya hum traka ham mam
    "I DEDICATE MYSELF TO THE UNIVERSAL DIAMOND   **65**
    BE THIS RAGING FURY DESTROYED"
And he will protect those who love woods and rivers,
Gods and animals, hobos and madmen, prisoners and sick
people, musicians, playful women, and hopeful children;
And if anyone is threatened by advertising, air pollution,   **70**
or the police, they should chant SMOKEY THE BEAR'S
    WAR SPELL:
    DROWN THEIR BUTTS
    CRUSH THEIR BUTTS

    DROWN THEIR BUTTS   **75**
    CRUSH THEIR BUTTS
And SMOKEY THE BEAR will surely appear to put the
    enemy out with his vajra[6]—shovel.

Now those who recite this Sutra and then try to put it in
    practice will accumulate merit as countless as the
    sands of Arizona and Nevada,   **80**
Will help save the planet Earth from total oil slick,
Will enter the age of harmony of man and nature,
Will win the tender love and caresses of men, women,
    and beasts
Will always have ripe blackberries to eat and a sunny spot
    under a pine tree to sit at,   **85**
AND IN THE END WILL WIN HIGHEST PERFECT
    ENLIGHTENMENT thus have we heard.

Szymborska's "The Terrorist, He Watches" (1976)

The bomb will explode in the bar at twenty past one.   **1**
Now it's only sixteen minutes past.
Some will still have time to enter,
some to leave.

The terrorist's already on the other side.   **5**
That distance protects him from all harm
and, well, it's like the pictures:

A woman in a yellow jacket, she enters.
A man in dark glasses, he leaves.
Boys in jeans, they're talking.   **10**
Sixteen minutes past and four seconds.
The smaller one, he's lucky, mounts his scooter,
but that taller chap, he walks in.

Seventeen minutes and forty seconds.
A girl, she walks by, a green ribbon in her hair.   **15**
But that bus suddenly hides her.
Eighteen minutes past.
The girl's disappeared.
Was she stupid enough to go in, or wasn't she.
We shall see when they bring out the bodies.   **20**

Nineteen minutes past.
No one else appears to be going in.
On the other hand, a fat bald man leaves.
But seems to seach his pockets and
at ten seconds to twenty past one   **25**
he returns to look for his wretched gloves.

It's twenty past one.
Time, how it drags.
Surely, it's now.
No, not quite.   **30**
Yes, now.
The bomb, it explodes.

---

[2]A hand gesture in Indian yoga and classical dance.
[3]The Law, or basic universal principles, according to Hindu and
Buddhist doctrine.

[4]In Indian thought, the last and most evil phase of the four cycles of
creation.
[5]A mystical formula recited by Hindus and Buddhists.
[6]A Sanskrit word meaning "thunderbolt."

Two of the leading voices of contemporary fiction, Chinua Achebe and Joyce Carol Oates, provide insight into the literature of social conscience. "Dead Men's Path" by Chinua Achebe (b. 1930), Africa's leading English-language writer, deals with ongoing bicultural conflicts that plague many parts of black Africa; at the same time the story probes larger, more universal tensions—those between tradition and innovation, between spiritual and secular allegiances, and between faith and reason—tensions which continue to affect and shape human values.

Joyce Carol Oates (b. 1938) deals with the violent underlayer of contemporary urban society. The story "Ace" is a highly concentrated kind of prose fiction that Oates calls the "miniature narrative." Its tale of random violence—the familiar fare of the daily broadcast television news—unfolds with cinematic intensity, an effect embellished by powerful present-tense narrative and vivid characterization.

READING 6.31 Achebe's "Dead Men's Path" (1972)

Michael Obi's hopes were fulfilled much earlier than he had expected. He was appointed headmaster of Ndume Central School in January 1949. It had always been an unprogressive school, so the Mission authorities decided to send a young and energetic man to run it. Obi accepted this responsibility with enthusiasm. He had many wonderful ideas and this was an opportunity to put them into practice. He had had sound secondary school education which designated him a "pivotal teacher" in the official records and set him apart from the other headmasters in the mission field. He was outspoken in **10** his condemnation of the narrow views of these older and often less-educated ones.

"We shall make a good job of it, shan't we?" he asked his young wife when they first heard the joyful news of his promotion.

"We shall do our best," she replied. "We shall have such beautiful gardens and everything will be just *modern* and delightful. . . ." In their two years of married life she had become completely infected by his passion for "modern methods" and his denigration of "these old and superannuated **20** people in the teaching field who would be better employed as traders in the Onitsha market." She began to see herself already as the admired wife of the young headmaster, the queen of the school.

The wives of the other teachers would envy her position. She would set the fashion in everything. . . .
Then, suddenly, it occurred to her that there might not be other wives. Wavering between hope and fear, she asked her husband, looking anxiously at him.

"All our colleagues are young and unmarried," he said with **30** enthusiasm which for once she did not share.
"Which is a good thing," he continued.
"Why?"
"Why? They will give all their time and energy to the school."

Nancy was downcast. For a few minutes she became sceptical about the new school; but it was only for a few minutes. Her little personal misfortune could not blind her to her husband's happy prospects. She looked at him as he sat folded up in a chair. He was stoop-shouldered and looked frail. **40** But he sometimes surprised people with sudden bursts of physical energy. In his present posture, however, all his bodily strength seemed to have retired behind his deep-set eyes, giving them an extraordinary power of penetration. He was only twenty-six, but looked thirty or more. On the whole, he was not unhandsome.

"A penny for your thoughts, Mike," said Nancy after a while, imitating the woman's magazine she read.
"I was thinking what a grand opportunity we've got at last to show these people how a school should be run." **50**

Ndume School was backward in every sense of the word. Mr. Obi put his whole life into the work, and his wife hers too. He had two aims. A high standard of teaching was insisted upon, and the school compound was to be turned into a place of beauty. Nancy's dream-gardens came to life with the coming of the rains, and blossomed. Beautiful hibiscus and allamanda hedges in brilliant red and yellow marked out the carefully tended school compound from the rank neighbourhood bushes.

One evening as Obi was admiring his work he was scandalized to see an old woman from the village hobble right **60** across the compound, through a marigold flowerbed and the hedges. On going up there he found faint signs of an almost disused path from the village across the school compound to the bush on the other side.

"It amazes me," said Obi to one of his teachers who had been three years in the school, "that you people allowed the villagers to make use of this footpath. It is simply incredible." He shook his head.

"The path," said the teacher apologetically, "appears to be very important to them. Although it is hardly used, it connects **70** the village shrine with their place of burial."

"And what has that got to do with the school?" asked the headmaster.

"Well, I don't know," replied the other with a shrug of the shoulders. "But I remember there was a big row some time ago when we attempted to close it."

"That was some time ago. But it will not be used now," said Obi as he walked away. "What will the Government Education Officer think of this when he comes to inspect the school next week? The villagers might, for all I know, decide to use the **80** schoolroom for a pagan ritual during the inspection."

Heavy sticks were planted closely across the path at the two places where it entered and left the school premises. These were further strengthened with barbed wire.

Three days later the village priest of Ani called on the headmaster. He was an old man and walked with a slight stoop. He carried a stout walking-stick which he usually tapped on the floor, by way of emphasis, each time he made a new point in his argument.

"I have heard," he said after the usual exchange of **90** cordialities, "that our ancestral footpath has recently been closed. . . ."

"Yes," replied Mr. Obi. "We cannot allow people to make a highway of our school compound."

"Look here, my son," said the priest bringing down his walking-stick, "this path was here before you were born and before your father was born. The whole life of this village depends on it. Our dead relatives depart by it and our ancestors visit us by it. But most important, it is the path of children coming in to be born. . . ." 100

Mr. Obi listened with a satisfied smile on his face.

"The whole purpose of our school," he said finally, "is to eradicate just such beliefs as that. Dead men do not require footpaths. The whole idea is just fantastic. Our duty is to teach your children to laugh at such ideas."

"What you say may be true," replied the priest, "but we follow the practices of our fathers. If you re-open the path we shall have nothing to quarrel about. What I always say is: let the hawk perch and let the eagle perch." He rose to go.

"I am sorry," said the young headmaster. "But the school 110 compound cannot be a thoroughfare. It is against our regulations. I would suggest your constructing another path, skirting our premises. We can even get our boys to help in building it. I don't suppose the ancestors will find the little detour too burdensome."

"I have no more words to say," said the old priest, already outside.

Two days later a young woman in the village died in childbed. A diviner was immediately consulted and he prescribed heavy sacrifices to propitiate ancestors insulted by the fence. 120

Obi woke up next morning among the ruins of his work. The beautiful hedges were torn up not just near the path but right round the school, the flowers trampled to death and one of the school buildings pulled down.

. . . That day, the white Supervisor came to inspect the school and wrote a nasty report on the state of the premises but more seriously about the "tribal-war situation developing between the school and the village, arising in part from the misguided zeal of the new headmaster."

READING 6.32 Oates' "Ace" (1988)

A gang of overgrown boys, aged eighteen to twenty-five, has 1 taken over the northeast corner of our park again this summer. Early evenings they start arriving, hang out until the park closes at midnight. Nothing to do but get high on beer and dope, the police leave them alone as long as they mind their own business, don't hassle people too much. Now and then there's fighting but nothing serious—nobody shot or stabbed.

Of course no girl or woman in her right mind would go anywhere near them, if she didn't have a boyfriend there.

Ace is the leader, a big boy in his twenties with a mean 10 baby-face, pouty mouth, and cheeks so red they look fresh-slapped, sly little steely eyes curling up at the corners like he's laughing or getting ready to laugh. He's six foot two weighing maybe two hundred twenty pounds—lifts weights at the gym—but there's some loose flabby flesh around his middle, straining against his belt. He goes bare-chested in the heat, likes to sweat in the open air, muscles bunched and gleaming, and he can show off his weird tattoos—ace of spades on his

right bicep, inky-black octopus on his left. Long shaggy hair the color of dirty sand and he wears a red sweatband for looks. 20

Nobody notices anything special about a car circling the park, lots of traffic on summer nights and nobody's watching then there's this popping noise like a firecracker and right away Ace screams and claps his hand to his eye and it's streaming blood—what the hell? Did somebody shoot him? His buddies just freeze not knowing what to do. There's a long terrible minute when everybody stands there staring at Ace not knowing what to do—then the boys run and duck for cover, scattering like pigeons. And Ace is left alone standing there, crouched, his hand to his left eye screaming, Help, Jesus, 30 hey, help, my eye—Standing there crouched at the knee like he's waiting for a second shot to finish him off.

The bullet must have come at an angle, skimmed the side of Ace's face, otherwise he'd be flat-out dead lying in the scrubby grass. He's panicked though, breathing loud through his mouth saying, O Jesus, O Jesus, and after a minute people start yelling, word's out there's been a shooting and somebody's hurt. Ace wheels around like he's been hit again but it's only to get away, suddenly he's walking fast stooped over dripping blood, could be he's embarrassed, doesn't want 40 people to see him, red headband and tattoos, and now he's dripping blood down his big beefy forearm, in a hurry to get home.

Some young girls have started screaming. Nobody knows what has happened for sure and where Ace is headed people clear out of his way. There's blood running down his chest, soaking into his jeans, splashing onto the sidewalk. His friends are scared following along after him asking where he's going, is he going to the hospital, but Ace glares up out of his one good eye like a crazy man, saying, Get the fuck away! Don't 50 touch me! and nobody wants to come near.

On the street the cops stop him and there's a call put in for an ambulance. Ace stands there dazed and shamed and the cops ask him questions as if he's to blame for what happened, was he in a fight, where's he coming from, is that a bullet wound?—all the while a crowd's gathering, excitement in the air you can feel. It's an August night, late, eighty-nine degrees and no breeze. The crowd is all strangers, Ace's friends have disappeared. He'd beg the cops to let him go but his heart is beating so hard he can't get his breath. Starts swaying like a 60 drunk man, his knees so weak the cops have to steady him. They can smell the panic sweat on him, running in rivulets down his sides.

In the ambulance he's held in place and a black orderly tells him he's O.K., he's going to be O.K., goin' to be at the hospital in two minutes flat. He talks to Ace the way you'd talk to a small child, or an animal. They give him some quick first aid trying to stop the bleeding but Ace can't control himself can't hold still, he's crazy with fear, his heart gives a half-dozen kicks then it's off and going—like a drum tattoo right in his 70 chest. The ambulance is tearing along the street, siren going, Ace says O God O God O God his terrible heartbeat carrying him away.

He's never been in a hospital in his life—knows he's going to die there.

Then he's being hauled out of the ambulance. Stumbling through automatic-eye doors not knowing where he is. Jaws so tight he could grind his teeth away and he can't get his breath and he's ashamed how people are looking at him, right there in the lights in the hallway people staring at his face like they'd never seen anything so terrible. He can't keep up with the attendants, knees buckling and his heart beating so hard but they don't notice, trying to make him walk faster, Come on man they're saying, you ain't hurt that bad, Ace just can't keep up and he'd fall if they weren't gripping him under the arms then he's in the emergency room and lying on a table, filmy white curtains yanked closed around him and there's a doctor, two nurses, What seems to be the trouble here the doctor asks squinting at Ace through his glasses, takes away the bloody gauze and doesn't flinch at what he sees. He warns Ace to lie still, he sounds tired and annoyed as if Ace is to blame, how did this happen he asks but doesn't wait for any answer and Ace lies there stiff and shivering with fear clutching at the underside of the table so hard his nails are digging through the tissue-paper covering into the vinyl, he can't see out of his left eye, nothing there but pain, pain throbbing and pounding everywhere in his head and the nurses—are there two? three?—look down at him with sympathy he thinks, with pity he thinks, they're attending to him, touching him, nobody has ever touched him so tenderly in all his life Ace thinks and how shamed he is hauled in here like this flat on his back like this bleeding like a stuck pig and sweating bare- chested and his big gut exposed quivering there in the light for everybody to see—

The doctor puts eight stitches in Ace's forehead, tells him he's damned lucky he didn't lose his eye, the bullet missed it by about two inches and it's going to be swollen and blackened for a while, next time you might not be so lucky he says but Ace doesn't catch this, his heart's going so hard. They wrap gauze around his head tight then hook him up to a machine to monitor his heartbeat, the doctor's whistling under his breath like he's surprised, lays the flat of his hand against Ace's chest to feel the weird loud rocking beat. Ace is broken out in sweat but it's cold clammy sick sweat, he knows he's going to die. The machine is going bleep-bleep- bleep high-pitched and fast and how fast can it go before his heart bursts?—he sees the nurses looking down at him, one of the nurses just staring at him, Don't let me die Ace wants to beg but he'd be too ashamed. The doctor is listening to Ace's heartbeat with his stethoscope, asks does he have any pain in his chest, has he ever had an attack like this before, Ace whispers no but too soft to be heard, all the blood has drained from his face and his skin is dead-white, mouth gone slack like a fish's and toes like ice where Death is creeping up his feet: he can feel it.

The heart isn't Ace's heart but just something inside him gone angry and mean pounding like a hammer pounding pounding pounding against his ribs making his body rock so he's panicked suddenly and wants to get loose, tries to push his way off the table—he isn't thinking but if he could think he'd say he wanted to leave behind what's happening to him here as if it was only happening in the emergency room, there on that table. But they don't let him go. There's an outcry in the place and two orderlies hold him down and he gives up, all the strength drained out of him and he gives up, there's no need to strap him down the way they do, he's finished. They hook him up to the heart monitor again and the terrible high-pitched bleeping starts again and he lies there shamed knowing he's going to die he's forgotten about the gunshot, his eye, who did it and was it on purpose meant for him and how can he get revenge, he's forgotten all that covered in sick clammy sweat his nipples puckered and the kinky hairs on his chest wet, even his belly button showing exposed from the struggle and how silly and sad his tattoos must look under these lights where they were never meant to be seen.

One of the nurses sinks a long needle in his arm, and there's another needle in the soft thin flesh of the back of his hand, takes him by surprise, they've got a tube in there, and something coming in hot and stinging dripping into his vein the doctor's telling him something he can't follow, This is to bring the heartbeat down the doctor says, just a tachycardia attack and it isn't fatal try to relax but Ace knows he's going to die, he can feel Death creeping up his feet up his legs like stepping out into cold water and suddenly he's so tired he can't lift his head, couldn't get up from the table if they unstrapped him. And he dies—it's that easy. Like slipping off into the water, pushing out, letting the water take you. It's that easy.

They're asking Ace if he saw who shot him and Ace says, Naw, didn't see nobody. They ask does he have any enemies and he says, Naw, no more than anybody else. They ask can he think of anybody who might have wanted to shoot him and he says, embarrassed, looking down at the floor with his one good eye, Naw, can't think of nobody right now. So they let him go.

Next night Ace is back in the park out of pride but there's a feeling to him he isn't real or isn't the same person he'd been. One eye bandaged shut and everything looks flat, people staring at him like he's a freak, wanting to know What about the eye and Ace shrugs and tells them he's O.K., the bullet just got his forehead. Everybody wants to speculate who fired the shot, whose car it was, but Ace stands sullen and quiet thinking his own thoughts. Say he'd been standing just a little to one side the bullet would have got him square in the forehead or plowed right into his eye, killed him dead, it's something to think about and he tries to keep it in mind so he'll feel good. But he doesn't feel good. He doesn't feel like he'd ever felt before. His secret is something that happened to him in the hospital he can't remember except to know it happened and it happened to him. And he's in a mean mood his head half- bandaged like a mummy, weird-looking in the dark, picking up on how people look at him and say things behind his back calling him Ace which goes through him like a razor because it's a punk name and not really his.

Mostly it's O.K. He hides how he feels. He's got a sense of humor. He doesn't mind them clowning around pretending they hear gunshots and got to duck for cover, nobody's going to remember it for long, except once Ace stops laughing and backhands this guy in the belly, low below the belt, says in his old jeering voice, What do you know?—you don't know shit.

Science Fiction

Science fiction has come to be one of our most entertaining genres. At its best, it evokes a sense of awe and a spirit of intellectual curiosity in the face of the unknown. It also is a vehicle by which writers express their concern for the future of the planet. During the twentieth century—a virtual golden age of science fiction—futurists contemplated the possibility of life in outer space, the interface between computers and human beings, the consequences of a nuclear disaster, and the potential for a bioengineered new species.

The beginnings of modern science fiction may be traced to the French novelist Jules Verne (1828–1905) and the British writer H. G. Wells (1866–1946). But the more recent flowering of the genre dates from the birth of space exploration—specifically the Soviet Union's historic launching of an artificial earth satellite (*Sputnik 1*) in 1957 and the American moon landing of 1969. These events triggered an energetic outpouring of fiction related to space exploration. In 1950, Arthur C. Clarke (b. 1917), one of Britain's most successful writers, produced the intriguing science fiction story "The Sentinel," which in turn became the basis for an extraordinary cinematic conceptualization of the Space Age, *2001: A Space Odyssey*.

SUMMARY

The last decades of the twentieth century witnessed a transformation from an industrially based world-culture to one shaped by mass media, electronic technology, space-travel, and advances in the biophysical sciences. Television and other electronic phenomena altered basic modes of communication and facilitated global homogeneity, while computer technology affected the structure and transmission of information itself. Propelled by high technology and by a condition of global homogeneity, the information age opened a new era in the arts—one that has persisted into the new millennium. The "postmodern

turn" accompanied the shift away from the anxious subjectivity and high seriousness of modernism, toward a skeptical and bemused attention to the history of culture and its myriad texts. Postmodern writers have examined language as verbal coding and as a vehicle for both parody and social reform. In the short stories of Isabel Allende, the empowering roles of language and of women are intertwined. Social conscience poetry and fiction manifest a deep concern for the ecological future of the planet, for world terrorism, and urban crime. Achebe and Oates illuminate the contradictory and violent aspects of contemporary life, while writers of science fiction work to construct a futuristic mythology of outer space. While stylistic diversity is the main feature of information-age literature, the search for a universal voice (the hybridized product of various vernaculars) is already apparent.

SUGGESTIONS FOR READING

Dunning, William V. *The Roots of Postmodernism*. Englewood Cliffs, NJ: Prentice Hall, 1995.

Gablik, Suzi. *The Reenchantment of Art*. London: Thames and Hudson, 1991.

Hassan, Ihab. *The Postmodern Turn: Essays in Postmodern Theory and Culture*. Columbus, Ohio: Ohio State University Press, 1987.

Harbison, O.B. *Disappearing Through the Skylight: Technology in the Twentieth Century*. New York: Penguin, 1989.

Kaku, Michio. *Beyond Einstein: The Cosmic Quest for the Theory of the Universe*. New York: Doubleday, 1995.

Loveless, Richard L., ed. *The Computer Revolution and the Arts*. Tampa, Fla.: South Florida Press, 1989.

Maybury-Lewis, David. *Millennium: Tribal Wisdom and the Modern World*. New York: Viking, 1992.

Mazower, Mark. *Dark Continent: Europe's Twentieth Century*. New York: Vintage Books, 2000.

Shlain, Leonard. *The Alphabet Versus the Goddess: The Conflict between Word and Image*. New York: Penguin/Arkana, 1998.

CHAPTER THIRTY-EIGHT

Image and sound in the information age

"Representing . . . information is going to be the main issue in the years ahead—how the world meets the mind, not the eye."
Bill Viola

The Visual Arts in the Information Age

In the last half century the visual arts have been overwhelmingly diverse in styles and techniques. Collectively, they are characterized by an indebtedness to mass media and electronic technology, by an emphasis on process and medium, and by such typically postmodern features as parody and irony. High-tech materials—fiberglass, Plexiglas, stainless steel, neon, and polyester resin—have become as commonplace in the artworld of the last fifty years as marble, clay, and oil paints were in the past five hundred. Performance and environmental art reach out of the studio and into daily life. The mixed media experiments of the early modernists have expanded to include film, video, television, and the computer.

The electronic media have revolutionized the visual arts of our time: computer-manipulated photographs, virtual environments, and mixed-media installations are among the more unique projects of the information age. The electronic synthesis of music, video, dance, and peformance constitutes new kinds of theatrical experience, some of which invite the participation of the audience. In the information age, the image has moved into a position of power over the printed word. Indeed, the visual image has come to compete—in value and in authority—with all other forms of cultural expression.

Artists of the information age have joined rock musicians and world-class athletes in becoming the superstars of contemporary society. The art of prominent living painters, sculptors, and performance artists may command fortunes comparable to those of former industrial barons. Critics and gallery owners compete with electronic websites to influence the marketing and commercialization of art, so that (for better or for worse) artists have become celebrities and art has become "big business."

Pop Art

The term *pop art* was coined in England in the 1950s, but the movement came to fruition in New York in the following decade—a time in which sixty per cent of America's population owned television sets. Pop art became the quintessential style of the information age in that it embraced the imagery of consumer products, celebrated personalities, and everyday events, as mediated by TV, film, and magazines. It presented commonplace goods and popular personalities in an overtly realistic style. Pop artists departed from postwar gestural abstraction, thus giving new life to the Western representational tradition. As Andy Warhol (1931–1987), the pioneer American pop artist, dryly pronounced: "Pop art is about liking things." Trained as a commercial artist, Warhol took as his subject matter familiar and banal supermarket products such as Brillo, Campbell's soup, and Coca-Cola (Figure 37.2),

WARHOL AND EXPERIMENTAL FILM

Andy Warhol pioneered some of the most novel experiments in postmodern film. He focused a fixed camera on a single object and let it "roll" until the film ran out—thus bringing to film the (uniquely cinematic) "dead time" between "events," as John Cage had brought to music the "silence" between moments of sound. In *Outer and Inner Space* (1965), he used a double-screen format to present multiple versions of his female "star" watching images of herself on televised videotape. Warhol also exploited the "long take": In the homoerotic film, *My Hustler* (1967), a single thirty-minute shot documents the interaction between two gay men who groom themselves before the bathroom sink.

American superstars like Elvis Presley and Marilyn Monroe (Figure **38.1**), and media-documented episodes of social violence (such as the civil rights riots of the 1960s). Warhol depersonalized images by enlarging them or by reproducing them in monotonous, postage-stamp rows that resemble supermarket displays. He employed the slick advertising techniques of **silkscreen** and airbrush, thus flouting distinctions between fine and applied art. Warhol's Coke bottles and soup cans exalt the commercialism of contemporary life even as they assault the consumer mentality of Ellul's "mass society."

Jasper Johns (b. 1930), an artist whose career has spanned more than half a century, shared Warhol's interest in manipulating commonplace objects in ways that pose questions about the imitative power of art and the growing commercialism of the art object. When Willem de Kooning quipped that Johns' art dealer could sell anything—even two beer cans—Johns created *Painted Bronze* (1960), a set of bronze-cast, hand-painted cans of ale (Figure **38.2**). Johns' beer cans, like his flags and targets, are at once neo-dada tributes to Marcel Duchamp (see Figure 33.5), whom Johns knew personally, and post-

Figure 38.1 (above) **ANDY WARHOL**, *Mint Marilyn Monroe*, 1962. Oil and silkscreen enamel on canvas, 20½ × 16½ in. Jasper Johns Collection © 2000 The Andy Warhol Foundation for the Visual Arts, Inc./ARS, New York and DACS, London 2000.

Figure 38.2 (left) **JASPER JOHNS**, *Painted Bronze (Beer Cans)*, 1960. Painted bronze, 5½ × 8 × 4¼ in. Private collection. © Jasper Johns/DACS, London/VAGA, New York 2000.

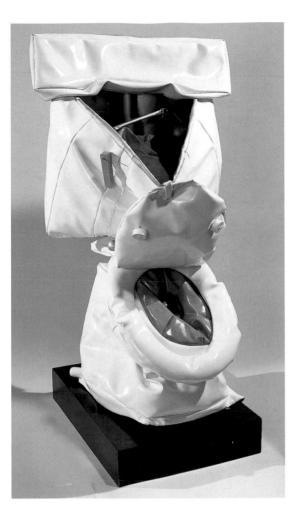

modern parodies of the cherished icons of contemporary life. But they are also mock-heroic commentaries on the fact that art, like beer, is a marketable commodity.

Among the most intriguing vehicles of pop parody are the monumental soft vinyl sculptures of Claes Oldenburg (b. 1929)—gigantic versions of such everyday items as clothespins, hot dogs, table fans, typewriter erasers, and toilets (Figure **38.3**). Often enlarged ten to twenty times their natural size, these objects assume a comic vulgarity that shatters our complacent acceptance of their presence in our daily lives. With similar bravado, the oversized paintings of Roy Lichtenstein (1923–1997), modeled on comic-book cartoons, bring attention to familiar clichés and stereotypes of popular entertainment. Violence and romance are trivialized in the fictional lives of Lichtenstein's comic-book stereotypes—superheroes and helpless women (Figure **38.4**). Like other pop artists, Lichtenstein employs commercial techniques, including stencil and airbrush; he even imitates the Benday dots used in advertising design to achieve tonal gradation. The resulting canvases, with their slickly finished surfaces and flat, bold shapes, are burlesque versions of mass media advertisements. With tongue-in-cheek humor, however, the commercial world of the 1990s has "reclaimed" pop art: Just as Warhol and Lichtenstein appropriated the images of popular culture, so the popular media and the world of fashion design continue to "quote" from the works of these two artists.

Figure 38.3 (left) **CLAES OLDENBURG**, *Soft Toilet*, 1966. Vinyl, Plexiglas, and kapok on painted wood base, 57⅛ × 2⅞ × 28⅛ in. Collection of Whitney Museum of American Art, New York. 50th Anniversary Gift of Mr. and Mrs. Victor W. Ganz. 79.83a–b. Photograph copyright © 1997 Whitney Museum of American Art.

Figure 38.4 (below) **ROY LICHTENSTEIN**, *Torpedo . . . Los!*, 1963. Oil on canvas, 5 ft. 8 in. × 6 ft. 8 in. Courtesy the artist, © The Estate of Roy Lichtenstein/DACS 2000.

Figure 38.5 ROBERT RAUSCHENBERG, *Buffalo II*, 1964. Oil on canvas with silkscreen, 8 ft. × 6 ft. The Robert B. Mayer Family Collection, Chicago, Illinois.
© Robert Rauschenberg/DACS, London/VAGA, New York 2000.

Assemblage

Art that freely combines two- and three-dimensional elements has a history that reaches back to the early twentieth century—recall Picasso's collages and Duchamp's modified readymades. Since mid-century, however, the American artist Robert Rauschenberg (b. 1925) has monumentalized the art of *assemblage* in works that incorporate what he wryly referred to as "the excess of the world." In creating bold, large-scale art objects out of old car tires, street signs, broken furniture, and other debris, he fathered artworks he called "combines." These creations attack the boundary between painting and sculpture and force us to examine ordinary objects in extraordinary new guises. Rauschenberg is a talented printmaker as well as a daring sculptor. For over half a century, he has experimented with a wide variety of transfer techniques, including collage and silkscreen, to produce provocative two-dimensional kaleidoscopes of contemporary culture (Figure **38.5**). These bits and pieces of cultural debris appear thrown together, as if all were equally valuable (or equally useless). But they are assembled with an impeccable sensitivity to color, shape, and form. Rauschenberg's sly juxtapositions of familiar "found" images—like the visual scramble of postmodern channel-grazing—startle, and occasionally disturb.

Numerous artists have used assemblage to bring attention to the random and violent aspects of contemporary society. John Chamberlain (b. 1927) has created seductive sculptures out of junked automobiles, whose corroded sheet-metal bodies and twisted steel bumpers suggest the transience of high-tech products and the dangers inherent in their misuse (Figure **38.6**). Louise Nevelson (1900–1988) collected wooden boxes, filled them with discarded fragments of found and machine-made objects, and painted them a uniform black, white, or gold. Like decaying altarpieces, these structures enshrine the vaguely familiar and haunting objects of modern materialist culture (Figure **38.7**).

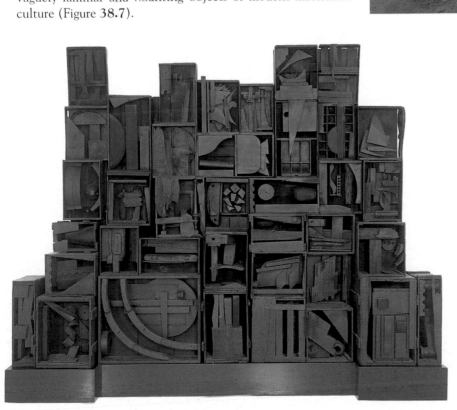

Figure 38.6 (above) **JOHN CHAMBERLAIN**, *Debonaire Apache*, 1991. Painted and chromium plated steel, 7 ft. 10 in. × 4 ft. 6¾ in. × 4 ft. 2½ in. Photo: Peter Foe/Fotoworks. Photograph courtesy of the Pace Gallery, New York. © ARS, New York and DACS, London 2000.

Figure 38.7 (left) **LOUISE NEVELSON**, *Sky Cathedral*, 1958. Black-painted wood, 9 ft. 7 in. × 11 ft. 3 in. Albright-Knox Art Gallery, Buffalo, New York. © ARS, NY and DACS London 2000.

Geometric Abstraction, Op, Minimal, Neon, and Kinetic Art

Not all contemporary artists have embraced the ironic stance of pop and assemblage art. Some have remained loyal to the nonobjective mode of *geometric abstraction*, first initiated in painting by Malevich and Mondrian (see chapter 32). Obedient to the credo of the Bauhaus architect Mies van der Rohe that "less is more," these artists have strived for the machinelike purity of elemental forms and colors, occasionally enlarging such forms to colossal sizes. Early in his career, the American artist Frank Stella (b. 1936) painted huge canvases consisting of brightly colored, hard-edged geometric patterns that look as though they are made with a giant protractor (Figure **38.8**). In place of the traditional square or rectangular canvas, Stella and others of the geometric abstract school constructed canvases shaped like chevrons or triangles, often fastened together or assembled into groups. Stella continues to reject value-oriented art in favor of a style that is neutral and impersonal. These features dominate even his more recent flamboyant three-dimensional pieces. "All I want anyone to get out of my paintings, and all I ever get out of them, is the fact that you can see the whole thing without confusion," explains Stella: "What you see is what you see."

The idea that what one sees is determined by *how* one sees has been central to the work of Hungarian-born Victor Vasarely (b. 1908) and Britain's Bridget Riley (b. 1931). Both Vasarely and Riley explore the operation of conflicting visual cues and the elemental effects of colors and shapes on the faculties of the human retina—a style known as *optical art*, or *op art*. In Riley's *Current* (Figure **38.9**), a series of curved black lines painted on a white surface creates the illusion of vibrating movement and elusive color—look for yellow by staring hard at the painting for a few minutes.

While Europeans pioneered optical abstractionism, Americans led the way in the development of *minimalism*.

Figure 38.8 FRANK STELLA, *Tahkt-i-Sulayman I*, 1967. Polymer and fluorescent paint on canvas, 10 ft ¼ in. × 20 ft. 2¼ in. Menil Collection Houston, Texas.

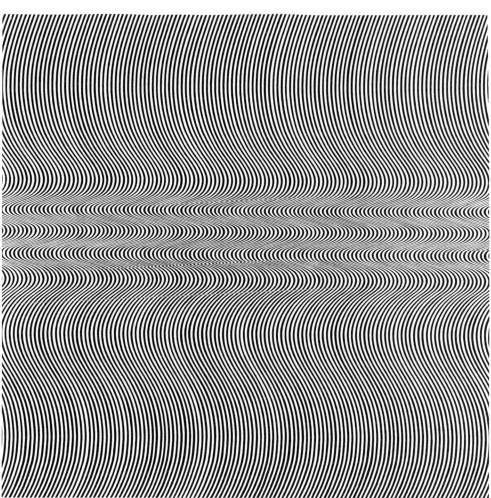

Figure 38.9 (left) **BRIDGET RILEY**,
Current, 1964. Synthetic polymer paint on
composition board, 4 ft. 10⅜ in. × 4 ft. 10⅞
in. The Museum of Modern Art, New York.
Philip Johnson Fund. Photograph © 1997
The Museum of Modern Art, New York.

Figure 38.10 (below) **DONALD JUDD**,
Untitled, 1967. Green lacquer on galvanised
iron, each unit 9 × 40 × 31 in. Museum of
Modern Art, New York. Helen Achen
Bequest and gift of Joseph A. Helman.
Photo © 1998 Museum of Modern Art.

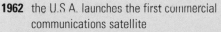

Minimalist sculptors developed a highly refined industrial aesthetic that featured elemental forms made of high-tech materials. The geometric components of minimalist artworks are usually factory produced and assembled according to the artist's instructions. The untitled stainless steel and Plexiglas boxes of Donald Judd (1928–1994) protrude from the wall with mathematical clarity and perfect regularity (Figure **38.10**). They resemble a stack of shelves, yet they neither contain nor support anything. The visual rhythms of Judd's serial forms create a "dialogue" between space and volume, between flat, bright enamel colors and dull or reflective metal grays, and between subtly textured and smooth surfaces. More monumental in scale are the primal forms of the Japanese-American sculptor Isamu Noguchi (b. 1904). Poised on one corner of its steel and aluminum frame, Noguchi's gigantic *Cube* (Figure **38.11**) shares the purity of form and the mysterious resonance of

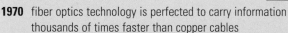

1962 the U.S.A. launches the first commercial communications satellite

1970 fiber optics technology is perfected to carry information thousands of times faster than copper cables

1977 the first international conference on Chaos Theory is organized

such monuments as the Egyptian pyramids and the crystal monolith in the film *2001*.

Minimalists have enthusiastically embraced the tools of modern electronic technology. The Greek artist Chryssa (b. 1933) transforms fluorescent lights into powerful shapes inspired by commercial lettering and industrial neon signs (Figure **38.12**). Others design anodized aluminum sculptures that move in response to currents of electricity or to the natural rhythms of wind and water. Constructed on the principle of movement, *kinetic* art looks back to the innovative mobiles of Alexander Calder (see Figure 35.13).

New Realism

During the 1970s, there emerged a new version of realism that emphasized the stop-action stillness and sharp-focus immediacy of the photograph. *New realism* (also called *neorealism*, *hyperrealism*, and *photorealism*) differs from previous realist strategies (including social realism and pop art) in its disavowal of narrative content and its indifference to moral, social, and political issues.

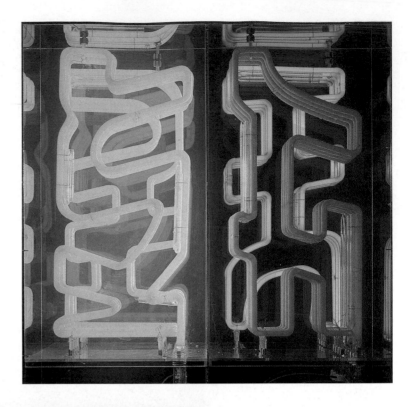

Figure 38.12 (above) **CHRYSSA**, *Fragment for "The Gates to Times Square,"* 1966. Neon, Plexiglas, steel, and painted wood, 75¼ × 34⅞ × 27⅝ in. Collection of Whitney Museum of American Art, New York. Purchase, with funds from Howard and Jean Lipman. 66.135a–b. Photograph copyright © 1997 Whitney Museum of American Art.

Figure 38.11 (left) **ISAMU NOGUCHI**, *Cube*, 1968. Steel subframe with aluminum panels, height 28 ft. Marine Midland Building, New York. Photo: Gloria Fiero.

Figure 38.13 (above) **RICHARD ESTES**, *Helene's Florist*, 1971. Oil on canvas, 4 ft. × 6 ft. The Toledo Museum of Art, Toledo, Ohio. Purchased with funds from the Libbey Endowment. Gift of Edward Drummond Libbey. © Richard Estes/VAGA, New York/DACS, London 2000.

Figure 38.14 (right) **CHUCK CLOSE**, *Big Self-Portrait*, 1968. Acrylic on canvas, 8 ft. 11½ in. × 6 ft. 11½ in. Walker Art Center, Minneapolis.

Although decidedly representational, new realism is as impersonal as minimal art. New realist artists do not imitate natural phenomena; rather, they recreate the artificially processed view of reality captured by the photographic image. Richard Estes (b. 1936), for instance, paints urban still lifes based on fragments of the photographs that he himself makes (Figure **38.13**). A virtuoso painter, Estes tantalizes the eye with details refracted by polished aluminum surfaces and plate-glass windows. In his early works, Chuck Close (b. 1940) used an opaque projector to transfer the photographic image to canvas after both photograph and canvas had been ruled to resemble graph paper; he then filled each square of the canvas with tiny gradations of color that resemble the pixels of a television screen (Figure **38.14**). The brutally impersonal tabloid quality of Close's oversized "mug-shots" is reinforced by his monochromatic palette.

High-tech materials and techniques have made possible the fabrication of new realist sculptures

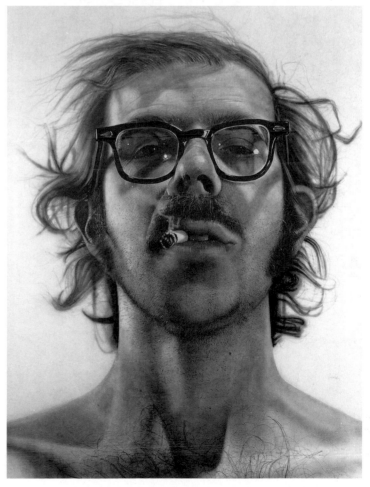

expressionism (see chapter 33). Kiefer draws his dark visions from the storehouse of German mythology and Nazi totalitarianism. Painted in dark, thick colors, mixed with latex, straw, and shellac, he conjures up memories of scorched earth and bombed villages—he achieves some of his effects with the use of a blowtorch. The ominous rectangular structure at the upper center of his paean *To the Unknown Painter* (Figure **38.16**)—at once a shrine, a gravesite, and a military bunker—suggests the painful ambiguity between humanity's creative and destructive forces.

Social Conscience Art

All art may be said to offer some perspective on the social scene; however, during the late twentieth century, many artists self-consciously assumed an activist, even missionary stance. Not overtly political nor even necessarily critical of the status quo, *social conscience art* seeks to transform society by awakening its visionary potential. Such art works holistically to reclaim the spiritual authority that art once held in ancient societies. Issue-driven art, like social conscience

Figure 38.16 (below) **ANSELM KIEFER**, *To the Unknown Painter*, 1983. Oil, emulsion, woodcut, shellac, latex, and straw on canvas, 9 ft. 2 in. × 9 ft. 2 in. Carnegie Museum of Art, Pittsburgh. Richard M. Scaife Fund and A. W. Mellon Acquisition Endowment Fund. 85,53.

Figure 38.15 (above) **DUANE HANSON**, *Tourists*, 1970. Fiberglass and polyester polychromed, 5 ft. 4 in. × 5 ft. 5 in. × 3 ft. 11 in. Scottish National Gallery of Modern Art, Edinburgh.

that are shockingly lifelike. Duane Hanson (1925–1996) used fiberglass-reinforced polyester resin to recreate the appearance of ordinary and often lower-class individuals in their everyday occupations (Figure **38.15**). Hanson cast his polyester molds from live models, then added wigs, clothing, and accessories. By comparison with George Segal's melancholic figures (see Figure 35.11), Hanson's "living dead" are symbolic of modern life at its most prosaic.

New Expressionism

Dramatically different from the new realism of Estes and Close, the paintings of Anselm Kiefer (b. 1945) manifest vigorous distortions of form and color that—in their brutal, emotional fervor—revive the tradition of early twentieth-century German

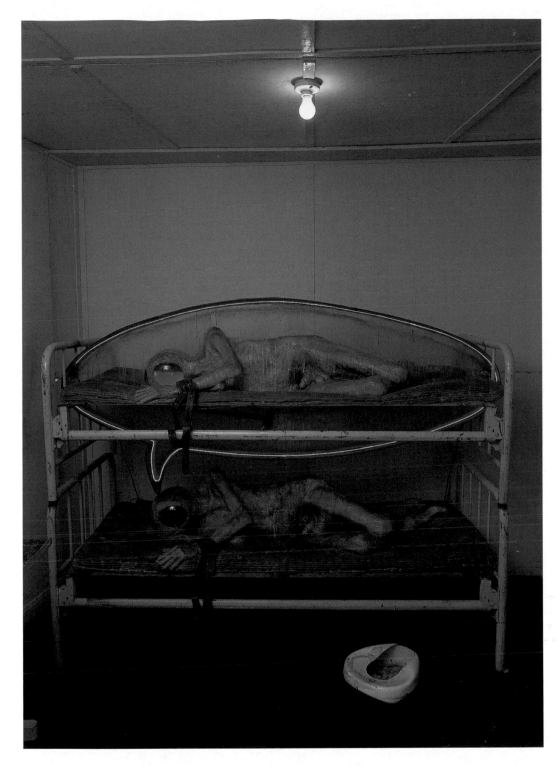

Figure 38.17 EDWARD KIENHOLZ, *The State Hospital*, 1964–1966. Mixed media, 8 ft. x 12 ft. x 10 ft. Moderna Museet, Stockholm. Photo: Statens Konstmuseer.

literature, draws attention to ecological ruin and widespread drug-use, to the threat of nuclear terrorism and the plight of marginalized populations, to decay in the quality of urban life and the erosion of moral values.

The Los Angeles based artist Edward Kienholz (1927–1994), brought attention to some of the most mundane and unpleasant aspects of modern American society. His room-sized tableaux, often filled with real furniture, manikins, and (taped) sound, are disturbing and intimate scenarios that invite the participation of the viewer. *The State Hospital* (Figure **38.17**) shows a man's naked, bony figure chained at the wrist to an institutional metal cot. A

glass bowl filled with two black fish replaces his head, from which emerges a neon "thought bubble" that surrounds his gruesome twin—the mental patient contemplating, perhaps, his own demise. Set in a large, gray room, complete with bedpan, the tableau requires the viewer to peer into the interior through a barred window in the door. Kienholz appended to the piece a detailed description based, in part, on first-hand experience —in 1948, he had worked briefly as an orderly in a mental hospital. A critic of the Vietnam War and a commentator on American politics of the 1970s and 1980s, Kienholz drew notoriety for his bitterly satiric tableaux.

The Cuban-born Luis Cruz Azaceta (b. 1942) combines figurative and expressionistic techniques to address the realities of arson, street crime, AIDS, and drug addiction (Figure 38.18)—the evidence of a universal social disorder. His huge canvases are often splotched with harshly colored paint, their surfaces blistered, burned, cut, or collaged with wire and debris. In the tradition of the gallows-humor comedians Richard Pryor and Woody Allen, Azaceta delivers grotesque and macabre images that convey the need for reform.

In contrast with the aggressive activism of Azaceta, social conscience artworks from postwar Eastern Europe are subtle and understated. The Polish sculptor Magdalena Abakanowicz (b. 1930) draws on traditional methods of weaving and modeling to cast hulking, monumental figures that stage the drama of the human condition (Figure 38.19). Sisal, jute, and burlap make up the substance of these figures, whose scarred and patched surfaces call to mind earth, mud, and the dusty origins of primordial crea-tures. Abakanowicz installs her headless, sexless figures in groups that evoke a sense of collective anonymity and vul-nerability, but at the same time underscore the kinship between human and natural forms. Abakanowicz, who regards art as potentially transformative and redeeming, brings to these highly concentrated works her experience as a survivor of World War II (and Poland's repressive communist regime).

With the successful mapping of the human genome in the year 2000 (see chapter 37), the human body and the ethics of genetic manipulation have come to preoccupy artists and scientists alike. Mapping the body with x-rays, MRI's (magnetic resonance imaging), DNA diagnostics, and endoscopic film, artists have revised the genre of por-traiture (traditionally, the record of the exterior self) to register an image of the body's inner mechanisms. Eduardo Kac (b. 1962) has gone even further: With the help of a geneticist, Kac altered the genetic makeup of a rabbit with a gene from a jellyfish containing a green florescent pro-

Figure 38.18 LUIS CRUZ AZACETA, *Coke Heads VIII*, 1991. Synthetic polymer paint on canvas, 8 ft. 11 in. × 10 ft. 2 in. Courtesy Frederick Snitzer Gallery, Coral Gables, Florida.

Figure 38.19 MAGDALENA
ABAKANOWICZ, *Crowd 1* (detail),
1986–1987. Burlap and resin, 50
standing life-sized figures, each 66⅞
× 23⅜ × 11¾ in. Courtesy
Marlborough Gallery, New York.
1997 © Magdalena Abakanowicz.
Photography © Artur Starewicz.

tein. By means of his "transgenic albino rabbit" (a glow-in-the-dark bunny), Kac aims to generate a public dialogue on the moral and social implications of bioengineering, or altering life forms. Clearly, contemporary artists have assumed the roles of scientists, educators, and social critics. If science is the art of our time, then the reverse may be true as well.

In the People's Republic of China, activist art emerged within (and in spite of) a dangerous set of circumstances. Despite communist efforts to modernize culture following the death of Mao Zedong in 1976, Chinese officials tightened control over intellectual and artistic expression: Resolving in 1983 to eradicate "spiritual pollution," the state forbade all artworks that propagated religion, embraced "bourgeois" humanist values, or included pornographic material. Despite the repressive measures, young Chinese artists, imbued with a keen sense of mission and historical consciousness, continued to write and paint, either in exile or at their own peril. In June 1989, at Tiananmen Square in Beijing, thousands of student activists demonstrated in support of democratic reform. With Beethoven's Ninth Symphony blaring from loudspeakers, demonstrators raised a plaster figure of the Goddess of Democracy modeled on the *Statue of Liberty*. The official response to this overt display of freedom resulted in the massacre of some protesters and the imprisonment of others. Since Tiananmen Square, literary publication has remained under the watchful eye of the state, but efforts to control music and the visual arts have been less successful. Chinese artists continue to pursue the traditional crafts of jade and porcelain, along with that favorite of Chinese genres, landscape painting. Others, however, have absorbed the styles of the Western avant-garde that continue to challenge the aesthetic mandates of the People's Republic.

The last decades of the twentieth century generated painting styles that deliberately mocked the conformist ideals of China's socialist society. Particularly popular among young Chinese artists was *cynical realism*—a style that utilized academic and commercial painting techniques to draw attention to social and political conditions. Cynical realism reflects the sentiments of post-Tiananmen artists who, having abandoned the idealism of the 1980s, use roguish humor to register a sense of powerlessness. Cynical realists share the humorously subversive tone of China's *political pop* painters, who seize on Western icons to glamorize the mundane aspects of contemporary Chinese life. Painters of political pop art are involved in a search for a new cultural rationale that might resolve the contradictions between ancient (Confucian) values and modern (communist) ideals, between Chinese holism and Western materialism, and between socialist realism and other, less conventional, modes of expression. One of China's most publicized artists, Wang Gangyi (b. 1956), united the conventions of old China—specifically, the propaganda posters of the Cultural Revolution—with the imagery of consumer-driven commercialism. His political pop art series, entitled *The Great Criticism*, combines flat bright colors and broad, simplified shapes in compositions reminiscent of the social realist poster art that was popular both in communist China and communist Russia (see Figure 34.3). Making visual reference to this style, his two soldiers, armed with an oversized pen, advance into the arena of commercial combat—an environment plastered

1981 lasers are utilized for the study of matter

1983 the first commercial cellular phones are produced by AT&T

1986 development of high-temperature superconductors

1990 the internationally-linked computer network (the Internet) becomes accessible to personal computers

Figure 38.20 WANG GUANGYI, *Great Castigation Series: Coca-Cola*, 1993. Enamel paint on canvas, 59 × 47 in. Hanart TZ Gallery, Hong Kong.

Total Art

The information age generated creative strategies that reached beyond the studio and the art gallery and into the public domain. With *total art*, process (and conception) became more important than product—the visual object itself. Somewhat like the Roman Catholic Mass or the African funeral, total art was a form of communal ritual that involved planned (though usually not rehearsed) performance. The beginnings of total art are found in the minimal and aleatory enterprises of John Cage (see chapter 35) and in the wildly experimental art of the postwar Japanese Gutai Group (see chapter 35), whose artist/performers engaged their materials violently—pounding the canvas with paint-filled boxing gloves or hurling themselves against wet canvases. In one of the earliest examples of *performance art*, a work entitled *Anthropometry* (Figure **38.21**), France's Yves Klein (1928–1962) employed nude women as "human brushes." Klein's contemporary Jean Tinguely (1925–1991) made a distinctive comment on twentieth-century technology with a series of machines he programmed to self-destruct amid a public spectacle of noise, fire, and smoke. The American pioneer of *happenings*, Allan Kaprow (b. 1927), shifted performance art from artist to audience. Kaprow called the "happening" a performance that occurs "in a given time and space." That space might be a city street, a beach, or a private home. During the 1960s Kaprow wrote and orchestrated more

with the official stamps of government approval (Figure **38.20**). Here, the collective idealism of Communism is replaced by the collective consumerism generated by popular commodities such as McDonalds hamburgers, Marlboro cigarettes, Coca-Cola, and Kodak film.

SOCIAL CONSCIENCE FILM

The late twentieth century was a golden age of cinematic creativity, an era in which the film medium (in alliance with television) reached a new level of social influence, its impact so great as to shape and even alter public opinion. The innovative films of the director/artists who emerged in the 1970s and 1980s reestablished the Hollywood film industry, which had faltered financially prior to the mid-1960s. The new directors, products of film schools rather than the Hollywood studio system, contributed to a reassessment of America's "master narratives" and dominant fictions: Arthur Penn's *Little Big Man* (1970), for example, exposed the myth of the Native American as "savage." Robert Altman, one of America's finest director/artists, launched a biting satire on the Korean War (and war in general) with the film *M*A*S*H* (1970). The image of the passive, male-dependent female was transformed in the film *Thelma and Louise* (1991), directed by Ridley Scott. Filmmakers of the late twentieth century worked to develop signature styles, using cinematic and editing techniques (as sculptors use their media) to create affect and audience response. So, for instance, Altman favored the telephoto zoom lens to probe the faces of his (usually) socially troubled characters; fractured sounds and bits of dialogue overlap or intrude from off-camera. To achieve lifelike spontaneity, Altman often invited his actors to improvise as he filmed. In *Nashville* (1974), he traded the single cinematic protagonist for some two dozen characters involved in a presidential election. Postmodern in style, Altman's films are vast kaleidoscopic scenarios, the products of judiciously assembled fragments. Issue-driven subjects were common fare in the history of late modern American film. But they have rarely been treated as powerfully as in Steven Spielberg's *Schindler's List* (1993), a story of the Holocaust adapted from Thomas Keneally's prize-winning 1982 novel. A virtuoso filmmaker, Spielberg made brilliant use of the techniques of documentary newscasting to create visually shattering effects.

Social conscience film is by no means confined to the United States. In *Salaam Bombay!* (1988), filmed in the brothel district of Bombay, one of India's leading filmmakers, Mira Nair, exposed the sordid lives of that country's illiterate street urchins. China's internationally celebrated filmmaker and cinematographer Zhang Yimou (b. 1951) lived among the peasants of Shaanxi Province prior to making films about China's disenfranchised rural population (*The Story of Qiu Ju*, 1992) and in particular its women, many of whom remain hostage to feudal and patriarchal traditions (*Raise the Red Lantern*, 1991). An admirer of Ingmar Bergman and Akira Kurosawa (see chapter 35), Zhang rejected the socialist realism of the communist era in favor of purity of vision and fierce honesty. His films, at least three of which have been banned in China, are noted for their sensuous use of color and their troubling insights into moral and cultural issues.

Figure 38.21 YVES KLEIN, *Anthropometry ANT49*, 1960. Photo: © Harry Shunk, New York. © ADAGP, Paris and DACS, London 2000.

the performance was itself the work of art. Happenings and performance pieces influenced the way the information age processed the semiritualized events of postmodern life—political demonstrations, street riots, rock concerts, and more recently "raves," became extensions of the total art enterprise. Clearly, however, happenings and performance pieces are ephemeral; hence, the only lasting "product" is the photographic or videotaped record of the event.

Like "happenings," *environmental art* involves a conceptualized modification or transformation of a specific space. The mixed-media tableaux of George Segal (see Figure 35.11) anticipated this type of total art. In the 1970s and 1980s, room-sized installations invited the physical presence of the spectator. Examples of such installations include a "walk-in infinity chamber" consisting of mirrors studded with thousands of miniature lights or filled with menacing, fur-covered furniture and floors.

Perhaps the most monumental type of total art is *earth sculpture*, a kind of sculpture that takes the natural landscape as both its medium and its subject. Earth sculptures are usually colossal, heroic, and temporary. Among the most impressive examples of this genre was the piece called *Spiral Jetty*, built in 1970 by Robert Smithson (1938–1973) at the edge of the Great Salt Lake in Utah (Figure **38.22**). Smithson's spiral—the snail-like symbol of eternity in ancient art—was 1,500 feet wide and consisted of over 6,000 tons of black basalt, limestone, and earth—materials which are virtually identical to the surrounding area. A

than fifty happenings, most of which engaged dozens of ordinary people in the dual roles of spectator and performer. *Fluids* (1967), a happening staged in Pasadena, California, called for participants to construct a house of ice blocks and then witness the melting process that followed. As in most happenings, chance played a key role;

Figure 38.22 ROBERT SMITHSON, *Spiral Jetty*, Great Salt Lake, Utah, 1970. Rock, salt crystals, earth algae; coil 1,500 ft.
© Estate of Robert Smithson/VAGA, New York/DACS, London 2000.

Figure 38.23 CHRISTO AND JEANNE-CLAUDE, *Running Fence*, Sonoma and Marin counties, California, 1972–1976. Fabric fence, height 18 ft., length 24½ miles. © Christo 1976. Photo: Jeanne-Claude, New York.

conscious reference to ancient earthworks, such as those found among the Native American cultures of South America (see Introduction), Smithson's project brought attention to the role of the artist in reconstructing the environment and its ecology. Earthworks like *Spiral Jetty*, however, which moved art out of the gallery and into nature, were often best appreciated from the air. Tragically, it was in the crash of a plane surveying one such sculpture that Smithson was killed. Smithson's heroic earthwork also disappeared; a part of nature, it fell subject to processes of dissolution and submersion beneath the waters of the Great Salt Lake. But Smithson's documentary drawings, photographs, and films of this and other earthworks have heightened public awareness of the fragile ecological balance between culture and nature.

The environmental sculptures of the American artists Christo and Jeanne-Claude (both b. 1935) are among the most inventive examples of total art. The Christos have magically transformed natural and human sites by enveloping them with huge amounts of fabric. They have wrapped monumental public structures, such as the Pont Neuf in Paris and the Reichstag in Berlin, and they have reshaped nature, wrapping part of the coast of Australia, for instance, and surrounding eleven islands in Miami's Biscayne Bay with over six million square feet of pink woven polypropylene fabric. One of the Christos' earliest projects, *Running Fence*, 1972–1976 (Figure **38.23**), involved the construction of a nylon "fence" 24½ miles long and 18 feet high. The nylon panels were hung on cables and steel poles and ran through Sonoma and Marin Counties, California, to the Pacific Ocean. The fascinating history of this visually breathtaking piece, which cost the artists over three million dollars and mobilized the efforts of a large crew of workers, is documented in films, photographs, and books. The fence itself, meandering along the California hills like a modern-day version of the Great Wall of China, remained on site for only two weeks. Unlike Smithson, the Christos do not seek to remake the natural landscape; rather they modify it temporarily in order to dramatize the difference between the natural world and the increasingly artificial domain of postmodern society.

Total art is essentially conceptual, since it is driven by ideas rather than by purely visual or formal concerns. Perhaps the purest kinds of *conceptual art*, however, are those that consist only of words. Since the 1960s, a variety of artists have created artworks that feature definitions, directions, or messages devoid of other visual images. Barbara Kruger's billboard-style posters (see Figure 36.12) combine photographic images and words that make cryptic comment on social and political issues. The superstar of conceptual art is the American sculptor Jenny Holzer (b. 1950). Holzer carves paradoxical and often subversive messages in stone or broadcasts them electronically on public billboards. She often transmits her slogans by way of light-emitting diodes, a favorite medium of commercial advertising. In language that is at once banal and acerbic, Holzer informs us that "Lack of charisma can be fatal," "Myths make reality more intelligible," "Humanism is obsolete," "Decency is a relative thing," and "Ambivalence can ruin your life." Holzer's typically postmodern word-art wryly tests the authority of public information, particularly information as dispersed by contemporary electronic media.

Video Art

In the 1950s, the Korean artist and musician Nam June Paik (b. 1932) predicted that the television cathode ray would replace the canvas as the medium of the future. The now-acclaimed father of video art was not far from the mark, for art that employs one or another form of electronic technology has come to dominate the artworld of our time. Video art had its beginnings in the 1960s, under the shaping influence of Paik himself. Paik began his career (under the combined influence of John Cage and Zen Buddhism) by creating performance pieces and electronic installations, some of which were among the first interactive experiments in sound and image. With the help of an electronic engineer, Paik designed and built one of the first videosynthesizers, a device that makes it possible to alter the shape and color of a video image. In the 1990s, Paik assembled television sets, circuit boards, and other electronic apparatus to produce the *Robot* series (see Figure 37.1). More monumental in scope and conception,

however, are the artist's multiscreen television installations. *Megatron* (1995), for instance, consists of 215 monitors programmed with a rapid-fire assortment of animated and live-video images drawn from East and West: the Seoul Olympic Games and Korean drummers, rock concert clips, girlie-magazine nudes, and quick-cuts of Paik's favorite artists alternate with the national flags of various countries and other global logos (Figure **38.24**). The animated contour of a bird flying gracefully across a wall of screens brings magical unity to this ocular blitz, while a two-channel audio track adds booming syncopated sound to the visual rhythms. Paik's wall of video monitors dazzles viewers with a kaleidoscopic barrage of images whose fast-paced editing imitates mainstream television and film.

In contrast with the dazzle of Paik's video projects, the art of Bill Viola (b. 1951) is subtle and profound. Viola uses rear-projected video screens to deliver personal narratives in the form of large, slow moving, mesmerizing images. Mortality, identity, and consciousness, Viola's central themes, draw inspiration from Zen Buddhism, Christian mysticism, and Sufi poetry. In *Stations* (a reference to the Stations of the Cross, Christ's journey to Calvary), a computer-controlled, five-channel video/sound installation projects the image of a male body (immersed in water) onto three vertical slabs of granite; the image is reflected onto mirrored slabs placed on the floor (Figure **38.25**). Viola wants the viewer to experience his work "insofar as possible, as a mental image"—in this case, as a motif that evokes the human journey from birth to death. Viola's art

Figure 38.24 NAM JUNE PAIK, *Megatron*, 1995. 215 monitors, 8-channel color video and 2-channel sound, left side 142½ × 270 × 23½ in.; right side 128 × 128 × 23½ in. Guggenheim Soho. Courtesy the artist and Holly Solomon Gallery, New York.

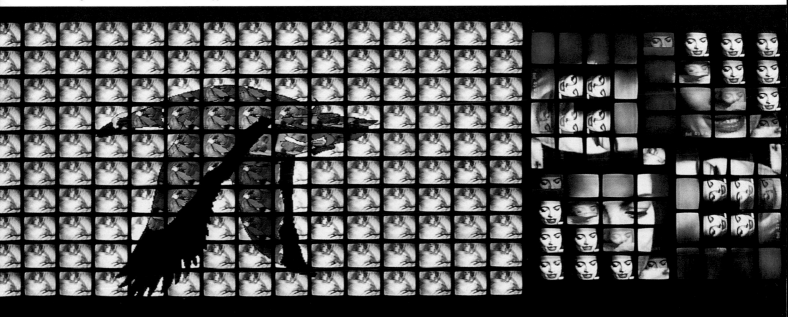

Figure 38.25 **BILL VIOLA**, *Stations* (detail), 1994. Video/sound installation with five granite slabs, five projections and five projection screens. The Museum of Modern Art, New York. Gift to the Bohen Foundation in honour of Richard F. Oldenburg. Photo: Charles Duprat.

is contemplative and deeply embedded in the exploration of conceptual reality. It makes reference to the current "crisis of representation and identity" in which new technologies leave viewers unsure as to whether an optical image is real or unreal. According to Viola, "representing information" will be the main issue in the arts of the future. Video and sound installations, which have become a major form of late twentieth-century expression, are related to the film experience. Both immerse the viewer in the moving image; but, as with Viola's work, video art works to concentrate experience in a way that film—especially film as entertainment—does not usually achieve.

Since the 1970s, video performances and video installations have moved in the direction of political theater. More elaborate in their staging, they may feature holograms, laser beams, moving pictures, television images, and computer-generated special effects, all of which may be projected onto screens and walls to the accompaniment of electronically recorded sounds. Some, like Mary Lucier's recent sound and video installation that recreates the disastrous effects of the 1997 flood in Grand Forks, North Dakota, are dramatic ruminations on personal and communal experience. Others are cast in the form of live theater. The leading American performance artist, Laurie Anderson (b. 1947), appropriates images from classic movies, newsreels, and other video resources and combines them with tape-recorded and live music. In one of her earliest performances, she played an electric violin with a neon-lit bow, waving the bow in the air to create not only sounds, but computer-generated images. For artists like Anderson, the computer has become a "metamedium"— a medium that transcends and transforms all other forms.

Computers and the Visual Arts

The computers of the last half century have become a unique means of reconciling the domains of art and science. In dozens of ways, digital devices are transforming the way in which art is made and experienced. Computers are commonly used in the design and construction of architecture and art: in fiberglass sculpture, for instance, the computer makes possible the execution of otherwise unachievable three-dimensional curves. New software programs allow artists to draw and paint electronically. At the same time, the use of the computer to manipulate old images and generate new images, a specialty known as *digital imaging*, has revolutionized the world of film, television, video, holography, and photography (Figure **38.26**). Digital imaging is of two varieties: one involves combining photographic images to create new images with the aid of special computer programs; the other involves generating entirely new photorealistic imagery by purely digital means. In the second approach, the artist gives the computer a set of instructions about the "look" of an image, which is then simulated by the computer. Among photographers, computer technology has inspired multilayered, futuristic artworks that could never have been achieved in the traditional darkroom.

Japanese artists have been particularly successful in using computer technology to generate provocative photographs and video projects. Yasumasa Morimura (b. 1945) transforms Western masterpieces into camp spoofs in which he impersonates the central figure. In *Portrait (Twins)*, Morimura turns Manet's *Olympia* (see chapter 30) into a drag queen decked out in a blond wig and rhinestone-trimmed slippers (Figure **38.27**). Using himself as the model for both the nude courtesan and the maid, he deconstructs and revisualizes the history of art. By "updating" Manet's *Olympia*, (itself an "update" of a painting by Titian), Morimura questions the authority of these

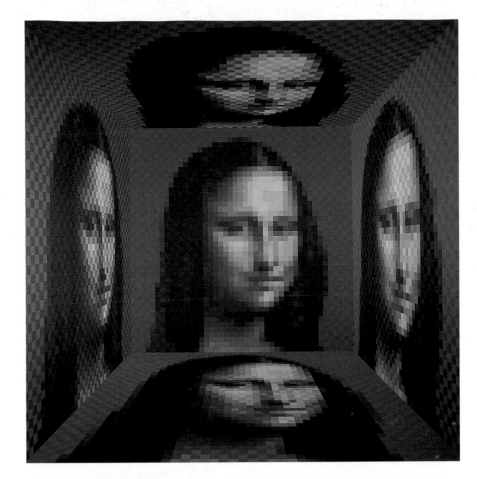

Figure 38.26 (right) **JEAN-PIERRE YVARAL**
Mona Lisa Synthétisée, 1989. © ADAGP, Paris and
DACS, London.

Figure 38.27 (below) **YASUMASA MORIMURA**,
Portrait (Twins), 1988. Color photograph, clear
medium, 6 ft. 10½ in. × 9 ft. 10 in. NW House,
Tokyo. Courtesy Luhring Augustine, New York.

Figure 38.28 MARIKO MORI, *Pure Land*, 1997–1998. Photograph on glass, five panels, 10 ft. × 20 ft. × 8 ft 5 in. Courtesy Deitch Projects, New York.

historical icons, even as he makes sly reference to the post-war Japanese practice of copying Western culture. *Portrait* is a computer manipulated color photograph produced from a studio setup—a combination of postmodern techniques borrowed from fashion advertising. Here, and in his more recent photographs in which he impersonates contemporary icons and film divas—Madonna, Marilyn Monroe, and Liza Minnelli—Morimura pointedly tests classic stereotypes of identity and gender.

Morimura's younger contemporary Mariko Mori (b. 1967) produces billboard-sized electronic installations, three-dimensional videos, and computer generated photographs that combine pop culture with self-spoofing autobiographical motifs. She employs sophisticated technologies for futuristic installations that combine image, music, and perfume—engaging all of the senses at once. In

Pure Land, (a reference to the Buddhist paradise of Japan's Pure Land sect), the artist appears as the Japanese goddess Kichijoten (see Book 2, Figure 14.22), floating in extraplanetary space among an assembly of alien cartoon musicians—which come alive in video versions of the piece (Figure **38.28**).

The use of the computer in making art is no longer exclusive to artists, however. *Interactive art* programs, available both in the art gallery and on the home computer screen, invite the viewer to become a partner in the creative act. In *Piano* (1995) designed by the Japanese media artist Toshio Iwai (b. 1962), the spectator creates a musical "score" by manipulating a trackball that triggers star-shaped points of light that travel along a scroll until they "strike" a piano keyboard; both visual and aural patterns are generated by the spectator—within limits

COMPUTERS AND FILM

Digital technology has transformed the world of filmmaking. Special effects, achieved by way of the computer, not only alter familiar images, but enable the filmmaker to juxtapose familiar images in ways that distort both history and nature. Robert Zemeckis' *Forrest Gump* (1994), for example, had its antihero shaking hands with the long-dead President John F. Kennedy. Like the docufiction that has become popular in the late twentieth century, cinema has found realistic ways of conveying what is not true. Digital technology is also capable of giving birth to entirely new images, or, as one film critic observed, film can realistically render things that do not exist in reality. Born of the computer, Steven Spielberg's dinosaurs (*Jurassic Park*, 1993) and James Cameron's liquid metal cyborgs (*Terminator 2, Last Judgment*, 1991) make use of "morphing" or shape-shifting techniques generated on the computer. In 1995 John Lasseter completed a four-year project that resulted in the first film (*Toy Story*) to be entirely computer-animated. These films are not notable for their lasting artistic value; rather, as vehicles of the hyperimages of our time, they raise questions about the differences between "originals" and "replicas," and between live-action and simulated reproduction. Even as entertainments, they probe distinctions between reality and illusion.

predetermined by Iwai. With *Electronic Eve* (1997), an interactive project conceived by Jenny Marketou (b. 1944), "image consumers" create their own multimedia environment by selecting (through direct touch on the computer screen) from a database of video sequences, still images, computer graphics, texts, and sounds. Other electronic installations invite the audience to turn words (the sounds of speech) into colored shapes and images. And the Internet provides a virtual theater in which one may assume an on-line identity—or more than one identity—in cyberspace.

Postmodernism's most intriguing fusion of media, often called *hypermedia*, is a powerful combination of high technology tools—computers, videotape, and photo-graphy—designed to generate a form of virtual reality. By means of optical discs, high-powered computers simulate artificial environments that are flashed onto a huge screen or onto the inside of a helmet. Donning the helmet, the spectator enters hyperspace and interacts with the simulated environment. Like a giant video game, virtual reality combines visual illusion, sound, and spoken texts. A synthesis of all retrievable informational forms, hypermedia offers an image-saturated playground for the mind.

The computer has put at everyone's disposal the entire history of art, as well as a vast assortment of electronic information in the arts. Sophisticated telecommunication systems facilitate collaborative electronic artworks and electronic art galleries, while the Internet provides access to the contents of more than 5,000 museums around the world.

The Visual Arts and the Global Paradigm

The emerging new framework for contemporary culture, known as the global paradigm, involves the reality of interdependence among cultures throughout the world. This new spirit of cultural and communal collectivity is readily apparent in the art of the information age. The cleverly designed installations of the Japanese-born Yukinori Yanagi (b. 1959), for example, call attention to globalism's "overarching system." Yanagi's *World Flag Ant Farm* (Figure **38.29**) consists of rows of transparent plastic boxes containing sand-poured flags that represent many different nations. The physical appearance of each flag is altered constantly, owing to the activity of thousands of ants who carry grains of colored sand from box to box (thus flag to flag). Yanagi identifies the ant as a natural "trickster" who defies the artificial rules and boundaries of geographic place. *The World Flag Ant Farm* reflects the typically Japanese respect for nature, and the Japanese philosophy of symbiosis, by which nature and culture thrive in a mutually beneficial relationship. But it is a striking visual metaphor for the interdependency of the global village. It portends, as well, by virtue of the plastic tracks that disclose the movements of its busy inhabitants, the "transparent society"* of the twenty-first century—in which privacy has given way to the free and immediate access to information on a global scale.

In a more flamboyant spirit, Chris Ofili (b. 1968) fixes heavily layered imagery (drawn from a wide variety of contemporary magazines) onto canvases that he ornaments with push-pins, sequins, elephant dung, and blobs of brightly colored lacquer. His paintings, usually mounted on varnished globs of elephant dung, are celebratory amalgamations of the world's diverse "stuff"—from African legend and Christian lore to pornography and comic-book

*See David Brin, *The Transparent Society: Will Technology Force Us to Choose Between Privacy and Freedom.* New York: Perseus, 1999.

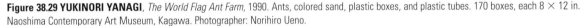

Figure 38.29 YUKINORI YANAGI, *The World Flag Ant Farm,* 1990. Ants, colored sand, plastic boxes, and plastic tubes. 170 boxes, each 8 × 12 in. Naoshima Contemporary Art Museum, Kagawa. Photographer: Norihiro Ueno.

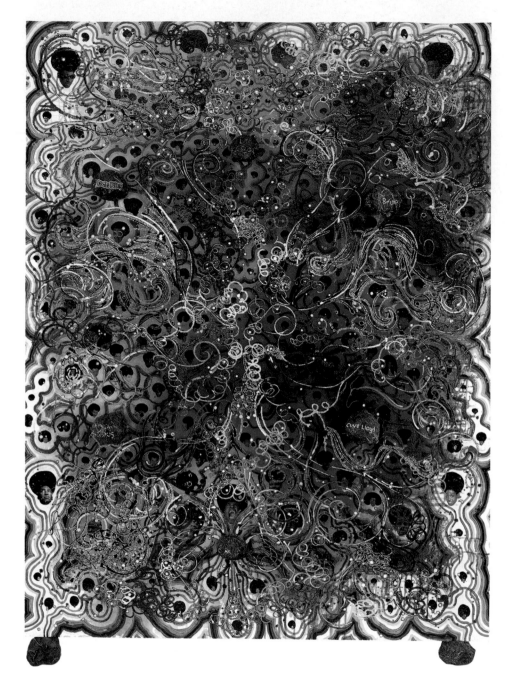

Figure 38.30 CHRIS OFILI, *Afrodizzia* (2nd version), 1996. Elephant dung, map pins, collage, resin and oil on canvas, 8 ft × 6 ft. Courtesy Victoria Miro Gallery, London

characters (Figure **38.30**). During his 1992 stay in Zimbabwe, for instance, Ofili learned the dot painting style of ancient African cave frescoes and the scarification designs of Nuba tribespeople. Ofili's work conflates the multiple (and hybrid) selves that populate the global arena. Born to Nigerian parents in Manchester, England, Ofili himself assumes the multiple identities of Roman Catholic, African, Westerner, and urban artist. His paintings capture the exoticism of the multicultural experience.

Architecture in the Information Age

Contemporary critics link the birth of postmodernism to the architecture of the 1960s and, specifically, to the demise of the international style. Robert Venturi (b. 1925), who first introduced architectural postmodernism in his book *Complexity and Contradiction in Architecture* (1966), countered Mies van der Rohe's dictum "less is more" with the claim "less is a bore." Venturi and others shunned the anonymity and austerity of the glass and steel skyscraper (see Figure 35.15) and the concrete high rise (see Figure 32.26), along with the progressive utopianism of modernists who hoped to transform society through functional form. Instead, postmodernists opted for an architecture that emphasized visual complexity, individuality, and outright fun. In contrast to the machinelike purity of the international style structure, the postmodern building is a playful assortment of fragments "quoted" from architectural traditions as ill-mated as a fast-food stand and a Hellenistic temple. Postmodern architecture, like postmodern fiction, engages a colorful mix of fragments in a whimsical and often witty manner. It shares with *deconstructivist* literary theorists (see chapter 37) the will to

Figure 38.31 PEREZ ASSOCIATES WITH CHARLES MOORE, RON FILSON, URBAN INNOVATIONS, INC., Piazza d'Italia, New Orleans, 1976–1979. © Norman McGrath, New York.

dismantle and reassemble "the text" in a search for its multiple meanings. Just as there is (according to deconstructivism) no single text for the whole of our experience, so there can be no unifying pattern or defining style in the design of any single piece of architecture.

One example of this postmodern aesthetic is the Piazza d'Italia in New Orleans, designed by Charles Moore (1925–1993). The plaza, which serves as an Italian cultural center, is a burlesque yet elegant combination of motifs borrowed from Pompeii, Palladio, and Italian baroque architecture (Figure **38.31**). Its brightly colored colonnaded portico—looking every bit like a gaudy stage set—

Figure 38.32 I. M. PEI & ASSOCIATES, Louvre Pyramid, Paris, 1988. Photo: © R.M.N., Paris.

is adorned with fountains, neon lights, and polished aluminum balustrades. Moore's parodic grab bag appropriation of the Italian heritage culminates in an apron (shaped like a map of Italy) that floats in the central pool of the piazza.

Postmodernism has engendered numerous architectural experiments in **geodesic** and modular design. One of the most inventive of these is the extraordinary glass pyramid that serves as the formal entrance to the Louvre Museum in Paris (Figure **38.32**). Built in 1988 by the Chinese-born American I. M. Pei (b. 1917), this monumental cage of stainless steel and Plexiglas opens up vast areas of interior space in the greenhouse style initiated by Paxton's Crystal Palace (see chapter 30). Pei has transcended national styles and periods by synthesizing the techniques of modern technology (including the glass-and-steel vocabulary of the international style) with the designs of seventeenth-century French landscape architects and the geometry of the Great Pyramid at Giza. His pyramid complex, despite its references to the historic past, is futuristic—a kind of space station for the arts.

The architectural giant of the late twentieth century, Frank Gehry (b. 1930), was born in Toronto, Canada, but lives and works in California. His early designs reflect an interest in humble building materials—plywood, corrugated zinc metal, stainless steel, and chainlink fencing—

which he assembled in serial units. These structures, in which facades tilt, columns lean, and interior spaces are skewed, reflect Gehry's deliberate rejection of the classical design principles of symmetry and stability. More recently, in monumental projects that combine steel, titanium, glass, and limestone, Gehry has developed a vocabulary of undulating forms and irregular shapes inspired by everyday objects: a fish, a guitar, a bouquet of flowers. A Gehry masterpiece, the Guggenheim Museum in Bilbao, Spain, is impressive for its bold, organic style (Figure **38.33** and Part II opener). Located at the river's edge of that Basque industrial port city, Gehry's Guggenheim, like a huge flagship with billowing metallic sails (an image particularly appropriate to Bilbao's maritime history) soars majestically into space. The vast, 260,000 square-foot museum, which includes nineteen gallery spaces linked by sloping ramps and metal bridges, is a showplace for art. A soaring atrium (which Gehry describes as a metallic flower) provides an ideal space for the monumental projects of late twentieth-century artists such as Richard Serra (b. 1939). Serra, whose minimalist steel-rusted plates often measure more than 13 feet tall and 50 feet long (and weigh well over 100 tons), shares Gehry's affection for organic design and geometric irregularity (Figure **38.34**). "There's an interconnection between the curvilinearity of Frank's building and the obvious torquing of my pieces," says

Figure 38.33 FRANK GEHRY, Guggenheim Museum, Bilbao. 1997. Commissioned by the Solomon R.Guggenheim Foundation. Photograph © Christian Richters Fotograf.

Figure 38.34 RICHARD SERRA, (from front to back) *Torqued Ellipse I*, 1996; *Double Torqued Ellipse,* 1998–1999; *Double Torqued Ellipse II*; *Snake*, 1996. Guggenheim Museum, Bilbao. Photograph © FMGB Guggenheim Bilbao. Photographer: Erika Barahona Ede.

Serra; "the ellipses play off the architecture and take on a new quality." Indeed, as Serra's sculptures are architectural in their space-defining capacity, so Gehry's architecture is sculptural. Gehry, like most contemporary architects, uses a computer to translate his original designs and (with the assistance of five aerospace engineers employed by his firm) to direct the cutting of the actual building parts.

Music in the Information Age

As with the visual arts and architecture, music since 1960 has been boldly experimental, stylistically diverse, and (with the exception of popular music) largely impersonal. Some late twentieth-century composers pursued the random style of John Cage (see chapter 35), while others moved in the opposite direction, writing highly structured music that extends Schoenberg's serial techniques to pitch, counterpoint, and other aspects of composition. In a field that has been dominated by men for centuries, women composers and conductors have become increasingly visible—witness the Pulitzer Prize-winning American composer Ellen Taaffe Zwilich (b. 1938).

The music of the late twentieth century was distinctly multicultural. Employing Western genres such as the string quartet, the versatile Japanese composer Toru Takemitsu (1930–1996) interwove silence and sound to approximate the effects of *haiku* poetry. His almost one hundred film scores reflect a synthesis of Eastern and Western instruments, forms, and techniques. In the West, many composers rejected the European emphasis on harmony and form in favor of experimentation with the rhythms, textures, and inflections of African and Caribbean music. They revived ancient and non-Western traditions of oral and instrumental improvisation, thereby breaking with the European dependence on the score instead of the ears.

Responsive to the influence of Asian musical practices, some composers have abandoned the Western harmonic system of dividing the octave into twelve equal parts in favor of **microtonality**—the use of musical intervals smaller than the semitones of traditional European and American music. In the microtonal works of the Hungarian-born composer György Ligeti (b. 1923), melody gives way to dense clusters of sound—subtle, shimmering currents that murmur in a continuous, hypnotic flow. Ligeti's choral *Lux Eterna* and his instrumental piece entitled *Atmospheres*, ♪ both of which are featured on the soundtrack of the film *2001*, achieve a new sonority that, as the composer explains, "is so dense that the individual interwoven instrumental voices are absorbed into the general texture and completely lose their individuality." While Ligeti's pieces are composed for traditional instruments, the microtonal works of other composers may depend on electronic apparatus that is capable of producing an infinite number of microtones.

♪ See Music Listening Selections at end of chapter.

Electronic Music and Computers

Electronic technology has shaped the sound of both popular music and music written for the concert hall. Indeed, electronics has affected all aspects of music, from its composition to its performance and distribution. Just as television has democratized the reception of visual images, so long-playing records, tapes, and digital recordings have brought the history of sound into every living room. At the same time, the cheap and ready availability of electronically reproduced music has worked to virtually eliminate the patronage system that governed musical composition in former eras.

Quite apart from the electronic technology used to record musical performance, there exists the phenomenon of electronic music. A product of the twentieth century, electronic music is not a style in itself; rather, it is a medium for creating new types of sound. While traditional instruments produce only seventy to eighty pitches and a limited range of dynamic intensities, electronic devices offer a range of frequencies from fifty to fifteen thousand cycles per second. This capacity provides the potential for almost unlimited variability of pitch. Further, electronic instruments can execute rhythms at speeds and in complex patterns that are beyond the capability of live performers. Because such features defy traditional notation, electronic music is often graphed in acoustical diagrams that serve as "scores."

Much like digital imaging electronic music may be created in two ways: by the electronic modification of pre-existing sound or by the purely electronic generation of sound. In the first method, electronic equipment is used to modify a wide variety of natural, instrumental, and mechanically contrived sounds, while or after they are performed. In the late 1950s, John Cage and other avant-garde composers began to employ magnetic tape to record and manipulate sound. By means of such techniques as splicing and reversing the taped sounds of various kinds of environmental noise—thunder, human voices, bird calls, train whistles, and ticking clocks—they produced a kind of music known as *musique concrète* (concrete music).

The second method for creating electronic music involves the use of special equipment to generate sound itself. "Pure" electronic music differs from **musique concrète** in its reliance on oscillators, wave generators, and other electronic devices. The pioneer in this type of music was the German composer Karlheinz Stockhausen (b. 1928). As musical director of the Studio for Electronic Music in Cologne, Germany, Stockhausen employed electronic devices both by themselves and to manipulate and combine pretaped sounds, including music generated by traditional instruments and voices. Stockhausen's compositions—atonal patterns of sounds and silence that lack any controlling frame of reference—renounce all traditional rules of rhythm and harmony. Editing taped sounds as a filmmaker edits footage, Stockhausen dispensed with a written score and composed directly on tape, thus assuming simultaneously the roles of composer and performer. Like a Kaprow "happening," a Christo environmental sculpture, or a jazz improvisation, a Stockhausen composition is an artform in which process becomes identical with product.

The most revolutionary musical invention of the late 1960s was the computerized **synthesizer**, an integrated system of electronic components designed for both the production and manipulation of sound. Stockhausen's American contemporary Milton Babbitt (b. 1916) was the first composer to use the RCA Synthesizer to control the texture, timbre, and intensity of electronic sound. 🎵 Since the 1970s, more sophisticated and portable digital synthesizers have been attached to individual instruments. The digital synthesizer allows the musician to manipulate the pitch, duration, and dynamics of sound even as the music is being performed. The synthesizer has facilitated the typically postmodern technique known as *sampling*. A sample is a short, "borrowed" segment of recorded sound, which may be stored digitally, manipulated at will (stretched out, played backwards, and so on), then reintroduced into yet another musical phrase or composition. Electronic sampling has generated sounds and strategies that, like the jump-cuts of postmodern film, capture the chaos and tumultuousness of postmodern life. As one critic points out, what one does with sounds has become more important than what the sounds are. While musical instruments can be manipulated by computers, computers themselves have become "musical instruments." Equipped with a miniature keyboard, faders, and foot pedals, the contemporary computer is not only capable of producing a full range of sounds but is also able to produce and reproduce sounds more subtle and complex than any emitted by human voices or traditional musical instruments. For better or for worse, such devices have now begun to replace musicians in the studio and in staged musical performances.

While computers have become an indispensable aid to the recording and manipulation of sound, they have also been utilized to generate original music. The American composer Barton McLean (b. 1938), for instance, composes music with a Lightpen that draws the contours of sound waves on the video screen of a sophisticated computer. His short piece *Etunytude* is the product of such a procedure. More recently, computers have been used to design interactive musical instruments that offer musicians (and nonmusicians) a new range of performance possibilities, as in the hyperinstrument projects of Tod Machover (b. 1953). Machover's hyperinstruments extend the range and sensitivity of traditional acoustic instruments. Multiple layers of sound, dense textures, and constantly shifting sound patterns characterize some of Machover's recent projects, such as the *Hyperstring Trilogy* (1993).

Minimal Music

Minimal music, like minimal art, reduces the vocabulary of expression to elemental or primary components. In the "stripped down" compositions of American minimalists such as Philip Glass, Steve Reich, and John Adams,

melodic fragments are repeated in subtly shifting patterns. In the instrumental and choral works of the Polish composer Henryk Górecki (b. 1933) and the so-called "mystical minimalists" of Eastern Europe, these fragments look back to folk songs and chantlike hymns. Minimal music is simple in tonality and melody, but it is often complex and innovative in its rhythms and textures.

Philip Glass (b. 1937) received his early training in the fundamentals of Western musical composition. In the 1970s, however, after touring Asia and studying with the Indian sitar master Ravi Shankar (b. 1920), Glass began writing music that embraced the rhythmic structures of Indian *ragas*, progressive jazz, and rock and roll. The musical drama *Einstein on the Beach* 🎵 (1976), which Glass produced in collaboration with the designer/director Robert Wilson (b. 1941), was the first opera performed at the Metropolitan Opera House in New York City to feature electronically amplified instruments. Like traditional opera, *Einstein on the Beach* combines instrumental and vocal music, as well as recitation, mime, and dance. But it departs radically from operatic tradition in its lack of a narrative story line and character development, as well as in its instrumentation. The opera, which is performed with no intermissions over a period of four-and-a-half hours, is not the story of Albert Einstein's life or work; rather, it is an extended poetic statement honoring the twentieth century's greatest scientist. The music for the piece consists of novel yet simple melodic lines that are layered and repeated in seemingly endless permutations. Mesmerizing and seductive, Glass' music recalls the texture of Gregorian chant, the sequenced repetitions of electronic tape loops, and the subtle rhythms of the Indian *raga*. Harmonic changes occur so slowly that one must, as Glass explains, learn to listen at "a different speed," a feat that closely resembles an act of meditation.

Historical themes have continued to inspire much of the music of Glass. In 1980, he composed the opera *Satyagraha*, which celebrates the achievements of India's pacifist hero Mohandas Gandhi (see chapter 36). Sung in Sanskrit and English, the opera uses a text drawn from the *Bhagavad Gita*, the sacred book of the Hindu religion. For the quincentennial commemoration of the Columbian voyage to the Americas, the composer wrote an imaginative modern-day analogue (*The Voyage*, 1992) that links the idea of great exploration to the theme of interplanetary travel.

Postmodern Opera

In the late twentieth century, opera found inspiration in current events such as international hijacking (John Adams' *Death of Klinghofer*), black nationalism (Anthony Davis' *X*), gay rights (Stewart Wallace's *Harvey Milk*), and the cult of celebrity—witness Ezra Laderman's *Marilyn* (Monroe), John Adams' *Nixon*, and Robert Xavier Rodriguez's *Frida* (Kahlo). Other composers turned to the classics of literature and art as subject matter for full-length operas: Carlyle Floyd's *Of Mice and Men* (1970) is based on John Steinbeck's novel of the same name; William Bolcom's *A View from the Bridge* (1999) is an adaptation of the Arthur Miller play; John Harbison's *Gatsby* (1999) was inspired by F. Scott Fitzgerald's novel *The Great Gatsby*; and Tennessee Williams' classic play *A Streetcar Named Desire* (1998) received operatic treatment by the American composer Andre Previn. Few of these operas attained the compositional sophistication of the century's first typically postmodern opera: *The Ghosts of Versailles* (1992) composed by John Corigliano (b. 1938). Scored for orchestra and synthesizer and cast in the style of a comic opera, *Ghosts of Versailles* takes place in three different (and interlayered) worlds: the eighteenth-century court of Versailles, the scenario of a Mozartean opera, and the realm of the afterlife—a place peopled by the ghosts of Marie Antoinette and her court. The score comingles traditional and contemporary musical styles, alternating modern dissonance and pseudo-Mozartean lyricism in a bold and inventive (although often astonishingly disjunctive) manner. In the spirit of postmodernism, Corigliano made historical style itself the subject; his multivalent allegory tests the text against past texts by having one of his characters in the opera suddenly exclaim, "This is not opera; Wagner is opera."

Rock Music

The musical style called *rock* had its origins in the popular culture of the mid-1950s. The words "rocking" and "rolling," originally used to describe sexual activity, came to identify an uninhibited musical style that drew on a broad combination of popular American and African-American music, including country, swing, gospel, and rhythm and blues. Although no one musician is responsible for the birth of rock, the style gained popularity with such performers as Bill Haley, Little Richard, and Elvis Presley. In the hands of these flamboyant musicians, rock came to be characterized by a high dynamic level of sound, fast and hard rhythms, a strong beat, and earthy, colloquial lyrics.

From its inception, rock music was an expression of a youth culture: The rock sound, associated with dancing, sexual freedom, and rebellion against restrictive parental and cultural norms, also mirrored the new consumerism of the postwar era. While 1950s rock and roll often featured superficial, "bubble-gum" lyrics, 1960s rock became more sophisticated—the aural counterpart of Western-style pop art. With the success of the Beatles, a British group of the 1960s, rock also became (like pop art) an international phenomenon, uniting young people across the globe. The Beatles absorbed the music of Little Richard and the rhythms and instrumentation of Indian classical music. They made imaginative use of electronic effects, such as feedback and splicing. Their compositions, which reflected the spirit of the Western counterculture, reached a creative peak in the album *Sergeant Pepper's Lonely Hearts Club Band* (1967). Although the electric guitar was in use well before the Beatles, it was with this group that the instrument became the hallmark of rock music, and it has remained the principal instrument of the rock musician.

During the 1960s, "establishment" America faced the protests of a youthful counterculture that was disenchanted with middle-class values, mindless consumerism, and bureaucratic authority. Counterculture "hippies"—the word derives from "hipster," an admirer of jazz and its subculture—exalted a neoromantic lifestyle that called for peaceful coexistence, a return to natural and communal habitation, more relaxed sexual standards, and experimentation with mind-altering drugs such as marijuana and lysergic acid diethylamide (LSD). The use of psychedelic drugs among members of the counterculture became associated with the emergence of a number of British and West Coast acid rock (or hard rock) groups, such as The Who and Jefferson Airplane. The music of these groups often featured ear-splitting, electronically amplified sound and sexually provocative lyrics. The decade produced a few superb virtuoso performers, like the guitarist Jimi Hendrix (1942–1970). The 1960s also spawned the folk-rock hero Bob Dylan (b. 1941), whose songs gave voice to the anger and despair of the American counterculture. Dylan's lyrics, filled with scathing references to modern materialism, hypocrisy, greed, and warfare—specifically, the American involvement in Vietnam—attacked the moral detachment of contemporary authority figures.

Music and the Global Paradigm

It is in the musical arts that the global paradigm is most apparent. Cultural interdependence and the willful (and often electronically synthesized) fusion of various musical traditions have transformed contemporary sound: Arabic chant, Indian ragas, and Latino rhythms are heard in jazz; rock and country blues give gospel music a new sound; Cuban brass punctuates contemporary rock; and shimmering Asian drones propel New Age music. The global character of contemporary music is also evident in popular genres that engage issue-driven lyrics. The Jamaican musician Bob Marley (1945–1981) brought to the international scene the socially conscious music known as *reggae*—an eclectic style that draws on a wide variety of black Jamaican musical forms, including African religious music and Christian revival songs. *Hip-hop*, which combines loud, percussive music (often electronically mixed and manipulated by disc jockeys), jarring lyrics, and breakdancing (an acrobatic dance style) has moved from its inner-city origins to assume an international scope. This "mutating hybrid" makes use of various musical traditions: modern (disco, salsa, reggae, rock) and ancient (African call and response). *Rap*—the vocal dimension of hip-hop—launches a fusillade of raw and socially provocative words chanted in rhymed couplets over an intense rhythmic beat.

While some critics lament that Western music has bifurcated into two cultures—art music and popular music—the fact is that art and popular music are becoming more alike, or more precisely: they share various aspects of a global musical menu. One example of this phenomenon is the orchestral suite *Portraits in Blue* (1995) by the American jazz pianist Marcus Roberts (b. 1963). Composed in what Roberts calls "semi-classical form," the composition is a "personal listening mix" that conflates Beethoven, John Coltrane, Chopin, Little Richard, Billie

Holiday, and George Gershwin. Other composers create an instrumental multicultural pastiche, achieving unique textures from the combination of electronic and traditional Western instruments, as well as ancient musical devices (such as the *balafon*, an African version of the xylophone). Jazz, a style that habitually "quotes" and parodies other music, continues to represent the postmodern sensibility. Wynton Marsalis (see chapter 36) combines the percussive rhythms of Afro-Caribbean music with the inventive polyphonies of instrumental jazz in "Marciac Fun," part of a thirteen-part suite Marsalis composed to celebrate the twentieth annual jazz festival held at Marciac, France. In the genre of free jazz, such musicians as John Zorn (b. 1953) borrow harmonic and rhythmic concepts from the domains of bluegrass, klezmer (Jewish folk music), and punk rock. Such fusions of Eastern and Western, urban and folk, tribal and lyric styles, constitute the musical mosaic of the new millennium. Moreover, new efforts to join music to theater, film, dance, and the visual arts move toward a productive interchange between word, image, and sound.

Dance in the Information Age

Created in conjunction with *Einstein on the Beach*, the choreography of Lucinda Childs (b. 1940)—who also danced in the original production—followed a minimalist imperative. In line with the hypnotic rhythms of the piece, her choreography featured serial repetitions of ritualized gestures and robotlike motions. Childs reduced the credo of pure dance to a set of patterned movements that were geometric, recurrent, and—for some critics—unspeakably boring. The role of improvisation in dance—the legacy of Merce Cunningham– has had a more successful recent history. Contemporary companies such as the Sydney (Australia) Dance Company, Pilobolus, and Momix have produced exceptionally inventive repertories that embrace the realms of acrobatics, aerobics, gymnastics, vaudeville, and street dance. The new dance projects of these and other companies, which utilize gymnastic or circus-related props, combine playful action and vigorous explorations of body movement.

Like postmodern opera, contemporary dance has drawn on social and historical issues and events, as for example in Paul Taylor's 1999 spoof of the Ku Klux Klan; Charles Atlas' meditation on death and decay in Bosnia (*Delusional*, 1994); and Ea Sola's choreographed recollection of war in her native Vietnam (*Sécheresse et Pluie* [*Drought and Rain*], 1996). The last of these works reflects the impact of the Japanese dance form known as *butoh* (*ankoko butoh* meaning "dance of utter darkness"). Butoh, which grew out of ancient forms of kabuki and theater, is a dance style that features simple, symbolic movements performed in a mesmerizingly slow and hypnotic manner. Butoh dancers, who perform with shaved heads and chalk-white makeup and robes, have had an increasing influence on the international dance scene of the last two decades.

SUMMARY

The visual arts of the information age have not assumed any single, unifying style. Rather, they are diverse and eclectic, reflecting the postmodern preoccupation with the media-shaped image, with parody and play, and with the contradictory nature of contemporary life. While pop artists glorified the commercialized image, assemblage artists appropriated imagery from the "historical dustbin." Some artists addressed social conscience issues, while still others pursued more abstract forms of expression made possible by commercial materials. With happenings and earth projects, the artist moved out of the studio and into the environment. Electronic technology and computers made possible new genres of video and cyberart. In architecture, the international style gave way to postmodern pastiche and zany designs; and finally, at the century's end, to a new kind of organic expressionism in the work of Frank Gehry.

The music of the information age deviated from traditional European modes of harmony and meter to incorporate microtonality, improvisation, and a variety of non-Western forms and instruments. Indeed, in the global marketplace a multicultural assortment of styles informs all aspects of music and dance. The minimal operas of Philip Glass feature hypnotic aural and visual effects inspired by Eastern forms of meditation. Contemporary issues mingle with historical motifs in postmodern operas. Electronic technology has had a massive effect on all phases of musical culture, from composition to performance and dissemination. The boundaries between concert hall music, jazz, and popular sound have faded considerably, and projects to unite the media—music, theater, dance, film, and the visual arts—work to expand traditional performance modes. The arts of our time, while ever more intellectually challenging, continue to remind us of the human responsibility for safeguarding the earth, ourselves, and the humanistic tradition.

SUGGESTIONS FOR READING

Carr, C. *On Edge: Performance at the End of the Twentieth Century.* Hanover, N.H.: Wesleyan University Press, 1993.

Danto, Arthur C. *After the End of Art: Contemporary Art and the Pale of History.* Princeton, N.J.: Princeton University Press, 1997.

Foster, Hall. *The Return of the Real: The Avant-Garde at the End of the Century.* Cambridge, Mass.: MIT Press, 1996.

Felshin, Nina, ed. *But Is It Art? The Spirit of Art as Activism.* Seattle: Bay Press, 1994.

Fineberg, Jonathan. *Strategies of Being: Art Since 1945.* Englewood Cliffs, N.J.: Prentice Hall, 1995.

Henri, Adrian. *Total Art: Environments, Happenings, and Performance.* New York: Oxford University Press, 1974.

Jencks, Charles. *The Architecture of the Jumping Universe.* London: Academy Editions, 1995.

Lovejoy, Margot. *Postmodern Currents: Art and Artists in the Age of Electronic Media.* Ann Arbor, Mich.: UMI Press, 1989.

Morse, Margaret. *Virtualities: Television, Media Art, and Cyberculture.* Bloomington, Ind.: Indiana University Press, 1998.

Rush, Michael, *New Media in Late 20th Century Art*. London: Thames and Hudson, 1999.

Shapiro, Gary, ed. *After the Future: Postmodern Times and Places*. Albany, N.Y.: State University of New York Press, 1990.

MUSIC LISTENING SELECTIONS

CD Two Selection 24   Ligeti, *Atmospheres*, 1961, excerpt.

CD Two Selection 25   Babbitt, *Ensembles for Synthesizer*, 1951, excerpt.

CD Two Selection 26   Glass, *Einstein on the Beach*, "Knee 1," 1977.

GLOSSARY

geodesic a type of space-frame employing light straight-sided polygons in tension

microtonality the use of musical intervals smaller than the semitones of traditional European and American music

musique concrète (French, "concrete music") a kind of music based on real or "concrete" sounds, such as street noises, human voices, bird calls, and thunder, that are recorded, altered, and assembled on magnetic tape

silkscreen a printmaking technique employing the use of a stenciled image cut and attached to finely meshed silk, through which printing ink is forced so as to transfer the image to paper or cloth; also called "seriography"

synthesizer an integrated system of electronic components designed for the production and control of sound; it may be used in combination with a computer and with most musical instruments

virtual reality the computer-generated simulation of three-dimensional imagery with which the viewer may interact (by means of special electronic equipment) in a seemingly physical way

CREDITS

Calmann & King, the author, and the literature researcher wish to thank the publishers and individuals who have kindly allowed their copyright material to be reproduced in this book, as listed below. Every effort has been made to contact copyright holders, but should there be any errors or omissions, Calmann & King would be pleased to insert the appropriate acknowledgment in any subsequent edition of this publication.

CHAPTER 19

Reading 3.25 (p. 492): from Michel de Montaigne, "On Cannibals" in *The Complete Essays of Montaigne*, translated by Donald M. Frame (Stanford University Press, 1958), © 1958 by the Board of Trustees of the Leland Stanford Junior University. Reprinted by permission of the publisher.

Reading 3.26, 3.27 (p. 498, p. 500): Footnotes for "The Tragedy of Othello", the "Moor of Venice" and "Hamlet" from *The Complete Works of Shakespeare*, 3rd edition, by David M. Bevington, © 1980 by Scott, Foresman and Company. Reprinted by permission of Addison-Wesley Educational Publishers Inc.

CHAPTER 20

Reading 4.1 (p. 510): From *The Spiritual Exercises of St. Ignatius*, translated by Louis J. Puhl, S.J. (Loyola Press, 1951). Reprinted by permission of the publisher.

Reading 4.2 (p. 513): From *The Complete Works of Saint Teresa of Jesus*, Vol. 1, translated by E. A. Peers, 1957. (Sheed & Ward, 1957), © 1957 Sheed & Ward Ltd., London. Reprinted by permission of Sheed & Ward, an Apostolate of the Priests of the Sacred Heart. 7373 South Lover's Lane Road, Franklin, Wisconsin 53132.

Reading 4.3 (p. 513): From *The Poems of Richard Crashaw*, edited by L. C. Martin (Oxford University Press, 1957).

Boxed Insert (p. 520): From *New Revised Standard Version Bible with Apocryphal/Deuterocanonical Books* (HarperCollins Study Bible, 1991).

CHAPTER 21

Reading 4.4 (p. 546): From *The Maxims of La Rochefoucauld*, translated by Louise Kronenberger (Random House, 1959), © 1959 Random House Inc., New York.

Reading 4.5 (p. 547): From *Molière, Le Bourgeois Gentilhomme (The Tradesman Turned Gentleman)*, translated by Curtis Hidden Page (modernized by the author). (G. P. Putnam's Sons, 1908).

Insert (p. 564): Matsuo Basho, five haikus from *An Introduction to Haiku* by Harold G. Henderson (Doubleday, 1958), © 1958 by Harold G. Henderson. Reprinted by permission of Doubleday, a division of Random House, Inc.

CHAPTER 22

Reading 4.6 (p. 568): The "Twenty-Third Psalm" from *Douay Bible*, reprinted in *The College Survey of English Literature*, Shorter Edition by Alexander Witherspoon (Harcourt Brace Jovanovich, 1951). Reprinted by permission of the publisher; The "Twenty-Third Psalm" from *Authorised Version of the Bible (The King James Bible)* (Cambridge University Press).

Readings 4.7 (p. 568), **4.8** (p. 570): From John Donne, *Devotions upon Emergent Occasions and Songs and Sonnets in The College Survey of English Literature*, Shorter Edition by Alexander Witherspoon (Harcourt Brace Jovanovich, 1951).

Reading 4.9 (p. 571): From John Milton, *Paradise Lost: A Norton Critical Edition*. Second Edition, edited by Scott Elledge (Norton, 1975), © 1993, 1975 by W. W. Norton & Company, Inc. Reprinted by permission of the publisher. (Footnotes.)

CHAPTER 23

Readings 4.10 (p. 585), **4.11** (p. 586): From Sir Francis Bacon, *Novum Organum* and *Of Studies* in *The Complete Works of Francis Bacon*, translated by James Spedding (modernized by the author). (Longman, 1960.)

Reading 4.12 (p. 587): From René Descartes, *Discourse on Method* in *Descartes Selections*, edited by Ralph M. Eaton. (Scribner, 1927), © 1927 Charles Scribner's Sons, © renewed 1955.

Reading 4.13 (p. 588): From John Locke, *Essay Concerning Human Understanding* in *The Philosophic Works of John Locke*, edited by J. A. St. John (modernized by the author). (George Bell & Sons, 1892).

CHAPTER 24

Reading 4.14 (p. 604): From Thomas Hobbes, *Leviathan*, edited by Herbert W. Schneider (Macmillan ,1958), © 1985, 1958 by Macmillan Publishing Company.

Reading 4.15 (p. 606): From John Locke, *Of Civil Government in The Works of John Locke* (modernized by the author). (Thomas Tegg, 1823.)

Reading 4.16 (p. 607): From *Thomas Jefferson, The Declaration of Independence* (1776).

Reading 4.17 (p. 608): From: *Adam Smith, An Inquiry into the Nature and Causes of the Wealth of Nations* (George Routledge and Sons, 1913).

Reading 4.18 (p. 611): From Denis Diderot, *Encyclopédie in Diderot's Selected Writings*, edited by L. G. Crocker and D. Coltman (Macmillan, 1966), © 1966 by Macmillan Publishing Company. Reprinted by permission of Prentice Hall, Inc., Upper Saddle River, NJ.

Reading 4.19 (p. 614): From Antoine Nicolas de Condorcet, *Sketch for a Historical Picture of the Progress of the Human Mind*, translated by June Barraclough (Weidenfeld & Nicolson, 1955), © 1955 George Weidenfeld & Nicolson Ltd. Reprinted by permission of The Orion Publishing Group.

Reading 4.20 (p. 109): From Mary Wollstonecraft, *A Vindication of the Rights of Woman* in *The Works of Mary Wollstonecraft*. Volume 5, edited by Jane Todd and Marilyn Butler (New York University Press, 1989).

Reading 4.21 (p. 618): From Alexander Pope, *Essay on Man* in *Poetical Works of Alexander Pope* (Little Brown, 1854).

CHAPTER 25

Reading 4.22 (p. 621): From Olaudah Equiano, *Travels*, edited by Paul Edwards (Heinemann Educational Books, 1970). Reprinted by permission of Reed Educational & Professional Publishing Ltd.

Reading 4.23 (p. 624): Phillis Wheatley, 'On Being Brought from Africa to America' from *The Poems of Phillis Wheatley*, edited by Julian D. Mason (University of North Carolina Press, 1989).

Reading 4.24 (p. 625): From *Jonathan Swift, A Modest Proposal* (London: 1729).

Reading 4.25 (p. 628): From Voltaire, *Candide* in *The Best Known Works of Voltaire* (Blue Ribbon Books, 1927). (with notes by G. K. Fiero; modernized and edited by G. K. Fiero.)

Reading 4.26 (p. 637): From Li Ju-chen, *Flowers in the Mirror*, translated by Lin Tai-yi (University of California Press, 1965). Reprinted by permission of Peter Owen Ltd., London.

Reading 4.27 (p. 641): From Jean-Jacques Rousseau, *Discourse on the Origin of Inequality among Men*, translated by Maurice Cranston (Viking Penguin, 1984), translation © 1984 by Maurice Cranston. Reprinted by permission of Peters Fraser & Dunlop Group Ltd.

CHAPTER 27

Readings 5.1 (p. 681), **5.2** (p. 682), **5.3** (p. 684): from William Wordsworth, "Lines Composed a Few Miles Above Tintern Abbey"; from Percy Bysshe Shelley, "Ode to the West Wind"; from John Keats, "Ode on a Grecian Urn," in *The College Survey of English Literature*, Shorter Edition, revised by Alexander Witherspoon (Harcourt Brace Jovanovich, 1951).

From Shen Zhou, "Written on a Landscape Painting in an Album," translated by Daniel Bryant, in *The Columbia Anthology of Traditional Chinese Literature*, edited by Victor H. Mairr (Columbia University Press, 1994), © 1994 by Columbia University Press. Reprinted by permission of the publisher.

Reading 5.4 (p. 686): From Shen Fu, *Chapters from A Floating Life: The Autobiography of a Chinese Artist*, translated by Shirley M. Black (Oxford University Press, 1960). Reprinted by permission of the publisher.

Reading 5.5 (p. 693): Ralph Waldo Emerson, "Brahma" from *The Complete Essays and Other Writings of Ralph Waldo Emerson*, edited by Brooks Atkinson (The Modern Library, 1950).

Reading 5.6 (p. 693): From Henry David Thoreau, *Walden* (Airmont Classics, 1965).

Reading 5.7 (p. 695): From Walt Whitman, *Leaves of Grass* (David McKay, 1900).

CHAPTER 28

Reading 5.8 (p. 708): From Napoleon Bonaparte, *The Corsican: A Diary of Napoleon's Life in His Own Words* (Houghton Mifflin Company, 1910).

Reading 5.9 (p. 709): From Mary Wollstonecraft Shelley, *Frankenstein. Or, the Modern Prometheus* (Oxford University Press, 1969).

Reading 5.10 (p. 711): Lord Byron (George Gordon Noel), "Prometheus" from *The New Oxford Book of English Verse*, chosen and edited by Helen Gardner (Oxford University Press, 1972).

Reading 5.11 (p. 712): From Alexander Pushkin, "Napoleon" in *Alexander Pushkin, Collected Narrative and Lyrical Poetry*, translated by Walter Arndt (Ardis Publishing, 1984). Reprinted by permission of the publisher.

Reading 5.12 (p. 713): From Frederick Douglass, *My Bondage and My Freedom in Frederick Douglass: The Narrative and Selected Writings*, edited by Michael Meyer (The Modern Library, 1984).

Reading 5.13 (p. 715): From Sojourner Truth, "Isabella's Marriage" in *Narrative of Sojourner Truth*, edited by Margaret Washington (Vintage Books, 1993).

Reading 5.14 (p. 717): From Johann Wolfgang von Goethe, *Faust: Parts 1 and 2*, translated by Louis MacNeice (Oxford University Press, 1951), copyright 1951, 1954 by Frederick Louis MacNeice, © renewed 1979 by Heidi MacNeice. Reprinted by permission of David Higham Associates and Oxford University Press Inc.

Reading 5.15 (p. 724): Heinrich Heine, "You Are Just Like a Flower" from *Heinrich Heine: Lyric Poems and Ballads*, translated by Ernst Feise (University of Pittsburgh Press, 1989), © 1961, 1989 by University of Pittsburgh Press. Reprinted by permission of the publisher.

CHAPTER 30

Reading 5.16 (p. 750): From Rudyard Kipling, "The White Man's Burden" in *Rudyard Kipling's Verse, 1885-1918* (Doubleday, 1920).

Reading 5.17 (p. 751): From Lin Tse-Hsu, "Letter of Advice to a Queen" in *China's Response to the West* by Ssu-Yu Teng and John King Fairbank (Cambridge, Mass.: Harvard University Press, 1954), © 1954 by the President and Fellows of Harvard College, © renewed 1982 by Ssu-Yu Teng and John K. Fairbank. Reprinted by permission of the publisher.

Reading 5.18 (p. 755): From Karl Marx and Frederick Engels, *The Communist Manifesto*, translated by Samuel Moore; revised and edited by Frederick Engels (London: 1888).

Reading 5.19 (p. 757): From John Stuart Mill, *The Subjection of Women* (Prometheus Books, 1986).

Reading 5.20 (p. 759): From Charles Dickens, *The Old Curiosity Shop* (London: 1841).

Reading 5.21 (p. 760): From Mark Twain, *The Adventures of Huckleberry Finn*. New American Library (Harper & Row, 1959).

Reading 5.22 (p. 762): From Fyodor Dostoevsky, *Crime and Punishment*, translated by Jessie Coulson, edited by George Gibian (W. W. Norton, 1975).

Reading 5.23 (p. 764): From Gustave Flaubert, *Madame Bovary*, translated by Francis Steegmuller (Random House, 1957), © 1957 by Francis Steegmuller. Reprinted by permission of the publisher.

Reading 5.24 (p. 765): Kate Chopin, "The Story of an Hour" in *A Vocation and a Voice: Stories* (Penguin, 1991).

Reading 5.25 (p. 766): From Henrik Ibsen, "A Doll's House" in *Six Plays*, translated by Eva Le Galliene (Random House, 1957), © 1957 by Eva Le Galliene. Reprinted by permission of the publisher.

CHAPTER 31

Reading 5.26 (p. 787): From Friedrich Nietzsche, *The Gay Science* and *Twilight of the Idols* in *The Portable Nietzsche*, edited by Walter Kaufmann, translated by Walter Kaufmann (The Viking Press, 1965), © 1954 by The Viking Press, renewed © 1982 by Viking Penguin Inc. Reprinted by permission of Viking Penguin, a division of Penguin Putnam Inc.

Reading 5.27 (p. 789): Stephané Mallarmé, "The Afternoon of a Faun" in *The Poetry of Mallarmé* (HarperCollins Publishers Inc., 1952), copyright 1952 The Estate of Aldous Huxley; Mrs. Laura Huxley, and Chatto & Windus Ltd. Reprinted by permission of Reece Halsey Literary Agency.

CHAPTER 32

Reading 6.1 (p. 820): Ezra Pound, "In a Station of the Metro" and "The Bathtub" from *Personae*, copyright 1926 by Ezra Pound. Reprinted by permission of New Directions Publishing Corporation.

Reading 6.2 (p. 821) Robert Frost, "The Road Not Taken" from *The Poetry of Robert Frost*, edited by Edward Connery Lathem (Jonathan Cape, 1969), copyright 1944 by Robert Frost, © 1916, 1969 by Henry Holt & Company, LLC. Reprinted by permission of Henry Holt & Co., LLC.

CHAPTER 33

Reading 6.3 (p. 844): From Sigmund Freud, *Civilization and Its Discontents*, translated by James Strachey (W.W. Norton, 1989), © 1961 by James Strachey, renewed 1989 by Alix Strachey. Reprinted by permission of W. W. Norton & Company Inc and The Random House Group Ltd.

Reading 6.4 (p. 847): From Marcel Proust, *Swann's Way* in *Remembrance of Things Past*, translated by C.K. Scott Moncrieff (Chatto & Windus, 1981), translation © 1981 by Random House Inc. and Chatto & Windus. Reprinted by permission of the Estate of Marcel Proust and The Random House Group Ltd.

Reading 6.5 (p. 849): From Franz Kafka, "The Metamorphosis" in *The Basic Kafka* (Washington Square Press/Schocken Books, 1979).

Reading 6.6 (p. 851). E. E. Cummings, [she being Brand] from *Complete Poems, 1904-1962*, edited by George J. Firmage (Liveright Publishing, 1994), copyright 1926, 1954, © 1991 by the Trustees for the E. E. Cummings Trust, © 1985 by George James Firmage. Reprinted by permission of the publisher.

CHAPTER 34

Reading 6.7 (p. 868): W. B. Yeats, "The Second Coming" from *Collected Poems* (Picador, 1990). Reprinted by permission of A. P. Watt Ltd on behalf of Michael B. Yeats.

Reading 6.8 (p. 869): From Erich Maria Remarque, *All Quiet on the Western Front*, © 1929, 1930 by Little Brown & Company; © renewed 1957, 1958 by Erich Maria Remarque. Reprinted by permission of Pryor Cashman Sherman & Flynn LLP on behalf of the Estate of the late Erich Maria Remarque.

Reading 6.9 (p. 878): Randall Jarrell, "The Death of the Ball Turret Gunner" from *The Complete Poems* (Farrar, Straus & Giroux, 1969), © 1969, renewed 1997 by Mary von S. Jarrell. Reprinted by permission of the publisher; Kato Shuson, three haiku from *Modern Japanese Literature: An Anthology*, edited by Donald Keene, © 1956 by Grove Press Inc. Reprinted by permission of Grove/Atlantic Inc.

Reading 6.10 (p. 879): From Elie Wiesel, *Night*, translated by Stella Rodway, © 1960 by MacGibbon & Kee; © renewed 1988 by The Collins Publishing Group. Reprinted by permission of Farrar, Straus & Giroux Inc.

CHAPTER 35

Reading 6.11 (p. 887): From Jean Paul Sartre, "Existentialism", translated by Bernard Frechtman (Philosophical Library, 1947), © Editions Gallimard, 1996. Reprinted by permission of Editions Gallimard and Philosophical Library.

Reading 6.12 (p. 890): From Samuel Beckett, *Waiting for Godot*, © 1954 by Grove Press; © renewed 1982 by Samuel Beckett. Reprinted by permission of Grove/Atlantic Inc.

Reading 6.13 (p. 892): T. S. Eliot, "The Love Song of J. Alfred Prufrock" from *Collected Poems 1909-1962* (Faber & Faber, 1963), © this edition by T. S. Eliot 1963. Reprinted by permission of the publisher.

Reading 6.14 (p. 893): Dylan Thomas, "Do Not Go Gentle Into That Good Night" from *Collected Poems, 1934-1952* (Dent, 1989), © 1952 by Dylan Thomas. Reprinted by permission of David Higham Associates and New Directions Publishing Corporation.

Reading 6.16 (p. 895): Iqbal, "Revolution" and "Europe and Syria" from *Poems from Iqbal*, translated by V. Kiernan (John Murray, 1955). Reprinted by permission of the publisher; Chairil Anwar, "At the Mosque" from *The Voice of the Night: Complete Poetry and Prose of Chairil Anwar*, translated by Burton Raffel (Ohio University Press, 1993). Reprinted by permission of Ohio University Press/Swallow Press, Athens, Ohio.

CHAPTER 36

Reading 6.17 (p. 912): Pablo Neruda, "United Fruit Co." from *Five Decades: Poems 1925-1970*, translated by Ben Belitt, © 1974 by Ben Belitt. Reprinted by permission of Grove/Atlantic Inc.

Reading 6.18 (p. 914): Langston Hughes, "Theme for English B" and "Dream Deferred" ('Harlem') from *Collected Poems* (Knopf, 1994), © 1994 by the Estate of Langston Hughes. Reprinted by permission of Alfred A. Knopf, a Division of Random House Inc; Gwendolyn Brooks, "The Mother" and "We Real Cool" from *Blacks* (Third World Press, 1991).

Reading 6.19 (p. 915): From Richard Wright, "The Ethics of Living Jim Crow" in *Uncle Tom's Children* (Harper & Row, 1937), © 1937 by Richard Wright, © renewed 1965 by Ellen Wright. Reprinted by permission of HarperCollins Publishers Inc.

Reading 6.20 (p. 917): Martin Luther King, from *Letter from Birmingham Jail*, © 1963 Martin Luther King Jr., renewed 1991 by Coretta Scott King. Reprinted by arrangement with The Heirs to the Estate of Martin Luther King, Jr., c/o Writers House Inc as agent for the proprietor.

Reading 6.21 (p. 919): From Malcolm X, *Malcolm X Speaks* (Pathfinder Press, 1965), © 1965, 1989 by Betty Shabazz and Pathfinder Press. Reprinted by permission of the publisher.

(p. 919) Bloke Modisane, "it gets awful lonely" from *Poems from Black Africa*, edited by Langston Hughes (Indiana University Press, 1963).

Reading 6.22 (p. 920): From Ralph Ellison, "The Prologue" in *Invisible Man*, © 1952 by Ralph Ellison. Reprinted by permission of Random House, Inc.

Reading 6.23 (p. 921): Alice Walker, "Elethia" from *You Can't Keep a Good Woman Down: Short Stories*, © 1979 by Alice Walker. Reprinted by permission of Harcourt Brace & Company.